George Melvyn Ella

The Practical Divinity of Universal Learning:

John Durie's Educational Pansophism

George Melvyn Ella

The Practical Divinity of Universal Learning:
John Durie's Educational Pansophism

WIPF & STOCK · Eugene, Oregon

THE PRACTICAL DIVINITY OF UNIVERSAL LEARNING
John Duries's Educational Pansophism

Copyright © 2014 Verlag fur Kultur und Wissenschaft. All rights reserved. Except for brief quotations in critical publications or reviews, no part of this book may be reproduced in any manner without prior written permission from the publisher. Write: Permissions, Wipf and Stock Publishers, 199 W. 8th Ave., Eugene, OR 97401.

This Edition published by Wipf and Stock Publishers in cooperation with Verlag fur Kultur und Wissenschaft.

Wipf & Stock
An imprint of Wipf and Stock Publishers
199 W. 8th Avenue, Suite 3
Eugene OR, 97401
www.wipfandstock.com

ISBN 13: 978-1-4982-0630-3
Manufactured in the U.S.A.

The Practical Divinity of Universal Learning: John Durie's Educational Pansophism

Dissertation zur Erlangung des Grades eines
Doktors der Theologie

(Dr. theol.)

im Fachbereich evangelische Theologie
der Philipps Universität Marburg

vorgelegt von

George Melvyn Ella

I. O.St.R. (Land NRW); I. Staatsprüfung Sek. I und II, (Duisburg);
II. Staatsprüfung Sek. I und II, (Essen); Översiktskurs in Theologie
(Uppsala); fil. kand. (Uppsala); BD, (London); PGCE (Hull);
Dr. phil. (Duisburg)

aus
Bradford, England

Gutachter: Herr Prof. Dr. Wolf-Friedrich Schäufele

Zweiter Gutachter: Herr Prof. Dr. Hans Schneider

Einreichungstermin
Dezember 2011

This book is dedicated to the great work of the staff, students, graduates and supporters of the Martin Bucer Seminar, Bonn.

Their world-wide outreach and devotion to education and the Great Commission would have thrilled Durie's heart.

Table of Contents (short)

Table of Contents (extensive) 11

Recommendations 17

Preface 19

Acknowledgements 23

CHAPTER ONE
John Durie and My Task 27

CHAPTER TWO
Durie's Life and Labours 47

CHAPTER THREE
Early Contributions to Durie Scholarship 105

CHAPTER FOUR
The 20th Century's reception of John Durie 131

CHAPTER FIVE
The Place of the Jews in Durie's Quest for Universal Learning 169

CHAPTER SIX
Discovering the Advantages of Universal Learning 209

CHAPTER SEVEN
The *Foedus Fraternum* of Durie, Hartlib and Comenius 247

CHAPTER EIGHT
Purpose, Method and Procedure in Academic Studies 287

CHAPTER NINE
A Parliamentary Agency for the Advancement of Universal Learning ... 331

CHAPTER TEN
Universal Reform through Practical Divinity 365

CHAPTER ELEVEN
Summing Up 407

Appendix 427

Bibliography 431

Biography of John Durie 489

Biography of George M. Ella 490

Table of Contents (extensive)

Recommendations 17

Preface 19

Acknowledgements 23

CHAPTER ONE
John Durie and My Task 27
    Rediscovering John Durie's importance 27
    Durie's sixty years' involvement in Continental Europe 28
    A prophet not honoured in his own country 32
    The refragmentation of a defragmenter's work 38
    Living in an ideal time for Durie scholarship 40

CHAPTER TWO
Durie's Life and Labours 47
    Born into a family of campaigners, ministers, diplomats, lairds and rebels 47
    Durie's youth and early adulthood in the Netherlands and France 51
    Durie at Elbing: First writings on universal learning and church union 53
    Durie the educationalist and irenist and the start of his international work 59
    Uniting the Protestants in war-torn Europe 62
    Work under Archbishop William Laud 64
    Further travels in Sweden, Germany, Denmark, the Netherlands and England 69
    Politician, educationalist and ambassador under Cromwell 72
    Representing the Republic in Sweden, Switzerland, Germany and Holland 80
    Triumphs turned to acute disappointments on returning to England.. 92
    Durie spends the rest of his life on the Continent 94

CHAPTER THREE
Early Contributions to Durie Scholarship 105
    The seventeenth to eighteenth centuries 105
    Mosheim and Benzelius 107
    The Nineteenth Century 110
    Essays by educationalists 125

CHAPTER FOUR
The 20th Century's reception of John Durie 131

CHAPTER FIVE
The Place of the Jews in Durie's Quest for Universal Learning 169
    The Jewish situation in England in the first half of the seventeenth century 169
    New trends in Jewish studies 175
    Popkin's three-point appraisal of Durie 179
    Durie and the 'lost tribes' 182
    Thoughts concerning founding a London University with a college for Jewish studies 189
    John Durie and Millenarianism 196

CHAPTER SIX
Discovering the Advantages of Universal Learning 209
    Filling the earth with true knowledge 209
    Durie's success in ecumenical activities 210
    Durie's early contact with universal learning 215
    Henry Oldenburg, Daniel Ernst Jablonski, Gottfried Wilhelm von Leibniz and John Durie's legacy 219
    Durie forms a solid basis for his future work 227
    Durie's first major efforts towards Protestant peace and Pansophy . 233
    Procuring the Public Good in Learning and Religion 241
    Teaching the organising and synergising of things presented to the senses 243

CHAPTER SEVEN
The *Foedus Fraternum* of Durie, Hartlib and Comenius 247
- Comenius' alleged influence on Durie re-examined 247
- Durie's acquaintance with Comenius through Peter Figulus 251
- Comenius was not *the* major 17th century educational trail-blazer .. 255
- The Pact between Durie, Hartlib and Comenius 263
- Durie's Pansophy more synergistic and comprehensive than that of Comenius 267
- Comenius' work for Sweden 271
- Comenius opts out of the *Foedus Fraternum* 273
- Cyprian Kinner's association with Comenius 276
- Durie's and Hartlib's disappointment with Comenius 281

CHAPTER EIGHT
Purpose, Method and Procedure in Academic Studies 287
- Right literary analysis as the handmaid of right learning 287
- Retracing the footsteps of a writer's understanding 289
- The first principles used in meditating on a given text 291
- Organising the acts of the mind in meditation 295
- The aim of right meditation 296
- Acts of ratiocination and the regulating principle 298
- Durie compared to his predecessor and mentor Bacon 301
- Durie's view of Scriptural textual interpretation compared with Grosseteste's 304
- The diversity of analytical methods and their inter-dependence 307
- Advising students how to study 310
- Understanding the Scriptures aright 315
- The place of the library and librarian in universal learning 319
- Durie's teaching recommended by today's information processors and librarians 325

CHAPTER NINE
A Parliamentary Agency for the Advancement of Universal Learning... 331
- Early attempts at finding private sponsors for an agency for advancing learning 331
- Petitioning Parliament again concerning reforms in Church and State 338
- Setting up a School Council to organise educational reform 344
- The grounds and method of reformation and its advancement 346
- Concerning the pedagogical or scholastical function of learning 350
- The need for a national curriculum for the advancement of universal learning 354
- Universities have their rightful place but no monopoly on learning 356
- The practical duties of an Office of Address 359
- Petitioning the Protector 361

CHAPTER TEN
Universal Reform through Practical Divinity 365
- Proposing a platform for Practical Divinity 365
- A Practical Divinity should be the whole doctrine of a life of Godliness in covenant with God 366
- The place of schools in confirming the Covenant in the life of the nation 369
- The Reformed School of Practical Divinity 370
- Concerning an Association or Society for the Education of Children 371
- Concerning proficiencies and the means and parts of learning 374
- Rules of teaching according to the ordinary degree of children's natural capacities 376
- A Supplement to the Reformed School 381
- How to find out the effectual way of advancing learning 382
- Reflections on how defects in learning may be rectified 387
- The need for a fundamentally different training for teachers 389

Education for public offices and leadership 391
Education for all children, youths and adults according to their abilities and calling 392
How Reform must start at once 395
The intellectual and practical truths to be taught in a Body of Practical Divinity 397
Appropriating data in theory alone is not knowledge, but doers of Practical Divinity learn how to activate data knowingly and usefully 398
Precognitions, Principles and Parts: Practical Divinity versus Case Divinity 400
Hartlib's thoughts break the *filum Ariadnes* 402
Durie's last stand in England 403

CHAPTER ELEVEN
Summing Up 407
Durie's Plans Seen as Realisable, Practical and Necessary in Twenty-First Century Thinking 407

Appendix
Copies of the two different title pages to Benzelius' dissertation and the title-page concerning Benzelius' inaugural Disputation 427

Bibliography 431
The major dated works of John Durie, including his reports and minutes used for this thesis in chronological order: 431
Published Collections of Durie's correspondence used in this thesis: 451
Undated works by John Durie either printed or published on the HP CDs 452
Schloß Ysenburg und Büdingen Records Repositor VI, p. 589, Section 26, 201, 1654-1670, in numbered order as per folder. 454
Original hand written mss, printed works, conference minutes and contemporary copies found in HStA, Marburg. 455
Sixteenth to Eighteenth Century Documents and Works consulted (originals, copies, reprints and microfilms) 458

Dissertations 463

General and specific works related to Durie's life and times 466

Published magazine, journal and review essays dealing with John Durie's life and times 479

Biography of John Durie 489

Biography of George M. Ella 490

Recommendations

'I highly recommend Dr. George Ella's insightful work *The Practical Divinity of Universal Learning*. Dr. Ella sheds new light on the pioneering work of John Durie (1596-1680) in early attempts at universal education and Protestant church unity. Dr. Ella convincingly proves that Durie's contributions to Europe's educational and political reforms in the late 17th and early 18th centuries are immense and often overlooked by modern scholars. Ella also helps the reader understand Durie's profound belief that all knowledge is of God, and as such, Practical Divinity cannot be considered mere theology, but life itself. Durie's use of the phrase "The Public Good" as a synonym for universal education is prophetic for me. After reading Dr. Ella's *The Practical Divinity of Universal Learning* a great deal of good will most assuredly come to the school and church over which I have influence.'

> WADE BURLESON, Chancellor of Emmanuel Christian School and Pastor of Emmanuel Baptist Church, Enid, Oklahoma, USA

'Scottish and English Christians are greatly indebted to George Ella for reviving and greatly expanding their knowledge of the tireless and many-sided work of one of their own Christian scholars, who lived in troubled times and laboured in many parts of Europe as well as in his own country to expand learning and to foster international Protestant understanding.'

> ROGER T. BECKWITH, M.A., B.D., D.D. Former Warden, Latimer House, Oxford.

'George Ella has written a rich and compelling account of a seminal seventeenth-century figure. Scholars of puritanism and its intellectual contexts across the disciplines will be enormously in his debt.'

> Prof. Dr. CRAWFORD GIBBEN, B.A., M.A., Ph.D., F.R. Hist.S., F.T.C.D. Trinity College, Dublin

'In the sixteenth century two great movements shook and woke up the European world: the Renaissance and the Reformation. The first was a movement of the mind, the last a movement of the Spirit. As the century progressed and knowledge, and the thirst for knowledge, increased, there arose a dichotomy between 'education' ('facts and figures') and 'theology' ('the religious realm'), which by the seventeenth-century were rapidly separating into two mutually exclusive, and mutually jealous, spheres. John Durie, above all other men, understood the danger and, realising that the fear of God is the beginning of wisdom, he strove tirelessly to ground *all* knowledge, *all* education, on its true foundation: the Almighty Creator God, and His will and plan as revealed to human minds in the Bible. Durie came to see that right views of our relationship to our Maker, instilled from earliest childhood, offered a foundation for true and uniform education (that could be built on to the highest level and encompass all available knowledge), and also a base for a uniform theology and united Church. Durie was a centuries ahead of his time. His God-given insights should be widely and seriously read today for they are of vital importance to the modern world.'

> Prof. Dr. STEPHEN P. WESTCOTT, M.A.C.S., Ph.D, Litt.D. Reformation International Theological Seminary

'Scotsman John Durie was an international statesman of the highest order during the reign of Charles I and under Cromwell's Protectorate. He served as ambassador to numerous European courts, laboured to create peaceful relations between war-torn European countries and endeavoured to establish union and common purpose amongst Continental Protestant and Reformed churches. For these labours alone Durie ought to be remembered and respected.

But, perhaps his finest achievement and most enduring contribution was in the arena of education. He systemised the nature and purpose of human learning and promoted a view of universal education that recognised the Divine source of all knowledge. He saw how all branches of human learning revealed the truth about God and all His works.

We are deeply indebted to Dr George Ella for reintroducing Durie's accomplishments to a new generation and for restoring to us one of Britain's and Europe's most comprehensive thinkers. In days when the whole purpose and practice of education is rightly being re-examined, John Durie's ideas may be about to prove their enduring usefulness.

> PETER MENEY, Editor of New Focus Magazine, Director of Go Publications

Preface

What awaits the reader of a book on John Durie's pansophism? „Pansophism" – that sounds like an esoteric secret science, like special occult teachings, like „Theosophy" and „Anthroposophy". In fact, the opposite is true. Not an exclusive secret knowledge for the few, but free access to the entire knowledge of mankind for all, regardless of race, social class, age and gender, is what a correctly understood pansophism aspires. It does not look for an exclusive knowledge of God, man or the cosmos, but rather for an integration and connection of all knowledge and its free distribution. Pansophism is not esoteric but exoteric, it is a comprehensive program of education and social reform. In this respect, the pansophical ideal is eminently modern. Many claims pansophical thinkers have raised over three hundred years ago are more relevant today than ever before, and only the technological achievements of our time make it possible to redeem them in full. Rightly so, this book reclaims the pansophical ideal as a model for the present.

At one crucial point, however, the pansophical program is decidedly non-modern, even anti-modern. For the totality of knowledge it seeks to integrate includes religious, theological understanding – and that not as an addition to other stocks of knowledge, but as the beginning and foundation. The core of pansophia must be the knowledge of God and its practical appropriation in life: a "practical divinity", as Durie called it. At this point the pansophical ideal constitutes a challenge, even a provocation for the modern secular thinking. Unlike as in Durie's days, the concept of a pansophism based on a theology of the Covenant of Grace nowadays cannot meet general acceptance in society and scholarship any longer. All the more it can and must serve as a necessary stimulus and skandalon for the secular society, but even more for theology, which is reminded that the knowledge about God must not became worldless, that it must never became a pious end in itself. Christian knowledge of God as the Creator, Preserver, and Redeemer of the world and of man cannot be without a comprehensive knowledge about the world and about man and an affectionate love for both of them.

Nowadays, usually John Amos Comenius is regarded as the main champion of pansophism. In fact, this credit must be attributed to John Durie. The author of this book, Dr. Dr. George Melvyn Ella, has clearly demonstrated his priority. As he could prove, in comparison to Comenius Durie has developed the more original, more comprehensive and more ambitious approach. So it is high time to make Durie step out of the long shadow of the famous Moravian theologian and educator.

Unlike in parts of anglophone scholarship Durie had never been totally forgotten in German church history. Above all he was known as a champion of pan-Protestant unity. As such, I became acquainted with Durie some twenty years ago in my own research on aspirations for Protestant unity in the early modern period without having the opportunity to spend more time on this fascinating personality. So when Dr. Ella approached me with the plan to write a doctoral thesis in divinity on Durie I gladly agreed to supervise his work and his graduation at the University of Marburg. Following Karl Brauer's essay of 1907, Dr. Ella's book is the second thesis on Durie presented to the University of Marburg – the State University of the Landgraviate of Hesse-Kassel which became Durie's most important operational base and his last asylum in Germany.

The book by Dr. Ella is something like the sum of a life's work. Since his student days in Uppsala half a century ago, he has been fascinated by Durie, and you can still feel this fascination in the pages of the present book. Through his varied biography Dr. Ella has acquired in a unique way all those skills which are necessary for a comprehensive assessment of Durie's concern and action. Like Durie, he is British with Scottish roots and has lived in England, Sweden and Germany. Like Durie, he is a polyglot and commands a wide range of antique and modern languages. Like Durie, he has worked as a clergyman, a teacher, a librarian and a writer, and like Durie he is a versatile polymath, a gifted theologian and an educator and irenicist of passion.

Dr. Ella's book cannot and will not be the last word on Durie research. It is intended as a guidance and expedient for further studies. Nevertheless, one can safely call this book a milestone in the history of research on Durie. Dr. Ella has used printed and manuscript sources from more than 60 libraries and archives, especially in Germany, Britain and Sweden. He has spotted and perused nearly 220 books and about 500 letters from Durie's pen and analyzed about 50 books and about 200 letters in detail. Thus, his work is based on a much larger amount of sources than any previous study of Durie.

In this way, Dr. Ella has greatly expanded the research material available for reconstructing the biography and thinking of Durie. Because of his knowledge of the sources he has been able to rectify a multitude of errors and misjudgments circulated in earlier publications. Most spectacular to me is his reassessment of the relationship between Durie and Comenius.

The most substantial achievement of this book, however, lies in the fact that Dr. Ella has presented for the first time a consistent, comprehensive interpretation of Durie's work in toto. Durie's amazing versatility and activity compelled all previous publications to single out only a few aspects of his work, mostly his irenicism or his contributions to education, but also his contributions to librarianship or his attitude toward Judaism. Actually, in all this Durie was conducted by one parent interest: the establishment of a universal, pansophic education on a Christian foundation. To have discovered this Archimedean point in Durie's will and action is the great merit of the present book. Any future research on Durie will have to deal with this thesis.

I wish the book a lot of interested readers, and many dedicated followers who will help to make the fascinating personality of John Durie so well known again as he deserves.

Marburg, on Ascension Day 2012
Prof. Dr. Wolf-Friedrich Schäufele

Acknowledgements

Over the past few years, whilst searching for John Durie's works and books and articles dealing with him, I have had the privilege of visiting, e-mailing and telephoning some seventy of Europe's archives and libraries both ancient and modern, most of which have provided me with very useful material. Space restrictions for a Dr. theol. thesis forbids an exhaustive individual analysis of the exact sources of all the works used but I would like especially to thank the staff of the following archives and libraries for providing me with copies of primary and secondary works in printed, digital and microfilm form:

- Augsburg UB
- Bayerische Staatsbibliothek München
- Berlin SU, Preußicher Kulturbesitz
- Berlin ZB and SB
- Bibliothek des Priesterseminars Trier
- Bibliothek für Bildungsgeschichtliche Forschung, Berlin
- Bielefeld UB
- Bochum UB
- Bodleian Library, Oxford
- Bonn UB and LB
- British Library, London
- Carnegie Library of Pittsburgh
- Carolina Rediviva Uppsala
- Codrington Library, All Souls College, Oxford
- Cologne UB and SB
- Diözesanbibliothek Cologne
- Domkapitlensarkiv Uppsala
- Dresden SB and UB
- Duisburg-Essen UB
- Duke Humphrey Library, Oxford
- Düsseldorf UB and LB
- Erfurt/Gotha UB and FB
- Essen UB
- Freiburg UB
- Friedrich-Alexander Universität, Erlangen-Nürnberg UB

- Harvester Press Microfilm Publications
- Heidelberg UB
- Herzog-August-Bibliothek Wolfenbüttel
- Hessisches Staatsarchiv Darmstadt
- Hessisches Staatsarchiv Marburg
- Hessisches Staatsarchiv Wiesbaden
- Kaiserslautern UB
- Koblenz LB
- Kommunarkiv i Stockholmslän
- Kungligabibliotek Stockholm
- Landsarkiv Uppsala
- Landesbibliothekzentrum Rheinland-Pfalz, Pfälzische Landesbibliothek
- Landeskirchliches Arkiv, Cassel
- Linköping and Vesterås Church Archives
- Marburg UB
- Media Haus, Mülheim
- Münster UB
- Museum für Stadtgeschichte Dessau
- Nederlands Archief voor Kerkgeschedenis
- Niedersächsische Staats und Universitätsbibliothek, Göttingen
- Radcliffe Science Library, Special Collections, Oxford.
- Riksarkiv Stockholm
- Rostock UB
- Saarbrücken UB
- Sächsische LB, Dresden
- Siegen UB
- Staatsbibliothek zu Berlin Preussischer Kulturbesitz
- Stadtarchiv Düsseldorf
- Stadtarchiv Hildesheim
- Stadtarchiv Marburg
- Strängnäs Domkapitelsarkiv
- Trier UBÅ
- Tübingen UB
- University Archive Sheffield
- Uppsala Domkapitelsarkiv
- Wolfgang Ernst Fürst zu Ysenburg und Büdingen (Private castle archive)

Acknowledgements

- Worms SB
- Wuppertal UB und SB
- Xerox University Microfilms, Ann Arbor, Michigan
- Zürich UB

Several hundred of the books, photo-copies and microfilms consulted have been in my own private library for over forty-five years and were procured from international sources now removed from my memory.

I am especially indebted to Frau Eilers, Herr Kirscheck, Herr Jordan and Frau Tscheschlok at the Medien Centrum in Mülheim for their weekly help in tracing works for me through the Inter-Library Loans Department and also Frau Keusemann and Herr Meiselbach of Duisburg University Library for their sheer endless assistance. So, too, without the help of Archive Director Dr. Fritz Wolff, Prof. Dr. G. Menk, Frau List and Frau Ried of the Hessische Staatssarchiv, Marburg, I would not have located some hundreds of printed and handwritten works by Durie and works appertaining to Durie. Pam Wood and Joe Maldonado of the British Library have been very helpful in my search concerning the Sloane mss, Benzelius and other earlier works by or on Durie. The staff of the Bodleian Library, Oxford has been of great assistance in guiding me through their vast collections of Durie works. Here, I would like to thank especially Mrs Rebecca Wall and Mr Oliver House for their patient guidance through OSIS, SOLIS and the Rawlings catalogues. I must also thank the staff of the Carolina Rediviva in Uppsala, where I took courses in Library management and archiving in the sixties, for providing me with the first glimpse of handwritten essays and letters by Durie and letters written by Gustav II Adolf, Queen Christina, Axel Oxenstierna, Johannes Matthiae, Johann Rudbeck, Paulinus Gothus, Sir James Spens and other friends and relations of Durie in Sweden. In this connection, I would like also to thank Archbishop Anders Wejrud, with whom I studied theology at Uppsala in the sixties, and his secretary Karin Åstrand for putting me in touch with people 'in the know' regarding Durie's Swedish sojourn. I am also most grateful to Wolfgang Ernst Fürst zu Ysenburg und Büdingen and his archivist Dr. Decker for allowing me to peruse through the Ysenburg family's private records. It is impossible to attempt any thorough research of Durie without consulting the Hartlib Papers and I would like to thank especially Jamie McLaughlin of the interdisciplinary Humanities Research Institute at Sheffield University for coaching me through the procedure of accessing them.

Shelf and stack marks will be given in the Bibliography for the Durie mss I have copied or had digitalised. Downloaded works will be given their full sources. Where I have used printed sources, I have altered nothing. However, as most of the Hartlib mss were edited by Hartlib and others, mostly with a view to publication, I have kept to the edited versions as with crossings out, corrections and omissions many transcriptions and mss do not facilitate useful reading. I have identified my main sources with HP for the Hartlib Papers; Bod L for the Bodleian Library; BL for the British Library; HStA for the Hessische Staatsarchiv, Marburg; and HAB for the Herzog August Bibliothek. The names of other archives and libraries are used in full.

I am also particularly grateful to my Marburg mentors Prof. Dr. Wolf-Friedrich Schäufele and Prof. Dr. Hans Schneider as also my friends Adrian Bradshaw, Prof. Dr. Stephen Westcott and Prof. Dr. Crawford Gribben for ridding my manuscript of many spelling and punctuation mistakes before it was ready for printing.

This book, now presented to a wide readership by the Martin Bucer Seminar, Bonn, started life as a Dr. Theol. thesis at the University of Marburg (Fachbereich Evangelische Theologie) in May, 2012. Prof. Dr. Wolf-Friedrich Schäufele, my 'Doktor Vater' and Supervisor has kindly provided the published work with a Preface.

CHAPTER ONE

John Durie and My Task

Rediscovering John Durie's importance

Most computer users have experienced hard disks full of jumbled, fragmented files which block spaces causing memory and retrieval problems. What a relief it is to switch on a defragmenter and have everything made ship-shape again. The Reformation in mid-seventeenth century Britain had reached such a fragmentation and a defragmenter was called for. The man for the job was certainly John Durie (1599-1680) who was possibly the most well-known personality in Europe at the time. Indeed, William Shaw, in his detailed two-volume *History of the English Church During the Civil Wars 1640-1660* speaks of Durie's 'ubiquitous original activity'[1] in campaigning for peace and union not only amongst England's Parliamentarians and Churchmen but throughout Europe. Pioneer Durie scholar, H. Tollin, claims that it would take a life-time to adequately evaluate Durie's Europe-wide activities.[2] The result of these activities was that countless crowned heads, universities, statesmen, church leaders, politicians, generals, educators, social reformers and humble men and women grew to love and respect Durie. Original letters are extant from English and Continental universities, Parliaments, Courts, Church Synods and International Disputations and Conferences proclaiming that Durie was acting as their representative. Indeed, in spite of the fact that Durie had worked closely with Archbishops Abbott, Laud, Ussher and Spottiswoode and had served under Charles I, Cromwell recognised his great value as an international diplomat and even identified himself for some fifteen years fully with Durie's aims for political and religious unity in Protestant Europe. He thus fitted Durie out with credentials making him England's Ambassador-At-Large in Europe. Thus we find Schröder's *Klassiker des Protestantismus* describing Cromwell as 'a fighter for freedom of conscience and promoter of a pan-Protestant thinking, which favoured John Durie's unionist poli-

---

[1] *A History of the English Church During the Civil Wars and Under the Commonwealth 1640-1660*, vol. 2, p 171.
[2] Johannes Duraeus, *Geschichtsblätter für Stadt und Land Magdeburg*, Band 32, 1897, p. 228.

cies.'³ No one else in this comprehensive work is placed so close to Cromwell. Indeed, though Cromwell is famed for his international diplomacy, without Durie's support and guidance, Cromwell would never have been taken so seriously in Europe. It was Durie who made Cromwell's political and religious aims in Europe palatable. Thus Roland G. Asch, the Thirty Years War expert, explains in his essay *Die Englische Republik und die Friedensordnung von Münster und Osnabrück* how Durie had published a pamphlet warning the German Protestants that the Peace of Westphalia of 1648 had left them at the mercy of Jesuit atrocities. Asch goes on to say:

> 'Dies waren nicht einfach unverbindliche Äußerungen eines Theologen ohne politischen Einfluß. Dury kann durchaus als einer der Vordenker der konfessionellen Außenpolitik Cromwells während des Protektorats gelten und bemühte sich mit Unterstützung des Protektors um eine Vereinigung aller protestantischen Kirchen unter englischer Führung'⁴

Durie's sixty years' involvement in Continental Europe

One of Durie's early major supporters was the mighty Gustav II Adolf of Sweden who conquered vast territories in the name of Protestant religion. Gustav never made much of the *Augsburg Confession*, though he ordered that theological students at Uppsala should be familiar with it. He had certainly no time for the *Formula Concordiae* that the Wittenberg Gnesio-Lutherans and those Swedes educated in Upper Saxony were striving to persuade Sweden to adopt. He preferred to reject the Romanising tendencies of his predecessors John III and Sigismund and rather carry on the policies of tolerance fostered by the then Duke Charles who was Regent between the reigns of John and Sigismund but became Charles IX in 1604. Though basically Reformed, Charles refused to call himself a Calvinist, claiming that he followed no man but the Bible. However, during Charles IX's reign, matters evolved that were to make John Durie's task in the future most difficult. In an effort to persuade the Swedish Lutherans to tolerate those of the Reformed faith, Charles called Scots Presbyterian, John Forbes to Sweden during 1608 to 1610, to discuss his theology with the Uppsala church leaders. Forbes, however, shocked the Swedish clergy by

---

[3] Band 5, *Der Protestantismus des 17. Jahrhunderts* (ed) Wilfried Zeller, Bremen, 1962, S. 419.
[4] Die Englische Republik etc., p. 433. For a brief overview of the opening years of the Thirty-Years War see my How the Thirty-Years War Started, *New Focus*, April/May, 2010, vii. 14, No. 06, pp. 15-19.

depicting God as the author of sin. The Swedish ministers quickly gained the impression that Forbes viewed salvation and reprobation as mere actions of God irrespective of the responsibility of man and Christ's redeeming work. Election, they argued, could only be understood within the atoning work of Christ and not independent of it. This was the view of Bullinger in his advice to John Calvin who, he felt, emphasised predestination outside of the realms of Christ's substitutionary and vicarious work. Forbes declared that he had been misunderstood and that the minutes of the meeting, preserved in the Stockholm archives with Forbes' annotations, gave a false picture of his views. However, when directly questioned on the issue, Forbes affirmed that he believed God did not merely permit the sin of Adam but fore-ordained it. Again, this was the interpretation of his hearers. Charles IX was greatly disappointed as he had hoped that Forbes would have broken a lance for inter-Protestant pacification. Forbes' visits thus left the Swedish clergy thinking that all Reformed Christians were compelled to believe as Forbes[5] and repeatedly accused Durie of believing the same. When Durie denied this, Hyper-Calvinists accused him of being an Arminian.[6]

When Gustav II Adolf became King in 1611, the Lutherans pressed him to accept the *Book of Concord* and exile all those of non-Lutheran faiths. Gustav refused point blank, claiming 'no sovereign has power to direct or coerce a man's conscience.'[7] As the bishops asked for more power, Gustav called a *Consistorium Generale* which was to include bishops, university theologians, ordinary ministers and laymen to rule the Church.[8] In this project, Johannes Matthiae, friend and correspondent of John Durie, became Gustav's right-hand man.[9] This planned synod never really materialised as neither the politicians nor the clergy could agree to what the responsibilities of the state were and what were those of the Church. Few were prepared to allow them to overlap.

---

[5] See Norlin, Andra Kapitlet, Karl IX och Svenska Kyrkan.
[6] See Norlin's account of Forbes' Swedish debates in his *Svenska Kyrkans Historia, Förste Bandets Andra Afdelning*. Durie corresponded with several members of the Forbes family, including John.
[7] Taken from *Johannes Matthiae and the Development of the Church of Sweden During the First Half of the Seventeenth Century*, p. 291 and footnote. See Bibliography.
[8] See Holmquist, especially 'Frågan om consistorium generale', p. 221 ff..
[9] Neither King Gustav nor Queen Christina, who shared his views, were permanently successful in establishing this body because of the independence of the local churches.

Sadly for Britain, the Swedes made it plain to the Protestant Stuarts that there was only room for one Protestant super-power in Europe and that was Sweden. So Sweden was always suspicious of James and Charles, not only because of their brand of Protestantism, but also because they were related to most of the Protestant crowned heads of Europe, and Gustav, who had taken control of almost all of them, did not want a rival whether popish or Protestant. He thus frowned on the, at times, quite substantial support for the Protestant cause that James and Charles gave to their Continental allies. He bargained that he would accept Charles' troops and money but not his interference. Axel Oxenstierna, who looked upon himself as Gustav's successor in Europe, continued Gustav's policies but after the Frankfurt Diet of 1634 in which Durie took part, the German Protestant Princes and Churches demanded more freedom and began to take the idea of cooperation with Charles, and even unity with the English Church, seriously.

When Cromwell came to power, Charles' Continental allies turned from 'the Protector', but with the help of Durie's many diplomatic visits to the Continental royal families, and Cromwell's openness to the idea of union in religion, science, politics and education, confidence was restored somewhat in British intentions and, once again the Protestant Continentals looked to Britain for more leadership. However, when Cromwell started bargaining with Spain and France, confidence in him again waned.

When Cromwell's Britain and Christina's Sweden were engaged in concrete discussions concerning political and ecclesiastical union, the Swedish Queen, her nobility, leading churchmen and statesmen, including her tutor, Bishop Johannes Matthiae, Prof. Ravius of Uppsala University and school reformers such as the Skyttes, all stressed that they wished for Britain to be represented first and foremost by Durie. Indeed, all Europe, with admittedly a few dissenting voices amongst Presbyterians in Britain and German Gnesio-Lutherans in Saxony,[10] felt that if anyone could knit together again what denominationalism, legalism, rationalism, political strife, opportunism and personal ambition had rent asunder, Durie was that man. Furthermore, when Charles was executed and many of the Continental heads of state and governments broke with England on that account, relations bettered largely due to Durie's frequent diplomatic tours of the Continent. However, some Gnesio-Lutherans and even Protestant Dutch

---

[10] After Luther's death, the Wittenberg Reformation split into two groups, the Gnesio-Lutherans or Flacians who were considered too rigidly orthodox by the Philippians, named after Philip Melanchthon. Actually both sides departed from Luther's doctrine of justification by faith in their belief that God did not make just but merely reckoned Christians as just.

Royalists, called Durie a King-Killer until his dying day, and even plotted to kill him, not realising that he had been one of Charles' staunchest defenders.

Happily, Durie was a brilliant linguist which made his arduous Continental journeys through war-torn Europe somewhat easier. Numerous original letters from Durie's pen in Latin, English, German, Dutch and French with also passages now and then in Greek or Hebrew are extant in Europe's archives. There is seldom a word crossed out or altered.[11] The German, English and Dutch reflect the chaotic spelling of the age but Durie's French and Latin letters are classical in their spelling, language and syntax. Contemporary witnesses remarked how Durie was so proficient in languages that he was taken as a native of England, Germany, Holland and France respectively. Because of his endeavours to have the Bible printed in Lithuanian, influential British authors even claimed that Durie was a Lithuanian![12] To encourage the harmless but very useful deceit that Durie was a native of whatever country he entered, he always adopted the clothing, languages, hair styles and beard forms of the areas he visited and altered his name to suit local usage. Thus John became Jon, Jhon, Jean, Jan, Johann or Johannes according to his country of sojourn and he used many variants of his surname, such as Dury, Durey, Duré, Durye, Dureus, Duraeus, Duräus or even, in the Netherlands, Du Reus.

James Reid's statement in his excellent *Memoirs of the Westminster Divines*, concerning Durie as: 'A Scotchman, and learned Divine, who was eminently distinguished by his indefatigable industry to promote union among Christians, and a member of the Assembly of Divines at Westminster', true as it is, it is quite an understatement concerning Durie's vast international outreach and pansophical learning. Up to recent times, however, when John Durie's former fame was mentioned in Anglo-Saxon theological, educational and general academic circles, the question was invariably asked, 'Who is John Durie?' It appears that the English-speaking world into which Durie was born had forgotten yet another of her greatest Christian heroes. On the Continent, interest in Durie had never died out. Nowadays, scholars worldwide are revaluating Durie's contribution to ecclesiology and learning and, in recent years, Durie appears to be finding general, world-wide appreciation at last.

---

[11] This does not go for Samuel Hartlib's editing of Durie's letters which was carried out with numerous alterations.

[12] Benjamin Brook, *The Lives of the Puritans*, vol. 3, p. 373.

A prophet not honoured in his own country

The probable reasons for this century-long neglect of a humble man who influenced the mighty reveal the little effort western churchmen and politicians have made towards national and international peace in subsequent ages. As Christ said, a prophet is not honoured in his own country, though this 'prophet' was truly an ambassador for Christ with a most godly message. Durie's energies and capabilities were, indeed, almost unbelievable and would appear to belong to the make-believe. One of Durie's earliest commentators, Carl Wilhelm Hering, in his 1838 work *Geschichte der kirchlichen Unionsversuche seit der Reformation bis auf unsere Zeit*, states with some humour:

> 'Duraeus ermüdete nicht, aber meine Leser würden ermüden, wenn alle die Reisen, die er unternahm, die Gespräche, die er führte, die leeren Versprechungen, die er erhielt, die Aussichten, welche als scheinbar günstig sich eröffneten und immer wieder trübten, hier geschildert werden sollten.'[13]

Happily, Durie's own accounts of his industrious endeavours are usually bright with optimism and not as pessimistic as Hering's. Mistaken Durie may have been at times, but tiring never. Even Durie's less tolerant contemporaries, who sneered in unbelief at his alleged activities, usually changed their tune on meeting him. His influence on people of all ranks was almost hypnotic and he could make friends of his fiercest, though honest, opponents within the duration of a single hour's conversation. This has caused Durie scholars such as Professor Gunnar Westin of Uppsala University to argue that Durie used his great charm and diplomatic skills unfairly in convincing his contemporaries to follow him. However, in his day, Durie's wit, intellect, general knowledge, diplomatic acumen and fervent faith made him a man to be admired. He was not only eagerly read by theologians, public servants and educationalists but also men of science such as Boyle, Oldenburg, Pell, Haak, Jablonski and Leibniz. Where, today, we must ask, is a modern man of God who is world-renowned as a great preacher, pastor, diplomat, educator, scientist, linguist, translator, man of letters, ambassador, library reformer, mediator and politician? Who today produces bestsellers at a breathtaking speed in the midst of many toils and travels? Who else addressed Parliament one day, spoke to a humble gathering of pilgrims bound for the New World the next, founded think-tanks and knowledge pools all over Europe, helped establish famous libraries such as

---

[13] *Geschichte der kirchlichen Unionsversuche*, Band II, pp. 124-125.

St. James' and Wolfenbüttel, wrote library manuals, text books, school curricula and campaigned for a reintroduction of the Jews to Britain, from whence they had been banned for generations, but also researched the possibilities of a national re-settlement for them in the Near East or the New World? Durie tutored the royal children, managed the Royal Library, kept the Commonwealth and Westminster Assembly records, reformed poor schools and rich men's universities, preached before Parliament and served as one of Parliament's official translators, sat on an endless number of governmental committees and sub-committees, consulted with Archbishops, Dukes and Generals and was often found at the Courts of great Continental Kings, only to leave them to take part in humble communal activities or sit at local synods. Durie, with the assistance of Samuel Hartlib (1600-1662) and some forty leading ministers, educators, scientists, men of letters and politicians was instrumental in setting up government departments for the classifying, pooling and distributing of world-wide knowledge. The Royal Society is said to have developed from the work of the so-called 'Invisible Societies' which were loosely formed around Durie and his circle. The above long list provides only a selection of Durie's Europe-wide activities. In all these fields, John Durie has been called 'great' or 'the greatest', yet it is indeed, almost beyond human imagination that such a man could have existed with such an encyclopaedic wisdom who was so diligent in absorbing and purposefully uniting all the knowledge of the world.

Pansophists, irenists and unionists such as, Böhme, Comenius, Fuhrmann and Kepler have received far more acclamation in scholarly works than Durie but, at best, they may be praised because 'they also ran' in their efforts to reach the same goal. Durie was clearly their master in the comprehensiveness of his field of learning and especially in Comenius' case, a mentor in the consolidation and peaceful use of universal knowledge and practical divinity. Minton Batten adds to the above list of irenists of Durie's day, Richard Baxter, George Calixtus, John Davenant, John Forbes, William Forbes, Hugh Grotius, Johannes Matthiae, Gerhard Molanus, John Owen, David Pareus and Edward Stillingfleet, but explains how Durie's work was so much broader and deeper in scope.[14] We could also add Cornelius Burges, Daniel Featley, Thomas Goodwin, William Gouge, Joseph Hall, Samuel Hartlib, Joachim Hübner, Philip Nye, Richard Sibbs, Sidrach Simpson, John Stoughton, William Twisse, Henry Oldenburg and James Ussher, to mention but some of those known to the English

---

[14] Batten's 1930 doctoral dissertation, *John Dury – Advocate of Christian Reunion*, p. 9.

speaking public of the day and who looked to Durie for leadership.[15] Hartlib, Nye and Oldenburg served as Durie's envoys in Britain, exchanging letters and literature with Durie and passing on donations from Durie's home friends. Most of these men remained faithful to Durie's cause throughout their lives and formed what Tom Webster of Edinburgh University in his *Godly Clergy in Early Stuart England* calls Durie's 'steering committee'.[16] The names of even more numerous Continental irenists, unionists and pansophists in Durie's campaign for universal knowledge and a pan-European Protestant pacification, concord and revival will appear throughout this work.

Perhaps the main reason why the English-speaking world, whom Durie served so long and well, has forgotten him is that Durie's work has had the least success in Great Britain and the United States where the situation is now radically different from Durie's day. The Church of England is no longer accepted as 'The Reformed Church of England', embracing all God-fearers and those who believed her Articles. She has been divided into several 'denominations' including the Church of England Continuing, the Free Church of England and the Evangelical Connexion and is no longer *the* Church in England. In the USA, the situation amongst the Episcopalians appears to be the same. The Presbyterians and Free Churches are also experiencing a decline and instead of pulling together, they are splitting up into numerous separate denominations. As William Cowper repeatedly said, the churches' worst enemies appear to be themselves.[17]

So, too, in Britain as in the rest of the so-called Christian world, the high educational aims of Durie are far from being realised and a State as a Christian community which fosters and finances education for all from the cradle to the grave by first educating church leaders, ministers, parents, educators, statesmen, employers and the ruling parties might be considered by some reformers more a Utopia now than in Durie's day in spite of Wikipedia and on-line know-how. Wisdom is still a matter of encyclopaedic and dictionary learning and not the universal synergism which Durie called 'Practical Divinity', although this situation, this writer believes, is rapidly changing for the better.

Trevor-Roper, speaking of the great deeds of Durie and his colleagues in his *Crisis of the Seventeenth Century* says 'the need produced the men'. It obviously did in the seventeenth century, but does it today? That need is

---

[15] See Webster, Part IV for names of lesser known men.
[16] Webster, p. 257.
[17] See my Dr, phil. thesis *Paradise and Poetry: An In-Depth Study of William Cowper's Poetic Mind*, p.174 ff.

greater than ever, but where are the men and women of Durie's calibre? Unlike today, in the seventeenth century, Durie's idea of a pan-European church and political union based on a consolidation of international Protestant thought in doctrine, natural and political sciences, education, culture and the arts was supported by the majority of Reformers and Puritans except for a few most ingrained intellectual rebels of his age such as the zealous pamphleteer, William Prynne, who appeared to be Durie's sole enemy at the Westminster Assembly. Nor was the idea new then, as the sixteenth century Reformers had held similar views. Indeed, Francis Bacon (1561-1626), who influenced Durie so much, carried the idea of universal learning from the sixteenth into the seventeenth century. The spiritual and intellectual movement of 1630-1680 in which Durie played a major role, was, however, also an inner reaction to the warring political and religious revolutions which were severely disrupting English and European society and national traditions.[18] As a result, an international hope arose amongst Protestants that a revival of religion and world-wide peaceful cooperation in religion, politics, science and education would arise out of the ashes of a ruined Europe and the knowledge of the Lord would cover the earth as the waters cover the sea.[19] Thus, when Durie wrote to Hartlib on 30 November, 1638 referring to an author's doubts concerning obtaining consensus between Christian minds, he said:

> 'The Chief matter then which your author doubteth of is this; that he telleth yow plainly, that hee neuer despaired half so much of the spontaneous motion of inanimate matter as of the conspiring agreement & unanimous nest of exasperated & disagreeing men: this I confesse I doe not so much despaire off as hee doth: for I know & haue found by experience, that the mindes of men although exasperated are more capable of agreeing thoughts then thinges inanimate of a freewilling inclination to moue. in these God hath not putte any principle of spontaneitie to action, but in those there is a facultie or principle which may bee brought <from potentia> to act, when it is fitly wrought upon & stirred up <by> meanes which God hath appointed. then also yowr author ought not to despaire twise so much of this, as of that, because the scripture hath promised unto us that this shall bee at last brought to

---

[18] It is often thought that the Thirty Years War was solely a Continental disaster where Protestants and Roman Catholics were in battle. In England, there was a very similar battle going on which, for many years, was equally bloody. In England, it was between the Church of the Reformation and the Monarchy on the one side and the usurping Presbyterian and Republican ideologies on the other. The world of England and the Continent became changed for ever.

[19] Isaiah 11:9.

passe in the Church of God & foretelleth us also of the meanes by which it shall bee accomplished: Esa. 11. 8, 9. wee there are told that the greatest enimitie & exasperation that is in nature shall bee taken away from amongst the creatures; & that there shall bee no hurting nor destroying any more in all the holy mountaine of God; because the earth shall bee full of the knowledge of the Lord as the waters couering the bottome of the sea. here the exasperat spirits of men are reconciled; & the meanes wherby God will bring this to passe is said to bee the abundance of his knowledge & the euidence of his will reuealed unto all those that shall bee in his Church.'[20]

Indeed, this view was common amongst the Puritans of Durie's age who spoke of making Britain a New Jerusalem which would prepare the world for that eschatological restoration of Eden called by many church historians The Puritan Hope.[21]

Foremost in his endeavours to have this hope realised in his time was John Durie, the non-party man.[22] Today, we have indeed the skeleton of a united Europe which Durie desired, but much progress must still be made before it is adorned with the spirit and cooperation with which Durie sought to enliven it. However, modern developments, which will be described throughout this thesis, make room for optimism.

Another major obstacle to Durie scholarship is that multi-linguist authors of Durie's calibre were few and far between even in his day and appear even less common nowadays. Although John Milton, for instance, was Parliament's Secretary for Foreign Languages, he was unable to write French like a native Frenchman and so John Durie was commissioned by Parliament to put Milton into French. Durie, like Cotton Mather in Massachusetts, with whom he had much in common and who praised Durie's work, wrote his books and pamphlets in some five different languages and Durie had his published simultaneously in several countries. To quote but one work among many, Durie's *Capitum de Pace religiosa* appeared in various forms and languages and was published almost simultaneously in London, Amsterdam, Stockholm, Berlin, Cassel, Frankfurt on the Oder, Bremen and several cities in Eastern Europe. The lack of sufficient linguistic accomplishments amongst Durie's author-colleagues in England caused Durie, supported by German and Dutch thinkers, to canvas throughout Britain for translators who would put English and Scottish works into the languages of the Continent. Amongst those forty or so who committed themselves were William Twisse, himself of German extraction, Samuel

---

[20] Ref: 2/6/12A-15B and passim, HP.
[21] See Iain Murray's excellent Banner of Truth book under the same title.
[22] Passim in Durie's works is the expressed desire to be 'a man without partialitie'.

Hartlib who was half Polish, the German Henry Oldenburg (Durie's Secretary and son-in-law who became the Secretary of the Royal Society), John Cotton, Henry Burton, Samuel Ward, Richard Sibbes, both Henry and Philip Nye, Jeremy Burroughs and Daniel Featley. A number of Durie's 'Committee of Foreign Language Speakers' like Philip Nye had picked up German, French or Dutch whilst living in exile on the Continent. These men began to collect material for a Body of Practical Divinity, in answer to a request from members of the 1631 Diet of Leipzig and 1634 Diet of Hanau, which could be translated into the Continental languages. The 'steering committee' as it has been dubbed by writers, asked Archbishop Ussher of Armagh to oversee the project. It almost failed to materialise as the 'steering committee' protested that the English theological language was so rich in vocabulary and eloquence that it just could not be translated easily. They also argued that English theologians had developed such a specialised theological language that there were no counterparts in other tongues. Of course, the Civil War years put a stop to many theological and educational reforms.

In conjunction with researching the work of this committee, it has become clear to this author that the work of many of Britain's major Puritans, whether Church of England, Presbyterian, Independent or Baptist, must be reassessed with a view to the strong influence John Durie had on them. Many of their long acclaimed works, over a period of almost fifty years, were written at the instigation of Durie or were translated into other tongues by Hartlib and Durie themselves and by other members of their circle. Future students of Durie will thus find his work an inspiring background to a very large amount of Puritan literature.

It has been mentioned how Durie was able to catch the attention of men from all walks of life and abilities. This, too, proved a problem for Durie. Amongst his supporters were high ranking Church of England men such as Abbott, Bedell, Davenant, Featley, Hall, Laud and Ussher, but also ministers such as Twisse and Burgess who had opted for Nonconformity and separation. Indeed, one might say that the bulk of Durie's followers such as Owen, Nye and Goodwin were of broadly-speaking Independent principles and others such as Milton had no denominational anchor at all. It is nigh on astonishing to find that Durie won the interest of most of the crowned heads of Europe, including Charles I, but he also gained a maximum of support and finance from Oliver Cromwell and the Republican Swiss. This meant that as long as these men and countries were directly approached by Durie, he could count on their support, but once Durie travelled further afield, which was very often, those left behind could rarely work with one another. They could not put into practice what, theoretically, found their joint approval. So, too, Durie's winning way of gaining friends caused great jealousy during his diplomatic service. Lutherans and Reformed alike became rivals in seeking his services. If he visited or wrote to one side before the other, cries of protest from the 'neglected' side would ensue. This was particularly the case in Switzerland where several cantons argued about whom Durie should visit first and who should chair the pan-Swiss meetings with him.

The refragmentation of a defragmenter's work

Sadly the very opposite approach has been followed in Durie research over the centuries to that actually pioneered by Durie himself. Though he sought to defragment and unite all strands of knowledge in his work as a Christian scholar and statesman, resulting studies based on his work have, to a large extent, been grounded in a fragmentation of Durie's own endeavours, which he believed were so necessary to the single cause of God and truth and the well-being of mankind. Either such writers have rejected any necessity in developing an overall concept of knowledge, or their own area of interest and studies was much less and that alone occupied their thoughts. So we find the earliest pioneers in Durie research, such as Tollin, bemoaning this lack of comprehensiveness in nineteenth century Durie research, but they would have also bemoaned this fact in the present century. Tollin, indeed, believed that so vast were Durie's accomplishments that writers, with all their energies, on dealing with the enormous scope of Durie's work could merely provide yet another 'Anregung' or stimulus to learn more about Durie. They could only point to one of the paths Durie took but not lead their readers on to explore all Durie's venues.

Perhaps, too, the fact that Durie's major aim in his Pansophism was to witness the fulfilment of Isaiah 11:9[23] is thought too naive or too impractical in our modern age. This, however, was the central pivot of all Durie's teaching of God's sure and certain Covenant with Christ on behalf of man. Speaking of the frustration and exasperation shown by those who sought for true knowledge in a world at enmity with God, and have given up the search, Durie declares that we should with patience and endurance keep up the quest until we find the knowledge of God the Revealer of all knowl-

---

[23] 'For the earth shall be full of the knowledge of the Lord, as the waters cover the sea.' Durie outlines his doctrine concerning the spreading of the knowledge of the Lord in his *A further discovery of the Office of Address* and *Some Proposals towards the Advancement of Learning*.

edge. Thus Durie continues his letter of November 30 1638 by writing that Isaiah 11:

> 'is one of the princpall conditions & promises which God bindeth himself to performe in the new Couenant Ier. 31. 34. why then should men so deeply despaire of such a matter which God so solemnely doth promise in his owne tyme to bring to passe? if wee looke upon the 76. psalme where the power of Gods name as it is knowne in his Church is sette forth: wee shall see that the chief effect of his glorious presence there: is to breake the instruments of warre; [v. 3, 4, 5, 6.] to daunt the stout hearted & cast them into a deep sleep: to cause [v. 8, 9, 10.] iudgment to bee heard from heauen for the saluation of the meeke of the earth; & to make the wrath of man to praise him & to restraine the remainder of wrath.'[24]

Yet those who have shared this aim in one way or another, or for one reason or another, such as Alcuin, the English and Continental Reformers, Moore, Hobbes, Bacon, Rutherford, Cromwell, Calixtus' Helmstedt and Alsted's Herborn *Johannea*, Comenius, Locke, Leibniz and Lessing have certainly helped in an enormous way to reform and mould society. Alsted's Reformed Herborn Hohe Schule alone, so familiar to Durie's circle, though thought unfit by the Emperor to grant degrees because of its Reformed status, drew scholars from England, Scotland, Scandinavia, the present day Czech Republic and Hungary and influenced the development of Western thinking in politics, theology and education to a high degree as Prof. Dr. Gerhard Menk has clearly documented in his numerous essays and books on the subject written whilst Archivoberrat at the Hesse State Archives. Reformed Academies formed on the Herborn proto-type were founded in Steinfurt, Danzig, Bremen, Zürich and Bern.[25] Several Herborn scholars such as Bisterfeld and Comenius were members of the Durie circle. Much of Durie's thinking, though generally not attributed to him today, has certainly had lasting results in ecclesiology, the Ecumenical Movement, international diplomacy, education and science. What has been neglected the most up to recent times is Durie's major interest in pooling and coordinating all knowledge and striving to establish a 'Practical Divinity' which would bring unity not only back to God's divided Reformation but a world divided by goal-less and uncoordinated education.

Thus, though a pioneer in European pacification of churches and states, Durie's strivings were but a peaceful means to a more practical end for

---

[24] Letter written to Hartlib 30 Nov. 1638, 2/6/12A-15B, HP.
[25] See Menk's 'Die Hohe Schule Herborn, der Deutsche Kalvinismus und die Westliche Welt.'

Durie and but a fraction of the work he undertook to do. Indeed, major and definite works on the full, comprehensive scope of Durie's work have still to be written. Just released whilst this present thesis was being made ready for presentation (2011), was Pierre-Oliver Léchot's sturdy work on Durie's comprehensive contribution to modern thought in his *Un christianisme 'sans partialité'*, which is worthy of close study. However, as Léchot's subtitle, *Irénisme et méthode chez John Dury* indicates, it is Durie's irenic activities which occupy Léchot's thoughts the most, though he scrutinises other areas of Durie's work. Thus Léchot's thesis is a good step in the right direction. Otherwise, it appears that research into Durie's main projects of pansophy, universal learning and practical divinity has been at a century long standstill. This is a blow against *Academia*, as the modern world is more able to realise and practise Durie's ideas of universal learning than ever before.

Living in an ideal time for Durie scholarship

Indeed, the present decade with its international inter-library loans system, state, city and community archives open to the general public, online catalogues, Wikipedia and free downloads provides an enormous potential in assisting the modern Durie researcher. There are now immense, freely-available resources waiting to be used in the libraries and archives of Europe alone. Recent visits to the State Archives of Hesse (Hessia) in Marburg, have revealed a huge parcel of loose, uncatalogued Durie mss in English, Latin, French, German and Dutch, including letters sent to Germany on behalf of Durie by the British universities and many multilingual, uncut printer's proofs of Durie's works, a number of which have not been referred to in Durie scholarship hitherto. Many are signed in Durie's hand and some have his hand-written notes in the margins. These were shelfmarked years ago as a labour of love by Professor Gerhard Menk, whose strong interest in Durie's life and works and Alsted's Pansophic centre at Herborn has continued for many decades to the present day. So, too, I have found important primary and secondary literature by and about Durie in many other German archives. During several visits to the Bodleian Library Oxford during 2010-2011, I found an enormous number of important manuscripts which were bound and shelfmarked in various collections without detailed title cataloguing. Old catalogues, some with hand-written entries, no longer point to the exact whereabouts of documents. Sadly only some 150 printed works in various versions are to be found in the new Bodleian Catalogue SOLIS which has now replaced OLIS leaving the majority of Durie works in the Bodleian not immediately discernable to internet users. However, other large archives give far less data though the material is on site. So, too, the high costs of library membership and enormous charges for each copied page plus extra charges for CDs, though paper is thereby saved, is a great barrier to ordinary students interested in writing theses on Durie. Now the Bodleian is further decentralising their stock, already spread throughout Oxford, to places as far away as Swindon. This is not how Durie foresaw and planned the work of the Oxford libraries which, he felt, should provide immediate access to all media centrally for poor and rich alike. The huge collection of Durie-Hartlib papers archived in Sheffield University, England, is also an enormous asset to Durie scholarship. So, too, the Harley, Lansdowne and Sloane mss of the British Library offer an abundance of material as does the multi-volume Calendar of State Papers. A copy of the rare 1744 biography and collection of Durie correspondence compiled by the Swede, Carl Jesper Benzelius, can be found in All Souls Library, Oxford.[26]. Though the Durie documents archived in Uppsala and Stockholm are comparatively few, there is a wealth of background material stored there relating to church and court contacts between Sweden and the rest of Europe in which Durie played a prominent part. The correspondence alone of Chancellor Oxenstierna and Lord Spens in the Riksarkiv is a vast mine of information. By the 1630s, academic works were being written at Erfurt, Wittenberg and Helmstedt Universities, copies of which are available through interlibrary loans. At present, this author has gained primary and secondary works on the subject from some seventy European libraries and archives listed above, some of which he has visited several times. Nevertheless, very little of Durie's work has been reprinted in modern times and very few works have been translated for publishing. The Hartlib Papers are still not made free to the public online as Sheffield University informed me they planned some years ago after they stopped their CD sales. Happily, I was able to make good use of the Hartlib Papers whilst they were more generally available. Many of Durie's original works are to be found on microfilms in the university libraries of America and Eastern Europe. Ann Arbor of Michigan is doing a fine job supplying the world with microfilms of this period. There are now a few smaller specialist publishing houses who are offering a 'print on demand' copying of Durie's works. Sadly, though methods of accessibility and organisation still do not live up to Durie's idea of a 'Reformed Library', we must be grateful for the splendid service offered by Google and Gutenberg Books. I needed a copy of Durie's *Reformed Librarie-Keeper* and his *Consideration Concerning the*

---

[26] Shelfmarked ASC Stack 2nd. 6:SR. 78. b. 13 (3).

Present Engagement and, to my great surprise, found them through Google as freebies to download. I then discovered many more seventeenth and eighteenth century documents and great works relevant to Durie studies such as Gottfried Arnold, Masson, Brauer, Rae and Murdoch as free downloads.

Only recently I found amongst a collection of eighteenth century dissertations online, a lengthy digitalised copy of the original printed invitation from Pro-rector and Dean Laurence Mosheim to Benzelius' inaugural Disputation on Durie and allied subjects which appears to have been a very high-profile and ceremonial examination and now kindly put online by the University of Halle.[27] In all the books and documents mentioned in my Bibliography, this most interesting document was not so much as mentioned. So, too, after visiting the Codrington Library, All Souls College, Oxford to study Benzelius' *Commentatio Historico-Theologica de Johanne Duraeo, Pacificatore Celeberrimo, Maxime de Actis eius Suecanis*, I discovered the Herzog-August Bibliothek on-line version of Benzelius' honorary doctor's thesis *Dissertatio Historico-Theologica de Johanne Duraeo*. This proved to be absolutely identical in decorations, pagination, printing and publishing to the Codrington version except for the title and the title-page text, the Codrington version having far less wording than the HAB version. It appears that the Codrington version was the one offered to the university for evaluation and marking and the more 'official' looking version, containing all Mosheim's titles, was the published work after the Disputation. Again, this was nowhere mentioned in literature on Durie and Benzelius.[28] I had been misled by the titles to think them two different works. The internet now helps spread Academia no end. Thus, in spite of a few setbacks, today, a student of Durie is in a far better position than ever before to attempt a more comprehensive work on every facet of Durie's personality, calling and achievements by means Durie himself foresaw.

The work now set before the examiners is an attempt to encourage Durie researchers to be more synergistic in their studies of Durie and to tackle his total concept rather than separated parts of it which present

---

[27] *Ad Cvrsorias, qvas Vocant, Lectiones et Inavgvralem Disputationem Viri Maxime Reverendi et Amplissimi M. CAROLI IESPERI BENZELII Sacra Regiae Mal Svecicae a Sacris Avlicis et Consistorio Professores Omnivm ordinvm Excellentissimos Cives Academiae Generosos Ac Nobilissimos Omnes Deniqve Sanctiorum Litterarvm Favtores Qvo Fas est Qvemvis Studio Invitat IO. LAVRENTIVS MOSHEMIVS Prector Academiae et Decanus, H. T. Ordinis Theologici.* See vd18-protobibliothek.uni-halle.de and Appendix for title-page.

[28] Copies of the two different title pages to Benzelius' dissertation are given in an appendix.

merely a lop-sided picture of little help to those researchers who come after us. I do not profess to write a definitive work on the subject but merely present a signpost for the guidance of future students who wish to dig deeper into the most productive mines of Durie's universal learning.

Before going on to attempt to give a wider and deeper insight into the full scope of Durie's teaching, it will be practical to review the continual progress made in Durie scholarship hitherto and also give a biographical overview of Durie's life and calling. This can be viewed as my own attempt to come to terms with the present state of Durie scholarship but also as a means of making the studies of those who come after me easier, as my list of sources will save them much of the detective work this author had to undergo. Such an overview will also demonstrate how international research into Durie's life and works, though it has not waned since the middle nineteenth century, has, nevertheless, produced a most fragmented picture of both its subject and its subject's aims. It is thus considered a most difficult and unnecessary task for any individual scholar representing a specific field of research to work out a comprehensive overview of the life and calling of this most successful scholar. The fact remains that though numerous writers have pronounced Durie to be of the very best in their own chosen fields, such scholars have not extended their research to examine all that Durie accomplished before describing him as either a pastor, diplomat, educator, scientist, linguist, translator, man of letters, ambassador, library reformer, mediator and politician or whatever.

In this thesis, I wish to demonstrate that one cannot rightly understand any of Durie's activities for unity without first taking into account the driving force behind all his work. This is not an impossible task as all the facets of Durie's life-long activities evaluated in different specific works can be found to merge under his theory, or rather doctrine, of universal knowledge or what his contemporaries called pansophism. However, this most necessary synergistic study of Durie's major motivation and calling remains merely hinted at in modern scholarship. This is surprising as Durie's age was one of widespread synergistic thinking, chiefly influenced through Durie's engagement. Durie's friends such as Joseph Hall, John Davenant, Jan Amos Comenius and Samuel Hartlib have been especially acclaimed for their works in this field, though they relied heavily on Durie's support and leadership as their published letters show. Indeed, it was Durie and Hartlib who encouraged and even published much of their writings and thus made their friends and supporters more well-known in this field than themselves. The result is that up to this present century, works on seventeenth century irenic pansophism have more or less ignored Durie's great contribution. For instance, Daniel Neval's post-doctoral work *Comenius Pansophie* does not once mention the man who arguably influenced Comenius the most in this direction. He also almost entirely ignores the vast assistance to Comenius' thinking provided by Samuel Hartlib, Durie's right-hand man and a sturdy contender for pansophism, mentioning him in one brief footnote only.[29] So, too, Winfried Zeller, in his contribution to *Klassiker des Protestantismus* concerning seventeenth century 'Einzelgänger, Ireniker and Pansophen', does not so much as mention Durie once in this context. This thesis, therefore, is merely an effort to point out how Durie played a major role in the development of practical divinity, universal learning and pansophy and also to serve as a *Janua* into Durie's life and works which will perhaps thus enable more thorough-going works on Durie to be penned.

Finally, a few words must be said about the Durie documents used in this thesis. Since Brauer's detailed list of available sources, it has become a tradition for researches to publish an exhaustive list of Durie's writings in their bibliographies. This has become much easier now that we have so many online-catalogues, which are easy to copy or download. This method has also become confusing at times as research students are given no indication whether or not the academic work being studied has actually been based on either some or all of these documents. So, too, titles have been listed which are either no longer extant or were never even written. Turnbull's record collection of 228 Durie works, which stood for decades, is now being complemented by today's scholars by another seventy or so. Furthermore, Turnbull has included a number of personal letters. If these were all included separately in an exhaustive Bibliography of Durie's works, it would run into over 1,500 titles. Turnbull has also listed works which are untraceable or which he has only found referred to in letters or catalogues. Nevertheless, Turnbull has not included important and lengthy works of Durie's which were easily available to him at the time of his studies at the Bodleian Library, for instance, *The meanes of Ecclesiastical Peace and Reconciliation amongst Protestants*, Rawlinson, A.427, Bod. L. and his *A true relation of the conversion and baptism of Isuf the Turkish chaous, named Richard Christophilus In the presence of a full congregation, Jan. 30. 1658. in Covent-Garden, where Mr. Manton is minister.* Imprimatur, Edm. Calamy, printed by S. Griffin, and are to be sold by John Rothwell at the Fountain in Cheapside, and Thomas Vnderhill at the Bible in Pauls Church-yard London, Bod. L. Turnbull says that he has read of an

---

[29] See Daniel Neval's *Comenius Pansophie*.

article called 'The Baptised Turk' in a letter to Hartlib of May 11, 1659[30] but says 'I do not know this writing.'[31] The reference must be to Durie's work '*A true relation*' of the previous year.

Merely quoting older catalogues, such as Rawlinson, as sources can be most trying for those following the information, as many items have been added, removed or revised on inset pages since then. So, too, listing works in bibliographies just because, say, Benzelius lists them, helps no one find where they are available now. Occasionally, as happened to me on several occasions, in England, Sweden and Germany, I came across uncatalogued or misplaced documents. Many items in archives are still only earmarked in packets as 'Letters' or 'Tracts' or bear a shelfmark or stack number but no catalogued titles. In this work, I have only listed documents and publications from Durie's pen which I have actually used. I spent a year reading through some 215 of Durie's major works besides some five hundred letters, as also the secondary works and biographies listed in my Bibliography before determining the exact path I was to take. I then concentrated on some fifty works and two hundred letters written by Durie which I felt were representative of the whole. Durie was an expert at repeating himself as also Hartlib was in publishing very similar works from Durie's pen. At a fair estimate and considering the almost-yearly new discoveries of Durie documents, students now have a choice of over 350 Durie mss to work on, not counting the letters, most of which were originally written for publication. Durie's letters alone would fill tomes rather than volumes. If future students wish to pursue their manuscript hunting far beyond what I present, they may think of starting with the list of 63 titles presented in Ref: 59/10/1A-2B in the Hartlib Papers, most of which I have been unable to trace as yet.

---

[30] Turnbull does not give the reference but it is Ref: 33/1/56A-57B, HP.
[31] *Hartlib, Durie and Comenius*, p. 302.

Chapter Two

Durie's Life and Labours

Born into a family of campaigners, ministers, diplomats, lairds and rebels

Durie was descended from a long line of adventurers, ministers, diplomats, lairds and rebels. His grandfather of the same name (1537-1600) was a former monk in Dunfermline and a close friend and distant relation of Andrew Melville (1545-1622). He also became a friend and fellow-minister of John Knox (1510-72), succeeding him at St. Giles, Edinburgh from 1574 to 1579. After he became a Protestant, Durie was sentenced to be jailed for life by his own cousin, George Durie who was Abbot of Dunfermline, but John Durie managed to escape. He was then banished twice by King James VI of Scotland, later James I of England, but was reconciled to the King and ended his life at Montrose on a substantial royal pension. John married Marion, the daughter of Sir John Majoribanks, the provost of Edinburgh and Robert Durie (1555-1616), our John Durie's father, was the second of three sons.[32]

Robert Durie became a member of the 'Famous Five Adventurers' who colonised the Island of Lewis. Robert was ordained a minister in Anstruther, Fife, which appears to have been a royal appointment, and evangelised the Orkneys and the Shetland Islands. He married Elizabeth Ramsey whose family provided many high-ranking officers for Gustav II Adolph's army. Sir James Ramsey (1589-1638), Durie's cousin, became a major-general in 1632 and Commandant of Hanau in 1634, his soldiers bearing the brunt of many of Gustav's campaigns. There are a number of Ramsey's letters to Axel Oxenstierna in the Uppsala archives. Robert and Elizabeth had seven children of whom our subject, John, was the fourth son. After differences with King James, Robert was found guilty of treason and exiled to France in 1606, when John was said by nearly all authorities to be ten years of age.

---

[32] For the information on Majoribanks, I am grateful to the anonymous author of the Biographical Sketch prefaced to the reprint of *The Reformed Librarie-Keeper* published in the Literature of Libraries in the Seventeenth and Eighteenth Centuries, Chicago, 1906. I have not found this substantiated elsewhere.

This supposition appears to have arisen merely from one scholar relying on another for his or her information. Most researchers tend to lean on either the multi-volume *Dictionary of National Biography* or on the *Concise Dictionary of National Biography* for their information but these works merely give the dates 1596-1680 for Durie without further explanation. Others references are made to Henke's and Brauer's works of 1806 and 1907 respectively but they, too, merely assume that 1596 is correct. *The Nieuw Nederlandsch Biografisch Woordenboek* (NNBW) states without further documentation that 1595 is the date of Durie's birth.[33] Friedrich Brandes in his 1882 work on Durie, dealt with in detail below as also the other works mentioned in this connection, gives 'the year 1595 or 1596', with no further details given. Tollin (1897) also takes it for granted that Durie was born in '1595 or 1596'.

My own research into documents referring to Durie's school days provides us with a more probable date. When speaking of Durie's birth, Dr. A. Eekof, the editor of *De Theologische Faculteit te Leiden in de 17de Eeuw*, refers to and quotes from the *Album Studiosorum Academia Lugduno-Batavae* in which Durie was registered as a student at Leyden in 1611. His age was then given as twelve, which means he was probably born in 1599, but Léchot gives 1600 based on this entry. According to my dating Durie would have been only seven when his family moved to France. According to Léchot, he would have been six. As the entrance list to Leyden University is the earliest reliable date ever documented giving evidence of John Durie's date of birth, though it might be a slip of the pen, it would be safest to assume that Durie was born in 1599 until more official evidence is forthcoming.[34] This means, however, that all traditional dating must be reduced by three years.

It is then usually surmised that sometime between 1606 and 1610, Durie studied at Sedan in France under the supervision of fellow-exile Andrew Melville, but if so, Durie would only have been of elementary school age. Durie then left for Holland, aged eleven, a year before matriculating at Leyden in 1611 at twelve, and not at the age of fourteen or fifteen as commonly reported. Thomas M'Crie is usually quoted to back up this early connection between Melville and Durie, where he says of Melville that 'Of all his friends, next to his nephew, he felt most attached to (Robert) Dury, and his letters to him are written in the most confidential strain, mingled

---

[33] Deel 8, pp. 443-444.
[34] See collection of documents in *De Theologische Faculteit te Leiden in de 17de Eeuw*, in particular Durie's correspondence with the university, pp. 349-357.

with a kind-hearted and familiar pleasantry.'[35] Melville, in his letters to Robert Durie, always addressed him as 'Right reverend and dearly beloved father in the Lord Jesus'.[36] However, the oft-mentioned friendship and correspondence between Melville and Robert Durie is no evidence that John Durie was actually educated in France by Melville at this time. Indeed, accounts of Durie's early years in Britain, France and Holland are most speculative, there being three major theories concerning Durie's possible time of tuition at Sedan under Melville. One claims that the tuition took place immediately after Durie's arrival in France, thinking Durie was older than he probably was, and the second claims that Melville taught Durie later at Sedan as a mature student. A third theory is supplied by Sabrina Juillet-Garzon in her essay entitled 'A Scottish-Style Universal Church? The Attempts at Religious Reconciliation of John Durie in Christendom, 1610-1653' (sic.), who claims that the Duries fled to Bordeaux to be sheltered by French Huguenots in 1606 when Durie was supposedly ten years of age. In 1609, they moved to Leyden where they lived for some time before returning to France to be with Andrew Melville at Sedan. Rae suggests Durie was in Sedan from around 1615 to 1620.[37] At some unspecified time, the family moved back to Leyden and Juillet-Garzon tells us that after finishing his studies there, Durie 'became a minister of a small congregation of English and Scottish Presbyterians at Elbing in 1624.[38] However, this misses out Durie's own testimony that he lectured in Cologne for some two years before moving to Elbing. As will be shown, Melville was no longer in France when many scholars place Durie under his tuition at Sedan but there is stronger evidence of a close connection between Du Moulin and Durie in France. We see, therefore, that fixing a time line for Durie during this early period is nigh impossible.

Clear evidence that Durie was in Leyden as a child is produced by Turnbull from a letter dated September 20, 1630 in which the writer, W. Wells, speaks of meeting Durie in Leyden during Durie's childhood, but no exact date is given.[39] So, too, there is evidence to show that Durie, very early in his career, was in touch with the select coterie of irenists, theologi-

---

[35] M'Crie, pp. 334-335.
[36] See, for instance, letter dated from Sedan 24th May, 1616, the year of Robert Durie's death, in M'Crie's collection, p. 487, annexed to his biography of Melville.
[37] *John Dury: Reformer of Education*, p. 14.
[38] *Scotland and Europe, Scotland in Europe*, ed. Gilles Leydier, Cambridge Scholars Publishing, 2007, pp. 13-17.
[39] *Hartlib, Dury and Comenius, Gleanings from Hartlib's Papers*, p. 127.

ans and poets such as Pareus, Bythner, Adam, Gruter and Durie who frequented the John Rosa workshops in Heidelberg and Frankfurt, hosted in Durie's day by Rosa's widow. There is an extant document in the Hartlib Papers dated 1618 from the Rosa workshop and clearing house in Frankfurt bearing Durie's monogram formed by the Hebrew letters yod, res, lamed and alef which he used as his autograph to mark his own compositions. The monogram is mentioned by most Durie scholars without explaining its origin and meaning. This author sought to solve the riddle by examining Durie's most often quoted Old Testament verses and found the solution in the opening words of Psalm 23 in his Hebrew Bible לא רעי יהוה אחסר. The monogram depicts the first letters of the four Hebrew words translated 'The Lord is my Shepherd, I shall not want'. Durie's manuscript thus signed is entitled *Exortationis Summa; quam pro consensu constituendo per Reformatas Ecclesias per Europam edidit pius qvidam Theologus nomine Fratrum Evangelicae Professionis in Regno Poloniae*. This fourteen page work outlines the principles Durie worked on until his death and shows a very early interest in Poland. It starts with a two paged summary of an irenic work by the Unitas Fratrum scholar Barthlomiej Bythner entitled *Fraterna & modesta ad homes per vniversum Europam reformatas ecclesias* etc., which ran into 258 pages. This is then supplemented by some 12 pages discussing the problems involved in inter-Protestant plans for union. Durie found inspiration for his own work in the 1570 Polish *Consensus Sandomiriensis* between the Lutherans, Reformed and United Brethren and the ensuing 1573 Warsaw Confederation which granted religious freedom. He saw in Bythner's work a further key to Protestant union and, when Comenius and the Protestant leaders in Poland turned to Durie for assistance, he urged that they reprinted Bythner's works. Durie remained a faithful friend of the Bythners throughout two generations, finding Bythner's younger brother Wiktoryn a fellowship in Christ's Church College, Oxford and Bythner's two sons Wiktoryn and Jan places as students at Oxford.[40]

Leyden University, however, was, and still is, proud of their student Durie and in the opening paragraph of Eekhof's *Inleiding* to the above-named work, we see how important his memory is to the university. Eekhof linking Durie with the success of the university writes:

---

[40] See Michael J. Rozbicki's '17th Century AD', *East European Quarterly*. Winter, 1996; also Wojciech Gajewski's 'Ugoda Sandomierska – swkces czy fiasko' in *Slowo I Zycie*, 2/2005.

'Niet licht zal men van vooringenomenheid of wetenschappelijk chauvinisme worden verdacht, wanner men de theologische faculteit der universteit te Leiden een van de meest beroemde en invloedrijke instellingen noemt, die er in de 17de eeuw zijn geweest; ja, men zal het Johannes Duraeus, die land en zee had vereisd, kunnen toegeven, wanneer hij van haar getuigt: "quae inter Protestantes velut primae magnitudinis stella eminet".'

Steve Murdoch's two books *Scotland and the Thirty Years War* (2001) and *Network North* (2006) have refreshed Durie scholarship with a good deal of personal and background material belonging to Durie and his circle. Though other scholars mention Durie's close cooperation with Sir James Spens (Spence or Spense) and Sir Robert Anstruther, they do not tell us that Spens had married an Agnes Durie and was also related to Durie's mother, a Ramsey. Anstruther, who was senior ambassador in Germany and Scandinavia for Charles I and worked with Durie during his German negotiations, was Spens' half-brother and also a relative of Durie's. Gustav Adolph's famous officer, Colonel Sir James Ramsey who provided Durie with military escorts and hospitality in Germany, was Durie's first cousin and Spen's son-in-law. According to Sabrina Juillet-Garzon, Durie was also closely related to the Leslies who led the Scottish army against England and the Swedish army against the Emperor's forces.[41] When Durie left Elbing around 1630 to consult Charles I, Archbishop Abbott and Bishop William Laud, he stayed with his mother's brother Sir David Ramsey who was Charles I's Gentleman of the Bedchamber and Master of the King's Clocks and his kinsman Spens was at Charles' court then as Swedish Ambassador.

Durie's youth and early adulthood in the Netherlands and France

By 1611, the Duries had lived a year in Leyden where they found a new home and where Robert took over a former British military church composed of two-hundred families as its first full-time pastor. Relations with the neighbouring Dutch Reformed churches were not the best, perhaps because as a demonstration of good will to Britain, the city magistrates paid the British pastors a salary. Turnbull informs us that Durie was 'brought

---

[41] *Scotland and Europe, Scotland in Europe*, Juilliet-Gazon takes a very independent line with her dating and arguments in seeing Durie as a Scottish agent in Europe, supported by his influential family. According to her title, Durie must have started reforming Europe at the age of around eleven.

up' in a 'French College' at Leyden but gives no exact source for this information.[42] Other commentators state, also without due sources, that Durie was tutored first in English, French, Dutch, German and Latin, adding Hebrew and Greek when he became a full student. The King pardoned Robert Durie in 1616, but the Scotsman died before the news reached Leyden. New to modern Durie scholarship, but revealed in the Leyden records, is that John's elder brother, Andreas, born 1594 in Anstruther where Robert was then Vicar, matriculated at Leyden in 1612 and studied Medicine there until becoming a surgeon on a Dutch East-Indies ship. After changing the spelling of his name to Andries van Duuren, John's brother settled in India and later in Batavia where he died in 1655.[43]

Accounts of John Durie's life between 1621 and 1626 are usually traced back to Tollin's *Johannes Duraeus* (pp. 330-23) who repeats what he calls 'traditions' relating to Durie. He relates how shortly after his father's death, John was chosen to give a Latin speech before the General Synod at Amsterdam for which he received fifteen Dutch pounds for his expenses. It would seem therefore that the synod still did not view Durie as a prospective candidate for the ministry, as they ruled that such candidates were not to be paid for their services. Perhaps the speech was within the framework of public recognition for Robert Durie's ministry. However, according to Tollin, shortly after completing his Leyden studies, John registered at an Amsterdam College with a view to taking a post-graduate probation course for ministerial candidates. Not being a member of a Dutch Reformed church, Durie was only officially recognised as a student a year later (1617) after the Dort Synod had given him an excellent testimony.[44] In 1621, a senior government official, Barthelemy Panhusen,[45] asked the Hague Synod to release Durie so that he might accompany his son to France as his private tutor during his studies. The Synod gave Durie a year's leave of absence and this was renewed in the following year when the Synod met at Utrecht. In 1624, Durie was called back to the Netherlands to take up a pastorate, but also Tollin suggests that Durie took an Ox-

---

[42] See *Hartlib, Dury and Comenius, Gleanings from Hartlib's Papers*, p. 127.
[43] Andreas died in Batavia-Jakarta and not Batavia-Netherlands or Batavia-Passau. See *The Nieuw Nederlandsch Biografisch Woordenboek,* Deel 10, pp.249-250.
[44] This was a year before the famous Synod of Dort of 1618-19.
[45] Also spelt Panhuysen and van Panhuys. Some sources say that Panhusen was a Huguenot merchant, others that he was a government Senior Civil Servant or treasurer. He may well have been all three. See the 1896 edition of the Synods of Wallon, La Haye.

ford doctorate in 1624. Thereafter, he moved to Elbing, Prussia. Sadly, Tollin gives no primary sources for these 'traditions'.

Another widely told 'tradition' is that between 1624 and 1626 Durie left to minister at Cologne. There is a vague reference to this in the Archiv der evangelischen Gemeinde in Cologne (Ca1) strengthened by Durie's own testimony in his *Narrative of his German Travels*[46] where he mentions that in 1631, he called on a Mr Justinus van Aschen at Cologne with whom he had left a trunk and books whilst a minister there some time earlier. It appears that Durie had succeeded Johannes Morian[47] who became a close associate of the Durie circle and was, in turn, succeeded by Peter Serrarius. Van der Wall in her essay *Petrus Serrarius (1600-1669) et le millénarisme mystic*, says that Serrarius, 'en 1628, il fut relevé de ses fonctions de pasteur, de la communauté wallonne de Cologne'.[48] Serrarius, who had studied with Durie at Leyden, must have also had a brief two years' ministry there. After Cologne, we read in the letters of Durie's kinsman Sir James Spens and Durie's own writings that he took on a work in Elbing, Prussia[49]. It appears that those such as Juillet-Garzon, mentioned above, who place Durie in Elbing in 1624 have missed the records both in the Cologne church books and Durie's own journals. This also goes for Swedish Church Historian Theodor Norlin who claims that Durie studied at Oxford after which he became priest (präst) to a small gathering of Englishmen and Scotsmen in Elbing in 1626. The members of this church, Norlin argues, were composed of former Lutheran and Reformed believers who had put away their differences.[50,]

Durie at Elbing: First writings on universal learning and church union

On 6 July 1626, King Gustav annexed the Prussian city of Elbing from Poland, making it the military, juristic, ecclesiastical and cultural capital of

---

[46] Ref: 60/5/ 1A-8B: 7B, 8B Blank, HP.
[47] See Journal tenu par Isaac Beeckman de 1604 à 1634. Tome 3: 1627-1634 (1635). Isaak Beeckman, editie Cornelis de Waard, Bron, 2007, p. 3. and C. de Waard's homepage at:
  ww.dbnl.org/tekst/beec002jour03_01/beec002jour03_01.pdf.
[48] Page 156.
[49] A substantial collection of Spens' correspondence is available in Sweden's Riksarkiv and as freebies online. I have used this collection extensively for my information on Spens.
[50] Norlin, p. 173.

his German territories.[51] In a lengthy caption to a contemporary picture depicting the event in Hjalmar Holmquist's classical study of the period, Holmquist explains that Durie was already in the city when Gustav took it.[52] In Durie's *Brief Relation*, published in 1641, his editor, Samuel Hartlib, shows that Durie had worked privately as a messenger of peace between Danzig and Elbing and won the clergy and Swedes over to his irenic ideas of Protestant unity. Furthermore, when James Spens wrote to Chancellor Oxenstierna from London in November 1626, he told him that there was a Scotsman in Elbing who had plans for peace terms with Danzig and ideas concerning the possibility of transferring the Elbing trade there which were worth considering.[53] In the light of what Hartlib writes, this appears to be a reference to Durie. Durie had realised that the future of the Elbing church was endangered because trade was interrupted through political unrest and most of the soldiers were only stationed there briefly. Eventually, the trade and church were transferred to Danzig, so the anonymous Scotsman's plans were successful. Commentators such as Thomas Rae usually link Durie diplomatically with Spens concerning Charles I's wish to send both of them as ambassadors to Gustav Adolf to create him a Knight of the Order of the Garter some time between 1624 and 1625.[54] However, this dating is certainly wrong. A letter from Spens dated 1626 in the *Carolina Rediviva* at Uppsala informs Oxenstierna that King Charles was planning to make Gustav Adolf an English knight but Durie was already in Elbing at this time. Archibald Duncan, who edited Spens' Riksarkiv letters,[55] says in his introduction:

> 'In 1627 Spens was charged with another important mission: Charles I sent him to the Swedish court in Elbing in the summer of 1627 to present the Order of the Garter to Gustav II Adolf and to try to persuade the King to come

---

[51] *Negotiations about Church Unity*, pp. 62-65.
[52] Holmquist, p. 197.
[53] *Relinquendo verba inania, hæc sunt, quæ Scotus a me petit, vt in me suscipere velim Sacræ Regiæ Maiestatis partim determinatum intentum partim suspectum contra ciuitatem Dantiscum ad amicam reconciliationem reducere. Qua in re (si successerit) gloriam et laudem acquirere potes ab omnibus, qui intellecturi sunt hanc piam et pacificam concordiam per te fuisse factam, et ab ciuitate Dantiscano gratias et præmium expectare potes, cum per me intellexerint rem vestro labore in effectum reductam esse.* RA/Oxenstiernska samlingen and *The Diplomatic Correspondence of Sir James Spens of Wormiston* (unpublished manuscript in Uppsala University Library, E 379 d:1).
[54] See Rae's *John Durie, Reformer of Education*, p. 14.
[55] There are some 90 letters between Spens and Oxenstierna in this collection. See also *The Works and Letters of Chancellor Axel Oxenstierna* in the Riksarkiv.

Durie's Life and Labours   55

to an agreement with Poland. If the war ended, the Swedes would be free to enter the war in Germany. Spens was also authorised to treat with the City of Danzig to ensure their neutrality. On his arrival in Elbing, Spens was told that Gustav II Adolf would prefer that he gave up his role as British ambassador for a time and started recruiting more soldiers.'

There is nothing in Spens' correspondence which connects Durie directly with the awarding of the British Knighthood to the Swedish King and no exact dating of either person's arrival in Elbing. However, we find Durie writing to Hartlib towards the end of 1628 saying, 'My Lord of Wirmoston (Spens) the Ambassador with whom I came first hither hathe beene a greate let vnto mee all the while hee was here, Now hee is gon & I will not bee able to fall to my former meditacions[56] till all my Letters bee written.' Here Durie speaks of when he 'first' visited Elbing as if it were some time before and that he had journeyed there with Spens. We are left to wonder where Durie and Spens were before they left for Elbing and when they 'first' arrived there.

Any visit to Elbing around 1624 or 1625 with Durie is hard to imagine as Spens was commuting between England and Sweden at the time and Elbing had not yet been taken. However, during this period, Spens was in discussions with several nations and we find from his letters in the Riksarkiv that he knew no foreign language and was lost without an interpreter.[57] Durie who was fluent in at least five languages including the languages of seventeenth century diplomats, French and Latin, would have been the ideal translator for him. Happily, there are at least four letters from Spens to Oxenstierna written throughout 1627 which are preserved in the Riksarkiv and which are unmistakably (because of Durie's most individual way of writing a letter 'd' and other factors) in Durie's hand. The reason for Durie's move to Elbing, if it were not on a diplomatic mission with Spens, and not the result of a direct church call, would still remain a matter for speculation.

In 1628, King Gustav revisited Elbing and was presented with a petition by Durie entitled *Le Treshumble Supplication d'un vray Fidele presentee Au tresillustre & trespuissant Prince* **Gustavus Adolphus** *Par la grace de Dieu Roy des Swedois des Goths & des Wandales. Grand Duc de Finlande; Duc d'Esthone & de Carele & Seigneur d'Ingre etcæt: pour obtenir Aide & Assistance necessaire en temps opportun Afin de recercher[altered] & restablir la Paix Ecclesiastique parmi les Eglises Evange-*

---

[56] Durie's *Treatys on Education*. The letter is taken from HP.
[57] See Spens' letter to Oxenstierna, 7 Oct. 1629, *Oxenstierna Collection*, Riksarkiv.

liques a la gloire de Dieu & l'auancement du Salut de tous Chrestiens. Matth. 5. v. 9. It was later republished several times in both French and English, the English title being, *The most humble Petition of a Minister of the Gospel for the obtaining of Aide; and Assistance in this seasonable time, to seek for, and restablish an Ecclesiasticall Peace among the Evangelicall Churches.* We read in *A Brief Relation of that which hath been lately attempted to procure Ecclesiastical Peace amongst Protestants* (1641), compiled by Hartlib from Durie's papers:

> 'To make a way for this purpose (Protestant reunification), he (Durie) had before hand through, Sir James Spense Lord of Oreholm, and General to the Scottish Nation, in the Swedish Army, given notice to his Majesty of Sweden, what his aime was in the business of Reconcilement, and how it might be affected.'[58]

Indeed, when Durie at last gained an interview with Gustav almost four years later, he was asked if he were the Scotsman whom Spens had mentioned to him. On answering in the affirmative, Gustav then told Durie that he was at his disposal and gave him two generous interviews though he was in the midst of preparing battles. This also agrees with Hartlib's version in *A Brief Relation* where he says that through Spens' intervention on behalf of Durie in 1628 'he found the King somewhat prepared'.

Durie's exact occupation in Elbing between 1625 and 1630 has caused a good deal of speculation. Steve Murdoch tells us that Durie 'preached to the British congregation in Elbing as an ordained Calvinist minister'.[59] Westin says 'En av tre prästerna i Elbing var John Durie', which might suggest that there was a less official kind of ministry there. Indeed, Westin goes on to say that Durie:

> "I sin tjänst i Elbing, ansåg han sig icke bunden till någon bestämd kyrka ock beskännelse, icke heller utförde han full prästerlig tjänst. Enligt hans egen uppgift ombesörjde han icke sakramentsförvaltingen.'[60]

This is accordance with Durie's own testimony. In his 1650 controversy with William Prynne, who had accused Durie of rejecting his alleged Presbyterian ordination for an Anglican one because of opportunism, Durie emphasises that he only served 'in the quality of a lecturer without obligation to a Pastoral Charge' at Elbing and thus not as 'an ordained Calvinist

---

[58] *A Brief Relation*, p. 4.
[59] *Network North*, p. 282.
[60] *Sv. kyrkan och de proteststant. enhetssträvandena*, p. 74.

minister'.[61] Only after his Church of England ordination in 1634 did Durie call himself a 'Minister of the Word'.

Th. A. Fischer says that Elbing was 'strongly garrisoned by Scotch troops' and the Scotsmen formed a church there in 1626 with which Durie is associated as lecturer. It appears thus that the Scottish troops joined the small number of British Christians gathered around Durie and at least two others. In these early Swedish campaigns in Germany, Gustav had used a large army of Scottish soldiers which Fischer estimates at some twenty to thirty thousand troops.[62] Indeed, as this writer found out whilst browsing through the Royal Correspondence in the archives at Uppsala and Stockholm, Fischer shows that during Charles I's reign, over 500 of King Gustav's and Queen Christina's most senior officers were Scotsmen, not counting the English and Irish officers, and many Swedish nobles had Scottish names. There were even several leading families named Durie in Sweden in our Durie's days that appear to have been long-established in that country. Sweden's own officers constantly protested that the royal family only allowed Scotsmen to guard them. Here, one also reads, how many English soldiers were sent to serve the Protestant nations on the Continent in the Thirty Years War. Charles I sent at least thirty thousand troops but a Parliament adverse to him stopped granting him the ship and soldier money needed for the project. The same Parliament, however, accused Charles of not doing enough for Protestantism, but by this time, they did not mean Old Protestantism but New Presbyterianism. According to Gunnar Westin, during the four years or so that Durie was in the city, Elbing's Reformed and Lutheran churches accepted his plans for unity of fellowship.[63] Elbing had very close connections with Britain and had opted out of her alliance with the Hanseatic League in 1620 in order to enter into closer trade negotiations with Stuart England.

Swedish control of Elbing secured a freer attitude towards denominationalism. At this time, Sweden had experienced a real indigenous Reformation so they did not feel obliged to accept any other major European Reformed Creeds whether Lutheran, Presbyterian, Congregationalist or Anglican.[64] Gustav Adolf set up his High Court at Elbing and appointed

---

[61] See Durie's *The Unchanged, Constant and Single-hearted Peacemaker*, p. 3. There will be a full discussion of this problem in my upcoming *John Durie: Defragmenter of the Reformation*.

[62] *The Scots in Germany*, Part II, The Army, p. 73.

[63] *Negotiations about Church Unity*, p. 73.

[64] A full discussion of this situation will be found in my work 'John Durie and the Defragmentation of the Reformation'.

Privy Councillor Casper Godeman as President of the Court of Appeals.[65] Godeman was also a fervent contender for a Lutheran and Reformed alliance and he and Durie pooled the studies which they had already made separately on a united Protestant Lord's Supper sometime between 1626 and 1630.[66] In 1629, Charles I sent Sir Thomas Roe (1581-1644) as England's ambassador to mediate in the Swedish-German-Polish peace treaties. Roe had been British ambassador to India from 1614-1619 and ambassador to Turkey from 1621-1628. From 1629-30 and once again in 1638, he was special ambassador at large for the Protestant powers in the Thirty Years War. Many of his letters have been preserved by Durie, Hartlib, Laud and Oxenstierna.

Durie and Godeman wasted no time in persuading Roe to use his talents as an ombudsman in the cause of Protestant unity. Roe saw, too, how such a union would be a bulwark against Rome and the Emperor. Indeed, Durie confesses in his 'Epistle Dedicatory' to his *A Summarie Discourse* that it was Roe who had first helped make concrete plans for Durie's negotiations for peace. At this time, Roe had free access both to King Gustav and Oxenstierna. Roe's major biographer Brown writes:

> 'The chancellor showed considerable interest and promised to use his influence to win Lutheran support for the project. Both he and Roe felt that the leadership should come from England, for since she had remained neutral in Germany's theological and political struggle, she could be expected to wield more influence over the various groups of German Protestants.'[67]

A further visitor to Elbing was Samuel Hartlib, who according to his Preface to the Reader in Durie's *Unchanged, Constant and Single-hearted Peacemaker* must have first met Durie there around 1626-27. Hartlib was the son of an Elbing citizen and his Grandfather had headed the British

---

[65] See *Copie D'une Lettre escrite a un prince de L'Empire; ou Brieve Information du Commencement, du Progres & de l'Estat present de la Negotiation De Jean Dureus, avec les Eglises Protestantes.*

[66] See Durie's *EXPLICATIO PHRASIUM QUARUNDAM IN DOGMATE DE SACRA DOMINI CAENA* which he presented to Uppsala University in 1637, HP, 19/11/106/1A-10A: 1B BLANK and 19/11/106/10A-18B: 18B BLANK.

[67] Brown's *Itinerant Ambassador*, p. 200. Brown is summing up pp. 21-22 of Batten's published thesis here, his university manuscript giving the details on p. 36. Batten gives Durie's Brief Relation, pp. 2-3 as his source but the pages, though dealing with Roe, do not give the information provided by Batten. Durie is referring to a wish uttered by the Danzig church that their English colleagues would join them in their efforts for a church alliance and Durie promptly informed Roe of this.

Durie's Life and Labours

Merchant's Association in the city. David Masson in his chapter on Hartlib, Durie and Comenius in Vol. III of his *Life of Milton* says:

> 'Among Durie's first disciples in the idea (of Protestant unity) must certainly have been Hartlib; and it does not seem improbable that, when Hartlib left Prussia, in or about 1628, to settle in England, it was with an understanding that he was to be an agent or missionary for Durie's idea among the English.'[68]

Hartlib was a great strength to Durie concerning both his educational reforms and his campaign for Protestant unity. He published *The Reformed Husbandman* as part of a series of publications aimed at the reformation of society. Durie's contributions were *The Reformed Schoolmaster; The Reformed Spiritual Husbandman* and The *Reformed Librarie-Keeper*. Hartlib also shared Durie's Pan-European views. Hartlib, like Durie, had also a passion for gathering universal knowledge and shared Durie's love for experimental science. He also agreed with Durie in advocating Practical Divinity as a university subject in the education of theologians and pastors. James Spens also played a most important part in this initial circle. He hoped for a peaceful union of Protestants and staunchly supported Durie until his death in 1632. He paved the way into many a Royal court for Durie and informed him concerning European politics of the day. So, too, we must mention several members of the Oxenstierna family present in Elbing who proved of immense help to Durie in his campaigns.

Durie the educationalist and irenist and the start of his international work

It is clear from Durie's preserved writings from this time on that he was captivated by the idea of education for all, including both sexes, young and old. He felt that the entire knowledge in the world should be placed at the service of all mankind for the common profit of all. He had envisaged founding educational institutions catering for all classes of society and ages providing equal chances for all to benefit from this learning. Indeed, Hartlib had already left for England by 1628 to contact people who might be interested in supporting such a venture and founding such educational establishments. In 1630, Durie's new friends begged him to resign his post at Elbing and solicit the English Court, Church and Parliament to send him out as England's negotiator-at-large in Europe for the procuring of peace

---

[68] Project Guttenberg download not paginated.

and cooperation between the churches and centres of learning. Armed with recommendations from Roe, Godeman and Spens, Durie travelled to Britain finding accommodation at the house of his mother's brother, Sir David, who was Keeper of the King's Bedchamber and had spacious quarters in London. Nor did he need to fear his reception at Court and Lambeth. Charles was well-informed concerning Durie's mission and his usefulness to Spens. Archbishop George Abbot, with the Bishop of London, William Laud, at his side, was immediately captivated by Durie's charm, faith and great sincerity. Laud was already acting as Abbott's independent spokesman as the Archbishop was in disfavour having accidentally killed a man in a hunting accident.

Whilst in England, Durie published his *Instrumentum Theologorum Anglorum* and *Problemata de Pacis Ecclesiasticae Consiliis Capescendis*[69] to which leading churchmen such as Richard Sibbes, John Davenport, Samuel Ward, Richard Holdsworth, Philip Nye, John White, Stephen Marshall, Henry Burton, Cornelius Burgess, Thomas Taylor, Thomas Edwards, Thomas Goodwin, Daniel Featley and Joseph Hall subscribed. Archbishop Abbot added a covering letter, signed by himself and Bishop Laud, recommending Durie and the aims expressed in his *Instrumentum* to the German and Dutch churches. Roe provided a covering letter to Lord Chancellor Oxenstierna, the Governor of Sweden's conquered territories. That this had the official sanction of Church and State is witnessed by the Calendar of State Papers, Domestic Series, of the Reign of Charles I, Vol. CXCIII for June 12, 1631 which states that 'John Dury was employed to effect a reconciliation between the Lutheran and other Reformed Churches and that all persons well affected to that work might safely subscribe a declaration to be left in his hands, that he had faithfully solicited this good cause, and that they would be willing to join with those of the like affection beyond seas.' Durie himself says in his opening words to *A Summary Relation Of that which Iohn Deury hath prosecuted, in the worke of ecclesiasticall Paciffication in Germany since the latter end of Iulij 1631 till the 26th of September 1633*:

> 'In the yeare 1631 after I had obteyned permission from my Lordes Grace of Canterbury who then was & him also that now is, who was then Bishop of London to goe over into Germany to try by way of private negotiation, how farr in the worke of ecclesiasticall Paciffication, matters might be ripened & brought about to a setled correspondency & consultation in that matter betwixt the Churches & haueing to that effect gotton leaue to take from cer-

---

[69] Presented to Archbishop Laud at the beginning of 1631.

taine divines in England whome I should thinke good to make choyce of a testimony subscribed by their handes to witnes for them in private that they desired not only to further for their owne part soe good & holy a purpose, but also entreated others to ioyne with them in it, I went from hence about the latter end of Iulij with a letter of recommendacion from Sir Thomas Roe vnto the Lord Chancellor Oxensterne, who a yeare before had vndertaken & promised both to Sir Thomas Roe & to my selfe to further & promote with all his might so pious & godly a worke.'

Thus, armed with passports, a limited finance and recommendations from the clergy, politicians, men of letters and scientists, Durie started out on his first major tour of the Continent. This first major journey is covered in great detail by Durie himself as witnessed by such works as the above mentioned *Summary Relation* of 1634 and *A Narrative of His German Travels* (1632); *A Briefe Relation of That which hath been lately atempted to precure Ecclesiastical Peace amongst Protestants of 1641*; *The Purpose, and Platforme of the Iourneyes that are vndertaken for the worke of Peace Ecclesiasticall and other profitable Ends* (undated) and *The effect of Master Dury's Negotiation for the uniting of Protestants* (1657), besides numerous letters from Durie's pen. Where other primary and secondary sources are used to give further evidence or comment, their full sources will be given.

March 1631 witnessed the end of the winter session of the Leipzig Colloquy where the Protestant Princes and Dukes and the Reformed clergy had invited the Saxony Lutheran clergy to a protest conference against Ferdinand II's Edict of Restitution of 1629. The Emperor had claimed Lutheran territories back for Rome, which had become Lutheran both before and after the Peace of Augsburg in 1555. The city had been captured without too much of a struggle by Scottish troops fighting for Sweden and the Protestant faith and the plans of their fellow-Scotsman John Durie had been put on the Conference agenda. Unlike Batten and Brown, Tollin argues that the main authorisation for Durie's own work for union and his influence at Leipzig came from neither the British King nor the Church of England but from an official invitation to take part in the Disputation sent to him by Court Chaplain John Bergius through the initiative of Casper Godeman.[70] The Leipzig Conference ended with the Lutherans agreeing to work for a general acceptance of the Reformed clergy as ministerial brethren. A full association was not reached immediately but the results were most promising. Though not present at the conference, Durie published its

---

[70] *Geschichtsblätter*, 1897, 32, p. 234.

findings as also those of the French National Reformed Synod held at Charenton, in September 1631.[71] The French reversed the anti-Lutheran transactions of the Synod of Dort, declaring that Lutherans were also Reformed because 'they do agree with the other Reformed Churches, in the Principles and Fundamentall points of true Religion and in their discipline, and form of Divine worship, there is neither Idolatry nor Superstition.'[72]

Uniting the Protestants in war-torn Europe

Durie's first aim was to gain Gustav Adolf's support for his European tour. The Thirty Years War (1618-1648) was in full swing and he had to travel through country ransacked by warfare. After arriving at a number of recent battle-scenes, Durie found that Gustav had already marched on but managed to reach him at Würzburg where the King gave him full support. Besides already being briefed by Spens as mentioned above, Privy-Councillor Godeman had kept King Gustav informed of Durie's plans and had passed on Durie's reports to the King.[73] However, his chief army padre in Germany, Johannes Botvidius, was against Durie's plans. When Durie complained to Oxenstierna, Botvidius was quickly replaced by Johannes Matthiae who became Queen Christina's tutor and Durie's life-long friend. Durie then travelled all through Germany, meeting important unionists and members of the Leipzig Conference such as Paul Tossanus, Johann Crocius, who wrote a most detailed account as an eye-witness of the Leipzig Conference, and Theophilus Neuberger who wrote a more brief account.[74] Durie was supported by the Protestant princes, especially by exiled King Fredrick V, the Landgrave of Hesse-Cassel and the Elector of Branden-

---

[71] See Durie's published accounts entitled *An Extract, out of the Nationall Synode, held by the Churches of France, at Charaton, in September 1631*; *Colloquium Lipsiae habitum inter utriusque partis Theologos ad Consensum in Doctrina contestandum: cui subjungitur decretum ordinum Euangelicorum ad Concordiae Conatum promovendum & praemittitur extractum ex Epistola D. Joh, Bergii, ad Duraeum de Colloquii Instituti scopo & usu; Extractum ex Epistola D. Dris. Joh Bergii ad Joh. Duraeum, qua cum Colloquii Lipsiae habiti Apographhum ei misit, Angliae Praesulibus & Theologis communicandum; Colloquium Lipsiae habitum anno 1631. Inter Lutheranos & Reformartos Theologos de reconciliandis Euangelicorum in Germania diffidiis*.

[72] See Durie's *An Extract, out of the Nationall Synode, held by the Churches of France, at Charenton, in September, 1631*.

[73] See Godeman's letter to Durie dated 27 March, 1631, Ref: 5/44/1A-2B, 1B, 2A Blank, HP.

[74] See the Hartlib Papers for correspondence between Tossanus, Crocius and Neuberger.

burg. After a meeting of the Protestant powers and leading churchmen at Cassel in June 1632, Durie told Roe 'I found the fulfilment of my wishes at last'.[75] Further conferences were planned for the following year with the Reformed and Lutheran church and state leaders, including Oxenstierna. However, three of Durie's major allies – King Gustav, Frederick V and Lord Spens – died in the autumn of 1632. Moving through territory held by the Emperor, Durie attended a conference called by the Earls of Wetterau and Count Ysenburg in Friedberg on 10th September 1632 which prepared negotiations with the Court and Church of England. After Friedberg, Durie visited the Dukes of Pfalz-Simmern and Zweibrücken-Kleeburg (Deux-Ponts-Kleeburg) whose families also promised their support.[76] Long letters to Sir Thomas, dated throughout December 1632[77] show that a large number of Protestant princes were supporting Durie, and he was being given many letters from the German courts and churches to send to Archbishop Abbot. Durie also made sure that copies were sent to William Laud, then still Bishop of London. A synod of Protestant ministers and court representatives was held at Herborn in January 1633 and the delegates voted unanimously to support Durie and sent a sixteen-paged account of the proceedings to the Archbishop of Canterbury, looking to him for support.[78]

Charles I now sent a gift of £15,000 to the Protestant powers in Germany, promising their troops a further £10,000 a year as Britain's contribution to Protestant defence in Europe. Oxenstierna, who now considered himself the Governor of Germany, told Charles' ambassador Anstruther that he did not want England's interference in Sweden's campaigns but would welcome British funds and British soldiers put under his command. Anstruther, now joined Durie in Hesse so that he might prepare the Heilbronn Colloquy of 1633 with him and profit from Durie's help in transactions with the Protestant states in general and concerning the Palatinate in particular. Chancellor Oxenstierna was to chair the conference. The Swedish delay in giving the Palatinate their full backing was apparently due to Ambassador Sir Henry Vane's *mal-entendu* (Queen Elizabeth's expression) with King Gustav, whereas both Frederick and Elizabeth, besides, of

---

[75] *Documents and Letters Written by John Durie*, Westin Collection, Uppsala, 1932.
[76] Simmern, Zweibrücken and Lantern were Palatinate principalities. Queen Victoria of England was in the seventh generation of a direct line from Countess Palatinate Eleonore Katharine of Zweibrücken-Kleeburg (1626-1692).
[77] See Westin's Documents and Letters 1628-1634 appendixed to his *Negotiations about Church History*, pp. 217-228.
[78] Ref: 59/10/92A-108B, HP.

course, Durie, felt that Roe would have been the better ambassador.[79] Durie, himself, served Elizabeth as a personal friend and ambassador, keeping her in touch with affairs in England and especially Poland where many Protestant Bohemian refugees lived.

At Heilbronn, all the Protestant delegates voted to adopt Durie's plans for union[80] as did further conferences at Mainz and Darmstadt. Now the *Concilium Formatum* of German Protestant states was set up and requested Oxenstierna to do all in his power to put Durie's plans into practice. Then Durie attended an even more important conference at Frankfurt, where he was allowed to address the four chambers of diplomats and clergy gathered and relates, 'The effect of this was that by generall consent they granted my desire'. After conferences at Hesse-Cassel,[81] Hanau, Wetterau, the free areas of the Palatinate, Heilbronn, Darmstadt and Frankfurt, which proved successful, Durie now felt that the time was ripe for more concrete action regarding Britain as Oxenstierna, the Marquis of Brandenburg and the Duke of Hesse had enough pan-European influence between them to work out a permanent union with Charles, Abbot and Laud. Durie left Frankfurt on the 26th or 27th of July 1633 and after perilous travels through war-torn territories and areas of religious and political upheaval, arrived at Utrecht on October 11.

Work under Archbishop William Laud

On his way, early in August, Durie heard that Archbishop George Abbot had died and in September, William Laud, the former Bishop of London, had replaced him in office. Obviously, Durie, who had been on good terms with Abbot, was now more anxious than ever to travel to England and find out if Laud were still willing to carry on Abbot's and Durie's irenic policies. At Utrecht, Durie talked with his old friend Buschoven and the Swedish agent in Holland, Hugo Grotius, whom he found gave a ready ear to his plans but wished to go further than Durie and bring the Roman Catholics closer into ecumenical talks. Durie then had brief conversations with Poliander and Rivet and was received by the Lord Mayor of Rotterdam, Lord Berkel, a fellow campaigner for peace amongst Protestants. He then visited

---

[79] *Calendar of State Papers, Domestic Series*, Addenda, Chas. I. p. 446. Also, see Everet-Green's *Elizabeth of Bohemia*, p. 292.

[80] See the findings of the Herborn Synod sent to the English Church on 10 Jan. 1633 signed by 21 delegates Ref: 59/ 10/82A-91B, HP.

[81] See statement made by the Cassel pastors and professors, 1 Jan. 1633, Ref. 59/10/113A-116B, HP.

Durie's Life and Labours 65

Middelburg where he found Hebrew scholar Adam Boreel very much open to his ideas of cooperation between the Lutherans and Reformed. The Dutch begged Durie to spend the winter in the Netherlands, but he was anxious to bring the good news to Archbishop Laud so he shipped from Flushing and arrived in London on November 8.

Durie spent his first few days in England writing *A Summary Relation of that which Jhon Dury hath prosecuted,* one of Durie's works from which this account is compiled. This he presented to the Archbishop during the middle of the month and secured an interview with him. He wrote to Thomas Roe from Westminster on 17th December 1633, telling him that he had briefed Laud on three topics concerning the state of the Protestant churches in Germany aiming:

'1. to show the state of their differences and subdivisions as well in Doctrine as affection & Church discipline one from another & amongst themselves.

2. to show their meannesse in goods, Authority & Learning.

3. & lastly to show their changeable conditions & y:t to agree them and to confirm their agreement a new government may be erected amongst them, & an uniformitie of divine seruice brought in, wherin they much differ.'[82]

Durie now consulted Secretaries of State, Sir Francis Windebank, suspected of being a Crypto-Romanist and Sir John Coke, a noted Puritan and senior member of the Privy Council, so as to gain the backing of as broad a front as possible. Durie kept up his correspondence with Oxenstierna and was overjoyed to hear that the Swedish Governor was planning a series of meetings with the Lutheran and Reformed states culminating in a Diet at Frankfurt on 24 February on the lines suggested by Durie. Oxenstierna was regretting his standoffish treatment of England and was sending his own son Johan Oxenstierna (1611-1657) to England as an ambassador of peace.

Laud was slow to fit Durie out with the credentials and introductory letters he needed, so Durie gave Laud a draft of what he expected. After Durie was officially ordained by Bishop Hall, Laud gave Durie the necessary documents. Durie examined them and told Roe in a letter written 12 March, 1633/4 that they were 'emphatic enough and full of strong expressions of love to the work, and some commendation of Durie's labours'[83]. Then Durie crossed the North Sea with British troops as their temporary chaplain, having no money for regular fares. At Hamburg, he found the

---

[82] Westin Collection, *Negotiations about Church Unity*, p. 276.
[83] *Calendar of State Papers*, vol. CCLXII, 1633-4, p. 509.

Lutheran clergy most willing to discuss unity with him. Then Durie travelled from Hamburg southwards with Ambassador Anstruther to the Frankfurt Conference. The Diet now seemed to be attracting more and more international interest so the King of France decided to send an ambassador there, though his only aim seemed to be to demand more territories from the German Protestants. The French and Swiss Reformed churches had sent Durie very encouraging letters, but Durie complained of disinterest in the Low Countries because of the wars. He was rather concerned for his safety through enemy territory as he was now carrying so many important diplomatic and ecclesiastical letters which, if lost or stolen, would destroy years of hard work on Durie's part and cause trouble with the Roman Catholic authorities he might meet up with. When Durie reached Frankfurt somewhat belatedly, he found that his friends had already started to debate his plans for unity and so he could say it 'will now giue me a better ground to worke upon then I could haue deuised if I hadde beene sooner here.'

Durie feared that the *Consilium Formatum* might break up because of Sweden's stern hand on the German states, so he decided to take the initiative once more, and after consulting with the influential ambassadors from the Palatinate, Brandenburg and Hesse who promised their support, Durie presented a paper to the Ambassadors of the sixteen states taking part. Durie found that all, including the Saxons, who asked for separate discussions, were keen to follow him. He then read letters to the Assembly from Archbishops Laud and Ussher; several English and Irish bishops; a number of Puritan divines, Oxford and Cambridge, besides letters of support from Sedan, Paris, Leipzig, Jena, Helmstedt, Zürich and Uppsala. The French Reformed present pointed out to Durie that they had already entered into peaceful cooperation with the Lutherans at the Assembly of Charenton. Indeed, the French who had been prevented from attending the Synod of Dort felt Durie's reforms did not go far enough and any agreement on doctrine and ceremonies was quite unnecessary. The Reformed Church of Anhalt,[84] who had not even been invited to the Synod of Dort, maintained that following Durie's proposals was the only way to peace.[85] The Conference quickly drew up an official Act beginning:

> First, 'That master Dury having been heard by a solemn Committee, and the Writs which he produced, taken into consideration by the rest of the States,

---

[84] In 1821, the Reformed Church of Anhalt entered into a 'Church Union' with the Lutherans.

[85] See Brandes, John Dury and his Work for Germany, *Catholic Presbyterian*, July, 1882, p. 30.

all of them with unanimous consent, did judge his Work most laudable, most acceptable to God, and most necessary, and usefull to his Church'[86]

In the further five points made, they suggested that those ambassadors who had agreed to the motion but had not received official authority from their Princes, should quickly report back to them to obtain permission to go ahead in preparation for a general international synod. This should be chaired by an organisational committee composed of the Electors of the Palatinate, Saxony, Brandenburg and Hesse. Divines should be called outside of the Empire and 'an agreement should be made in a Common Confession of Faith containing all the Fundamentals of Religion necessary for Salvation, setting other points of Scholasticall dispute aside.' Meanwhile, the states undersigned should do nothing to hinder the peace in religion and politics and that prayers to this end should be said in both Reformed and Lutheran churches.

Durie quickly posted off his proposals to the Princes who still had to give their agreement. Durie told Ambassador Roe that he would use the Frankfurt Fair to make sure that the good news of the Diet would be broadcast. He also informed Roe that he was facing large printing bills, obviously hoping that Roe would settle them for him. Durie was also keen to print and circulate the letters of Bishops Hall and Davenant as they had taken a very active part in the Synod of Dort. He thus published these in pamphlet form alongside recommendations of Bishop Thomas Morton. For the sake of the Dutch brethren, bishops Morton, Davenant and Hall had their supporting pamphlets and letters reprinted in Amsterdam in 1636. Further editions followed. Davenant emphasised in his Preface that he had undertaken the work after thorough discussions with Durie. Davenant's covering letter to the material he sent Durie has been preserved and shows the close fellowship and trust the two men enjoyed together:

> 'Salutem in Christo.
> I haue now at last sent you vp what you desired. You had receaved it much sooner had j not in vaine expected the returne of my absent Chaplain whom j had thought to haue vsed in writing it out fairer. You must now bee content to take it as it is written with mine own bad hand and worse eyes. I wish it may in some degree answer your expectation. But howsomever take it as a testimony of my love towards yourselfe et good affection towards that busines wherin you are imploied. Thus wishing you et it all happy succes j commit you to the God of Peace and only Author of all happines resting ever
> Your loving frend and Brother in Christ

---

[86] See *A Brief Relation*, p. 11.

Salisburie Io. Sarum.
May the 5th 1634
When you haue receaued the writing signifie so much in a word or 2 that j may bee assured it is come to your hands.
To his loving friend Mr. Iohn Durie.'[87]

Whenever Durie felt that his life's ambition to see peace amongst the churches was reaching fulfilment, something happened to prevent him from reaching his aim. The next letter in the Westin collection dated 18 July begins with the words 'I have dolefull news to tell you'. Durie had already related how, after a number of victories, the Protestant forces suffering from hunger and exhausted after a long march to relieve Ratisbon, lost 15,000 of their 24,000 troops and were utterly defeated by an army three times their size. He had, however, thought that reinforcements were on their way but these, too, were almost annihilated by the Emperor's forces, and at the Battle of Nördlingen there was a further defeat and massacre. This was a nigh fatal blow to the Protestants as the Protestant League had been founded at Nördlingen where the Emperor was now in power. All the foot soldiers were killed or taken prisoners, the cavalry was destroyed and the few survivors fled. Whole brigades were wiped out. Durie's cousin Ramsey was now totally surrounded by vast enemy forces with only 200 men left to command. Durie knew that the Scotsmen's policy in battle in Germany was to fight until their last man was killed as an example to the enemy but also to their German and Swedish allies. Most of the Protestant officers from Colonels downwards were killed or taken prisoner and the few spared blamed their Generals for their negligence and timidity rather than the enemy Emperor. Durie, too, blamed the Protestant leadership, as there was no necessity for the confrontations when hopes of peace between the Protestant states, France and the Emperor were high.

With Germany closed for a while, Durie visited the Netherlands with recommendations from Bishops Hall and Davenant to their fellow Dutch member at Dort, Johannes Bogermann. Durie met Hugo Grotius, Sweden's ambassador, again. At the time, Grotius was sounding out the prospects of a political union of England and Sweden and preparing a Swedish-English confession of faith which was to include the other Scandinavian countries and be used as a basis for Reformed and Lutheran unity in general. The Walloon Churches welcomed Durie and the Utrecht Synod came down fully on Durie's side. Durie met Comenius' son-in-law Peter Figulus, who became his secretary for the following seven years.

---

[87] Ref: 5/24/1A-2B, HP.

Further travels in Sweden, Germany, Denmark, the Netherlands and England

When Oxenstierna moved to Sweden in 1636 to take up his office of Chancellor, Durie decided to follow him with his secretary Figulus and seek further support from Protestant Europe's most powerful leader and ally. Durie first visited Bishop Johannes Rudbeck at Västerås who was perhaps the hardest man in Sweden to convince of the wisdom of Durie's plans. He was himself an ardent educational reformer and founded Sweden's first grammar school besides being an Uppsala Professor and one of the first Swedes to be awarded the newly instituted doctorate at Uppsala. Durie gave a most balanced pen-portrait of Rudbeck with all his pros and cons in a long report to Hartlib in October 1636, preserved in the second Westin collection. Durie explains that they agreed to disagree and became 'pretty intymate friends'. Rubeck did not differ from Durie over his ideas of universal learning but could not agree with Durie's plans for church union, which Rubeck thought were too totalitarian and against local church independence. Durie then informed Hartlib that he had made for Strängnäs to contact Bishop Laurentius Paulinus whom he describes as 'a godly plaine dealinge old man'. Paulinus was soon to become Archbishop. There were several candidates but they all stood back to let Paulinus have the honour. Though he first opposed Durie, he later accepted Durie's plans and the two became 'very great friends'. Paulinus was a Ramist and thus open to the ideas of the British Puritans. He was also interested in Astrology and eschatological speculations which were shared by many Lutherans and English Puritans at the time.[88]

Durie was delighted to receive Uppsala University's agreement on an eight-point plan for Church unity. Again, when all seemed to be going well, the University of Aberdeen through Archbishop Spottiswoode, under great pressure from the Presbyterians, wrote to Uppsala University challenging Durie's wisdom in affiliating with even the mildest of Swedish Lutherans. Again, memories of John Forbes were awakened. In 1637, Oxenstierna took Durie with him for further consultations with Rudbeck and Paulinus. The former refused to consider the fifty suggestions for peace that Durie gave them, but the latter accepted them without question. Now it was Queen Christina's and her Privy Council's turn to give Durie their

---

[88] We find an almost day to day account of Durie's sojourn in Sweden in Westin's and Turnbull's collections besides the Hartlib Papers and Durie's published journals and the Uppsala and Stockholm archives. Apparently, further mss were lost in the great archive fire of 1669.

support and Durie was allowed to attend the final discussions of the June Synod of 1637 and present his plans for union. Influential Rudbeck, however, made it clear that he wanted Sweden's local churches to be free of central state control. However, he demanded many a state right for his local church, including allowing authors to print or not. So, too, at this time, leading bishoprics Västerås and Strängnäs held strongly to their ancient rights and Uppsala was trying to steer a *via media* course between them. Durie's lack of knowledge of these traditions sometimes caused him to appear quite tactless. For instance, in the face of church opposition, Durie appealed to the Privy Council, and made the strategic mistake of criticising Rudbeck, who was a much loved and respected bishop, even by those who did not share his views. This divided Church and government so the Council (not the Church) demanded that the clergy accept the *Augustana invariata* and young Christina, who was for Durie's plans, was forced by her advisors to pronounce an edict on 7 February 1638 compelling Durie to leave the country. The trouble was, with all his love for union and even compromise, his suggestions appeared too extreme for the Swedes. Their main problem was to refrain from being too one-sided in their acceptance or rejection of the Augsburg Confession. Durie brought new problems with him which were not 'Swedish'. Thus, he was officially told that he was to be censored for not holding to the *via media* promoted by Uppsala that ruled, 'wåra församblingar icke komme vthi mistanka hoos andre wåra Troosförwanther, likja som wij icke stadighe wille blifwa widh wår gamble mening.'[89] Durie was told that if he became a member of the Svenska Kyrka, then he could argue from inside and not outside.

Though Tollin gives Rudbeck's intervention as the main reason for Durie's sudden unpopularity,[90] this writer, well familiar with the life of Rudbeck through his studies in Swedish Church History at Uppsala, would suggest that the reason Sweden suddenly changed its mind must be sought not with Rudbeck but in the great doctrinal and confessional controversy between Uppsala and Åbo Universities at the time and the rivalry between Oxenstierna and Christina and also between Johannes Elai Terserus and Christina which thwarted any chances of success on Durie's part. Assessments of the lengthy Uppsala/Åbo debate on inter-Protestant union are nigh absent in works on Durie. So, too the role of Terseus who moved from views similar to Durie's to a conviction that Sweden should become a Catholic Church but without Rome and the pope, need to be taken into consideration. Nor does Tollin explain how, shortly after Durie left Swe-

---

[89] See Sven Göransson, *Ortodoxi och Synkretism in Sverige*, 1647-1660, p. 169.
[90] See Tollin, 243-44.

den, the tide turned back in Durie's favour. This is easily explained when one knows that when Uppsala sought reform, rival Åbo blocked it and vice versa.

Durie returned to Germany in October 1638, finding more backing amongst the Lutheran secular powers than amongst their clergy. However, in 1639, Durie met a man of like vision in Prof. George Calixtus of Helmstedt University who had the backing of Duke August of Brunswick. The latter utilised Durie's comprehensive ideas of library management in developing and organising his famous Wolfenbüttel Library. When Durie left Germany in 1641, the country was more divided on the issue of church union than Sweden was.

Now Durie turned to Denmark where King Christian IV had spoken out in favour of union. Again Durie's hopes were dampened as Christian said he could not move unless Germany, France, Holland and Poland moved with him. His clergy, however, still demanded that the Calvinistic churches should openly repent of their alleged errors and anti-Lutheran propaganda.[91] After his disappointing visit to Denmark, Durie was given a warm welcome in the Netherlands, entertained by church and state leaders such as Heinrich Alting, Johannes Coccejus and William II of Orange. Calls from England now grew stronger and Durie had to leave his haven of rest in the Netherlands and return to England to join Comenius and Samuel Hartlib and consult with Archbishop Ussher and Bishops Morton and Hall and Parliamentarian John Pym. Meanwhile, political revolution was aiming at the end of the monarchy and the outlawing of the Reformed Church of England. In 1641, Durie was made tutor to Princess Maria and her chaplain when she married William II of Orange. Durie now left England for The Hague with the royal couple. Immediately, Durie became active in the work of the Dutch synods, and the Synod of Delft held in September 1641 ruled that they would strive towards a pan-Protestant alliance. Durie commuted regularly between England and the Netherlands and kept up his international correspondence. This was especially the case with his Swedish friends, and when Comenius and his son-in-law departed for Sweden through Durie's initiative, Durie issued them with recommendations and letters to Johannes Matthiae, now Bishop of Strängnäs, and Chancellor Oxenstierna. He also continued a long correspondence with rich merchant and Huguenot, Louis de Geer, one of his long-time supporters, now hosting

---

[91] Several letters are extant in the Hartlib Papers from Durie to Thomas Roe describing the state of the churches in Denmark and their attitude to Durie's plans. These are from 1638-1640.

Comenius in Sweden, and looked after the British church in Rotterdam where he met and married his wife, Dorothy Moore.

Politician, educationalist and ambassador under Cromwell

Since 1640, Durie had been granted access to Parliament both as a petitioner and preacher. In 1641, he petitioned first the King and Parliament with *A Memorial concerning Peace Ecclesiasticall: To the king of England and the pastors and elders of the Kirk of Scotland meeting at St. Andrews* and *Petition to the Honourable House of the Commons in England now assembled in Parliament*; then *A Discourse concerning Peace Ecclesiasticall* and the year after *Petition to the House of Commons, for the Preservation of True Religion* and *Petition to the House of Commons; whereunto are added, certain Considerations, showing the necessity of a Correspondence in Spiritual Matters, between Protestant Churches*. It was in this petition that Durie included a description he had sent to Alexander Henderson and the Scottish Assembly concerning his views for a common Practical Divinity to be used throughout the British and European Protestant churches.

These documents led to Durie being proposed as a member of the planned Westminster Assembly. They also help to solve the mystery fostered by W. M. Hetherington in his *History of the Westminster Assembly*. Hetherington argues that not Durie but Alexander Henderson was the British divine who pioneered the work of peace and union amongst the churches.[92] As we see from Robert Baillie's letters, Durie had been petitioning the Scottish ecclesiastical leaders in general and Henderson in particular since 1635. The evidence Hetherington produces for this theory can only be called worse than scanty. He builds it on one document allegedly from Henderson's pen which is fiercely intolerant and most unlike Henderson. Hetherington confesses in his Preface that he has not discussed alternative research and has merely 'perused' a few essential documents but found it 'impractical' to study the largest collection of minutes and reports extant in Dr Williams Library.[93] He obviously has no first-hand knowledge of the verbatim minutes of the official Assembly scribe, Adoniram Byfield,

---

[92] *History of the Westminster Assembly*, p. 363. See also pp. 362-364; 376-384. See my John Durie: Defragmenter of the Reformation for a full rebuttal of this theory.

[93] More research must be done in determining which works Henderson actually wrote. He was either a Janus or several works attributed to him are not from his pen.

a friend and supporter of Durie's and about the only Presbyterian Cromwell trusted after Pride's Purge.[94]

Durie continued to publish on church union and educational reform throughout 1642. He planned international theological colleges in London and Heidelberg under British supervision and a chain of schools throughout Britain based on his, Comenius' and Hartlib's system. Johannes Matthiae and Queen Christina, his most faithful Swedish contacts, planned the same for Sweden and Germany. Durie was praised repeatedly before Parliament as a man who 'well advanced the peace and unity of the Reformed churches' and linked with Bacon and Comenius as a 'pioneer of a new age'.[95] However, the political unrest in Britain and the growing rebellion limited Durie's philanthropic and ecclesiastical endeavours greatly as monies were reserved for the war game that put a stop to the natural progress of Reformation. Durie then published his *Motion Tending to the Public Good of this Age and Posteritory* which late nineteenth and early twentieth century Foster Watson called 'the best model'[96] for a child's education ever put forward in the seventeenth century. Last century's J. M. Batten went further and called it 'a landmark in the history of English education'.[97]

In 1643, Durie was voted in as a full member of the Westminster Assembly; a fact which received strong criticism from the Scottish representatives who were not given full voting rights as he was. Indeed, Durie was also the only member whom Charles I had urged to join the Assembly. The Scots spread the rumour that Durie was a royal spy, which Durie soon contradicted in various pamphlets. However, once Durie was established in England, the Scottish members looked to him to do them favours. Samuel Rutherford, for instance, wrote to Durie around 1647, saying:

> 'Sir
> The Gentelman whom I entreate yow to recomend is William Hamilton Esquire Son to Sir Robert Hamilton of Goswick not farr from Barwick he suffered the loss of his estate by the Kings residing at his Fathers house when he went to Dunslaw for his Father was & he himselfe hath always beene for the Parliament cause. His abilities for learning are more then ordinary: he hath beene a Regent in the Colledge of Glascow, and with much credit taught the course of Philosophy whiles he stayed there: & since he left that station & came hither partly to see what subsistence God would provide

---

[94] These are soon to be published in transcribed and edited form by the Westminster Assembly Project, a Post-Doctoral Fellowship work at Cambridge University.
[95] See, for instance, John Gauden's 1640 Fast Sermon before Parliament,
[96] *Educational Review*, 'Dury's 'Public Good' and Education', vol. 1, p. 776.
[97] Batten, p. 168.

for him instead of his losses for which he doth expect some reparation partly to improove his abilities in some parts of humane & Divine Learning: he hath lived in very good credit in the acquaintance of some of the chiefe Ministers of the Assembly soe that besides the consideration of his losses for the Parliament and his faithfulnes to the cause, and the services which he may in dve time doe in it, I am sure that his parts will be very vsefull for the Vniversitie in respect of his piety & learning & may proove in dve time a speciall Ornament thereunto. For which causes I entreate yow to recommend him to some preferment: for thereby yow will doe the Public good service, and oblige a man off worth.'

Durie obliged Rutherford and, at first was quite naively taken in by Hamilton's promises of cooperation and the offer of writings which he professed to have which would enhance their work. Partly because of their 'first impression' and partly because of a wish to live in peace with the Scottish Presbyterians, Hartlib allowed Hamilton to sign a pact which he and Durie had drawn up with Comenius as a replacement for the latter who had withdrawn himself from this cooperative project. So the 'Triumvirate' of pansophists was reinstated, to use Trevor-Roper's term for the signatories.[98] The full story of this pact will be dealt with in Chapter VII of this thesis. Durie warned Hartlib not to give Hamilton too much attention on hearing that the Scotsman was in debt. However, the two men obtained a post for Hamilton at All Souls College, Oxford, which he did not keep long, though he did once lend Hartlib and Durie £10 from his salaries. However, thereafter, Hamilton immediately became something of a financial burden to Hartlib and Durie as he could not stand on his own feet and always reminded them of their obligations to him. He would either not keep or find employment either in Britain or abroad and did not contribute to Durie's and Hartlib's research and publications. It soon became clear that Hamilton was something of a Presbyterian 'mole' in their undertakings, claiming that Durie had no right to meddle in any work of pacification amongst ministers as he was apparently no lawful minister (i.e. a Scottish-type Presbyterian) himself. After his first smiles and bows, he became most insulting and intolerant, complaining that Hartlib and Durie had not opened the doors for him to the top university posts he fancied though they had the influence to do so. Hamilton now treated Hartlib and Durie as enemies of the Presbyte-

---

[98] *The Crisis of the Seventeenth Century*, p. 234. See Chapter VII of this dissertation for the background and results of this pact.

rian Church,[99] and, as he would not, like Durie, sign the 'Engagement' in support of Cromwell, he was compelled to flee to the Continent in 1650.

Baillie's own much published animadversions against Durie[100] seem to have been only of an intolerant political kind as he wrote to William Spang, his cousin who pastored a Scottish church in Middelburg, Zeeland, in 1637, saying:

> "Concerning Durais business, when ever I hear of the advancement of it, I am refreshed; yow neid put no questione on our side, for we did ever earnestlie sute (petition for) it. I marvell of your Hollanders that does oppose it now. The best of them, Voetius, I am sure, and, as I remember, Rivet and Valle, has declared in print their judgement for that Unione. I fear the Saxon divines shall now retract their Leipsick Conference. I wish Durae would turn his Hypomnemata[101] into a full storie, like that of Hospinian, in Re Sacramentaria. His answers that he has gotten from Divines and Princes, if they were in print, would be much for edificatione. I was much bettered by the wreit of the thrie Inglish Bishopes. I wish yow sent to the Colledge some wrytes of that kinde, such as Paraei Irenicon, and Crocii Assertio Augustana, with Menzeri Anticrocius, and one Christophorus Massenus, or some other, who writes well on that subject. However, it be now two years since Durae wreit to St. Andrewes of that purpose, yet never did I hear of any such purpose, no, not to this day, bot from yow, albeit, in such purposes, I am curious of intelligence."[102]

Indeed, Baillie regularly asked his cousin to send him copies of any writings to and from Durie which he could get that had to do with peaceful connections between the Protestant churches on the Continent.[103] In a very lengthy letter dated August 20th, 1641 to Spang, Baillie gives a report of the meeting of the Scottish Assembly in which a letter from Durie concerning 'assistance to his *Negociation of peace among Protestants* was read by the Moderator. Here, Baillie clearly took Durie's side and so praised the motion that it was accepted. Baillie, Andrew Ramsey, Blair and Gillespie were asked to formulate a reply to Durie and Blair was chosen to write it. The letter was read to the ministers in a further meeting and approved.

---

[99] See Hamilton's correspondence with the Durie circle in the Hartlib Papers, mostly with agent Hartlib but especially his letter dated December 17, 1649, Ref: 9/11/18A-20B, HP.

[100] See Carruthers' *The Everyday Work of the Westminster Assembly*, p. 187 where he quotes alleged critical evidence from one, of Baillie's letters to Spang.

[101] *Hypomnemata de studio pacis ecclesiasticae*, Amsterdam, 1636.

[102] Baillie, vol. 1, p. 9.

[103] See, for instance, Baillie, vol. i., p. 117.

Durie was asked to keep the ministers of Edinburgh briefed about his transactions.[104] Several letters are extant from Durie to Henderson soliciting support from him and his Scottish brethren for Protestant union. However, with the Rebellion and after Baillie's invitation to Westminster in 1641, Baillie wrote a number of aggressive pamphlets regarding taking vengeance on alleged 'delinquents' of a non-Presbyterian persuasion, so Durie felt compelled to tell him and his fellow delegates to keep to the peaceful agreement they had made with England and:

> 'God grant that yow all may remember yowr oath & and the Declaration of yowr intention in coming into England; & that by seeking a nationall union yow may not giue occasion unto some that will no doubt seeke occasions with aduantage, to sowe the seeds of a nationall division. my heart doth tremble when I consider the possibilities of mens intentions; & unmaske the actions of tymes past: yet I hope all will be well; & that God will direct yow, that yowr wayes may be equall in the ende as in the beginning; & that yow may not trust to your strength nor be lifted up by success but feare, to this effect yow shall haue continually my prayers, who am yowr brother & fellow seruant in the Gospell of Christ.'[105]

Naturally, Durie sent his countrymen copies of his proposals for pan-Protestant peace especially to Baillie, Ramsey and Henderson for their consideration.

Durie gladly accepted membership of the Westminster Assembly and saw it as a further opportunity to foster international church and political union, especially his campaign for a state agency for the advancement of learning and an alliance of European protestant churches. He was told to keep a base on the Continent to this end, so he accepted a call as a commuting chaplain to the English traders in Rotterdam. Durie immediately not only gained Cromwell's and Parliament's full backing but also that of the leading Puritans. He was appointed to chair, sit on and speak before numerous joint committees, sub-committees and petition groups. He found that men of science and letters such as Robert Boyle, John Pell, Theodor Haak and John Milton were happy to work with him. Parliament ordered Durie to translate Milton's book *Eikonoklastes* into French.[106] Indeed, Durie, Hartlib and their close supporter Katherine Viscountess Ranelagh, Boyle's sister and Durie's wife's niece, and close correspondent, formed

---

[104] Ibid, p. 364.
[105] Ref: 2/3/3A-4B, HP.
[106] *Eikonoklastēs, ou, Réponse au livre intitulé Eikon basilikē, ou, Le pourtrait de Sa Sacrée Majesté durant sa solitude & ses souffrances.*

the heart of Milton's famous Petty France group of educational reformers.[107] In 1645, Durie became Member for Winchester and minister of the Cathedral Church and was told 'to reform that place.' Durie promptly prepared a catechism of Christian doctrine and drilled ministers and congregation in the doctrines of the Reformation. Winchester School moved him to produce further bestsellers on education and reform such as his *Reformed School*.

Though Durie did his best to keep up his writings on Universal Learning and Practical Divinity, he found he was drawn into politics, especially as a mediator between the Presbyterians and the Independents. During these controversies, he published a series of pamphlets which have been little researched. Tollin, for instance, argues that Durie's 1644 pamphlet *Epistolary Discourse on Toleration* was *against* toleration and for the Presbyterian way only. Actually, in the work, Durie is arguing for toleration regarding Independents and urging both Presbyterians and Independents to learn from each other. In his classical, two-volume work *Memoirs of the Lives and Writings of those Eminent Divines who convened in the Famous Assembly at Westminster*, James Reid even makes Independent Philip Nye the author of Durie's 1644 work, claiming Nye was assisted by Thomas Goodwin and Samuel Hartlib. Durie wrote the work to compel Goodwin and Nye to put their politics on a sound Biblical basis.

In 1645, Durie, now aged forty-six,[108] married Mrs Dorothy Moore, widow of Viscount Moore of Drogheda's son. Mrs Moore brought two young boys into the marriage and had a son and a daughter by Durie. In 1646, Durie was given the task of tutoring the King's children, James, Elizabeth and Henry and worked as Librarian in the ex-King's library. Though Durie was widely employed fostering relationships between the Assembly and the Continental churches, he was also given the responsibility of cataloguing and archiving the Westminster Assembly's records. Durie fulfilled these tasks with meticulous care and his ensuing works on librarianship are still claimed to be sound, practical and revolutionary. During the years 1645-49 Durie co-worked on the *Westminster Confession* and the *Westminster Catechisms*. He, however, was unsatisfied with the outcome and, after Pride's Purge, worked with a committee appointed by Cromwell on a full revision. Whilst at Westminster, he published many works in English, French, German and Dutch, including expositions of Revelation, a rarity at the time. One of Durie's best known works is his *Israel's Call to march out of Babylon unto Jerusalem* (1646) based on Isaiah

---

[107] Dorothy Durie also wrote a treatise on the education of girls.
[108] If he were born in 1599.

52:11 preached before the House of Commons on Nov. 26, 1645. Durie felt that the Puritan tendency to savour their preaching with party politics was not being faithful to the gospel and so denounced this mixing of pulpit with Parliament in his *A Case of Conscience concerning Ministers meddling with State Matters in or out of their Sermons* (1649). His French works were widely appreciated by Continental readers.

Durie also wrote a number of works defending Cromwell's rule. His 'common sense' attitude to Parliament was that any government is more use to God than no government at all and ought to be obeyed. As Cromwell's system worked, nobody had grounds for complaint. This pragmatic approach caused him to accept Cromwell's *Engagement* which required his loyal subjects to affirm, 'I Declare and Promise, That I will be True and Faithful to the Common-Wealth of England, as the same is now established without KING or House of LORDS.' Soon, two groups of Westminster Assembly members were formed, the one calling themselves 'The Old Puritans' and the other 'The Old Protestants'. Ever Durie's opponent, William Prynne took the 'Puritan' side, condemning 'Protestant' Durie. In December 1648, Prynne was banished from Parliament during Pride's Purge. Cromwell found Prynne almost as troublesome as Charles I and Laud and, like them, imprisoned him.

Now Durie became a most active member of the Assembly's Accommodation Committee for pan-Protestant tolerance, which the Presbyterians boycotted. He was instrumental in founding special government institutions for the teaching of Universal Learning but these were short-lived. Parliament became increasingly critical of the work being done in the Westminster Assembly and Durie was chosen to defend that work before Parliament. He thus wrote his *A Discourse concerning the Queries of the House of Commons to the Assembly of Divines touching the Divine Right of the Presbyerie*.[109] The work is undated but the contents require a date before 1648. Here we find Durie in a firm and outspoken mood, telling the Commons:

> 'The Great cause of our Miserie, is that men of public employments have noe public Spirits; few there are that walk in the light openly, according to the Royall law of libertie; for allmost all are snared in Holes and hid in prison houses. The holes are their privat Interests & Endes, without which nothing allmost is done for the Public by any body. & the prison houses are the Parties to which they are engaged; for most men act by the Rule of prejudice; rather, to crosse an opposit partie; then to advance the Universall

---

[109] Ref: 17/9/1A-10B, HP.

good af all. Therefore matters which are named Public are caryed rather by strife and debate, then in a peacable way: & destruction is found to be the path of many, rather then Edification in Love. But seeing yow are inabled to raise your mind above the thoughts of such; as are led by the sense of their flesh to runne into parties; and doe not enquire soe much after the miscariages of others to lay them open and to Clamour against them, before the world; as after the wayes of righteousnes; wherby all men may come unto the accknowledgment and apprehension of that Truth which is after Godlines; seeing I say this is your commendable Endeavour and studie: I think it my duetie to contribute what I can to yowr furtherance therin; & for this cause shall bee at this tyme willing to let yow know my true sense of the doubts which yow make; concerning the Questions which are offered by the Parliament, unto the Assembly of Divines to bee resolved.'

Durie goes on to argue that one cannot hope for any spiritual and just reform in the country so long as the 'Higher Sphere of Government' is unjust and prejudiced against the lower and uses its strength to persecute the weaker. The conscience of rulers must be governed by the Word of God and when that government is settled inwardly on God's Word, they can operate outwardly to settle the nation. At present in England, where even civil conversation is out of order, the young are in revolt against the elder, the base against the honourable and everyman appears to want to oppress his neighbour through prejudice, personal advantage and a seared conscience. Where are the people who are willing to deny themselves for the common good, Durie asks.

This was an indictment against the entire Presbyterian order of society and obviously well-appreciated by Cromwell as the Presbyterians had branded Cromwell as a Usurper and led the campaign against the Engagement. Pride's Purge was thus inevitable and now Durie, former Anglicans and independents pressed on with their campaign for tolerance in reforming Britain under Cromwell. After Pride's Purge of the Presbyterians from Parliament, Cromwell relied more and more on peaceful minded ministers like Durie, Nye, Goodwin and Owen as his advisors. Now foreign Protestant ambassadors felt more liberty again to support Durie and campaign for church unity.

However, that support was more ideological than material and Durie and his wife, Dorothy, found themselves almost penniless as promised benefits, legacies and salaries for Durie never materialised and after the Irish Rebellion, Dorothy Durie lost the rent from her property. They now had also three children to care for, two boys which Mrs Durie had brought into the marriage and a son by Durie who was born in 1649. By 1650, Mrs

Durie was reduced to opening a shop selling oils and herbs as a means of earning a little money. Even members of Durie's circle were quick to criticise Mrs Durie, a Gentlewoman, for becoming 'common'. Hamilton, who had profited greatly from the Duries' benevolence, told Hartlib in his letter of December 17, 1649 amongst his long list of 'discontentments' that he felt Mrs Durie had descended to 'the sordidness of a hostess' and 'stooped' far too much for her station.[110] In spite of such insults, he still demanded firmly that Hartlib and Durie should aid him, pointing out what monies he imagined Hartlib had and what influence he allegedly had in high places. He was obviously jealous that though Hartlib and Durie could not keep a pound without sharing it, at the time, they were helping foreigners and Jews (Boreel and Ben Israel) instead of Hamilton.

Representing the Republic in Sweden, Switzerland, Germany and Holland

Westin cites Samuel Puffendorf's 1686 work *Commentariorum de rebus Suecicis, Libri XXVI* concerning a possible visit of Durie to Sweden in 1652, which, he says, was hitherto unknown to Swedish church historians. Westin had found a letter from Dalerö, dated 7 May, 1652 to Oxenstierna in which Durie asks him how he should proceed as Queen Christina was not in the capital and he wished to announce the arrival of the English ambassador. *The Journal of the House of Commons* for 1652 and Durie's own letters from Stockholm during 1652[111] help us to reconstruct the events. In January, 1652, Queen Christina of Sweden sent a number of letters to the English Parliament, and during the following months several Swedish delegates visited England. The Swedish Ambassador, Silvercron, died whilst in England and caused such embarrassment that on 10 February, Sir Henry Mildmay, Sir Henry Vane and Mr Strickland 'or any two of them' were dispatched to Sweden to report to Queen Christina on the matter. On 25 February, Parliament ruled that the Council of State, under Bulstrode Whitelocke's leadership should compose a fitting letter to Queen Christina and chose a trustworthy man to deliver the letter personally. On 11 March, Whitelocke read out the letter in Latin and French to Parliament and it was accepted. The Speaker signed the letter and it was sealed with the new Parliamentary seal. Then Whitelocke suggested that Daniel Lisle Esquire

---

[110] Ref: 911/18A-20B, HP.
[111] See letters from Stockholm during May and June 1652, 4/2/33A-36B; 4/2/24A-25B; 4/2/22A-23B and Prof. Ravius' letter from Uppsala to Hartlib dated June 12, 436 f. 172AB-172B, HP.

should deliver the letter and be fitted out with all 'Necessaries' for the journey. One of these 'Necessaries' was John Dury, well-known to Queen Christina. This did not delight vindictive Lisle, who told Durie to his face that he did not agree with his aims and methods.

In Durie's report to Lord Commissioner John Lisle, Daniel Lisle's brother, Durie explains that Lisle, who was taken ill in Sweden, had objected to Durie continuing transactions without him. Lisle made terrible accusations against Durie who thus wished Lord Lisle, Richard Bradshaw, the English Resident in Hamburg, and Hartlib to have his side of the story. Durie had been conferring with his old friends the Queen, Chancellor Oxenstierna, now aging rapidly and Prof. Ravius of Uppsala University, a coworker in Durie's circle.[112] The sick Lisle imagined they were plotting behind his back, though Durie gave him full reports of all that was said. Durie was obviously so disturbed by Lisle's attitude and the conviction that there was a spy in the contingent that he asked Hartlib to pass on papers he was sending via Fleming, Cromwell's kinsman, to Bradshaw's Hamburg address to keep them safe 'in case God takes me out of this life before I return'.[113] As both Durie and the Commons refer to 'Mr. Lisle' and not Viscount Lisle, there has been some confusion amongst scholars regarding the two characters.

Mr. Daniel Lisle is next referred to in the House of Commons on his way back from Sweden via Hamburg on 19 June when a letter from him was read out. However, before Lisle's return, Queen Christina sent several angry letters to the English Parliament complaining of Britain's warships attacking 'almost all' Swedish ships and confiscating both the ships and their cargoes, including two gold-transporters.[114] She demanded that England restore all confiscated ships and cargoes to the Swedes and warned Parliament that they were jeopardising the welfare of English citizens residing in Sweden and her territories. Parliament confessed to Christina soon afterwards that the British navy had been looking for prize money and the Swedish ships had not shown them certificates of safe conduct. Sweden, however, as Durie points out had used at least one Swedish ship, disguised as a Dutch vessel to carry goods to Holland for the support of the exiled English King Charles II.[115] After Parliament had listened to these letters being read, Lisle was 'immediately ordered' to present himself on

---

[112] Ref: 4/2/19A-B, HP.
[113] Ref: 4/2/9A-B, HP.
[114] Thurloe's *State Papers*, vol. ii, p. 500.
[115] See also here Durie's *Memorandum: A case to be weiged*, concerning the capture of a Swedish boat by the English for prize money in 1653. Ref. 4/4/13A-B, HP.

Friday 30 July before the Commons. Thurloe's State Papers for the next few days show that England believed their action agreed with international law but decided, this time, to send a more senior ambassador to Sweden to discuss the matter with the Queen. It would seem, therefore, that Lisle's good-will visit to Sweden was not very successful.

However, contrary to what Batten and many other scholars assume, Durie did not visit Sweden in 1653-54 with this delegation. Though various authors have linked Durie's name with that of Lord Viscount Philip Sidney Lisle during this alleged visit, Viscount Lisle backed out of the mission when all had been prepared.[116] Perhaps this was because Sweden had notified the English Parliament that the plague was raging in Stockholm. Lord Commissioner Bulstrode Whitelocke, however, replaced Lisle. Ruth Spalding in her biography of Whitelocke comments: 'Parliament was still smarting from their earlier blunder in sending a callow youth with letters to Queen Christina; unaccustomed to Scandinavian toasts he had disgraced himself in front of the hard drinkers.' The 'illness' of which Durie diplomatically spoke was apparently caused by the wrong kind of 'medicine'. However, Spalding neither mentions Durie in conjunction with Lisle, nor in conjunction with the preparations for sending Whitelocke to Sweden. Nor does Spalding so much as mention Durie when referring to Whitelocke's responsibilities for the St James Library.[117]

Thurloe lists all the conditions Whitelocke was told should be met for a friendship-pact with Sweden. These were rather bullying on England's part, but not one single paragraph related to obtaining any kind of church union between the two countries. Whitelocke had to report regularly to Cromwell and State Secretary Thurloe, the latter being closely connected with Durie, but neither Thurloe nor Whitelocke mention Durie in their correspondence.[118] Sir Robert Stapleton, who assisted Whitelocke, does not mention Durie either. Whitelocke feared the Swedes would do him mischief as they complained that England was still confiscating Swedish ships. To intimidate Whitelocke, drunkards (as Whitelocke calls them) stood outside his Swedish residence calling 'Come out you English dog.'[119] Bradshaw, now Resident in Hamburg, passed on information to Parliament that

---

[116] See Guernsey Jones' Introduction to his thesis Diplomatic relations between Cromwell and Charles X. Gustavus of Sweden entitled, *Relations between England and Sweden before the Beginning of the Northern War*. Jones does not mention a 1652 visit. Jones is obviously relying on Puffendorf as also Westin.
[117] See Spalding, p. 140.
[118] Thurloe, vol. ii, pp. 263-66.
[119] Thurloe, vol. ii. p. 353, Feb-March, 1554.

Durie's Life and Labours 83

the English navy was molesting Swedish seamen and imprisoning their captains. After four months of waiting, Whitelocke was told that in Sweden, representatives of kings were given pre-eminence and others such as Whitelocke had to wait. When Whitelocke was eventually given an audience with Christina, the Queen told him that she was about to abdicate. He was then told to wait until Charles, Christina's successor, was crowned, but he pressed for a quick agreement. The Swedes gave him a much different agreement than the one Parliament had told Whitelocke to bring back. Both sides signed the pact on 28 April 1654. The Swedes were promised fishing rights in British waters and would receive compensation for the plundered Swedish fishermen. After Whitelocke signed, he was promised a safe escort to Travemunde. On 13 May, however, Whitelocke quarrelled with the Swedes concerning compensation for the Swedish ships lost to the English navy, jeopardizing the agreement. A few days later, the Queen abdicated and the new King, Charles Gustav, took the initiative of writing to Cromwell to tell him that Sweden was under a new ruler.

Durie's own correspondence shows conclusively that Durie did not accompany Whitelocke. In a letter to Richard Baxter dated 27 October, 1653, Durie says that he had helped to prepare Whitelocke's visit but could not accompany him because of illness.[120] Cromwell did not delay the diplomatic mission because of Durie as he needed him in Holland, Germany and Switzerland. Whitelocke, though he made quite a figure showing off the latest English fashion in dancing, failed to reach the detailed agreement Cromwell had hoped for, and Durie's plans had not even been discussed. Queen Christina told Whitelocke that she was surprised to find him a Cavalier. This may not have been as complimentary as it sounded as she, her tutor Johannes Matthiae and Professor Ravius at Uppsala had expected Durie and not a court beau. It is perhaps then no wonder that Ruth Spalding names her biography of Whitelocke *The Improbable Puritan*. Before Whitelocke returned from Sweden in April, 1654 old-style, we find Durie writing to Secretary Thurloe from The Hague on his way to Switzerland under orders from Cromwell.[121]

Cromwell was in danger of losing his Dutch and German Protestant allies, and even staunch Swiss support for Cromwell wavered because of their own inner quarrels and fear of France. Johann Jakob Ulrich, Head

---

[120] *Calendar of the Correspondence of Richard Baxter*, Keeble/Nuttall, Vol I, 1638-1660, OUP, 2002, p.114.

[121] See Vaughan's collection of letters in *The Protectorate of Oliver Cromwell and the State of Europe*, 2 vols, p. 1 and passim. Whitelocke returned from Sweden in May, 1654.

Pastor at Zürich, had become a close friend and enthusiastic correspondent of Durie's, so in 1653, he told the Swiss envoy in London, von Schaffhausen, to include Durie in his consultations. This move was so successful that Cromwell decided to send Durie and another member of the Durie circle, John Pell the mathematician, to Switzerland early in 1654 as ambassadors. Pell was to take care of the political side and Durie the ecclesiastical. At times, such as when dealing with the Swiss envoy, Stockar, both men received the Swiss representatives together. Durie was then to tour Germany and the Netherlands. Besides credentials received from Cromwell, Durie received authorisations from the Vice Chancellors and professors of Oxford, and Cambridge Universities and the ministers of London to speak on their behalf.[122] By this time, both Durie and his wife were officially receiving life pensions from the Commonwealth Treasury with all expenses paid.[123] This allowance, however, met with opposition from the member of the Council in charge of the monies.

Brauer writes of Durie being accompanied by his wife and John Pell to The Hague. There the Duries alleged left Pell and proceeded to Amsterdam where Mrs Durie obtained quarters. Thereafter, Durie allegedly visited his wife in Amsterdam from time to time. Brauer cites no evidence for this information which strictly contradicts letters between Dorothy and John and from Durie to Hartlib and other people in England, where Mrs Durie was obviously still living. Durie speaks of the comfort her letters are to him and how concerned he was when he heard she was ill as she was expecting a child (born around May 1654); the girl later became Mrs Oldenburg. Perhaps Brauer was misled here by Durie's references to a Moore (Mr) who lived in Amsterdam, assuming that this was a home belonging to the Mores of whom Mrs Durie was a member. Durie also complains in these letters of a new man in the Great Council called Mr Cressit (also called 'Cresit') who had been harassing his wife in England with threats of withdrawing Durie's income and recalling him to England.[124] Cressit also sought to persuade Jessey to break with Durie as seen in Chapter Five. Durie took up the matter with Henry Lawrence, the Lord President of the Great Council

---

[122] Copies are extant in the Hesse State Archives in Marburg, 22a 1 Nr. 10, as also itinerary and documents related to Durie's Swiss, German and Dutch visits.

[123] Full details of Cromwell's warrants for the support of Durie and his wife are found in A. 62. 10; 260. 4; 261. 2b-4; 326. 13 at the Bodleian. Copies of documents appertaining to Durie's passport and recommendations from Cromwell are also given in an appendix in Brauer's *Die Unionstätigkeit John Duries unter dem Protektorat Cromwells*.

[124] See letter for 1654 and 1655 in Refs 4/3/7A-B; 4/3/13A-B; 4/3/75 A-B; 4/3 93A; 4/3/ 118A-B in the Hartlib Papers.

in a very diplomatic way and we hear nothing more of Cressit,[125] though now Durie found it an impossible task to appropriate the funds promised him.

After the Netherlands had been reconciled to England through Swiss and other European mediation, Pell moved to Utrecht and Durie visited the international churches in Amsterdam and consulted with Irenists such as Gaudery Hotton, pastor of the French Church. William Hamilton had continued to insult Hartlib in his correspondence, so when Durie was in Amsterdam in April 1654, he visited Hamilton whom he found unemployed and sought to reconcile him to Hartlib and gave him some money to assist him in seeking work. Durie's friend Morian found work for Hamilton but it was refused. Hamilton returned to England thinking he could receive his old post at All Souls, Oxford back, although Durie had warned him in Holland that his chances of employment would be greater in that country. Once again, in England without employment, Hamilton insisted that Hartlib should help to finance him, though he continued to criticise Hartlib and Durie massively. Hartlib wrote to Hamilton in 1657, enclosing a pamphlet from Durie's pen entitled *An Answer to the Proposall of Doubts, made by Mr. Hamilton Concerning his Engagement with Mr. Durye and Mr. Hartlib, to prosecute public aimes.*[126] The bone of contention appeared to be the *Foedus Fratrum* which he had signed as a substitute for Comenius, outlined in detail in Chapter VII of this thesis. The three original subscribers had believed in a covenant as taught by the Protestant churches in 1642, before the major dominance of the Presbyterian movement. Hamilton had understood the theological statements in the pact to refer to the Solemn League and Covenant as interpreted by the Hyper-Presbyterians. Durie's paper apparently put an end to Hamilton's hostilities and his unfruitful correspondence.

Once again, the work of peace amongst the Protestants was drawing England, Germany, Holland and Switzerland and possibly France together. Once in Zürich, the canton took Durie's side with *laude atque applausu*, and a joint colloquy at Aarau was organised before individual consultations

---

[125] Ref: 4/3/85A-86B: 86A, HP.
[126] Ref: 9/11/31A-34B, HP. Turnbull reproduces the article as an appendix to his Hartlib, Dury and Comenius.

at Bern, Basel and Schaffhausen.[127] Basle was not very communicable because Durie had gone to Zürich and Bern before consulting with them.[128]

After returning to Zürich, Durie travelled via St. Gallen to the eastern Swiss churches. Everywhere, Durie received official documents from politicians and churches who agreed with his plans. Now Durie moved through Biel and Neuchatel to Geneva and Lausanne. To commemorate Durie's visit to the Academy at Lausanne, Peter d'Apples, wrote:

> 'Ecce Duraeus adest quo non sapentior alter
> Qui pietate parem vix saecula nostra tulerunt
> Aethereum cujus spirant praecordia numen
> Qui rem restituit nobis duce et auspice summo
> Numine quo molitur opus memorabils saeclis,
> Jam jam aderit qui summus oves compellet in unum
> Pastor ovile suas solida qui foedere jungat
> Pectora qui firma compagine membra redempti
> Corporis infuso connectat flamine sacro.'[129]

Durie was now so popular that the cantons were quarrelling over who should be next in Durie's schedule. Various cantons produced a *Declaratio* or *Judicium* of their own but at last on 21 April 1655, the Protestant cantons presented Durie with a joint *Judicium* and *Declaratio* and a letter to Cromwell saying that Switzerland was now moving towards union with other Protestant states with all speed. France, who claimed ownership of the French-speaking Reformed cantons, especially Geneva, was furious and threatened military action but feared to interfere because of Cromwell, who was now pledged to protect Protestant Switzerland. Durie's life was now in grave danger and he had to travel under the pseudonym of Robertson (Son of Robert Durie), Pell adopting the name of Adrian Peters. State Secretary Thurloe used these names in his letters. The Swiss gave Durie a secret code so that he could keep up his vast correspondence undisturbed. Before leaving Switzerland, Durie wrote to a number of German nobility and clergy, forwarding copies of his successful transactions with Switzer-

---

[127] See Durie's description of these events in his report to State Secretary Thurloe preserved in the Hartlib Papers, Ref: 4/3/63A-64B.

[128] For further particulars concerning Durie's service under Cromwell, I have used Durie's preserved letters in the various collections listed, including Vaughan's, and reports of Durie's agenda in Pell's diary from 1654 to the beginning of 1659. I have gathered material from the numerous Durie publications and minutes listed in the Bibliography, also his *Syllabus documentorum* and *Supplementum Syllabi*.

[129] Taken from *Berner Beiträge zur Geschichte der Schweitzerischen Reformationskirchen*, p. 307.

land and asking for leave to discuss inter-Protestant cooperation with them. Ten such letters to Solms-Braunfels alone, from Durie in German and Latin have been preserved and are outlined with copies of further correspondence with William Otto Solms and church dignitaries by Oberpfarrer Himmelreich of Braunfels in his 'Die Einigungsbestrebungen des Johannes Duraeus zwischen den evangelischen Konfessionen und die Klassen des Solmser Landes'. This is a further example of how enormous Durie's correspondence still was. Durie now travelled through Germany and Holland with the Swiss *Judicium* in his luggage as a sound argument for a wider union.

After the Treaty of Westphalia (1648), which came principally into being through the diplomacy of Queen Christina, Germany had enjoyed seven years of relative peace before Durie's 1555 visit. Pan-Protestant talks seemed to be progressing. Durie, however, found his going tough, as many of Germany's states were ruled by relations of Charles I to whom they had looked for relief against both the Roman Catholic Emperor and Protestant Sweden. They now ranked Durie with 'King-Killer' Cromwell as an enemy of the Protestant Stuarts, so Durie found his Commonwealth credentials were often scorned. So, too, Cromwell was under suspicion by the Reformed churches of allying with Roman Catholic Spain and France. The Swiss *Judicium* found, however, general interest. So, first of all, Durie decided to storm the citadel of now greatest opposition, the Palatinate, the Lords of which were of Stuart stock, thinking that if he first re-won their support, the rest would be easier. However, Elector Carl Ludwig, once Durie's supporter, now refused to meet him. Durie then made for Württemberg where Lutheran Duke Eberhard III was seeking a Protestant union. Eberhard accepted Durie's plans and promised him that he would win over the Palatinate. Johann Mellet, the Württemberg court-preacher, supported him.

In June 1655, Durie visited his old friend Mattieu Rouyer at the Walloon church in war-devastated Hanau. Amongst the Lutherans, a second generation of peace-lovers promised their support and on 31 July, a conference at Hanau provided Durie with backing that rivalled that of Zürich. Durie also found support still strong in Frankfurt, Wetterau, Hesse and Brandenburg. Now Friedrich von Zweibrücken supported by Eberhard of Württemberg, entered into negotiations with Durie again. Numerous church and state leaders now signed the Swiss *Judicium*. Sweden again showed strong interest in Durie through Schnolsky, who declared that Ambassador Christian Bonde was in London ready to enter into union with Britain. Bonde arrived in England with no less than 200 attendants ready to do business with England on behalf of Carl X Gustav. However, the Dutch Ambassador moved Cromwell to be suspicious of Bonde who he feared would clinch a deal with England against Dutch interests. Bonde found out that whatever he suggested to Cromwell in the way of co-lateral cooperation, other European states wanted a hand in it. Once envisaging a union of politics, military powers and religion with Sweden when Holland and France were at enmity with England, as pan-European peace grew, Cromwell grew less interested in co-lateral agreements with Sweden. Bonde's mission became something of a failure, chiefly because of the fact that Sweden would not give up claims on Denmark, Prussia and Holland.

Professor Hottinger, originally of the Palatinate, now representing Zürich, at last persuaded Elector Carl Ludwig to work with Durie, who found the Dukes of Wetterau and their clergy still on his side and also influential Hesse-Cassel, Brandenburg and Nassau. In a conference at Marburg University, Durie was given full backing. Now, however, complications arose in Anhalt through false rumours that the royal signatures on Durie's documents were fakes and Durie was a crypto-republican. Durie dashed over and soon re-won Koethen, Dessau and Bernburg and their Ascanian rulers to his plans on 30 November, 1655. Letters of introduction and recommendation were now given him for the other eastern states, and Durie made for Lutheran Thüringen and Weimar where he hoped to consult brothers Wilhelm IV of Weimar and Ernst von Gotha, Duke of Saxe-Gotha and Altenburg. Ernst von Gotha has gone down in history as 'Ernst der Fromme'.[130] It was now March 1656. The Duke of Saxe-Gotha insisted on discussing with Durie from 8.00 a.m. until 6 p.m. for two whole days. The stones of stumbling were the Book of Concord on the one side and the Synod of Dort on the other. Thereafter, the Duke brought senior members of the Court and leading theologians into the talks. Though no official documents were drawn up, Durie had found two lasting allies in Eastern Germany.[131]

Now Durie journeyed to Rotenburg an der Fulda to report to Landgrave Hermann and then to Eschwege to consult Landgrave Friedrich and the Swedish ambassador Horn, who promised to instruct the new King of Sweden, Charles X concerning Durie's progress. This Dr. Horn or Horneius is to be distinguished from Thomas Horn of the Durie-Hartlib circle of educators. Dr. Horn, though he spoke of an ecumenical council of Protestant churches in a paper sent to Hartlib, appeared to have had merely

---

[130] Ernest the Pious.
[131] A visit to the Museum for Stadtgeschichte, Dessau, Saxon-Anhalt proved very worthwhile regarding this period.

a political or even warring target in mind. Durie was worried about the way he was being associated with Horn and wrote in August 1655, probably to Worsely:

> 'The iudgment which your freind makes concerning Dr Horn's designe; seemes modest, although it is seuere enough; how farre it may glance also at my endevours I cannot well coniecture; because I find nothing directly mentioned of the busines I haue in hand; except hee meanes by his oecumenicall Counsell & Confederation of all the Protestants & their Princes, that which I haue in hand; as if my endevours did tend to nothing else, but to vnite them, that they might the more powerfully destroy & slaughter Papists; so that it seemes hee doth melt & mix our workes into one mould, to make my busines subordinat unto his undertaking; if by this oecumenicall Counsell & Confederation my worke bee understood, as only intended to that effect.
>
> How farre hee may bee mistaken in Dr. Horn's designe I know not; but if that bee his notion of mine; I am sure that hee is as farre wide, at least, as wee are distant one from another: that is, some hundreds of miles.'[132]

After consulting Horn, Durie reported back to Cassel keeping up correspondence with all the places and people he had visited thus far. Durie's friends at Cassel had good news for him from all over Germany. On 8 May, Durie left Cassel for Rinteln to speak with the Lutheran theologians at the university there, three of whom, Henichius, Eccardus and Musaeus were Calixtus' followers and made Durie most welcome.

Now, Durie duly reported to State Secretary Thurloe, enclosing a letter from the landgrave of Hessen. His memorandum for his communication with Thurloe is extant. Durie wanted a collection to be made in England for the Protestant churches and their seminaries in Poland, Hanau, Hessen, Deux Pont (Zweibrücken) and Anhalt which had suffered much under the Roman Catholic-Protestant wars. He asked that Thurloe would move Cromwell to allow him free access to the universities on returning to England, his intention being to internationalise education in Europe. He also requested that Thurloe would look into the matter of his income authorised by the Great Council which did not appear to be forthcoming. Then Durie wrote concerning his decade-long campaign for a Body of Practical Divinity to be used in education, saying:

> 'That his Highness would be pleased to encourage the Compilement thereof by recommending it to the universities: that at the request of forraine Churches it might at last bee taken in hand.'[133]

---

[132] Ref: 4/3/121A-B, HP.

The ministers of Hanau and the Consistory at Cassel had repeatedly approached England through Durie asking for financial support for their churches and schools, and it is sadly obvious that when such support was not forthcoming, though often promises had been made, interest in England's leadership in church and educational life waned and also interest in Durie.[134] However, Durie's campaign to raise money for the Polish churches certainly bore fruit, as Turnbull in his *Hartlib, Dury and Comenius*, speaks of some £11,000 being collected for the Polish and Bohemian Protestants in 1658.[135]

Next, Durie visited Philipp von Schaumburg-Lippe who, with his clergy, promised to back Durie's campaign. At Detmold, Durie attended a conference with the local clergy who were critical of his methods and which did not produce any written agreement. At Tecklenburg, Durie met Count Moritz von Bentheim and his clergy who gave him written testimonies of their support, as did the clergy at Emden. Zig-zagging back, Durie concluded successful visits to the Weser and Ems regions and found that even his old opponent Samuel Mareus, who had caused trouble for him in the Netherlands by calling him a 'King-killer', now signed an agreement drawn up at Groningen to back Durie's plans.

Durie then moved to the Lower Rhine, via Wesel. The leading clergy were at a conference in Duisburg, so Durie followed them and asked them to hear him out. The delegates were so interested that they dropped their planned agenda and debated with Durie for two whole days. The University then published a written endorsement of Durie's views with their own suggestions for Protestant unity.

Durie then visited Cleves and moved back into the Netherlands via Nimegen where the ecclesiastical problems caused by the Synod of Dort were still troubling the Protestants. During his six months' tour of the Netherlands, Durie was accompanied by the Amsterdam minister, John Rulice (Johann Rülz) who appears to have pastored the English there. His next goal was the Synod at Dort of the Dutch Southern Provinces but the delegates told him that he had no authorisation from the civil authorities. More cautious now, Durie asked for permission to attend the Synod of Geldern and joined the conference on 23 July presenting them with no less than twenty-seven recommendations from royalty, public officials and churches.

---

[133] Ref: 15/7/20A-21B, HP.
[134] See letter from the ministers of Hanau dated 29 Feb. 1656 and letter of 1 May, 1656 from the Cassel Consistory in HP.
[135] Turnbull. See his discussion of this topic in Chapter VI.

The result was that the southern reformed churches decided to follow Durie on all points, confident that the civil authorities would accept their plans.

Durie now proceeded to The Hague to speak with the government, but he made no headway. He therefore visited his *alma mater,* Leyden, in the province of Holland but found only Hoornbek who rejected Durie's irenic ideas. Then Durie attended a synod at Utrecht where he was given a warm welcome by clergy and professors. Encouraged by this, Durie moved up to Alkmaar via Amsterdam and attended the Northern States Synod. Here, the civil authorities banned Durie from addressing the gathering for want of Church backing. Thus Durie wrote to the General Assembly of Dutch States enclosing an overview of all his work. The Assembly refused to act on the grounds that the secular arm could not tell the individual civil authorities and churches what to do. They suggested that Durie should visit each Province and each church separately to gain their agreements. Of course, this was the very method Durie had been following all the time but it had not worked. Nothing daunted, Durie attended the Synod of Utrecht and laid all his problems and difficulties before them. After checking that all the written documents Durie presented to the Synod were correct (there had been rumours of forgeries), the Synod heartily endorsed all that Durie was doing and promised to seek for open doors on the issue in the other provinces and ecclesiastical districts.

Ever learning from his mistakes, Durie decided to tour Zeeland, starting at Middelburg, after informing the Dutch and French churches of his plans and gaining their agreement. Various churches helped him by calling all the surrounding presbyteries to a larger gathering but their enthusiasm was limited. The French Reformed churches gave Durie a greater welcome. After a conference of presbyteries at Goes and a meeting with the secular powers at Middelburg, Durie was now given official backing in his approach to the Zeeland churches. However, weeks went by before he received any concrete support from those in secular or ecclesiastical power. At last, in October 1656, an official *Judicium* was given Durie to take back to Cromwell. Now Durie received the backing of Utrecht, but Dort and Leyden argued that there was no proof that the Lutherans would take advantage of any offers of peace. Thus Durie had all the documents he had received from German, Danish and Swedish Lutherans copied, printed and distributed, hoping that he would now be received more positively at Leyden.[136] Durie found old friends now present there who immediately gave him a written promise of cooperation. This led Durie to make another tour

---

[136] See Eekhof's collection of Durie's letters appertaining to Leyden in his *De Theologische Faculteit Te Leiden* for a coverage of these events.

of all the Dutch Provinces, hoping that he would now receive a general pan-Dutch backing. His efforts were successful and he suddenly found new irenic winds blowing through The Netherlands. Durie lost no time in distributing copies of all the agreements gained to all his friends in Eastern, Western and Northern Europe.

Whilst Durie was in Holland, Richard Bradshaw, still the British Resident in Hamburg, remembered his correspondence with Durie during his 1652 visit to Sweden, and wrote to State Secretary Thurloe on 24 March 1656 to say that he was planning to visit Sweden as a mediator and wanted a multi-lingual diplomat to accompany him. He goes on to write:

> 'The council of state were pleased to send mr. Durie with mr. Lisle to Sweden: I should be glad of such a friend and companion, if he would undertake it, being now in London, as I heare he is. He is one whom I love and honour for his eminent parts and good affection; but if he cannot be prevailed with, then to have some other gentleman suitably qualified.'[137]

However, Durie was not finished in the Netherlands and Germany where he stayed another year.

Triumphs turned to acute disappointments on returning to England

Now that Cassel[138] had become the German centre of Durie's European endeavours, he asked his old friend Vice-Chancellor Johann Henrich Dauber, one time pupil in the Herborn High School, Professor in Sedan and Rector in Breda, to translate and distribute his documents in High German. Dauber had received a great interest in Pansophy from his godfather Johann Henrich Alsted after whom he was named. At the beginning of 1657, King Carl X's brother, Prince Adolf of Sweden, wrote to Durie, promising that he would do all in his power to rally the Lutherans to support his Scottish friend. On 14 February, after three years of intense but successful labours, Durie set sail from Zeeland to Margate, England. Immediately on arrival and accompanied by a German ambassador and a young Swiss teacher, who hoped Durie would find him a good post, Durie dashed to London to report to Cromwell who immediately gave him audi-

---

[137] Thurloe's *State Papers*, vol. vi. pp. 138-139.
[138] See *Durie's Consultationum Irenicarum Prododiorthosis*, p. 128, the *Gothaer Verhandlungen*, the list of publications and letters from Cassel mentioned in the Bibliography and the Ysenburg Papers for Durie's transactions in Cassel.

ence and told Durie how pleased he was and he would hear more at a later date.

Cromwell's time was now taken up with reforms in Parliament concerning the monarchy and wars with Spain, so Durie was left to build a deputation and appeal directly to Parliament in order to persuade them to put his plans into practice. A committee of five was appointed by Parliament in his support. Just as they planned to sit, war broke out between Denmark and Sweden, the very two nations that Durie had hoped would lead the Lutherans into union with the Reformed churches. Denmark strove to take Sweden's north German territories from her and thus the war began to involve Germany, too. The Emperor Ferdinand III died, and the Roman Catholic states went through something of an upheaval. In England, there was only talk of war and, once again, Durie's campaign for European peace and union seemed suddenly unimportant to the nation. Then, when Durie sought to claim his wages for the last three-quarters of a year which he had left in England in the hands of 'friends' because the Swiss and Germans had been financing him, he found that they had squandered his money. Now left penniless, Durie was reduced to knocking at the doors of 'old friends' who owed him money but they turned their backs on him. Even worse, Durie had placed funds in 'friends' hands so that they could pay the bills accumulating in England but he found that these bills had not been paid. Now, too, the Continental Protestants were asking why the British churches and Parliament were doing nothing for the Continental cause. Actually, this was unfair, as Durie had published more than sixteen pamphlets soliciting support for them between leaving Switzerland and 1658,[139] but, as so often, Durie now stood alone.

Oxford University, once the flagship of Cromwell's educational reforms, formally rejected Durie's plans for introducing science into the general school curriculum, arguing that the subject was only of interest to mature scholars. The problem was that premature old age had overcome Cromwell and now with all royal honours and privileges except the title of king, though Cromwell was actually referred to in Thurloe's State papers as the King of England, and £2,000 per annum salary besides extra royal perks, Cromwell wanted comfort, peace and quiet with no Parliament to disturb him. Preaching was falling out of vogue, the stage was as popular as ever, the press more frivolous and worldly and, after peace returned to Europe with the Swedes, Danes and Germans patching up their quarrels, Britain was in a party mood. Again, 'mixed dancing' was allowed in

---

[139] Sixteen is only the amount I have traced, copied and used. There are more publications in the Bod. L and HA collections.

Whitehall with one-hundred-man-strong orchestras trumpeting and drum-banging away until the following morning. Durie and Hartlib were just not required any more and left to spend their old age without their pensions.

To cap all, Cromwell became ill and died without having supported Durie in any way since his successful trip to the Continent. The news of his death caused the Dutch to dance in the streets, and it was business as usual in Switzerland which looked for other allies. Tumble-down Dick, as Cromwell's son Richard was commonly called, put his faith in the army rather than a stable Parliament. He was so much in debt himself that he had nothing to give to others and did not think of paying Durie and Hartlib their pensions. The army soon grew tired of a man who had never fought in any battle and forced him to resign. Richard spent the rest of his long life half a fugitive and half a scrounger until his death in 1712. His only fame was that he had been the longest living ruler England had ever produced, though he had reigned as the Second Protector for only nine months.

Durie spends the rest of his life on the Continent

When Charles II was called back by those Presbyterians who had dethroned his father, Charles' demands for an Edict of Toleration were ignored and neither he nor Parliament had any real sympathy for Durie's and Hartlib's proposals, and turned a deaf ear to their pleas for financial support in their work. The offices they held, including Durie's position of Librarian at the St James' Library, were taken from them. It is interesting, however, to note that Durie's successor was a Scotsman by the name of Ross, a member of a family that became distinguished for their inter-Protestant work in Germany. Durie defended his position in his *A Declaration of John Durie, to make known the Truth of his Way of Deportment in all these Times of Trouble*, but he received no backing. England had turned her back on the troubled past. For a number of years, this author thought that this was reason enough for Durie to leave England, but there was another motive quite unlike Durie behind it. On February 6, 1661, we find Durie confessing to Hartlib:

> 'the Truth is that I am not moued to go abroad for any thing which I feare from the Bishops for I haue hitherto no Cause (for ought I can discerne from any of them; nor doe I think my self so considerable as to bee minded by them, they haue other cares which take them up; but the true Causes of my retirement are the danger of beeing arrested for the Arreares of all the liuelihood which I haue had out of Hartland: to auoid which inconvenient till a composition bee made; & till I may know how to subsist in these parts I

think it will bee expedient for me to bee out of the way, & whiles I am abroad & retired I hope to haue an opportunitie to set upon the Historie of my worke, & the Taskes which lye upon my hand. you see that in this letter I speake my thoughts of the Bishops that I am no enemie to them in regard of their office; nor haue I yet found any enemitie from them; & will not suspect any such thing of them, till it otherwise appeare: yet I leaue the euent to Gods prouidence, & if this other pressure of Lawe sute commended did not lye upon me I would not sturre, but rather then to bee Cast in prison I am willing to prouide for my safetie & libertie. in the meane time I desire you not to Communicate these Causes of my retirement to any but to Confiding freinds till I bee gone: & when I am gone I leaue you to your Libertie.'[140]

The usual method of paying those in the service of Cromwell's various Parliaments or Great Councils, was to utilise the rent on property taken from royalists or outlawed Anglican ministers, teachers and university professors which was then re-distributed by the Committee for Plundered Ministers. As there was no permanent rule of law and order, this was a most arbitrary affair and it was most unclear which ministers were 'plundered'. When Durie was appointed to represent Winchester on the Westminster Assembly, he was granted a salary of some £200 per annum from these monies and further wages for educating the King's children. It appears from a statement in his *The Unchanged, Constant and Single-hearted Peace-maker drawn forth into the World* (p. 14), that none of the funds promised him materialised. Not could Durie rely on his wife for financial support. A military garrison had been stationed on Mrs Durie's Irish property, though she had not been involved in the war, which led to the loss of her rents which had been her sole means of maintenance. A few days before his commission to represent Cromwell on the Continent, Charles Cavendish, Viscount Mansfield had been 'allowed' by the Act of Pardon and Oblivion on 6th February 1654 to write over the lease of the Hartland Rectory and living to Durie as part of his payment. The first instalment was given him on March 31 so that Durie could pay off some costs due to postage fees and a few other overheads. However, the powers of the act were only temporary and after September 1654, other temporary committees and acts took over. Again, Durie had to spend his precious time writing to this public servant or that to find redress. When Charles II took over, another legal broom began to sweep and those who had funds from the outlawed and oppressed were called to give an answer for their conduct. Durie was in a difficult position as most of his income gained in England had been

---

[140] Ref: 4/4/3A-3B, HP.

placed in the hands of others who were found to have 'misplaced' it. Durie was, however, made responsible for the Hartland funds which he had scarcely enjoyed. So, too, Durie was expected to pay many a bill which had accrued at Hartland. He was now faced with a debtors' prison with no hope of pacifying the new system, so he felt bound to go into exile.[141]

Durie, therefore, decided to return to Germany where friends still backed him. Hartlib, suffering under the same financial difficulties, was compelled to stay in England and suffer poverty and ill-health until his death in 1662. Durie headed for Cassel, where he found Landgrave William VI (1629-1663), a Reformed believer, ready to patronise his old friend, make him a court chaplain and ambassador and give him a pension for life, though Durie outlived that pension, too. William came from a line of most popular and beloved rulers who lost huge domains to the Imperialists in the Thirty Years War but were able to gain them back and add more territories after the Peace of Westphalia. The Hesse-Cassel line was closely related to the Electors of Brandenburg and the Swedish royal family. William had recently inherited Lutheran areas from the Duke of Schaumburg and he needed Durie's help to keep the peace between Rinteln (Lutheran) and Marburg (Reformed) where he knew Durie was welcome as a mediator. So William immediately called the professors of theology at his universities in Marburg and Rinteln to a conference featuring Durie as chief speaker. Here the church leaders formally promised that they would live in peace together and not criticise each other from their pulpits.

The Lutherans of Brandenburg and Saxony, however, refused to accept the Hesse-Cassel findings and felt that Great Elector Frederick William would be unwise to follow it. Modern Gnesio-Lutheran Gaylin R. Schmeling gives his interpretation of the conference thus:

'The Conference in Hessen-Kassel in 1661 was a meeting between the Reformed theologians of Marburg and the so-called Lutheran theologians of Rinteln. Here it was agreed that the Reformed and the Lutherans did not differ in fundamental articles of the faith. Also these Lutherans agreed to the removal of the baptismal exorcism and the fractio panis in the Supper. The results of this conference were rejected by the universities of Wittenberg, Jena, and Leipzig where pure Lutheran doctrine was taught. However this conference gave the Great Elector the incentive to work for the same agreement in Brandenburg-Prussia.'[142]

---

[141] See The Ordinances of 1653-54 in *The 1654 Union with Scotland*, www.olivercromwell.org/Scotland_union.pdf.

[142] *Paul Gerhardt: Pastor and Theologian*, pdf, p. 12. See also Bodo Nischan's *The "Fractio Panis." A Reformed Communion Practice in Late Reformation Germany*.

However, Frederick William, though a contender for Protestant unity, had been alienated from Durie because of the latter's services to Cromwell. Nevertheless, when Durie heard that Frederick William was visiting the Lower Rhine for a conference with other Protestant princes, he dashed over to seek audience with him and renew connections with the university at Duisburg which Frederick William had founded in 1655. Even though his brother-in-law, William, had fitted Durie out with the best of recommendations, Grand Duke Frederick William refused to give him an interview but told him to put his proposals into writing. Durie obliged and wrote his *Irenicorum tractatuum prodromus* in preparation for a new thrust in Germany, and found that the clergy of Cleves and Moers and the theologians at Duisburg were ready to back him. Frederick William, however, remained aloof. William of Hesse now died but his widow Hedwig Sophia, Princess of Brandenburg, kept Durie on as court chaplain and supported all his endeavours. Without the backing of William, however, Durie found criticism from Reformed hardliners in Hesse who thought Durie compromised too much with the Lutherans.

Durie now found an even fiercer opponent in Aristotelian Lutheran Johann Konrad Dannhauer (1603-1666) of Strasburg University. He called Durie and Calixtus 'Syncretists' and campaigned against any form of tolerance or cooperation between the Protestant churches. This moved Durie to travel extensively in Southern Germany in defence of his plans for peace now challenged by Dannhauer. Durie also visited Switzerland and Holland to keep up the strong connections he had there. When Great Elector Frederick William called a conference in Berlin to discuss Protestant union from September 1662 to May 1663, Durie was unable to be present as he was campaigning in the Solms-Braunfels state but his friend Otto von Schwerin represented his views. However, the Lutheran participants, Paul Gerhardt and Georg Reinhardt refused to give up an inch of Lutheran beliefs and practice and refused to accept Frederick William's Toleration Edict of 1664.

In 1666, we find Durie spending several months in Switzerland where he was able to relax from the growing criticism he was receiving in Germany. Here, he was able to consult people of like-mind such as Johann Heinrich Ott who was Professor of Church History at Zürich and was in touch with a number of Durie's Dutch friends. Leonard Forster in his *Unpublished Comeniana* has recorded seven letters between Ott, Durie and Comenius between 1666 and 1669. Their topic is Ott's hope that Comenius would assist him in compiling a dictionary of German loan words in the French language. Thinking that Durie still had his old influence on Comenius, Ott wanted him to persuade Comenius to join his project.[143] At least this was a break for Durie from Germany's Protestant quarrels.

Durie still did not give up in Germany and after obtaining backing from Prince Frederick of Anhalt and furnished with letters of recommendation from Hesse's Regent, Hedwig Sophia, Durie travelled to Berlin to ask Frederick William if he could mediate between the Lutherans and the Reformed who were arguing that they represented two different religions. In August 1668, he presented a Harmony of Confessions to be used as a basis but received little interest. Indeed, a Reformed court chaplain named Bartholomäus Stosch wished to have nothing to do with Durie because of his allegedly strict views on predestination which Durie had never held. So, too, Frederick William began to think it under his dignity to have a 'private man' as his discussion-partner, although Durie was his sister's chaplain and diplomat. On 15th November 1668, Durie was given 100 Thaler for his expenses and dismissed unwanted. However, he decided to stay the winter in Berlin and lobbied Frederick William and his ministers of both confessions until the Great Elector finally gave Durie a letter of recommendation, wishing him well in his enterprise.[144]

On Durie's return to Cassel, he still had no thoughts of giving up but continued to lobby and petition the rulers of Europe and their clergy, publishing Latin works such as *De Mediis ad Scopum Evangelicae Unionis Obtinendum Reqvisitis* (1667); *Carmen Gratulatorium In Reditum Serenissimae Matris Serenissimique Filii Celsissimorum Hassiae Principium cum Serenissima Sponsa Churlandica Cassellas* (1669); *Brevis Narratio de iis, quae in negotio irenico acta fuerunt Gothae*; *Extractum ex harmonia Confessionum* (1670); *Brevis disquisitio de Doctrinis Veri Christianismi Fundamentalibus* (1672); and *Acta Collationis Amicae Antehac Privatim per literas institutae* (1672), and other irenic works in German and French. Copies of these works were sent to all Durie's former contacts, including de la Gardie, now Sweden's Chancellor. Durie was obviously conscious at this time that he, himself, would never gain the success he desired, but he pressed on, believing in a better future.

In 1672 at Cassel, Durie made another great effort to rally all the Protestant churches around the common basis for discussion listed in Chapter Six which had been accepted by the Svenska Kyrka as early as 1636. This time, however, Durie added a detailed explanation of each point, preserved by Arnold, who also printed lengthy extracts from Durie's private letters in

---

[143] See Leonard Forster's essay, *Philip von Zesen, Johann Heinrich Ott, John Dury, and Others.*

[144] I have this from Brandes, *Geschichte*, p. 299.

his 1700 work which ran into many editions.[145] Though Dury kept up his flow of pamphlets until 1675, his work appeared to be in vain.

Now the Lutherans began to openly attack Durie for all kinds of base deeds of which he was quite innocent with John Meisner now leading the fray with his *Irenicum Duraeanum de Articulis Fidei Fundamentalibus*. For the Lutherans, Durie was too Reformed and for the Reformed, Durie was too Lutheran, both sides viewing Christianity through the narrow spectacles of their creeds. Durie complained that the education of the young was to blame, as they were taught to adhere to creeds without having the Scriptural background to understand them; to criticise whatever was new before they learnt what it was all about. They learnt that the secular philosophy of the day should rule their Practical Divinity. He further complained that students were merely fed with notions and not taught how to practise piety. He thus says:

> 'Sie werden von ihren Magistris mit den principiis der zänkischen Philosophie alsbald von jugend auf eingenommen, und also geschickt gemacht alle dinge streitig zu machen, wissen auch nichts anders als in blossen speculationen die wörter und redens=arten aufzufangen, darwider sie mit einiger wahrscheinlichkeit hernach fechten können, auch in der praxi selbst difficultäten machen, und von anderer leute actionen urtheilen. Sie sind auch darinn noch ärger als die alten Scholastici, weil sie sich noch in mehr dingen mengen, da unser seculum ohne dem immer was neues vorbringet: Sie vermessen sich immer mehrere dinge, widersprechen noch hitziger, gehen auf personalia u.s.w..'[146]

Durie had no easy, triumphant old age, nor could he be said to be the proverbial old tree that continued to bear much fruit. Hartlib died in 1662, so he had lost his closest friend and agent in England who had always collected his letters and manuscripts and prepared his works for publication. Though Prince Adolf of Sweden had assured Durie of his continued backing, Charles X did not follow in Christina's footsteps and in 1664 Johannes Matthiae was deprived of his bishopric. Dorothy, Durie's wife, died in 1664. Comenius and also Durie's first secretary and travelling companion, Peter Figulus, died in 1670. Durie's daughter and her husband, Henry Oldenburg, followed them in 1677. One of Durie's last letters relates how he is trying now to look after his orphaned grandchildren. Happily, his

---

[145] Taken from Arnold's 1729 copy in his *Unpartheyische Kirchen- und Ketzer Historie*, vol. 1, pp. 1009-1011.

[146] See Arnold's extracts from Durie's letters and articles in his *Unpartheyische Kirchen- und Ketzer- Historie*, pp. 1009-1016.

friend and relation by marriage, Robert Boyle the famous scientist, took custody of the children.

By 1677, vicious and most untrue reports were circulated by Durie's enemies concerning him so that, according to Brauer,[147] the Reformed Church in Cassel, worried about their own reputation, turned him from their churches. Many Reformed men now called Durie openly an Arminian, whereas the Lutherans accused Durie of being a Hyper-Calvinist. It is difficult to find unity amongst Christian brethren.

Durie is thought to have died in Cassel, which had become the Scotsman's home-from-home amidst his international tasks and toils. Just as Durie's exact date of birth has never been definitely confirmed in Durie scholarship, we do not know the exact date of his death, though it has been variously given as either 26 September, as per Klähr, or 28 September, 1680 as per Tollin. Professor Turnbull in his 1947 definitive work *Hartlib, Dury and Comenius: Cleanings from Hartlib Papers*, merely refers to MH VI 70 as the source of his knowledge concerning Durie's death. This must be a reference to Theodor Klähr's 1897 essay entitled 'Johannes Duraeus' in the *Monatshefte der Comenius-Gesellschaft*, Volume Six, p. 70. Klähr, however, merely states, 'Am 26 September 1680 starb der vielgeschäftige Theologe in Kassel mit der bitteren Klage über die Erfolglosigkeit seiner mühevollen Lebensarbeit.' Neither Tollin's statement nor Klähr's is given a source reference. A visit to the Cassel church-records and repeated searches in the Hesse State Archives at Marburg have produced no confirmation of this dating. Bombing during the Second World War sadly destroyed most of the Cassel archives. As a former court chaplain, and trusted friend of Hedwig Sophia, William VI's widow, one would have expected him to be buried as a member of the Hofgemeinde but their extant records do not mention Durie's death. Indeed, Durie's name is not to be found at all in the Cassel church archives, as this writer found to his dismay in the spring of 2011 when assisted by knowledgeable archivists very eager to help. Suggestions have been made that Durie became a member of the French Church in Cassel but their records are no longer extant. Most late twentieth and twenty-first century writers have dropped giving an exact date. However, the latest major writer on Durie, Pierre-Olivier Léchot, returns to the traditional dating of 26 September 1680 in his Conclusion and Time-Line, though naming no source. Prof. H. Schneider of Marburg University has pointed out to me that an unknown scribe has added a four-lined later gloss inserted in the one-line space between the records of September 30 and October in the Church Book of the Freiheiter Gemeinde zu

---

[147] Brauer, p. 229.

Kassel claiming that Durie died on 28 September, aged 85. However, the entry is obviously not by the scribe who entered the particulars for September and October being written in another much later hand and by one who did not keep to the normal entry specifications for which special columns are provided. Such later glosses which are sadly to be found in many documents pertaining to Durie merely continue the problem of dating Durie's birth and death. If he actually died aged 85 then the data given by the Leyden Album Studiosorum giving Durie's matriculation at the University for 1611 as aged 12, is wrong by four years. As the last we hear of Durie writing at all was in 1678 to Pell and Barclay, we can only presume that Durie died some short time later. Though Rae favours the date 1680 in his *John Dury: Reformer of Education*, when summing up Durie's life on page 281 of his *John Dury and the Road to Piety*, he supposes Durie could have lived until 1685, saying:

> 'One can but guess at Dury's state of mind from 1676-1685 and at its elements but it is not improper to postulate a sense of physical and increasing frailty; a sense of acute intellectual loneliness; a consciousness of the passing of time with ever increasing speed; feelings of regret for a life mis-spent alternating with the contrary conviction that it had all been worthwhile, together with the worry of not really knowing.'

After relating the above account of Durie's endeavours, this writer wonders at such pessimistic speculation, also aired by Turnbull and Klähr. Tollin seeks a more balanced position and says that Durie was 'von den Theologen seiner Zeit unverstanden, von den Obrigkeiten aller Lande gewürdigt als der kommende Mann.'[148] It might appear a human tragedy that a man who did more for the cause of God and truth and the education and edification of the human race than perhaps any other of his day died unwanted by his church and no grave or even marker reminds us of his selfless life in the service of universal learning and practical divinity. However, Durie realised perfectly that his one-man ministry could not reform the world in his time and accepted this fact with confidence that the future would vindicate his work. In his *A Discourse tending to Peace Ecclesiasticall* written in Hamburg in 1639, Durie made it clear that he had:

> 'a task for my whole life, and therefore will make no haste to rid myself of it, nor ever think of being weary, or of taking any other thing in hand, which is not either collaterally helpful or subordinate unto it. For when I enter seriously within myself to consider what course of life I must from henceforth

---

[148] Johann Duraeus, p. 283.

follow, that I may be able to perform the vows and promises which I have made to Almighty God, I find that I must resolve before all things to be no more mine own man in any thing, but a servant to the work and to such as will help to further it; whereupon this consequence followeth, that as I must resigne and give up myself unto the work, so I must resolve to be at full libertie and free from all occasions, obligations and relations which may divide and distract my thoughts from it.'[149]

Fourteen years later, Durie opens his proposals to a Parliamentary Committee on the advancement of learning by saying:

'As there is cause to hope, that the manifold sollicitations & endeavours for the Reformation of the improfitable, & advancement of the profitable wayes of learning which we have put ourselves upon, shall not altogether invaine through the hand of God upon our Leaders, in publick places; whose Spirits (we hope) are now raised (for which we blesse the Lord) unto most noble undertakings; so we are loath to be wanting to the opportunity which now is offered for the obtaining of our wishes. For which cause in all humility we shall crave leave to make some Proposalls unto the Honorable Committee to whom this eminent worke is referred, that if these suggestions may be allowed, & found practicable in this our generation, we may rejoyce with those that shall reap the benefit thereof; have this comfort to our Consciences, that we have with faithfullnesse performed our dutie, in a time, wherein it was accepted.

Durie never departed from the course of gaining satisfaction from doing his duty and could thus also say, thirty two years later, in 1671:

'Ich habe schon längst gesehen, Gott wolle sich den ausgang dieses wercks selbst vorbehalten, uns aber nichts übrig lassen, als daß wir das unsrige thun, wir mögen nun einen erfolg sehen oder nicht; Wir werden doch die frucht unserer arbeit von dem Fürsten des friedens selber erlangen, dem wir dienen. Ich habe alles gethan, was ich gethan zu haben gewünschet, und worauf mein gemüth gerichtet worden. Nun überlasse ich Gott den ausgang, was er durch seine innerliche würkung in eines jedweden Geist schaffen will. Denn das stehet nicht in unserer gewalt, kömmt uns auch nicht zu, darinne zu grübeln sondern wird seiner vorsehung überlassen.[150]

The Regent of Hesse, Princess Hedwig Sophia, stood by Durie and his dedicatory letter to her in 1676, prefaced to his *Rayons de L'Esprit de*

---

[149] *A Discourse tending*, p. 18.
[150] *Epist. Mista ad Forstnerum*, Arnold, ibid, p. 1016.

Grace Donnant Conseil, Lumiere, vie & consolation a L'ame fidele, as also the entire tract, witnesses to a man who is as confident as ever in the comforting counsel and illuminating work of God's Spirit on the trusting soul.

Today, Durie, as a man of the future, could not complain of any lack of attention. Though he did not live to see the ripe fruit of his labours, he certainly ploughed, sowed, watered and weeded throughout the Protestant churches and schools of Europe with confidence, trusting that his labours would not remain in vain in the Lord. Like Abraham, he looked to a time when God's promises would be fulfilled on Earth as in Heaven. His hope and trust was that others would soon start harvesting where he had sown. This is certainly happening today. Here, the words of Bishop Reginald Heber certainly apply to John Durie, the first true European:

They climbed the steep ascent of Heaven,
Through peril, toil, and pain;
O God, to us may grace be given
To follow in their train!

CHAPTER THREE

Early Contributions to Durie Scholarship

The seventeenth to eighteenth centuries

The seventeenth century produced a wide range of irenic works on church unity. Pareus (Paraeus) led the debate with his *Irenicum sive de unione et synodo Evangelicorum* of 1614, followed by such thinkers as Davenant, Morton, Borroughs, Stillingfleet, Calixtus and Leibniz, besides John Durie. At the same time, there was an increased interest in studies in the purpose and art of learning in both secular and ecclesiastical circles and though all of the above named men were also interested in epistemological, empirical and gnosiological studies, writers such as Bacon, Alsted, Hartlib, Comenius, Kinner, Crocius, Bergius and, again, Durie, were more concerned with didactical tools for universal learning against a background of a united Protestant Church.

Foremost in the history of scholars who have devoted themselves to Durie studies is Samuel Hartlib who was Durie's advisor, editor, publisher and agent from 1628 or earlier to his death in 1662. Tollin refers to scholars having to devote their lives to Durie research if they want to adequately describe all Durie's achievements. Hartlib is without a rival in this respect and his name is thus *passim* in this thesis. One of the first works in Germany contemporary with Durie's own writings on the subject of church unity was that of Erfurt's Pro-Rector and Professor of Theology, Johann Matthew Meyfart entitled *Dissertatio Academica de concilianda Pace inter Ecclesias per Germaniam Evangelicas* which he presented to his university in 1636 during the aftermath of the Leipzig and Frankfurt Diets which Durie influenced so much.[151] It is a critical and outspoken work on the Early Fathers, typical of one who believed that the universities and education in general were in a state of decay. In condemning the *rabies theologorum* of the times, Meyfart added extensively to it, lacking the objectivity which *Academia* ought to produce. After this, and referring particularly to Durie's impact on the German scene, came Johan Meisner's work, *Johann, Irenicum Duraeanum De Articulis Fidei Fundamentalibus, Et Consensu Ac*

---

[151] HA, 22al, Nr.10, Mappe 1, in sheet form numbered p. 32-3 with four pages to a sheet

Dissensu Inter Lutheranos ac Reformatos presented to Wittenberg university in 1675 which sought to weigh up the pros and cons of Durie's irenic work in a less than irenic spirit.[152] Though Meisner was critical of Durie's 'Calvinism', he recognises the value of Durie's practical divinity.

Pierre Bayle's gigantic *Dictionaire Historique et Critique* of 1697 still features as a pioneer study into many seventeenth century stalwarts' lives and work, including John Durie's. It was reissued in various complete and abridged forms throughout the eighteenth and nineteenth centuries in Rotterdam and Amsterdam as well as in England and Germany and has been reprinted several times in recent years. Bayle can rightly be called the man who internationalised Durie's fame as his work was widely circulated and translated, appearing in many editions throughout Europe and the British Isles. The *Dictionaire* is not a dictionary as such but a collection of essays, mostly biographical, in alphabetical order.

Gottfried Arnold, son of a schoolmaster and close friend of Spener's, painted a most objective portrait of Durie in his work *Unparteyische Kirchen- und Ketzer Historie* published at Frankfurt a. M. in 1700. He also worked in a number of later letters, pamphlets and transactions from Durie's pen. Scholars as far apart in time as Benzelius and Westin have profited greatly from Arnold as also this writer.

1716 saw the publication of a work by another 'Arnold', of quite a different persuasion. George Henry Arnold wrote a thesis on Durie under the guidance of Professor Johan Christoph Colerus of Wittenberg University. Wittenberg had hardly ever a good word to say about Durie because of their gnesio-Lutheran and anti-Swedish ideas. Arnold's thesis, entitled *Historia Joannis Duraei, qua ea inprimis, quae P. Baelius et G. Arnoldus tradiderunt/diligentius investigantur et explicantur*,[153] was thus an attempt to contradict the findings of Gottfried Arnold and Bayle. His references from Durie's works are, however, very useful to scholars wishing to pursue the early eighteenth century debate.[154]

---

[152] A copy is in the Herzog August Library.
[153] Also available at the HAL.
[154] In 1728 appeared *Epistolae diversi argumenti maximam partem a Variis ad clarissimum multorumque meritorum Virum Lucam Lossium illustris Lycei apud Luneburgenses dum viveret Pro-Rectorem & post eum â Duraeo, Langwedelio, Boeclero, Portnero, Berneggero, Freinshemio aliisque ad alios exaratae, partim excerptae, & in compendium redactae, partim vero integrae ex autographis descriptae / Nunc primum in lucem protraxit ac Dissertationem de multiplici Eruditorum studio epistolis hactenus impenso praemisit Adamus Henricus Lackmannus, Hamburgi: Felginer*. I have not yet had the opportunity of reading this thesis but was notified of it by the Herzog-August Library.

Mosheim and Benzelius

The eighteenth century also produced the works of John Lawrence von Mosheim's *Institutionum historiae ecclesiasticae libri*, and Carl Jesper Benzelius' work *Dissertatio Historico-Theologica De Johanne Dvraeo, Pacificatore Celeberrimo, Maxime De Actis Eivs Svecanis / Qvam ... In Illvstri Academia Ivlia Praesidente Magnifico Prorectore Io. Lavrentio Moshemio ... Pro Svmmis In Theologia Honoribvs Conseqvendis In Ivleo Maiori Horis Ante Et Pomeridianis Consvetis D. XXIX. M. Maii MDCCXLIV*. Mosheim's work came out in various extensions and editions from 1721 to 1768. Oddly enough, the first German edition of 1771 was translated from the English which had been translated from the Latin.

Mosheim, justly called 'The Father of Church History', was a skilled church historian but also a fine Lutheran theologian and educator and did much to mend the breeches between the Reformed and Lutheran parties. He put his Durie-like ideals into practice as General Inspector of Schools in Brunswick-Wolfenbüttel and as university professor and Chancellor of Göttingen University. In his *Institutes*,[155] Mosheim describes the fragmentation of Protestant churches and their need for church cooperation outlining the neglected work of James I of England and his close associate French Puritan Du Moulin of the Academy of Sedan. Du Moulin was also an associate of Durie's. Had Du Moulin and the French contingent been allowed by Luis XIII to take part in the Synod of Dort, that synod would certainly have become a wider standard than merely for the stricter Calvinists and would have boosted the Reformed nature of both Lutherans and Calvinists alike and made of both churches one truly Evangelical Church. Though Du Moulin did not actually take part in the Synod's proceedings, supported by James I and other irenicists, he campaigned for an understanding of the Reformation which would include Luther's part. In a letter to the English ambassador to the Netherlands, Sir Dudley Carleton, dated December 8, 1618, Du Moulin wrote,

> 'Il y a une autre affaire non moins importante, sur laquelle il feroit a desirer, que la synode de Dordrecht travaillast; qui est de faire un project d'accord et reconciliation entre nous et les eglises Lutheriennes.'[156]

---

[155] For English purposes, I use the Reid Edition, London, 1849, here Vol. V.
[156] Sir Dudley Carleton's Letters from January 1615/16 to December 1620, London 1775, pp. 325-326.

Though King James urged the synod to consider Du Moulin's plea, the Dutch majority were against it.[157]

Mosheim sees the Conference at Leipzig in 1631 as a milestone pointing to the unification of the Protestant cause but reminds us that it fell short of the French Reformed Colloquy at Charenton meeting in September of the same year where:

> 'an act was passed by the Reformed doctors of that respectable assembly, declaring the Lutheran system of religion conformable with the spirit of true piety, and free from pernicious and fundamental errors. By this act, a fair opportunity was offered to the Lutherans of joining with the Reformed church upon honourable terms, and of entering into the bonds both of civil and religious communion with their Calvinistic brethren.'[158]

Turning to Durie, Mosheim comments:

> 'The most eminent of the Calvinistical peace-makers was John Dureus, a native of Scotland, and a man justly celebrated, on account of his universal benevolence, solid piety, and extensive learning; but, at the same time, more remarkable for genius and memory than for nicety of discernment and accuracy of judgment, as might be invinced by several proofs and testimonies, were this the proper place for discussions of that nature. But that as it will, never, perhaps, was there such an example of zeal and perseverance as that exhibited by Dureus, who, during the space of forty years,[159] suffered vexations and underwent labours, which required the firmest resolution, and the most inexhaustible patience; wrote, exhorted, admonished, entreated, and disputed; in a word, tried every method that human wisdom could suggest, to put an end to the dissensions and animosities that reigned among the Protestant churches.'[160]

Mosheim then refers to:

---

[157] Readers may care to look up my account of the Synod of Dort in Part Five of my More Mountain Movers, Go Publications, 2005. In view of the negative write-up James I has received, especially from the Presbyterian side for his work with the churches, it is refreshing to read W. P. Patterson's 1997 work entitled *King James VI and the Reunion of Christendom*, Cambridge University Press, which, though far from solving all the problems concerning James' campaign for Protestant unity, is a great step in the right direction.

[158] Mosheim's *An Ecclesiastical History*, Book 4, Part II, p. 231.

[159] Mosheim is thinking particularly of the years 1631 to 1674.

[160] Ibid, p. 232.

'an account of Duraeus, published under my direction at Helmstedt, in the year 1744, by Benzelius, and entitled *Dissertatio de John. Duraeo, maxime de Actis ejus Suecanis*. This dissertation contains a variety of anecdotes drawn from records not yet made public.'[161]

Carl Jesper Benzelius was a Swede who had grown up in a family of archbishops and bishops. He spent some time during 1744 in Helmstedt where Mosheim had him granted an honorary Doctor of Theology. This, together with his family background, helped boost Benzelius' career so that he soon became a Swedish university professor, bishop, court preacher and Member of Parliament. One of the requirements for the honorary doctorate was that he should prepare a dissertation to be presented before the faculty. It would appear that Mosheim provided Benzelius with the necessary material concerning the life of John Durie and asked him to put it into Latin and defend it in order to receive the title. Thus, the work is usually referred to merely as Benzelius-Mosheim.[162] Brandes therefore writes in his opening words to his essay 'John Dury and his Work for Germany', that he is referring to one whom 'Benzelius, or rather Mosheim, the renowned theologian of Göttingen, in his commentary on Durie's proceedings in Sweden, characterised under the honourable name of 'the most celebrated peacemaker.' Both the British Library and All Soul's Library, Oxford have copies of this work which deals, as Brandes says, mainly with Swedish material, but is superseded by Westin's and Turnbull's works. Nevertheless, it has become customary to drop Benzelius' name in works on Durie. As mentioned above, a printed invitation to and description of Benzelius' inaugural disputation has been preserved by Halle University. After all criticisms and scepticisms have been aired concerning Benzelius' thesis, it still remains the Mother of all Durie biographies. It gives a balanced, concise overview of Durie's life and works and is of great importance in presenting us with the titles of very early works on Durie. Benzelius' Latin is simple and unpretentious yet elegant. He has a story to tell and sticks to its ingredients without the ostentatious displays of classical learning employed by many of his theological contemporaries. Students, who are less proficient at Latin like this author, should tackle Benzelius as an 'easy reader' before going on to Durie's 'advanced readers'.

Returning to Mosheim, he believes that Durie and his supporters were weak in theology for allegedly reducing Christianity to the Apostles' Creed; the Ten Commandments and the Lord's Prayer. This is to misun-

---

[161] Ibid, 277.
[162] See, for instance, Tollin's 'Johannes Duraeus', p. 241, (fn.), and p. 260.

derstand Durie. Davenant, Calixtus and Durie were not guilty of a *reductio ad absurdum* but used these elements as a didactic starting point on which to build their wider Practical Divinity. As good educators, they worked from the most generally known and accepted factors to areas where their readers and hearers had had hitherto no knowledge at all. They were good educators besides being good theologians

Mosheim mentions the Swedish irenist and tutor of Queen Christina, Johannes Matthiae and George Calixtus of Helmstedt whom Durie 'had animated with a portion of his charitable and indulgent spirit' but points out that both suffered in the cause of unity and concord. Thereafter, Mosheim relates the great difficulties Calixtus had when Durie left Germany and similar difficulties Matthiae had when Durie left Sweden in 1638.

The Nineteenth Century

Ernst Ludwig Henke

An early assessment of Durie's impact on 17th century thought is found in the three volumes of Henke's *Georg Calixtus and seine Zeit* which appeared in 1853.[163] The analysis of Durie's work it contains has served as a starting point by most Durie scholars and provides much background information concerning negotiations between the universities of Uppsala and Helmstedt and the various international conferences in which Durie proved so influential. Henke describes Durie's early connections with Godeman, Roe and Oxenstierna, his authorisation by Archbishop Abbott and how he quickly grew in international significance. Henke skips over Durie's non-too successful early missions to Holland, Denmark and Sweden but outlines in detail Durie's greater success in Brunswick in 1639 especially after meeting Count August who had succeeded Friedrich Ulrich. The chief reason for Count August's acceptance of Durie's plans for Protestant union, however, was not so much irenic, according to Henke, but a means of blocking the progress of the Neophotinians and Socinians. Henke points out that Duke Georg of Brunswick-Calenberg (1590-1649), one of King Gustav's generals, proved a great supporter of Durie, Calixtus and Horneius (Horn) in their discussions throughout 1639-40.[164]

Though Henke provided thought-provoking ideas for further Durie studies, his main thrust was to outline specifically German problems and

---

[163] See vol. 1, pp. 500 ff., vol. 2:1 pp. 106-110 and vol. 2:2, p. 35 and p. 252 ff..
[164] See Henke 2:1, p. 109 and fn.

he made no attempt to summarise the results of Durie's life-time's work or to discuss the motivating factors behind it.

David Masson

In 1859, David Masson published his *The Life of John Milton: Narrated in Connection with the Political, Ecclesiastical and Literary History of his Time*. In this eight volume work, Masson deals with Durie briefly in his second and fifth volumes but in detail in over 400 pages of his third volume, chiefly in association with his friends Samuel Hartlib, John Amos Comenius and John Milton. Masson calls this section 'Milton Amongst the Sectaries', though at the time, just who was Orthodox and who was a Sectarian had not been worked out by the various Parliamentary and Westminster Assembly committees appointed to deal with this question. In November 1645, Durie was chosen by the Assembly as spokesman to sit on a Lords' committee appointed to deal with this very problem.[165] Masson goes into great detail concerning Durie's connections with the Church of England, the Presbyterians, the Independents and his work of Pan-Protestantism. Indeed, Masson has guided many a Durie scholar such as S. Levy, to discover a deeper appreciation of Durie.[166]

Modern scholars often isolate Durie, Comenius and Hartlib from each other, claiming that their 'favourite' was the leading figure in the trio's work. Masson believes Durie was the initial source of influence behind both Hartlib and Comenius, calling Hartlib 'Durie's first disciple' and viewing Comenius as merging his own plans for a union of Protestant churches with Durie's and developing his own Pan-Protestantism ideas into Pansophism from theirs.

Theodor Norlin

Norlin's 1864 work has already been referred to in Chapter Two. The first volume of his *Svenska Kyrkans Historia efter Reformationen* deals with the problem of uniting the different elements in the Swedish churches in which he sees Durie as playing an important, but unsuccessful part. Norlin views himself as Benzelius' interpreter, though fitting his work on Durie into the history of the post-Reformation Swedish Church. He shows how Durie's connections with Sweden from 1626 on came as a continuation of English, Scottish and German friendships at a time when Sweden was moving from

---

[165] See Shaw, vol. 2, p. 48 ff.
[166] See Levy's John Dury and the English Jewry.

a strongly patristic background to a more open Reformed one. Though Forbes attempts to mend the breaches between the Reformed and Lutheran clergy were not successful, Paraeus more irenic work of 1631 was received with favour and it was in the spirit of Paraeus that Durie developed his work. The Swedes were still of various minds how their own Reformation should develop. Some wished to carry on the status quo but without Rome's interference, others were for allowing the various bishoprics and centres of learning a good deal of independence including receiving their own legal system as was the case in Uppsala; yet others wished to put Sweden under the firm hand of a sternly orthodox Lutheranism. On the whole, the ruling nobility wished to see both Reformed and Lutheran elements in church life which would reflect the political claims Sweden had on a united Protestant Europe under their control. Happily for Durie, a number of leading clergy wished to cooperate, though with noted exceptions such as Rudbeck and Botvidius.

Norlin's account must be viewed as a most individual one-sided interpretation of facts which, though outlined by Benzelius, are made to tell rather a different story to the detriment of both Durie and the Swedish Church. Moreover, Norlin, though mentioning few names, deals with the Swedish clergy as if they mainly opposed Durie, whereas his views were widely accepted by leading churchmen, educators and politicians. Norlin relates how various members of the Oxenstierna family who governed captured Prussia were for a union of the Protestant churches even in 1626 when Durie moved to Elbing and ordered Johann Botvidius to cooperate. Botvidius refused to depart from a rigid Lutheran position. This would explain why Axel Oxenstierna, a man who read his Bible daily, removed Botvidius from his post when he opposed Durie in 1631. Norlin also judges Durie's being sent to England by Oxenstierna, Godeman and Roe to gain the backing of Church and State positively and claims that Durie returned to his work of pacification on the Continent with their full backing and authority. Norlin describes Durie's two interviews with King Gustav at Würzburg as successful but explains how Gustav's chaplain, Jacob Fabricius, accepted Durie only with caution whereas his other chaplain, Johannes Matthiae, received Durie's ideas with 'all the more enthusiasm'.[167]

Norlin further relates that when doubt in the Swedish churches arose in 1662 concerning Gustav's and Christina's plans for church unity amongst Protestants, Gustav Adolf's close friend Per Brahe, who knew Durie from his German campaigns, reminded Parliament of Durie's talks with Gustav and the King's enthusiasm for the cause. Brahe was Lord High Steward,

---

[167] 'Med desto större ifver', Norlin, p. 174.

Privy Councillor, and Governor of Finland and admirer of Durie. Amongst his educational reforms was the founding of Turku (Helsinki) University. Norlin claims that Oxenstierna was slow to give Durie the necessary written recommendations for his work in Sweden which has probably given rise to the much repeated idea that Oxenstierna would not give Durie his full support. However, the facts relate that when Durie needed Oxenstierna's backing, he received it and often Oxenstierna took the initiative in supporting Durie.

Though Norlin describes Laud as 'den fanatiske ärkebiskop', he nevertheless says that he favoured Durie's venture. By 1636, however, Norlin admits that Oxenstierna was backing Durie and provided him with the recommendations King Gustav had promised him five years previously, shortly before Gustav was killed in battle. In Sweden, Oxenstierna reintroduced Durie to Matthiae and also to the minister of Stockholm's Storkyrka, Jakob Zebråzynthius, who also became a close supporter of Durie's. Zebråzynthius, who became Bishop of Strängnäs in 1539, is overlooked by the bulk of Durie researchers. Another Bishop of Strängnäs, important in Durie studies, was Carl Jesper Benzelius on whose work Norlin relies as almost a sole source.

Now backed by Oxenstierna's recommendations, Durie sent a lengthy letter to the Uppsala theological faculty, outlining broadly his plans for inter-church cooperation, though he did not go into much detail. He explained that he would await Uppsala's suggestions before airing his own.[168] The positive reply included the eight points mentioned in Chapter Two and outlined in Chapter Six which were to serve as a basis for further discussions. Durie accepted wholeheartedly these recommendations and wrote to Hartlib saying he would probably settled down in Sweden for a number of years as there were many signs of blessings on his work 'which scarce could be imagined'.[169] However, Durie made the mistake of suggesting that Sweden should follow the example of Poland in uniting the protestant churches. Poland at the time was seen as something of a rebel state in Sweden's eyes and Uppsala viewed Durie's idea as a modern Chinese statesman might view the suggestion that China should be ruled on lines suggested by Taiwan. The Swedes thus stressed that a syncretistic solution as made by the Poles was not their desire. Nevertheless, they agreed that a General Synod might help find a solution which would leave all with a

---

[168] A copy of this letter is found in Benzelius p. 130 ff. with the theological faculty's immediate, positive reply.

[169] Westin collection, *John Durie in Sweden*. See Westin's more cheerful account and Durie's letters of 1636 which bubble over with optimism and enthusiasm.

good conscience. Durie would have been satisfied if the Swedes had pressed for union with each side reserving his own faith and practice but Uppsala aimed for a union in which each Christian doctrine would be accepted by all. This was an ideal practised nowhere in Sweden and not what Durie demanded. Yet Uppsala told Durie that the Swedish churches were entirely one in doctrine, which must have come over to Durie's ears as most wishful thinking indeed. His aims were less idealistic and he emphasised that discussions should take place as a *via practica* rather than a *via scholastica*.

Oxenstierna, according to Norlin, took the faculty's reply positively and encouraged Durie not to give up but press on. Happily, Johannes Canuti Lenaeus, who had formulated the eight points of agreement,[170] was asked to lead the discussions with Durie but Lenaeus fell out with Christina who held her protecting young hand over Durie, so in the end, Durie lost him as an ally, too. Lenaeus wanted to turn Sweden into a Theocracy. Durie now thought he should tour the various Swedish dioceses but sadly, enemies went before him, spreading the rumour that Durie had only one aim in mind and that was to make 'Calvinists' of the Swedes. Even at Vesterås, however, Rudbeck greeted his 'Broder Duraeus' heartily, declared his honest opinion that Durie was on the wrong track but gave him his blessing in visiting the other bishops. Paulinus in Strängnäs thought the findings of Uppsala now would cause Lutherans and the Reformed to work together. Durie quickly published the results of his irenic discussions with Paulinus on 7 October 1636,[171] but expressed his wish that those who were not for irenic cooperation between the churches and condemned their brethren in Christ for holding different views of externals, should be disciplined by their churches which, Norlin points out, was hardly in the spirit of peace and expresses astonishment at Durie's 'intolerance'. This is to misunderstand Durie whose policy was always 'live and let live' and who always dealt fairly with 'cases of conscience'. It was one thing, however, to have convictions and another to rail against either 'Calvinists' or 'Lutherans' from the pulpit and engage in denominational squabbles.

Durie now turned to Stockholm still writing to Rudbeck in an effort to move him to change his mind which brought no fruit. Durie wanted to call a synod as Uppsala had suggested but Rudbeck thought Durie should seek agreement in brotherly discussions with each bishop separately. Rudbeck was always wary of centralising church policy. Durie appealed repeatedly to the Privy Council for support as mentioned above, thinking that a major-

---

[170] See Benzelius, p. 120.
[171] See Benzelius for Durie's publication of 7 October 1636 on p. 92 ff.

ity vote taken at a synod could push through Durie's plans irrespective of Rudbeck's opposition but the Privy Council respected Rudbeck too much to go behind his back.

Norlin seeks to explain what he feels is Durie's uncompromising stand by pointing out that every time Durie seemed to feel he was reaching his aim, his target moved further away.[172] Oxenstierna now intensified his support of Durie and in March 1637 invited him to his home estate at Tidö in Westmanland for consultations. From there, Durie revisited Vesterås and Strängnäs with a special letter from Oxenstierna to Rudbeck. Durie's hand was also strengthened by a letter from the theological faculty at Uppsala who were anxious to proceed in the dialogue concerning inter-Protestant cooperation. In his letter to Rudbeck, Oxenstierna gave him an ultimatum. He should accept Durie's plans or reject them at once with no beating about the bush. However he should decide, Oxenstierna demanded an explanation in writing. Rudbeck ignored Oxenstierna's letter but received Durie as a friend and colleague, though still differing from him. Next, Oxenstierna and Durie proceeded to a meeting of the faculty at Uppsala in May 1637 and another at Stockholm in June to discuss both Durie's ecclesiastical and educational plans. Oxenstierna was thinking of establishing schools on Durie's lines and the Skyttes and de Geer favoured Durie's approach but the Uppsala and Stockholm synods had more on their agenda than Durie who was given little attention. Durie pressed for a meeting of clergy and professors to examine his proposals and this was held on 10 July 1637. Norlin describes the meeting as something of a farce. It was certainly not what Durie expected. In the morning session, Durie was tested like a young student on the soundness of his theology. Though the clergy and professors were pleased to find Durie came so close to themselves, they argued that his own views were in contradiction to what they held to be Calvinism. Again, Forbes' ideas were still working against Durie who could only defend himself by saying that there were different opinions amongst Calvinists. Rudbeck then spoke up provokingly and obviously with his tongue in his cheek, suggesting that if all Calvinists were prepared to sign the Book of Concord, a union of Lutherans and the Reformed would be guaranteed. Durie responded honestly that neither he nor the Calvinists would be prepared to do that. In the afternoon, Durie was examined as to his method of interpreting Scripture and the Biblical passages concerning the Lord's Supper, which was the main cause of difference between the Reformed and the Lutherans, were given him to expound. Durie received harsh criticism for his apparently too rational or 'scientific' ap-

---

[172] Norlin pp. 183-184.

proach to text analysis which neither suited the dogmatic standards of his examiners, nor their piety. A copy of Durie's defence can be read in Benzelius, p. 146 ff. and there is a full official report of the entire sessions on page 160 ff.. Durie's system of text interpretation will be discussed at length in Chapter Eight. The meeting ended with the Professors rudely telling Durie to go home to those of his own faith and teach them how to better it. In his published account of the 'examination',[173] Durie complained that Rudbeck never gave him a chance to explain himself and kept interrupting him with irrelevant questions. Durie replied to Rudbeck personally in writing on five and a half quarto pages which is also preserved in Benzelius. He also distributed two tracts at the meeting of Parliament (Riksdagen) in 1638 but these led to a counter-pamphlet from various clergymen denouncing Durie's efforts at church unity and demanding that he should be expelled from the country. Her Majesty's government reacted most oddly. For the sake of peace, they commanded Durie to leave the country but gave him a glowing testimony to his irenic character and work which quite refuted the opinions of those clergy who had condemned him. Both the girl Queen, Christina, rapidly taking over powers hitherto given to regents, and Oxenstierna were probably behind this document and they openly criticised the way Durie had been misrepresented by the clergy who had acted contrary to Christian decorum and diplomatic acumen.

As to be expected, Durie broke down under the weight of the hard work and intense criticism and disappointments he had suffered over the previous two years and became very ill but was allowed to stay in Sweden until his usual good health returned. During this time, the tone of many a critic, including Rudbeck, altered and many church men were sorry to see Durie leave Sweden in the late summer of 1638. Norlin mentions that when Durie left Sweden, he recommended that Comenius should be allowed to visit the country and help them in their school reforms. Oxenstierna and de Geer had suggested that Durie should take on this task but he did not want to be dependent on their pockets and opinion. He realised that it was time that he went further afield with his teaching.

Frederick Brandes

Brandes' two works *Geschichte der evangelischen Union in Preußen* (1872) and his two-part essay on 'John Dury and His Work for Germany' in the *Catholic Presbyterian* (July, 1882) are of special interest to the Durie

---

[173] See Benzelius' *Historica relatio contracta colloquii etc. ab ipso Duraeo exarata*, p. 152 ff.

Early Contributions to Durie Scholarship

researcher. Brandes appears to have no access to Durie's separate works except through Hering. However, he has provided the backbone for numerous Durie studies, in particular, Batten's work discussed below. In Chapter Seven, entitled *Georg Wilhelm's letzte Zeiten 1631-1640*, Brandes relates that one of John Bergius' principle efforts was:

> '. . . die Bestrebungen eines Mannes zu fördern, der in dieser Zeit des ärgsten confessionellen Haders die Betreibung der Union zur Aufgabe seines lebens gemacht hatte: Johann Duräus. Dieser merkwürdige Mann, von dem später noch des Weitern wird zu reden sein, hatte nicht bloß an dem Leipziger Gespräche den lebhaftesten Antheil genommen, sondern er war mit dem Dr. Bergius auch in engere Verbindung getreten und fand durch denselben Fürsprache und Unterstüzung, so viel dieser sie irgend zu gewähren im Stande war. Durch ihn wurde Gustav Adolf der anfänglich gegen die Reformierten genugsam eingenommen war, auf andere Gedanken gebracht, durch ihn namentlich auch der Kanzler von Schweden, Oxenstierna, für die Sache des confessionellen Friedens gewonnenen, und immer begleitete Bergius das Unternehmen des Duräus mit all der angelegentlichen Theilnahme, die da stattfindet wo man in des Anderen Arbeit seine eigene Angelegenheit erkennt.'[174]

Concerning the state of the churches leading to the Peace of Westphalia in 1648, Brandes describes how Durie's activities in Germany moved Sweden to put more trust in the Reformed churches and demand that in their peace negotiations with Roman Catholics, Lutherans should also make their peace with the Reformed churches.[175] Indeed, Brandes calls Durie 'the most famous peace-maker of his century',[176] devoting Chapter Twelve entirely to him, under the title, 'Ein Friedensmann um Gottes Willen (1668-1680)'. He points out that Frederick William was most sympathetic to Durie's views, but had to reject them because they went further than the political necessities of the day. Brandes, indeed, claims that Durie was two hundred years ahead of his irenic contemporaries.

Brandes maintains that Durie was educated in 'English or Scottish universities', mentioning in particular Edinburgh. He places Durie on the Continent first in 1628 at Elbing. Though he mentions the support given to Durie by Archbishop Abbott, three bishops and twenty Doctors of Theol-

---

[174] *Geschichte*, pp. 124-125.
[175] Ibid. pp. 165-166.
[176] Brandes is quoting Benzelius here. In the second Brandes' work mentioned, he attributes this to Mosheim, probable to indicate the nearness of Benzelius authorship to Mosheim's.

ogy, Brandes still argues that Durie was neither backed by the King nor the 'strengen Episkopalen'. However, both Abbott and Laud endorsed Durie's project after consultation with Charles I and Durie's earliest supporters such as Ussher, Hall and Davenant were strong contenders for the episcopate in its ancient form[177] and assisted Laud in drawing up an apology for it. Hall, Davenant and Carleton defended the Episcopacy at Dort. During the Engagement Controversy, it was the Episcopalians, not the Presbyterians, who formed pressure groups in sixteen English counties and Ireland, putting forward ideas for a united Protestant Church built on Durie's lines but without a King and the House of Lords.[178] Brandes leaves out Spens role as a link between Durie and Gustav II Adolf but recognises Roe's. He also belittles Oxenstierna's role believing he denied Durie the support Gustav Adolf had promised him.[179] Brandes is on more certain ground when he explains how Durie sought to remove discussion from mere doctrines and dogmas of faith and centre them in the entire active worship and caring outreach of the churches. In other words, 'zu echter Schriftforschung und zu Untersuchungen über die Übereinstimmung der ersten Kirche mit dem Fundamente der Schrift, sowie auch zur Wiederherstellung der leider ganz vernachlässigten praktischen Theologie'.[180] Brandes believes that Durie's plans for a practical piety pointed the way to the Pietism of Spener. However, he also outlines Durie's method of combining his faith with a scholarly appreciation and application of it.[181] Brandes argues that those theologians and ministers in opposite camps who start controversy are the last to heal the wounds made by it. Referring to the Leipzig, Wittenberg and Jena position that union could only mean accepting the Augsburg Confession lock, stock and barrel and the 'Zwinglians' were to blame for all quarrels, Brandes says this must have seemed 'fast wie Hohn' for Durie.

Brandes claims that Archbishop Laud was suspicious of Durie's Presbyterianism, and used 'Feuer und Schwert' against all Presbyterians. This

---

[177] See William Abbott's 'James Ussher and "Ussherian" Episcopacy, 1640-1656; The Primate and His Reduction Manuscript.'

[178] See the report of one of these meetings entitled *The Judgment and Advice of the Assembly of the Associated Ministers of Worcester-Shire, Held at Worcester Aug. 6th 1658. Concerning the Endeavours of Ecclesiasticall Peace, and the Waies and Meanes of Christian Unity, which Mr John Durey doth present; sent unto him in the Name, and by the appointment of the aforesaid Assembly*. By Richard Baxter Pastor of the Church at Kiderminster. The report is also undersigned by John Boraston, Thomas Wright, Giles Collyer, George Hopkins and Joseph Trebell.

[179] *Geschichte,* pp 278-279.

[180] Ibid. 279.

[181] Ibid, p. 281.

was never an issue between the two men as Durie had gone to England with a view to being ordained into the Church of England and, in Germany, had already corresponded with Bishop Hall, who eventually ordained him, to this end. Furthermore, Durie left England for the Frankfurt Diet of 1634 with even stronger credentials from Court, the universities and leading churchmen than he had received from Abbot, though Abbott had also had Laud's signature on his own letter of support for Durie. Durie was always a neutral man in matters of church orders. However, when dealing with the 1634 Frankfurt Diet of Protestant powers, Brandes claims that Durie and his message were in their proper place. On following his subject to Sweden, Brandes compares Durie's disappointments with Jena, Leipzig and Wittenberg as on a par with those of Uppsala. He admits, however, that Durie spoke rather of the successes which gave him new hope.

Brandes now returns Durie to England where he is made chaplain to the King's daughter, petitions Parliament and becomes a member of the Westminster Assembly. Brandes says Durie rejoined the Presbyterians from whom he had never really departed. However, most of Durie's contacts were either Episcopalian or Independent. Though the difference between the factions only came gradually. Jumping over many years, Brandes has Durie back on Continental soil in 1654 as Cromwell's agent of peace in Europe. He relates how Durie returned to England in 1657 with a success story concerning his mission which was brought to nought by Cromwell's death. However, Cromwell dropped Durie shortly after his return from the Continent. Brandes claims that Charles II would have nothing to do with Durie because he was a Presbyterian.

Brandes now brings us back to the year 1661 with Durie's returned to Cassel and the subsequent death of Landgrave William in 1663. Returning to the subject of the Berlin Colloquy of 1668, he points out how Court chaplain Stosch saw no hope in Durie's 'syncretism'. He might have added also that Lutheran Paul Gerhardt looked on Stosch and his Reformed men as 'Dickköpfe' who would never be converted to Lutheranism.

In his *Christian Presbyterian* paper, Brandes quotes Mosheim as calling Durie 'the celebrated Peacemaker', the appellation which appears in Benzelius' title. Brandes shows how the *Formula of Concord* was a veritable declaration of excommunication for those of the Reformed faith.[182] He sees the *Formula* as breaking the power of the Evangelical Church in Germany which made the counter-reformation easier for the papists. Brandes account here of William Laud's lack of support for Durie contradicts

---

[182] John Durie and his work in Germany, p. 23

Laud's own correspondence with Ambassador Sir Thomas Roe and Durie, and ignores contemporary biographies such as that of Heylin, Laud's chaplain and the various accounts of Laud's attitude to Durie recorded in the *Calendar of State Papers* from 1634-5. The best source for Laud is his own letters, diary and writings. John Bruce, who wrote the prefaces to the Calendar of State Papers during the reign of Charles I, tells us that it is through Laud's dealings with Durie that we come 'peculiarly near' to the Archbishop. He appears to be surprised that Laud was on such friendly terms with Durie, of whom Bruce says erroneously was 'a clergyman of the Church of Scotland'.

Brandes emphasises the urgency of Durie's work because contemporary Protestants realised that their lack of unity was their undoing and reunion would be the salvation of the Evangelical cause. He concludes that the major, if not only, reason why Durie's success was not greater in Europe was that he visited the royal houses of Europe as ambassador of Oliver Cromwell, the King-Killer. Concerning Durie's plans to see Practical Theology courses in all university and colleges throughout Europe, Brandes adds the interesting information overlooked in modern studies that Durie urged for multi-lingual textbooks to be used in Europe's schools. So, too, Brandes comments on Gustav II Adolf's political shrewdness in realising the advantages of ruling over a united Evangelical Church in Germany as proposed by Durie. However, at the same time, Brandes plays down the importance of Durie's connections with King Gustav and believes that the support of Calixtus and the Helmstedt theologians 'could not be of great importance'.[183] He thus fails to take into full account the Swedish royal family's continued interest in both Durie and Helmstedt. Indeed, Queen Christina's policy was to set up theological training colleges based on Durie-Helmstedt principles in Gnesio-Lutheran areas of Germany and call together a committee of classical scholars and theologians to undertake a new German translation of the Bible, thus challenging the unique position of the Lutheran Bible in Germany.[184] So, too, Brandes conclusion that Durie's aim was to work out a formula on a Presbyterian basis to which all sides should agree is a misunderstanding of Durie's Presbyterian-Independent mediation and connections with the Church of England. Nevertheless, Brandes' account is one of the most comprehensive overviews of Durie's life and work written to date.

---

[183] Ibid, p. 30.
[184] See Göranson, *Orthodoxi och Synkretism I Sverige 1647-1660*, Chapters I:iii; II:v; and IX.

C. A. Briggs

In 1887, the *New Yorker Presbyterian Review* carried an article by Briggs on Durie's *A Summarie Relation of that which John Durie hath Prosecuted in the Worke of Ecclesiastical Pacificacon in Germanie since ye Latter End of Julie 1631 till 26 September 1633*, believing it was hitherto unknown. It is accompanied by an introductory essay entitled 'The Work of John Durie in Behalf of Christian Union in the Seventeenth Century'. Briggs opens by saying of his subject:

> 'John Durie was the great peacemaker of the seventeenth century. He did a noble work in behalf of Christian union during the evil times of the thirty years' war on the Continent of Europe, and the great civil wars of Great Britain. He persevered in his peacemaking notwithstanding every obstacle for half a century.'

Briggs describes the rapid development of Durie as an irenist from 1628 on, mentioning his usual co-workers cited by scholars but adding Richard Baxter, William Gouge, George Walker, Adoniram Byfield, Sidrach Simpson, Obadiah Sedgwick, John White, Richard Sibbes and John Cotton. Briggs deals with conferences held at Leipzig (1631), Hanau (1633), Frankfurt (1633-34), Hamburg (1634) and Helmstedt (1639) and that 'they did judge his work most laudable, most acceptable to God, and most necessary and useful to the Church'.

Briggs relates how in 1640, Durie presented a petition to the House of Commons arguing 'that the blessed and long-sought-for union of Protestant churches might be recommended unto the publick prayers of the church' and called for a General Synod of Protestants of all nations. He also sent letters to the King and to the Scottish General Assembly meeting at St. Andrews. Briggs, calling William Prynne 'that bitter partisan', speaks of his intolerance of peace overtures within Protestantism such as those Durie made. Briggs sees Durie's overall work as 1. A plea for a full body of practical divinity to be taught to all who 'seek the truth which is after godliness'. 2. To abolish all denominational and party names within the Protestant churches, merely referring to them as 'The Reformed Christians' of England, France, Germany etc.. 3. Discontinue controversial writing amongst private persons and 4. Each Christian should be free to follow his Christian faith in his own way and not have it determined by 'the dictates of other men'.

Between 1654 and 57, we find Durie, armed with letters from Cromwell, the heads of Oxford and Cambridge universities and the joint-ministers of London, touring the courts, universities, governments and churches of Europe with his message of peace and unity. At the restoration, Durie made his permanent address in Hesse-Cassel as Chaplain to Princess Hedwig Sophie and died there probably in 1680. The author sees Durie as teaching 'a full body of practical divinity, which instead of the ordinary philosophical jangling school divinity, might be proposed to all those that seek the truth, which is after godliness.' Of Durie and his circle he comments:

> 'These are the men of the seventeenth century who have the most to say to the men of the nineteenth century who are preparing to enter the twentieth century. The disunion of Protestantism has continued long enough. It is high time that we should set our faces towards a realization of that ideal of Christian Union for which these heroes of the seventeenth century labored so faithfully and so well.'

Briggs has not researched Durie's early years in Scotland, France and Holland and in his *Schaff-Herzog Encyclopaedia* account argues that though Durie was 'supposed to have been born in Scotland', he suggests 'he was born of Scottish parents settled in Germany'. He also believes that we first know of Durie through his 1628 letter from Elbing in Prussia to Gustav II Adolf. Briggs is not alone in thinking Durie was a German. Henry Reeve, in his introduction to Bulstrode Whitelocke's *Journal of the Swedish Embassy*, refers to Durie as a 'German Librarian', having taken over this without question from Whitelocke.

H. Tollin

In 1897, Dr. H. Tollin sent a monograph to the *Verein für Geschichte und Altertumskunde des Herzogtums und Erzstift Magdeburg* for publication in their *Geschichtsblätter*, entitled simply 'Johannes Duraeus'. This work was a major step forward in Durie research. Tollin uses international church and synodal records concerning Durie's early life in Holland and France not used by other researches and still most difficult to trace. Tollin believes Durie was twenty-one years old when he gave a Latin oration in 1616[185] before the Amsterdam Synod and refers to his connections with the Synods of The Hague and Utrecht. He shows how Durie commenced his theological studies at Amsterdam in 1617 and took the 'Proposant Examen' in 1620. He claims that in 1624, the Synod at Dort called back Durie to the services of the Dutch Church so that he could pastor a church in Elbing,

---

[185] Several other sources make him from five to three years younger.

Prussia. Tollin holds that Durie gained a doctor title in 1624 at Oxford. He does not mention Durie's ministry in Cologne before he moved to Elbing. Tollin also maintains that Durie had no authority to serve as a representative of the English Church and Court which is why Durie sought a closer contact with Oxenstierna, Sweden and Germany. The main authorisation for Durie's work for union, he argues, came with an invitation to take part in the Leipzig Disputation of 1631 from Court Chaplain John Bergius through the initiative of Casper Godeman. Tollin believes Durie took part in the Leipzig Disputation but admits that this is a mere 'Vermutung' or 'opinion'.[186]

Tollin discusses Durie's contacts with Gustav Adolf and his chaplains and Chancellor Oxenstierna, tracing Durie's early transactions at conferences in Hanau, the Palatine, Hesse, Wetterau and Nassau before returning to England after the death of Archbishop Abbott in 1633 to consult Abbott's successor. Tollin is harsh on Laud, calling him an 'inveterate Episcopalian',[187] who regarded Durie as a heretic. The author claims that Durie was a 'renegade' Presbyterian who became an Anglican out of opportunism. He mentions, however, that Puritan Archbishop James Ussher and like-minded bishop and Bible translator William Bedell backed Laud in promoting Durie's journey to the Frankfurt Diet of Protestant States in 1634 after his being invited by the Prince of Orange and Duke William of Hesse. At this Diet of all the Protestant rulers in Germany, their ambassadors and senior clergy in August, 1634, Durie gave a paper entitled *Judicia Theologorum Anglorum et aliorum de Pace Protestantium sacra* backed by the highest Anglican dignitaries. On 14 September 1634 and encouraged by Axel Oxenstierna, the colloquy unanimously declared they would follow Durie's proposals. Bishops Davenant and Hall published their strong support for Durie in these transactions.

Tollin refers to Durie's meeting with Johannes Bogermann who had been the Chairman of the Synod of Dort and had appointed Durie's supporter Davenant as its spokesman and contender against Cameronism in the French churches. Because Durie consulted with Hugo Grotius, Tollin concludes, by association, that Durie was an Arminian. Grotius, however, was consulted in his office as Swedish ambassador to Paris and one whose task was to prepare a political union of England and Sweden. Grotius also requested Durie's help concerning a Swedish-English confession of faith which was to include the other Scandinavian countries and used as a basis for Reformed and Lutheran unity. As Henk Nellen shows in his *Grotiana*

---

[186] Johannes Duraeus, p. 234.
[187] 'Eingefleischter Episkopale'

paper 'Hugo Grotius' Political and Scholarly Activities', Grotius 'kept his distance from the Scot John Durie' and was more for a reunion with Rome rather than Canterbury, Wittenberg, Zürich or Geneva.[188] Furthermore, the scores of godly Calvinist ministers who backed Durie resolved to do so as an antidote against Arminianism.[189] Tollin then speaks of Durie's great welcome and success in the synods of the Walloon Church in 1636 and that the Utrecht Synod came down fully on Durie's side.

Tollin mentions the correspondence between a changing Scottish church and Sweden during Durie's visit there which is often overlooked. He blames Bishop Rudbeck for Durie's expulsion from Sweden towards the end of 1638. Tollin's account of Durie in Germany and Denmark and in 'sein Adoptiv-Vaterland' Holland, and especially his transactions at Helmstedt and Wolfenbüttel makes excellent, well-documented reading but Tollin's constant apparent dread of English and Anglican influence on Durie and Durie's alleged 'opportunism' reveals his own national and confessional bias. However, Durie was now busy commuting between England and the Continent and planning further works with what Tollin calls his *Geheimen Gesellschaft der Naturphilosophen*,[190] in which he counts Samuel Hartlib, Bishops Thomas Morton and Joseph Hall, Archbishop Usher and John Pym. Though Tollin argues that Durie's alleged opportunistic Anglican connections made his fellow Puritans suspicious of him, he nevertheless relates how the Long Parliament did not hesitate in 1645 to make Durie a preacher to the Parliament and 'enthusiastic' co-author of the Westminster Confession and the Westminster Catechisms. Tollin mentions how through many petitions, Durie strove to save Charles from the martyr-maker's axe.

Tollin claims that Durie could not be happy in the guise of an Anglican chaplain at the Hague royal court. However, in September 1641, the Synod of Delft stressed how important it was for the Dutch Presbyterians to accept Durie's plans for peace. Tollin mentions Durie's marriage to Dorothy More, the widow of an Irish Puritan, at Rotterdam merely by the way. He describes Durie's reception in Switzerland as a march of triumph through the cantons and he was given special honours at the pan-Swiss *Kirchentag* at Aarau in 1654. The Swiss gave Durie generous financial support and heaped him with letters of recommendation and good wishes to the British Republic. Tollin describes how Durie's popularity continued throughout

---

[188] See Nellen's paper pp. 19-20.
[189] See Tom Webster's *Godly Clergy in Early Stuart England*, especially the chapter 'John Dury and the godly ministers'.
[190] Secret Society of Natural Scientists.

1654 and 1655. A similar tour of Germany and Holland provided Durie with many documents from the various Protestant churches to testify to their British brethren that they were willing to form a universal brotherhood of Protestants. Thus a very happy and satisfied Durie returned to England in 1657 to place his findings before the gathered political representatives of England, Scotland and Ireland who ruled that Durie's plans were fully acceptable to Parliament and he should be appointed as the official Parliamentary representative to organise and enforce this great task. Immediately, Durie began conveying the good news to the British and Continental Protestant churches. Then Cromwell died and his son Richard reigned for a short time and preparations for the end of the Republic began. Durie's great work was placed on ice.

Essays by educationalists

Friedrich Sander

In 1894, Sander, a Bremen teacher, wrote his *Comenius, Duraeus, Figulus: Nach Stammbüchern der Familie Figulus-Jablonski* in the *Comenus-Gesellschaft*'s magazine for 1894. He gives helpful insights into the fellowship of these three men, dealing particularly with Durie's secretary and Comenius' ward and thereafter son-in-law Petrus Figulus Jablonaeus (Jablonski). The Figulus-Jablonskis were instrumental in founding the Comenius Society and sat on its governing board. They donated their family collections of manuscripts and letters to the society, including the autograph albums and diaries of Durie's secretary. Sander also describes Durie's education as being solely British and that he left Oxford in 1624 to become pastor of an Elbing church. The author rejects the commonly held view that Godeman in Elbing put the idea of becoming an ambassador of peace amongst Protestant churches into Durie's head or even worked two years with him on a mutual project. He claims they pooled their mature individually made proposals and presented them jointly to Oxenstierna in 1630 at Elbing. He affirms that Hartlib agreed to visit England in 1628 to prepare the way for Durie's visit. Sander writes positively of the backing Durie received from Archbishop George Abbott, Bishop Joseph Hall and Bishop John Davenant and in Germany from John Bergius, John Crocius and Theophilus Neuberger. In contrast to Tollin, Sander tells us that Oxenstierna continued to support Durie's irenic task enthusiastically and that Durie received credentials and financial help from Archbishop Laud and Archbishop Ussher. Sander also speaks of Durie's connections with the

Bohemian Brethren, a much neglected part of Durie scholarship. He especially mentions Durie's influence at the Synod of Thorn in July 1636.

Sander records how Figulus visited Sweden with Durie in 1636-38, referring to Figulus' diary and Benzelius as his sources. Sander shows that entries in Jablonski's scrap-book for June 1638 in Oxenstierna's, Petrus Wibe's and Rudbeck's hands were very friendly and collegial but we are otherwise told that Durie was forced out of Sweden by Johannes Rudbeck's bitter opposition and lack of support by Oxenstierna in 1638.

Sander describes Durie's and Figulus' work in Lübeck, Hamburg, Brunswick, Hildesheim, Celle and Luneburg, believing that if it were not for the Swedish military presence and the German-French treaties, these friends would have put Durie's plans into practice there and then. Most of 1640 was spent in Denmark where Durie was warmly received by King Christian IV who Benzelius says was impressed by Durie's plans. In the autumn of 1640, Durie and Figulus journeyed to Groningen where they stayed until July 1641. Figulus' album preserved the names of the dignitaries they met including the signature 'Elizabeth', i.e. Elizabeth Stuart, sister to King Charles I. Figulus' account of Comenius' England visit as Durie's and Figulus' guest blows fresh wind into the debate concerning the teamwork of Durie, Comenius and Hartlib.

Theodor Klähr

Educator Klähr published his 'Johannes Duraeus: Sein Leben und seine Schriften über Erziehungslehre' in the Comenius-Gesellschaft's periodical in 1897. He introduces his subject as a shining light against the darkness of the Thirty Years War, uniting the quarrelsome Protestants with true Christian disposition so that they would be one fold with one Shepherd. Klähr appears to disapprove of Durie's irenic activities, concentrating on Durie's educational thoughts and also places Durie at Oxford in 1624. Klähr relies much here on secondary sources for his rather questionable biographical data and Tollin gives quite a different account of this period in his Magdeburg work though he used both Sander and Klähr.[191]

Klähr, using Kvačala as his source, refers to three untitled works Durie allegedly authored on the subject of Protestant unity at Elbing, claiming they are no longer extant. However, there are at least four extant works from this period, three in printed form. Klähr sees Sir Thomas Roe as the first to recommend Durie to King Gustav Adolf. However, in Durie's

---

[191] See Tollin's 'Johannes Duraeus, especially pp. 231, 235, 240, 246, 249, 252, 256

Briefe Relation,[192] he claims that James Spens first acquainted the Swedish King with Durie. Roe came to Elbing two years later.

Klähr also argues that Durie had no Church of England backing in his endeavours for peace amongst Protestants and even plays down Durie's quite triumphant success in the Frankfurt Diet of 1634. That the Battle of Nördlingen put an end to much hoped for union, as Klähr stresses, did not affect the quality of Durie's work and acceptance amongst so many Continental states.

We are told that Johannes Matthiae invited Durie to Sweden and Klähr gives the Scotsman four years in Sweden rather than three. He contradicts both Durie and Hartlib in claiming that Oxenstierna refused to give Durie a letter of recommendation to the Swedish Church and to Uppsala University. Klähr believes Bishop Rudbeck had an 'irreconcilable hate' against the 'damned Calvinists', but found Archbishop Laurentius Paulinus (1565-1646) friendly in his attitude towards Durie.[193]

Klähr does not mention Figulus in connection with Durie, though he is writing for the Comenius Society and suggests, quite without evidence, that in order to stand as a Presbyterian, Durie witnessed against Laud. On the whole, Klähr views Durie's work as fruitless, unclear and impractical, but nevertheless admits he knows too little about him.

On education, Klähr sees 'the enormous figure of Comenius' behind Durie and Hartlib, claiming that Comenius' fruitful activities and great influence is still not acknowledged in England. Klähr ends his survey by adding a brief overview of Durie's *A Seasonable Discourse* and adding Hartlib's Foreword to Durie's *The Reformed School*, followed by an appendix by John Durie. He then gives a multi-paged analysis of Durie's *Reformed School* reprinting Durie's suggestions for a reformed syllabus and curriculum.

Foster Watson

The 1899 and 1900 issues of *The Educational Review*, featured Watson's two essays on John Durie's works, 'John Dury: The Public Good and Education' and, 'Seasonable Discourse'. In the first essay, Watson examines

---

[192] Printed 1641.

[193] Alias Lars Pålsson. See Holmquist's *Svenska Kyrkans Historia*, vol. 4, *Svenska Kyrkan under Gustav II Adolf* for a detailed analysis of Paulinus Gothus' work. For a brief biography, consult *Svenskt biographisk handlexikon*. For a more legthy appreciation see Lindström's *Laurentius Paulinus Gothus: Hans lif och Verksamhet* (2 vols), 1893.

Durie's three point inquiry into what is the public good and how it may be advanced. Durie finds true goodness in the life of God in man, a goodness thus common to God in its universality. Though this goodness is made available to all men, it is to be used in its universal capacity for the good of all. Thus all self-seeking is inconsistent with goodness. The means to attain God is through the medium of the Lord Jesus Christ who illuminates our souls with divine knowledge. Man's duty is to live a blameless life according to this knowledge, doing good to all by making known to all the rules and grounds of the spiritual life and conversation. Watson explains Durie's theory that good teaching is necessary for the rightful development of the natural man and this rightful natural development is necessary for his rightful spiritual development.

Watson sees Durie's *Reformed School* as one of the most able works of the 17th century in reaching this goal, pointing out contemporary defects in education and aiming first at instructing parents as the first and principle educators of their children. To this end, Watson underlines Durie's demand that the teaching of reading and writing must be reformed but does not elaborate on this. Children should be instructed in things present to the senses before going on to think in abstract terms. Religion, languages and science must be the three pillars of a reformed school education. Here Watson outlines Durie's detailed plans for all three, claiming that Durie was 150 years before other educational reformers with such ideas.

Shortly after Charles I's execution and the enforcement of a rigid party-line imprimatur, Durie was nevertheless given permission to publish his *Seasonable Discourse* which Watson believes helped make Durie 'the very centre of the movement for a reconciliation of all the Churches of Christ'. Watson demonstrates further how education and religion are merely two aspects of the same human need. Both are steps in making the knowledge of God cover the earth, thus creating peace within all men. It is a view, when seen admittedly from its best side that is held by the three great universal religions Christianity, Jewry and Islam. Durie, as Watson points out, saw his hope best fulfilled in a Protestant Christian environment.

Watson explains how Durie sees his tiered school system as serving two purposes. Primary and secondary education is to teach what must be known and practised by the pupils and higher education is to instruct people to teach and educate others. Then Watson outlines Durie's theories of acquiring universal learning and meeting the human need of universal communication.

In order to put his ideas into practice, Durie explains the need of increasing the number of elementary and secondary schools in the nation and of waking up the universities to reconsider their position, purpose and calling as academic leaders. Watson ends his account by saying that:

> 'Of Dury's three treatises combined – the *Public Good*, the *Seasonable Discourse*, and the *Reformed School*, it is not too much to say that they are (though so short) among the most philosophical utterances on education in our language.'

Watson's essays come nearest of all the writings here discussed to my own appreciation of John Durie. Nineteenth century works tended slowly to move their focus from the mere biographical and irenic to the topic of Durie's practical divinity and universal learning.

CHAPTER FOUR

The 20th Century's reception of John Durie

Karl Brauer

In 1907 Brauer presented a dissertation to the University of Marburg entitled *Die Unionstätigkeit John Duries unter dem Protektorat Cromwells: Ein Beitrag zur Kirchengeschichte des siebzehnten Jahrhunderts* for which he was awarded the title of Lizentiat. This well-prepared, well-documented and well-argued thesis not only underlined Durie's importance in striving for political and religious unity between the Protectorate and the Landgraviate of Hesse and her Protestant churches but also went into great detail to explain Durie's pioneering pan-Swiss, pan-German and pan-Dutch endeavours to foster union between Republican England under Cromwell and the Kingdoms, Dukedoms and Cantons of the Continent.

Brauer claims he has mostly used hitherto unknown sources but his contents and footnotes reveal a strong dependence on Henke's *Georg Calixtus and seine Zeit* (1853) and Tollin's *Johannes Duraeus*. Brauer also used Mosheim's, Kvačala's, Klähr's and Sander's works besides a large number of general historical studies. In his list of sources of Durie mss, Brauer merely names shelf-marks and collection titles but does not give individual names, titles, dates etc.. Personal visits to several of the archives Brauer lists as also online and telephone research connected with the others prove sometimes disappointing as references are often to mere snippets or title pages or damaged and even missing documents. Contrary to Brauer's claims, his list is far from exhaustive. He did not consult the Uppsala and Stockholm archives, nor had the Hartlib Papers become common knowledge in his day. Though Brauer mentions the Wolfenbüttel Staatsarchiv, whilst at Wolfenbüttel, he appears not to have consulted the large collection of Durie works at the Herzog August Library. Nor does Brauer refer to the great Oxford libraries such as Bodleian and Codrington, which even in Brauer's day contained a great number of Durie mss. This author misses reference to and comments on a few notable secondary works such as those of Brandes. Indeed, though Brauer's footnotes are profuse, most of them refer to secondary works or contemporary writers other than Durie himself. No bibliography of books used is given.

Nevertheless, any scholar treading in Brauer's footsteps might be able to attempt a wider work but would have great difficulty in being as specific and detailed as Brauer in his own area. Brauer has, for instance, used sources now in the Hesse State Archives in Marburg which were hitherto almost untouched by scholars. So, too, he wisely drew up definite Lockean-like borders around his field of study leaving out many geographical, chronological, ecclesiastical, political, scientific, social and educational aspects. These areas, thanks to the modern technology of data processing, library management, defragmentation of knowledge and online information, which Durie partly foresaw, are now easier to cover.

After a six page overview of Durie's pre-Commonwealth period by way of introduction, Brauer divides the remaining 247 pages of his thesis into two major parts. The first 'Hauptteil' is entitled 'The History of Durie's Work for Unity under Cromwell's Protectorate'. This is divided into five sections (Teile), the first dealing with how Durie prepared his work and made plans for his first endeavours in Switzerland. The second deals with Durie's actual work in Switzerland. This is divided into five sub-sections (Abschnitte). The first deals with Durie's transactions with the four Protestant centres Zürich, Bern, Basel and Schaffhausen. The second deals with Durie's work in Eastern Switzerland. The third deals with his work in Western Switzerland. The fourth deals with ecclesiastical law in Switzerland and Durie's successes and the fifth sub-section deals with Durie's general reception in Switzerland and his plans for the future.

The third section deals with Durie's work in Germany; one sub-section deals with the South and West; one with the East and one with the North. The fourth section deals with Durie's work in the Netherlands and the fifth section deals with the situation in Britain under Cromwell.

The second main part is far shorter than the first and deals in 29 pages with Durie's unionist aims. The twelve final pages are taken up with appendices relating to Cromwell's letter of recommendation for Durie and his special diplomatic passport (1-2). A letter from Durie to Landgrave William von Hesse-Cassel. (3). A letter from Johann Crocius to Durie (4). Official statements and pronouncements concerning Durie's work from the Theological Faculty at Marburg (5-6) and an official statement concerning Durie's work from William von Hesse-Cassel (7).

The forty chapters and appendices of this most informative work mostly concern themselves with Durie's biography and his work as a Unionist and diplomat. Switzerland has become a neglected area in Durie scholarship, perhaps because Brauer has apparently said the last word on the subject. Scholars hoping to fill in the few holes Brauer has left will find abundant material in the Bodleian and Hesse State Archives, including Durie's own detailed itinerant agenda and schedules used throughout this work. However, Durie's plans for universal learning and practical divinity are almost absent in the work. Nevertheless, this thesis cannot possibly be ignored by anyone looking for detailed information on Durie concerning the middle sixteen-fifties.

John Wordsworth

After naming a row of irenic spirited men including Bucer, Wängler (alias Paraeus), Grotius, Casaubon, Melanchthon and Calixtus in Bishop Wordsworth's Hale Lecture for 1910, published the following year under the title *The National Church of Sweden*, Wordsworth went on to say:

> 'Of even more interest to us than these great scholars and theologians, whose work in other departments of theology is recognized by those who care to explore the treasures of our old libraries, is a man of less commanding ability, who deserves recognition for the whole-hearted devotion with which he applied himself to the cause of re-union. I mean the Scotsman, John Durie, who gave up the last fifty years of a life of eighty-four years (1596-1680) to this work. From the year 1628 he laboured unceasingly in the North and West of Europe to promote the reconciliation, or at least to secure, the intercommunion and co-operation of the Evangelical Churches. He visited courts and statesmen, bishops and clergy, he attended synods, he held disputations, he entered into personal correspondence, he published elaborate treatises, in the interest of a confederation in which England and Scotland, and the Netherlands, and the reformed Churches of France and Germany, especially in the Palatinate, and Switzerland, were to cooperate with the adherents of the Confession of Augsburg.'

Wordsworth is basing his findings chiefly on an article in the *Christian Remembrancer*[194] and on an account in Norlin's *Svenska Kyrkan's Historia* which was more or less a Swedish rendering of Benzelius' Latin work for Professor Mosheim with Norlin's own, individual position maintained throughout. Wordsworth argues that Durie did not wish to found a universal church institution but a co-operation and fellowship of Protestant churches who were in communion together, though they respected one other's national identities and even church traditions. Contrary to many critics of the Church of England, Bishop Wordsworth emphasises the warm reception Durie received from the Archbishop and Bishops of that church

---

[194] January, 1855, Vol. 29, pp. 1529.

and how they willingly and effectively encouraged him to go on with his work. Few, too, give the exact date of Durie's ordination by Bishop Hall of Exeter which was 24th February, 1634. He also mentions that Bishop Bedell gave Durie an annual pension. Following Grubb's *Ecclesiastical History of Scotland*, Wordsworth shows that Archbishop Spottiswoode provided Durie with 'credentials' to the German states. Usually, we only read that Spottiswoode hindered Durie's transactions at Uppsala. Concerning Rudbeck's alleged disagreement with Durie regarding the *Book of Concord*, Wordsworth points out that the *Formula Concordiae*, 'was merely an attempt to unite the followers of Luther and Melanchthon, and was, therefore, of no use in conciliating Calvinists. Indeed, it was an exposition of developed Lutheranism, coloured by references to all the controversies of the day, and, therefore, more hard for Calvinists than the vaguer language of the original confession (Augsburg). Wordsworth maintains that the move towards a lasting union of Lutherans and Reformed in Germany at the beginning of the nineteenth century was a direct outcome of Durie's work.

Hans Leube

In 1928, Lutheran Hans Leube published his two-volume analysis of *Kalvinismus und Luthertum im Zeitalter der Orthodoxie*. He deals with Durie's work, especially in Germany, at length in the first volume 'Der Kampf um die Herrschaft in protestantischen Deutschland'. Leube is one of Durie's major critics. His main and repeated argument is that Reformed Durie was forced into a life's work which overtaxed his abilities. Then, in view of his failure, Durie, as a last resort, turned in bitterness to eschatological speculation. Leube strives to prove that though Durie's contemporaries never doubted the purity of Durie's conduct, he was actually guilty of duplicity and dishonesty. In spite of this highly negative, unsubstantiated view, Leube devotes some sixty pages to Durie's work of peace in Germany, recommending Karl Brauer's Marburg Dissertation *Die Unionstätigkeit John Duries unter dem Protektorat Cromwells* as the best study so far on which he has obviously leaned heavily, especially for quotes from Durie's contemporaries. Leube campaigned for renewal within Lutheranism as a means of ending what he calls the 'the war for supremacy in Protestant Germany' and thus cannot be expected to be too enthusiastic about a man who spoke of Lutherans and Calvinists pulling together. Indeed, Leube's entire criticism of Durie is because Durie was allegedly on the 'Calvinist' side.

Though Leube relates how the Continent was ripe for Durie's ideas in the sixteen-thirties, he feels Durie's success in Heidelberg, Würzburg, Heilbronn, Frankfurt and Upper Germany amongst all ranks and kinds of Protestants was in vain. Leube accuses Durie of trying to deceive Oxenstierna who thus, Leube alone argues, turned from him. Leube also claims that all the written agreements Durie was given by both Calvinists and Lutherans on the Continent had no official validity whatsoever[195] and when he presented them to Archbishop Laud and King Charles they refused to back Durie's project.

Leube argues that Durie made many enemies working for Cromwell, ignoring the fact that he turned most enemies into friends. So, too, Leube accuses Durie of campaigning 'leidenschaftlich' against Independents, yet most critics rank Durie with the Independents. Leube gives the interesting piece of information, however, that Staupe of Switzerland told Gilbert Burnet that the Protector planned to establish an international council for the Protestant religion to rival with the Roman Catholic congregation *de propaganda fide* at Rome. This would be under England's control and divide Europe and the rest of the world into four zones which would include Turkey and both the East and West Indies. Two of Cromwell's ambassadors to this end were John Durie and his friend John Pell the mathematician. It is strange, however, that though Leube claims Durie was ignored and a failure, he yet affirms that he was Cromwell's right-hand man in uniting the known world under a Protestant flag. Few Scotsmen, or Englishmen for that matter, reached such pre-eminence in Commonwealth times. Again, Leube argues against all the documented evidence that Durie was without success in his mission to Switzerland, Germany and Holland in 1654-1657 and returned to England as a failure.

Leube relates that Durie was unable to convince the Restitution government that he was not a co-plotter in the execution of Charles I, and thus left England in 1661 to continue his work on the Continent, relying on his old Swedish, Dutch, German, French and Swiss allies to help open doors for him. Though many doors were opened and many positive results achieved, Leube plays down all by arguing that Durie not only changed his coat but his character to suit the prevailing political and religious winds, faking his reports. He argues that Durie's work failed in Germany because the Germans saw through his deceit and thus rejected Durie's person. Yet, shortly before, Leube had confessed his surprise that the bulk of Reformed ministers in Germany accepted Durie as genuine.[196] Then Leube argues

---

[195] Strangely enough although they came from the highest sources.
[196] Leube, P. 221.

that the Reformed ministers had never thought of being allied with the Gnesio-Lutherans but only with the moderate followers of Calixtus. The Lutheran apologist quotes Geneva's Phillippe Mestrezat, as saying that the Swiss would not give up their Reformed Confessions for some general inter-church *Harmonia confessionum*. However, Durie never asked for a church to give up its confessions. He wished to form a fellowship of churches around basic Reformed doctrines which would enable them to accept one another as brethren and perhaps take communion together. This was also the view of Crocius, Bergius and Calixtus. Durie's *Harmonia confessionum*, like similar works written by Calixtus and Matthiae, merely showed in what measure the different Protestant churches could find agreement up to that time. Durie wanted a free *correspondentia evangelica* or exchange of views in brotherly fellowship and not a Super-church rivalling Rome.

Leube even sees Durie as acting against Davenant's teaching and claims that he left the doctrines of the Reformation and Cromwell and that his doctrines would have been acceptable to Rome. He then challenges Durie's doctrine of the Word of God and its exegesis, linking him with the Pietists, especially through his work *Le véritable Chrétien*, probably meaning Durie's *Le Vrai Chrestien* published in 1676. Leube seeks an ally in Philipp Jacob Spener but does not consider all the evidence given in Spener's letters and writings. Actually, he does not consider much evidence at all.

Now taking a more positive line in his treatment of Durie, Leube says that he sought for a tolerance amongst Christians which could lead to a deeper mutual understanding. He relates how Durie greatly influenced Bishop Matthiae in his work for union in Sweden via the latter's *Ramus olivae septenrionalis*, published in eleven expanded editions between 1656 and 1661.[197] Nevertheless, Leube maintains that Matthiae was the only Lutheran to take Durie seriously, and that Calixtus and the Helmstedt moderate Lutherans never became his friends. Leube closes his evaluation of Durie with several pages of discussions concerning Lutheran doctrines essential for salvation and concludes that for Lutherans the person and work of Christ is the essential doctrine of all doctrines but for the Calvinists it is predestination. If this were so, it ought to have opened Lutheran hearts to Durie who had a more Bullingerite view of predestination than Calvin and believed, as the British Reformers, that predestination was the result of Christ's atoning work on the cross and not irrespective of it as if it were a mere fatalistic *fiat dei*.

---

[197] These were republished by Durie in the sixties.

Gunnar Westin et al.

Whilst studying theology at Uppsala University in the nineteen-sixties, I was immediately confronted with Durie's enormous impact on European Protestant thought through the work of Prof. Gunnar Westin (1890-1967), then already officially Emeritus, and his successor, Prof. Sven Göransson (1910–1989). Gunnar Westin's studies such as *Negotiations About Church Unity: John Durie, Gustav Adolf, Axel Oxenstierna* (1934); *Svenska Kyrkan Och De Protestantiska Enhetssträvandena Under 1630 Talet* (1934) and *John Durie in Sweden 1636-38* (1935) as also his numerous articles on Durie's correspondence and his times in the *Kyrkohistoriska Föreningen Skrifter* and the *Kyrkohistorik Årsskrift* helped me rid myself of denominational intolerance. This common-sense tolerance formed an essential background to Westin's *I den Svenska Frikyrklighetens genombrotstid* (1963). Prof. Westin was the only non-Svenska-Kyrka Professor in the theological department and his constant buffeting with anti-free-church prejudice had made him come to cherish cooperation and fellowship amongst Protestants. Westin's laborious research into and publication of two large collections of Durie letters has made the work of subsequent Durie scholars much easier.

Nevertheless, though more positive than Norlin, Westin displays a marked pessimism in evaluating Durie's influence, even when analysing the documentary evidence underlining the frequent periods of success Durie experienced. For instance, when Durie was basking in the knowledge of a great work, well done, at Frankfurt in 1634 where his influence had now extended from the Reformed to the Lutherans, Westin feels the conference was a disaster. Nor can Westin apparently accept that the great and the learned of Britain and the Continent were genuinely moved by a most persuasive and influential Durie. He feels that they were merely mesmerised by Durie's charm until the talks and discussions were over. Thus in his Introduction to his *John Durie in Sweden 1636-1638*, Westin's very first words summarising the findings of his two previous books concerning Durie's mission in England and the Continent are, 'John Durie had not been successful in his efforts to gain the support of the Swedish king, Gustav Adolf, and Oxenstierna, the Lord Chancellor, for his work for church unity. His exertions 1628-1638 had been futile'. Later, he admits that Durie had both English and Swedish royal and ecclesiastical backing but still claims that 'Laud's struggle for church conformity in England was no good omen for a reconciliation of the churches on the continent', and that 'the Swedish clergy would never tolerate union with Calvinists in religious matters.' However, Westin's over-sober introduction to *John Durie in Sweden* stands in stark contrast to his own detailed description of the events leading up to Durie's Sweden visit in 1636 with all its diplomatic, political and ecclesiastical implications in his *Svenska Kyrkan och de Protestantiska Enhetssträvandena*.[198]

Steve Murdoch feels it is 'quite surprising' and 'unsatisfactory' that Westin failed to examine the relationship between Durie and Oxenstierna that kept the two men in close contact for over many decades. Murdoch thus claims that 'Westin, unaware of the significance of many of the family connections which underpinned it, sometimes takes us in the wrong direction when trying to work out John Durie's network.'[199] He is commenting on the fact that many of the names Westin drops in his works as isolated individuals with no immediate connection with Durie were indeed his close kinsmen and friends in tight association with one another. So, too, Murdoch accuses Westin of not understanding the significance of Durie's association with Anstruther and not realising how important Anstruther was. However, during 1631-34 when Anstruther was of particular help to Durie, his position at Whitehall had been weakened. Murdoch points out that Spens' authority was behind Durie at the decisive Frankfurt Diet and Durie was grateful for help from whatever legitimate source it came. Notwithstanding, the evidence concerning the success of the Frankfurt Diet shows that Murdoch overestimated Anstruther's and even Spens' importance. Murdoch's aim is, however, to show that 'it was not Laud, nor was it Roe, but kith and kin that gave Durie his platform at the conference'.[200] Durie's own account was rather different. He made very much at the conference out of the letters he had in support from the English Church and as his major target group were theologians, this move proved the most effective. So, too, it was the English bishops and Roe who were financing his enterprise, though Durie did get a free lift in Anstruther's coach from Hamburg to Frankfurt.

In the 1930s, Hjalmar Holmquist and Hans Cnattingius did fine research into the 17th century consolidation of the Swedish Church, outlining its former very loose diocesan structure and the struggles between the 'Evangeliska' and 'Lutherska' sections and especial the great rivalry between the theological departments of Uppsala and Åbo who constantly changed their theological colours to represent the opposite of what the other party taught. Durie played a major part in these controversies. Queen

---

[198] See especially pp. 106 ff..
[199] *Network North*, pp. 280-285.
[200] Ibid, p. 295.

Christina, Chancellor of Uppsala and a strong supporter of Durie, called the Swedish Church in her edicts 'Evangeliska' and not 'Lutherska', declaring where she herself stood in the quite fierce religious debates during her father's and her own reigns. Durie followed this practice using the term *evangelicos* or 'evangelicals' to describe the Protestant churches.[201] In Holmquist's two volume work in the series *Svenska Kyrkans Historia* ((IV-V) dated 1938, he deals in detail with Durie's part in the development of the Svenska Kyrkan under Gustav II Adolf and Johannes Rudbeck whose firm hands helped to stabilise the Church in Sweden and her Empire. Holmquist, however, gave the seventeenth century theological debates concerning Durie's plans for unity an international perspective. Cnattingius' 1939 work *Den Centrala Kyrkostyrelsen i Sverige 1611-1636* features eight valuable pages of primary sources and eight pages of secondary sources on the period leading up to Durie's Anglo-Swedish endeavours. Göransson's specific study *Ortodoxi och Synkretism i Sverige 1847-1660* followed in 1950 and his *Den Europeiska Konfessionspolitikens Upplösning 1654-1660*, published in 1956, dedicated to Gunnar Westin, was printed both in Uppsala and Wiesbaden and has a summary in German appended. In this volume, Göransson deals so prolifically with Durie that he is merely listed as passim in the Index. Berndt Gustafsson dealt with Durie's importance to Sweden in his University text book *Svensk Kyrkohistoria* published in 1957. Though these Swedish works deal more specifically with Durie in his international setting and take a broader look at his multi-talents, they are very much national and Swedish in their interpretations, written from the nostalgic position of a country very much aware of being once a great political and military power in Europe. Thus the work of Durie is seen more as an auxiliary movement in Sweden supporting the expansionist plans of King Gustav II Adolf, Queen Christina and King Carl rather than that of a British diplomat and theologian sent by Charles I and Cromwell to a nation they wished to win for their side.

Joseph Minton Batten

In his doctoral thesis, *John Dury – Advocate of Christian Reunion* presented to Chicago University in 1930, Batten declares that Durie's activities 'furnish material for a unique chapter in the history of Christian irenics.'[202] His thesis goes a long way in raising Durie from his contemporary

---

[201] See, for instance, his various works which begin: *De Pacis Ecclesiasticae Rationibus inter Evangelicos usurpandis*, etc..

[202] Preface.

irenists and demonstrating his outstanding individual contribution towards freeing the Protestants from their denominational shackles. However, as his title indicates, Batten's main goal is to present Durie as an incomparable campaigner for Christian union without outlining in detail the practical outworkings of such a union and its usefulness for the modern generation. He thus opens his thesis in Chapter One with the title 'The Churches in an Age of Discord' by proclaiming that:

> 'The following pages will indicate that John Dury occupied a unique position among these irenic leaders. Certainly the range of his irenic efforts was broader than that of any other leader who attempted to heal the divisions of Christendom in the 17th century. In fact, he is the only irenic leader of the period who presented overtures of peace in an effort to settle each of the eight major types of ecclesiastical controversies prevailing at the time, viz. – the alignment of Catholics against Protestants; of the Lutherans who accepted the Formula of Concord against the Lutherans who rejected it; of Lutherans against the Reformed; of Calvinists against Arminians; of Anglicans against Scottish Presbyterians; of Puritans against strict Anglicans; of Anglicans against Separatists; and the alignment of English Presbyterians against English Independents.'[203]

In stressing that Durie's aims were 'broader than any other leader who attempted to heal the divisions of Christendom in the 17th century,' Batten shows the strengths and weaknesses of his work. He presents a most vivid picture, full of biographical detail, of Durie's efforts for peace from the twenties to his death in 1680, not neglecting the latter twenty years of Durie's life which are usually less researched. However, there is little comparison with 'the other leaders' Batten mentions. At times, Batten relies solely on biographers who have not given their sources themselves, though he has sound documentary coverage for other periods such as Durie in Switzerland already covered so well by Brauer. For Durie's years in Sweden, Batten relies on Brandes, Wordsworth and, very occasionally Benzelius, but Batten was writing a few years before the publication of Westin's detailed research. Batten, however, relates how Durie visited Sweden in 1653 with Bulstrode Whitelocke showing how Durie made good use of his time there. As mentioned in Chapter Two, Durie had helped to prepare Whitelocke's 1653-4 visit but did not accompany him and was sent to Switzerland instead.

Batten follows most of Brandes' interpretations in detail, though he also uses Wordsworth, Hering, Henke and Spinka where he could have

---

[203] *John Dury - Advocate of Christian Reunion*, pp. 9-10.

consulted Durie's own autobiographical writings directly. However, even when these are before him, he opts for a different version or interpretation to Durie's. This is especially the case when Brandes deals with Durie's alleged 'chilling' reception in England and Durie's ordination. When one reads in Durie's 16 paged extract of how Laud made several attempts to find Durie a church and living until success crowned his efforts, this takes off most of Brandes 'chill'.[204] Even in his main field of church union, Batten highlights certain features only which can hardly be analysed separately from Durie's other activities and Batten never really gives the whys, wherefores and whereuntos of Durie's major aims outside of Batten's one subject. Thus, when Batten says 'Dury's efforts were, in most cases, unsuccessful,'[205] this is a generalisation which certainly does not describe Durie's success in, say, library management, education, political reforms, practical divinity, England's policy regarding the Jews or popularising the natural sciences. Even in his own sphere of church union, Batten fails to account for the fact that Durie's goal, albeit on a modified basis, was already gaining world-wide recognition in Batten's own day.[206]

Batten places Durie at Sedan under Andrew Melville after his Leyden studies. However, Melville left Sedan in 1622 but Du Moulin was there in 1621-23 and 1625-1659.[207] This would suggest that Durie either visited Sedan before 1622, and before ending his Leyden studies, or that he sat under Du Moulin and not Melville afterwards. As Melville was in Sedan when Robert Durie was exiled to France before moving to Leyden in 1610, it could be that Melville helped with John's elementary education then. However, Batten claims that in 1624 and after being called to serve the Merchant Adventurers Church at Elbing, Durie was ordained in Holland in the Presbyterian manner.[208] This seems rather inconsistent with the fact that English Merchant Adventurer churches abroad came under the jurisdiction of the Archbishop of Canterbury at this time and the Dutch Presbyterians had no ecclesiastical authority in Prussia. Nor had Durie performed the requirements for a Presbyterian ordination, which was to a particular local church only in the Netherlands and her foreign possessions. Batten claims he is following Tollin, but Tollin is uncertain as to the time and place of

---

[204] See Durie's explanation of the situation in *An Extract pf Mr. D. letter written long ago to S.H*, Ref. 6/10/1A-16B, HP.
[205] Ibid, p. 14.
[206] See Rouse-Neill, *Geschichte der Ökumenischen Bewegung 1517-1947*, Erster Teil, p. 137 ff. 'John Durys Lebenswerk im Dienste ökumenischen Handels'.
[207] Batten, p. 23.
[208] Ibid, p. 25.

Durie's move to Elbing and this is one of his several clearly expressed 'Vermutungen'. Furthermore, Tollin merely refers to Durie's taking the Proposant Examination in Amsterdam in 1620. This was a theological course for those training for the ministry but graduates were not automatically ordained but had to serve some time in a Dutch or affiliated congregation before being called as its pastor first. Batten also suggests a friendship at this time between Durie, Comenius and Andreae which he does not back up by evidence. So, too, Batten refers to the Leipzig Colloquy of 1631 solely through modern secondary sources though Durie published several eye-witness accounts written by delegates as also did Crocius.

Leaning on Matthew Spinka, Batten sees a change in Durie's views concerning Protestant Alliance. First he sought for 'pacification' amongst German Protestants only, then a union of Reformed and Lutheran churches, then the union of all Protestant churches. The latter, however, was Durie's aim from the start but he could only put it into practice as his success grew and widened. Incidentally, Batten sees Durie's demand for a common declaration of faith as first fulfilled in Philip Schaff's *Harmony of the Reformed Confessions* of 1887. However, Durie followed up his demands for a 'Harmony' by publishing several versions, especially his *Extractum ex harmonia* of 1671.

Where Batten sidesteps into the realms of education, he sees Durie's concept as a development of Bacon's and Comenius', but believes that Durie and Calixtus both went beyond Comenius in constructing a moral philosophy.[209] It is obvious from Durie's letters after 1636 that Durie was comparing Comenius' proposals with his own. Both men at this time were teaching that sound education could only lead to sound theology and international peace. So, too, Durie's works on the advancement of learning and his disdain of systematic theology and Aristotelian logic certainly reflect Bacon's influence.

Batten refers briefly to Durie's Practical Divinity,[210] seeing it as 'a theological discipline' which was to be introduced as a subject into schools. Though he calls Durie's views 'a landmark in the history of the whole educational system', except for a comparison with modern Kindergarten work, he limits his description to Bible teaching. Here he has obviously misunderstood Durie who was quite against subject teaching and saw in Practical Divinity a synergism of all the worlds 'sciences' or wisdom which was to be introduced to the pupils as a means of appropriating universal knowledge. He was even against teaching 'theology' or 'the Bible'

---

[209] Ibid, p. 238.
[210] Ibid, pp. 58-59; 92-93; 238.

as a separate subject and not as part of a coordinating and merging of subjects into one practical and usable whole.[211] Batten suggests that Durie was more successful at this time in publishing treaties on church union backed by Davenant, Morton and Hall but this was the very spade work necessary to set up an international Body of Practical Divinity as requested by the Continentals after 1633-34. At least Durie's views on Practical Divinity and Universal Learning became official Parliamentary strategy for a brief period. So, too, Batten spends several pages, leaning on Kvačala, trying to prove that Durie was indebted to Comenius for linking the topic of church union with his educational plans. However, from the twenties, when Durie laid the foundations for his future work, he had emphasised that he had no one to help him and the 'proof' Batten finds of Comenius influence on Durie is the letter already mentioned above written ten years later in which Durie promises to send Hartlib a comparison of his own findings and those of Comenius saying 'I will elaborate my own and some of Comenius Pansophical tasks as God shall enable me.'[212] Here, the reference is to works of Comenius recently received which he aims to compare with his own views. This is insufficient evidence to argue for a strong Comenian influence on Durie.

Durie's work on Library Management which is part and parcel of his teaching on Universal Learning and Practical Divinity is merely touched upon briefly.[213] Batten tells us that in his last years Durie renewed his interest in Practical Divinity and education, publishing his views in 1676 in *Le Véritable Chrétien*.[214] However, he does not attempt an evaluation of this work and does not indicate that he has studied it. This writer, in keeping with his contemporary fellow-researchers, has failed to find a copy of this work.

In his account of the Frankfurt Colloquy of 1634, Batten leans heavily on Brandes' pessimistic account instead of the original documents he lists. For Durie, Frankfurt 1634 was very encouraging. When, Batten quotes Durie on his warm reception on his return to England in 1634 by the King and Archbishop Laud, he adds a footnote declaring 'most of the writers who have presented accounts of Durie's labours have over-estimated the amount of support which he received from Laud.' Batten's story of the difficulties Durie encountered in the 1660s and 1670s and how he remained

---

[211] Ibid pp. 166-168. See Durie's letter to Hartlib on Practical Divinity, April 13, 1633 and my discussion of the topic below.
[212] Batten, p. 122.
[213] Battern, p. 231.
[214] Ibid, p. 357.

true to himself and his calling is most moving and the author ends his dissertation with a fine tribute to Durie's life's work.

Wilbur Abbott's 1945 review of Batten's dissertation and later publication is of considerable interest as Abbott draws conclusions from Batten's thesis which go beyond those of the author. Abbott sees Durie's work as 'the history of a failure, though a magnificent failure' which 'accomplished virtually nothing in his great task of bringing together the various Protestant communions into anything like the semblance of unity which the Roman Catholic church offered.' Though Batten did speculate on whether Durie's unification of Protestants might lead to union with Rome neither Durie nor Batten envisaged a Protestant organisation and hierarchy as in the Roman Catholic Church. Durie's aim was to unite those of the same faith in that faith and not in any external form of denominational discipline and order. He saw the latter merely as a utility of local tradition and practice which had virtually little to do with the piety of the individual. Abbott criticises Durie in this way believing that 1945 was a year in which 'other and more successful efforts are being made to complete the great task to which he (Durie) set himself.' Abbott does not give documentation for this statement but tells us that Durie was not even successful in uniting the English and Scottish churches let alone those of the Continent. This statement, too, must be qualified as cross-border British fellowship, even on an organised basis, has become a common occurrence nowadays. Even before Durie's day, real efforts were made to bridge the gap between Lutherans and the Reformed on the Continent with great success. Durie built his wider efforts on this basis. In modern Germany, the Lutheran and Reformed churches are closely united under a common leadership. In Sweden, one can take a thoroughly Reformed stance through the entire theological preparation for the ministry without fear of being 'disciplined', as this writer experienced.

Hugh Redwald Trevor-Roper (Lord Dacre)

1940 saw the publication of H. R. Trevor-Roper's biography of Archbishop Laud which included a chapter on 'The Church Abroad'. Here, the author deals in some detail with John Durie's relationship to Laud. Lord Dacre sees Laud as an Arminian who was, as far as Continental churches were concerned, 'completely uninterested in ecclesiastical affairs'. He claims that Durie was, 'an earnest apostle of Protestant unity' but an embarrassment to Laud who objected to Durie 'badgering him'. Trevor-Roper claims that 'Durie was an idealist who based the activities of a life-time upon the mistaken assumption that people really care about religious doctrines.' He maintains that especially theologians had no use for Durie and 'turned him out of doors'. Trevor-Roper's evidence seldom catches up with his conclusions. Where he is most assertive in his negative interpretations, he is less so in documenting their validity and is often self-contradictory and drops into journalese. Though branding Laud as an Arminian, Trevor-Roper has to confess that many of the men with whom Laud associated, such as Sibbes, Gouge and Davenport, were staunch Anti-Arminians. We may add Hall, Ussher and Durie's circle, who were all firm believers in the doctrines of grace. Trevor-Roper also speaks of Laud's support of the Palatine Calvinistic clergy. For diplomatic reasons, of course, this affinity could not be emphasised in Commonwealth times. However, this keeping his cake and eating it pervades all Lord Dacre's comments on Laud and Durie. He describes Durie's great success amongst British and Continental divines and refers to Latin letters of Laud to the Continental Lutherans and Reformed expressing the Archbishop's great interest in their cause. He points out that Laud claimed to be 'overwhelmed with delight' at the work of peace going on between the Protestant churches.[215] He also relates how the Reformed churches of Cassel and Hesse in Germany and Sedan in France appealed to Laud for support in their strivings for unity amongst Protestants. To this we may add Laud's own personal correspondence with divines of all categories from several European countries many of whom supported Durie's thinking. Laud's letters simply do not show that Laud was 'unconcerned' about what happened on the Continent as Trevor-Roper postulates. Indeed, after telling us how troublesome and even 'badgering' Durie was to Laud, he quotes the Archbishop as saying that his prayers for the success of Durie's project were continually besieging God.[216]

In 1967, Trevor-Roper published his *Religion, Reformation and Social Change* which contained an essay, also published separately, entitled 'Three Foreigners: The Philosophers of the Puritan Revolution'. The 'philosophers' Trevor-Roper has in mind are Durie, Hartlib and Comenius. This essay was so well received in one quarter, that it was described as giving a 'large perspective' in 'a luminescent essay' showing 'masterly detail'.[217] Such praise reflects Trevor-Roper's popularity rather than sober

---

[215] The two Latin letters are found in Laud's *Works*, vi. p. 410 and vii. p. 112.
[216] Laud's *Works*, vi., p.410.
[217] See Mark Greengrass, Michael Leslie and Timothy Raylor in their joint Introduction to the book *Samuel Hartlib and Universal Reformation*, and also Howard Hotson's contribution to the book entitled, 'Philosophical pedagogy in reformed

facts. The essay is a brief introduction to the commonwealth of ideas shared by Durie, Hartlib and Comenius and gives little attention to their great differences in thinking and in their individual ambitions and aims. The work merely portrays a simplistic, black and white sketch of the three reformers, leaving others to provide the exact contours and colouration. Trevor-Roper's material on Durie in the essay is scanty. His evaluation of Durie's historical, philosophical, religious, political and social setting is too cramped and his historical interpretations questionable.

Trevor-Roper views Cromwell as a 'Leveller'. It is true that the Protector was all for restricting, even abolishing the powers of the Lords and his other royal rivals, but anyone who had himself called 'His Highness', took upon himself every royal power bar the title of King, lived in the Royal Chambers and had a proud delight in travelling around in the beheaded King's coach can hardly be thought to further decentralisation and especially laicization as Trevor-Roper implies. Furthermore, there are enough speeches and letters of Cromwell extant to prove that he made it clear to everyone that he regarded himself as King by nature, though not in name. When Durie wrote from Westminster to inform his fellow ambassador to Switzerland, John Pell, of the new Settlement, he explained that the only difference between Cromwell's new status and that of a king was that the title had been merely changed to Supreme Magistrate and that now Cromwell could 'administer the laws of the state to all intents and purposes with as much authority and right as ever any king before him did.'[218] So, too, Trevor-Roper's 'laicization' was not the word to describe how Cromwell gave secular powers to the clergy who supported him and legal powers as judges to the senior military. As for Cromwell's alleged de-centralisation, he did place local military governors in various districts, but they were all very much subject to his central command and did not have the local independence of the former alleged 'malignant' Lords whom they succeeded.

Trevor-Roper's idea that Cromwell followed a policy of anti-professionalism must also be questioned. Cromwell's Westminster Assembly strategy was certainly to professionalise religion under his model government control. He certainly professionalised the military Overlords in his model army who often took the law into their own hands and were even used by Cromwell to chastise church leaders and educators. Indeed, Cromwell's cooperation with Durie certainly meant a professionalisation of education which was quite in agreement with educators of the day. Mil-

---

central Europe between Ramus and Comenius: a survey of the continental background of the 'Three Foreigners'.

[218] Vaughan's *Protectorate of Cromwell*, vol. 2, p. 174.

ton, Durie, Hartlib and Comenius all wished to have education reorganised on a national, social, religious and international scale and placed under teachers who had been given the most professional of training. State and even European control of educational establishments was part and parcel of their view of universal learning, granting that Comenius was suspicious of too much state control, though he, too, placed himself under it in his years of work under Oxenstierna and de Geer.

Trevor-Roper's words 'And as for the "Presbyterian" clergy, we know how they fared. "Old priests writ large," they were used and thrown aside; they never, at any moment, controlled the Puritan Revolution,' need serious qualification. The Solemn League and Covenant alone was sufficient to create a Big-Brother-is-Watching-You totalitarian society. The Scottish army called to support it under General Leslie was composed of the most skilled, war-proven veterans of the European wars. Parliament invited them to promote faith by force. Indeed, when the rebel Parliament invited Leslie's mercenaries to put down the King's loyal subjects, they claimed this was the way towards a Reformation of England according to the Word of God. The Presbyterians had lobbied Parliament continually from Elizabeth's days on with their revolutionary and reforming plans after failing to impress Church Convocation. Like Cartwright and Travers, the Presbyterians' 'spiritual' parents, rule by Parliament was counted higher than the rule of the Church by the Church. Their decade-long pleas for the abolishing of Episcopalianism and the Reformed Book of Common Prayer were, however, first taken seriously by Parliament towards the end of Charles I's reign for purposes of their own. Oliver Cromwell's plans for his new-bureaucracy, military power and total control of church and state were engendered by Presbyterian political and religious revolution. Cromwell was thus swept into power on Presbyterianism's long-prepared stormy wave. No sooner was Laud executed than the Presbyterians began their 1645-6 'Accommodation' debates in which the Hyper-Presbyterian Baillie accused the Independents of being Lutherans alias Libertines, and the Independents rejected all ideas of synods and classes and demanded free congregational ordination. The writing was now clearly on the wall for the Presbyterians, especially as Leslie and his troops began to reveal themselves as Independents at heart. Here Durie took no sides. He remained where he stood before the Usurpation with such as Hall, Morten, Davenant and Ussher.

It is thus true, of course, that Presbyterian power did not last long. Cromwell's personal quarrels with the Presbyterians and the Scots through the Earl of Manchester started before the end of the Civil War. Always opportunistic in his demands, Cromwell did not wish to be too long dependant on anyone and swiftly took his chances for a time with the Independents, which meant the end of the Presbyterian, equally opportunistic, party. Pride's Purge in 1648 was the end of the Presbyterians' plan for absolute power. The army they had backed was suddenly an army of Independents. Cromwell now reaped criticism enough from the most moderate of Presbyterians, and the Independents, to whom he looked for the most support, grew tired of him. The Scottish Presbyterians had quickly crowned Charles II King after his father's murder and the opportunism of both the English Presbyterians and Independents forced them to claim they had never had regicidal ambitions and called Charles II back to England. However, not only the strong centralised power of the Presbyterians failed but also that of the Independents who would not bide by any set doctrinal system, discipline or order. Thus the entire Commonwealth idea itself failed.

So, too, Trevor-Roper's comments on Bacon's alleged, 'simple, rational approach to religion—the religion not of Puritanism, which could so easily become a new clericalism, but of latitudinarianism, whether Anglican or Puritan: the "layman's" religion of Chillingworth or Hales,' must be challenged. Bacon was the man who wrote passionately on Biblical religion, being pleased to have his good friends Lancelot Andrewes, John Donne and especially George Herbert to advise him on his religious and scientific works. Bacon, as a Member of Parliament was highly political in pleading for his strictly Church of England, orthodox faith which was not the religion of the Latitudinarians by any means. For instance, Bacon in his *Advancement of Learning*, a title that Durie used for his own work, clearly refutes the natural religion which was rapidly becoming a major pillar in the Latitudinarian humanistic canon, taking the same line as Hooker, Donne and Herbert that fallen man is blind to the appeal of nature and needs the Word of God as spectacles in order to gain a clear perception of knowledge and the will of God. Here, the Baconian School, of which Durie was a protagonist, differed from Comenius'. Indeed, Bacon's nigh-utopian pansophic views of an all-inclusive commonwealth, finding a key to all knowledge via a simple formula and his efforts to advance learning were reminiscent of the dreams of Laski, Cranmer, Bucer, Bullinger, King Edward VI, Calixtus, David Paraeus and the Jonathan Edwards to come. These all shared Durie's vision of a Reformed commonwealth of nations with a common doctrine of knowledge in an eschatological setting where swords would be made into plough shares, wars would be abolished, the Protestant religion would triumph and commerce, education and scientific discoveries would unite the whole world in peace.

The fact is that research on Hartlib, Durie and Comenius has followed different paths with separate histories and emphases, not all of which by far have been covered by Lord Dacre. This was also instanced in a conference entitled *Universal Reformation: Intellectual Networks in Central and Western Europe 1560-1617* held at St. Anne's College Oxford on 21-23 September, 2010, where Howard Hotson gave his paper *Three Foreigners Revisited*, showing for other reasons than mine listed above that Trevor-Roper's account is 'less than wholly satisfactory' because the essayist shows no familiarity with either Comenius' writings or the Hartlib Papers. Indeed, he claims that the conference will present an alternative account which is: 'less as an episode in a purely English narrative of the history of science between Bacon and the Royal Society, and rather more as the transplantation to England of a set of assumptions and aspirations deeply rooted in central Europe, only some of which found favour and bore fruit in the British Isles.'

G. H. Turnbull

Howard Hotson, sees G. H. Turnbull's sterling work on Hartlib, Durie and Comenius as a pioneer accomplishment paving the way for a deeper interest in the study of Trevor-Roper's 'Three Foreigners'.[219] Hotson is obviously thinking of Turnbull's intimate connection with Sheffield University's Hartlib Papers but Turnbull's own work on Durie leans heavily on Gunnar Westin's and Brauer's publications. Nevertheless, Turnbull in his *Hartlib, Dury and Comenius* published in 1947 merely drops, without comment, the names of Westin's *Negotiations about Church Unity* of 1932 and Westin's second collection of Durie letters published in 1933. He neither refers to Westin's first large collection of Durie correspondence published in 1932, nor to Westin's English Preface and Introduction to his 1935 republication of documents formerly published in the *Kyrkohistorisk Årskrift* entitled *John Durie in Sweden 1636-1638*. Nor does he refer to the work of Prof. Linderholm who edited them, or any other pioneer Swedish studies for that matter.[220] Nor does Turnbull follow the usual highly neces-

---

[219] See Hotson's essay, 'Philological pedagogy in reformed central Europe between Ramus and Comenius: a survey of the continental background of the 'Three Foreigners', in *Samuel Hartlib and Universal Reformation: Studies in Intellectual Communication*.

[220] There is one reference to Westin's *Svenskakyrkan och de protestantiska enhetssträvandena* in a footnote on page 250 of Turnbull's collection of Durie letters pub-

sary custom of placing the names of scholars he refers to or quotes from in the index. This makes checking his sources most difficult. Indeed, in the writings of Brauer of Germany, Westin of Sweden and Minton Batten of America are to be found a far greater topographical richness concerning Durie's commonwealth of ideas than that mapped out by either Turnbull or Trevor-Roper, two names often praised in modern Durie research.

This does not mar the excellence of Turnbull's work as his aim was to place his three subjects against the set background and limitations of their work together and not to examine the wider motives and fields of Durie's individual endeavours. Indeed, producing the CD version, based on Turnbull's editorial work, of the Hartlib Papers, which include many letters from and to Durie was a mammoth task. The transcribing alone must have been a great labour of love, judging by all the bracketed readings in the texts and suggestions where the manuscripts are damaged. Turnbull's detailed, almost day-by-day examination of Durie's works is a masterful example of sound research in a readable and highly informative style.

In *Hartlib, Dury and Comenius*, Turnbull mentions 'well over a hundred letters' in his possession written by Durie during the period 1654-1657, but sees them as merely supplementing and correcting Brauer's account. Nevertheless, neither Turnbull nor Brauer provide a list of anywhere near 'well over a hundred letters' from this period. These would have been of enormous help to subsequent Durie scholars. In 1949, Turnbull published a number of Durie letters with a brief introduction in Sweden's *Kyrkohistorisk Årsskrift* but these were letters not included in Westin's collections and written between 1636-1638 only.[221] Perhaps Turnbull was thinking of the upwards of a hundred letters and small pamphlets written in Durie's hand during the fifties found in the Hesse State Archives, Marburg. So, too, there are well over a hundred letters, some in copy form and some in Durie's hand in the British archives other than the Sheffield, German and Swedish collections which are awaiting editing and cataloguing, many of these being written in the fifties.

Of great help, to scholars is Turnbull's list of 228 works known to have been written by Durie; twenty-four which may have been written by Durie and sixty-seven letters and documents either written to Durie or are concerned with his work. This is a great improvement on former lists which have merely contained up to 100 works. Lord Delaware's *Hartlib Papers*, edited by Prof. Turnbull and published by Sheffield University on two

---

lished in 1949 concerning Swedish opposition to the proposed marriage of Queen Christina to Carl Ludwig of the Palatinate.

[221] *Kyrkohistorisk Årsskrift*. årg. 49., vol. 49, pp. 204-251. 8vo.

CDs, contain many mere extracts or snippets and collections of title pages, raising the questions of where Lord Delaware found these documents and where the full originals are and what efforts Turnbull made to procure the full works whether in original or copied forms.

Charles Webster

Webster has enhanced Durie scholarship with his *Samuel Hartlib and the Advancement of Learning* published in 1970 and his *The Great Instauration* of 1975. However, Webster's titles are somewhat misleading as most of the essays discussed in his work on Samuel Hartlib, including *Some Proposals to the Advancement of Learning*, published in 1653 and used for Webster's title, are from Durie's pen and not Hartlib's. There would thus have been more point in naming the book *John Durie, Samuel Hartlib and the Advancement of Learning*. Durie's work, taken up in Webster's title of 1970 goes back to Bacon's scholarly initiative in his two books entitled the *Advancement of Learning*. However, on other occasions where it is difficult to determine whether Hartlib or Durie authored a work, Webster comes down on Durie's side. Webster makes much of 'The Great Instauration', again leaning on Bacon's *Instauratio Magna* dealing with a period of six ages until Paradise is regained in the seventh. This Webster combines with Milton's thoughts in his *Prolusion*, but he forgets at times that Durie and Hartlib were there to reform the here and now of the seventeenth century and not a future Seventh Day. Indeed, Webster sees the major trend in the seventeenth century as merging millenarianism with educational learning, a factor which is more spoken about in works such as Webster's than in those of many of the scientists, philosophers and men of letters from whom he quotes as evidence. Especially in Durie's case, his universal learning was to reunite man with God in a steady progress until that knowledge filled the earth. It was not seen as a Seventh Day which would come after the Six Days of history but as the outworking of the Day of the Lord which had started with the first spreading of the gospel. God's covenant, he believed, had been with man from eternity, actualised since the creation.[222]

Webster's first work features an Introduction of 72 pages which is mostly devoted to Hartlib who is rather isolated from his co-work with Durie which lasted over thirty-six years. He thus leaves a rather unbalanced impression. The Introduction is followed by reprints from the Durie

---

[222] See both his *Platform* and *Earnest Breathings*.

circle: a four-paged letter from Hartlib to Durie written in 1630; the *Description of the Famous Kingdom of Macaria* (1641), attributed to Hartlib; *England's Thankfulness* (1642) which Turnbull thinks is Durie's but Webster Hartlib's; *A Motion Tending to the Publick Good of this Age* (1642) by Durie which reflects the contents of *Englands Thankfulness*; *The Parliaments Reformation* by Hartlib written four years later; *Considerations Tending to the Happy Accomplishment of Englands Reformation* (1647) by Durie; *The Reformed School* (1650) by Durie; *The Advancement of Learning* by Durie; *The True and Readie Way to Learne the Latin Tongue* (1654) compiled from various authors by Hartlib; and two letters from Samuel Hartlib to John Worthington (1660), one referring to Hartlib's *Macaria* and Comenius' neglect to finish his promised work on Pansophism and the other to *Antilia* and Durie, concerning the conversion of the Jews. These are followed by brief notes on the various pamphlets.

In his Introduction, Webster airs the fragile theory that Britain did not enter the Thirty Years War owing to her own Civil War. So the despairing Europeans, he argues, had to rely on Sweden's king Gustav Adolf. History shows that the Thirty Years War started in 1618 and Gustav forbade Britain to enter Sweden's war. Nevertheless, during James I's and Charles I's reigns Britain had many thousands of troops in Germany. The Swedish King fell in battle in 1632. The British Civil War started nine to ten years later. In Webster's Preface, Webster says, 'Dury gave literary expression to the educational ideas of the Hartlib circle, while Hartlib himself was the publicist and coordinator.' In the Introduction, however, Durie is given a most subsidiary role, though referred to as Hartlib's 'closest collaborator'. Webster sees Hartlib's alleged leading pioneer activities in education in the fact that Hartlib wrote the Preface to Durie's *The Reformed School* and that educationalist Foster Watson viewed Hartlib as the central figure in the Educational renaissance of the Commonwealth. These views must be challenged. In his *The English Grammar School in 1660*,[223] Foster Watson claims that the pioneering educational work of the period centred in Durie, not Hartlib. In his *Juan Luis Vives: On Education*, it is Durie's *Reformed School* (not Hartlib's Preface), that Watson compares favourably with Vives' Academy, with no reference at all to Hartlib. In his two *Educational Review* essays on Durie's works, Watson refers to Durie's *Motion Tending to the Public Good of this Age and Posteritory* as 'the best model' for a child's education ever put forward in the seventeenth century'. Webster does not appear to have consulted these publications.

---

[223] Pages 117-118.

In the circle surrounding Durie and Hartlib which Webster calls 'The Spiritual Brotherhood', Webster says, 'Anonymity was almost certainly an intentional guise of their Christian Association, although it was always clear that Hartlib and Dury were themselves the chief agents, Hartlib being the primary organiser and instigator, while Dury drafted the majority of their tracts'. Webster refers to Durie's perhaps earliest educational work *De summa curae paedagogicae seu spirituali agricultura exercitiato* of circa 1628. However, when commentating on Durie's original suggestions for improving education, Webster constantly refers his reader to examples from Comenius' works, thus giving the impression that Durie has gained his ideas from Comenius. Neither the dates of Comenius' works nor their contents back this up.

Webster's second volume on the *Great Instauration* is a far more lengthy and ambitious work and depicts quite a pansophical panorama of the mid-seventeenth century, weaving Durie's story expertly into the general warp and woof of that period. Whereas this thesis centres on comprehending the entire scope of Durie's ageless work, Webster's aim is to merger Durie's one voice into the *Grand Finale* of the great choir of seventeenth century thinkers. In this, he is followed by Léchot whose dissertation on Durie was published this year.

Karl Adolf Stisser

In the *Jahrbuch für Stadt und Stift* published by the Hildesheim city archives in 1988 appeared a fine, well researched essay of 12 pages entitled 'Ökumenische Verhandlungen in Hildesheim i. J. 1640: Johannes Duraeus und Georg Calix am Hof Herzog Georgs'. Stisser deals solely with the events of 1639-40 in Lower Saxony, starting with Durie's enthusiastic use of the '*Decretum*' that he received from the Protestant States at the 1634 Diet of Frankfurt in which his views were officially adopted by the delegates. Since shortly before the conference, Duke Frederick Ulrich had been discussing ideas of unity between the Protestant churches and the principalities with Professor Calixtus at Helmstedt on the basis of Duries' correspondence with them. The Helmstedt churches had answered Durie in the words, 'We praise and love more than we can confess with words all those who are working towards repairing the House Of God which is falling apart.' Durie had long wanted to visit Calixtus but was delayed until December 1639, partly because the Emperor had occupied the Duke's territories and he had to flee from Wolfenbüttel. Now, a meeting was arranged between Durie, Calixtus, General Superintendent Heinrich Wideburg and, out of consideration for the Emperor's military presence in the district, the Abbot of Marienthal, Johannes Haspelmacher and Duke August the Younger's political advisors. August had succeeded Frederick Ulrich as head of the dukedom. The delegates soon came to a joint understanding and even an agreement but this was not so much a decision to accept one another's orders and discipline but to draw up a common union against the somewhat fanatic sects who were spreading at the time, in particular the Neophotinians and Socinians. Stisser's work provides an excellent bird's-eye view of the progress made in one small corner of Durie's pan-European interests.

Writers on Durie from Eastern Europe

Though Durie began his campaign for European unity in Eastern Europe, scholars from these countries have been given relatively little coverage by English-speaking authors though a number of important works have been translated into or even authored in English, German, French and the Scandinavian languages, making them more accessible to those of us who do not understand Polish, Hungarian, Czech and the Baltic languages. Eastern European writers on Durie appear not to be hindered by such language barriers as they quote widely from English, French and German studies and use these languages themselves. Thus Arnold Starke in his *Reformation in Europa* chapter 'Im Kampf um Glaubenseinheit (Polen)', writes:

> 'Der im 16. Jahrhundert nicht wirklich durchgeführte Zusammenschluß der Reformierten und der Böhmischen Brüder in Polen kam 1633/34 doch endlich zustande, gefördert durch den schottischen Friedensboten John Durie (Duraeus) und durch Johan Amos Comenius.'

However, Durie tends to be less covered in Eastern European works than their own Hartlib and Comenius, though it is constantly stressed that Durie began his mission of unity in the former Polish town of Elbing, then recently annexed by Gustav II Adolf. Éva Petröczi in her essay 'Samuel Hartlib, A Man for all Countries, Including Hungary and Transylvania',[224] after reading Trevor-Roper and mentioning Hotson's *Samuel Hartlib and Universal Reformation*, Ján Kvačala and a brief mention of Durie in Ember-Lampe's *Historia Ecclesiae Reformatae in Hungaria et Transylva-*

---

[224] Károli Gáspár University of the Hungarian Reformed Church.

nia,[225] outdoes even Hotson by calling Trevor-Roper's brief overview of his 'Three Foreigners', 'The probably best and most accurate description of their personality and intellectual-spiritual service'. Keeping to the hyperbole, she calls the three Unionists repeatedly 'The Holy Trinity' and the 'legendary triumvirate'. Petröczi deals very summarily with her 'Holy Trinity', viewing particularly their joint influence on Hungarian-Transylvanian matters but does not adequately analyse the individual contributions of the three men. Though the three 'foreigners' did work together for a brief period, none of them kept within such a tiny clique. Rather, they formed separate alliances with a number of like-minded men and women in Europe and the New World and each influenced circles far outside of the interests of the other two.

Starke's reference to Durie's cooperation with the Moravians reminds us that in Eastern Europe there is more emphasise on Durie's connection with the budding free churches and the Moravians and early Calvinistic Baptists. Jeremy Dupertuis Bangs' and Keith Sprunger's findings show how Durie was much concerned in supporting the Dutch Mennonites' efforts to help their German and Swiss brethren.[226] Sadly, Durie's Dutch connections, in spite of him having lived in the Netherlands for many years, have yet to be intensively researched. Not only the Continental Mennonites but also the early Particular Baptists of England looked to Durie for cooperation and support as in the case of the Hebrew Scholar Henry Jessey who was an associate of Durie's in persuading Cromwell to allow the Jews to return to England.

There is very little information on Durie's influence in the Baltic States other than Sweden and Finland but a recent Ph.D. dissertation by Andrej Kotljarchuk from Södertörn University, Stockholm[227] provides us with a

---

[225] See Petröczi's 'Samuel Hartlib', pdf, fn. 4, www.theroundtable.ro/journals/cultural_studies/eva_petroczi_samue... 'DEBRECENI EMBER Pál, Friedrich LAMPE, *Historia Ecclesiaie Reformatae in Hungaria et Transylvania,* Trajecti ad Rhenum Apud Jacobum van Poolsum M.D.CCXXVIII. in the chapter dedicated to the 1634 Synod of Alba Julia, p. 379.:' *cum hac temperate consilia Irenica Johannis Duraei totam Ecclesiam Protestantem pervaderent...*According to these words, the tempestuous Ireneic counsels of J. Duraeus penetrated all the Protestant churches.' Petröczi's tempestuous rendering of *temperate* would appear somewhat exaggerated.

[226] See Bangs' *Letters on Toleration: Dutch Aid to Persecuted Swiss and Palatine Mennonites 1615-1699,* Rockport, Maine: Picton Press. 2004. Pp. 489. With CD-ROM of transcriptions and Sprunger's review in *The Mennonite Quarterly Review,* 289, 2004.

[227] Södertörn University, Stockholm, 2006.

few 'extras' hitherto disregarded by Durie researchers. In his thesis entitled *In the Shadows of Poland and Russia: The Grand Duchy of Lithuania and Sweden in the European Crisis of the mid-17th Century*, Kotljarchuk writes:

> 'Comenius, Hartlib and John Durie were, at this point, the spiritual leaders of Protestant Europe. They dreamed of a single unified Church between the Lutheran and Reformed branches, under the patronage of the Swedish Crown. The GDL[228] was given a significant place in these plans. The interest in Lithuania was caused by the existence, there, of a church organization, which united Protestants of all denominations. This was seen as a prototype for a future, unified Protestant Europe. Sweden had been interested in the preparation of plans for a great Evangelical Alliance that would serve as a counterweight to the Catholic counter-reformation. The brother of Karl X Gustav, Adolf Johan av Pfalz, was a supporter of this unification of Protestants.'

Kotljarchuk reveals something of the Durie circle's plans to put their work of pacification among Protestants into practice by actually founding Protestant settlements in the Eastern States where they could live in sheltered peace. He says:

> 'The idea of founding the colony of Antilia – a land where all Protestant refugees could live together – made up a considerable part of Comenius', Hartlib's and Durie's philosophy. Hartlib, the central figure in the proposal of a utopian brotherhood, had many correspondents among the Lithuanian Lutherans. One of the projects was to found the colony in one of the Radziwills' cities. In another project, the colony of Antilia was to be established on the island of Rune in the Riga Bay, under the protectorate of Jakob De la Gardie. Comenius, Hartlib and Durie kept in touch with the Lithuanian and Swedish political and intellectual leaders. Among these were Krzysztof II and Janusz Radziwill, Jakob and Magnus De la Gardie, Johan and Bengt Skytte, Axel Oxenstierna and Louis de Geer. Thus, prior to the 1655 war, the Swedish political elite was well-informed on the situation in the GDL.'

Educational twentieth century writers

Even in the 20th century, Durie research concentrated more on Durie's biography and irenic work rather than on his ideas of universal learning and Practical Divinity. Typical of the high praise for Durie's piety was that of Tom Webster writing in 1997 in his *Godly Clergy in Early Stuart England*,

---

[228] Grand Duchy of Lithuania

Webster starts his chapter entitled 'John Dury and the godly ministers' with the words:

> 'The first activity to receive our attention is something of a footnote to the monumental labours of John Dury. His design was amongst the grandest: from 1628 to the year of his death, 1680, he strived in the cause of 'ecclesiastical pacification' between the disparate branches of the Lutheran and Calvinist churches, initially in the context of the Thirty Years War, but struggling on in the changed conditions of Europe after the Treaty of Westphalia. In the main, his projects have been as a curious sideline to the period, the activities of an eccentric idealist, working against the grain of his times. While his reputation is now being rescued from whiggish ecumenical historians, what is of present interest is his relationship with the godly ministers of England.'[229]

Two authors, Harry Scougal and Thomas Rae, however, opened the doors to wider research in the field of Durie's system of learning, the one at the beginning and the other at the end of the century.

Harry J. Scougal

In 1905, Scotsman Harry J. Scougal gained his Dr. Phil. at Jena University for a thesis entitled *Die pädagogischen Schriften John Durys (1596-1680): Ein Beitrag zur Geschichte der englischen Pädagogik*. In his Foreword, Scougal complains of the difficulty of tracing Durie's works but found all the scanty material for his thesis with one exception in the British Museum (now British Library). He obtained a copy of Durie's *Reformed School* from the Glasgow University Library. Scougal's bibliography of only twenty-eight secondary works, mostly encyclopaedias and general works, gives neither publishers nor publication dates. A number of further sources referring to brief quotes are listed in the footnotes. No bibliography of primary literature is given, but Scougal devotes a few sentences to Durie's *A Motion tending to the Public Good* in his biographical overview in Part II and then in Part III, he devotes two pages to the work. In this section, he spends three pages on *A Seasonable Discourse* and eight pages on *The Reformed School*, which he calls 'die bedeutendste und umfangreichste der pädagogischen Schriften Durys'.

In Part I, A Historical Overview, Scougal deals with the history of education from the Reformation period to Durie's day mentioning the contributions of Comenius, Lubrinus, Ascham, Sturm, Vives, Erasmus, Mul-

---

[229] *Godly Clergy*, p. 256.

caster and Coote. Durie's name is mentioned merely in the last three sentences as a companion of Comenius 'and other men' who stood on the threshold of modern scholarly education.

In Part II, The Life of Durie, Scougal gives as original sources Briggs' copy of Durie's *A Summarie Relation*, a letter from the Calendar of State Papers, Durie's *Motion Tending to the Public Good*, Hartlib's *A Brief Relation* and Wood's *Athenae Oxenienses*. This is insufficient material for a biography. Scougal passes on a quote from Masson regarding Durie which he appears to have obtained from Dircks' *A Biographical Memoir of Samuel Hartlib*, but gives neither the original nor secondary source in Masson's work. Otherwise, his biographical material is mainly taken from Benzelius-Mosheim.

Scougal passes over Durie's own education apart from mentioning a probable visit to Oxford to consult the libraries before continuing with his work in Elbing 'four years later'. He claims that it was Godeman who interested Durie in a 'union of all Protestant sects' and Godeman and Ambassador Roe persuaded him to visit England to receive the backing of King and Church. He writes that Laud sent Durie back to Germany under his 'protection and authority' and mentions Durie's successful tour of many Diets and Conferences. When all was going well for Durie, his great ally, Gustav Adolf, died. Scougal does not mention that here there was a triple loss as Friedrich V of Bohemia and the Palatinate and his friend and kinsman Sir James Spens, died within days of Gustav. Scougal emphasises that the credentials which Durie received from Laud, Ussher, Hall, Morten, Davenant 'and other famous church and statesmen' in 1634 were quite 'according to his wish' so that he might attend the Frankfurt pan-German Diet of rulers and the churches. Scougal writes of a disappointing time in Holland and covers Durie's 1636-1638 visit to Sweden in just a few lines, though he puts forward Benzelius as a major source.

Scougal relates that Hartlib invited Comenius to England in 1640 in connection with Hartlib's translation and publication of Comenius' *Prodromus Pansophiae* which, he claims, brought into being the idea of a Scientific Society. Next, Scougal maintains that in 1642, Durie joined the Royalist party without further explanation. Scougal speculates as to whether or not Durie met Descartes in Holland. Under the Cromwellian regime, he relates how Durie served a merchants' church in Rotterdam; spoke before Parliament; was a member of the Westminster Assembly; and a co-author of the Westminster Confession and Catechisms. He also authored a number of pamphlets or lectures on education. As Durie was made Member for Winchester, Scougal believes the evidence points to a lectureship at the college there. In 1647, Durie was appointed Librarian of the Royal Library and the King's collection of medals under the supervision of Bulstrode Whitelocke. In 1649, Durie published his *A Seasonable Discourse on Reformation* in which he pleaded for both a reformation of learning and religion. This was followed by his *Reformed School* in 1650 or 1651.

Scougal describes how in 1654, Durie returned to the Continent assigned both by Cromwell and the English universities to carry on his mission of peace amongst Protestants and, together with his old friend John Pell the celebrated mathematician, set up concrete proceedings leading to a union with the Swiss cantons which was very successful as were visits to Germany and Holland in 1655-1656. When Durie returned with his mission accomplished, he found the Republic in dire need of money and was told that his work could not be financed. After Cromwell's death, Durie found no backing from Archbishop Juxon and settled down in Cassel, Germany where he died in 1680.

In Part III, 'Durie's Educational Writings', Scougal gives a helpful overview of a mere three of Durie's educational works similarly to the way Klähr handled them. Part IV, A Critical Overview is the longest section and deals first very briefly with world events in pre-Durie days, arguing that the spirit of the age always influences attitudes to learning. Scougal describes the empiricism of Bacon and his efforts to free the spirit of youth from the shackles of mere rote learning and scholastic methods, recommending inductive learning by using all the senses. He sees Durie as taking Bacon's *Advancement of Learning* a step further, showing that learning is not so much a collection of facts but a training of the mind to associate them and apply them productively. Here, Scougal demonstrates that Durie went beyond Comenius' pansophism which was based more on an encyclopaedic collection of knowledge. He sees Durie as also transforming Bacon's empiricism and Descartes rationalism. Scougal also emphasises the 'green' nature of Durie's school curriculum seeing an awareness of the union of mankind with the natural world going hand in hand with the awareness of super-sensory, metaphysical and religious experiences. So, too, Scougal shows how Durie pioneered education for all sorts and conditions of men in all social states so that a land-worker's son could one day become a university don. He sees Durie as going way beyond Comenius here, too. Furthermore, Durie paved the way for women to reach the top of the academic ladder, arguing that they were quite as capable as men for academic studies. Scougal argues that Durie's school curriculum stood in sharp contrast to the curricula of his age. A brief look at the scope of subjects Durie strove to introduce into primary and secondary education such as basic medicine and surgery, commercial languages, aesthetics, ethics and bodily fitness would amaze many a modern teacher as Durie aimed to educate the whole being of man, body, soul and spirit. However, in all these projects, Scougal maintains that Durie remained a Realist and trod paths where Comenius and Milton could not follow.

Scougal feels, however, that, like Comenius, Durie comes short of literary appreciation which is seen as the highest goal of humanistic learning. He calls this a 'great deficit' (großer Mangel). What Scougal is getting at is that, in keeping with many of the Christian educationalists and literary figures, such as William Cowper, he did not emphasise art for art's sake. This would have been disfunctional to his wider view of complimentary and comprehensive knowledge. To balance off this alleged deficit, Scougal shows how Durie exhibits great progress (einen großen Fortschritt) in going far beyond such as Comenius and even Mulcaster, in correctly observing what Scougal calls the psychological development of children and what their aims in education should be. Indeed, Scougal finds it difficult to find the tiniest trace of influence on Durie by former and contemporary educators.

After praising Durie's teaching system, Scougal surprisingly reaches three extraordinary conclusions. First, he maintains that Durie was merely a learned dilettante in matters of education. Scougal is obviously not using the term in the old sense of a lover and promoter of the fine arts but in the newer sense of an amateur. Secondly, he claims that education in learning was merely a side-track in Durie's life's work and thirdly, he argues that Durie himself never realised the significance and range of his educational reforms. These conclusions cannot stand. Durie began his pioneer educational work in the 1620s, producing works on the subject throughout the following five decades. Scougal has used only a very bare minimum of Durie's works on which to build his thesis. His limited view of Durie's educational policy can only lead to blind-alley scholarship. He fails, for instance, to give a complete overview of Durie's comprehensive doctrine of universal learning or his Practical Divinity. Perhaps this is why J. M. Batten, claims that Scougal gives 'an unsatisfactory account of his (Durie's) educational interests,'[230] though Batten himself in his dissertation, as shown, centres on Durie as an advocate of Christian union and only sidesteps into education. Nevertheless, Scougal, on the positive side, argues that Durie was the first in England to advocate a comprehensive cur-

---

[230] See Batten's *American Society of Church History* article, 'John Dury, Advocate of Christian Reunion', 1932, p. 224, and his dissertation of that name.

riculum embracing all the educative needs of children. He claims that Comenius and Milton felt that Durie demanded more than was practicable, but this was because Durie had a wider vision than these men. He also understood a child's psychology better, and was more practical and democratic in his plans for education. Last but not least, Scougal says Durie practised a magnanimous love for mankind without distinctions. These are hardly the characteristics of a dilettante! The scholar sums up his dissertation by saying:

> 'Mr James Oliphant hat Mulcaster den 'Vater der englischen Pädagogic' genannt; aber wenn wir die Erziehung in ihrem modernen Sinne auffassen, als ein algemeines nationales System der geistigen, sittlichen und körperlichen Bildung, aus ihrem wahren Zweck abgeleitet, und in der Anwendung durch eine Kenntnis der Gesetze der geistigen Tätigkeit geregelt, dann gebührt dieser Titel vielleicht mit besserem Recht dem puritanischen Geistlichen John Dury.'

Thomas Rae

Rae's work *John Dury Reformer of Education* was published in Marburg in 1970. The author has done much to capture the 'intellectual ferment in the world of Durie's thought' showing great ability in going behind Durie's own words to examine the concepts they represent. Rae sees Durie's emphasis as dealing with the political, moral and religious state of the 17th century nations. He entertains the theory, however, that the Reformation began in England as a royal and political movement and only very slowly in the seventeenth century became a popular and religious one. On the other hand, Rae believes Reformation began on the European Continent as a popular religious movement and became, by the time England was becoming more religious, a scholastic and political movement which favoured the ruling classes and neglected the ruled and underprivileged. One cannot flank Durie's enormous pan-European activities against such a simplistic theory. Durie's great work towards unity and peace must be seen against a background which demonstrates that England was more thoroughly and nationally Reformed under Wycliffe, Tyndale, Latimer, Bullinger, Bucer, Lever, Jewel, Grindal, Cox, Ridley, Hooper and Coverdale than Germany was under conflicting Reformed, Lutheran and Roman Catholic states. So, too, England had embraced a more friendly form of what came to be known as Calvinism a matter of decades before Calvin finally and hesitantly accepted this teaching himself. On the other hand, the Reformed pietism with which Durie so closely identified himself grew contemporarily and internationally with Durie's engagements with Germany. Besides, Germany was not the sole foreign sphere of Durie's labour as Sweden, Switzerland, Holland and Eastern Europe were enjoying a popular upsurge in Reformed and Lutheran piety and to a certain extent also Protestant France under the ministry of such as Du Moulin. Indeed, the Thirty Years War in Europe, though it polarised Protestant and Roman Catholic political aims, it also served as a catalyst for more intensive popular piety. This can also be traced in Roman Catholic educational Reforms, not merely in those of the Protestants.

Though Rae says at the commencement of his book that education must be seen as a mere part of the reforms hoped for at the time, he does not look at this Pan-European interest in 'all the issues and institutions of corporate life' but to that of education alone, although Rae happily often breaks the restrictions which he has placed on himself. However, in isolating education from the general thought processes, aims and ambitions of the times, Rae hardly gives a balanced picture of what was going on. However, in contrast to Batten, who believes that Durie built his educational ideas on those of Comenius, Rae emphasises how Durie developed his own views on a completely independent footing.[231]

This writer is deeply indebted to this first of Rae's books on Durie because of its list of Durie's earlier pedagogic works such as his *Capita rerum quae fusius in cura paedagocica sunt tractanda*; his *Summa Curae Pedagogicae* and his *De Murum Puerilium Disciplina*. These strengthened his conviction that Durie must have started on his educational reforms as early as the late twenties.

In 1998, Rae's *John Dury and the Royal Road to Piety* was published for the Institut für Wissenschaftliche Irenik Universität Frankfurt/Main, by Peter Lang of Frankfurt. The book strives to place Durie against the background of a fragmented Protestantism, believing he performed 'the greatest irenic effort' in history. In Rae's well-researched material the author centres his attention on Durie's school and university reforms and his accompanying views concerning library management and science. He stresses, however, that these reforms were secondary to Durie's view of the will of God to which he subordinated all else. Rae obviously thinks highly of Durie's ecumenical ideas but is perhaps going too far in hiding behind Batten to promote Durie's alleged hope of a Roman Catholic-Protestant merge. Gunnar Westin, in his *Negotiations* also hints vaguely at this ideal possibility. At times, Durie is extremely sharp in his condemnation of

---

[231] See Rae's *John Dury and the Royal Road to Piety*, p. 73. Rae gives Batten's quote as p. 135.

Rome, especially in his reports as Continental ambassador to State Secretary Thurloe. Writing in May 1955 from Danzig, Durie tells Thurloe:

> 'The Bohemian Exiles at Lesna in Poland are in a very miserable & dangerous Condition for the present. For though they have cause to expect a more favourable vsage from the approaching Swedish Army then the Papal Idolaters (who are the most venemous Enemies of the Truth, as can bee found in the World) yet its mightily feared, that the Papists in those Qvarters upon suspicion, that they will bee spared, will bee the first that will fall upon them to kill & destroy them all in those Countries, before the Swedes shal bee able to protect or deliver them. I am intreated likewise by some great Ones in this place to signifie the jealousy of the Reformed party which they have against the Swedes least their King (in case hee prevaile) give more priviledges to the Lutherans, then to the Reformed. Therefore you are most earnestly entreated in the name of all the Reformed in this Towne & Country, that you will please to insinuate their Case unto his Highness (whom God seemes to have raised not only to bee the Protector of the Commonwealth of England but likewise of the Gospels Cause, & of the true Protestant Religion) to oblige the said King in his Treatises with him, that the Reformed in this Towne may have their ancient & former rights, restored to them to exercise freely their Religion in those Churches, which have beene taken from them, & generally to shew a due & eqval right to both parties in all other places, wherof hee shal become master. And as in all likelihood the King of Sweden will bee willing to embrace such a temperament, so it will bee a great addition of honor & happines to my Lord Protector for having beene Instrumentall in so blessed a worke.'[232]

In a letter which appears to be written to Worsely before the Siege of Drogheda, Durie argues that we must distinguish between overthrowing the Papacy and warring against ordinary Roman Catholics. He is discussing the views of Dr Horn which he feels have been misinterpreted by Ultra-Protestants. He writes:

> 'Dr Horn can lay open his owne purpose in this undertaking better then any man else: the extracts of letters which you haue imparted unto me; I confesse seems to import nothing but a Politicall designe of warre; to ouerthrow the power of the Pope; which to mee seemes quite another thing then to make a slaughter of Papists; for the first signifies to me; the deposing of a Tyran, & the breaking of his usurped power & counsell of wickednes; & the last signifies the killing of men only because they haue beene brought up in Poperie

---

[232] See British Library Add. MSS 4365 ff. 3A-4B, included in a volume of the Birch Papers, mainly relating to the Swiss Cantons (Add. 4365).

as the Papists of late in Ireland, & in Savoye haue massacred the Protestants because they were Protestants, which beeing an Abominable designe in them, would bee more execrable in us then in them by how much wee haue more light to discerne the will of God both in respect of Christianitie & humanitie then they haue. now your freind seemes to take up the Dr his scope to bee only this; which I am not apt to belieue; because I think wee ought not to construe anything in a sense which is the worst it can bee taken in; when it can beare one that is good or tolerable. but the truth is that some men use alwayes to doe so; & most men are naturally inclined so to doe. some use to doe it by Policie, to draw out the secrets of mens intentions & the knowledge of matters, in disputing against them, as Chimists sometimes or Alchimists use to doe when they would diue into the secrets of nature which others pretend to haue; & states men when they can argue & debate matters to bee resolued upon, & suspect secret plots. some use to doe it out of an humour of Censuring, hauing a good opinion only of themselues & not of any thing which others take in hand; & therefore intend to contradict & discredit it; which is another kind of peruerse Policie; which is naturall to all proud men.'[233]

Even modern ecumenically minded scholars see Durie's strivings for unity as strictly 'Protestant' as witnessed by the various co-authors of the book *Union-Konversion-Toleranz: Dimensionen der Annäherung zwischen den christlichen Konfessionen im 17. und 18. Jahrhundert*,[234] and Harm Klueting's collection of essays by various modern authors entitled *Irenik und Antikonfessionalismus im 17. und 18. Jahrhundert*.[235] Rae apparently builds his optimistic view of Durie's future hopes on his *Touchant L'Intelligence de L'Apocalypse par L'Apocalypse même* written in Hesse, 1674 and his *Le Véritable Chrétien* of 1676, yet he only knows of these books through Batten mentioning them almost by the way. Perhaps, too, he might have been thinking of Durie's memorandum written for Hartlib on February 2, 1661 where he said,

'I intend also to looke after the Popish negotiation of a Reconciliation with the Lutherans and to see how farre that is likely to proceed.'[236]

This cautious remark of Durie's was accompanied with a request that Hartlib should keep the information to himself and would rather express doubt

---

[233] Ref: 4/3/121A-B, HP.
[234] Published and edited by Heinz Duchhardt and Gerhard May, 2000.
[235] Georg Olms Verlag, Hildersheim - Zürich - New York, 2003.
[236] Memorandum in full from the Hartlib Papers in Turnbull's *Hartlib, Dury and Comenius*, p. 292.

rather than delight. A more sober and balanced interpretation is found in Jean Ségun's article *Les Oecuménismes du XVIIe Siècle et les relations internationales de l'époque* in which he says concerning Durie's idea of church unity backed by Hartlib and Comenius:

> 'Au premier plan de ses idées il plaçait le souci de réunir tous les chrétiens protestants en une seul Eglise sans dogmes obligatoires ni organisation. Les catholiques finiraient par se joindre à ce nouveau christianisme devant l'évidence de la vérité, et la papauté disparaîtrait comme par enchantement, dans l'excès de lumière accordé aux derniers temps.'[237]

Pierre-Oliver Léchot and Un christianisme 'sans parialité

One lecturer at the Oxford conference on 'Universal Reformation' mentioned above which announced a new approach to Durie, Comenius and Hartlib in contrast to Trevor-Roper's account, was Pierre-Oliver Léchot, a young French-speaking scholar who gave a paper entitled *Reason, Sanctification, and the Restoration of the Image of God in Man? John Dury's Relationship to Bartholomaus Keckermann*. Léchot maintained that 'Throughout the first half of his life, John Dury—irenicist, theologian, pedagogue and 'intelligencer'—was in constant dialogue with the work of the 'post-Ramist' philosopher and theologian Bartholomäus Keckermann (c.1570–1609).' The only concrete reference Léchot gives to back up his argument is that Durie, in 1647, aged around fifty, recommended Keckermann's works to 'a budding student in theology' as a platform for more detailed study.

At the Budapest 2010 Conference on 'Encyclopaedism, Pansophia and Universal Communications 1560-1670', Léchot gave a paper entitled *Dianoia versus Pansophia: John Dury's Relationship to Bartholomew Keckermann'*. This time, he did not speak of Keckermann's influence on Durie *during the first part of his life* but now claimed '*Throughout his entire life*[238] John Dury (1600-80) theologian and irenist, maintained an ambivalent relationship to the thoughts of Bartholomew Keckermann (c.1570–1609) and his encyclopedic project.' Again much was made of the scanty evidence associating the two scholars' works.

Then, in the summer of 2011, a dissertation by Léchot entitled *Un christianisme 'sans parialité: Irénisme et méthode chez John Dury (v.*

---

[237] Article in *Archives des sciences sociales des religions*, 1967, vol. 23, Numéro 1, p.p. 180-181.

[238] My emphasis.

1600-1680) was published in Paris, based on a thesis presented to the University of Geneva in 2009. The writer first expresses his dependence on the two CDs containing some 25,000 pages from the original 10,000 documents contained in the Hartlib Papers published at Sheffield University in 1995 which are now being studied by a consortium of researchers at Oxford of which Léchot is a co-worker. Here, again, Léchot's aim is to trace Durie's position against the background of irenic, post-Ramistic thought. He touches, however, on Durie's concept of universal learning in part of Chapter II, 'Le Discours de la Méthode D'un Iréniste du Grand Siècle' under the multi-lingual subtitle "Methodus Analytica', 'Practicall Divinity' et Démarche Irénique", and in Chapter V entitled 'A Rational Way of Interpreting the Sense of the Scriptures', Léchot, dealing admirably with this neglected side of Durie's insistence on both a spiritual and rational approach, presents a comprehensive compendium of different scholars' views. Mapping this area out, however, with such emphasis on other scholars has resulted in losing much of the chronological and logical development in Durie's own thought-process. So, too, much of Durie's essential contribution to learning is merely placed in footnotes or appendices without due comment, analysis and evaluation in the body of the text.

Rather than follow Durie's own outline and comments on both a rational and spiritual way of interpreting Scripture via rules of experience applicable to all knowledge-acquirement, Léchot tends to interpret Durie's views through his own wider, interpretive reading of Mead and Richard Popkin and not primarily and directly through Durie's own specific and fundamental instructions to Culpeper, St Amand and N. Smart. Indeed, Léchot dwells on eschatological interpretations which, at times, as will be shown in the following chapter, contradict Durie's own assessment of his position. This is seen, too, where Léchot discusses the *Clavis Apocalyptical*, which was not from Durie's pen and Durie's own *Touchant L'Intelligence de L'Apocalypse*. Hypotheses concerning Durie's eschatology can hardly be seen as a motivating factor in his quest for scholarly text interpretation and learning. Rather, Durie was concerned with the education of both Church and State according to the needs of his day in preparation for whatever future might come.

Léchot presents the views of numerous academic writers whose affiliation of thought to Durie's is not established. Again, Léchot allows much space for a discussion of Bartholomäus Keckermann, naming nine works from his 1614 collection. Léchot then concludes that 'sans doute', Durie stood in the ideological 'héritage' of Keckermann's thoughts. However, a definite link between these works and Durie is not demonstrated. Though

Durie and Hartlib mention Keckermann very rarely indeed, Léchot gives Keckermann more attention than he does any of Durie's immediate circle including Hartlib and Comenius. However, the organ of that circle, *Ephemerides*, concluded in 1639 that Comenius' work on logic was far superior to Keckermann's. Indeed, Léchot bases the bulk of his direct evidence on but one Durie reference to Keckermann, where Durie tells N. Smart, the son-in-law of his friend Mr Clough, to read Keckermann *and* Alsted as a basis for commencing studies on 'Logick and Rhetorick, Physick, Ethick, Politick oeconomick, & Metaphysick'. The two scholars are thus merely mentioned here as a prolegomenon to further studies and Smart is told he should not spend too much time on them. Furthermore, the fact that Alsted is mentioned far more often in the works of the Durie circle than the hardly-mentioned Keckermann is not given like attention by Léchot. Indeed, Durie never deals with Keckermann in any detail or depth. So, too, Durie also mentions Ames but once in his instructions to Smart but Léchot uses this to dwell on Ames throughout over thirty pages. Léchot also spends much time on Ramus' logic which Durie admittedly praised in the thirties, but it is clear from remarks in *Ephemerides* that the members of the Durie-Hartlib circle were quite aware of Ramus' limitations, feeling he was inferior to Jung. Léchot's references to Bisterfeld are far more helpful to Durie scholarship as he was an associate member of the Durie-Hartlib circle and is referred to some 50 times in the Hartlib Papers. Like Léchot on Keckermann, I admittedly spend a whole chapter on Durie and Comenius, discussing who influenced whom the most. However, these two contemporaries and friends were in a pact together concerning their joint work whereas such a strong association cannot be shown concerning Keckermann. So, too, I have dealt with Kinner at length so as to show the personal relationship he had to both Durie and Comenius and how he influenced the latter.

CHAPTER FIVE

The Place of the Jews in Durie's Quest for Universal Learning

The Jewish situation in England in the first half of the seventeenth century

Much has been written about the undeniable fact that Durie's contemporaries in Church, Parliament and State, on the whole, denied the Jews any rights to live in England. Robert M. Healey in his article *The Jew in Seventeenth-Century Protestant Thought*,[239] points out that Jews in Britain in the early seventeenth century were classified as 'aliens' and 'perpetual enemies' and could not even be heard as witnesses before a court as no Jew was to be trusted. Indeed, the Jews had been banned officially from England since the thirteenth century. Even Christian academics suspected of reading the Hebrew Scriptures were punished for being Judaisers. When Menasseh Ben Israel arrived in England as Cromwell's guest in 1655, chiefly through the instigation of Durie, a conference at Whitehall called by Cromwell found no reason why Jews should not be permitted to dwell in England. However, Parliament denied the Jews that right. A report of this conference was penned by H. Whitefield, Ed. Calamy, Simon Ashe and J. Arthur.[240] Pro-Jewish Henry Jessey was also a member, but Durie was not present as Cromwell had sent him as an ambassador to Switzerland. A. M. Hyamson in his *History of the Jews in England*, names Thomas Fuller, the Church Historian, in one breath with Durie and Jessey as also pleading for a resettlement of the Jews in England. However, Fuller criticised the views of Menasseh in his *A "Pisgah Sight" of Palestine*. Hyamson also maintains that Jessey, too, had certain reservations. Possibly this was because Jessey was more interested in a resettlement of the Jews in the near East.[241] Hyamson writes that Jessey suggested as a compromise at the Whitehall Conference that the Jews should only be admitted to decayed ports and cities, and that they should pay double customs duties on

---

[239] *Church History*, vol. 46, 1977, No. 1, March.
[240] *Harleian Miscellany*, vol. 6, pp. 445-454, A Narrative of the Late Proceeding at Whitehall Concerning the Jews.
[241] Hyamson, pp. 168; 198; 203

imports and exports. Indeed, there was a large section of those who pleaded for a resettlement of the Jews in England who merely felt that they would enrich England through their trade and wealth. Nevertheless, the conference came to naught as there was a massive protest in the country against the admission of Jews, so Cromwell dropped the idea. However, in 1656, Cromwell began to give Jews a measure of recognition in an experiment which granted them permission to build a synagogue with an adjoining cemetery. With this move, Cromwell was acting in opposition to his own Parliament of 1648-1649 which claimed that toleration should only be shown 'to those who profess faith in God by Jesus Christ'. After 1667, Jews were, however, allowed to be called as witnesses in courts and an extension of Cromwell's 'experiment' was gradually accepted by the British public.

Perhaps with this parliamentary situation in mind, oft-quoted Daniel Neal (1678-1743) in his *History of the Puritans* has helped to create the idea that Durie was anti-Semitic. He tells his readers, 'The famous Mr Prynne, and Mr. Dury, a Presbyterian minister, wrote fiercely against the admission of the Jews to England.'[242] However, in his coverage of the growth of Presbyterianism and Nonconformity, Neal often allows his personal convictions to cover the facts. This is seen in his handling of the Hampton Court Conference in comparison with Bishop Bankcroft's, Strype's and Fuller's accounts. Also, in his description of the imagined Knoxian conflicts with the Coxian exiles at Frankfurt in the 1550s who fled from Queen Mary's persecutions, Neal claims repeatedly that the entire Frankfurt church became 'Knoxian' and left with Knox *en bloc* to join an English church at Geneva.[243] Actually Knox departed alone from Frankfurt with Scotland as his destination, not Geneva, though he called at Geneva very briefly on his way to Dieppe, his port of departure for Scotland. Some Coxians did leave Frankfurt six months later but they settled in Basle and Aarau. The few so-called Knoxians actually joined Bale in Basle. Even Knox's one time closest ally, Whittingham, in contradiction to Neal's account, remained in Frankfurt for some time after warning Knox not to cause a schism. He then moved to Basle with Coxians Bale, Sampson and Foxe.[244]

In stating his views concerning Durie, Neal mentions particularly the visit to England of Menasseh Ben Israel who pleaded with Cromwell to

---

[242] Neal, vol. 11, p. 652.
[243] *History of Puritanism*, Vol. I, pp. 80-81.
[244] See my *Troublemakers at Frankfurt*, Chapter Ten, The Aftermath of Knox's Retreat. Also Appendix II in the book.

allow the Jews to re-settle on British soil. Neal has missed the fact that Durie was one of the prime instruments in inviting Menasseh Ben Israel to England. Concerning the pamphlet war fought in England over the Jewish problem, Neal's research must have brought him in touch with three of the main publications of this rather hot debate. Prynne's pamphlet entitled *Short Demurrer* was, as its name suggests, against allowing the Jews back into England. Durie's pamphlets in the middle fifties, such as his *Concerning the Question Whether it bee lawfull to admit Iewes to come into a Christian commonwealth* and *A Case of Conscience, whether it be lawful to admit Jews into a Christian Common-Wealth?* argued for the readmission of the Jews. So, too, Durie had published works in the thirties and forties urging British educators to examine Jewish scholarship more closely so that they may profit from it. Durie was on the Continent at the time of the English and Whitehall debates as Cromwell's ambassador for peace but sent his views to Hartlib for publication.

Mordecai L. Wilenski, of the Hebrew Teachers College, Boston, describes how Durie was attracted by the ideas of the Millenarians and the mystics in his essay 'Thomas Barlow's and John Dury's Attitude Towards the Readmission of the Jews to England'.[245] He concludes, however, that he 'did not completely endorse the ideas of these radical dreamers'. Nevertheless, he says:

> 'Dury was regarded as one of the most important theologians, and many of England's scholars corresponded with him when he was both at home and abroad. It is therefore not surprising that in 1655 those concerned with the question of the admission of the Jews, which necessitated a practical solution, turned to him and asked him to express his views on the matter.'

These views were expressed by Durie in the various works considered in this chapter, but Wilenski has, in particular, Durie's *Concerning the Question Whether it bee lawfull to admit Iewes to come into a Christian commonwealth* written from Cassel, Hesse in mind, though he does not quote from it.[246] Wilenski shows how radically different are the interpretations made on reading this work. Scholars such as L. Wolf and C. Roth are 'of the opinion that this work is mainly an attack upon the Jews,' whereas S. Levy in his 'John Dury and the English Jewry', sees the same work as pro-Jewish. It is interesting to note that Wilenski found a manuscript in the British Library entitled *Concerning the Jewes Reception into the Territo-*

---

[245] *The Jewish Quarterly Review*, 50, 3, pp. 256-268, 1960.
[246] Ref: 68/8/1A, HP.

ries of the Landgrave of Hessen which did not bear its author's name but Wilenski says, 'I have definitely identified him as Durie.' On turning to the work in question, we find Durie saying:

> 'Speaking of the situation in Germany. I know none of the Reformed Churches or Divines who makes their admission to bee unlawfull: but it is a worke which the Civil Magistrat takes wholly into his owne consideration to doe or not to doe therin, what he finds expedient for the aduantage of the state: nor doe I remember to haue redde or heard; that the case hath euer beene put to any of the Churches; to bee scanned as a matter of Conscience. There is one of the Chief Reformed Divines Dr. Alting who in his Problematicall Theologie part 2. problem. 21. puts this Question, <u>Vtrum Judæi in Societate Christianorum tolerandi sint</u>? & hee doth answer it affirmatiuely & I am cleerly of his opinion, that it is not only lawfull, but if matters bee rightly ordered towards them, expedient to admit of them; nay to invite & encourage them to liue in Reformed Christian commonwealths: how farre it may bee a sinne to refuse them admittance when they doe desire it upon lawfull termes; & in a reasonable way; is a further question; which cannot bee decided till the former points of the lawfulnes and expediencie of admitting of them bee made out.'[247]

After discussing the pros and cons, Durie concludes that the Jews should not be admitted to England merely because of any eschatological millennial speculations but solely for their own sakes as a people who have so much in common with Christians. This is repeated in Durie's *Cases of Conscience* which is even more positive concerning the expediency of re-admitting the Jews. Durie states quite dogmatically that eschatological speculations should not affect our decisions concerning the Jews because, 'the times and seasons of their deliverance is in God's hand alone and that we are very much inclined to mistake in conjectures of that nature.'[248] Christian charity should be our sole concern. However, they are to be re-admitted only if they are prepared to share with Christians the gifts they have and be prepared at least to enter into dialogue with Christians about their faith and learning and to be instructed in their ways. He envisages an educational exchange whereby knowledge of Hebrew texts, traditions and culture was to be received in exchange for knowledge of the Christian gospel. This exchange should be on the German model of public lectures for the education of both parties. However, as we see in the case of Neal, Batten is not exaggerating when he says in his *John Durie - Advocate of*

---

[247] Ref: 68/8/1A-2B, HP.
[248] *A Case of Conscience*, Harleian miscellany, vo. 6, p. 444.

Church Reunion that Durie has been misrepresented 'by many writers', concerning his association with the Jews.[249] Prynne and Durie, for instance, were old political and religious opponents and could hardly be thought to agree on anything. Christopher Hill is thus on firmer historical ground when he says in his *Intellectual Origins* that Durie 'Practically started the first agitation in favour of admitting the Jews to England'. This had long been the conviction of earlier Jewish writers such as Hyamson who wrote in 1907 that Durie 'took a prominent part in the Jewish Re-settlement movement.'[250]

In her essay *Cromwell and the "Readmission" of the Jews to England, 1656*, Barbara Colton of Lancaster University, wrote in 2001:

> 'While in Holland in the 1640s Dury, who wished for the conversion of the Jews as well as the reconciliation of all Protestants, met Menasseh; he corresponded with him in 1649 on reports that the legendary 'lost tribes' of Israel had been identified in the Americas; this was important to the messianic dream of Menasseh and other Jews.'[251]

Though Durie was a leading Philo-Semite of his age, he desired their conversion to Christianity from a simple utility point of view. Before the world turned back to God, he believed, all nations must come under the gospel, the Jews included. Furthermore, he believed that the Jews had linguistic traditions and knowledge which were essential to interpreting the Hebrew Scriptures aright. He was not alone as there was a growing interest in the study of Hebrew in Britain and The Netherlands, spreading into other European countries such as Sweden. This could not be separated from the various millennial interests present in their governments and universities. For Durie, all knowledge was ultimately based on following the ways of God as illustrated in Scripture, so in a letter written to Hartlib in 1646, concerning Adam Boreal, the Dutch Hebrew scholar, Durie says of his friend in relation to the Jews:

> 'I know his zeal will not suffer him to rest till he hath brought the matter to some period, for although hee hath not such meanes of his owne as will beare the charges which are requisite in prosecuting this designe, yet there is hope that God will raise instruments to assist him; for no doubt the tyme doth drawe neere of their calling; & these preparatives (H alters from preparats) are cleer presages of the purpose of God in this worke, for when hee

---

[249] Batten, p. 257.
[250] *A History of the Jews in England*, p. 181.
[251] *Cromwelliana*, The Journal of the Cromwell Association, 2001.

doth beginne to fitte meanes for the discoverie of their errors & for the manifestation of the Truth of Christianitie, upon more vniversall (H alters from universall) grounds then as yet have beene offered to them, it is a cleer token that hee intends to take the vaile from of their faces; & the many wayes which are now intended for the facilitating of the studie of the Orientall languages amongst Christians, is another token of the same purpose of divine Providence.'[252]

The many seventeenth century pamphlets written on the resettlement of the Jews in England, including a number from Durie's pen, were soon out of vogue. A much smaller renewed interest in the Jews arose at the end of the nineteenth century and the beginning of the twentieth through authors such as S. Levy, Lionel Abrahams, Lucien Wolf and Albert Hyamson; but this was of short duration, most likely due to the highly speculative tone of these works. On May 18, 1903, Hyamson gave a 33-page paper to the Jewish Historical Society of England on the subject of 'The Lost Tribes and the Return of the Jews to England'. Hyamson goes briefly through all the various theories of how ten tribes were lost (if they ever were 'lost'), looking at the Chinese, the Tartars, the Hottentots, Gog and Magog, the Cumanians, the Scythians and adding the Queen of the Amazons, the English and the Irish to his accounts into the bargain. Amidst this apparent confusion of theories, Hyamson turns to Menasseh's *The Hope of Israel*, a work which developed through Menasseh's correspondence with Durie. Much of this correspondence had to do with the eschatological idea that God had ordained that the Jews would be scattered all over the world and that when their Messiah came, he would draw the Jews back from the four corners of the earth to some Near Eastern State. Thus when rumours came from the New World, that the Native Indians were descendants of the Ten Lost Tribes, it appeared that now the Jews were present in all known countries and their re-gathering could begin. It was then pointed out to Menasseh and his Messianic followers that this prophecy had not been quite fulfilled as Jews were banned from Britain. Thus, they must be resettled in Britain for the sake of the fulfilment of prophecy. Then the Messiah, a descendent of David, could come. Various 'British Israelite' views were aired by both Jews and Christians who began to speculate on whether the Kingship of England was of the heredity Davidic line, though even Cromwell was suggested as a candidate for Messiahship.

This was welcome news for many British Christians who believed that the conversion of the Jews and their world-wide recognition of a Messiah

---

[252] Ref: 1/6/7A-10B: 9B, 10A BLANK and Ref: 3/3/32A-33B, HP.

must precede the Second Advent of Christ and that this mass-conversion would have its centre in the New Eden of the Commonwealth. Others, such as Semi-Separatist Henry Jessey, also joined the Durie-Hartlib campaign for the resettlement of the Jews in England, but tended to place their Messianic hopes in a resettlement in Jerusalem. Durie, a friend of the Jews with or without immediate millenarian Messianic hopes, campaigned for a resettlement of the Jews both in England and the Near East. Richard Henry Popkin sees Durie as a co-initiator of collections for the poor Jews of Jerusalem alongside Jessey.[253] Popkin also in his 'The Fictional Jewish Council of 1650: A Great English Pipedream' cites Jessey as one whose ideas, he believes, helped to form the background to the myth that in 1650 three hundred rabbis met in Ageda, Hungary, to debate on whether the Christ had come or not. The work, on which Popkin is commenting, was published in 1655 by Richard Moon and was said to be an eye-witness account by Samuel Brett. Katz describes it as 'a sort of Jewish Whitehall Conference whose results were favourable to the adoption of Christianity'.[254]

New trends in Jewish studies

Towards the end of the last century and into the opening decade of this century, new trends in Durie studies have developed and, once again, much attention is being paid to Durie's works relating to the Jews. This, however, is based on surer historical grounds and on a more academic approach to the peculiar situation of the Jews. We can also look back on the seventeenth century from the hindsight of having the modern state of Israel which has proved a home for millions of Jews. Durie still features centrally in the modern debate. It is, however, still to be determined to what extent Durie really identified himself with the Jewish-Christian concepts of his day and whether modern Jewish-Christian scholarship has placed Durie in the correct historical, theological and millennial niche. Pioneers in this new area are the late Richard Henry Popkin; David S. Katz; Ernestine G. E. van der Wall; J. Van den Berg and Jonathan Israel. These scholars appear to be so close together in their thoughts and use of one another's works that they might be said to build a society or school of interpreters concerning Durie's attitude to the Jews. Ernestine van der Wall calls this group of whom she is a very active member, 'the Popkinites'.[255]

---

[253] The Lost Tribes, p. 225.
[254] David S. Katz, Philosemitism and the Readmission of the Jews to England, pp. 105-106.
[255] Henry Jessey and his 'The Glory and Salvation', p. 184.

Though whole books are being written on the subject, these are mostly collections of essays such as *Jewish-Christian Relations in the Seventeenth Century: Studies and Documents*, edited by J. van den Berg and Ernestine G. E. van der Wall (1988) and *Sceptics Millenarians and Jews*, Brill, Leiden, edited by Katz and Israel (1990). Other material is to be found in individual essays in collections of works dealing with related, topics such as *Samuel Hartlib and Universal Reformation: Studies in Intellectual Communication*, edited by Mark Greengrass et al (1994). In this work, we find Popkin's essay 'Hartlib, Dury and the Jews.' The bulk of works concerning Durie and the Jews are individual essays found in magazines and journals such as *The British Library Journal*; *The Journal of Ecclesiastical History*; *The Journal of Jewish Studies*; *Hîstôrya yêhûdît*; *Jewish Quarterly Review*; *Revue des études juives*; *Church History* and *Cromwelliana*. The subject-matter of these articles is often widened to include Durie's teaching on eschatology and his efforts to prepare the world for 'the restitution of all things' and the coming Second Advent. So, too, Durie's views on Jewish and especially Hebrew studies into the ordinary school curricula has proved a welcome subject to modern scholars interested in Jewish religion and culture.

On the heels of this new focus on Durie's work, and developing in a large measure from it, we find an increasing awareness of Durie's let's-start-now reforms in universal learning, the sciences, Pansophy and Practical Divinity. As a prelude to examining Durie's epistemology of Universal Learning and his pansophical cosmology in more depth, it is, however, fitting that we examine Durie's attitude to the Jews. This 'nation', to use Durie's expression, played a substantial role in his plans for educating all nations in preparation for a global acceptance of his vision of a world where the one knowledge of the God-Only-Wise would unite all mankind. The conversion of the Jews and the spread of universal learning were thus all part of Durie's one plan towards the Puritan Hope of an Eden restored. This was not essentially a millennial project. Nevertheless, van der Wall writes in her essay *Petrus Serrarius (1600-1669) et Le millénarisme mystique*:

> 'Le millénarisme était surtout en vogue en Angleterre, en Allemagne et dans les pays d'Europe centrale. Aux Provinces Unies également, le chiliasme jouissait d'une grande popularité. John Durie remarqua que beaucoup de gens en Hollande cherchaient l'accomplissement des prophéties qui se trouvaient dans l'Apocalypse, de même que Friedrich Breckling constata qu'aux Pays-Bas le millénarisme était prêché publiquement du haut de la chaire. C'était surtout grâce à la présence d'étrangers, des bannis pour qui la Répu-

blique hospitalière était une seconde patrie, que le chiliasme y prenait un essor particulier.'[256]

Mario Caricchio in his 25-page study of 2006 entitled *John Dury, reformer of education against the radical challenge*, comments on the growing interest now shown in Durie's works. He points out especially how Jewish scholars are rescuing Durie from the side-tracks of history, saying that the noted Jewish scholar Richard H. Popkin has viewed Durie's works as being part of the 'third force of the seventeenth century', and that his 'blending of rationalism and millenarianism can be considered crucial to the understanding of the construction of modern scientific thought.[257] As a corollary, attention has been paid to Durie's interest in the readmission of the Jews into England, which was widely shared in the millenarian climate of the 1640s and 1650s.'[258] Popkin thus became very interested in Durie's educational programme with a view to comparing Durie's eschatology with that of the Jews. In 1983, he helped to bring out a reprint of Durie's *Reformed Librarie-Keeper* with Thomas F. Wright, saying in his Introduction, 'This work, with its quaint sentiments and its grim picture of what librarians were like in the mid-seventeenth century, is more than a curiosity. John Durie was a very important figure in the Puritan Revolution, offering proposal after proposal to prepare England for its role in the millennium. *The Reformed Librarie-Keeper* is an integral part of that preparation.'[259] Popkin, however, does not appear to have seen the practicability of Durie's Reformed Librarie-Keeper for not only his own day and age but for all time as Popkin reads the work as an instrument to further millenarian views rather than library science.

---

[256] Openaccess.leidenuniv.nl/bitstream/8261/1/3_908_020 pdf. Van der Wall's Doctor's thesis was entitled *De mystieke chiliast Petrus Serrarius(1600-1669) en zijn wereld*, Leiden, 1987. See also Van der Wall's Three Letters by Menasseh Ben Israel to John Durie: English Philo-Judaism and the 'Spes Israelis'; The Dutch Hebraist Adam Boreel and the Mishna Project: "Six Unpublished Letters and Without Partialitie Towards All Men": John Durie on the Dutch Hebraist Adam Boreel. Then there is her joint treatment with Popkin of Samuel Hartlib, John Worthington and John Durie with regards to 'Adam Boreel's Latin Translation of the Mishna (1659-1661)

[257] Caricchio is referring to Richard Popkin's essay, The Third Force in Seventeenth Century Thought: Scepticism, Science, and Millenarianism, in *The Third Force in Seventeenth Century Thought*, Leiden 1992.

[258] *Les Dossiers du Grihl*, http://dossiersgrihl.revues.org/3787.

[259] Published for William Andrews Clark Memorial Library, University of California, Los Angeles, 1983.

In keeping with this aim, Popkin then tells his readers, who would mostly be librarians or other book-lovers, that Durie wrote the work so 'that the prophecies in the books of Daniel and Revelation could be fulfilled'. As will be shown below, Librarians today view Durie as a man with twenty-first century views which are, moreover, timeless and ageless in their practicability. Furthermore, Durie in his outline of the library's function in what he calls 'the trade of learning' never so much as mentions Daniel and Revelation and the nearest he gets to a future millennium is by speaking of Christ's injunctive to spread his Kingdom on earth, which Christians have been doing since Christ's day. On the other hand, we can view Durie's work as suggested by Malcolm Oster who sees the Durie circle as following Bacon's vision of true religion going hand in hand with natural philosophy albeit with 'apocalyptic colouring' rather than 'millennial eschatology'.[260]

One of the questions thus to be discussed in this chapter is whether Durie's educational reforms were indeed in preparation for a future akin to the way modern Jewish writers on Durie view it. It is noticeable, however, that most of the modern Jewish scholars mentioned here have not found their knowledge of Durie in seventeenth century Jewish studies but have been strongly influenced by Trevor-Roper and Charles Webster which has caused them to look back on history through particularly coloured reading glasses. Especially Trevor-Roper in his far too strict and narrow view of his 'Three Foreigners' has strongly influenced Popkin's interpretations.

Another legitimate question is whether or not one can identify Durie's views of eschatology with those of Comenius in the way that Popkin does. To say that 'In a long series of pamphlets and tracts, Hartlib and Dury turned Comenius' theory into practical applications to the situation then prevailing'[261] needs evidence which Popkin merely assumes is there from the fact that the three met in 1641. The facts show that very little indeed came of this meeting. In tracing Durie's and Hartlib's publications for the advancement of universal learning in the second half of the forties and first half of the fifties, continually dropping Comenius' name, Popkin is ignoring the fact that Comenius' writing at the time, as will be shown in Chapter VII were counterproductive to this aim. More interesting, and possibly true, in Popkin's discussion is his remark that Henry Oldenburg, Durie's

---

[260] Malcome Oster, Millenarianism and the new science, in *Samuel Hartlib and Universal Reformation*, M. Greengrass et al, p. 140.

[261] Popkin's Introduction to the 1983 reprint of the *Reformed Librarie-Keeper*, my online version p. 2.

son-in-law at the creation of the Royal Society, 'helped bring about some of the scientific reforms Dury had advocated.'[262]

Popkin's three-point appraisal of Durie

In his 1994 essay, *Hartlib, Dury and the Jews*, Popkin relates how Charles Webster put him in touch with the Hartlib Papers and opened up new dimensions of research to him. He now understood that Hartlib, Durie and Comenius 'were key figures in understanding the extraordinary philosemitism that developed in England and Holland towards the middle of the seventeenth century.' However of over 300 printed works from Durie's pen and the numerous essays extant in manuscript form, very few have to do with the Jews other than with reference to their conversion or to their languages and learning as a means of extending universal knowledge. Nevertheless, Popkin records that after two relatively brief visits to Sheffield to study the Hartlib Papers, he was able 'to piece together a most unusual picture of the ways in which Christian millenarianism and Jewish messianism interacted from about 1640 onwards in England and the Netherlands.' After two years' intense hands-on study of these papers in all their aspects, I believe it is wrong to isolate the relative little Durie and Hartlib, say concerning the Jews from the bulk of the general issues discussed in them. Durie's teaching on the value and future of the Jews must be studied in that general context only to be understood best. Comenius' views concerning the Jews do not find much utterance in the Hartlib Papers per-cent wise at all. Popkin then refers to the visit of Comenius to England in 1641, claiming the three 'were ready to reform everything in preparation for the millennium, the thousand-year reign of Christ on earth'. Popkin gives three reasons for his claim that Hartlib, Durie and Comenius presented a hitherto 'most unusual picture' concerning their interest in the Jews and their 'reform of everything'.

First, Popkin mentions the college for Jewish Studies which had been Durie's desire many years before Comenius visited England. However, a college for Hebrew studies was only one of a number of closely integrated colleges in Durie and Hartlib's planned university, all dealing with hitherto different 'sciences' and all following Durie's central aim of a synergisation of all knowledge promoting universal learning. Evidence for a pioneer participation of Comenius in these plans does not exist. In 1628, Hartlib and Durie were already working on such plans expressly stating that they were

---

[262] Ibid, p. 4. page 4.

not building on the ideas of others save Bacon. So too, these plans could not be realised in Durie's day.

Popkin's second point was the Mishna project which was indeed a pioneer work regarding Jewish Christian cooperation. However, neither the initiative for the project nor its carrying out had much to do with Comenius. Nor was this a main project of the Durie-Hartlib circle. This was mainly the work of Boreel who struggled with the translation for forty years, assisted by Rabbi Judah Leon. The latter moved in to live with Boreel so that they could work long hours together on the translation. Durie's connections with Boreel, Leon and the Mishna project in general were merely those of encouragement and mediation. Indeed, the connection, at times was something of an embarrassment as witnessed by a letter from Hartlib to John Worthington, a former Vice-Chancellor of Cambridge University. Hartlib tells him:

> 'I shall write to Dr. Horn about the Elzever Josephus, as likewise to Mr. Adam Boreel the author of ad Legem et Testimonium, who hath left above 200 copies of the Mishnaioth in my hands, of which I have not been able to sell one copy for him, so that I fear they must all be returned upon his hands.'[263]

Popkin's third point was the mere fact that Durie's circle was interested in 'the construction and description of an exact model of Solomon's Temple' which Rabbi Judah Leon and Adam Boreel were undertaking in Holland. Here, too, Comenius had little if anything to do primarily with Durie's and Hartlib's interest. This arose initially from a hint given them by a Jew domiciled in England named Moses Wall which came at a time when Durie's circle were corresponding on an enormous number of projects and discussions on science and literature which is quite astonishing to read. Especially John Worthington's Cambridge reading seems to have been enormous and highly academic. The Jewish Theologian S. Levy, in *John Durie and the English Jewry*, calls Worthington 'a great theologian'. So also, Popkin has overlooked the enormous difference between Durie's Christian teaching concerning the Temple and the views of 17th century mainstream Jews. Writing to Hartlib in a long, undated, letter concerning the advantage of a universal knowledge to the spread of the gospel, Durie says that he had seen Judah Leon's reconstruction of the Temple and he thought it could be used as an 'inlett' or visual aid to help raise man's thoughts to

---

[263] *The Diary and Correspondence of Dr. John Worthington*, 1847, vol. I, pp. 130-132.

true worship.²⁶⁴ Perhaps Durie's most detailed discussion of Solomon's Temple and the construction and description of a prophesied New Temple is to be found in his reply to rather harsh criticisms from Edward Lane written 13 October, 1651. Here Durie tells Lane that all prophesies of the Temple to come and its measurements refer to the Antitype of the Old Testament Type found in Solomon's Temple. The Type in the OT points to the Antitype in the NT which is the People of God and the gifts of the Holy Spirit bestowed on them. The OT Temple was made with hands but the NT Temple is a spiritual building made without hands.²⁶⁵ Nevertheless, Popkin continues to assume that when Durie was told by such as Serrarius about, say, Rabbi Shapira's allegedly nigh-Christian views, or anything else to do with a Jewish-Christian common undertaking, Durie automatically accepted them 'enthusiastically' as his own. Indeed, Popkin, contradicting what he had said in former years, claims in his 1992 *Jewish-Christian Relations in the Sixteenth and Seventeenth Centuries* that Durie first heard of Shapira's alleged nigh-Christian views in 1657 and immediately published a work saying that the Jews were about to convert to Christianity. The footnote Popkin provides, however, does not give the title of this work but merely refers to another essay from Popkin's pen, 'Rabbi Shapira's Visit to Amsterdam.' Popkin does add in a footnote however, that Rabbi Shapira allegedly 'made very un- and even anti-Christian remarks' but added, 'So far I have not been shown any of these sermons.'²⁶⁶ In his 1992 work, Popkin says he has heard of Shapira's anti-Christian statements from a Moshe Idle. Actually, Durie and Serrarius were part of a large international group of correspondents including many Englishmen such as Boyle, Milton, Thomas Goodwin, Comenius, de Labadie, Hettinger, Essenius, Oldenburg, Christian and Johann Ravius and Hübner who passed on such pieces of information as the newspapers of the times. It could never be concluded that all were equally adherents of the views they passed on and discussed unless certain evidence were given. Though van der Wall relates Durie with Rabbi Shapira by association with Serrarius, she does hint that when rumours of the Lost Ten Tribes had reached Europe, Serrarius, Durie and their many correspondents suddenly dropped Shapiro and discussed the evangelisation of the Americas.²⁶⁷ A new topic had arrived. When the

---

²⁶⁴ Ref: 1/6/11A-14B, HP.
²⁶⁵ Ref: 132/23A-28B, HP
²⁶⁶ Hartlib, Dury and the Jews, p. 131.
²⁶⁷ Van der Wall's, A Precursor of Christ or a Jewish Impostor? Petrus Serrarius and Jean de Labadie on the Jewish Messianic Movement around Sabbatai Sevi, p. 114 ff.

name Abate Levi was on Serrarius' tongue, his vast number of correspondents 'chatted' on the 'snail-mail' lines with him on the subject and the Americas were nigh forgotten.[268] Popkin's understanding of Moses Wall also needs modification. Because, it appears, of his keen, sober, interest in everything Jewish and his interest in Boreal, Serrarius and Menasseh Ben Israel, Popkin calls Wall in his 1991 *History erudite* work on the fictional Jewish council of 1660 a 'wild millenarian'.

Durie and the 'lost tribes'

Although Menasseh and Durie were equally interested in the news coming from the American colonies that the Indians were the alleged Ten Lost Tribes of Israel, their interpretations were different. Thus invariable attempts by modern writers such as van der Wall to emphasise the beliefs Menasseh and Durie had in common do not serve to prove that both men took a common stand concerning their eschatology. It was, however, because of the Lost Tribes theory that Durie wrote to Menasseh in the first place and also discussed and corresponded with his fellow Westminster Assembly member Thomas Thornwood on the subject. Thornwood published his *Ewes in America or Probabilities that the Americans are of that Race* in 1650 with an Introduction by Durie. However, to the title, they added the words, 'earnest desires for the effectual endeavours to make them Christians.' Two years later, Durie published a joint work with Thornwood and Menasseh entitled *Digits dei: nevv discoveryes: with sure arguments to prove that the Jews (a Nation) or people lost in the world for the space of near 2000 years, inhabite now in America; how they came thither; their manners, customs, rites and ceremonies; the unparallel'd cruelty of the Spaniard to them; and that the Americans are of that race. Manifested by reason and scripture, which foretell the calling of the Jewes; and the restitution of them into their own land, and the bringing back of the ten tribes from all the ends and corners of the earth, and that great battell to be fought. With the removall of some contrary reasonings, and an earnest desire for effectuall endeavours to make them Christians. Whereunto is added an epistolicall discourse of Mr John Dury, with the history of Ant: Monterinos, attested by Manasseh Ben Israell, a chief rabby.* In the early fifties, Durie produced his *Concerning the Question Whether it bee*

---

[268] See Popkin's 'Three English Tellings of the Sabbatai Zevi Story', *Jewish History*, vol. 8, Numbers 1-2. where he claims 'John Dury, based in Germany and Switzerland, spent much time trying to figure out where Sabbatai Zevi fitted in the expected Christian scenario about 'the end of the days'.

lawfull to admit Iewes to come into a Christian commonwealth. Durie then, in 1656, published his *A Case of Conscience, whether it be lawful to admit Jews into a Christian Common-Wealth? Resolved by John Dury.* This was followed two years later by his joint work with Henry Jessey and Petrus Serrurier entitled *An information concerning the present state of the Jewish nation in Europe and Judea: wherein the footsteps of Providence preparing a way for their conversion to Christ, and for their deliverance from captivity are discovered.*

Present-day Jewish Studies have closely related Durie's name with that of Menasseh Ben Israel, Henry Jessey and Peter Serrarius. These friends' names are indeed of importance in the history of seventeenth century Jewish-Christian relationships as the four men from quite different backgrounds became allies through their interest in Hebrew studies. Jessey and Serrarius have been comparatively neglected until the turn into the twenty-first century, but Jessey especially has now been highlighted for his contribution to Jewish research by a number of modern writers. Barbara Coulton in the above mentioned article in *Cromwelliana* continues her remark on Durie by saying:

> 'Another philo-semite, the English Baptist divine Henry Jessey, addressed his book *The Glory and Salvation of Jehuda and Israel* to the 'dear' and 'eminent' nation of the Jews, in particular Menasseh. Jessey drew on rabbinic and kabbalistic prophecies to prove that these authorities supported Christian views about the Messiah; he believed that the Jews would be converted by 1658. He corresponded regularly with Menasseh who sent him a copy of his book *Esperanca de Israel – The Hope of Israel*; this work, also drawing on prophecy, aimed to show 'that the day of the promised Messiah unto us doth draw near.' Both books were published in 1656.' Van der Wall states that 'Jessey's treatise bore the imprimatur of four famous divines: John Dury, Joseph Caryl, William Greenhill, and Nathaniel Homes. Dury expressed the wish that the tract might be spread among all Jews in the whole world, while Homes stated that he believed that this treatise would be most profitable for Jews and gentiles alike.'[269]

Jessey was born in West Rowton in the North Riding of Yorkshire where his father was the Church of England minister. He was brought up from childhood to study the Scriptures which had a lasting effect on his life. He matriculated at Cambridge in 1618, gaining his B.A. in 1623, after which, according to Neal, he became Master of Arts. At this time, he testified to a change of heart and a strong desire to enter the ministry. Here stories about

---

[269] Sceptics, Millenarians and Jews, p. 163.

Jessey become rather muddled, some accounts saying he studied Hebrew and Rabbinical literature until his ordination in 1627. Yet other stories send him to the New World for a brief period. Jessey appears to have assisted at his father's church after being ordained a deacon and after his ordination as priest received a Yorkshire living in 1633 left vacant by one expelled for Nonconformity. Soon suspected of Nonconformity himself, Jessey was patronised by Sir Matthew Boynton of Barneston in Yorkshire who kept a protecting hand over him and eventually took him to London and Uxbridge where he continued his ministry in Semi-Separatist churches such as those led by Henry Jacob and John Lathrop. Jessey preached alternately at former Anglican churches now disestablished by Cromwell and at the Savoy where the Church Historian Thomas Fuller also preached. Jessey was also high in demand at the various inter-confessional meetings in London. He very gradually accepted the tenets of the Seventh Day Baptists and, under Cromwell he became a Trier, determining the suitability of ministers for appointments to former Anglican livings whose vicars had been ejected. He gradually became a Fifth-Monarchy man and a Sabbatarian. He had qualms of conscience on worshipping on Sunday as the Lord's Day. Not realising for all his knowledge of the Scriptures that the old Jewish week was not the Roman week used in the New Testament, he counted from Sunday through to Saturday (days which formerly did not exist as such), believing that Saturday dated back to the true Seventh Day after Creation when God rested. As in the Scriptures, the Sabbath began on the evening before the morning; he felt that one should set aside Friday night to Saturday night as the Sabbath. This view gained him favour with the Jews. Jessey objected to the Authorised Version of the Bible, merely because he felt it was enforced on the people and prelatal. He thus worked on his own translation which he does not appear to have completed. Jessey never married and loved his studies more than company, writing on his study door the words:

Amice, quisquis huc ades;
Aut agito paucis, aut abi,
Aut me Laborantem adjuva.

It is not easy to describe Jessey's ecclesiastical preferences as he mixed equally with Episcopalians, Presbyterians, Independents and Baptists. Van der Wall perhaps hits the right note by saying, 'He was among the most prominent Independent clergymen of his day and is considered as the foremost representative of "respectable nonconformity".' He does not seem to have been a close acquaintance of the Dury-Hartlib circle, judging by the paucity of extant references, but Hartlib describes him to John Worthington as one who is 'a very loving and hearty man'. Hartlib rejects the suggestion that Jessey should help with a work on the French Reformed Churches on the grounds that he lacked the ability. This might mean that Jessey either knew no French or that his own Baptist theology might hinder him. Durie's troubled letter to Jessey concerning the latter's friend 'Mr. Cresit, Master of Suttons Hospital', indicates that there was strong opposition to Durie's work from those of Jessey's communion.[270] However, Hartlib tells Worthington that Jessey and Philip Nye possessed knowledge of the Masoreths of Tiberias which would be useful in that sphere.[271] An undated letter addressed to both Hartlib and Durie from Jessey, probably written at the end of 1659, is extant in the Hartlib Papers, indicating Jessey's interest in the Jewish people. Jessey wrote:

'For Mr Hartlib or Mr Durie, or both
   The bearer, a Iew-borne, being directed unto me by some; and I can understand but litle of his Language: Because he seemes expert in the Hebrew; and to beleev the Messias is come, & that Iesus is He: and seemes plain in his profession, and believes not ther are 3 Gods, as he thinks Christians do: he saith, he is not a Christian. But he seemes to be ingenuous & docible. I entreat you not to be offended with me, that thus I send him to you, to do for him, according to his Petition, what in you is. Compassion to Banished Iews from Poland, will not be forgotten by the LORD at the day of Recompences. So beleevs,
   Your Loving friend
   H. Iessey.'[272]

This letter is followed up by one dated in the old style, 19th of XI Mon. Ianu., in which Jessey says:

'By such understanding of the bearer Meyer Isaac, as by a litle broken discourse with him, I have had I judge him to be a IEW, banished or rather fled from the persecution of Iews in Poland that seemes more convinced that Iesus is the Messias, then any, that yet professeth to be a Iew, and not a Christian in Religion. For he thinks Christians beleev their are 3 Gods. & Iews confess but one. & beleev in one God. And he beleevs not in Iesus.
   I judge he is ingenuous, & docible: and therefore I should be glad if any may further him to imployment, that he may have good and raiment, & not

---

[270] Ref: 4/3/103A.-104B, HP.
[271] See Hartlib's letters to John Worthington dated 30 Jan. 1659/60 and a year later on 11 Jan. 1660/61.
[272] Ref: 15/8/15A-16B: 15B-16A BLANK, HP.

be discouraged amongst us. But that he may be helped spiritually & temporally: which wilbe no greef of heart to any at the great day of Recompences.'

Jessey's views concerning his agreement in certain fundamentals of religion with the Jews and especially concerning the Messiah, which he published in 1650 in his *The Glory and Salvation of Jehuda and Israel,* were translated into Dutch by Petrus Serrarius. However, van der Wall states, 'A year before, similar thoughts had been brought forward by Durie, who maintained "that the Christian Religion doth teach nothing, but that Truth nakedly, which of old was darkly spoken of, and believed by the chief Doctors of the Jews themselves, and from the beginning by Moses and the Prophets"'.[273] Van der Wall says she has this quote from Popkin's *The First Jewish College,* giving pp. 351-64 in his work as her source.[274] Actually, the thought in context, as Popkin points out, is from Durie's *A Seasonable Discourse.* On page 15 of that work, Durie is speaking about the benefits of learning other languages to universal learning in general and science, trade and commerce in particular. On page 16, he goes on to consider Hebrew and other 'Oriental languages', dealing now particularly with the future promises to the Jews in the Old Testament. As Jews know little about Christianity and Christians know little about the Hebrew writings, a trade in knowledge is here, too, desirable, says Durie. He writes further:

> 'For the benefit of the Trade will be reciprocall, at least very much for our advantage, by the confirmation of that Truth whereof God hath made us partakers above them; and according to the promises made of old unto them, seeing not only a clearer understanding of the things delivered by the spirit in the old Testament, will be granted by this means; but also many of the Mysteries of the new Testament, and chiefly that of the desire of all Nations, the *Messias*, will be opened more fully to us by them, and by us unto them: because it is evidently found of late by some that have traded, with their most ancient Rabinicall writers, (men with them of unquestionable credit) that they speake plainly from the words of Moses and the Prophets, the same Truths which are revealed unto us by the Apostles and Evangelists.'

Another person whom modern writers on Jewish Studies link closely with Durie and Jessey is Scoto-Dutch Peter Serrarius[275] about whom Popkin,

---

[273] The Amsterdam Millenarian Petrus Serrarius, p. 76. See R.H. Popkin, 'The First College for Jewish Studies', *REJ* CXLIII (1984), 351-64, esp. 361.

[274] The original quote is found at the bottom of page 16 in Durie's *Seasonable Discourse.*

[275] The NNBW, Deel 10, pp. 911-912 claims that Serrarius was born in Flanders.

van der Wall and Katz have written in great detail. Again, van der Wall believes it was Durie and his circle who introduced Jessey to Serrarius and persuaded him to work with them. Serrarius was born in London and matriculated to Christ Church, Oxford in 1617. One of Serrarius' earliest letters to Durie is addressed to Monsieur Ian Durêe, F. Ministre de l'eglise Engloise a Elbeing and is dated 26 February, 1629 in which the subject is Serrarius' brother Philippe who was at the time a merchant in the city.

Serrarius commuted through most of his life between England and Holland and was host to Durie several times on the latter's visits to the Netherlands. Besides his connections with Durie, Hartlib, Boreel and Jessey, he also worked closely with Spinoza and Menasseh Ben Israel and many scholars of Jewish Studies. Of a strictly Reformed persuasion and a contender against Moses Amyraut, it was, nevertheless rumoured owing to his messianic studies that he had become a follower of Sabbatai Zevi who claimed to be the long-awaited Messiah though he converted to Islam in 1666. Other scholars point out similarities in Serrarius' beliefs with the Quakers. Van der Wall says:

> 'Serrarius belonged to the small circle of philo-Judaists, whose members were mainly to be found in England and the Dutch Republic. Among its prominent representatives were John Durie, Henry Jessey, Nathaniel Homes, Samuel Hartlib, Benjamin Worsley, and John Sadler. They knew each other well and kept in close contact with each other, cooperating if necessary. John Durie, whom he had known since the early 1620s when both studied theology at the Walloon College at Leiden, was one of Serrarius' intimate friends.'[276]

Of this group of friends of the Jews, van der Wall relates:

> 'Most of the members of the Anglo-Dutch philo-Judaists were in personal contact with 'the father of Judéo-Christian friendship', the Amsterdam Rabbi Menasseh ben Israel. Jessey, Durie, Hartlib, Homes, Sadler, Worsley, Serrarius: they all were acquainted with the Rabbi, by letter or by face. When in 1655 Menasseh went over to England to plead the readmission of the Jews he met several of his English Christian pro-Jewish friends in person. Jessey was the man behind the scenes of the Whitehall Conference on the readmission of the Jews to England, held in London in December 1655. He wrote an eye-witness report about the Conference. It was as a result from Menasseh's correspondence with Durie in 1649 on the lost ten tribes of Israel that arose

---

[276] The Amsterdam Millenarian Petrus Serrarius (1600-1669) and the Anglo-Dutch Circle of Philo-Judaists. pp. 75-76.

the Rabbi's famous *Spes Israelis* (1650), which soon was translated into English and other languages. Menasseh and Serrarius knew each other quite well. Serrarius had a great admiration for his Jewish friend of whom he spoke in terms of the highest esteem. Of course he found it greatly to be deplored that Menasseh would not believe that the Messiah had already come. On the other hand, he rejoiced at the fact that Menasseh knew of the coming kingdom of the Messiah upon earth, a fact of which, to Serrarius' deep regret, most Christians were ignorant. During the discussions between Serrarius and Menasseh, held in December 1654 at Serrarius' home, in the company of the Bohemian chiliast and philo-Judaist Paul Felgenhauer,[277] Menasseh's views regarding the coming Fifth Monarchy came to the fore. Shortly afterwards these messianic ideas were published by him in his *Piedra Gloriosa* (1655).'[278]

Concerning Paul Felgenhauer, the Durie-Hartlib circle was far from agreeing with him in his theology. Felgenhauer was born in Bohemia, the son of a Protestant minister and studied at Wittenberg. He had to flee from Bohemia with Comenius after the Battle of the White Mountain and settled in Northern Germany where he succumbed to mystical and chiliastic teachings. He taught that Roman Catholics, Lutherans and the Reformed were all harmful sects and was pronounced a heretic himself. He is first mentioned in the circle's *Ephemerides* in 1640 where we read 'Ruarus hase refuted Felgenhauer. This is worth the seeing. For these sects bee quite opposit one to the other, the one maintaining only the Humanity the other only the divinity of *Christ*.'[279] Felgenhauer was imprisoned for his views. The last reference to him in the Hartlib Papers is in a letter dated 26 April 1658 written by John Morian to Hartlib in which Morian says, 'Felgenhauer ist seiner gefängnis erledigt, des landes zue ewigen tagen verwieszen und seine schrifften durch den scharpffrichter verbrandt.'[280]

Of Serrarius' connection with Durie, van der Wall says:

> 'In 1660, Serrarius was involved in another project of the kind, for which he asked support from Durie and Hartlib. A well learned Rabbi - of unknown identity – had presented himself to Serrarius to translate the Dutch New Testament into Hebrew 'to make it legible and intelligible unto his Nation'. The Rabbi had heard some sermons by the Lutheran minister Justus Brau at Kampen and he had had some conversation with Brau and others, such as the

---

[277] Durie and his circle were to contend strongly against Felgenhauer who appeared to deny the humanity of Christ.
[278] Ibid, p. 76.
[279] Ref: 30/4/53A, HP.
[280] Ref: 31/18/17A-18B, HP.

Hebraist Matthias Drudius, by which he had found himself very much convinced. Brau was deeply interested in Jewish matters, being well versed in the Hebrew language. The translation by the Rabbi had to be 'wrought out secretly in our Houses, under the Inspection of some of our Christians', Serrarius wrote to Durie. He told him that he and his friends were about to procure a stock for that work in order to relieve the Rabbi from his poverty and to allow him an honest salary, all the while he would be at work. Furthermore, money was needed, presumably even from Jews, to have his translation printed or written out several times. Serrarius asked for financial support from Durie and his English friends: 'we shall see it well bestowed, and endeavour by it to provoke others also . . .'[281]

Dury immediately travelled to Holland to stay with Serrarius in Amsterdam and he must have been in Holland by the beginning of January 1661 as Hartlib, who had been seriously ill, complained to Mrs Dury that 'I am now risen but am full of horrible pains occasioned by the famed medecin sent by Mr. Serrarius upon good Mr. Dury request for my ease & relief; but it hath pleased the Lord to lett me find quite other effects And it is noe small mercy that I am yett in the land of the living.' On 11 March, Durie was still with Serrarius but planning to travel with him to their alma mater Leyden University. We find Durie still at Serrarius house, though he might have been to Leyden and then returned, when he wrote on 19 November asking Hartlib if the medicine had helped which he and Serrarius had sent him.

Thoughts concerning founding a London University with a college for Jewish studies

Within his programme for introducing society to his universal learning of Pansophy, it was most desirable for Durie that Jewish scholars should be appointed as teachers of Hebrew in English schools so that they could help Protestants to study the Scriptures which revealed their joint future with converted Jews. This is why he worked closely with the Dutch Hebraist Boreel on his Mishna Project and with Menasseh on his messianic work *Spes Israelis*. With a view to resettling Jews in England and with Durie's backing, Menasseh dedicated his major work 'To the High Court, the Parliament of England, and to the Councell of State'.[282] Van der Wall writes:

---

[281] Ibid, pp. 79-90.
[282] See Hyamson, p. 191.

'In 1649[283] Durie put forward another plan to promote the study of Oriental languages: he proposed to establish a college of Jewish studies, which would deal with Oriental languages and the mysteries of Jewish learning. One of the points of his programme was "to advance the printing of the New Testament into those languages at easie rates, to be made common amongst the Orientals and chiefly the Jewes'. Both English and Dutch philo-Judaists were occupied with the realisation of this proposal. It was thought that the knowledge of the Jews about Christianity ought to be increased first of all by making the New Testament available to them. A good and complete Hebrew translation was needed. Several times in the seventeenth century - the age in which so many Bible translations were published - plans were made to have the New Testament translated into Hebrew, but most of them fell through. This was also the case with the plans of the Anglo-Dutch Philo-Judaists. According to them there could be no greater preparation for their conversion than when the Jews could read the New Testament 'as a true History in their own Hebrew Dialect'.[284]

The idea of teaching what Durie calls the Oriental tongues had been with Durie since the early thirties when the Bohemian and Polish Protestants formed a union during the early part of the Thirty-Years' war. In a 6,900 word paper sent to Hartlib on 'touching the worke of pacification' in which he outlined his early plans for Universal Learning and Practical Divinity, he said of these Eastern European Protestants, among whom were experts in the Hebrew language:

> '1. I could labour to bring them in here with our uniuersities; in respect of the meanes of Learning & good order kept in them; that seeing most of all their owne academies are either ouerthrowne or destitute of learned men they might bee mooued to send hither their sonnes to bee bredde & instructed, by which meanes they would bring home at least the knowledge of the language which is the facultie to make use of our bookes.
>
> 2. I could giue them an Impression of the usefulnesse of our bookes exstant in Practicall Divinitie to stirre them uppe to desire the benefit of them.
>
> 3. I could take notice of all the rare gifts which God hath bestowed upon the most eminent men in any of those parts, in any kind of learning or facultie; to bring the benefit of it hither either in bookes or treaties exstant or in M.S. or by way of some setled correspondencie to bee entertained that that effect;

---

[283] During this time Durie was corresponding with Mennasseh concerning such projects.
[284] Jewish-Christian Relations in the Seventeenth Century, p. 79.

as for example I might draw Schikkardus[285] his peculiar gifts in the orientall tongues to the profit of our Schooles & Iongius his facultie of teaching Sciences, & searching naturall thinges might also bee gained; & whatsoeuer Docemius or any other hath in a Singular kind might bee ripened, drawen forth & improoued to a publick good by some way of correspondencie & communication.'[286]

John Beale, a clergyman and scientist and one of the Royal Society's first Fellows, on hearing that Durie and Hartlib were planning to start a college which would include Jewish studies, sent them a 'Memo of a College' in which he said that part of its education should be to train, 'Some to bee Students & Professours of the learned Languages Latine, Greeke, Hebrewe, Arabique & other Orientall tongues; To the plaines of teaching such as come thither to learning & to the elegancy of delighting & perfecting such as are skilld in it.[287]

Mario Caricchio, warns here of misunderstanding Durie's interest both in planning an all-comprehensive education and in his peace work aimed at Protestant union. These were merely facets of Durie's wider plans and have sadly taken researchers' gaze from the comprehensive nature of Durie's work. Of Durie's wider endeavours, he writes:

'Theoretical and practical efforts for the reform of schools and universities certainly occupied a conspicuous place in Dury's activities. He regarded them, indeed, as an integral part of his schemes for advancing Christian unity. By giving too much credit to his self-portrait as an 'unchanged peacemaker' standing above 'parties', however, twentieth century studies have generally relegated Dury's involvement in the politics of revolutionary England to the margins.'

Caricchio shows how little attention has been paid to the fact that Durie was 'one of the most important voices in buttressing obedience to the *de facto* power' of the Commonwealth.[288] He believes that Antony Milton was the first to challenge the one-sided image of Durie as an 'idealist irenist'. However, Caricchio leaves all ideas of Durie's universal learning and global importance to centre on one brief difficulty he had politically with John Saltmarch who did not appear to want any ordered government of ei-

---
[285] Wilhelm Schikkard (1592-1636)
[286] Ref: 1/9/1A-6B: 6A BLANK, HP.
[287] *Memo of a College*, John Beale, Ref: 31/1/77A-80B, HP. Beale (1608-1683), a clergyman and scientist, was a close associate of the Durie-Hartlib circle and became one of the Royal Society's first Fellows (1663).
[288] John Dury, reformer of education against the radical challenge, §2.

ther state or church but a state of individuals, each minding his own business. Durie's plans brooked no dissecting of society. For him, the function of an ordered state was to lead its citizens for the common good which meant primarily towards the knowledge of God and His creation. Thus, any distinction between Church and State, the material and the spiritual, merely meant that the person who believed in such a distinction was lacking in his education. The ideal state was Pansophical. It was this didactic element in his faith which had caused many Swedish ministers and Professors in 1636 to misunderstand Durie.

Notwithstanding the strong Christian background to Durie's plans for Hebraic Studies in England's schools and colleges, Prof. Richard Popkin, in the opening words of his 1984 work *The First College for Jewish Studies*, sees John Durie and Samuel Hartlib as taking a positive stance towards the Jewish religion by pioneering Judaic Studies where they had hitherto been fully disregarded. He further points out that educational writers such as Charles Webster and historians such as Trevor-Roper had overlooked the fact that the two friends planned to found a university for Judaic Studies which was the first proposal of its kind in western history. Actually, the proposals worked out by the Durie-Hartlib circle were not for a university solely based on Jewish Studies but for a University of London including multi-lingual colleges for universal learning; for Baconian experimental philosophy (experimental science); for the teaching of statesmanship and Jewish Studies together with the advancement of Oriental Languages.[289] They also planned colleges for the Irish but also Greek and other foreign nationals. Durie wished to learn from the Greek Orthodox Church as much as from the Jews. There was a strong hope that the Greek Orthodox Church would become reformed in Durie's day because of the writings of Cyril Lucaris 1572-1638.[290] The Hartlib-Durie Circle's own Chelsea College, founded around 1628 to propagate Durie's reforms, should furnish as a centre of correspondence between London University and foreign universities.

One decorative printed paper on the founding of the university under the title *Motives Grounded upon the Word of God, and upon Honour, Profit, and Pleasures for the present Founding an University in the metropolis London* published by Durie's circle in 1647, stated the need of a School of the Prophets as related in Numbers Chapter 4, where instruction was given until a student's thirtieth year. Durie's main purpose was to raise

---

[289] See Popkin's *The First College*, p. 353.
[290] See my Cyril Lucaris: The Reformed Patriarch of Constantinople, *New Focus*, October/November, 2010, vol. 15, No. 03, pp. 17-19.

20,000 ministers to furnish churches, chapels, armies, navies, noble families, foreign plantations and merchant enterprises with correct Christian teaching, whereas Oxford and Cambridge together had only produced 5900 students when 'in their prime' and their education and calling was insufficient for their tasks. The authors also envisaged 80,000 being educated in trade, navigation, land warfare and seamanship. As Episcopacy was abolished, the authors say that there is little incentive now to study for the ministry and generous grants for poor scholars must be raised. The authors explain that if the affluent in England gave up one meal a week and gave the money saved to the University, then 20,000 students could easily be taught through the money thus saved.

These departments were, however, not subject-oriented but catered for the universal needs of all students from all parts of the world. Nor were these colleges for one stream of education only but during their studies, students could partake of some or all of the work done in the various colleges which were places for lectures and practice in languages rather than the traditionally one-faculty colleges. The students could thus move through one college where only Greek was spoken to another where only Hebrew was spoken, and visit another where Latin was the main language and another where English was used. This should be seen as preparation for learning other languages such as Italian, Spanish and French. Transfer Training was high on the university agenda. The languages taught by foreign experts would be for the benefit of the English-speaking students and the English language would be taught foreigners as they moved through the university during their seven-year courses. It appears that those who planned London University envisaged the courses as including what we would call Secondary and Tertiary Education today. They should be open to 'strangers (foreigners), natives and citizens', and the Professors should be chosen both from 'outlandish' and English scholars. Durie made it clear, as will be pointed out in further chapters, that the University should be open to non-matriculated students for special basis educational tuition. Today, in North-Rhine-Westphalia, this idea has been recently implemented and one can receive tuition in Chemistry in, say, English, French or Russian according to the qualifications of the teachers available. Russian, Chinese, North African, Turkish and Japanese staff are employed in several schools. English, French, Russian and Chinese are being taught in elementary schools, some offering two foreign languages to their young pupils. The plan for a London University states:

> 'Then all forraigne Protestants of worth in this western World would send their sonnes to the University of London, and our elder Brethren the Iewes,

now, their conversion to the Christian Faith is at hand, some of them perhaps shall live to see many of them come out of the East, and also hear them sing David's Psalmes, and Hebrew Songs joyfully with us their westerne English brethren here in London.'

In a three-page undated manuscript entitled *London University*,[291] the authors discuss the buildings necessary for such work. Former bishops' houses; Charter House, Hatton House; Gresham College, Chelsea College, Paul's Church House and Sutton Hospital could be taken over as their Anglican use had been abolished. One college should be reserved for theological studies and *propaganda fide* open to both Jews and Gentiles. The library in Paul's Church with Bishop Ussher's library were 'to be given' for a foundation of the future University Library. We notice that the Durie-Hartlib circle dropped the 'St' when referring to former Anglican churches as befitted the Commonwealth times.

Popkin, however, interprets Durie's educational aims fully in terms of a Millennium to come when a Messiah would reign. He centres his interest almost exclusively on Jewish Studies which were only a part of Durie's concept of Universal Learning. So, too, in the four or five papers extant outlining the work of the London University, millennial thoughts play no role whatsoever, nor is a Messianic reign so much as mentioned. However, Popkin also repeats his interpretation of Durie's founding a millennialist Jewish College in his 1992 work 'Jewish-Christian Relations in the Sixteenth Centuries: The Conception of the Messiah' in which he argues that in 1640, 'two leading millenarians, John Dury and Samuel Hartlib (proposed) that a college of Jewish studies be established in London'. He also writes of his close connection with Hebraists Johann Stephanus Rittangel (1606-1652) at Königsberg and Christian Rave (Ravius) of Berlin and Uppsala. These two scholars had influenced Comenius and encouraged him to write on Pansophy. The Durie circle, however, though pleased to have Ravius work with them, were very sceptical about Rittangel. Durie writing from Amsterdam on 24 October 1647, says:

'The Conversion of the Iewes might very much bee advanced by their Caballisticall Bookes and the paines of such Learned Linguists, who have not only a smattering of the language, but are likewise thoroughly acquainted with all the tearmes of Art used by any of them. But of those there are so few amongst the Professors of Christianity, that as yet I have met with none suf-

---

[291] Ref: 47/9/16A-17B, HP.

ficiently qualified this way, but only Rittangel. But the Man is of such an vntoward and humerous disposition, that there is no dealing with him.'[292]

Popkin then goes on to speak of Comenius' interest in Hartlib and Durie's plans for a new college of universal learning in London and his visit to England to be informed of this progress. This was some 12 years after Chelsea College was formed but six years before plans for a University began to take more concrete forms. When, in 1642, Durie and Hartlib[293] published their proposals concerning 'religion, learning and the Preparatives for the conversion of the Jewes', Comenius' name was not mentioned, though he was in England whilst it was being written. Popkin calls this work 'super-optimistic', perhaps as a Jew contemplating on attempts to convert him.[294]

Popkin shows how Durie, Boreel and Ravius cooperated with Menasseh on a translation of the Mishna and other Hebrew writings with a view to using them towards the conversion of the Jews. Concerning London University, Popkin emphasises, quoting Webster, that Durie felt that if the knowledge of the Jews was added to that of the gentiles, 'we would know more distinctly the ancient ways of God towards the first inhabitants of the world.'[295] Though Popkin claims that Hartlib first aired the proposal for the university, he refers to it, nevertheless, as Durie's work. One interesting point Popkin makes is Durie's wish to have the New Testament translated into Hebrew, also pointed out above by van der Wall. Popkin, however, adds that this was undertaken by William Robertson in 1661 and was 'very scholarly'.[296] Judging by the correspondence of Dr. John Worthington, another central member of the Durie-Hartlib circle and Vice-Chancellor of Cambridge under Cromwell, that circle did not share Popkin's view. In August, 1661, Worthington wrote to Hartlib saying,

---

[292] Ref: 1/6/1A-2B, HP.
[293] Popkin refers to Hartlib and/or/ Durie as the author.
[294] Full title: *England's Thankfulnesse, or An Humble Remembrance presented to the Committee for Religion in the High Court of Parliament with Thanksgiving for the happy Pacification between the two Kingdomes. By a faithful well-wisher to his Church and Nation. Wherein are sumarily discovered a naïve and most subtle Plot of the Pope and his conclave against Protestancy. Their true method and policy how to undermine the same. The best and principle meanes of reestablishing the Palatin House and preserving all Evangelical Churches. As likewise three special Instruments of the publique good in the ways of Religion, Learning and the Preparatives for the conversion of the Jewes.*
[295] Ibid, p. 355.
[296] Ibid, 360.

'What you write in the postscript about Mr. Worsley (to whom, I pray, return my remembrances) that he told you the New Testament is extant in Hebrew, is rare news. You do but hint it. One would desire to know such things more particularly. Is it printed? Where and when? What is said of the edition? Where was the Hebrew copy found? Who had the MS.? There is indeed extant of the Gospel of S. Matthew in Hebrew one edition by Munster; and a better by Mercer; but neither of them thought authentick. What is therefore the reputation of this Hebrew copy of the New Testament?'[297]

Worthington looked further into the matter and told Hartlib a month later:

'I was in hopes, when you first mentioned the New Testament being extant in Hebrew, that it signified more than a late production of one Robertson. If it be he that went about teaching those that knew not Latin to construe Hebrew, I am not solicitous about enquiring any further after it. To perform this undertaking well, requires the best labours of one thoroughly acquainted with the Hebrew in the Old Testament, and in the Jewish Records; of which several proofs are given by the late more accurate interpreters. Among the several translations of the New Testament published in two volumes by Elias Hutterus, there is an Hebrew translation. I was in hopes, that the Evangelium Nazarzeorum (or Evang. secundum Hebræos) had been discovered; out of which Ignatius, Justin Martyr, Clemens Alex., S. Jerom, &c., quote some passages not extant in our Greek copies.'[298]

It appears thus that Robertson's translation was something of a disappointment to Worthington who was a most well informed man in Semitic and oriental languages.

Popkin ends his essay on Durie's proposed Jewish college by stating that it was first realised two hundred years later. Then, he adds, the college was financed by the Jews for the Jews and thus all aims at converting them to Christianity were dropped. Popkin still thought in terms of Jewish Studies alone.

John Durie and Millenarianism

In his review of James Jacob's work on Henry Stubbe and radical Protestantism published in 1986, Popkin discusses the alleged millenarian views of the leading members of the Royal Society and their association with Durie which ought to have been qualified by producing evidence. After

---

[297] *The Diary and Correspondence of Dr. John Worthington* ed. J. Crossley. Vol. I. (Chetham Society Vol. XIII: Manchester, 1847). pp. 353-356, also HP.
[298] Vol. II. Part I. (Chetham Society Vol. XXXVI: Manchester, 1855). pp. 2-13.

dealing with the presumed millenarian views of Hobbes, Wilkins, Boyle 'and many lesser lights,' again giving no documentary evidence, Popkin goes on to write:

> 'Henry Oldenburg was Boyle's close associate and secretary of the eminently respectable Latitudinarian Royal Society. In his case, we can see from his letters that he clung to his Millenarian ideas. In 1666, he hoped that the news was true that Sabbatai Zevi was the Jewish Messiah. He collected and passed on to Boyle every scrap of news he could get from the Dutch Millenarians and Christian followers of Sabbatai Zevi. Oldenburg and Boyle were respectively the son-in-law and the nephew of John Dury, one of the leading Millenarians of the Puritan period and one of Cromwell's chief agents on the Continent. But Dury was not allowed to return to England after 1660. Had his son-in-law and his nephew disowned his views in part or in toto? Boyle Boyle and Oldenburg in 1663-65 got the Dutch Millenarian, Peter Serrarius, to make them a copy of the work of Adam Boreel, the Collegiant Millenarian, on Jesus, the lawgiver of the human race. There is evidence that Oldenburg was taking care of Dury's affairs through the late 1660s and 1670s.

Prof. Popkin has here selected one relative small item of news and information passed between members of the Royal Society and Durie, amidst many hundred others and placed more meaning in it than should have been intended by one familiar with their works. Popkin's use of the word 'Latitudinarian' as an umbrella term for the Royal Society members' theology, and that related to millenarianism, ought also to have been qualified. The one thing that really united the Royal Society and Durie was as related by Oldenburg in a letter to Lubienietzki in July 1666 saying that they had 'taken to taske the whole Universe' and their joint pursuit was universal learning[299]. Yet in the same year, Popkin claimed in his essay 'The Lost Tribes, the Caraites and the English Millenarians' in the *Journal of Jewish Studies* that 'the leading Puritan Millenarian' was John Durie, giving as evidence Durie's discussions concerning the Caraites. Although Popkin quotes five secondary 'authorities' to back up his initial argument, including himself, he does not produce a single immediate reference to Durie's own words here. So, too, when Popkin speaks of Durie's doubts concerning Menasseh which he has obtained from Durie's *Tract on Admitting Jews to a Christian Commonwealth*, written when the Whitehall discussions were taking place, Popkin nevertheless maintains that Menasseh Ben Israel was not at all interested in millennial speculations until Durie encouraged him with great enthusiasm to think of the return of the Jews to the Holy

---

[299] Oldenburg's *Correspondence*, vol. iii, pp. 191-2.

Land and the relationship of the Jews to the Native Americans in conjunction with the Millennium. However, this idea is merely one of the very many arguments from 'may be' which cover Popkin's pages making it difficult to deduce what his view of Durie's relationship to millenarian thinking really is and what was his relationship to the Caraites.

By 1992, Popkin had dropped his opinion that Menasseh had received the idea of a Millennium from Durie and in his 'Jewish-Christian Relations in the Sixteenth and Seventeenth Centuries', he argues that Menasseh first became a believer in an imminent Millennium after the newly abdicated Christina of Sweden received Menasseh in her Belgium residence in 1654 and told him about the Millennium soon to come. Then Menasseh rushed to the home of Peter Serrarius to tell him that the coming of the Messiah was at hand. From thence, Menasseh journeyed to England to spread the new tidings there. Popkin tells his readers that if they take Durie's description in his appendix to Thorowgood's account to its logical conclusion, 'we will find a new role emerging for the Caraites as a judgement of the failings of the Jews.' Yet Popkin never clearly defines what this 'new role' is. Popkin argues that Durie gained his knowledge of the Caraites from Johann Stephanus Rittangel yet the letters of Morian and Comenius during 1641 and 1642 are full of complaints concerning Rittangel's bad temper and untoward behaviour and it is quite clear that Rittangel is not liked by the Durie-Hartlib circle. However, Morian says that Rittangel is one of the very few who could possibly make a good translator of Hebrew texts and that to get at that honey, one must accept a sting or two.

There is some obvious truth in Popkin's statements concerning Durie, the Caraites, Rittangel and millenarianism but not quite as he expresses it. Most other Jewish scholars portray Menasseh as a millenarian but more evidence is needed before assuming that Durie was the compelling influence behind Menasseh's eschatology. Durie was indeed very wary of the Rabbi's plans for the future of the Jews and especially how he wished for his own sect of the Jews to settle in England but not others. Durie wanted all Jews to be free to enter England which would not happen in a millennial apocalyptical 'twinkling' but only under strict, cautious and patient control over a period of time. As Popkin shows, Menasseh changed his views on the Millennium at least twice whereas, as Gibson demonstrates, Durie kept to the views he had worked out in his early years. Writing from Switzerland in January, 1656 under his pseudonym John Robertson as the French had put a price on his head, Durie told Hartlib:

> 'In the busines of receiuing the Iewes the state doth wisely to go warily & by degrees. Menasseh Ben Israel his demands are great, & the use which they

make of great priuiledges is not much to their commendation here & elsewhere: they haue wayes beyond all other men, to undermine a state, & to insinuate into those that are in offices & preiudge the trade of others, & therefore if they bee not wisely restrained they will in short time bee oppressiue, if they bee such as are here in Germany, to call in the Caraites would fright away these; for they are irreconcilable enemies: time must ripen these designes & Prudencie may lead them on.'[300]

Popkin seems to be arguing that it is principally the pro-Menasseh branch of the Jews, who were far from orthodox, whom Durie wanted to settle in England and not the Caraites. These would, because of their narrow keeping to the Pentateuch, alarm the pro-Menasseh Jews who would then stop settling in England. However, when reading all that Durie has to say about the Menassehites and the Caraites it would seem that he saw the latter as a corrective to the former, though they went to different extremes. It was not that he did not want the Caraites to settle in England, as Popkin presumes, but that he wanted all representatives of the Jews there but on peaceful terms with one another. Hartlib wrote to Worthington on 12 Dec. 1655, saying:

'This day is the great Meeting about the Jews, but I had rather hear the issue from your relations, than give it to you. I suppose our friends that are members of it will write freely & impartially of that business. I am for Mr. Borel's Judaical studies and undertaking and that the Caraites might be invited hither and encouraged, being such as begin to look towards their engraffing again.'[301]

What the Caraites claimed for the Pentateuch as alone authoritative in discerning matters of faith, Durie claimed for the entire Christian Bible. However, Durie accepted Jewish writings such as the Talmud and the Mishna as aids to interpretation whereas the Caraites totally rejected all other ancient Jewish writings and especially the Talmud. It was Durie's aim to collect the very writings which the Caraites rejected for common study for the educational benefit of both Jews and gentiles, linguistically, spiritually and practically.

This century has profited from a new introduction to Rittangel and the Caraites through Daniel J. Lasker's long essay (117 pages) in the *Renaissance Quarterly*[302] entitled 'Karaism and Christian Hebraism: A New

---

[300] Ref: 4/3/147A-B, HP.
[301] Worthington's Diary, vol. 1, p. 78, taken from HP.
[302] Vol. 59, 2006, pp. 1089-1116.

Document' which is a commentary on a transcribed and translated letter of Rittangel's in Hebrew to John Selden (1584-1654). Lasker, however, emphasises that Durie did not fancy working with Rittangel and the scanty reference Lasker gives relating Durie with the Caraites and Rittangel, taken from Turnbull and Webster (who influenced Popkin) does not indicate that Durie was dependent on Rittangel for his views of the Caraites. So, too, Lasker points out that the documents preserved in the Hartlib Papers, here Ref: 1/33/63A-B, contradict the information Rittangel gives Selden. Lasker also believes that Rittangel confused the Caraites with the Samaritans. Such a relationship, however, is commonly believed. Though Lasker does not prove that there is either a strong theological or ideological link between Durie and Rittangel, he nevertheless states, 'John Dury seems to have had less hope for the Rabbanite Jews of Western Europe, since, in light of his contacts with Rittangel, Dury's millenarian expectations were focused on the Karaites.' Thus, though using the same scanty evidence, Lasker comes to opposite conclusions to Popkin's, bringing us no further in analysing Durie's true position which was quite independent of extreme eschatological speculations.

Indeed, most 20 and 21st century writers on Durie's alleged millenarian enthusiastic views concerning the Jews rarely spell them out and even less often produce documentary evidence of any substantial weight. They also tend to refer uncritically to one another's writings to back up their commonly held theories, linking Durie with other campaigners under the common heading of 'Millenarians'. This appears to be for want of a more precise term, though Durie's ideas were markedly different from most others they place under this label. Thus a number of modern writers have taken it for granted that Durie was a Premillenialist if not a Dispensationalist without detailed examination of such claims. Durie was always too scholarly and practical to allow himself to roam into Chiliastic speculation where no grounds in practical, textual, studious exegesis were to be found.

Durie suffered all his life from those who were all too quick to label him through his association with others. This was especial the case in his honest, objective search for dialogue with all who disagreed with him. He found that as long as Christians discussed their problems with one another, there was no bar to fellowship. This did not mean he agreed with all his closest correspondents and even friends. He disagreed even with Hartlib on several issues, including Pansophy. Writing to Hartlib in 1661, Durie objects to the labels that the Dutch have given him by association, and accuses the Synods of South and North Holland of blocking peace negotiations between the Reformed and Lutherans. He is particular concerned with the complaint of his old friend, Johann Rulice that Durie cannot speak on behalf of pan-Protestantism as he has friends such as Serrarius and Boreel whom they suspect as being unorthodox on eschatology. Durie tells Hartlib:

> 'I told him that I had that authoritie by which hee counted himself a minister of the Gospell, & that if hee were a true Minister hee should doe in his place the same thing which I did towards all; & to satisfie him more fully I sent him a copie of the Epistolicall Discourses written to Mr Goodwyn & Mr Nye where in the Second Epistle I giue them an account of the Authoritie by which I act; since which time I haue found him Shye to meet with me, but yesterday I did discourse with him at his house familiarly of the affaires of England; & I belieue hee is gladde that I go into Germanie. as for the thing he blames me, for conversing with suspected persons Serrurier Boreel[303] &c. that is a part of the disease wherof I must endevour to cure him & some others, namely to let them see how they ought to Converse as Christians with others although there may bee some different opinions between us, & not to persecute men by politic power & practise without euer speaking to them or dealing with them to reclaime them. in a word all that which wee Condemne in others & Complaine ouer; is done here by our Synods & Combined parties against those whom they suspect. & thus wee are euery where ripe for a iudgment which Certainly the Lord will bring about & wee are here ripe for it.'[304]

Durie concludes that in spite of Rulice's recent aggression 'yet I am not the lesse his freind for that'.

In April, 2010, Kenneth Gibson of Derby University wrote a most informative account for the *Journal of Ecclesiastical History* (No. 2) entitled 'John Dury's Apocalyptic Thought: A Reassessment'. Gibson explains that in modern works anyone speaking about the 'Last Days' or universal reformation or a renewed and purified society is thought immediately to hold millenarian beliefs. This was not the case in the seventeenth century when theological terminology was more exact and a distinction was drawn between millenarian and non-millenarian views concerning the end of the world and how it was to be understood. This Aristotelian-like over-analysis of millennial views even caused new denominations to spring up all over England and the New World. Gibson is thus not exaggerating here as most of the modern works mentioned in this chapter, for want of a closer scrutiny of the seventeenth century situation, associate Durie's sound, objective

---

[303] See Durie's fine and lengthy pen-portrait of Boreel in Ref:1/6/11A-14B, HP.
[304] Ref: 4/4/36A-B, HP.

and practical convictions regarding the spread of knowledge with millenarian schools of thought to which he was a complete stranger. Nevertheless, for the benefit of universal learning, he was eager to study and document them. He wished to know what was going on in the world at large. Gibson thus argues for a more rigorous definition of millenarianism before examining any eschatology, apocalyptic or millenarian beliefs between, say, 1600 and 1647.

As a case in point Gibson deals especially with John Durie views. He quotes Richard Popkin as saying Durie 'was actually pursuing the millennium for at least fifty years.'[305] Gibson then argues concerning the Durie-Hartlib circle, including Joseph Mead (Mede), that the conclusions drawn from this association by such as Charles Webster and Richard Popkin who picked up many ideas from Webster, obscure more than clarify Durie's eschatological position.[306] He emphasises Howard Hotson's words in his *Paradise Postponed*, stating that 'we still lack careful accounts of the genesis of Hartlib and Dury's millenarianism' but nevertheless he still believes that both were indeed millenarians: but of what kind? In his own analysis of Durie's position, Gibson includes views which were not strictly speaking Durie's. For instance, he claims that Durie believed in the 'binary theory of the war between good and evil, ungodly people and godly people.[307] This was demonstrably not Durie's view as he taught that God had immediate access to the minds of all men and had prepared for their right education towards their common good. It was not a question of being good for the sake of being good or bad for the sake of being bad but of how far sinful man had a knowledge of God. Goodness was where God was at work in man. Gibson here merely refers to Peter Lake's references to William Bradshaw, concluding without evidence that Durie 'retained such a (black and white) view'. This does not mean that Durie took no notice of his brethren's prophecies. When reporting to State Secretary Thurloe in June 1655 from Amsterdam, Durie is speaking of Charles Adolf's wars and says:

> 'I thanke you very kindly for the things communicated, & if it may be should crave the continuance especially concerning the intentions to assist the poore Waldenses, & the certainty you have of the intention of the Swedes. I wish I were with you a day or two, to open my heart unto you

---

[305] Gibson, p. 301, Popkin's Third Force in Seventeenth Century Thought, Leiden, 1992, p. 95.
[306] John Dury's Apocalyptic Thought. p. 301.
[307] Ibid, p. 308.

concerning these times wee live in: The Peace of Germany I feare will be as Monsieur Bisterfeld one of the P. of Transylvania's privy Counsellours long agoe prophecied, for the sinnes (the causes of destroying plagues) continuing yea increasing in the highest degree. But doe you remember what Mr Mede hath prophecied hertofore, concerning the Swedish warre, that it should bee the destruction of the House of Austria, & of the Romane Empire?'[308]

Gibson explains how Durie refused to speculate as to which worldly powers were to be identified from Scriptural prophecies, claiming merely that all governments and religious bodies who have no rule or law apart from their own tyranny are 'the Dragon's Vice regents on earth.'[309] Though Durie obviously saw the Roman Catholic Church as apostate, he would not call their pope 'The Antichrist'. Far from speculating on the 'Last Day', he was more concerned about bringing peace to the churches and nations and educating a people who would be well-prepared when those days came. As, Gibson mentions on p.312, Durie was critical of the radical millenarianism of his day, saying in a letter to Hartlib from Zürich in December 1654, 'The Millenary men in due time God will beat off from extrauagancies & what I can Contribut shall not bee wanting if God giue life & leisure.' We note, too, that Hartlib criticises the Fifth Monarchy men in a letter to Worthington dated 10 March 1655-56 and points out that Amyrald has written to demonstrate the fallacies of the 'Millenaries' views which is looked on by many to be unanswerable.[310] In a letter written to Worthington dated 17 Dec. 1660, Hartlib demonstrates how learned and devoted Christians did not necessarily equate the conversion of the Jews with millenarian views. He writes:

> 'By the adjoined Letter of Mr. Borel's to Mr. Dury you will see how he methodizes the great affair of God's kingdom. The world may not expect any great happiness before the conversion of the Jews be first accomplished. But many tell me that Mr. Lightfoot can find no such truth revealed nor promised, either in the Holy records, or in any of the Jewish writers. Till it be known what grounds he doth alledge, we can oppose the authority of the late learned Dr. Ames, who professed to his dying day the conversion of the

---

[308] British Library Add. MSS 4365 ff. 3A-4B. Included in a volume of the Birch Papers, mainly relating to the Swiss Cantons (Add. 4365).
[309] Ibid, p. 309.
[310] *The Diary and Correspondence of Dr. John Worthington*, vol. I, Manchester, 1847, p. 79-84.

Jews to be a most liquid scriptural truth, but could not approve of any of the Millenary tenets.'[311]

Gibson, however, explains that Durie's school reforms were worked out as a social, educational and religious basis for people who would honour God and work for the common good of all mankind. Here, Gibson is one of the few modern writers to devote a few lines to the importance of Durie's Practical Divinity in understanding his major initiative and aims.[312] However, Gibson appears to agree with Joseph Minten Batten (whom he calls John Batten) in his dissertation reviewed above that Durie's Practical Divinity was more of a practical rather than scholastic importance. Perhaps there is a misunderstanding here. Durie used the term 'scholastic' in his works on Practical Divinity for 'scholarly' and he insisted that his aim was to educate good practical scholars so that they might be versed in universal learning.[313] Scholarship is, for Durie, part of the method of appropriating the good, here and now. Thus Chloë Houston can state in her Cromohs Virtual Seminary article 'Could "Eutopian politics (...) never be drawn into use?"[314] Utopianism and radicalism in the 1640s', that ' Dury not only called for institutional improvements to be undertaken, but published a variety of texts detailing exactly how they might be implemented.' She thus concludes 'For Dury the City of God is not only a spiritual idea, but one that can be fostered here and now.'[315]

Turning to Durie's Foreword to the *Clavis apocalyptica*, Gibson makes a statement essential to a right understanding of Durie. He claims that Durie was merely presenting the work as a librarian would comment on a new book put in the library. This is quite evident from the German version of Durie's preface preserved in the Hartlib Papers where Durie does not go into the speculations of the book but says soberly that it can be used as a platform for further study and comment. That this was often the method of Hartlib and Durie is clear from their remarks in *Ephemerides* and Durie's co-authorship with Thorowgood. In this joint work, Durie claimed he was giving his material as he had received it merely for the wider needs of the debate going on and to interest people in supporting John Elliot's work amongst the Native Americans. Gibson sees Mead's influence on the

---

[311] *The Diary and Correspondence of Dr. John Worthington*, vol. XIII, Manchester, 1847, p. 250.
[312] Ibid, p. 303.
[313] Ibid, 304.
[314] Houston is using a truncated quote from from Milton's *Areopagitica*.
[315] See Houston's lecture, pp. 6-7.

Clavis apocalyptica but Mead certainly did not agree with the methods of dating stated in it. Because of Durie's connection with the work, a number of authors argue that Durie believed that the Millennium would come in 1655, others, like Edward Lane told Durie that because he had written such a Preface, 'Seducers haue deriued somewhat from your Epistolicall Discourse to Foment their Errours, & doe make it their Boast that you doe fully agree with them in their Opinion concerning the Nullitie of a Visible Church in these times, and withall I declared how my Spirit was troubled within mee that your Name should bee made vse of in the carrying on of so pernicious a Tenet, fearing too as I afterwards told you that you had giuen too iust an Occasion vnto them to Triumph as they doe'.[316] It is clear from Durie's correspondence with Lane that Durie had misgivings about writing the Preface as he would not write off the idea of a visible church and sincerely believed that there was still leaven in the churches waiting to rise.

Joseph Mead[317] is often cited to prove that Durie was a Chiliast of the Premillennial type. In his *The Effect of Master Dury's Negotiations for the uniting of Protestants in a Gospel Interest*,[318] Samuel Hartlib places Mead with Daniel Featley as 'the best of the Prelatical men' close to Durie, dealing with him in the section 1628 to 1641 and we can count Mead as a close associate of the Durie-Hartlib circle at this time. Mead is said to be the father of the synchronism method of interpreting Revelation. The events recorded after the blowing of the trumpet beginning at Rev. 1:10 then Rev. 4:1 and then Rev. 10:8 all refer to the passage of one period of time seen from various aspects, according to Mead. Thus, instead of a continuous timeline going all through the book, Mead sees a set period of time up to the end of time which runs in consecutive accounts to be taken as different aspects and viewpoints of the same events.[319] Though Mead has been called a Premillennialist, his methods are more used today by Post and Amillennialists to describe their eschatologies. This is witnessed by Amillennialist William Hendriksen in his 1939 work, *More than Conquerors: An Interpretation of the Book of Revelation*, still in print, which divides Revelation onwards into seven blocks which are to be interpreted as 'recapitulations'. Mead, however, preferred the three-fold method of Scriptural

---

[316] Letter from Edward Lane dated Aug. 26 1651, Ref: Ref: 1/32/7A-22B: 7B, 22A-B.

[317] See my Joseph Mead: Cloistered Cleric of International Fame, *New Focus*, April/May, 2011, vol. 15, No. 06, pp. 16-20.

[318] Undated (last date mentioned 1657), Ref: 14/2/1A-6B, HP.

[319] This is explained in Robert Clouse's, The Apocalyptical Interpretation of Thomas Brightman and Joseph Mede.'

interpretation, taught also by Durie, of viewing the Book of Revelation literally, rationally and spiritually. Hendriksen's interpretations were decidedly allegorical, a form of interpretation Mead very rarely used.

Mead campaigned for reforms in the Church of England with his colleagues Ussher, Bidell, Hall, Davenant, Morton, Featley and Durie. When going through his vast post, he always read correspondence to do with Durie's progress first before going on 'to others of lower rank'.[320] He was disappointed that the Church of England did not give Durie more ecclesiastical and educational backing. He said of Laud's modest support of Durie in his life-long work for Christian unity:

> 'It grieves me not a little, yea perplexes me, to hear that Mr. Dury is come off with no better success from my L. -- I am loth *malè augurari*, but I like it not. I fear it is *mali ominis*, and that our State and Church have no mind to put their hand to this Work: *Deus avertat omen*. But our Church you know, goes upon differing Principles from the rest of the Reformed, and so steers her course by another Rule than they do. We look after the Form, Rites and Discipline of Antiquity, and endeavour to bring our own as near as we can to that Pattern. We suppose the Reformed Churches have departed farther therefrom than needed, and so we are not very solicitous to comply with them; yea we are jealous of such of our own as we see over-zealously addicted to them, lest it be a sign they prefer them before their Mother. This, I suppose, you have observed, and that this disposition in our Church is of late very much increased. Well then; If this Union sought after be like to further and advantage us in the way we affect, we shall listen to it. If it be like to be prejudicial, as namely to give strength and authority to those amongst us who are enamour'd with the foreign Platform, or bring a yoke upon our own by limiting and making us obnoxious; we'l stand aloof and not meddle with it, lest we infringe our liberty. This I have always feared would be no small Remora on our part; and I pray God it may fall out beyond my expectation.'[321]

Mead refused to accept the nigh-occult future speculations of many Puritans. Few in the middle of the seventeenth century could escape the impact of astronomy into the Christian faith, especially after William Lilly produced his best-selling *Christian Astrologer*. Reformed university Professors, for instance, demanded the day and the hour of their students' births so they could work out their horoscopes. As Melanchthon, they started the day by consulting the constellations and sects arose which combined the

---

[320] John Worthington's *Works of Joseph Mede*, 4th Ed., Book IV, pp. 868-70.
[321] Ibid, 4th Ed., Book IV, pp. 865-6.

language of Sion with the spells of Nostradamus. Female dissenting clergy skilled in dukkerin pestered the 1653 Saints' Parliament with prophetic petitions signed by over 6,000 sisters and ex-Leveller John Cadbury consulted the planets for the Royalists whilst William Lilly star-gazed for the Republicans. In many ways, the Civil War was a Star War.

Mead condemned the general occult astrological political and religious visions and visionaries of his day. Accepting that the heavens, climate and seasons could affect the moods, manners and character of man, he denied that they could predict a person's future; a prerogative of God's alone. Nevertheless, he diligently studied the Book of Revelation, chiefly because there were so many current Jesuit theories concerning it which were helping the Roman Catholics to divide and rule the British Babel of Protestant split-offs. Thus Mead told the early Methodist Perfectionists that it was idle talk to say that the Devil was bound in past history during Constantine's reign and had lost his power. He will be bound when the Lord comes and we shall sin no more. He also rejected the ancient postulate that the resurrection was merely a metaphor to be spiritualised as per Brightman's commentary on Revelation. Mead stressed that Christ rose physically from the dead and we shall likewise follow Him. Such doubters always cut out huge passages of the Bible, claimed Mead. Nor did Mead believe in judaising Christianity as many of his Premillennialist colleagues did. He rejected the Parenthesis Theory outright whereby the Jews are replaced for a season by the gentiles but when Jesus comes they will all suddenly be converted 'by sight' and all will reign with Him for a thousand years. Mead says that the Apocalypse is a prophecy given to the universal church during the time of the gentiles and thus the final Catholic Church will produce a harvest mainly from the more numerous Gentile stock. Of all the redeemed, Jews will remain a minority. He also rejected the Hyper-Premillennialist teaching of two millenniums with two future Advents of Christ. The Vice-Chancellor of Cambridge, John Worthington, who had studied under Mead and became his biographer and collector of his letters, was also a close contact and correspondent of the Durie-Hartlib circle.[322] Writing in 1661, Worthington, told Hartlib, whilst complaining of Tongue's eschatology, 'I have seen none since Mr. Mede's *Clavis Apocalyptica*, that hath brought forth to the world what hath been much observable, but what has been lighted at his flame.'[323]

---

[322] See especially Mede's letter to Hartlib dated April 16 1638 in Worthington, Book IV, p. 880.

[323] '*The Diary and Correspondence of Dr. John Worthington*' ed. J. Crossley. Vol. II. Part I. (Chetham Society Vol. XXXVI: Manchester, 1855). pp. 68-71 and HP.

Gibson closes with Richard Popkin's remark concerning Durie's *Touchant l'intelligence* that Durie became dispirited at the end of his life and so gave up his 'activist millenarianism'. As Gibson rightly points out, Durie's views displayed in this work are identical with the views he had been maintaining since the 1630s. Gibson's well-founded remarks may be compared with Leube's unfounded, opposite thoughts aired above that in his old age, when Durie had failed in his life's work of promoting peace amongst the churches, he fell into eschatological fantasies.

CHAPTER SIX

Discovering the Advantages of Universal Learning

Filling the earth with true knowledge

After editors Ruth Rouse and Stephen Charles Neill published their one-volume *History of the Ecumenical Movement 1517-1948* in 1954, a need was immediately felt for a German translation which would also include a more detailed analysis of the ecumenical work done on the European Continent during the 17th and 18th centuries. This conviction gave rise to a two-volume edition, *Die Geschichte der Ökumenischen Bewegung,* published in 1957. For this version, Martin Schmidt worked over and extended his English contribution presenting John Durie in a fuller and more accurate light. After dealing with ecumenical ideas, he moved to ecumenical action, starting with the section *John Durys Lebenswerk im Dienste ökumenischen Handelns*. His opening words are:

> 'John Dury (1595-1680) bietet das einmalige Beispiel eines Lebens, das keinen anderen Inhalt kennt als die Befriedigung und Einigung der Christenheit. Auch bei den leidenschaftlichen Verfechtern des gleichen Zieles, bei Grotius, Jablonski und Leibniz, auch bei einem bewußt darauf hinarbeitenden Gelehrten wie Calixt füllen noch andere Aufgaben den Tag – Dury kannte nur sie.'

In this evaluation, Schmidt has obviously projected his own single, deep interest in the Ecumenical movement onto one branch only of Durie's lifework, thus making a statement which is at best a half truth and at worst a misrepresentation of Durie's major aim in life. Those who have tackled multi-tasking Durie on a host of other individual subjects have made similar mistakes. As Durie was so versatile and comprehensive in his writings, we find literally scores of works on special Durie studies in numerous branches of knowledge which present him as the ecumenist, the educator, the theologian, the politician, the linguist, the diplomat, the social reformer, the scientist and the man of letters. Actually, Durie turned to working for peace within the churches as a practical means of forming a basis for his educational plans to reform society through pansophical and world-wide organised learning. He believed however, that it was no use introducing unity in godly learning where godless chaos existed. He thus decided that the churches must be reformed before society in general could follow their leadership.

Durie's success in ecumenical activities

Having said this, the great ecumenical success Durie had in England for a time and on the Continent for probably all time must be admitted and stressed. The biographical section in Chapter Two has served to emphasise this.

Charles Augustus Briggs,[324] who was noted in Chapter Three, one of the USA's pioneers in the history of the ecumenical movement, was a Professor at Union Theological Seminary in New York from 1874 to 1913. He was a leading authority on the history of the Westminster Assembly and called 'the most prominent figure' in the fierce theological controversies of the day. The irenist was acquitted of the charge of heresy by his Presbytery in January 1893 but, nevertheless, the General Assembly in March of the same year, condemned him as a heretic and removed him from his ministry in the Presbyterian Church for holding views similar to Durie's, who, we remember, was also removed from his English and German ministries, because his time had not yet come. Biggs was found guilty of questioning the Westminster Standards, which he believed had become the Presbyterians' Bible. He supported Durie's ideals and gave much of his energy to the reunion of Christendom as a basis for the further welfare and advancement of mankind. Biggs triumphed over all opposition and subsequently was given the chair of Irenics at his Seminary, using Durie's work to express his ideals and aims.[325] Of Durie, he said:

> 'John Durie died without seeing the fruit of his lifelong labors, but he did not live and work in vain. Like Richard Baxter, James Ussher, and John Davenant, he was a prophet of a better age of the world. He was sowing the seed and preparing the germs of Christian toleration, liberty, and union that have

---

[324] See *Cambridge History of English and American Literature*, vol XVI, §4, 1907-21.
[325] *The Cambridge History of English and American Literature* in 18 Volumes (1907–21). VOLUME XVII. Later National Literature, Part II, XVI Later Theology, §4. Charles Augustus Briggs.

unfolded in later times and are still unfolding with rich blessings for our time and richer promises for the future.'[326]

Briggs is speaking here with the bulk of writers on Durie listed in Chapters Three and Four. There is thus no doubt, judging by the many scholars who have testified to this with cast iron proofs, that Durie was the leading irenist of his age whose influence has been strongly felt since the seventeenth century. First of all, we must ask, after centuries of irenic work between the Protestant churches, if such a union is now possible or merely a reverie of a too idealistic mind? Developments since the 17th century have shown that Protestant amalgamation has looked like the Alchemist's attempt to make diamonds out of stones. However, it is now possible through detonation synthesis, and other syntheses with the right pressure and temperature, to create diamonds harder than the 'original' product. It is all, just as in Durie's irenic plans, a matter of methodology and, as Durie also realised, a question of finance. Many attempts have been made to 'reunite Protestants' but have failed because they were under the 'süße Wahn' that Protestants were once united, which, of course, they never were. Indeed, attempts at any kind of union such as the Synod of Dort, the Westminster Assembly and the modern Ecumenical Movement have demonstrably produced stronger divisions than those previously existing. The way the Synod of Dort turned former Reformed brethren into 'heretics' to be stamped out and their church buildings pulled down is a case in point. The Westminster Confession could only be built on the ruins of an outlawed Reformed Episcopalian Church, though that church was based soundly on the Book of Common Prayer and the Thirty-Nine, Irish and Lambeth Articles. However, though Independents and Congregationalists have had some success in Britain, the Reformed Church of England and the Presbyterian churches are as far from each other today as they were in the years before Pride's Purge. Nevertheless, there have been strong attempts made at church unity internationally amongst Protestants, especially in Scandinavia, Poland, Holland and France and in several East European Churches before, after and in spite of Communist regulations. Germany, the centre of Durie' main activities, has perhaps gone further than any other European State in seeking for Protestant peace. Switzerland cannot be counted here as most of her Protestant churches were 'Reformed' from the start and there were very few Lutherans to fall out with.

---

[326] The Work of John Durie in Behalf of Christian Union in the Seventeenth Century VII pp. 297-309, *The Presbyterian Review*, No, 30, April 187.

Traditionally, not even the Reformed churches had any formal church unity as they were split by their various histories and different forms of government. The Lutherans were at sixes and sevens concerning doctrine, order and discipline throughout the seventeenth century as the rivalries between Saxony and Sweden illustrate and Johann Georg's campaigns in Bohemia. Added to the divisions of the strict Gnesio-Lutherans and the Philippites were the Helmstedites or those Lutherans who rejected the *Book of Concord* and each tiny dukedom had a different form of church oversight, often purely secular. After the Peace of Augsburg, the faith of the people was determined by the authority of the nobility who, at times, but by no means always, put political convenience and personal gain before religion. Even amongst thorough-going, genuine Lutherans like Paul Gerhardt, there were those who signed the *Augustana Invariata* and those who agreed only to the *Variata* and those who signed the entire *Formula Concordia*. Some signed only one document, others two, some all. Durie gave over fifty years of his life to solving these problems.

Because of this, the Protestant churches of the German Federal Republic can now be regarded as major role-players in a success story because that country has made enormous progress in the integration of Protestant churches which certainly can be traced back to the initial influence of men like Paraeus, Calix and their inter-state and international coordinator, John Durie in whose days tradition and political history had made them Lutheran, Bullingerite, Bucerite or Calvinistic. However, though all the German federal states have benefitted more or less from such unions, the amalgamation of Lutherans and Reformed churches in the former territories now called North-Rhine-Westphalia, this writer's home state, serves as a special example of successful influence through the policies of Durie and those who followed him.

North-Rhine-Westphalia (NRW), is a modern combination of most of Westphalia and part of the Rhine area,[327] and has seen different forms of unity between the Reformed and Lutheranism since Durie's days, albeit marred by political and military upheavals, especially in the wake of the two World Wars. There are now, however, more union churches than old-type Lutheran or old-type Reformed churches in the federal state. One of the pioneers in this direction was Frederik William (1620-1688), Landgrave of Brandenburg and Duke of Cleves who had occasionally given Durie an unready ear when it did not suit his politics but at other times was most eager to cooperate with him. Wishing to combat the spread of the Jesuits on the Western border of his kingdom in 1655, the Landgrave

---

[327] Rheinland.

Discovering the Advantages of Universal Learning 213

founded Duisburg University, which he placed under the oversight of the clergy at Cleves, so that Protestant ministers could be educated there. This is why, as soon as Durie heard of the university's founding, he visited Cleves and Duisburg and won the cities and university for the cause of Protestant union. Duisburg was the first German city to celebrate the Lord's Supper in the Reformed manner due to the many English, Dutch and Belgian Reformers who had sought asylum in the city when forced into exile by Mary the Bloody of England. From Duisburg, they branched off into Wesel, Emden, Frankfurt, Strassburg and Aarau.[328] Durie could build on this international background.

Lasting plans for the modern union were drawn up in 1817 with at least three members of the Krummacher family, well-known in the English-speaking world, playing an important part. Frederick William Krummacher, who did much for church union in present North Rhine Westphalia, was brought up near Duisburg[329] where his father Frederick Adolf (1767-1845) was Professor of Theology. Frederick William tells in his autobiography how much his father was imbibed with the spirit of the Great Brandenburg Elector and the Prussian Eagle who fell to the Gallican birds of prey in the Napoleonic Wars.

True to strong Scottish influence in NRW since Durie's pioneer activities, the first General Superintendent of the churches in former Rhineland and Westphalia was William John Gottfried Ross, an offspring of Scottish seventeenth century refugees like Durie. The Ross family, however, had commuted between Scotland and Germany ever since the Middle Ages. Ross studied at Duisburg, after which he pastored a unionist church on the Lower Rhine and became famed for his preaching, educational work and for his orphanage. This came to the ears of the Prussian King William III and his chaplains and in 1835, Ross was invited to Berlin by the King to discuss his work. Ross' cousin, John Ross, had already been made a Count for saving the King's life at the Vienna Congress and William John was also offered such a title, but he refused it. The year after, Ross was made the first unionist General Superintendent of Westphalia and the Rhinelands. William III's successor, William IV was not of the same persuasions and Ross was compelled to resign his post and retired back to his pastorate at Budberg. On his gravestone in the church cemetery, we find 2 Corinthians 1:24 inscribed with true Protestant unionist spirit: 'Not for that we have dominion over your faith, but are helpers of your joy: for by faith ye stand.' Thomas Alfred Fischer, a German who settled in Edinburgh and

---

[328] See my *Troublemakers in Frankfurt*, 2003 for the history of this phenomenon.
[329] Born in Moers 1796. Died 1868.

wrote his *The Scots in Germany* in 1902, notes how on August 31st, 1647, that is when rumours of union with the Lutherans were rife, the Moderator of the Scottish Assembly, an enemy of religious toleration, Robert Douglas, wrote to the Scots in Germany, reminding them to stick to their Presbyterian heritage and not 'compromise'. He could use this authority as the Douglas family had played a prominent part in German trade and finances for centuries. It was a Douglas who represented Britain at the famous International Diet of Frankfurt in May-August, 1634 to discuss a common Protestant policy for Europe. Durie had hoped that Sir Thomas Roe, who had pioneered Britain's diplomatic work in India and Asia and was at times as much a missionary as he was a statesman, would have been chosen for the post.

The Protestants of Westphalia and the Rhinelands now supported nation-wide cooperation. Friedrich von Bodelschwingh was elected Reichsbischof by the 28 state churches in 1933 but quickly deposed for opposing Hitler's inhuman policies. Hitler then founded his 'Deutsche Christen' on strict party lines which the Bekennender Kirche opposed, campaigning for a more traditionally Christian view as stated in the Barmer Erklärung of 1934. After the Nazi period, the political division of Germany hindered pan-German inter-church cooperation but the Western churches allied under the mantle of the Evangelische Kirche Deutschland (EKD) with the Eastern churches joining after Germany's reunion. Over a million individual EKD and Free Church members have joined the Evangelische Allianz Deutschland.

Scottish influence was still present in Germany when on August 23rd, 1946 the solid Protestant districts of Westphalia and the Rhinelands were broken up and parts were joined together and new borders were drawn under the name of North-Rhine-Westphalia (Nord-Rhein-Westfalen) by the Scottish Military Governor representing the British occupying forces. His name was Air Chief Marshal Sir Sholto Douglas, kinsman and clansman of the above named Robert Douglas'.[330] He called his action 'Operation Marriage'. For this and other services he was made First Baron Douglas of Kirtleside, Dumfries.

The post-war EKD, (Evangelische Kirche Deutschland), an alliance of Lutherans and Reformed, was brought into being by men such as Theophil Wurm, Martin Niemöller and the strongly evangelical Gustav Heinemann, who later became Federal Germany's national President. Again the EKD

---

[330] Regulation 46 (Verordnung 46.) covering this celebrated the occasion as being a 'marriage contract'. The newspapers referred to it dramatically as a 'shot-gun marriage'.

was pioneered in Westphalia and the Rhinelands shortly before Baron Douglas 'married' the two districts. The editor of the main Berlin Evangelical newspaper *Die Kirche*, wrote last year (2010) to tell this author that she had placed a copy of his paper on the irenic policies of Reformer Henry Bullinger, Zürich, towards the British and German churches on the desk of each member at the latest synodal meeting. The EKD still lives in the spirit of John Durie. Happily, Durie's influence is not limited to being but a pioneer at the start of one state church enterprise. This can be equally paralleled, as this thesis has shown, all over Germany.

Durie's early contact with universal learning

Having established Durie's success in fostering inter-church cooperation, this was but a necessary step before going on to a far wider work. Durie's aim was not to diversify himself or knowledge in the many special areas in which he excelled, but to consolidate all and unify all, merging all the supposed varied factors, ecumenical, political, social, theological, educational, scientific and moral in the observed world around him. Such a method, he believed, would help restore edenic structures in the fallen world which sin, banishment from Eden and Babel's confusion had created. Like Englishman William Cowper (1731-1800):[331] Germans Johan Georg Hamann (1730-1788)[332] and Johann Gottfried Herder (1744-1818:[333] and Dutch Willem Bilderdyke (1756-1831),[334] Scotsman Durie wished to trace all language and learning back to its original roots. However, the above mentioned writers and poets aired their views in the century following Durie and did not base them on the Scotsman's all-embracing view of Pansophy.

Starting with the basic conviction found in Romans 16:27 that all knowledge (Pansophism) is found in 'God only wise', Durie's Christian, irenic and educational target was the fulfilment of Isaiah's prophecy, 'They shall not hurt nor destroy in all my holy mountain: for the earth shall be full of the knowledge of the Lord, as the waters cover the sea.'[335] Nor was this a lone idea of Durie's as almost the entire Puritan movement, whether Anglican, Presbyterian, Independent or Baptist, at this period of troubled

---

[331] See my Dr. Phil. thesis *Paradise and Poetry: An In-Depth Study of William Cowper's Poetic Mind* for Cowper on language and learning.

[332] See his Aesthetica in Nuce, Kreutzüge der Philologen and Konxompax, Metakritik über den Purismum der Vernunft.

[333] See his Abhandlung über den Ursprung der Sprache and Kritische Wälder, oder Betrachtungen die Wissenschaft und Kunst des Schönen Betreffend.

[334] See his essay-poem *Der Ondergang der Eerste Wareld*.

[335] Chapter 11:9.

British history were talking about the Puritan Hope and the Restitution of All Things.[336] Men like Davenant, Hall, Morten, Owen, Jessey, Comenius, Matthiae, Thomas Goodwin and especially Joseph Mead and Oliver Cromwell, besides Durie, sincerely felt that prophecy was being realised in their day and age. They believed that knowing the mind of God in all things was a most viable and necessary preparation for improving man's state before God's Kingdom was set up and perfected once again on the earth, making it ready for heaven. This had also been the vision of previous generations of Reformers and thinkers such as Tyndall, Hutchinson, Bradford, Nowell, Bullinger and Bacon who saw God working His purpose out in His covenant agreement with His Son to restore all things. But first, we must see how Durie came to combine a reunification of the churches as part and parcel of his endeavours to revolutionise human learning.

Durie gained his first experience of universal learning as a young refugee of six or seven years of age.[337] He was compelled by his situation to go through schooling and university work in three or four different countries, early gaining a command of English, Latin, French, Dutch, German, Hebrew and Greek. A precocious child, he matriculated at the age of twelve at Leyden University and after long intensive and varied studies, he began his occupational life as a lecturer and private tutor in France. Thereafter, the scanty records show that he accompanied his near relation Sir James Spens on diplomatic missions, serving as a scribe and translator and ministered in a French-speaking church in Cologne for two years or so. After around 1624/5, he worked as a 'lecturer' in a Merchant Adventurers' church[338] in Elbing, Prussia. It was in Elbing that Durie commenced writing on education, probably based on his own experience as a teacher in France as he wrote that he had no one to teach him. During this time, Durie took up the then seldom used term *Practical Divinity* to express his ideas of Universal Learning. This led to his friend and colleague Samuel Hartlib (c.1600-1662), who was, until his death, Durie's right hand man and agent, leaving Elbing around 1627-8 to found Chelsea College and other educational projects in England which could work on principles devised by Durie. By the time Durie moved to England for a brief period in 1630,[339] Hartlib had won

---

[336] See Iain Murray's excellent volume on this topic *The Puritan Hope*, BOT, Edinburgh, 1975.
[337] See discussion concerning Durie's date of birth at the beginning of Chapter Two.
[338] Durie only called himself *Verbi Dei Minister* after his Church of England ordination in 1634.
[339] Schmidt gives 1636 incorrectly as the date in the English edition, p. 98. Durie visited Sweden in 1636.

over a large circle of clergymen, educators, scientists, politicians and men of letters to their side.

An extract of a letter is preserved in the Hartlib Papers which Durie wrote to Hartlib from Elbing in November 1628, telling his friend of the difficulties he is facing in putting his ideas of educational reform onto paper. He confesses:

> 'As for Pædagogicall affaires they have hitherto taken vp all my spare houres for I am almost entred into a Labirinth seeking to enter into a particular consideracion of the whole duty of a Tutour how hee ought to bee fitted & prepared for the Charge & what hee ought to doe to leade a Child from his infancy as it were by the hand through an insensible Custome of well doeing vnto a perfect degree of all vertues I did allmost loose my selfe in the variety of things that did offer themselves to bee considered & therefore was forced to breake off in the midst & to gather the generall heads of the whole Pædagogicall care that I might have a filum Ariadnes to order my thoughts This generall meditacion is here sent vnto you . . . . This particular Treatise as you may see is neere halfe done wherin first I shew the difference of a christian & naturall direccion of manners then I set downe the summe of a naturall Ethicke then I begin to shew what prudency & care a Tutour must vse to move little Children that are vncapable of the Precepts of Christianity to a Custome of naturall vertues of this I make 2 parts viz. the care to judge of the persons & accions of Children & the care to order all by way of Correccion & direccion Concerning the judgment of persons that is done & that which doth belong to the judgment of actions is onely begun & besides the intricatenes of the meditacion wherein I have noe helpe of any Authour.'[340]

Here, Durie is obviously envisaging something quite new in education whereby the 'whole duty' of a teacher is required in leading a child through 'well-doing unto a perfect degree of all vertues' and he himself is amazed at all the particulars this entails whilst 'gathering the heads of the whole Paedagogicall care'. However, Durie finds the going hard because he knows no educational authors who could help him in his pioneering work. Of special note here is Durie's use of the term *Filum Ariadnes* in his endeavours to lead his pupils through the Labyrinth of knowledge. Ariadne, daughter of King Minos of Crete had fallen in love with Theseus of Athens and given him a thread to unwind secretly through the labyrinth when led as a sacrificial victim to the Minotaur. Theseus managed to kill the brute and escaped back through the labyrinth by following the thread. Durie modified this 'thread' theory to make it a *Filum Meditandi* method of study

---

[340] Ref: 1/12/1A-4B, HP.<^^1

linking the various parts of the 'labyrinth' of knowledge together, thus gaining an overview of the entire construction.

Ideas of a *Filum Ariadnes* and a *Filum Meditandi* in epistemology and education are with us to stay. These terms, or rather ideas, have become part of the standard thought process in modern communication science, knowledge engineering, telecommunications and electronic publishing. Hewlett Packard researchers John Tillinghast and Giordano Beretta explain what a modern *Filum Ariadnes* entails:

> 'The skill of grasping a large body of information has always been an important one in human societies, from storytelling in the pre-historic ages, to Gottfried Leibniz[341] in the modern ages. Leibniz — the inventor of scientific journals — described the value of being able to find a linear order in a set of information and creating knowledge in the form of a linear thread, which he called filum Ariadnes. More recently, Vannevar Bush has expanded on these ideas and described how a number of threads can be combined in a graph, building the foundation for hypertext systems. Finally, Ikujiro Nonaka has brilliantly exposed the spiral from tacit knowledge to explicit knowledge and again to tacit knowledge, showing how difficult but important the step from an intuitive form of justified true belief is towards knowledge that can be expressed and communicated. Our quest is for tools that can help users in performing this step.'[342]

Nonaka's way of expressing the step from 'an intuitive form of justified true belief towards knowledge that can be expressed and communicated', was the very method Durie used in his teaching on text analysis and takes the words almost directly out of Durie's mouth. Philippe Godognet of Paris University in his undated web article *The Semiotics of the Web* also links *filum Ariadnes* with Leibniz' theory of epistemology, claiming he defined the term as 'a perfect knowledge of the principle of all sciences and the art of applying them'. However, neither of these authors gives the source of Leibniz' alleged statements.

These writers appear to believe that the idea of a logical *filum Ariadnes*, helping to find a guiding line through the labyrinth of all knowledge, originated with Leibniz, though the idea is as old as the original story itself. It

---

[341] Gottfried Wilhelm Leibniz (1646-1716). See *Studia leibnitiana Supplementa: Leibniz' Auseinandersetzung mit Vorgängern und Zeitgenossen*, ed. by Ingrid Marchewitz & Albert Heinekamp, Stuttgart: Franz Steiner Verlag, 1990, pp. 277-312.

[342] *Structure and navigation for electronic publishing*, John Tillinghast, Giordano Beretta, Computer Peripherals Laboratory HPL–97–162, December 1997.

was especially a vogue term in logic, theology, alchemy and chemistry towards the end of the seventeenth century. Durie, however used the terms in his very special, novel way in the early seventeenth century. It is thus interesting to note that Leibniz applies his *filum Ariadnes*, *filum meditandi* and *filum cogitandi* in the sense Durie used forty years before him. This was quite different to the way other correspondents and mentors of Leibniz such as Comenius used the term. Leibniz worked out his ideas of the different threads of learning to help formulate his epistemological theories between 1668 and 1675, whereas Durie had used the term with even wider educational connotations than Leibniz in the sense of discovering and applying a key to universal knowledge, knowledge organisation and management since the sixteen-twenties. Nevertheless such scholars as Witold Marciszewski in his *Two Leibniz' Legacies and their Implications Regarding Knowledge Engineering*,[343] feel that this is a pioneer discovery of Leibniz' alone.

Reference was made in Chapter VII to Martin Schmidt's citing of Jablonski and Leibniz as having similar aims to Durie and it must tempt the student of Durie to ask what connections might be found. It soon becomes clear that Leibniz circle of friends, colleagues and correspondents overlapped with Durie's and, as Leibniz neither coined such terms as *filum Ariadnes* and *filum meditandi*, nor filled them with a radical new meaning, it is thus not wild speculation to consider the possibilities of Leibniz having been influenced by the Durie-Hartlib Circle, the English Invisible Society and the Royal Society, all organisations springing up from Durie's, and his close associates such as Robert Boyle's and Theodor Haak's, work.

Henry Oldenburg, Daniel Ernst Jablonski, Gottfried Wilhelm von Leibniz and John Durie's legacy

Though writers in such inter-church magazines as *The Ecumenical Review* and the *Journal of Ecumenical Studies* tend to see Leibniz as the great ecumenical pioneer in Germany, Durie is, nevertheless, being linked with him more and more as his forerunner and even mentor. Not only Protestant writers but also Roman Catholic and Greek Orthodox writers now see Durie as a pioneer of the modern international ecumenical movement. Vladimir Kharlamov in his article 'Vatican II on Ecumenism and the Eastern Orthodox Church' writes:

---

[343] http//www.calculemus.org/MathUniversalis/2/marcisz/leibniz.html.

'In the seventeenth and eighteenth centuries, we see no official church-to-church attempts to search for unity. Instead, ecumenical witness was initiated by some individuals such as John Amos Comenius, who developed a plan for union among Protestants that was based upon scripture as a ground for all doctrine and state structure as well as the integration of all human culture. Others, such as John Dury and Richard Baxter in England, George Calixtus in Germany, and Nicholas von Zinzendorf in Moravia, also attempted to unify some Protestant denominations. Gottfried Leibniz made a great effort to reconcile Protestants and Roman Catholics. Even in Russia in the nineteenth century, Metropolitan Philaret of Moscow and Russian Orthodox theologian Aleksey Khomyakov expressed enthusiasm for Christian unity. However, all these attempts accomplished nothing of significance.'[344]

Markku Roinila in *The Reunion of the Churches*, an essay on Leibniz' contribution to ecumenism starts by discussing irenic pioneers in Germany who preceded Leibniz. Of these, he writes:

'The Thirty-years-war gave a new burst to the enterprises of church reunion. Hugo Grotius failed completely in his undertaking, but others, like the English John Dury, Baron von Boineburg, Landgrave Hessen-Rheinfels, the solicitor Herman Conring and the theologian George Calixtus (who was part of the Helmstad syncretist school), were not discouraged. In Germany the ecumenical movement flourished – surprisingly? – in Mainz and in Hanover, where Leibniz was active. The movement had had some substantial projects, like the ecumenical congress in Poland in 1645'.[345]

There are several clear links between Durie and Leibniz. The major ones are through Durie's secretaries, Henry Oldenburg and Peter Figulus-Jablonski. Oldenburg (1618-1677) was born in Bremen, Germany, the son of a teacher who later became a Professor at Dorpat University. Oldenburg studied Theology before spending a number of years in England tutoring noblemen's children. On his return to Bremen, he was sent back to England to represent Bremen in the city's transactions with Cromwell concerning Sweden's intervention in Northern Germany. In England, Oldenburg became a member of Durie's circle and, according to Christopher Hill,[346] subsequently became Durie's personal secretary. He worked closely with Durie on theories of learning and pan-education. He also played a major role in looking after the Hartlib-Durie circles foreign correspondence from

---

[344] *Journal of Ecumenical Studies*, 2001.
[345] www.helsinki.fi/~mroinila/reunion.html
[346] *Intellectual Origins of the English Revolution Revisited*, p. 96. Hill gives three secondary sources to substantiate his claim but no primary sources.

around 1652 and archiving their scientific, educational and theological documents. Indeed, as the circle gradually developed through the so-called Invisible Society into the Royal Society, Oldenburg stayed on as its secretary, and became the founder editor of the *Philosophical Transactions of the Royal Society*. Thus, in spite of what Tillinghast and Beretta say concerning Leibniz being the father of scientific journals, such can be found seminally in the publications of the so-called Invisible Society which bore fruit in the pioneer work of Oldenburg in that field. The *Philosophical Transactions of the Royal Society* was established as a journal in 1665, so this makes Oldenburg's publication the oldest scientific journal in the world, not Leibniz'. Here, too, we may mention the information presented by the Herzog August Bibliothek on their website (http:www.hab.de) in which they claim:

> 'Die bedeutendsten Bibliothekare in Wolfenbüttel waren Gottfried Wilhelm Leibniz (von 1691 bis 1716) und Gotthold Ephraim Lessing, der von 1770 bis zu seinem Tode im Jahre 1781 hier wirkte. Leibniz ließ unter anderem den ersten alphabetischen Katalog anlegen und regte auch den Bau eines neuen Bibliotheksgebäudes an.'

Durie beat both these feats of Lessing's by some fifty years. In his First Letter concerning his Reformed Librarie-Keeper which he shortly afterwards became, Durie says:

> 'therefore I would have a peculiar place appointed for such Books as shall be laid aside to keep them in, and a Catalogue of their Titles made Alphabetically in reference to the Author's name, with a note of distinction to shew the Science to which they are to be referred.'

In 1663, widower Oldenburg married Katherina Durie, John Durie's daughter and only child. Oldenburg and Katherina had two children, Rupert and Sophia. After Oldenburg's and Katherina's early deaths, Durie took custody over his grandchildren for a brief time until Robert Boyle, his relation by marriage, took over the task because Durie was confined to Germany. Both Oldenburg and Leibniz read and quoted from each other's works, with Oldenburg becoming Leibniz' friend, correspondent, host and advisor. Through Oldenburg, Leibniz gained contact with the Durie circle, including Theodor Haak, Robert Boyle, Isaac Newton and John Pell. It was Oldenburg who campaigned for Leibniz' acceptance as a member of the Royal Society, though John Pell and Isaac Newton opposed the idea. So, too, it was Oldenburg, according to Leibniz' correspondence, who passed on to him John Wilkin's ideas of universal language and *Ars characteris-*

tica on lines dealt with by the Durie-Hartlib circle a generation before.[347] Martin Schneider, the current editor of Leibniz' letters, confirms this. Oldenburg, who was privy to all Durie's works and custodians of his documents, conversed freely with Spinoza, Leibniz, and Boyle on the subject of universal learning, organising knowledge and a right use of the *filum Ariadnes* and *filum meditandi* until his death in 1677.[348] Thus Meyer, of Zürich University can say, 'Henry Oldenburg (1626-1678), first Secretary of the *Royal Society*, kept him (Leibniz) constantly informed on all the scientific and philosophical topics discussed in England at the time.'[349] After Oldenburg's death, Leibniz continued to correspond with his successor Theodor Haak, another member of the Durie Circle and co-founder of the Royal Society. Haak was a close confident of Durie's and stood with him on pansophy in the form of universal learning and also in the matter of a universal language. He also translated and distributed Durie's works, though not always with Durie's permission.[350] Leibniz could not accept the Durie-circle's and the Royal Society's idea of knowledge being open in its growth and beyond systematising and scorned Oldenburg's, Newton's and Boyle's Durie-like theories as revealed in Oldenburg's correspondence with Leibniz, Spinoza and Newton.[351] Indeed, Professor Stephen Gaukroger in His work *The Unity of Knowledge* comments on letters from Leibniz and Spinoza to Oldenburg,[352] saying they 'both thought Boyle *perverse*[353] in not offering a 'systematic' account of his views'.[354]

---

[347] See Leibniz' *Philosophischer Briefwechsel*, Erste Reihe, p. 373.
[348] See Leibniz' *Philosophischer Briefwechsel*, Erster Reihe, with its many references to *filum Ariadnes, filum meditandi* and *filum mechanicum.* especially N. 117 pp. 373-381. See also *The Correspondence of Henry Oldenburg*, Hall and Hall, 1986, 13 vols.
[349] *Leibnitz and the Seventeenth-Century Revolution*, p. 62.
[350] See Durie's letter to Hartlib, 15 July, 1655, Ref: 4/3/108A-B, HP.
[351] See Leibniz to Oldenburg, 5 July 1674 (vol. 11, 46) and 10 May 1675; Spinoza to Oldenburg, April 1662, vol. 1, 462, Oldenburg to Newton, 18 Jan. 1673, vol. 1, 255-6. (Hall and Hall, 1965-75).
[352] Leibniz to Oldenburg, 5 July 1674 and 10 May 1675, in *The Correspondence of Henry Oldenburg*, ed. A. Rupert Hall and Marie Boas Hall (13 vols., Madison, 1965-75), vol.11, 46; Spinoza to Oldenburg, April 1662: ibid, vol. 1, 462.
[353] My emphasis.
[354] Gaukroger, S. (2009). 'The Unity of Knowledge: Natural-Philosophical Foundations of Spinoza's Politico-Theology'. in V. Alexandrescu (ed.), *Branching off. The Early Moderns in the Quest for the Unity of Knowledge.*, Zeta Books, Bucharest, pp. 140-166. Separate pdf of The Unity of Knowledge, p. 15. See 25/5/06 12:56 PM.

Leibniz, like Hartlib and Comenius, sought true knowledge by separating what they thought were essential elements from the inessential and judging the other less essential elements by them. This was the very method which Durie condemned as blind-alley reasoning, placing him before in time and beyond in scope Spinoza and Leibniz in his universality of approach to learning.

A second factor in linking Durie with Leibniz is the Figulus-Jablonski family. Peter Figulus Jablonski was Durie's first long-term secretary. His son, Daniel Ernst Jablonski and other relations placed Figulus' diary, recording his service to Durie, and other works appertaining to Durie in the hands of the Comenius-Gesellschaft which they founded. Daniel Ernst Jablonski studied at Oxford, became a royal chaplain and corresponded with Leibniz for a number of years concerning church union. Building on Durie's work, Jablonski strove for a union of Anglicans with the United Brethren, the German Reformed and Lutheran Churches, especially in Poland, based on treatise influenced by Durie such as that of Thorn. As Jablonski was connected with Comenius through his father who was Comenius foster-son and son-in-law, Jablonski inherited a double interest in pansophical education. He founded the Brandenburg Scientific Society with Leibniz in 1700 (later the Berlin Academy of Sciences) and became a member of the Royal Society in 1713. Following Durie, Jablonski argued that instead of using the terms 'Reformed' and 'Lutheran', the German Protestants should be called 'Evangelicals' which is the term still used today. However, Jablonski was more interested in an outward display of unity in the form of common rites and liturgies than a common faith. He even strove to prove that the United Brethren upheld the Apostolic Succession in the form that High Anglicans and Roman Catholics did.[355] This separated him from Durie and united him with Leibniz who had a more philosophical approach to religion rather than doctrinal. We know from Leibniz' correspondence with Daniel Jablonski that he was anxious to deepen his knowledge of Durie's works. In his paper 'Daniel Ernst Jablonski und Gottfried Wilhelm Leibniz – Kirchen und akademiegeschichtliche Beobachtungen zur Frühaufklärung' presented to the Leibniz-Sozietät in 2009, p. 15, Hartmut Rudolph relates how Jablonski grew up from his youth in the spirit of Hartlib and Durie which was the same spirit that grew in Leibniz. He continues:

'Von daher ist es eben kein Zufall, dass beide, Leibniz wie Jablonski, 1696/97, als sie voneinander noch nichts wussten, und bevor sie durch

---

[355] See Meyer, 'Daniel Ernst Jablonski und seine Unionspläne.'

politische Vorgaben des Berliner Hofes zur Zusammenarbeit veranlasst werden, bevor sie miteinander korrespondieren, in ihrer jeweiligen Korrespondenz auf John Dury zu sprechen kommen. Dieser habe, so schrieb Jablonski 1697 an den englischen Theologen Patrick Gordon, in ihm das „Feuer", nämlich der Kirchenunion, „entfacht"; und 1698 wünscht sich Jablonski einen Phoenix, der aus der Asche Durys aufsteigen sollte, um mit gleicher Begabung und Intensität, aber mit glücklicherer Hand und mehr Erfolg das Werk der Union vollenden zu können.'

In October 1697 Leibniz heard from the Reformed Professor of Theology at the Berlin Court, Gerhard Meier that Jablonski was thinking of publishing and editing Durie's works but wondered whether Jablonski was the man for the task as he had not been very successful in bringing out an edited work of Richard Bentley's sermons against atheism. So, too, Leibniz had felt he was himself placed under suspicion by Bradley's clerical friends in England. Leibniz not only greeted the fact that Durie was to be published but also uttered the wish that someone should publish a résumé or abstract of Durie's teaching for the use of scholars. According to Rudolf, Leibniz was won over for Jablonski's idea that some kind of amalgamation with the Church of England would prove a sound basis for plans for church union.

Jablonski was ignored as an influence on Leibniz until very recently, but in November, 2007, the Leibniz-Sozietät decided to correct this neglect by issuing a Jablonski Medal twice yearly, beginning in 2008, to members of the society who had provided outstanding support. Perhaps they might now consider a Durie Medal?[356]

Prof. Dr. Lutz Danneberg of Humboldt University in his essay *Der Ordo Inversus in Hermeneutik und Natur Philosophie*, defines *ordo inversus* as 'Mit ordo inversus ist allgemein die Bewegung gemeint eines Ausgehens von etwas, das sich mit dem Zurückkehren zum Ausgangspunkt verknüpft.' This he associates with Bonaventura[357] and also with Leibniz' theory of the *filum Ariadnes* in his historical overview. Danneberg sees the *ordo inversus*, however, as working not only backwards but forwards. It can be thus seen as *regressus* or *revolutio*. There are certainly parallels here between Durie's going back to the roots of knowledge and then advancing from there to his educational *revolutio* of universal learning as he describes in his treatise given to Smart, dealt with below. It is also interesting to note that Danneberg starts his analysis of knowledge-acquirement by

---

[356] *Mitteilungen der Leibniz-Sozietät*, Nr 37, 21 Nov. 2007, pp. 3-4.
[357] Giovanni di Fidanza (1221-1274).

discussing methods of Scripture interpretation before branching out into wider fields in an almost identical way to Durie. However, Dannenberg gives so many examples of the use and abuse of the *ordo inversus* that he makes it mean anything and nothing. Durie used the logic of the *ordo inversus* merely to start with the idea revealed in Scripture, go back to the known in the experience of God as the source of all knowledge and then use the insight gained to comprehend the known universally in nature. This is the difference between Durie on the one side and Bonaventura and Leibniz on the other. Bonaventura spoke of the *rationes aeternae* or the idea of all things in God. Durie saw God as not only containing the idea but the reality and creation of the 'Ding an sich'. God was not only the source of ideological knowledge. He was also the Realiser and Creator of the knowledgeable. The Bible, to Durie, was the handbook of all practical, utility knowledge-engineering. Leibniz was far more metaphysical than Durie and, though he emphasised the possible harmony of knowledge, his was a harmony of separate bodies without intersection or interaction. Durie's Pansophy saw a harmony of unity, including interaction, interrelation, interconnection and intersection. Knowledge to him was one because it was of the essence of the one God.

Leibniz followed the kabbalistic idea that *bereshiit* in the opening words of Genesis means 'in the mind' not 'in the beginning'. He soon put human mind and idealism where Durie found the mind of Christ. Leibniz' pansophism thus became a bundle of parts. Glenn Alexander Magee, who re-founded the Invisible Society, nevertheless, in his *Hegel and the Hermetic Tradition* says that Durie's Pansophism was a dream which Hegel put into practice. Hegel merely turned Comenius' parallelogramic dream, not Durie's sober analysis, into a triangular one. His theory is defined in his never-ending triangular dialectic outlined in his *Encyclopaedia of Philosophical Science* as:

> The *thesis*: 'God is God only so far as he knows himself.
>
> The *anti-thesis*: His self-knowledge is a self-consciousness *in* man and man's knowledge *of* God.
>
> The *synthesis*: This proceeds to man's self-knowledge *in* God.

This leaves us back where we started with the question how complete is God's knowledge of Himself and how does man partake of it? Hegel compares at best three parallels but does not give new information gained from them. So he goes on like a dog chasing its tail setting up further never-ending triangles. This again, is the kabbalistic eternal logoic triangle, but Hegel calls it 'the eternal idea' or 'absolute mind' but only as 'fundamental concepts of the particular sciences.' Thus his 'eternal idea' was a mere collection of ethical, logoic and magical ideas on departmentalised cultic knowledge. Eric Voegelin thus rightly calls Hegel's scientific mysticism a 'grimoire' or book of magic. No government set up a Parliamentary committee to study Hegel's cabbalistic gnosticism, but Cromwell's Parliament actually set up a Committee to put Durie's Christian 'dream' into practice. One of Cromwell's very last letters was to give the project his blessing and say that funds had been made available to finance the project. Modern communication scientists and socio-linguists are now praising John Durie's input, but they still lack his comprehensiveness and synergism.

Frank and Frizie Manuel in *Utopian Thought in the Western World*, criticise the *filum Ariadnes* in Durie's Pansophism. Using Aristotelian logic, which Durie, following Francis Bacon, rejected as 'unscientific', they back-track through the Labyrinth of knowledge, cutting up the all-vital thread so as to analyse it 'logically', but actually examining only selected parts. They appear to believe that destruction makes for construction. This, by the way, is what our Protestant and supposedly 'Reformed' Systematic Theologies do, following 'Calvinistic' Aristotelianism. Frank and Frizie Manuel see Durie's wholeness as an unrealistic dream but regard their own cognitively chaotic creation as 'Science'.

A further link between Durie and Leibniz is that both were librarians and library reformers and both were connected with the Herzog August Bibliothek in Wolfenbüttel. Durie published a work entitled *The Description of one of the chiefest Libraries which is in Germany, erected and ordered by one of the most Learned Princes in Europe* in 1651. In this work, Durie describes the Herzog-August-Bibliothek Wolfenbüttel which Durie had discussed with Duke August in its pioneer stages and which was continually referred to and praised in Durie's writings. It is also thought that Durie based his work in the St. James Library on ideas he and Duke August developed in Wolfenbüttel. Durie also published his *Reformed Librarie-Keeper* in 1651 which was very much appreciated abroad. Leibniz became librarian of the Herzog August Bibliothek in 1691 and though his methods of cataloguing and processing books and documents are supposed to be unique for his time and original to him, they simply reflect Durie's rules for library management which we shall see below. Indeed Leibniz' views of a library as a knowledge centre and think-tank closely reflect Durie's *Reformed Librarie-Keeper* which, however, went further because of Durie's wider and more comprehensive pansophistic ideas.

In search of more insight into pansophy and ecclesiastical union, Leibniz begged Jablonski who spoke Polish and could understand Czech to find Comenius' works for him in German. Jablonski replied from Berlin on 3 Sept. 1715:

> ‚Sein (Comenius) Labyrinthus Mundi ist ein sinnreicher Apologus, und zugleich ein Meister-Stück in der Böhmischen Sprach, welche Comenius ungemein besessen, und wird es schwer seyn, wegen der besonderen Derivationen und Compositionen, derer die Böhmische Sprache sich gebrauchet, gewisse Worte in die deutsche oder andere Sprachen zu übersetzen; und ob wohl selbiges Büchlein in die Polnische Sprache übersetzt, zu Dantzig vor einigen Jahren gedrukt worden, hat doch die Übersetzung (obgleich die Polnische Sprache eine Schwester der Böhmischen und der Übersetzer ein Gelehrter und Geschickter Mann) keinen sonderlichen Applausum gehabt. Ich schliesse mit hertzl. Anwunsch alles erspriesl. Wohlseyns, absonderlich dass ich das Glük haben möge, von der guten Societät etwas Angenehmes und Vergnügendes fördersamst melden zu können, Der ich inzwischen mit allem respect verharre Eurer Wohlgeborenen, Meines Hochgeehrten Herren Geheimbten Rahts Gehorsamster und Ergebenster Diener D. E. Jablonskj.'[358]

Durie forms a solid basis for his future work

When one considers Durie's extant educational writings en bloc from 1628 on, as will be adequately demonstrated in this thesis, it is clear that he was captivated by the idea of propagating education for all irrespective of gender, age or background. He felt that the entire knowledge in the world should be placed at the service of all mankind for the common profit of all. He had envisaged founding educational institutions catering for all classes of society and ages providing equal chances for all to benefit from this learning. It was in 1628, however, when he was hoping to complete his *Treatyes on Education* that Durie realised that he could not possible find a *Filum Adriadnes* through the Labyrinth of learning when the Reformed churches in which he lived and moved were so disunited that any common approach to education was out of the question. He realised that he must first achieve a mutual understanding of doctrine and inter-church cooperation amongst Protestants before providing them with a reforming educational programme which could only be built on such a basis. He thus wrote

---

[358] Taken from *Monumenta Germaniae paedagogica*, Berlin, 1886. This work also contains several letters of Joachim Hübner to Comenius in the sixties, especially a letter explaining Durie's leaving England finally for Germany.

on 8 December from Elbing to Hartlib who had already made concrete plans for a college and found like-minded people who were prepared to follow Durie's vision, telling him of his widened plans. Sadly, only an extract of this letter has also been preserved which reads;

> 'Then you come to Pædagogicall affaires entreating mee to send what I have in readines & to bee large in that Subject. But since I wrote vnto you I have done nothing in them because another matter of farr greater moment wherevnto one of the King of Swedens Privie Counsellours hath provoked mee doth take place before them that is concerning the pacification of the Churches troubled with needles & endlesse Controversyes in these meditacions I have beene both perplexed & comforted greately & am still as with child till I satisfye my mind by Gods Grace in them The things belonging to this Subject are soe wonderfull diffused intricate & obscure & my desire is soe earnest to prosecute them & I have none to helpe mee in them and I find my selfe by reason of my manifold weakenesses and sins soe vnfit for them that I am oft tymes in greate Straites and extreame impatiencye & sorrowe The former troubles of my mind concerning the Pastorall care were ever heretofore the cheife but now they are swallowed vp by these I thanke you for your bookes & MS. which through your wonted care you have sent mee but I desire not that you should send any other things vnto mee till I see you Except it bee something to this effect whereby I may bee helped in these Counsells of peace For till I see some greater light in the particulars of this whole matter I have determined to thinke vpon nothing save onely the Texts of my ordinary 3 Sermons And if ever the Lord send mee into England I hope it shall bee not onely with a full informacion concerning those new Reformatours in Germany but allsoe with the glad Tydings of peace that reformacion of Schismes & Scandalous practizes & fruitles intentions may easily bee procured and established vnchangeably in the Churches of God which in these latter ages have beene called out of Babilon The Lord Stirre vp many labourers in this worke for the harvest is <very> greate And if I bee longer absent from you then I intend I suppose it will bee because I shall not bee well fitted for this worke, but I hope that by your prayers & the supply of the Spirit our joy & expectacion shall be fullfilled For indeede I must confesse that the Lord hath assisted mee evidently in some thoughts beyond my expectacion soe that in regard of his favour offered to invite mee to prosecute this worke I have greate inward assurance & noe occasion at all to feare but in regard of my continuall indisposicion on the other side whereby I doe neglect or abuse the good motions of his holy Spirit & the assistance or rather provocations comeing from his grace I am altogether discouraged & scarce dare hope that ever I shall bee worthy to bee an Instrument of soe good a worke But if it please God to blesse mee in this project but soe farr that I may bee able to provoke others more able & worthy to take this Subject to

heart & the worke it selfe in hand then at better leisure I will Stretch my selfe out vpon the things belonging to the education of Children [another hand?: Mr Williamsons] Tutour comes not neere mee & I am sorrye for it though I thinke not expressely vpon this matter now yet I would not care now & then to have some occasions to fall abruptly vpon them for oft times incident & abrupt thoughts are noe lesse materiall then others which have beene long sought out.'[359]

It was to this end that he decided to address King Gustav Adolf of Sweden, the mightiest monarch of the Protestant world, and solicit his assistance in bringing peace to broken Protestantism.[360] He believed that what Gustav was doing in a military way was of no avail if spiritual unity was not aimed at. In an astonishing and daring frank petition, Durie reminds Gustav of his Christian duties in bringing spiritual peace to the nations and even tells him that the civil and temporal peace that Gustav is aiming at could do more hurt than war. His reason for saying this is his conviction that the spiritual disunity in the churches is the true cause of all the disasters that are tearing Europe apart. Thus Durie, once banned from Britain by Royal Sovereign James VI because of the alleged sins of his grandfather and father in challenging the King, says with the same courage as his forebears, to the monarch of the vast Swedish empire:

'You that are the Kings and Rulers of the world, you are gods amongst mortall men. God hath lent you his authority, his hand, and power to make use of, and employ your Subjects, who are all the servants and children of God, as well as your selves. If you do not his work, and refuse to favour those that do it, you shall give account unto him, as well as the meanest of your Subjects; for with him there is no respect of persons.'

Nevertheless, Durie was also a diplomat of diplomats and adds:

'Sir, the world knows, That God hath singularly favoured, elevated and preserved you; your self do acknowledge the same with thankfulnesse, your friends recount it with joyfulnesse, your enemies confesse it with admiration and astonishment: For by his power it is, you possesse the gates of your enemies, and by his favour you enjoy the hearts of your friends, but more especially by His Providence, you seem to take up the longings and expectations of all the oppressed throughout all Germany; the oppressed (I say) and such as are persecuted now for witnessing the truth of the Gospel. I do not exhort you to warre, Sir, under the pretext of the cause of God (God forbid)

---

[359] See 1/12/1A-4B:, HP.
[360] See *A Copy of a Petition As it was tendered by Mr Dury to Gustavus, the late King of Sweden*, Bod L

but I do humbly petition, and offer my self unto you, and Summon you by the Grace of God, to Councels of Peace, in the proper cause of God himself.'

Through this petition and the testimony of Sir James Spens to Durie's character and gifts which accompanied it, the mighty king of warfare was won for the cause of Protestant unity and peace. King Gustav was also encouraged on the home-front by his former tutor Johan Skytte who became Chancellor of Uppsala University. Princess Christina's tutor, Johannes Matthiae, gave the princess a pan-Protestant education, relying on Durie and Hartlib to supply him with a suitable syllabus and media. Thus, when Durie visited Sweden in 1636 to present his programmes of church unity and education to Chancellor Oxenstierna and the professors of Uppsala, then Sweden's only university,[361] a joint understanding of the way future cooperation should develop was quickly concluded. This stipulated:

'1. That a full agreement should be made in all fundamental Articles of faith.

2. That all errors overthrowing the foundation, or tending to overthrow the same, should be condemned.

3. That in matters Ceremoniall and of indifferencey, there should be a mutuall toleration.

4. That betwixt the parties united, sincerity and uprightness should be maintained, lest ancient errors might be upheld under doubtful speeches.

5. That when peace is made, none should be suffered to maintain, excuse, or spread any more the errors once condemned.

6. That ambitious and needlesse disputes and brablings should be inhibited on all sides.

7. That former reproaches and injuries should be put to oblivion.

8. That the Church government should be setled according to Apostolic Rules.'[362]

---

[361] Lund University was founded in 1666 as a Swedish University after the South's occupation by Denmark. There had, however, been a Studium Generale there since 1438.

[362] See *A Brief Relation of That which hath been lately attempted to procure Ecclesiastical Peace amongst Protestants*, London 1641, p. 17. A copy of the Latin original sent from the Theological Faculty on 13 September 1636 and signed Decanus Professores Fac. Theol. in Academia Vpsaliensi is found in Benzelius p. 135.

On hearing of Durie's progress, there was some murmurings in the ranks of the hardliners on both the Reformed and Lutheran sides in Europe but many English and Irish Churchmen such as Davenant, Hall, Morten, Ussher and, in particular, Joseph Mead (1586-1638), felt Durie's first step to full union was wise. Joseph Mead (or Mede) was a Pansophist after Durie's heart. A Fellow of King's College, Cambridge, he was a classicist, philologian, historian, mathematician, physicist, botanist, anatomist, astronomer, Egyptologist and expert on ancient Semitic religions but was able to merge all his vast knowledge for the public good. These are the kind of allies Durie needed and cultivated. That pansophy and universal learning was Durie's aim above and beyond ecclesiastical factors relating to inter-Protestant cooperation is clear from Durie's many letters referring to both the topic of pansophy and the need for pacification and concord to promote it. One example amongst many is found in a relative early letter of Durie's sent from Hamburg on 9. February, 1639 to Hartlib in which Durie writes about finding the right men to cooperate with him, saying:

> 'For the Spirituall good which wee seeke to advance towards all Men must bee advanced Spiritualy by whose who are able to giue assistance therunto. You see that I am here fallen vpon a Subject wherin much might bee said to rule and direct your way and mine also of Sollicitation in Pansophical and Pacifical endeavours.'[363]

In the same letter, Durie tells Hartlib how he is looking for a method with Tassius of teaching the sciences more effectually and that he is trying to find sponsors interested in supporting Comenius and pansophical studies. A month later, we find Durie writing to Hartlib from Bremen saying what pleasure he is having by reading Hübner's thoughts on pansophy and Comenius' letters.[364]

Commentators have missed much of Durie's educational teaching by concentrating on his works which bear either the word 'education', 'school' or 'learning' in their titles. Durie, however, continually described his view of universal knowledge from 1628 on as *Practical Divinity*, believing all knowledge was of God, reflecting the Being of God and was therefore to be used to the glory of God and the preparation of His People for Eternity. Like Bacon, he refused to analyse and separate one supposed strand of learning from another. Divinity, to Durie never meant merely 'Theology' or 'Religion' but 'Man's Being in God's Being' in service to

---

[363] Ref: 9/1/73A-76B. HP.
[364] Ref: [9/1/79B, HP.

Him and mankind. Thus, another synonym used by Durie to describe his Pansophy was *The Public Good*. True education for Durie is therefore the product of practical divinity aimed at the public good. This pansophical side of Durie's plans to bring back Edenic standards to the religious, social and political society of mankind has been seriously neglected in Durie studies. Thomas H. H. Rae, for instance, sees Durie's Practical Divinity merely as a 'solvent of religious disunity'[365] and surprisingly claims that Durie wrote little on the subject. Actually, most of what Durie wrote in public or private form is expressed in terms of Practical Divinity, Universal Learning or the Public Good. Though Rae's two major works on Durie are enormously deep-sighted and informative, he has simply not researched this area as adequately as he has others, though he seeks to present Durie as a reformer of education. Rae thus never mentions Durie's publication and translation of *Ecclesiarum Magnae Britanniae atq: Hyberniae Patronis & Antistibus Primariis, Eximiis Dei servis etc.*; nor his 1654 work *A Summarie Platform of the Heads of a Body of Practical Divinity which the Ministers of the Protestant Churches abroad have sued for, etc.*, nor his 1658 work *The Earnest Breathings of Forreign Protestants, Divines and Others: to the Ministers and other able Christians of these three Nations, for a Compleat Body of Practical Divinity and Cases, wherein the Grace of God hath more Eminently appeared amongst us in these Islands, then in the rest of the World besides*. Here Durie describes the basis and outworking of his pan-educational Practical Divinity in great detail, applying it to all areas of life both private and public. Nor does Rae list these fundamental studies in his forty-four works from Durie's pen consulted, though Rae has packed into his list obviously all he found. These include as separate mss a copy of Durie's signature which otherwise adorns scores of Durie's extant letters, printers' proofs etc.; very brief notes and several titles which Rae claims are not extant or may never have been written. Yet he leaves out major works dealing with Durie's overall teaching such as his 1671 *Extractum ex harmonia* of 191 pages and his *Irenicorum tractatum Prodromus in quo Preliminares Continentur tractatus de Amsterdami* of 1662 which fills 548 pages. These published books and especially Durie's many autobiographical works besides Hartlib's important contributions must be studied alongside Durie's *A Motion tending to the Publick Good of this Age* (1642) as also those titles which obviously refer to methods of universal learning such as *The Reformed Librarie-Keeper* (1650); *The Reformed-School* (1651); *The reformed spirituall husbandman: with an humble*

---

[365] See his *John Dury and the Royal Road to Piety*, pp. 132-3, 207, 209 and index 350.

memorandum concerning Chelsy Colledge, and a correspondencie with forreign Protestants (1652) and *Some Proposalls Towards the Advancement of Learning* (1653). Furthermore, contrary to Rae's suggestion, Durie did not teach practical divinity as a basic means of healing the wounds of Protestant division. For him, it was a synergism of all knowledge and an enterprise only considered practical once a united Protestant Church was established. That Durie's ideas of practical divinity also encouraged church unity is, nevertheless, true and important.

Durie's first major efforts towards Protestant peace and Pansophy

Early in 1631, Durie outlined his detailed schedule for his first major Continental tour under the title The Purpose, and Platforme of the Iourneyes that are vndertaken for the worke of Peace Ecclesiasticall, and other profitable Ends. In this pamphlet, Durie explains that he would be travelling under the auspices of Chancellor Oxenstierna and King Gustav Adolf of Sweden and the Dukes of Brandenburg and Hesse of Germany and that:

> 'By the Gratious assistance of God, I intend in passinge through the cheife places of Prussia, and Germany, to laie a ground, and settle a waie of Correspondencie betwixt vs, and the Reformed divines of Germany. That wee, and they maie bee able to Communicate in all spirituall things; But cheifelie in our Councells, and Meditations for the advancement of peace in the Churches, and for the buildinge vpp of one another in the power, and truth of Godlines.'

His aims therefore were:

> 'First, to act the rest of the divines in Germany, to set them, (soe many as are fitt) vpon this worke.
> Secondlie, to gather from them, that labour seuerallie in it, the fruite of their Meditations, to bringe it into the common stocke.
> Thirdlie, to giue from tyme to tyme notice, and intelligent vnto vs, howe things passe, what the cheife lets, and impediments and which maie stopp our worke of Pacification, or in generall hinder the course of the Gospell.
> Fourthlie, what helpes are requisit, or maie bee made vs of in all respects of persons, of books, of M.S.'

This visit was to be the first of many such journeys to various countries so Durie goes on to say:

'Afterwards when I shall haue seene England againe, and giuen vpp an account of my spent tyme, My purpose is further to see Ireland, Scotland, Fraunce, the Grisons,[366] and Polonia,[367] where the cheifest men will not bee wantinge vnto vs (as I hope) to stirr vpp, and set vpon this worke, as many as shalbee fitt for it; And thus all the Eminent men of the Reformed Churches, maie bee prouoaked, and Combined in thoughts, and Endeauours, and the fruite of all their Councells, and Meditations maie bee reaped, which nowe by distraction is last.'

Durie relates how these journeys are not merely for the sake of ecclesiastical peace but for the spreading of mutual knowledge. Thus he intends to 'gather' all the rare books he can find and record all the inventions he comes across and how all the foreign 'sciences'[368] are practised. Concerning the books, he wishes not only to catalogue them but to list their contents in the language used and secure either the right to reprint them or even obtain the original manuscripts and copyrights. He explains that he will be particularly looking for ideas and inventions which will advance learning and good manners in the universities and schools and provide for the common good. He also plans to research all ideas concerning public health, the increase of wealth by trade and the mechanical industries whether they apply to sea or land, war or peace.

Durie also relates how he aims to compile all the works on international and ecclesiastical peace he can find in their various languages so that their ideas and conclusions can be added to what is already known and practised in England. This will include their views on teaching Scripture and the Oriental languages. He hopes to find new methods of communicating with Jews 'whose callinge is supposed to bee neere at hand'. Here we have the first hint that Durie is interested in the future of the Jews and their place in the global preparation for a Paradise regained. He will then go on to research, 'Arts, and Sciences Philosophicall, Chymicall, and Mechanicall, whereby not onlie the secrets of disciplines, are harmonicallie, and compendiouslie deliuered, but alsoe the secrets of nature are thought to bee vnfolded; Soe that Gods wonderfull power, wisedome, and goodnes is to bee seene more apparantlie in bodilie things then euer heretofore.'

Next, Durie reveals his interest in what was then called a 'magical language'. Scholars, educators and politicians alike were at this time looking for means of international communication in a utility language which was

---

[366] The Grey Leagues of Switzerland or Graubünden.
[367] Poland.
[368] Contents of and methods of attaining knowledge.

more exact and precise in its expression and could easily be taught and understood on a 'no rules' basis. Much of Leibniz' correspondence with the Durie circle and the Royal Society was on this subject. Hartlib's and Durie's friend, the scientist Cyprian Kinner had already begun to work on such a language which also gained the interest of John Amos Comenius (1592-1670). Since then, many poets and linguists have sought to create a *lingua generalis* or a natural language of the senses whether it be Esperanto, Interlingua or Newspeak but none of these attempts have found widespread usage. Leibniz, motivated by Wilkins and Oldenburg, worked hard on his *ars characteristica universalis*, adding his *ars combinatoria* and *ars inveniendi*. It is still an in-built desire in mankind to get back to the language of Eden and to pre-Babel thinking. It would appear that only a person who has perfected universal knowledge can hope to found a new, ideal language and our schools need much reforming before that goal can be approached. Durie, however, was also thinking here of a secret or codified language to preserve information from those who would censor or hinder it. Indeed, when travelling in countries which had placed a price on Durie's head such as France, Durie used a codified language which he had worked out with the Swiss. This explains, too, the Durie's circles interest in Steganography as, at first, a *Scribendi methodus Secreta, arcana, obcultaque, nulli mortalium quantumcunque Studioso vel eruditoi patula*, which, even then combined para-linguistic, meta-linguistic and socio-linguistic features and has now become such an integral part of modern digital communication and advertising.[369] One of Durie's major interests in travelling through Europe was to study their methods of organisation and administration of people who came from different walks of life with different skills. Thus he was eager to find out more about the Continental clubs, societies and corporations and how they dealt with arts and industries, both rational and mechanical.

Durie's thoughts now move from the educational to the ecclesiastical, still keeping to a pansophical approach, so he needs to know about:

> 'the state of the Churches in Germany, to knowe all the Sects, divisions, and subdiuisions of them that professe Christ in those places, with their perticuler, and different opinions, and the Circumstances, Occasions, Causes, and effects of their controuersies; As for example of the Socinians, Arrians, Anabaptists, Swenkfeldians, Famelists, Weigelians, Nagelians, and to purchase the cheife bookes of all their Tenents, and to obserue the difference of

---

[369] See Memo On Trithem's Work On Cryptography, In Latin & English, Ref: 8/47/1A-2B, HP.

their Churches, Orders, and Customes, seruinge, either for decencie, or discipline. . . . the relatiue Estate of the Church, and Common wealth in Germany each to other, to knowe what Authoritie the Civill Magestrate hath, or hath not in seuerall places ouer the Ministerie, and by what meanes the Ministers maintenance is raised vnto them. . . . the notable, and Eminent men, either in Sects, as Ring-leaders of the rest, or in the Church as lights to others, Or in the Common wealth as nursinge Fathers, that wee maie knowe them, and what vse maie bee made of them to good, or what Euill maie bee feared from them. Concerninge all these, I purpose to haue Epheride obseruations, out of which Collections beinge made, in due tyme, wee shalbee able to Iudge of the state of forraine Churches, lookinge vpon them as on pictures, wherein all the Lineaments of their faces are represented.'

In the Hartlib Papers, there is preserved a journal of comments on British and Continental works dealing with education, theology and science entitled *Ephemerides*. It appears that many of the earlier entries deal with Durie's findings during his 1631-32 journeys when he avowed to make general 'Epheride obseruations'. Hartlib's *A Briefe Relation of that which has been lately attempted to procure Ecclesiastical Peace amongst Protestants* printed in 1641 also deals with this time of Durie's harvesting of Continental thought.

Though Durie began writing on universal learning in the late sixteen-twenties, it was the interest of German, Dutch and Belgian theologians, educators and statesmen between 1631-1633 which really gave him encouragement and impetus. These learned, church and university men had asked their English colleagues for an introduction of Practical Divinity into Continental universities. In the letter-pamphlet of 1633 *Ecclesiarum Magnae Britanniae*[370] mentioned above, the seventeen signatories, all Continental theologians and educational leaders, wrote:

'Haec eo spectant, illustres, clarissimiq; Viri, Reverendissimiq; atq; Reverendi in Christo patres & Fratres, ut cum nobis certo innotuerit inter Ecclesias magnae Britanniae, Doctrinam Theologiae Practicae multorum pie Doctorum Ecclesiae vestrae Antistitum publicis scriptis egregie excultam esse, atq; ad usum Popularem insigniter accomodatam, atq; eam solummodo linguae vestra Cancellis tanquam reconditum ab exteris Nationibus thesaurum contineri, & asservari maximamq; utilitatem ad omnes Ecclesias Christianas, praesertim autem Evangelicas redundaturam, si quae vobis in hoc genere peculiaria sunt, publicentur, ita ut ab iis quoq; legi & intelligi possint, ut (inquam, cum haec ita se habeant) Illustritatibus

---

[370] Prefaced to the *Earnest Breathings of Foreign Protestants, Divines and Others*, London, 1658, Bod. L.

atq; Reverentiis Vestris votum nostrum ac desiderium aperiamus; atq; per sancta Communionis in Christo vinculum, fraternaq; libertatis Parrhesiam rogemus, vos presertim quotquot inter Ecclesiarum Rectores, Protectores & Fautores, estis aedificationis Publicae vere studiosi, ne permittatis hoc Talentum tam pretiosum ulterius abscondi & occultari ab Exoticorum manibus & oculis, sed velitis pro prudentia vestra, pro ferventis erga fraternas Ecclesias Charitatis, ac liberalis studii erga Dei gloriam in Evangelii propagatione, pio zelo & affectu vestro rationem aliquam inire commodam, qua Medulla Auctorum in illo genere apud vos extantium & eminentium ex omnibus collecta in volumen aliquod conjiciatur, sive locorum communium, sive Systematis Theologiae practicae, quod publici juris sit, & doctioribus communi.'

This led Durie to form a committee of men composed of William Gouge, John Stoughton, John Downam, Henry Burton, George Walker, Nicolas Morton, Sidrach Simpson, Adoniram Byfield, Richard Culverwell, Obadiah Sedgwick, George Hughes and Joseph Symonds who promised to co-operate in producing suitable English writings on Practical Divinity to be translated into foreign tongues. These approached Archbishop James Usher with a request that he should lead them in compiling a *Body of Practical Divinity*.[371] Most of these men became leading divines in the Commonwealth period.[372] Durie had also hoped that Sir Thomas Roe could help with soliciting suitable men for the task. *The Calendar of State Papers* for 1633 record that on April 2/12 of that year, Durie wrote to Sir Thomas Roe from Heilbron, asking him to support Hartlib, his agent in England, 'with a petition of Divines of those quarters concerning an edition of a Body of Divinity, gathered out of English authors, a work which will be exceeding profitable, but will require divers agents and an exact ordering of the work, for which no one is fitter than Roe.' Sadly, this project initially came to naught because of the troubles of the wars on the Continent and then in Britain and the fact that Sir Thomas lost favour for several years with the King and was ill for a lengthy period. So, too, the translators appointed who included German-born William Twisse and other Continentals; British ministers who had served abroad such as Nye and scholars who had found refuge in England such as Joachim Hübner of Cleves, found the niceties of English almost impossible to put into German and Dutch. Though Durie

---

[371] See *The Copy of a Letter which was written by several Godly Ministers, Undertakers in this Work of compiling a Body of Practical Divinity, to Doctor Usher the Primat of Armach in Ireland* (undated) appendixed to Durie's *Earnest Breathings*.

[372] Letter to Usher enclosed in Durie's *The Earnest Breathings of Forreign Protestants*.

himself was a brilliant linguist, he insisted that theological and educational works should be in the languages of the people. Many English scholars and their Continental counterparts, brought up on Latin, were not yet competent enough for this move. Durie was obviously very disappointed by the fact that most of those who supported him enthusiastically concerning a Body of Practical Divinity pulled out of the agreement owing to one reason or another. He wrote to Thomas Roe from Stockholm on 3 December, 1636 saying: 'The excuse of such as remaine at home for doing nothing in the Worke of Practical Divinity or Pacification show their irresolutenes and needles fears. But what shall I say? God hath all things in his owne hand, so also Mens hearts.'[373] Durie was particularly interested in receiving the help of Dr. Prideaux, so he asked Roe in the same letter:

> 'if you could bring him to show either that there is no fundamental difference betwixt us and the Lutherans even in the Schoole-questions, or supposing there were a fundamental difference in the same then to show How that it ought to bee taken away his judgment might be of great worth and profit. Also if hee would insist upon the grounds laid in the Conference of Leipsigk and show How that the agreement found there is either sufficient or may further bee accomplished and made up it would bee very steadable.'

Durie also wrote to Hartlib on 3 December, explaining that he was battling with attacks on his reputation as a peacemaker at the time. Enemies were writing to Oxenstierna telling him that Durie wished to turn Sweden into a Reformed-only country and his arguments for a union of the Lutherans and Reformed were only a step in that direction. Durie feared that one letter of slander containing six lines would ruin six months of hard work.[374]

It is clear from the petition sent to England by the Continental clergy stating that on hearing Durie's words concerning a Practical Divinity, they had assumed that this was something already well-established in England from which they could benefit. The idea, however, was as rare in England as on the Continent. England had indeed given birth to Francis Bacon (1561-1626) and his works on the *Advancement of Learning* in 1605 and *Novum Organum* in 1620, but Germany had produced Johann Heinrich Alsted (1588-1638) with his *Compendium philosophicum* in 1620 and his seven-volume *Encyclopaedia Cursus Philosophici* of 1630. Comenius had matriculated from Alsted's High School at Herborn to Heidelberg and was deeply influenced by this theologian and educator as many others through-

---

[373] Turnbull's collection, p. 227.
[374] Turnbull's collection, pp. 228-229.

out Europe. It is quite surprising what influence this educational institution which was not even allowed to grant degrees had on 17th century Europe. It was Durie's and Comenius' aim to combine and build on both the traditions of the Bacon school and that of Alsted; Comenius following Alsted more closely and Durie Bacon. However, both found that works to do with practical divinity or Pansophia from Alsted's pen and especially Peter Lamberg's Rostock *Pansophia* published in 1633 were mere compilations of other men's thoughts put together without any coordinating principles. However, as we shall see, Joachim Hübner in his comments on Comenius' allegedly Pansophic *Janua* which Comenius had written on the pattern of the Spanish Pansophists, was hardly an improvement on Alsted's and Lamberg's works.[375]

As an encouragement and even basis for a more thoroughly synergistic work on universal learning and practical divinity, Durie often quoted the above mentioned *Ecclesiarum Magnae Britanniae* and he determined to return to the Continent in 1634 armed with credentials from the English court, state and ecclesiastical authorities to build on the cooperation he had gained between 1631 and 1633. In a pamphlet entitled, *Touching the worke of Pacification*, written at Westminster on 31 March, 1634, Durie related to his supporters his aims in revisiting Germany to gain statements of agreement from the leading Princes, educators and clergy concerning matters of education and pacification. These were:

'1. The substance of all the best treatises & counsells of ancient & moderne authors may bee compiled & drawen together in one bodie & put forth with especiall recommendations from those that are in authoritie.

2. Polemicall writes & chieflie inuectiues may bee prohibited by common consent & the authors censured.

3. The examples of the Agreements of the Churches of Polonia & of Bohemia may bee urged as a president in this kind, & the necessitie of the like practise may bee shewed in these Churches at this tyme.

4. but because the agreements of Polonia & Bohemia haue not fully reached to the effect which may bee attained by reason of the loosenesse & confusednesse of their gouvernments & Leiturgies, & some other defects under which they lye a remedie for all this may bee suggested, & conveniently insinuated which in due tyme might take effect to the great advancement of the

---

[375] See Bergmann's 1896 work 'Zum Gebrauche des Wortes „Pansophia" vor Comenius' for a detailed overview of this problem.

Gospell, & preseruation of it from the incroachments of Popish superstition, & to the building uppe of all the Churches in the true beautie of holinesse.'

Durie continues:

'These are the purposes which by the grace of God in using the meanes I think I could bring to some effect; besides which I could intend collaterally some ends which perhaps would proue no lesse aduantagious for the publick good then some of the verie chief.

1. I could labour to bring them in here with our uniuersities; in respect of the meanes of Learning & good order kept in them; that seeing most of all their owne academies are either ouerthrowne or destitute of learned men they might bee mooued to send hither their sonnes to bee bredde & instructed, by which meanes they would bring home at least the knowledge of the language which is the facultie to make use of our bookes.

2. I could giue them an Impression of the usefulnesse of our bookes exstant in Practicall Divinitie to stirre them uppe to desire the benefit of them.

3. I could take notice of all the rare gifts which God hath bestowed upon the most eminent men in any of those parts, in any kind of learning or facultie; to bring the benefit of it hither either in bookes or treaties exstant or in M. S. or by way of some setled correspondencie to bee entertained that that effect; as for example I might draw Schikkardus his peculiar gifts in the orientall tongues to the profit of our Schooles & Iongius his facultie of teaching Sciences, & searching naturall thinges might also bee gained; & whatsoeuer Docemius or any other hath in a Singular kind might bee ripened, drawen forth & improoued to a publick good by some way of correspondencie & communication.

4. The historie of the true state of the Churches in those partes, containing the diuersitie of their Schismes, divisions & subdivisions, the true causes of these, & the differences of all their gouvernments & leiturgies might bee set forth; to shew what the fundamentalls are wherin they all agree or disagree; & what possibilitie there is of reforming in due tyme those euills that giue so great aduantage unto the publick ennemies of the Gospell to preuaile & ouerthrow those Churches.'

Durie then concludes his pamphlet by asserting:

'for if the end & aime bee from God, hee will find meanes to bring it to passe one way or an other sooner or later; & if I can not bee made use off in so reddie & currant a way as this seemeth to bee, I will not leaue off to seeke out some other way; neither shall it bee losse of tyme or labour, for I know that I serue a Master who is faithfull & is able to reward me; therefore also I shall straine to bee faithfull unto him & constant in this course resoluing to creep when I can not go; & flutter when I am not able to flye; so I know that God his power will bee so much the more manifest in my weaknesse; & if it fall out that the iealousies of opposit factions lye heauie upon me & presse me downe on both sides whiles I striue to walke in a Royall way betwixt them both & will not side with either partie in particular practises: I must resolue to endure that extremitie of partiall mens iudgments with patience, striuing to giue offence to none, & to worke upon that which is effectually good in both; hoping that this will bee both an easie & a pleasant taske if God support my spirit under the burden of outward wants, & endue me with discretion to converse with all men without partiall & priuat intentions. Yet for all this if in this miserable & distracted age, (for who knoweth what light God may bee pleased to bring out of those stormie clouds of darknesse) a man should bee soe happie as to meet with some publick & resolut spirits <left margin: in this countrie aswell as in forraine parts who should bee> reddie to ioyne in these endevours of our spirituall calling; I should bee most entirely bent to contract a holy [2 words deleted] <league> of fraternitie with them; & devot my self as a sacrifice unto their seruice, to bee directed by their counsell & giue them constantly account of all my proceedings.'[376]

Procuring the Public Good in Learning and Religion

Thinking success was near, Durie published *A Motion Tending to the Publick Good* in 1642 composed of introductory thoughts and views aired in two letters to Sir Cheney Culpeper. The work was to demonstrate 'how by the best means of reformation in learning and religion it may be advanced'. Its further aim was given in the extended title, as encouraging text book authors 'to set forward Pius and Learned Works'. In his Introduction, Durie explains that nobody can do any good to posterity unless he has served his own generation aright in doing that same good. Goodness, in order to be goodness must be to the public good; otherwise it is good for nothing. However, this raises the questions of what is truly good and how this goodness is attained. As true goodness can only come from Christ the Giver of all things wise and good, a truly good man must have found his way into Christ's Kingdom and discovered the substance and matter of goodness there. So Durie goes on to discuss the aims of a public good which are:

---

[376] HP, Ref: 1/9/1A-6B: 6A BLANK

1. Public good is the universal private good of every man who has his being in the life of God. As this goodness is universal, none can grasp it for himself. It is for everyone. A goodness which serves merely some is not a public good.

2. No one can procure this good for others if he does not search it for himself and attain to the true love of it. He cannot however, enjoy goodness by himself, as true goodness is public goodness, it is to be enjoyed and shared by all who have been given their being by God. That which makes anything good at all is that it serves for the benefit of all.

3. There can be no self-seeking in propagating the public good. God cannot be made to serve any man's ends as knowledge of God and His works is for all. The means leading to this public good are:

   a. Education for all: By educating the whole natural and spiritual being of all mankind and rejecting methods below this standard. Natural education must precede spiritual education. A person who is not educated naturally, cannot be educated spiritually. Thus a most laudable work of public good is to provide a right course for the education of children and the perfection of human learning.

   b. The setting up of Agencies; Spiritual Counsellors and Agents should be appointed to work out a foundation of evangelical religion for educational purposes, avoiding the scandals and differences of denominationalism and showing the benefits of ecclesiastical pacification. Unblameable and peaceful conversation with all men should be taught, even when opinions differ. A lively correspondence should take place between the Protestant churches concerning pan-educational matters and this should be printed for general distribution.

   c. Chairs appointed in Practical Divinity and Colleges: Professorships of Practical Divinity should be set up in all universities and one each at Sion and Gresham Colleges in London, teaching the practical application of public good. Works on Practical Divinity should be compiled from the practical writers of the age. By 'practical writers', Durie means those who use their knowledge of whatever kind for the public good.

   d. General public Lectures and Bible Studies established: General lectures should be arranged in London for the common people, teaching them how to make use of Scripture and Christian meditation. It must be added here that a filum meditandi for Durie was more a course of study rather than merely 'pondering about things.' These courses should be graded according to the abilities of the learners. A whole or half a chapter should be dealt with per lecture. Here, Durie was actually pioneering what the English call 'Night Schools' or Colleges for Further Education.

Durie then speaks of the need for treaties or special works dealing with both the human (humane) and the divine aspects of knowledge. These should be:

1. To discover defects: Defects and disorders in teaching and educating children should be revealed and suggestions made for their remedy and how they may be best applied. Such works must be detailed but brief.

2. To educate parents: Parents must be taught how to implant seeds of virtue in their children and create in them an eagerness and enjoyment in learning.

3. To evolve new methods of learning: New ways of teaching children must be developed especially in alphabeticism, reading and writing. Durie recommends learning by enjoyment in doing in the form of games, playing together and pastimes.

Teaching the organising and synergising of things presented to the senses

Teaching starts with the general preparation of discerning and being able to name things immediately present to the senses, so enriching the children's imagination and preparing the pupil for learning based on these observations such as religion, language, and science. This includes:

1. Religious education
   a) A brief overview of the Bible is to be taught according to the capacities of the children.
   b) Bible examples should be used to point out the ends for which God has given them.
   c) The marrow of Biblical doctrines should be taught, graded to the age and understanding of the pupils.

Prior and in conjunction with these three stages, the teacher should be taught how to teach them and be provided with correct directing literature.

2. Linguistic education
   a) Direction must be given in the use and properties of the mother tongue as a basis for learning other languages.
   b) Then directions for learning, say, Latin or Greek or Hebrew must be given. This requires four further helps:

i. The presentation of the foreign language with its basic uses and its various declensions and conjugations.
ii. The body of the language, containing all its vocabulary with its special features in their derivations and compounds with an easy to use grammar and dictionary.
iii. The 'periodicall doctrine' of language should be now taught. This is Durie's terminology for structure, syntax and style.
iv. Again, Durie stresses the need for teacher's manuals so as to portion the volume of teaching didactically and methodically.

Durie uses the word 'science' here in the sense of the accumulation of learning. Here there are four degrees in teaching:

3. Scientific education
   a) Knowledge of the history of human learning.
   b) Knowledge of structured learning with its principles and fundamental truths.
   c) Knowledge of the body of science 'containing all the precepts and branches of humane learning and the deductions which are infallibly evident, and truly drawn already by other men's labours from universall principles.'
   d) 'Knowledge of the universal method of ordering the thoughts, to finde out by our own industry any truth as yet unknown, and to resolve any question which may be proposed in nature, as the object of rational meditation.'

These proficiencies lead the pupils from the first steps of learning to the perfecting of the use of reason in discovering by their own efforts all that can be found in nature. Here we see that Durie felt that knowing how to learn and finding things out for oneself was quite as important as what to learn through the instructions of others. To these reforms in education, a treatise needs to be added concerning a re-ordering of secondary education, the colleges and universities and introducing fitting curricula. Textbooks need to be written both building on the research of others and paving the way for new research. The faults and defects of establishments of learning must be revealed and the poor quality of text books rectified. Durie maintains that even if good textbooks are available, poor teachers cannot do much with them. He gives the example of the Bible, 'which few make good use of now adaies'. Thus the treatise he wishes to have written must of necessity be the material and lesser part of teaching. The main part is instilled in the pupils by teachers of the correct spiritual and mental stature who know their business and calling. He confesses that it is a vain idea to think that the common run of Doctors and Masters of Science will be able to do much with reformed textbooks. Public authorities must be won over to invest in a new type of college and university instruction so as to make new men for new tasks. New wine must be put into new bottles. Thus the King and State should both be persuaded to fill the breach in education. He trusts that Culpeper will be diligent in explaining this need in Parliament. Durie had indeed, been recommended to Parliament by John Gauden, alongside John Amos Comenius, in 1640, as those able to reform Britain's education. Durie himself had already petitioned Parliament and the King twice during 1641 and now probably felt that such a move need not be futile. Durie, however, confesses that he has not yet discussed the matter of finding political and private sponsors with his close friends Comenius and Hartlib and must do so before informing Culpeper concerning his plans, adding the words, 'For we are bound to doe things with mutuall advice.' Such humble statements from Durie's pen have moved the greater number of researchers into seventeenth century education to feel that Durie took his educational cue from Comenius and both Hartlib and he trod the same paths as Comenius, thankful for his guiding hand. This, as the next chapter will show is far from being the case and in fulfilling his ideas and ideals of universal learning, practical divinity and pansophy, Durie blazed tracks where no one had gone before.

CHAPTER SEVEN

The *Foedus Fraternum* of Durie, Hartlib and Comenius

Comenius' alleged influence on Durie re-examined

Scholars have often argued that it was John Amos Comenius who first set Durie on the path of pansophical learning and served as his mentor in his campaign for Protestant unity. Harry J. Scougal in his Jena dissertation *Die pädagogischen Schriften John Durys* sees Comenius' hand in guiding Durie through the labyrinths of learning, and writes concerning Comenius' visit to England in 1642, 'in diesem Jahr richtete DURY zum ersten Male seine Aufmerksamkeit auf die Frage der Erziehung'.[377] So, too, Theodor Klähr of the *Comenius-Gesellschaft* claims that Durie's plans for church unity brought him in contact with 'seinem grossen Zeitgenossen Comenius' and that, 'diese Verbindung hat wohl das Interesse Dury's auch auf pädagogische Fragen gelenkt'.[378] Indeed, after referring to Durie's writing on education in 1658 almost as if this were a maiden attempt, Klähr claims that behind him and Hartlib stood, 'die gewaltige Gestalt des Comenius, der in England eine fruchtbarere Thätigkeit auf pädagogischen Gebiete geweckt hat, als bis jetzt allgemein bekannt ist.'[379] Other scholars take it for an axiom not to be doubted that Comenius' influence on Durie started not in England in the early 1640s but in Elbing in Prussia in the late 1620s. So, Thomas H. H. Rae writes:

> 'Another friendship was equally important, his (Durie's) meeting and friendship with Comenius, who was at Elbing by 1628 and a friend of Dury by 1628 or 1629 at the latest. Their friendship was not, therefore delayed till 1635 as some have previously believed, an error that is in part responsible for the common belief that Durie was merely a disciple of Comenius with no independent contribution to make.'[380]

---

[377] *Die pädagogischen Schriften John Durys*, p. 23.
[378] Johannes Duraeus, *Monatshefte der Comenius-Gesellschaft*, VI Band, 1897, pp. 65-66.
[379] Ibid, p. 71
[380] *John Dury and the Royal Road to Piety*, p. 52.

These words are puzzling as one would think that the sooner Durie met Comenius, the more scholars would tend to think that he was influenced by the Moravian. The later their meeting, the more likely it would be that Durie and Comenius developed their ideas independently. However, evidence of an Elbing meeting in the twenties has not been forthcoming and Durie could hardly have met Comenius personally in 1635 as he was in Holland for most of the year and then journeyed to Sweden carrying a letter of recommendation from Charles I,[381] and one from Archbishop Laud[382] via Germany and Denmark whilst Comenius remained in Poland. Nor can they have met at the Synod of Thorn in July, 1636 as often postulated as we know from Durie's numerous letters that he was in Sweden at the time. Furthermore, his 1635-8 correspondence refers to the clergy at Leszno and Thorn, including Comenius, asking Durie to advise them and not to give Durie advice either in ecclesiastical or educational matters. So, Rae's rather inconsistent claim in 1998 that 'No written evidence of any exchange of ideas actually in 1628 exists, no proof of sufficient intimacy for such influences exist,'[383] certainly still holds good. Even though Rae predates the meeting of Durie and Comenius by many years, he shows how strong influence from Comenius' side on Durie is historically impossible. Rae blames Scougal for saying concerning Durie, 'there is not the slightest doubt that the first impulse came from Comenius'[384] in educational matters, but Scougal continues the sentence by saying that Comenius had apparently very little influence on Durie *as the Scotsman differed from Comenius in almost all essential points.*[385] He also argues that Comenius' works evolved from discussions with Durie and Hartlib, not vice versa. Batten refers to the alleged evidence Johann (Jan) Kvačala gives in his much cited *J. A. Comenius* of 1914 to show that Durie was working with Andreae and Comenius at Elbing. Kvačala's words, however, do not support this interpretation. He does refer to all three men but as men going different ways, though at the same time. What Kvačala actually says is:

---

[381] Dated Greenwich, 29th May, 1635, Oxenstierna Collection in the Riksarkiv and Appendix in Westin's *John Durie in Sweden*.
[382] Dated London, May, 1635 also in the Oxenstierna Collection and in Westin's *John Durie in Sweden* appendices.
[383] *Ibid*, p. 52.
[384] *John Durie and the Royal Road to Piety*, p. 52. Rae is referring to Scougal's *Die pädagogischen Schriften John Durys*, p. 64. See also p. 49 where he says more or less the same thing.
[385] My emphasis.

'In demselben Jahr wo sich Comenius mit seinen Genossen *an* J. V. Andreae um Aufnahme in seine Freundschaft *wandte*,[386] erschienen bei dem Prediger der englischen Mission in Elbing, dem Schotten John Dury, zwei Männer, ein Schuldirektor und ein Hofrat, und baten um die Begutachtung einer von ihnen verfaßten irenischen Schrift. Dies wurde für Dury Anlass über das Heilige Abendmal eine selbständige Abhandlung zu schreiben, die dem schwedischen Residenten Godemann sehr gefiel.[387]

It appears that Batten and others have read into Kvačala's 'seine Freundschaft' a reference to Durie and not to Andreae. But Kvačala first mentions Durie after referring to Comenius' seeking Andreae's friendship and is obviously merely comparing Andreae's cooperation with Comenius with Durie's cooperation with his friends at Elbing. Nor does Kvačala tell us which year he is writing about or where Andreae and Comenius were at the time. Nevertheless, they were obviously acting independently of Durie. Who the Headmaster and the Privy Councillor were, who were so interested in the Lord's Supper, Kvačala does not say, but the headmaster was obviously Johannes Mylius who, the rector of Elbing Grammar School who died in 1629, so Kvačala's meeting must have been before Mylius' death. The Privy Councillor was obviously Godeman. Kvačala says Godeman persuaded Durie to leave off working at his school (seine Arbeit an der Schule aufzugeben) which is strange as Durie does not appear to have worked as a teacher, but this may mean merely to leave off writing his *Treatise on Education* which Durie was working on at the time. However, Durie did not get on too well with Mylius whom he found a carping wrangler and not interested in the practical application of education.[388] Thereafter, Kvačala describes Durie's six Pansophical tasks on his 1631 visit to Germany, to gather scientific material; to foster the study of oriental languages in preparation for a mission to the Jews, to study keys to opening up prophesies, to enquire into philosophy, Chemistry and Mechanics to gain a better world-view; to examine what was then called 'magical languages', which meant attempts at a world language like modern Esperanto in which all the world could correspond and which would aid universal enquiry, and to organise a perfect society where all the above gained knowledge could be synthesised. These aims had nothing to do with a Comenian influence though Kvačala explains that Comenius' sole aim in his discussions with Andreae was to work on reorganising society which was merely

---

[386] My emphasis.
[387] See Kvačala's *J. A. Comenius*, p. 26.
[388] See letter written to Hartlib 1 January 1629, Sloane MSS, 654.

one of Durie's alleged six aims. Kvačala then relates how Hartlib had given up his former tasks to help realise Durie's aims, of which, he adds, Comenius probably knew nothing.[389]

Westin argues that both Durie and Hartlib, must have been in touch with Comenius during their time in Elbing but quotes disbelievingly Johann Kvačala in his *Die Schicksale der Grossen Unterrichtslehre des Comenius* where he claims that Durie completely abandoned his interest in education in 1628.[390] So here we have Kvačala maintaining that Durie abandoned education in 1628 whereas, as we have seen, Scougal and Rae argue that he first started writing on education in the forties and fifties. Westin, obviously with a smile on his face, corrects all and putting the matter historically right says, 'I verkligheten uppgav varken Hartlib eller Durie sina pedagogiska studier och intressen. De voro en del av deras verksamhet även in den kyrkliga förbrödringens tjänst.'[391] This quite fits the facts revealed in the two friends' correspondence such as when, in 1636, Durie writes from Sweden, asking Hartlib to send him anything he has penned on universal learning and languages as his friend Matthiae is educating young Queen Christina pansophically and he needs all he can obtain on the subject.[392] Furthermore, Durie tells Hartlib that he has been promised funds to finance the printing of a Practical Divinity so the English team already working on it should not fail in their duty. Practical divinity, as will be shown further, included for Durie his educational reforms and was a synonym for universal learning or pansophy.

Juillet-Carzon, continues her individual suppositions concerning undocumented dating by claiming that around 1627, Hartlib and Comenius persuaded Durie to leave Elbing and work for inter-church peace in Britain with Hartlib remaining the 'intermediary between the two men'. She also speaks of Comenius' strong support for Durie between 1633 and 1634.[393]

Actually, the first extant certain references to Comenius made by Durie were made in letters from Sweden to Hartlib preserved in the Westin collection for the years 1636-38. Here, Durie speaks of Comenius at Leszno and Albert Niclassius, a Reformed minister at Danzig soliciting help for their United Brethren Synod of Thorn.[394] Durie mentions that Comenius has sent him some books to his Swedish address but he must postpone

---

[389] Ibid, p. 27.
[390] This is also claimed, as already mentioned by Kvačala, in his J. A. Comenius.
[391] *Svenska Kyrkan och de Protestantiska Enhetssträvandena*, p. 110, fn 45.
[392] Letter dated 29 May, 1636. Turnbull Collection, Kyrkohistorisk Årsskrift.
[393] Scotland and Europe, pp. 15-17.
[394] Westin Collection, *John Durie in Sweden*, pp. 35; 61.

reading them till a later date. Turnbull, in his *Kyrkohistorisk Årsskrift* collection of Durie's correspondence adds in a footnote to a letter of Durie's dated 29 October 1636 concerning correspondence sent by Niclassius from Leszno, 'At the Synod of Thorn, in July 1636, they agreed to support Dury's work of ecclesiastical pacification.'[395] This was also the finding of Sander as seen above. In letters preserved in the Westin Collection, Durie speaks of post from Poland 'with many subscriptions promisinge to Ioyne further my worke, likewise from Comenius in the name of the Synod held at Thorn.'[396] Here, again, the reference is to Comenius following Durie, not the other way around. Otherwise, we find Durie telling Hartlib on 7 Jan, 1638, in another letter preserved in the Westin Collection 'I have a mind to retire my selfe to a setled way of writing and meditation to elaborate my owne and some of Mr. Comenius Pansophical taskes soe farre as God shall enable me.'[397] This would indicate that Durie was about to compare Comenius' pansophy views with his own. Westin claims that Comenius first mentioned Durie in one of his irenic writings 'as early as the late thirties' but does not give the source.[398]

Durie's acquaintance with Comenius through Peter Figulus

When Comenius was banned from Bohemia in 1628, he sought refuge in Polish Leszno (Lissa) where he became a teacher under John Rybinski, who was Headmaster until 1638. It is often pointed out that as Leszno is only a stone's throw from Elbing, nothing hindered the two friends from visiting each other around 1628/9-1630. Four hundred kilometres as the crow flies is a long way and though a modern train covers the distance in little over five hours, it was a journey of several days through most uncertain, dangerous territory during the Thirty Years War. Moreover, it must first be established that Comenius and Durie were, indeed, 'friends' at this time and sufficiently interested in each other to travel such a long way through Prussia with few decent roads. Comenius, indeed, apart from the undocumented reference mentioned by Westin, first mentions Durie's name in his autobiography and correspondence in conjunction with John Garden's fast sermon entitled *The Love of Truth and Peace* preached in 1640 which he was first shown in 1641 after reaching England. I find nei-

---

[395] Turnbull Collection, p. 220.
[396] *John Durie in Sweden*, pp. 34-35.
[397] *John Durie in Sweden*. Letter written 7 January 1638, pp. 96-97. See also letter written 18 October 1637, p. 78.
[398] *Negotiations about Church Unity*, p. 39.

ther records of correspondence with Comenius in Western's first collection of Durie's letters up to 1634, nor in the Hartlib Papers, nor in the many other archives listed in my Acknowledgements. We do find a letter from Comenius addressed to Hartlib in October, 1634, thanking him for sending money to finance his Pansophical studies. Then Comenius answered 'Since you have made provision for the cost of boarding an amanuensis, I shall make sure to send you part of my Pansophical writings as soon as I may.'[399]

Comenius is mentioned occasionally and rather critically in the yearly Durie-Hartlib Circle's debates reported in *Ephemerides* from the mid-1630s on. In *Ephemerides* Part 3, 1635-36, where pansophism is being discussed, we find the comment recorded 'To have the one and selfe-same Method in all things with Comenius cannot bee and is absurd'. In Part 5, there is an entry referring to a suggestion from Sir Christopher de Berg that something must be done to help Continental exiles of whom Comenius was one. Sir Christopher then suggested, 'But Mr Dury <or Comenius> should make a Paraenesis to contribute Meanes to it.' The addition '<or Comenius>' appears to be a later editor's comment as usually any parenthesis in the transcript is included in normal curved brackets but latter additions thus <. . . >.[400] Reference to Durie's own didactics and educational reforms are far more numerous and positive in the *Ephemerides* think-tank. Indeed, though England was in the know concerning Comenius and considered his works critically, Comenius was obviously not aware of the many reformers in England who were thinking pansophically.

It is certainly most likely that Durie first became more deeply knowledgeable of Comenius' life and work through his secretary of many years, Peter Figulus, who was Comenius' former foster-child and later son-in-law and was with Durie in Sweden during 1636-1638 and was to bring Comenius and Durie together in 1641.[401] One interesting detail in this connection shows that Comenius and Durie were at least both well known to third persons, though not linked.[402] In a letter from Germany dated 18 December 1634 in the Hartlib Papers giving no sender's name, we are told that

---

[399] Ref: 7/103A-B, HP.
[400] Refs: 29/3/50B-65B: 30/4/18B-27B, HP.
[401] See Sander, Friedrich, Comenius, Duraeus, Figulus. Nach Stammbüchern der Familie Figulus-Jablonski, in *Monatshefte der Comenius-Gesellschaft*, Dritte Band, 1894, Heft 9 und 10, pp. 307-326.
[402] In *A letter from Germany* dated 18 December 1634 preserved as a copy in the Hartlib Papers Ref: 11/1/22A-B, neither the sender's name, nor the recipient's, is mentioned.

'Comenius ist vergangenen September nach der Wilda gezogen auff den littawischen Synodum, welcher zu dem ende angestelt, auff dz die littawische kirchen, so bisher Helveticæ confessionis gewesen, sich auch geben sollen vnter pacem Sendomiriensem.' After relating what other mutual friends were engaged in, the writer devotes most of his letter to news of his relationship with Durie, writing:

> 'H. Duræus ist erstlich vor 2 tagen anhero kommen. Es hatt mier seines ad quæstiones Docem. communicieret, weil ich ihn nicht sagen darff dz miers der H. geschickt hatt. Ich beginne seine sachen woll gnug zuverstehen, aber 1. kan sie noch nicht imitieren allerdinges. 2. Kan nicht persuadieret werden, dz es commodus modus sey, sed video [scripturam?] saepe torqueri. Er hatt hier wenig zeit, vnd ich auch. Ich versiere ihn in meiner technologia generali, vnd kan absque jactura die meditation nicht interrumpieren. Mus deshalben noch ein 14 tage sparen, als dan will ich meine difficultates zu papier bringen vnd ihm nachschicken. Der H. urgire alsdan responsum. Insonderheit bitte ich der H. wolle mier fleissig communicieren seine analysos die er hin vnd wieder über varia scripturæ loca gemacht hatt. Der H. soll sehen wie sehr ich meinen circulum generalem verändert brevius, plenius, et accuratius omnia. Will ihn abschreiben lassen vnd den H. mit ersten zuschicken, wirdt mier als dan ohne zweiffel mehr occasiones geben können. Bitte [delition] er lasse mier doch wissen wz doch Comenij Pansophia sey, obs Logicum oder physicum etc sey. In physicis et grammaticis agnosco illum excellere, sed non possum adhuc capere eius Logicalia [quod?] eò pertinet. Mein principalste vnd schwerste arbeit wirdt sein 1. in Logicis, da ich sehr grosse vnd schwere concepten habe, vnd viel weiter sehe als zu vor. 2. in his ad Theologiam specialim accommodandis. Wen dz geschehen (:hoffe es soll innerhalb 3 monden gethan sein), als dan will ich hernach in theologicis particularibus in sonderheit bleiben. Wz aber angehet Comp. dogm. et historicum, müsse wier sehn vnd hoc fiat nostra non operâ sed directione. Si Angli vestri nolunt facere systema, dent nobis aliquid pecuniæ, facilè faciemus systema. Iudico consultissimum, ut, quemadmodum Comenius singularum vocum dedit januam, ita et conficiatur aliqua omnium Latinarum elegantiarum, formularum, idiotismorum, flosculorum. Ich meine Mr Goodin, vmb dessen stucke ich ihn gebeten. Aliâs plura. Vale.'[403]

Amongst the remarks of a number of British and Continental authors listed under the title *Desiderata Theologica* preserved in the Hartlib Papers and Sloane MSS, there are three extracts of letters from Gaspard Streso dated 27 November, 4 December and 18 December 1634 respectively. The 18

---

[403] Ref: 11/1/22A S.H., HP.

December letter is partly identical with the letter quoted above which mentions both Durie and Comenius, so the author who is not named in the above quoted letter must have been Casper Streso. Here, Streso says in the first two extracts:

> 'Eben izo kan ich vom H. Duræo vnd bin den gantzen tag mit ihm in arbeit gewesen Seine Analysin etc. zu lernen. Succedit et laudo deum ipsi ac Tibi gratias post hac plura - Iam in modo Analyseos me parumper exercebo et tum meis elaborandis me accingam. . . . . Nach dem Duræus von mir gezogen habe ich beginnen zu Examiniren seinen Modum Analyseos. Sed reperio me non rectè percepisse. Cum redieris de difficultatibus percunctabor. Non judico hanc esse Verum illum aut sufficientem Analyseos docenda [et? margin obscured] dum, sed hoc spero me meis objectionibus et Occasionibus ipsum ita exercitaturum vt se bene [excuti cado? margin] Modum rectum demum [inveniat? margin]. Dum abest Bibliothecam eius perscrutor vbi inter alia in [illeg.] physicam incidi quam vt rerum [fatiar?] tanta [cum anditate?] et delectatione [typ.? margin] vix præter Theologica quicquam Commode admodum incidj dum ad [illeg., margin] Circulum me præparo. [Vatoe? abbrev.] [illeg., margin] viri ingenium. In doctrina de [Ratione?] et Hominis Intellectu [p...cula?] [quapiam? margin] desidero. Id.'[404]

These extracts show how deep Durie's involvement in universal learning was even at this early date. Streso mentions his particular interest in Durie's *Modum Analyseos*. This is no doubt because in the previous year, Streso had published his own *Technologia Theologia* which had to do with '*Doctrina analyseos & geneseos Logicae particularius elaboratur & ad Theologiam applicatur.*' As he wrote on Pansophism, he was obviously curious to know how both Durie and Comenius approached the subject. Streso was an early addition to the Dury-Hartlib circle, with other Transylvanian connections. It was through him, Comenius gained the idea of soliciting financial support from several Princes of Transylvania including free postage to and from the Principality. Durie regularly kept Streso furnished with his works from the early thirties on and the Durie-Hartlib circle reviewed Streso's works regularly.[405] However, Durie was rather critical of Streso's 'typographicall faults'.[406]

---

[404] Ref: British Library Sloane MSS 638 ff. 46A-54B: 46B, 47B, 48B, 52B BLANK.
[405] See for instance, Westin's *John Durie in Sweden*, pp. 4-5 where Durie tells Hartlib, 'Vrge mr Streso to print the thinges I left with him, I wish I had already here 100 of each of the things to be printed.'
[406] See letter dated October 1636 in the Turnbull Collection.

Comenius was not *the* major 17th century educational trailblazer

The older tradition that Comenius was *the* trailblazer of universal learning in seventeenth century educational teaching is aired by Professor John William Adamson in his *Pioneers of Modern Education* preface.[407] He relates, however:

> 'While much of the story gathers about the thought and activity of Comenius, there were also educational pioneers in England now forgotten or, if not forgotten, remembered by reason of achievements in other fields. To these and especially to Samuel Hartlib, a name which should be honoured by all friends of Education, some of the following chapters are devoted.'[408]

Hartlib, as Durie, who is strangely not mentioned at this point by Adamson, had Francis Bacon's ideas concerning the advancement of learning to build on and, according to John Milton in his 1644 work *Areopagitica*,[409] the country was bubbling with educational reform and 'so pliant and so prone to seek after knowledge', so that if 'some great and worthy stranger should come among us, wise to discern the mould and temper of a people', he would be thrilled with what was going on. Milton had long been an associate of the Durie-Hartlib circle, though not a leading member. He, however, played a major role in the Petty-France circle with which Durie was closely associated, which campaigned for educational reforms. Milton responded to a request by Hartlib by sending him his views on education entitled simply *Of Education* which, he says, he had been working on for a number of years and were thus based on older authors. Nevertheless, Milton's reforms are now being accepted as a breakthrough in modern educations. It is thus interesting to note that when reforming educator Oscar Browning introduced Milton's treatise to his colleagues in the latter half of the 19th century, the Senior Latin Master used it as proof that Milton must have been wrong in his head. Cambridge University published a facsimile reprint of the 1673 edition[410] of Milton's work under Browning's editorship in 1890. Milton's ideas are more literature-based than the practical divinity of Durie. In his work, Milton indirectly but clearly discloses

---

[407] Cambridge, 1921.
[408] P. viii.
[409] Found in a separate essay entitled 'A Vision of England' in an anthology *A Book of English Prose 1387-1649*, edited by Henley and Whibley, 1894, ppp. 358-362.
[410] The first edition was published by Hartlib in 1644.

the fact that Comenius was the 'great and worthy stranger',[411] he mentioned in *Areopagitica* however, he tells Hartlib, 'And, as I hear, you have obtain'd the same repute with men of most approved wisdom'. So Milton does not see Hartlib as being in any way inferior to Comenius. Furthermore, he again gives an indirect allusion to Comenius by saying that 'to search what many modern *Janua's* and *Didactics* more then ever I shall read, have projected, my inclination leads me not.' As Milton's educational views are not the subject of this thesis but a passing piece of evidence concerning it, it is sufficient to say that Milton takes an independent stand, sometimes agreeing with Comenius, sometimes agreeing with Durie but showing no major dependence on either.[412] We must also bear in mind that Comenius claims frankly and honestly in his *Continuatio Admonitionis Fraternae* that he visited England with the sole intention of profiting from what was going on there. Other letters suggest that Comenius viewed his visit to England as a fund raising trip. Indeed, the Durie circle and especially Hartlib who had done all the preparatory work were as disappointed with the outcome of Comenius' visit as Comenius himself was. Both sides had expected more. Keatinge, in his Introduction to Comenius' *Great Didactic* explains the whole problem in a nutshell:

> 'Uppermost in the minds of Hartlib and his friends was the formation of a Universal College for physical research, on the lines suggested by Bacon in the New Atlantis. Now at last in Comenius they thought they had discovered a man competent to found a 'Solomon's House,' if only sufficient assistance were given him by Parliament. This was their chief object in urging him to come to England, and it was on the establishment of the college that the conversation turned. As we have seen, Comenius was totally unfitted to organise a collection of laboratories for physical research for that was what the proposal practically amounted to. He was, as he himself confesses, primarily a theologian, and, though he could talk glibly and attractively of enlarging the boundaries of human knowledge, he had no conception of the tedious processes of experimentation that were necessary, and flew off to vague generalisations at every opportunity. If proof was necessary, he supplied it from the Scriptures, and as a means for verification valued a text from Genesis more than all the paraphernalia of the chemist and the physicist.'[413]

---

[411] 'I see those aims, those actions which have won you with me the esteem of a person sent hither by some good providence from a far country to be the occasion and the incitement of great good to this Island.'

[412] See *Of Education* in the 1673 edition of *Poems etc. Upon Several Occasions*, Guttenberg Books.

[413] See Keatinge's Introduction to Comenius *Great Didactic*, p. 45.

This would explain why Durie and Hartlib continued to publish their educative ideas during Comenius' visit without any contributions from the Bohemian. Indeed, there was not even a single 'joint-statement' on education issued during that time It was clear that Comenius visited England as a learner not as a teacher.

In his chapter 'Hartlib and Pansophia', in *Pioneers of Modern Education*, Adamson says '*It has been suggested[414]* that Hartlib and Comenius got to know each other between 1625, when Comenius perceived that the Moravian community must suffer permanent exile, and 1628, when Hartlib quitted Prussia for London.' More concretely, he goes on to say that the first known connection of Hartlib with Comenius is found in a manuscript letter in Amsterdam dated March 1636 which refers to the 'first Author of Janua Linguarum' and gives a list of five names of people who helped publish a Latin course worked out by Comenius, the first of whom is described as 'Mr Samuel Hartlib in royal London'. The reference to 'the first author' is unclear as *Janua* appeared either anonymously or under the name of John Anchoran in the sixteen thirties. However, Adamson mentions that Hartlib published Comenius' 60-paged work *Conatuum Comenianorum Praeludia* in 1637, which was designed to pave the way for a lengthier work on pansophy. Comenius in his Preface to his *Great Didactic*, however, does not say specifically that Hartlib published the work but a 'worthy man' in England did. Whoever published the work, he appears, nevertheless, to have been disappointed with it or with its limited reception. Nor does Comenius, himself, seem too pleased with the publication of this seminal work which was never really finished. Adamson quotes Comenius as saying:

> 'I sent to him what I aimed at in the form of a preface to be prefixed at some time or other to a book. Quite beyond my expectation (indeed I was not consulted at all) this was printed at Oxford under the title *Conatuum Comenianorum Praeludia*. The intention was of the best, to facilitate the knowledge of the project amongst many of the learned, and to seek their judgment thereon: but the result did not in all respects answer to the expectations of my excellent friend'.[415]

M. W. Keatinge in his Introduction to Comenius' *Great Didactic* again links Hartlib with Comenius, saying, 'At the beginning of 1632, greatly struck by Comenius' didactic venture (*Janua Linguarum*), and especially

---

[414] My emphasis.
[415] Pioneers of Modern Education, p. 84.

by its Encyclopaedic features, he (Hartlib) sent him a friendly message with a copy of Streso's *Of the use and abuse of reason*. He also hinted that it might be possible to procure him some monetary aid in England to enable him to carry on his work with greater ease.'[416] Keating does not mention any deeper or further cooperation between Hartlib and Comenius at this time. On the contrary, he writes that now Comenius left educational work for a while to write a history of the Bohemian Brethren and works on Physics. Comenius' English friends were obviously anxious to encourage him to write more thoroughly about his Pansophy, by publishing the *Preludium* of his views. However, caution is required in interpreting these events. Adamson and others emphasise Hartlib's cooperation with Comenius here, though Kvačala tells us that Comenius was not knowledgeable of what the English were doing themselves towards Pansophic learning at the time. Actually, the mediating link between England and Comenius, as Kvačala shows, was the young German Scholar Joachim Hübner, now studying at Oxford. Hartlib did not have Comenius' *Preludium* printed but passed on the copy he had received to Hübner wondering if it might interest him. Hübner, a Pansophist himself, thought the overview of a possible future work had potential and took out an Oxford license to have it printed in 1637. Kvačala relates how Descartes had complained that Comenius ideas on Pansophy were merely an anthology of other men's works that he had put together rather than written an original work. The Durie-Hartlib circle had been compiling such anthologies in their yearly *Ephemerides* since the middle thirties in which Comenius' *Janua* was occasionally mentioned and at times severely criticised. Kvačala relates how Comenius, on being notified that Pansophist Hübner had given him a hearing in England, sent him an overview of his planned *Great Didactic*. Hübner, according to Kvačala, made it look very tiny. As an introduction to Pansophy it was quite useless, he argued, and betrayed its title. Comenius had not graded his learning to suit the age and abilities of the pupils and indeed, though there were elements that would be of interest to teachers, there was little in it for the learners and the art of learning had been left out in a work allegedly to be about universal learning. Parents were left out of the educational picture, too. There was no structure in the work and no linking subject with subject. One did not know where to begin and where to end. Material which belonged together had been cut into pieces. Comenius wrote much about 'nature' but never explained what he meant.

---

[416] See Ref: 26/23/1A-8B in HP. This is a letter of 16 pages soliciting financial aid for Comenius.

Kvačala says of Hübner's criticism, 'zu einem grossen Teil ist sie berechtigt.'[417] Though he believes Hübner has emphasised the weaknesses in Comenius' work rather than its strengths, he also says, 'Von panharmonischen Normen sieht man in dem Aufbau und auch in den Details der Didaktik kaum etwas.' Perhaps it was no wonder that Comenius, after this, took up writing plays for the stage, Latin text books for schools and prophetic mysteries for those interested in speculating about the future. This is all written to show that Kvačala, who is invariably pushed forward as the champion of a Comenius who totally out-paced Durie, was certainly no one-sided propagandist for Comenius. Indeed he demonstrates how Comenius relied on many other friends to provide him with substance for his works and confessed that without the help of philologists, philosophers, historians and those skilled in polymathy, he could not compile his works.[418] So, too, co-workers with Comenius such as Kinner and Ravius, and even fellow Bohemian George Ritschel, fell out with him concerning either the alleged misuse of their contributions or because Comenius was slow to come up with the fully-fledged pansophy he spoke about for decades and and to which they had contributed. Judging by the letters preserved in the Hartlib Papers, jealousy and an exaggerated sense of personal professionalism upset their working together.[419] Nevertheless, Comenius' *Janua Linguarum*, as Durie testifies in a letter written from Stockholm on 26 Nov. 1637, had already been printed in Stockholm and 'received in all schools'.[420]

1637 was also the year that Comenius published his *Faber Fortunae Ars Consulendi Sibiipsi Quæ est Pansophiæ Christianæ particella non postrema. Illustribus Dominis, Comitibus Leschnensibus, strenæ loco oblatus*, which will be considered when comparing Durie's pansophy with Comenius' later in this chapter. It is sufficient here to say that the work has little to do with pansophy with its teaching of every man for himself first and an alleged Pansophy gained from generalising on particulars. Comenius self-styled 'present' to the Polish Lords appears to be a rather blunt and unimaginative way of courting sponsors. Durie's Pansophy was always for

---

[417] See pp. 38-40.
[418] Kvačala, p. 42.
[419] See especially Kinner's letter to Hartlib of 9 Oct. 1647 in which he outlines his and Comenius' differences with Ritschel, Ref: 1/33/16A-17B and 1/33/4A-18T. For Ravius, see below.
[420] Turnbull's *Letters Written by John Dury in Sweden*, 1636-1638, Svenska Kyrkohistoriska Årsskrift, vol. 49, 1949, p. 227.

the common good and a means of encountering problems with a synthesis and synergism of knowledge, not a particularisation.

Concerning Comenius visit to England in 1641, Adamson says frankly, 'Particularly what Hartlib's precise relationship to Comenius was when he invited the latter to England in the summer of 1641 is a question which has baffled research.'[421] However, Comenius stresses in his *Continuatio Admonitionis Fraternae*, Sections 49 and 50 how Hartlib had sought for a meeting with him concerning the setting up of a Pansophic school and had gathered a number of men who wished to discuss this matter with Comenius in either England, France or Holland as he chose. However, Kvačala, without giving alternative sources, claims that it was Hübner who made this suggestion, not Hartlib.[422] He also suggests that Hartlib was not happy with Comenius keeping aloof from the English research into Pansophy and that Hartlib scolded him into visiting England by telling him that he should forget flesh and blood and think of God's honour. Comenius replied that he would come but remain incognito. However, he complained in his farewell letter quoted from below that he was given too much public attention which hindered him in doing what he wanted. If one works, however, for the public interest one must attract public attention. These facts must be taken into mind when reading the numerous exaggerated theories of what great reforms Comenius set in motion during his visit to England, chief of these being his supposed influence in founding the Royal Society. In meticulous detective work, Dorothy Stimson sifts all the scanty evidence and concludes in contradiction to Robert Fitzgibbon Young, 'It does not seem probable, therefore on the basis of the existing evidence that the visit of COMENIUS to England in 1641-2 marks an "important stage in the development of the idea of a great institution for scientific research."'[423] So, too, G. H. Turnbull when examining R. H. Syfret's idea that Comenius was involved in the founding of the Royal Society through his alleged influence on the Durie-Hartlib circle from 1638-40 via Thomas Haak, comments:

'So far as I know, however, there is no evidence, either among Hartlib's papers or in the published correspondence of Comenius that Haak was himself a collaborator in that scheme; and it is relevant to note that he is not among

---

[421] *Pioneers of Education*, p. 88.
[422] Kvačala, p. 43.
[423] Comenius and the Invisible College, *Journal of the History of Science Society*, Cornell University, vol. 23,2, 1935, pp. 373-288. See also Robert Fitzgibbon Young's Comenius in England, the visit of Jan Amos Komensky the Czech Philosopher and Educationalist to London in 1641-1642, its bearings on the Origins of the Royal Society, etc., Oxford, 1932.

the helpers who were to cooperate with Comenius in carrying out his plans for his stay in England, plans which included the working out of Pansophia.'[424]

Turnbull might have added that there was also no evidence to call the Durie-Hartlib circle 'the Comenian group' as he does, either.

In Section 52 of his *Continuatio Admonitionis Fraternae*, Comenius, however, writes, *Dedi ergo me itineri, Londinumque ipso aequinoctii autumnalis die ingressus, demum quid fieret cognovi: Nempe me Parlamenti jussu vocatum fuisse.*' This reconstructed conviction that the English Parliament had called Comenius was apparently merely based on the fact that after his arrival in England, he had been shown a transcript of Gauden's speech before Parliament recommending Durie and Comenius to the nation, so there was no official invitation from Parliament at all. Webster calls Comenius' conviction a 'misapprehension'.[425] Scougal suggests that Comenius was disappointed at what England had to offer him, but claims that: 'In einer Hinsicht aber war sein Besuch nicht ohne allen Erfolg gewesen', seeing the success of his venture in encouraging Durie to write on education.[426] As mentioned above, this quite ignores Durie's co-work with Hartlib on the subject from 1628 on. Indeed, Kvačala says that it was Comenius who was anxious to adopt Durie's system, not the other way around.[427] This was also the case, as we have seen, regarding Durie's plans for ecclesiastical peace accepted at Thorn in 1636.

When Comenius was called to Sweden on Durie's initiative, and after discussions with Durie and Hartlib, whilst in England, he wrote down notes on a planned work *Via Lucis* as a means of introducing his ideas to the Swedes. Much in this work reflects Durie's and Hartlib's views of the early thirties. Thus Scougal rightly claims that the elements of Durie's *Notions Tending to the Publick Good* of 1641-2 are to be found in Comenius' *Via Lucis*, which was finally published as late as 1668 in Amsterdam. Scougal therefore argues on internal evidence that *Via Lucis* was initially composed by Comenius 'und seine Freunde' in England.[428] However, it does appear that Comenius sent his *Via Lucis* preview to De Geer without

---

[424] Notes and records of the Royal Society of London, Samuel Hartlib's Influence on the Early History of the Royal Society, London, 1953, Vol. 10, pp. 101-130. See pp. 104-105 for my quote.
[425] *The Great Instauration*, p. 42.
[426] Die pädagogischen Schriften John Durys (1590-1680): Ein Beitrag zur Geschichte der englischen Pädagogik, p. 23.
[427] Kvačala, p. 45.
[428] Scougal, p. 28.

the knowledge of Durie and Hartlib. This would explain why, in the same year, Durie wrote a critical review of the work entitled *De studio Comeniano Consultones Exercitationes Exercitatio: 1 De Viæ Lucis capitibus prioribus*. Though Durie confessed that Comenius' subject was a good one, he thought the Bohemian had approached it from a most impractical and far too general angle. He then went on to give practical advice about setting up reform schools and describing the education they should give, emphasising true virtue and its practical application to the various professions practiced. About the same time, he also campaigned for setting up such schools on the Continent as in his *A Proposal that 2000£ per Annum may be set apart out of the Dean & Chapters Lands, towards the erecting & mantaining an English College at Heidelburg*, according to plans he had laid in the early thirties. Durie was most eager that the right kind of universal learning might be promoted Europe-wide.

Scougal claims that Comenius himself confessed that his *Via Lucis* was a joint work in his Introduction to his *Great Didactic*. As Comenius does not mention this in his own Introduction, Scougal is probably referring to the Introduction in the English text he used which is from the pen of Keatinge.[429] However, in the final production of *Via Lucis* there is a display of intolerance against other 'sects' most unlike Durie and Hartlib. This was unfortunate as De Geer, who was financing Comenius' trip, belonged to one of the so-called Reformed 'sects' that were not tolerated in Sweden. Furthermore, the work is highly philosophical. Comenius writes of a three-fold light which enlightens the learner, the eternal, the outer and the inner, whereas for Durie the Lux was the one pansophical light found in Lux Mundi, Christ, the Light of the World. So, too, striving to be scientific, Comenius describes his three-fold light in terms of waves or flux which are constantly moving. Durie looked to one Light as the standard of all knowledge. He also rejected Comenius' constant use of his Rule of Three. Christ was All in All and besides God's Word and Works, there was no third, man-centred revelation.

From this point on, Kvačala leaves his comparison of Comenius and Durie as each goes his own way.[430]

On Comenius' departure from England, he left a general letter of thanks addressed 'to the Supporters of Pansophical Study in England.' However, in the letter, there is no word about any joint work on Pansophy having been undertaken or plans for such. There is also no mention of a planned

---

[429] See Keatinge's translation *The Great Didactic*, pp. 45 and 96 and Scougal's Bibliography on page 67.
[430] Kvačala, pp. 43-45.

college for universal learning. Comenius is, indeed, full of complaints. He writes, 'I may do nothing here in quiet,' and that 'I was not allowed to do those things which were my first intention.' He believes that things would have been better if 'unpropitious times had not come over us' and that he wishes that 'our designs may not always be mere designs but may be transmuted into works.' Then he adds, 'Cease not to put your trust in my faith and sincerety.' Nothing is said that is more concrete apart from Comenius thanking his friends for all the gifts he has received but also saying, 'For my own purpose I ask for nothing, or nothing that may be a burden, except that certain debts, contracted here for my needs and the needs of my people, may be expunged with your help.' This all underlines the fact that Comenius had looked on his trip to England as a fund-raising expedition. De Geer had already sent money to Comenius before his England visit and financed Comenius admirably in Sweden. As soon as Comenius told his Swedish sponsors that he was in Elbing and ready to start the philological work for which they had hired him, he was sent 1,000 Thaler as a down-payment for his services. He received financial aid from Sweden until his death but also from his trusty English and Dutch friends.

The Pact between Durie, Hartlib and Comenius

In an 'aside', in his work *A Motion for the Publick Good* published in 1642, Durie explains to Culpeper the precise relationship between himself, Comenius and Hartlib as it stood whilst the three were together in England, saying:

> 'Though our tasks are different, yet we are all three in a knot sharers of one anothers labours, and can hardly bee without one anothers helpe and assistance. But it is no new thing to such as serve God without respect to private ends, to spend and be spent and receive no incouragement from the world. Therefore also we can have patience, and waite upon God's providence till hee shew what use he will make of our talents, which we have dedicated unto his service, to be imployed and set a worke in any place where we shall perceive the overture to be made by him, onely our end must alwaies be answerable unto the guift bestowed upon us, viz, publique and universal, because we know that God's intention is, that his goodnesse and glory should not be concealed nor ingrossed by any, but made common to all that can partake thereof.'

Durie can write in this vein because in March 1642, he, Comenius and Hartlib had signed a joint secret and solemn pact, sealed with a vow, concerning their mutual aims and literary cooperation entitled *Foederis frat-*

erni Ad mutuam in publico Christianismi bono promovendo aedificationem sancte in conspectu Dei initi.[431] The full text is given to show the most detailed scope of the mutual course the three men pledged, under God, to follow in the interest of Protestant unity and Christian education.

> '*Foederis fraterni. Ad mutuam in publico Christianismi bono promovendo ædificationem sanctè in conspectu Dei initi*
> *Tabulæ.*
> *Nos qvorum hîc infra subscripta sunt nomina, postquam misericordiâ Dei nos eodem spiritu agi, cordaque nostra ad gloriam Dei & Proximi in publico utilitatem omnibus Christianæ vocationi nostræ consentaneis vijs promovendam, Zelo non fucato inflammari animadvertimus: in conspectu Dei ter Optimi Maximi qui secreta cordium scrutatur constituti, & invocato sacro sancto ejus nomine, hæc fraterni Foederis pacta inviolabiliter in timore nominis ejus servanda inter nos sancivimus; ad arctiorem animorum in vero amore fraterno coalitionem, ad ardentiorem Zeli à mundanis affectibus puri mutuis monitis & exemplis inflammationem, & ad efficaciorem consiliorum qvæ suggerit & suggeret Deus, ope mutuâ exseqvutionem.*
> *Vovemus itaque, & elatâ in cælum manu nostrâ juramus, atque Deo & nobis invicem coram ipso promittimus hæc seqventia.*
> *I. Qvòd scopum divinæ gloriæ manifestandæ, Proximorumque publicæ ædificationis promovendæ, unicè nobis propositum habebimus: qvem ad vnicam revelatæ nobis in Verbo Evangelij Veritatis normam, sine omni humanarum nostrarum vel alienarum quarumcunque particularium opinionum præconceptione & præjudicio componemus. Ac proinde qvòd nihil privatim nobis in studio publico qværemus, aut captare studebimus (puta gloriam, aut emolumentum aliquod externum) præter id qvod ad finem jam propositum omninò necessarium esse comperiemus.*
> *II. Hunc finem ut cum bono Deo asseqvamur, proponimus nobis, & eos qvi jam ad agnitionem Christi vocati sunt, ad meliorem & pleniorem in Religionis professione consensum revocare; & eos qvibus nondum Christus illuxit, Evangelij luce collustrandi omnes legitimas atque possibiles vias qværere; tandemque inter omnes, vocatos & vocandos, Pietatis & Charitatis veræ vera excitare studia. Idque omnibus vijs, qvas ostendit hactenus, & ostendet posthac, misericordia Dei: nominatim verò,*
> > i. *Per procurationem Pacis Religiosæ inter dissidentes.*
> > ii. *Per educationem Juventutis Christianæ veri Christianismi scopo magis conformem.*
> > iii. *Per Reformationem studij veræ Sapientiæ, ad qvod capessendum publicè alij, hoc præsertim fine excitandi erunt,*

---

[431] HP 7/109/1A-2B.

ut omnes & facilius consvetas mundi vanitates animadvertere, & veras veræ felicitatis vias dilucidè agnoscere, possint.

III. In hoc autem proposito ut propitium habeamus Deum, qvotidianis precibus apud eum certabimus, cùm pro nobis invicem, tùm pro alijs omnibus, qvos ad similia studia ubicunque locorum, aut jam (conscijs vel inscijs nobis) excitat, aut posthac excitabit, Deus: ut omnes nos spiritu suo ducat, & conjunctos perpetuò regat, ad omne beneplacitum suum perficiendum.

IV. Ipsi interim nos nobis invicem spondemus, non nisi mutuo consilio & consensu omnia in hisce acturos: nec ullum nostrûm de seipso & actionibus majoris momenti suscipiendis constituturum, qvoad hæc, seorsim: sed communicatis invicem (sive coram, sive per literas) consiliis, qvotiescunque id fieri poterit. Si autem non poterit, tum verò rem ipsam gestam, cur & qvomodo gesta sit, nobis invicem communicaturos.

V. Pollicemur, neminem nostrûm alteri sua ad propositum hunc scopum facientia ulla cogitata, etiam intime qvæque, celaturum: sed in Dei conspectu apertè omnia qvæ Deus suggeret de qvolibet ad deliberandum hactenus proposito, aut dehinc proponendo casu, declaraturum.

VI. Neminem etiam nostrûm consentientibus reliquorum consilijs præfractè restituturum, sed alijs cessurum: etiamsi forsan non illicò ratio num qvæ allegabuntur validitatem & momenta plenè perspicere qveat. Qvodsi tamen qvispiam rationes suas omninò validiores esse credat, ideò qvod satis evidenter convelli neqveant; [deletion] is ad seqvendum alienum potius qvàm proprium sensum cogi non debebit: sed res in suspenso relinqvenda, ac precibus Deo commendanda erit.

VII. Promittimus, nos non tantum in spiritualibus consiliorum momentis ad mutua studia (qvæ publico omnium bono subordinabuntur) promovenda unanimiter fovendis, nobis invicem omnem fidelitatem præstituros; sed etiam in externis vitæ adminiculis temporalis, qvibus mutua societas nostra confirmari, defectus si qvi incidant suppleri, & infirmitates sublevari, qveant, communicandis, re & operâ, id qvod fratres intimos, & in Christo vera ejus membra decet, facturos.

VIII. Recipimus qvoque nos liberè nos invicem, sed tamen amicissimè, de erroribus (si qvi per imprudentiam humanam committantur) monituros: nec monitionem alteri ab altero (aut etiam à pluribus uni, vel ab uno pluribus) factam, etiamsi acrior forsan fuerit, ægrè laturos.

IX. Visum autem est, & datâ fide spondemus, pacta hæc foederis nostri (conscientiæ potissimùm nostræ causa in conspectu Dei initi) non vulgare ad alios, nisi communi consensu: atque id ijs solis, qvos ejusdem foederis socios fore idoneos confidamus: nempe qvos similiter intentiones universales corde pio & simplici in timore Dei fovere & promovere velle ac posse certis indicijs constet. Nisi forsan & Patronis ac promotoribus, qvos suscitabit Deus, eadem hæc patere opus videatur, ad intentionis nostræ integritatem demonstrandam.

> *X. Tandem, si qvid amplius huic Religiosæ in Deo consociationi nostræ ex usu fore communi consilio deprehensum fuerit, his ipsis pacti hujus nostri articulis subscribi, eundemque cum illis valorem habere, debebit.*
> Actum Londini 3./13. Martij 1642
> Johannes Duræus
> Johannes A. Comenius.
> Samuel Hartlibius.'

Here we see in paragraph II, sub-sections i-iii, that Comenius, Hartlib and Durie were one in first seeking religious peace before establishing a system of education which would prosper only on such a basis. So, too, paragraphs IV and V make it quite clear that nothing should be undertaken by the three friends that was not by mutual design and consent and no decisions should be made without mutual agreement. The three men swore that even their most inner thoughts on their joint projects should not be kept from one another. It is thus always useful to compare Durie's writings with those of Hartlib and Comenius, especially in their proposed two main endeavours to achieve a Protestant union and to reform education. Most scholars appear to be in no doubt as to the relationship between Hartlib and Durie within their circle of friends and would thus agree with Webster's statement 'Anonymity was almost certainly an intentional guise of their Christian Association, although it was always clear that Hartlib and Dury were themselves the chief agents, Hartlib being the primary organiser and instigator, while Dury drafted the majority of their tracts'.[432] Again, Webster says in his Preface 'Dury gave literary expression to the educational ideas of the Hartlib circle, while Hartlib himself was the publicist and co-ordinator'.[433]

Concerning John Amos Comenius, the matter is rather more difficult. Durie and Hartlib brought Comenius into their fellowship as they did Hamilton as one needing their support and one who had the potential to work for their cause. In both men, they were disappointed. When comparing Durie's work with that of Comenius, one finds possible mutual influence and cooperation, especially around 1641-1642. However, Comenius' influence on Durie, in the light of the evidence available, must be seen to be lesser and later than Durie's influence on Comenius. Durie was the leading influence behind Comenius' visits to both England, according to Figulus, and Sweden, according to Blekastad, and it is obvious that his earlier writings influenced the later writings of Comenius. So, too, Comenius view of universal learning in its more philosophical components differed from that

---

[432] See Webster's *Samuel Hartlib*, p. 8..
[433] Ibid, p. vii.

of the team of Durie's followers who, as mentioned above, approached Archbishop Usher so that he might compose a Practical Divinity which backed Durie's ecclesiological and educational plans. Durie preferred to call his pansophical system either 'Universal Learning' or 'Practical Divinity' as it was to be taught as a practical project to educate body, soul and spirit, and fit the pupil or student out to make a maximum contribution to the welfare of the world.[434] Comenius' teaching was more philosophical, encyclopaedic and dialectical, leaning more towards Rosicrucianism[435] than Durie's more utilitarian, Biblical approach, though Comenius did speak of learning by doing. The real difference was that Durie approached his work with a fully-developed concept whereas Comenius worked in faith towards such a concept which never found realisation in his own mind.

Durie's Pansophy more synergistic and comprehensive than that of Comenius

When in 1637, Comenius outlined his views concerning Pansophism in His *Faber Fortunae sive Ars Consulendi Sibiipsi Quæ est Pansophiæ Christianæ particella non postrema. Illustribus Dominis, Comitibus Leschnensibus, strenæ loco oblatus, Anno 1637*, he criticises Bacon for his irrelevancy and poetical flair in his Pansophy outlined in his *Advancement of Learning* and writes:

> '*Cùm ergo nobis in Pansophiæ opere adornando necessariò fuerunt exhaurienda omnia, obvenit etiam illud suo loco tractandum: sed ad cæterorum formam et normam, pleniùs et solidiùs. Eò namque Pansophicis nostris moliminibus tendimus, ut Eruditionem, hactenus ferè sine termino diffusam, vagam plerisque partibus vacillantem, in pauciora, sed fixiora, et solidiora contrahamus: ne opus sit scientiam jactare, sed scire: & scire non multa, sed bona, et necessariò profutura, idque certò et infallibiliter.*'[436]

This is not Pansophy in Durie's understanding of the word. Here, Comenius shows he is still of the old school which generalised from case studies

---

[434] See Durie's *A General Discourse touching a concurence of the work of Peace Eclesiasticall with the aim of a civill Confederation amongst Protestants* (1641) pp. 1-4 for a discussion of the necessary balance in activity of the body and soul and their spiritual necessities.

[435] See Young, *Faith, Medical Alchemy and Natural Philosopy: Johann Moriaen, Reformed Intelligencer and the Hartlib Circle*. pp. 19; 104.

[436] Ref: 35/3/1A-14B, HP.

of particulars. By this means, one cannot possibly view the factors which hold knowledge together. The only time Durie and Hartlib were of two different minds, as will be shown in more depth below, is when Hartlib, at least for a time, favoured case studies to be generalised in amalgamated knowledge-engineering. Durie could not accept the idea of synthesising mere isolated case studies but campaigned for synergising all knowledge from the start of education. So, too, Comenius was obviously very much influenced by the prophetical visions of Christoph Kotter, Mikulas Drabik and Krystyna Poniatowska in forming his theories in contrast to the more level-headed empiricism of Durie. J. T. Young argues, without being too convincing, that Hartlib also had his roots in at least 'quasi-Rosicrucianism' because of his interest in Antilia, the legendary island where Christians lived in unity.[437] Hartlib's views on Antilia were most pragmatic but he held them for only a brief time. However, the Swedes, moved by Hartlib and Durie, planned to materialise the idea in their Lithuanian Protectorate.[438] Young, however, is on more certain ground when defining Comenius' Pansophy as a departure from the 'two books' theology of Bacon. The latter, as Durie after him, spoke of 'the book of God's word' and 'the book of God's works'. Comenius, Young argues, added 'The book of Man's mind', keeping to his rule of three, believing that because man is made in the image of God, true divinity starts off with man's contemplation of himself.[439] This probably explains why Comenius was made so much of in the German Democratic Republic where the hypothesis that man is the measure of all things reigned. Pfarrer Otto Riedel of Zwickau wrote from the German Democratic Republik in 1984 as part of a discussion concerning Comenius' basic educational thinking. Commenting on Comenius' appeal to an anthropological based 'Lebenspraxis' Riedel says:

> 'In diesem Zusammenhang sei darauf hingewiesen, daß die Formalstruktur der Gesamtpädagogic von Comenius in der Pädagogik der Deutschen Demokratischen Republik zur Grundlage, gemacht worden ist, ohne daß die geistig-religiösen Inhalte der Comeniuspädagogik als konstitutive Elemente übernommen worden sind. Allein Comenius ist in der DDR hoch geachtet. Es gibt zahlreiche Strassen, Plätze und Schulen, die seinen Namen tragen'.[440]

---

[437] *Faith, Medical Alchemy and Natural Philosophy*, p. 104.
[438] See Kotljarchuk, Andrej, *In the Shadows of Poland and Russia: The Grand Duchy of Lithuania and Sweden in the European Crisis of the mid-17th Century*. See also Webster's study of Antila and Macaria in his *Great Instauration*, p. 46 ff.
[439] *Faith, Medical Alchemy and Natural Philosophy*, p. 110.
[440] *Der Convent*, Heft 12, 1979, p. 301.

The Foedus Fraternum of Durie, Hartlib and Comenius

Durie believed that fallen man, as he explains in his two major works on Practical Divinity and Universal Learning, cannot possibly contemplate divinity and attain to universal knowledge without reconciliation with God through faith in the Lord Jesus Christ. Thus finding a true knowledge of God in this way is the beginning of wisdom.[441] Riedel, however, sees Comenius' gift as been able to recognize the 'man in man'. Thus in a recent study of Comenius' educational principles by Czech Jan Hábl, pastor and lecturer in pedagogical theory at the University Hradec Králové, the author entitles his book, *Lessons in Humanity from the Life and Works of Jan Amos Comenius*.[442] Durie did not neglect this aspect but emphasized the need to recognize God for the benefit of man, in a practical divinity. Such thoughts probably led J. T. Young to conclude concerning Comenius' adherence to the Durie-Hartlib circle:

> 'At its nexus, it was an association of personal friends. Hartlib and Dury were the two key figures: Comenius, despite their best efforts, always remained a cause they were supporting rather than a fellow co-ordinator. Around them were Hübner, Haak, Pell, Moriaen, Rulise, Hotton and Appelius, later to be joined by Sadler, Culpeper, Worsley, Boyle and Clodius. But as soon as one looks any further than this from the centre, the lines of communication begin to branch and cross, threading their way into the entire intellectual community of Europe and America. It is a circle with a definable centre but an almost infinitely extendable periphery.'[443]

In his essay 'Comenius, Light Metaphysics and Educational Reform' in *Platonism at the Origins of Modernity*, Jan Rohls begins his sub-section on Forerunners of Philosophy by stating:

> 'Despite having already composed a slim work with the title of *Prima philosophia* at the beginning of his Lissian Exile, Comenius' own philosophical system developed only gradually, in ever new programmatic drafts. In the second half of the 1630s, he sketched out his Platonically inspired Pansophia in various different texts as a philosophico-theological reform programme. The incentive came from his contact and friendship with a circle of English scholars: the Scottish theologian John Dury, Samuel Hartlib from Elbing, and his young friend Joachim Hübner.'

---

[441] Ibid, p. 110.
[442] VKW, 2011.
[443] See Young's *Faith, Alchemy and Natural Philosophy*, p. 248.

Rohls also claims that it was under the leadership of Hartlib that Comenius carried on Bacon's idea of an *instauratio magna*.[444] Thus Comenius and his two friends were influenced alike by Bacon rather than Comenius being the instigator of such views in the minds of Hartlib and Durie. Indeed, Rohls places the influence of Durie and his friends on Comenius before Comenius' visit to England in September 1641. Figulus implies in his diary that Comenius came as Durie's and his special guest and says the three of them remained in intimate contact from Comenius' actual arrival in England in September 1641 until their joint departure for the Continent in June 1642. Figulus also speaks of numerous meetings with influential people to whom Comenius was introduced by Durie and Hartlib.[445]

There is, however, as Rohls hints, much difference in the theology and philosophy behind Comenius' work compared with the similar works of Durie on the subject. Rohls calls *Prodomus Pansophiae* 'a fusion of Platonic light metaphysics with educational reform.'[446] It is also worthy of note again here that Durie's work *Notions Tending to the Publick Good* came out ten years before Comenius' *A Pattern of Universal Knowledge*. Durie's work emphasises strongly the connection between universal learning and practical religion, void of any Platonism or Neo-platonism. By 1651, Durie, Hartlib, Streso, Cyprian Kinner and Johann Ravius and several other friends of Durie had written widely on the subject, being far more precise than Comenius. Indeed, as we have seen with reference to Rae's views of Comenius above, Hartlib and Durie introduced one of their own circle, Cyprian Kinner, an expert on the subject, to Comenius as they were keen to encourage and help him. Johann Ravius also worked closely with Comenius at Elbing, hoping Comenius would develop his Pansophy on lines pioneered by the Durie circle.

Durie kept to his plans concerning natural and spiritual learning being brought into a single whole throughout his life, whereas Comenius considered the idea as a main educational goal only for a few and scattered number of years. So, too, much of Comenius' supposed pioneering, educational work including logic, mathematics, science and language learning came after Durie, Hartlib, Pell, Kinner and Ravius had widely published their more synthesising thoughts on the subject.

Durie centred his Practical Divinity in the Being of God as revealed in Scripture as a harmony of all knowledge, whereas Comenius set up a tri-

---

[444] Springer, *The Netherlands*, p. 63 ff.
[445] See Sander's Comenius, Duraeus, Figulus. Nach Stammbüchern der Familie Figulus-Jablonski.
[446] Chapter 5, p. 63.

partite system of Wisdom, Nature and God as three equal parallels to be compared. His rule-of three incorporating Analysis, Synthesis and Syncrisis often verged on Neo-Platonism or Near Eastern Cabbalism and paved the way for Leibniz and Hegel to build their triangular dialectic on it. So, too, especially in the early forties, Comenius, as seen in his autobiography and communications with Durie's circle, was torn between working on a theoretical Pansophy and hack-writing single-subject text-books for schools as a means of earning a living. Durie, supported by his closest friend Samuel Hartlib,[447] had no such problems as all knowledge was integral for him. He also firmly believed that teaching should not be hindered by subject-orientation.

A major cleavage between the views of Durie and Comenius was that the former saw the mother tongue as the initial conveyor of knowledge with language learning developing afterwards based on this foundation. Comenius still saw Latin as the pathway to knowledge.[448] This was probably because his native Bohemian tongue had no serious international appeal and a *lingua franca* was needed. Much of Comenius' work has only been internationally appreciated in relatively modern times as it had not been widely translated, not even into English or German as his *Great Didactic* illustrates. One of the many reasons why Comenius was pleased to allow Cyprian Kinner to help him in his work was that scientist Kinner had already researched the acceptance of a model *lingua franca* that would make learning easier and more effective internationally.

Comenius' work for Sweden

During his 1641-1642 stay in England, Comenius was invited by Cardinal Richelieu to teach his views of pansophy in France, but also invited for various other reasons to the American colonies, Holland, Poland and Sweden. Comenius, was, however, not yet ripe for the task demanded of him in France as he had to revise his views, incorporating Hübner's criticism and also his main financial sponsor in France died. Comenius thus asked Hübner if he would like to travel to France and introduce his pansophism there. Hübner was pleased to accept the offer. It appears that Oxenstierna's promise to Comenius not to rest until Bohemia was liberated from the papists clinched the deal with Sweden. However, we know from Johann Morian's letter of 23 Dec. 1641 in the Milada Blekastad collection of letters first

---

[447] See Webster's *Samuel Hartlib and the Advancement of Leaning*, p. 8.
[448] Comenius was to change his mind on this issue several times. Whilst working for the Swedes, it was learning through Latin which he supported.

published in 1976 that De Geer had already been supporting Comenius most generously. This had caused Morian in Amsterdam, always a little critical of Comenius, to withdraw his own financial support as Comenius was in more financially secure hands. However, during the following March, we still find kind-hearted Morian following Comenius plea for help in supporting his wife and family left in Leszno, though Comenius was now on a generous fixed income.[449] Indeed, according to Blekastad's Introduction to *Comenius' Självbiografi*, Sweden's interest in employing Comenius arose in Sweden between 1636 and 1638 through Durie's visit with his secretary Peter Figulus.[450] Skytte and other educators had hoped that Durie would drop his emphasis on universal learning and pansophy and help in providing their reformed schools with Latin textbooks as the gateway to learning. This was contrary to the Durie circle's plans as, like Alsted, Comenius' first major teacher at Herborn, the Durie circle taught the need to perfect one's mother tongue before becoming multilingual and the beginning of all wisdom was the knowledge of God alone so that education must be homogenous and not built on a monographic education. The Swedes obviously hoped that Comenius could be persuaded to do what Durie refused to do. Durie had been very careful not to let De Geer's financial offers influence his projects. Writing to Hartlib at the beginning of his stay in Sweden on 3 June 1636, Durie tells Hartlib, 'I have nothing to add but to entreate you, not to suffer me for want of supply, so to bee forced to depend on this Man, that hath called me hither, that hee should make any advantage upon me to engage me further to him then perhaps otherwise I would.'[451] Indeed, Durie was unpopular for a while in Sweden because of his reluctance to toe every line the Swedes dictated or to be persuaded by offers of money, needy as he was. The Swedes wanted to use Durie for their own ends but Durie merely wanted Sweden to campaign for Protestant unity and universal learning. Comenius, initially also refused to consider Sweden's demands on him but nevertheless weakened when quite enormous sums were mentioned to him by way of encouragement.

Happily, Comenius has left us with a clear account of his connections with Elbing in his diary which was built into his autobiographical account *Continuatio Admonitionis Fraternae de temperando Charitate Zelo . . . ad S. Maresium*, published in 1669 in Amsterdam. On leaving England in 1642 Comenius journeyed through Holland and Germany to Sweden, a

---

[449] 37/106A, HP.
[450] Comenius' *Självbiografi*, p. 15.
[451] Letters written by John Dury in Sweden, ed. Turnbull, *Kyrkohistorisk Årsskrift*, 1949.

schedule organised for him by Durie. In Sweden, Comenius came under the patronage of Louis de Geer who had supported Durie in 1636-38. He also met Durie's old friend Johannes Matthiae, Durie's former sponsor Axel Oxenstierna and young Queen Christina. The Queen surprised Comenius by conversing in perfect Latin. De Geer immediately begged Comenius to drop his plans for a pansophical work and write text books for Sweden's schools to reform and promote the teaching of Latin. Comenius, thinking of the Swedish aversion to foreigners, especially those with connections in enemy Poland, and that his family were still in Leszno, agued that it would not be appropriate for him to settle in Sweden and work for the Swedish schools system. Furthermore, as Comenius tells Maresius, Mrs Comenius refused point blank to go to a country whose language she did not know. Indeed, Milada Blekastad, in her Introduction to Comenius' *Självbiografi*, says that Comenius was frightened by this time that he would be forced against his will to stay in Sweden. De Geer, however, arranged for a meeting between Comenius and Chancellor Oxenstierna so that they could talk over the project and discuss an alternative to Comenius' remaining in Sweden.

Oxenstierna told Comenius that de Geer would finance everything both for him and a team of writers. He then recommended that Comenius should settle down in Pomerania or Prussia but not Poland where he had lived since his expulsion from Bohemia. Oxenstierna thus wanted him in a more accessible, Swedish-controlled place. Comenius said he would rather go to Prussia than Pomerania and work in either Thorn or Danzig. Oxenstierna said, 'Why not Elbing?' Comenius answered, '*Locus iste ignotus est mihi, nunquam visus.*'[452] This claim alone from Comenius' pen shows that he could not have been in Elbing during 1626-30, not even for a brief visit. Oxenstierna told Comenius that he knew Elbing well and found it a lovely place. Thus Comenius journeyed to Elbing and arranged for his family to move from Leszno and settle there. If this occurred, it must have taken some time as letters are extant from Elbing referring to his wife being still in Poland. De Geer financed Comenius admirably both in Sweden and in Elbing

Comenius opts out of the *Foedus Fraternum*

There was much disappointment in the Durie circle concerning Comenius departure from his English vows. Indeed members of the Durie circle started to complain about Comenius lack of input as early as 1643. Johann

---

[452] *ContinuatioAdmonitionis Fraternae*, p. 24.

Morian, who had supported Durie since his earliest launch into education and work of pacification in the churches, wrote saying:

> 'Herr Comenius hat vnsz vff ein Iahr ein stillschweigen aufferlegt das ist nun furuber vnd höre Ich das Er nur seine Ianuam vnd Vestibulum revidirt vnd auff einen andern schlaag gebracht haben soll, welches ob es zwar ein gut werkh sein möchte so ists doch das Ienige nicht darauff man so lang gewartet vnd den leuthen hoffnung gemacht/ Ich hoffe Ia es werde was anderes dabej sein sonst müste man sich fast schämen das auch nach Iungst gegebener hoffnung (das Er sich nun fort an ad realia begeben vnd innerhalb Iahrs einen gustum Ianuæ rerum geben wolle) gleichwoll nun nichts anders als solche schuhl sachen herausz kommen solten. Zuemahlen weil mir leuthe wiszend sind die da fur halten Comenius könne nichts weiters præstirn als etwan in diesen vnd der gleichen puerilibus darumb hette Ich woll gewunscht das Er auch nur ein geringen anfang in realibus gemacht vnd damit seinen ansehen das Er berait gemacht auch erhalten hette. Vechneri vestibulum auctum wird fast von Iederman seiner Ianuæ furgezogen.'[453]

In 1647, when petitioning Parliament concerning his ideas for universal education, Durie declares Bacon's works to be still being useful but says that Comenius' methods of learning and education must first be 'perfected' before they can become practical.[454] This was after the publication of Comenius' provisional *Pansophiae Diatyposis* in 1643, criticised above by Rohls, and Kinner's 1647 *Diatyposis Pansophiae* which probably led to Comenius falling out with him.[455] In subsequent editions of Durie's 1647 work such as *A Seasonable Discourse* of 1649, Durie drops mention of Comenius altogether, though he still recommends Bacon. Comenius was quite aware of Durie's disappointment and also tells us in his *Continuatio Admonitionis Fraternae* that his friends in Britain did not approve of his going it alone. M. W. Keatinge, in his introductory biography of Comenius to his *Great Didactic*, which he first translated into English in 1849, sees Comenius' silence and inactivity as a major betrayal of Comenius' agreement with Durie and Hartlib and comments frankly:

> 'In the history of great renunciations surely none is stranger than this. We have a man little past the prime of life, his brain teeming with magnificent if somewhat visionary plans for social reform, a mighty power in the commu-

---

[453] Ref. 37/116A-B, HP.
[454] See Durie's *Considerations Tending to the Happy Accomplishment of Englands Reformation in Church and State*, sub-section 'Of the Office of Address'.
[455] Kinner produced several works of his own which differed little in their titles from Comenius' works which were written with strong help from Kinner.

nity that shared his religious ideas, and an object of interest even to those who may have shrugged their shoulders at his occasional want of balance. Suddenly he flings his projects to the winds, consigns his darling plans to the dust-heap of unrealisable ideas, and retires to a small sea-side town 'not to meditate, not to give definite form to latent conceptions or to evolve new ones, not to make preparations for the dazzling of intellectual Europe with an octavo of fantastic philanthropy or of philosophic mysticism, but to write school-books for the little boys in Swedish schools. True, he was paid. He was bartering his inclinations against coin of the realm, against the good gold that streamed from de Geer's Dutch counting-house. He was going to do useful work. Europe gained far more advantage from his school-books than from the Pansophia that did but impart a certain dignity and finish to his didactic method. None the less, Comenius was martyrising himself. Money, sufficient for his daily wants, he could always obtain, and with ease. Of school-books he had written enough, and of school method he was sick unto death. It was the old story. The old inability on the part of a versatile man, to realise his true vocation.'[456]

Keatinge, using sources he does not give, continues by quoting Comenius' 'English friends', writing:

'You have devoted sufficient attention to school-books,' they wrote; 'others can carry on the work you have begun. The world will gain far more advantage from having the paths of true wisdom opened to it than from any study of Latin.' "Quo moriture ruis? minoraque viribus audes?" added Hartlib, more disappointed than any of them at the dissipation of their Pansophic dreams of the previous winter.'

S. S. Laurie in his Preface to *John Amos Comenius Bishop of the Moravians his Life and Educational Works*, (p. 46) in 1884 tells the same story, perhaps borrowed from Keatinge saying:

When he (Comenius) communicated his resolution to his friends in England, he received a strong protest. They complained of his too great facility in yielding to his Swedish advisers, and of his unfaithfulness to the great Pansophic scheme. "Quo moriture ruis?" wrote Hartlib. "Minoraque viribus audes?" He was much shaken by these representations'

Laurie, like Keatinge does not give his source, nor have I been able to trace it. However, though not conclusive evidence, it does fit in with my comments supplied by named original sources.

---

[456] *Great Didactic*, pp. 51-52.

Cyprian Kinner's association with Comenius

It was then that Comenius approached Hartlib's old college friend and Durie's correspondent, Dr. Cyprian Kinner (d. 1649). Research concerning the contributions of Kinner to the development of pansophical thinking in general and a supplier of material for Comenius' works in particular has been sadly neglected. Kinner was a former Privy Councillor who held doctorates in both Law and Medicine. He had been a co-worker with Alsted and Johan Heinrich Bisterfeld and had written widely on education and perfected a system for cataloguing plants. He was also a member of a group of eminent scholars such as Marin Mersenne, John Wilkins, John Delgarno and Johann Heinrich Bisterfeld who were bent on the reform of languages to facilitate learning. Comenius, on the look out for a scientist to enrich his own work, persuaded Kinner, with Durie's help, to work with him. Durie praises Kinner as a pioneer educationalist in his *Petition, John Dury to the Christian Lovers of Learning*. This work is undated but internal evidence shows that it was written around 1648 after Comenius had worked with Kinner for several years and then opted out of the partnership. Durie points out that Comenius, on first hearing of Kinner's successful work, begged him to join him at Elbing in a well-financed project under the guidance of Chancellor Oxenstierna and Louis de Geer. Kinner left all to help Comenius who eventually broke with him because of feelings of jealous rivalry which left Kinner without an income. This is why Durie strove to organise support for Kinner who, Durie says, had followed pansophism, 'from his youth', but could not live by it, so he trained as a lawyer and physician.[457] It was because Comenius was receiving financial support from De Geer and still spoke of researching into pansophism that Hartlib and Durie recommended Kinner to Comenius as one proficient in the subject. This was one of their stratagems to win Comenius back to their working agreement. Comenius was only too eager to jump at the offer. As Kinner had far wider qualifications than Comenius, and was a man who had made his name in far wider fields, it is rather inaccurate of Benjamin DeMott to refer to Kinner as 'a disciple of Comenius' in his *Comenius and the Real Character in England*. Indeed, Kinner was disappointed to find Comenius merely producing Latin text books for Swedish schools, though Comenius assured him at once that this was only a temporary task. Kinner's numerous letters extant show he thought he was giving Comenius far more input than was being turned into output. Nevertheless, Kinner continued to supply Comenius with ideas on the organisation and classification of

---

[457] *Petition John Dury to the Christian Lovers of Learning*, undated.

learning, the world of the natural sciences to which Comenius was a stranger, and advice on didactics. However, he became increasingly exasperated with Comenius' instability of purpose and almost servile dependence on De Geer, believing that such a gifted man could easily make his own way. Kinner claimed, too, that Comenius was not even doing his work for De Geer properly and felt that Comenius was making a fool of De Geer by taking his money but not delivering the necessary work.[458] Kinner was uncertain also about what is own position was in the eyes of De Geer and Oxenstierna.

Some dozen letters from Kinner sent to Hartlib are full of criticism of his partner in authorship, Comenius. Admittedly, much of this criticism is of a very petty nature and given under the guise of a benign friendship with Comenius. Nevertheless, he accuses his co-worker of being unbalanced, of being at times most enthusiastic in what he was doing for Sweden and at others most uncertain and saying he would give up the work and return to publishing on pansophy, which he, however, did not do. Kinner wrote that De Geer was wrong to think that Comenius alone was equal to the task of producing text books on Latin to order and complained that Comenius was not publishing anything at all on pansophy. It is obvious, however, that Kinner wished for more recognition for the part he was playing in his joint work with Comenius and felt overlooked by De Geer who apparently considered him to be a mere assistant to Comenius.[459] Kinner seemed particularly keen on stating that Comenius' *Linguarum Methodus* ought really to be called Comenius and Kinner's *Linguarum Methodus*. Kinner's mention of this work is especially interesting because in Kvačala's sole reference to Kinner in conjunction with another of Comenius' co-writers, Johann Ravius, Kvačala says of their joint works which appeared only under Comenius' name, 'wieviel daran dem Comenius, wieviel anderen gehört, ist nicht zu entschieden'. Of *Linguarum Methodus*, however, Kvačala claims that this must have been Comenius' own work.[460] Kinner's statement puts even that in doubt. Both Kinner and Johann Ravius who were co-workers on pansophy with Comenius at Elbing, published their own works on pansophism after breaking with their partner as Comenius pursued other literary schemes, neglecting the pansophy which he always said was his major love. Comenius had thus quickly broken the pact which Durie and Hartlib in which he had declared, '*Vovemus itaque, & elatâ in cælum manu nostrâ juramus, atque Deo & nobis invicem coram ipso pro-*

---

[458] See Ref: 1/33/39A-42 B, HP.
[459] See Kinner's correspondence with Hartlib from 1646-1648, HP.
[460] Kvačala, p. 61.

mittimus hæc seqventia,' and eight years later, he still had not returned to the partnership. However, against the will of Durie and Hartlib, he, recruited Johann Ravius, the younger brother of Christian Ravius, an old friend of Durie's, by persuading him that he was joining the *Foederis Fraterni* with Durie and Hartlib. Ravius now felt that he was a central member of the Durie circle and was now in Durie's and Hartlib's team working for universal learning. Durie, however, had always been most suspicious of Johann whom he compared negatively with his brother Christian. Johann, too, became frustrated when he found that Comenius had promised him mere bubbles and the younger Ravius began to publish on his own.

Both Durie and Hartlib stood by Kinner who in 1648, published via Hartlib his *A continuation of Mr. John-Amos-Comenius school-endeavours, or, A summary delineation of Dr. Cyprian Kinner Silesian, his thoughts concerning education, or, The way and method of teaching exposed to the ingenuous and free censure of all piously-learned men ... : together with an advice how these thoughts may be succesfully put in practice / translated out of the original Latine, transmitted to Sam. Hartlib, and by him published.* It cannot be denied that Comenius relied on Kinner to a great extent for ideas concerning language and science in writings which came out under Comenius' name only, and so it was this document coming so soon after Kinner's works on several of Comenius' planned themes which hailed the final break between the two men. Kinner claimed that he was enlarging on what he and Comenius had produced together and made sure that his own name was placed advantageously against Comenius'. This break is carefully recorded in two extant documents in the Samuel Hartlib Collection. The first is a formal declaration of separation sent to Lord De Geer: It reads:

Copia Instrumenti Discessionis nostræ.

Quandoquidem a Magnifico Domino Ludovico de Geer, Mæcenate suo benignissimo, Dominus Iohan Amos Comenius impetraverat ut Dominus Cyprianus Kinnerus [Medicinæ Vtriusque?] Doctor in elaborandis Didacticis suis (opere annorum aliquot) sibi ad biennij tempus adjutor esset; illud autem tempus jam elapsum est, et responsum Patroni, utrum videlicet nos diutius cohabitare vellet, emansit; Kinnerus ob rem angustam domi, de alijs subsidijs sibi dispicere necesse habuit. Quanquam autem ad finem usque operarum Comenius eum habere optasset, et ipsemet manere voluisset, cùm maximæ porrò etiam difficultates supersint: necessitate tamen hâc, iste ut discederet, ille ut eum dimitteret, uterque coactus est. Satisfacto prius illi, quicquid de salario pactum erat. Vltro tamen pollicitus est Dominus Kinnerus, etiam absens, si quâ possit, residuas operas juvare, et optimo semper affectu prosequi. Dominus Comenius verò eundem, ob navatam diligenter operam, ubi ubi opus fuerit, commendare. Atque sic amicè ab invicem discessum est. Quod subscriptione hîc manus suæ uterque testatur.

Actum Elbingæ.

17. Septemb. 1647.[461]

The second is a copy of a letter from Peter Figulus to Kinner and a copy of Kinner's reply to Figulus sent to Hartlib and now preserved in the Hartlib Papers. Though Figulus only addresses Kinner by name, he is referred to as representing several of Comenius' former co-workers. The letter is given in full but the reply, written on the day of reception, is three pages long, but can be summed up in a paragraph.

Copia Epistulæ Petri Figuli, hodie ad me missæ.

Reverendo Domino Comenio illa, qvæ volebas, significavi. Displicet consilium, subsuntque ejus rei rationes multæ et multi/ponderis. Certè confusio magna conceptuum et rerum inde metuenda: nempe qvi non diversis solummodò, sed et planè contrariis, Didacticæ structuræ vestræ nitimini fundamentis, eamque deducitis principiis: ipsa etiam Methodus planè non erit una sed longè varians. Dixit etiam possibile non esse, ut Tu tua illa ad horum rationem accomodare ullo modo possis: qvippe qvi jam tantis locorum intervallis separati estis: sua autem in dies mutantur in melius, et limatiora ordinatioraque fiunt: et qvod magis obstat, addidit, Tibi illa penitius inspicere, et illorum intima penetrare viscera, nunqvam fuisse integrum; imo qvædam ne legere qvidem, aut etiam videre contigisse: dum toto illo biennii tempore, tantùm in elimando Lexico, et perficiendo Ianuæ Textu fuisse occupatos vos, imò omnes nos, nemo est qvi ignoret, nostrorum aliqvantùm gnarus. Sed produxit insuper schedulam tui chirographi; qvâ aliqvando eum certiorem esse jubebas. Tibi non deesse vias, quibus cum Tuis illis de Didacticâ Conatibus, citiùs per universum orbem, qvàm ille per Sveciam suam, inclarescere [posses?]. Hîc Optimus Vir commotior factus, infit: Inclarescat ergò, qvantum volet, cum suis, meque sinat latitare cum meis; nollem meas umbras ipsius obscurare lumina. Ita vides, Vir Excellentissime, non satis convenire vobis cogitationes vestras. Et me judice præstat, ut sua qvisque agatis pro virili, alter alterius qvasi inscij: ne plurium capitum conjunctio plures pariat sensûs, et inde contradictiones enascantur. Cæterùm condolet morbidæ tuæ valetudini: utque revalescas precatur: plurimumque [I. ˙˙tem?] per me salvere jubet. Salveat et ex me

---

[461] Ref: 1/35/13B-14B: 14B BLANK, HP.

Uxor nobilissima, filiola mellitissima, atque filioli svavissimi. Deus vos custodiat ab omni malo, repleatque omnimodâ benedictione suâ. Raptim, Lessnæ. 26. October. 1648.[462]

Here Figulus points out how Kinner and his father-in-law have come to differ in both the foundation and structure of their educational programmes. Kinner had obviously blamed Comenius' attachment to his Swedish projects and Swedish money as the real reason behind their breaking fellowship with each other. Thus Figulus advises each former partner to mind his own business and live as if the other did not exist. These are hard words concerning former intimate friends and co-authors. Kinner only outlived the break by a year.

Kinner's main criticism is that Comenius had broken his word concerning working in cooperation in all things with him and in their agreement to exchange copies of their written work for mutual consultation and adoption, such as their jointly planned *Didactica*. This is similar to Durie's and Hartlib's criticism of Comenius though they did not show the same bitterness. Kinner seems to think that Comenius is aiming at fame for himself without considering this ought to mean fame for his co-workers, too. But he rather spoils his argument by boasting that he is now becoming more famous than Comenius now that he is left alone. In this connection, he mentions his *Cogitationum Didacticarum Diatyposis summaria* which became a most popular educational work. This is because Kinner bases his pedagogics on a broader fundament including the natural sciences, an area in which Comenius confessed he was a novice, though he wrote on the subject with the aid of such as Kinner. The latter concludes that Comenius is a theorist and schoolman whereas he, Kinner, deals with the practical realities of life as he is employed as lawyer, doctor and botanist besides Councillor and Prefect of the Ducal metal mines.

Most of Comenius' friends still hoped that after Comenius had returned to Poland in 1648, he would take up the one theme of universal learning, pansophy and practical divinity again but on leaving Elbing, Comenius, using Figulus as his agent, was most anxious to keep receiving funds from de Geer whom he promised to keep supplying with four to ten sheets of finished work a day. He however, still dreamt of completing his pansophic '*Realia*', as he had been telling friends and co-workers such as Bisterfeld since 1643, if he could only be released from his text-book work.[463]

---

[462] Ref: 1/33/1A-2B, HP.
[463] Ref: 7/105A-B: 5B BLANK, letter to Figulus dated August, 1648, HP.

Durie's and Hartlib's disappointment with Comenius

In a letter from August 3rd, 1646 Durie confesses his liking for the Hebrew Scholar Christian Ravius whom he had invited, with Kinner, to head his planned College for the Advancement of Universal Learning and for Jewish Studies. Of Johann Ravius, however, he says:

> 'As for his Brother Iohannes Ravius, I will take notice of that which yow tell me; that hee hath underwritten our tabulas foederis, which I Conceiue at first wee intended rather to bind our selues one to another & Comenius to his taskes in following our Counsells then to oblige others to us; yet what Comenius hath done in this kind, although it should bee done imprudently by him, wee must beare with; & I think that Ravius when hee entered in league with us by Comenius meanes should haue in Discretion acquainted us with his Resolution & shewed his sence of the ende for which wee should bee leagued in our labours. his Tabula Pansophiæ wherin hee shewes the Idea of Comenius & his owne aimes is as all that hath beene done hitherto only to make poeple gaze, & raise expectations; therefore I would make none other use of it; but only to impart it to such as understand the Principles of Humane & Divine knowledge, without recommending the authors unto them. I am ashamed of so many promises & so little performance & it is no difficult matter to make euery weeke a new Idea of thinges possible to bee elaborated, but that will not doe our turne nor saue our credit which alreddie doth lye too deeply at the stake in this matter; & if this Ravius hath beene alreddie false to the worke & to Comenius in it by deserting him, who shall assure us that hee will bee henceforth Constant therunto. what Age hee is of Learne if yow can; for if hee bee young & giuen to Companie & loytering, I feare wee shall not haue much good of him, & what hee will doe, will come from him by flashes, & as the fitt doth take him, & so wee shall neuer bee able to make any reckoning of him further then a priuate interest with a shew of his owne parts & Contriuances will leade him to cooperate. but enough at this tyme of him; I wish wee knew distinctly what Mr. Comenius is about, & where Peter[464] is, but in due tyme I hope wee shall know all that is expedient for us, & what the Swedes will doe for Comenius.'[465]

Hartlib certainly always hoped that Comenius would produce the 'great work' on pansophy that he was always promising, but complained that Comenius always let less important matters get in his way. Hartlib wrote letter after letter to Comenius after 1643 up to the early 1660s with Comenius replying that he was not wasting time and that he could not work if he

---

[464] Durie's former secretary, Peter Figulus, Comenius' son-in-law.
[465] Ref: 3/3/32A-33B, HP.

were disturbed, but since making himself independent of Hartlib and friends 'many things in my Pansophical studies have been better observed and I have become altogether more clear-sighted than ever in the Didactics'.[466] In May 1646, Comenius told Hartlib; 'I see you, friend Hartlib, as being offended, or saddened, or pained by continually entreating me in vain for editions of works that are in demand or, at least, for specimen pages; since in your country there are such great opportunities of displaying these works of divine talent on a public stall and for a very rich profit to return to the Lord.' Comenius confesses that his pansophical studies are overwhelming him and he cannot continue unless he has a staff of assistants and De Geer's approval. However, though Comenius gained skilled help, as outlined above, it was his assistants who complained that Comenius was dilly-dallying with the work. Towards the end of the 50's, we find Comenius still saying he 'could not find retirement' and was looking for his 'strangely scattered Pansophic concepts'.[467]

As an excuse for his neglecting Pansophy, Comenius always mentioned De Geer as hampering him in his work through lack of support. This can hardly have been the case. Hartlib wrote to Ambassador Pell on March 25, 1658 to tell him that De Geer had just called Figulus and his family to Sweden with a view to persuading him to finish off his father-in-law's *Pansophia* should Comenius' die.[468] Other factors were at work in hindering Comenius. When writing to John Worthington on 30 January 1659/60, Hartlib explains that Comenius was so busy meeting criticism of his translation of prophetic visions *Lux in Tenebris* that he had no time to finish his work on pansophy. A young Dutch Professor, Nicholas Arnold, had challenged Comenius' imaginative interpretations and what Comenius claimed were his 'New Revelations' and Comenius had responded in great anger, asking Arnold who he thought he was to have the cheek to contradict a person of such respected status and that Arnold should not undertake the task of challenging a man of Comenius' high standing. In his haughtiness, Comenius maintained, that the task of criticising him could only be undertaken by an official, general Church Council. This was sadly typical of Comenius. Kvačala explains in his *Schlußwort* to his pedagogical appreciation of Comenius how Comenius felt he had perfected a system which must be either accepted as a whole or ignored to carry the consequences. Anyone, like his fellow clergyman University Professor Arnold, who

---

[466] Ref: 7/72/1B, HP.
[467] See letters to Hartlib dated July, 1654; Jan. 1655; Jan. 1656; Dec. 1656; Sept. 1657. All under 'Pansophical' in the HP.
[468] Vaughan's *Collection*, vol. 2, p. 453.

wanted to argue over this or that part, was counted an ignoramus, as former school Headmaster Comenius hotly claimed Professor Arnold was. Such a method, Kvačala concludes, has 'keine Aussicht auf Verwirklichung'.[469]

On April 8, 1661, Hartlib wrote again to Worthington to tell him that Comenius was still working for De Geer and had just finished his (second) refutation of Zwicker's *Irenicum Irenicorum* and would then continue with his pansophia.[470] Hartlib related how Comenius was then seventy years old, adding, 'I believe or rather fear, we shall see little of Pansophia; indeed many excellent inventions, sweet discourses, we may have, but no solid piece of what I always desired.' Two weeks later, Hartlib told Worthington that he wished Comenius had left Zwicker alone and finished his work on pansophy, believing that his old friend would shortly be no more.[471] Comenius, however, outlived Hartlib, who died in 1662, by another eight years. In spite of Arnold's criticism of Comenius' dabbling in the visionary, he could not put the idea of *Lux versus Tenebris* out of his mind and worked on the theme until 1667. His final *Lux e Tenebris*, just as his multiple revisions of his *Janua* in the fifties, showed that in his old age, he was returning to some of the themes of his youth.[472] However, though Comenius' first letter to Hartlib, a rather long one, was full of thoughts on his *Janua*, didactics and especially pansophy,[473] the four short letters Comenius wrote to Hartlib after his disappointments of 1661 carried no mention of them.

Immediately on taking up his Swedish tasks, Comenius, besides turning to Kinner, Ritschel and Ravius, asked Johann Heinrich Bisterfeld (1605-1655) of Siegen, if he could 'light his lamp from his'. Bisterfeld had also been tutored with Alsted at the Herborn High School and became Professor

---

[469] *J. A, Comenius*, pp. 174-175.
[470] In Comenius' overview of his life and works placed under the title J. Comenius Petro Montano S. pp. 233-245, dated 10 December 1661, Comenius lists two works against Zwicker under *Polemica etiam implicari (vel invito) contigitas*: 3. Adversus Danielem Zwikkerum Pseudo-Irenicum (hoc est: de conditionibus pacis a Socini secta reliquo Christiano orbi oblatis) ad omnes Christianos facta admonitio. Amsterdami apud Henricum Bekium 1660. 4. De iterato Sociniano Irenico iterata ad Christianos admonitio, sivi Pseudo-Irenici, veri autem Christomastigis, Zwikkerii, superbus de Christo aeternitatis throno dejecto Triumphus, virtute Dei dissipatus.
[471] Comenius' *Korrespondence*, p. 221.
[472] See, for instance, *The Revelations and Visions of Christopher Kotter* (1625) and his *De veris et falsis prophetis* (1629) and his versions of *Lux in/et Tenebris* from the mid fifties to late sixties. Also his *Opera Didactica Omnia*, which he worked on from 1627 to 1657.
[473] *Korrespondence*, undated but placed before 1640, p.p. 19-21.

of Philosophy there in 1629. He was a close friend of Kinner's and Hartlib's. Bisterfeld became Head of the Academy at Walsenburg, Transylvania and was well known for his research into logic and Pansophy of the encyclopaedic kind besides the construction of a universal language. Bisterfeld, like Durie, Hartlib and Kinner, had also repeatedly urged Comenius to use his talents for more important work than writing school books and dictionaries and Comenius replied complaining that he found his tasks at Elbing sheer drudgery, saying:

> 'De me nunc non aliud possum quàm seposuisse me omnia realia, insudare Vestibulo et Ianuæ à fundamento reformandis: quia id a variis variè sollicitor, urgeorque. Et verò semel me istis exoneravero, ut si quid vitæ supererit, realibus tota mente incumbere liceat. Tædet equidem tam diu luctari cum verbis.'[474]

Comenius was eventually called to teach in Siebenbürgen, Transylvania in 1654 and was told that if he had arrived their 30 years previously, he would have found barren soil but thanks to Alsted, Piscator and Bisterfeld he would now find a well-developed educative and academic life in the school.[475]

In this connection, Adamson in his *Pioneers of Modern Education* introduces Durie's name, hitherto kept out of the discussion, as probably being of the 'one or two' who were interested in setting up a pansophic college, the other being Hartlib. From this stage on, however, Adamson writes more of Durie's pansophic work than Comenius' as if one star had faded and another has taken its place. Hartlib, too, appears to have dropped Comenius after the 1643 disappointment and he now not only published his own utopian, if not pansophic, work, *A Description of the Famous Kingdom of Macaria* but well over a dozen works from Durie's pen concerning international cooperation on a pansophic basis. Hartlib also published several works such as *A Brief Relation of That which hath been lately attempted to procure Ecclesiasticall Peace amongst Protestants*, outlining Durie's work in the pacification of the churches, education, politics and theology from the late twenties on. By this time, however, Durie was publishing ideas of a total synergism of knowledge in his pansophy with which even Hartlib, let alone Comenius, could not keep pace. Durie, who always spoke in the most tender terms to Hartlib, as we shall see below, was to

---

[474] Letter from Elbing dated 20 May, 1643. Ref: 7/63/1A-2B, HP.
[475] See Menk's *Das Restitutionsedikt*, p. 62 and Comenius' *Självbiografi* (Blekastad), p. 256.

criticise Hartlib's generalising of case studies, in a similar way to Comenius', in the name of pansophy as 'ridiculous'.

The only probable reason why it is commonly thought that Comenius influenced Durie on educational pansophy is that narrow research into Comenius and the works carrying his name has progressed far ahead of Durie scholarship in recent years to the detriment of not only historical accuracy but also of a number of other reforming educators who ought to at least share Comenius' laurels. It is reserved for modern authors to reverse this trend. May this thesis help to move others to take a new look at John Durie's pansophy.

CHAPTER EIGHT

Purpose, Method and Procedure in Academic Studies

Right literary analysis as the handmaid of right learning

Unlike Milton who saw literary analysis in general as the key to training the mind for academic studies, Durie maintained that the true basis for such literary education and methodology, indeed, education in general, must start with knowing God who is the source of all wisdom. The most practical and effective way of knowing God is through a comprehensive study of the Word of God which reveals the God of all knowledge to mankind. The disciplines gained through such a study will train the mind for all subsequent textual work in whatever occupational field the student enters. It will also fit the student out to be able to utilise knowledge practically from whatever source it comes. Thus Durie wrote several pamphlets and many letters on how to interpret the Word of God aright.

In 1637, whilst Durie was in Stockholm, Hartlib had passed on a letter to him from a noted Christian benefactor named John St. Amand who was interested in Durie's way of analysing Scripture. Durie replied in four letters on various allied subjects but his letter of 9 December dealt specifically with text analysis. He also employed his secretary, Peter Figulus, in looking up the works he mentioned and copying out relevant passages to pass on to St Amand. Durie called his system of Scripture analysis the *Demonstrative Method* which consisted of first writing down a *structural analysis* of the axioms or sense units of the passage under scrutiny. He uses, as an exemplary analysis via the Demonstrative Method, Acts 2:39, which he divides as follows:

'First main axiom: repent

Second main axiom: be baptized

Dependent axioms: every one of you

         in the name of Iesus Christ

	for the remission of sinnes
Third main axiom:	ye shall receive the guift of the holy ghost
Fourth main axiom:	for the promise is unto you
Dependent axioms:	to your Children
	to all that are a farre of
	to as many as the Lord our God shall call.'

This served to provide the mind both with an overview of the text, fixing it more firmly in the memory, and as a basis for the further analysis necessary. In his *Discourse on a Method of Meditation*, Durie argues through *Postulata*, *Definitiones* to *Axiomata*, defining his *Postulata* as 'suppositions conceiued to bee true & taken up as most universal grounds of the whole matter.' *Definitiones*, Durie explains are 'expositions of our conception touching the nature & being of the matter,' and *Axiomata* are 'propositions, which wee concieue either to bee undeniably evident, or may bee undeniably prooved.'

The next stage is the *Literal Analysis* which works out the proper grammatical, syntactical and literal sense and function of each word used. When the literal sense of the text has been firmly established, the student goes on to the *material analysis* of the text. This is a study of all the information in the text concerning factual knowledge and what learning can be derived from it. What the text says must be qualified by what it means in terms of both self-evident and derived knowledge. This information gathered in the material analysis Durie calls the *matter* of the sentence. Text analysis is not a case of identifying knowledge with learning by rote but having the rational and spiritual faculties activated by its message to put this knowledge coherently to use after merging it with knowledge already appropriated.

This point was one of Bacon's initial arguments in Book I of his *Advancement of Learning*. In Part IV, Section 3 he wrote in his Address to the King:

'Here, therefore, is the first distemper of learning, when men study words and not matter; whereof, though I have represented an example of late times, yet it hath been and will be SECUNDUM MAJUS ET MINUS in all time. And how is it possible but this should have an operation to discredit learning, even with vulgar capacities, when they see learned men's works like the first letter of a patent, or limned book; which though it hath large flourishes, yet is but a letter? It seems to me that Pygmalion's frenzy is a good emblem or portraiture of this vanity: for words are but the images of matter; and except they have life of reason and invention, to fall in love with them is all one as to fall in love with a picture.'

Scripture must therefore be read as communication of matter for the understanding. Each axiom, self-evident truth or sense-unit must be synthesised and synergised so that the true utterance of the text bedded in the entire context can be understood and merged with the pre-knowledge of the student and reflected upon. Thus, concerning this three-fold analysis, Durie says:

> 'the end of such a resolution in the text of Scripture is to dive into the true meaninge thereof, or rather to apprehend the whole wisdome and science of the discourses which the spirit of God vttereth in the scriptures to instruct vs vnto salvation, I say that the end of all Analysis is to apprehend the wisdome which is in scripture vnto salvation, And the end of this Method which I vse is to apprehend it demonstratively that is infallibly./ Soe that a man shal be able to demonstrat every thinge which he doth apprehend to be certainly true a priori noto et infallibili till he come to the first principles of infallibility which noe man can deny, soe that by a continuall orderly concatenation of apprehentions the vnderstandinge is ledd by infallible degrees from one intellectuall obiect to another till it gather them all vp together in one summe soe that it can all at once apprehend the whole, and all the parts thereof distinctly & conionctly in theire severall relations each to other and each to the makeinge vp of the whole,'

Retracing the footsteps of a writer's understanding

Durie claims that the best way to illustrate his analytical procedure is to explain it in terms of mathematics in which one sum added to another makes a third and many sums added together make the sum total. In text analysis, one object is added to another to make a third common to both and thus total sums are obtained leading to total conclusions regarding the intellectual matters examined. This is based on a *postulatum* which no rational man can deny. If simple axioms are rightly understood and correctly combined, then the resulting compound cannot be falsely understood. All rational discourses are merely systems of simple axioms or sentences joined in a certain frame together towards some fixed scope. The aim in considering any discourse under examination is to frame the same thoughts in the understanding that the speaker or writer had in mind when he uttered or wrote his discourse. So to conceive the understanding and knowledge (wisdom and science) of a man, we must know his thoughts and to know his thoughts, we must analyse what he says and writes, that is, his discourses. This can only be done by retracing the footsteps of his understanding in framing his line of thought in words, following how he began and how he continued. All prejudices and party-mindedness must be laid aside and the statements of each discourse broken down into their basic axioms which are then analysed one by one. One may not hazard a guess at what this that and the other meant but one must keep to the statements 'as uttered' in their context.

What Durie is expressing here is his theory of knowledge *in toto* which is his Practical Divinity or Pansophy. True knowledge or wisdom is never there to exist in divided elements but in its universal utterance and application. This, for Durie, is 'rightly dividing the Word of Truth,'[476] He maintains in this letter that what is to be seen in the verbal sense is *suo modo* in the material and what is in the outward part of the material sense of knowledge is also *suo modo* in its inward or spiritual part. This is because the material sentences of Scripture as expressed in outward corporate things also express inner spiritual and incorporate things which are as really and truly meant, the one as the other. Thus Durie concludes:

> 'Soe that by this you may nowe conceive howe many partes or rather kindes of Analyses there be in my conception the first is of the words, the second is of the matter, and in this matter I conceive the sensuall and bodily parte which every rationall man may conceive from the scripture, and the spirituall and truely intellectuall parte which none but such as God enlightneth in openinge theire vnderstandinge to conceive and theire harte to beleive, can apprehend./. In each of all these kindes is a severall Analysis not differinge in the Method but in the obiects to be considered vnderstandingly and rationally, for the spirituall obiects in the last kinde are considered alsoe rationally, although the light of that reason is from the spiritt and not from the naturall facultie.'

Durie warns his readers that if they feel they know what the text says and means in its full proportions before going on to a deeper and more contextualised analysis, they can easily deceive themselves:

> 'because our vnderstandinge is too nimble and deceiveth vs with a faire showe of some truth which satisfieth the desire of knowledge in some kinde

---

[476] 2 Tim. 2:15.

and soe we rest contented, & because we are in love with our owne conceptions we can hardly be ever brought backe againe from such conceptions which are thus taken vp, but standinge in defence of them, least we should seeme to have erred in our interpretation (which is a disparagement for a Learned man before the world) or be ignorant of the truth, we bend our witte to make the first thought which was taken vp to appeare the only true and proper meaneing of a place.'

This is what has caused, according to Durie, all the strife and quarrels concerning the meaning of Scripture. Thus, for him, no Christian should quarrel with a brother unless both have followed the pattern proposed by Durie and researched every jot and tittle of the text and pooled all common knowledge regarding it and resolved to study on together in the great enterprise of learning. Doctrines are not thus to be taught and learnt in the individual's private chamber but with representatives of all Christians seeking to appreciate each axiom of God's Word for the common good and from the common source of the universal wisdom gained in studying it rightly. The skill Durie is thus eager to impart to St Amand here, and to a number of others in England and especially Holland who asked for Durie's advice, is not to fly off with interpretations based on partial utterances of the text. First the entire sense context is to be studied analytically, grammatically, lexicologically and semantically. If this is not done, the eye will merely look 'vpon a greate heape of different things standinge togeather' which cannot possibly represent to the untrained imagination what the true meaning of the 'heap' is. The eye must be trained in considering these parts to look for coherence in the whole so the mind can examine the matter backwards and forwards, up and down from all angles *'per minutissima et maxima'* and find all the rational and spiritual relations in it. It is a further step in combining what has been learnt with what is being learnt. Durie describes this as a *Methodus procedendi a simplicissimis ad composita et demonstrandi rem quamlibet a priori cognito.*

The first principles used in meditating on a given text

One of Durie's more intimate correspondents was Sir Cheney Culpeper (1601–1663), a wealthy Oxford graduate, Inner Temple lawyer and landowner who was keenly interested in theology, chemistry, alchemy and scientific inventions and greatly supportive of new ways of universal learning. Though open to church reforms, he strongly opposed the Presbyterians' efforts to impose Presbyterian government on the English. Durie acknowledged that through Culpeper's correspondence, he had come to understand true scientific contemplation and meditation all the better, saying, 'I thinke myselfe a debter more to yow therein, then vnto others because your zeale doth leade yow to more vniversall conceptions then others are capable of.' It was in a lengthy undated letter to Culpeper containing these words that Durie revealed his position regarding what he and Culpeper called 'The Method of Meditation' or *via meditandi*.[477] This 5,100 word treatise in a private letter appears to have developed into a much larger work entitled A Discourse *Shewing a Method of spiritual meditation in Holy Matters which are Scriptural truthes & persvasions, how the same may bee apprehended by us, & made knowne unto others most conveniently for edification*, which Durie dedicated to Sir William Waller. The copy, catalogued as *Dury's Discourse on a Method of Meditation* found in the Hartlib Papers and dated 1640 with a question mark, however has been badly damaged by water and is partly in fragmented form with missing pages, though 26 pages including 7,400 words have been preserved. As the methodological line in the larger work has been broken because of losses in the text, the shorter, complete work will be used here as our main guide.[478]

In the treatise sent to Culpeper, Durie explains how he organises his thoughts when consulting any new work so as to obtain the maximum information and benefit from it. On first approaching a text, Durie states, the reader must observe:

> '1. That a Man is able to order his owne thoughts.
>
> 2. That the meanes to order them is a certayne Rule by which he should walke.
>
> 3. That this Rule hath certayne Principles of which now I am cheifely to speake.
>
> 4. & that the ends or rather the objects towards which the thoughts are to be ordered are the Acts of Meditating & consulting.'

Commenting on his first point, Durie explains that he does not mean that man has any great proficiency or natural talent in ordering his own thoughts. He refers his reader to Prov. 16:1 and Jer. 10:23 which teach that the first motions in learning are not from man, neither can man, even when placed on the right path, attain to any perfection of himself. Man's steps always need to be directed by God. However, it is self-evident, Durie ar-

---

[477] Ref. 1/4/9A-18B: 18B Blank, HP.
[478] Ref: 26/4/1A 10BMS, HP.

gues, that the understanding of man has a reflexive faculty to consider itself and its own actions and to organise and structure them to a certain degree. This capacity needs to be trained meaningfully as all are by their fallen nature children in its use. The faculty of learning must be cultivated and regulated to fulfil proper God-given ends for the common good.

The second point indicates that once a man realises that he has a reflexible faculty in his understanding and has a basic capacity to order his thoughts and free them from confusion, he must necessarily conclude that he needs some rule or order to work by.

Durie argues in his third point, that once any person is aware that a rule is called for, it will be concluded that certain principles must be followed in setting things in a relationship of presidency and consecution to each other. This must follow to show why one order should be used and not another. As all forms and frames naturally arise from the nature of the thing under study, there must be rules and principles governing why this matter is so and not otherwise.

In his 1640 *Discourse on a Method of Meditation*, Durie also covers this ground but starts by defining what he means by 'method'. Durie sees 'method' not so much as a door or gate to learning as in contemporary didactics such as Comenius' *Janua* but as a path by which one is led by a disciplined and trained mind from one area of knowledge to another, using each newly gained experience to blend with and enhance the already observed and understood. Durie defines the rules of proceeding along this path as:

> '1. That hee which doeth sette himselfe to profitte by meditation, must know of his owne thoughts, that they proceede not at Randome, but orderly. For if hee bee not able to know this of the action of his mind, hee shall neuer bee sure of any thing which hee knoweth, that it is either full or demonstrable, but shall easily bee deceiued. And to bee able to know this of his owne thoughts, hee must before hee beginne to thinke upon any subject, forecast & settle with himselfe what kind of meditation hee will undertake, & in that kind what order of thoughts hee will obserue; both in respect of the matters, to bee thought on; & in respect of the way of thinking thereon.
>
> 2. That the order of thoughts bee alwayes with some connexion & coherence of one to another & so bee raised one from another To which effect in all meditation some maine ground, & as it were primo cognitum in that matter must needes bee taken up from whence inferences may be by rule of reasoning.

3. That hee labour to make the connexion of his (thoughts?) & the progresse thereof unto the aime which hee hath in the matter, if not fully demonstrable at least apparently without exception. Which may bee done if hee can finde the way how to make one thought haue that relation unto another, which a cause hath to its effect. And this may bee done if hee obserue reflexiuely within himselfe, whence notions & conceptions arise, whereof they are made up, & how from the former a succeeding thought either should or occasionally doeth flow.

4. In all meditations it is safest to proceede from simple thoughts unto compounds in the same nature, as it were by addition of one to one, as they are subordinat unto the same ende of knowledge. For hee that doeth know & can reckon up all the things which make up an ende of knowledge, & then knoweth with what order, those things should stand together one by another to make up that ende, & lastly can finde the way to follow in his thoughts that order of the composure of those things, hee cannot faile of the true knowledge thereof. And indeede this Rule is the chief ground of Demonstration & of trueth: for if a man can shew that hee hath not failed, in proceeding from simple notions to compounds, of the same kind, by perpertuall Degrees of conceptions hee doeth Demonstrate â priori cognito all his thoughts. And this is the Method which in searching & deliuering Scripturall Truethes wee thinke most fitte to bee obserued.'[479]

Once that is settled, Durie goes on to recapitulate on his 'lesson' concerning what meditation is by saying:

'Yow have now already vnderstood that by Principles I meane the grounds of Rules by which a man is to walke in his thoughts of Meditation & consultation; the end then to which we drive is to Meditate & consult aright; by meditating I conceive the act of the minde reflecting vpon the nature of any thing to dive into the true properties & vses thereof. By consulting I vnderstand the act of the mind reflecting vpon the Actions which are to be vndertaken or left of or not vndertaken about any thing; to gaine some good end wherevnto they should be directed according as it may be conceived to be or not to be posssible or vsefull. from whence yow may gather that the Acts of the mind which are to be regulated (which we call Meditation & consultation) are not now to be considered in respect of the subjects whereupon they are to reflect (which we have called the natures of things & the Actions which may be intended by vs for some good end) but in respect of the Reflection it selfe, that whether we meditate or consult we may have a Rule to order the reflection of our mind, vpon any subject whatsoever.'

---

[479] Ref: 26/4/1A 10BMS, HP.

Purpose, Method and Procedure in Academic Studies 295

Durie is here saying that the rules which one uses for meditation on one subject are not limited to that subject but they are usable in a transfer of training to fit any matter under meditation. One has worked out a tool which is universally applicable and useful. He is not talking about particular facts to be discovered and observed but general acts of the mind which can be used to understand all observable phenomena. The rule then is not gathered from the nature of the objects observed but from the acts of the mind which are applied to any object brought before the senses.

Organising the acts of the mind in meditation

Durie now progresses in his Culpeper letter from the realisation that thoughts may be organised to consider:

> '1. What the Acts of the mind of man are & how they are distinguished?
>
> 2. How they stand in relation one to another in their seuerall inward propertyes?
>
> 3. What the end of this relation is? & how it must be gayned? for this Relation is the grounds of the Reflection; & the end of that Relation is the first inward Principle of goodnesse & of that well being wherevpon the nature of the soule of Man hath bin framed & constituted; & from which all the well ordered Acts thereof must naturally flow & what soever is not answerable therevnto in the agitation of thoughts & motion of the mind is to be judged irrationall & void of vnderstanding.'

Next, Durie asks what man essentially is and what his mind is. He concedes that a man is a creature distinguishable from all other creatures in body and soul made after the image of God. This image of God, however, has been lost since the Fall, according to the Scriptures and has become as unknown to man as it is unknown to nature in general. This means that through natural reason, no man can know himself truly except from what is revealed of him in Scripture, which teaches that man is partly of the earth, but has become a living soul under subordination to God who has placed all other creatures in subjection to him. Though Durie admits that these things are indiscernible to the nature of a fallen being, Scripture enlightens him with the new principle of knowledge that man has the capacity to act sensually, rationally and spiritually. This, he analyses as:

> '1. The sensuall arise from the body & its outward or inward senses,

2. The Rationall arise from the facultyes of the Naturall soule in the imagination of the mind, in the memory, in the discerning & judging facultyes & in the will.

3. The spirituall arise from the conscience bearing witnesse of the will of God & of our agreement or disagreement with the same.'

Durie goes on to argue that in educating man, none of the three sources of acts in man should be neglected as man can only be fully educated when he exercises each part aright. Nevertheless, he feels that the acts of the spiritual are supreme and predominant over the natural senses and what Durie calls 'the memorative understanding' and 'willing faculties'. If the sensual is allowed to dominate over the rational then the balance is out of order and man becomes beastly or devilish.

The aim of right meditation

Durie believed that the right end of all education must be to return man to his original Edenic roots. Mankind must be reformed to express the life of God in the soul of man, enabling him to regain his status as God's steward on earth, working for the universal happiness of all creation. Durie sees this working out when once the true relations in which God has set us has been realised and understood. These are:

'1. That our spirits should be in our Conscience wholy subjected vnto his spirit & dependant from him (who is the father of spirits) in all things so with out his leave and the knowledge of his will by reflecting vpon his word ingrafted in our hearts we should not presume to thinke say or do anything

2. That our Reason should in all things be a servant vnto the enditement of the spirituall word made manifest vnto our Conscience to obey it & to make the truth and goodnesse thereof plaine & evident to our selves & others.

3. That our sensuall motions should be a servant vnto the prescripts of Reason to helpe our rationall facultyes to expresse the will of God & apply it vnto those with whome we have to deale outwardly.

When this Edenic situation, once present in man but lost, is regained, Durie envisaged all mankind as being new Adams and Eves, going out into a world restored as its steward, cataloguer and administrator, thus bringing it again under the dominion of the God Only Wise. Once the fountain has been found, to use Durie's imagery, it will run out and irrigate the whole world. With this in mind, each teacher-cum-learner must make sure that the wheels of his mind are function aright because God 'doeth not giue true Wisdome & Understanding, but unto such as come to him to seeke it.' Durie comments:

> 'So that wee see the first Principle & preparatiue unto Meditation, must bee the composing of the heart towards God; to sette our selues to thinke of that which is to be thought upon, as in his presence through his feare depending upon his word, & desiring his direction; that not onely with his leaue & permission, but by his order & according to his will wee maye doe all thinges, & thinke all our thoughts. This predisposing of the mind towards God, to reflect first upon him in all our meditations, is like unto the Tuning of an Instrument before a man doeth beginne to playe a piece of good Musick: so by drawing neare to God, with a good conscience, in cleansing it from all superfluitie of naughtinesse & calling upon him by Faith for grace & direction; the strings of the soule are tuned & sette in a good Harmonie, that the spirit of wisedome which proceedeth from him maye playe some harmonious melodicall piece upon the same: which without this tuning of the soule cannot bee done: And this Tuning cannot bee perfourmed, except the conscience bee brought neare unto God, & bee able to looke upon him, that it maye bee inlightned. For by looking to him & comparing it selfe to his will & Livinge word, it receiueth light, first to see & judge itselfe in what estate it is; & then to judge other thinges alsoe: for then it reflecteth upon all thinges (& chiefly upon the inferiour faculties, which are subordinate unto the motions of the Spirit:) with a commanding power: so that they all stoope & yeeld to it, to become answereable unto the Intentions of the spirit, which are conceiued by a good Conscience, to bee aimed at in the worke of meditation & consultation: And lett euery man who desireth to go safe in any businesse of consequence, bee sure that hee neuer fall to worke without this preparatiue: For without it hee may runne himselfe into errours & those very daungerous, & hee cannot possiblely walke by true light & Rules, as longe as the great Maister Rules & principle of light is not made use of, which is the subordination of the Intents & purposes of the heart unto God to sette it in a frame, which maye bee answereable unto his Will. This then is the first maine Principle of true order, to bee settled in the Thoughts to bring the conscience to reflect upon God, & settle itselfe, towards him in the businesse which is to bee minded.
>
> The second maine Principle is, to haue a care to cleare the naturall understanding, from prejudices & forestaled opinions, which are like filmes ouer the eyes of the mind through which it cannot looke soe as to discerne the right shape of thinges, otherwise in themselues sufficiently apparent. These prejudices arise from a narrownesse & stinting of the thoughts unto thinges too particular. Therefore before wee beginne to meditate or consult, wee

should abstract from particulars & state the Question whereof wee are to thinke in generall tearmes; which should comprehend the true nature of particulars. Which being done, the Termes of the Question are to bee considered & examined; that the properties thereof maye bee discouered. To which effect the Acts of Ratiocination should bee obserued & rightly ordered; which are:

1. To discerne distinctly the differences of matters belonging to the tearmes of the Question.

2. To compare those distinct matters together with the thinge enquired after; that from their agreement or disagreement, the judgement maye gather the Resolution of the Question.

3. To applye the Question Generally resolued, unto the particular matter in hand: where the circumstances of the particular are to bee lookt into; to finde how farre they answere or answere not, unto the Generall determination of the Question.'

Acts of ratiocination and the regulating principle

Though Durie rejected Aristotelian logic like his mentor Bacon, he argued that all learning must follow a logical course. In acts of the mind, progress can only be made when one moves from things already known to things still unknown. Single observations must be made before compounding them. The generals now known and understood can be used to acquire particulars unknown. Particulars already known can be used to gather generals unknown in that the reader compares them with elements in the particulars with which they agree. The procedure in Durie's words is thus:

'1. To state the Question which is to bee made the subject of meditation, by summing up the particulars foreknowen; into one Generall head & propertie of their Agreement.

2. To resolue that Question into its distinct matters, to discerne the properties thereof.

3. To compare those properties with the thing sought after, to see what they will discouer of it in Generall.

4. Lastly to applye that which shall bee discouered in generall to the particular, as it standeth under its circumstances. And to this last Act of Reasoning, which concerneth the circumstances of particular matters, the use of sense doeth concurre to enquire, obserue, discerne & helpe to compare thinges to-

gether by their outwardly perceptible Realities, which leade the understanding, to the apprehension of more inward properties.'

The principle whereby acts of sense are regulated is that the thoughts should be kept from confused wanderings and made to reflect purely on the observation of ordered circumstances compared with one another as the trained reason and memory suggest. The aim is to find truth in the objects of meditation and goodness in the objects of consultation when examining all matters and actions. Neither should be neglected as a search for goodness alone, for instance, can be limited to selfish sensuousness. This is because there are three kinds of people in the world. Those few who seek the goodness which comes from God in the life of the Spirit who are citizens of Heaven; those who seek a moral-rational way who are satisfied with natural knowledge who are the rulers of this world and those who seek merely to satisfy sensuous appetites who are the slaves of this world. None put such who in acts of meditation and consultation raise their thoughts first to spiritual good which leads to life eternal and then comprehend subordinate matters as objects of reason and sense order their thoughts correctly. The one who seeks the Kingdom of Heaven in this way will find many other things will be added to his knowledge according to Matthew 6:33.

Durie cannot help complaining here that the majority of his ministerial friends do not set the Kingdom of Heaven first but that which is earthly and seek profit, honour and credit for themselves. This is why, he says, he cannot find a patron for his work, 'because I doe not sette my minde to serue endes & particular interrests, unto which all parties nowadayes are wedded; & can relish nothing but what is subordinat thereunto.' Durie wants to bring mankind, and especially ministers and teachers, from private aims and advantages to a truly general good which alone is God-honouring. This is a problem Bacon also had to struggle with. In his *Advancement of Learning*, Book I, V:11 he bemoans the fact that academic pursuits are undertaken for reasons which are not for the public good, saying:

'But the greatest error of all the rest is the mistaking or misplacing of the last or farthest end of knowledge: for men have entered into a desire of learning and knowledge, sometimes upon a natural curiosity and inquisitive appetite; sometimes to entertain their minds with variety and delight; sometimes for ornament and reputation; and sometimes to enable them to victory of wit and contradiction; and most times for lucre and profession; and seldom sincerely to give a true account of their gift of reason, to the benefit and use of men: as if there were sought in knowledge a couch whereupon to rest a searching and restless spirit; or a tarrasse, for a wandering and variable mind to walk up and down with a fair prospect; or a tower of state, for a proud mind to raise itself upon; or a fort or commanding ground, for strife and contention; or a shop, for profit or sale; and not a rich storehouse, for the glory of the Creator and the relief of man's estate. But this is that which will indeed dignify and exalt knowledge, if contemplation and action may be more nearly and straitly conjoined and united together than they have been; a conjunction like unto that of the two highest planets, Saturn, the planet of rest and contemplation, and Jupiter, the planet of civil society and action: howbeit, I do not mean, when I speak of use and action, that end before-mentioned of the applying of knowledge to lucre and profession; for I am not ignorant how much that diverteth and interrupteth the prosecution and advancement of knowledge, like unto the golden ball thrown before Atalanta, which while she goeth aside and stoopeth to take up, the race is hindered.'

Here Durie shows himself as a true son of Bacon. Finally, after a rather lengthy 'aside' outlining his aims in seeking peace in the churches and universal learning, Durie sums up and lists three other matters which proceed from his system which should provide material for future correspondence, writing:

'These are the generall Principles of Meditation, & Consultation which a man by the Grace of God is able to make use of, for the ordering of his thoughts in all particular objects: & according to these grounde Rules maye bee giuen, concerning these following matters: whereof I hope I shall gette by me to spreade more at large hereafter.

1. Of Scripturall Interpretation; to shewe the waye both of finding out Analytically the true Litterall, Materiall & Mysticall sense thereof, & of demonstrating & delivering, the same unto others according unto the seuerall Degrees, of their capacitie compositively.

2. Of Humane Speculation to shewe the waye; How men should order their thoughts, to finde out hidden Trueths in naturall thinges; and to propose orderly unto others, that which they haue found.

3. Of Spirituall & Humane consultation: To shewe how in Spirituall matters doubts of conscience, may bee resolued: or thinges belonging to the Edification of others prosecuted & proposed. And how in Humane affaires the wayes of Prudencie, to finde out & followe the best courses of doinge businesses should bee intended:

And you shall neuer bee more willing to putte mee upon these taskes, then I shall bee to elaborate the same, according to the Abilitie which it shall please God, to graunt unto mee with tyme & leisure; which I am desirous to spend upon Your edification, as being the Trueth'

In all this, as has been hinted at, Durie showed how he was working on much material inherited from Bacon. Durie, like Bacon saw true knowledge and wisdom as originating in the knowledge of God. Bacon says in his *Advancement of Learning*:

'First therefore let us seek the dignity of knowledge in the archetype or first platform, which is in the attributes and acts of God, as far as they are revealed to man and may be observed with sobriety; wherein we may not seek it by the name of Learning; for all Learning is Knowledge acquired, and all knowledge in God is original: and therefore we must look for it by another name, that of Wisdom or Sapience, as the Scriptures call it.'[480]

Durie compared to his predecessor and mentor Bacon

The difference between Francis Bacon's and Durie's view of Divine knowledge is that Bacon hardly seems to distinguish between the Scriptures and the Classics and the Church Fathers as sources for discerning the Divine will. He explains that Luther in his reforms had no contemporary to guide him, so he resorted to the ancients and this is the course he wishes to take himself. However, Luther looked to the Church Fathers who, he believed, looked to Scripture whereas, Bacon, though a man of the Bible, used his classical learning to illustrate Biblical truths. On reading Bacon's address to the King in Book 1 of his *Advancement of Learning* it is noticeable that he had to establish and prove to James that he was learned, and in those days learning was seen almost as a monopoly of the ancient Greeks. Thus, Bacon begins his appeal for an advancement of learning in Book I, with a mixture of Scriptural acumen and deep knowledge of Classical literature and history, using both to guide him, often allegorically, through the labyrinth of learning.[481] Thus, after writing the above appeal to the knowledge of God, Bacon, demonstrates from Dionysius, the senator of Athens, how knowledge radiates variously from the Seraphim who are angels of love, then the Cherubim who are angels of light, then the angels of Thrones and Principalities, then the angels of Knowledge and Illumination

---

[480] Book I, VI:1, ff.
[481] See Comenius' early work, *The Labyrinth of the World and the Paradise of the Heart*. Comenius puts forward his ideas via allegory.

and lastly the angels of Office and Domination each group descending in emanations. This is more a Gnostic understanding rather than Durie's division which does not refer to the emanations of sources but man's God-given facilities to comprehend them when they are there displayed before the senses. It is correct that Durie wished to understand the spiritual alongside the rational and material but it was most different from Bacon's Gnostic idea that knowledge is emanated from God via a descent from 'Spirits and Intellectual forms to Sensible and Material Forms'.[482]

Durie teaches that spiritual forms are immanent and immediate, not emanated, in sensible and material forms as Scripture is the Spirit-breathed, holy Word of God speaking to fallen man at all times. Thus Durie can say in his *Discourse on a Method of Meditation*:

> '1. That matters contained in the holy Scripture, being delivered to us by the word of God, are all fit objects of holy meditation & fitted also for our edification.
>
> 2. That God's intention in deliuering these matters by scripture is the same knowen to us: & that consequently they are so clearly deliuered; that they may be understood by us, if we rightly consider the same. Therefore if wee meane to profite by the Scriptures, we must needes learne how to consider rightly the same . . . . . & to propose the same demonstratiuely unto others, that they also may bee edified.'

The appeal to bygone writers is seen, too, in Comenius' brief work, *A Reformation of Schools*, published by Hartlib in 1642 which contains something of Durie's proposals but without their comprehensiveness. Comenius, refers to Bacon's words, 'Let it therefore be agreed: That there is no booke so bad, wherein some good thing or other may not be found: and if nothing else, yet it may occasion us to amend some errour.' This was also typical of Durie's philosophy so misunderstood by Gibson as seen above in his otherwise excellent critique of Durie's supposed millenarian views. However, Comenius opens his work with an appeal to a mixed medley of mentors such as Aristotle, Cicero, Solomon, Seneca, Job, Elephaz, Elihu, Mercurius Trismegistus, Socrates, Epictetus, Ritterus, Glaumius, Coecilius, Andreae, Campanella and others whose names, unlike Bacon who uses Classical authors as windows, throwing light onto what he means, Comenius merely drops as 'gateways to wisdom' and 'ladders to God'. They are, however, merely names named with no indication as to how they function as ambassadors of knowledge and what may be gained from their teaching.

---

[482] See Book I, VI:4.

Furthermore, in spite of his own advice that one may gain something from each writer, Comenius repeatedly tells his readers that, in order to work out a pansophy, they must specialise in knowledge of the few rather than lose themselves in the many. Although Comenius does place Scripture as one of the few, he yet flanks it with Latin as a major gateway to learning. However, Comenius closes his pamphlet, which he claims is a book on pansophy, by stating that his aim is not to expound what pansophy is but to create an awareness that a pansophy is needed. Nevertheless, the work falls between two stools as it neither demonstrates how God seeks to educate mankind methodically and didactically, nor does it show how linguistic analysis via Latin affords transfer of training. Durie always deals with such necessary tools of learning in his many demonstration of how true knowledge is attained.

Durie resembles Bacon in seeing unfallen Adam as a man of meditation and contemplation whose duty it was to compass and catalogue nature and to understand what true knowledge of God and His world is.[483] So, too, Durie, as Bacon, sees Adam's fall in his wishing to acquire God's knowledge of good and evil outside of his subordination to God and his stewardship for Him and to make himself independent of God. Bacon emphasises the great and speedy development made in discovering arts and craft in the ancient world until the confusion of tongues came 'whereby the open trade and intercourse of learning and knowledge was chiefly imbarred.'[484] Bacon sees Job as indicating universal learning, especially in natural philosophy and knowledge of a round world.

In Chapter VI: 16 Bacon shows he stands four-square with Durie when he says:

> 'Wherefore, to conclude this part, let it be observed, that there be two principal duties and services, besides ornament and illustration, which philosophy and human learning do perform to faith and religion. The one, because they are an effectual inducement to the exaltation of the glory of God: for as the Psalms and other Scriptures do often invite us to consider and magnify the great and wonderful works of God, so if we should rest only in the contemplation of the exterior of them, as they first offer themselves to our senses, we should do a like injury unto the Majesty of God, as if we should judge or construe of the store of some excellent jeweller, by that only which is set out toward the street in his shop. The other, because they minister a singular help and preservative against unbelief and error: for our Saviour saith, YOU ERR, NOT KNOWING THE SCRIPTURES, NOR THE POWER OF GOD;

---

[483] See Book I, VI:6.
[484] Ibid VI:8.

laying before us two books or volumes to study, if we will be secured from error; first, the Scriptures, revealing the Will of God; and then the creatures expressing His Power; whereof the latter is a key unto the former: not only opening our understanding to conceive the true sense of the Scriptures, by the general notions of reason and rules of speech; but chiefly opening our belief, in drawing us into a due meditation of the omnipotence of God, which is chiefly signed and engraven upon His works. Thus much therefore for divine testimony and evidence concerning the true dignity and value of Learning.'

Durie's view of Scriptural textual interpretation compared with Grosseteste's

Beryl Smalley in her essay 'The Biblical Scholar'[485] poses the question why Robert Grosseteste (c.1170-1253)[486] failed in his own age but succeeded in another. This question could certainly be asked concerning John Durie whose contemporaries and immediate successors quickly forgot him but modern scholars in many different branches of *Academia* are giving him more and more pre-eminence in their various spheres of service. Durie's correspondence with St Amand on Scriptural analysis continued for several years and on 14th February, 1640 Durie wrote to Hartlib, congratulating him on receiving a measure of recognition from Archbishop Laud and telling his of new correspondence with St. Amand. He writes:

'I am gladde that my Lord primat doth beginne to mind yow & his debt unto yow. I purpose to doe as yow bidde me when I shall write unto him. I approoue of your Counsell Concerning a Narratiue of my proceedings, & God willing I will putte it in execution when I come backe from Gluckstat in the meane tyme yow haue these copies which I pray yow to keep by yow till yow heare further from me; yow may cause some coppies to bee made therof which according to my desire afterward may bee distributed. I pray yow salute Mr St Amands from me & thanke him for his letter & the extract of Bishop Grossete his discourse of which Godwilling by the next I will tell him my iudgement & perhaps send him another piece of my begunne discourses to him about the Analyticall Method for there is a second discourse begunne more then six moneths ago & hath lyen imperfect all this while by reason of my distractions & perpetual interruptions of thoughts partly proceeding from the attendance required of me in this state I am, partly from the varietie of other pressing thoughts, partly from my trauels & negotiations

---

[485] Robert Grosseteste Scholar and Bishop, edited by D. A. Callus
[486] Called also Greathead, Grossetête or Grossete. See my *More Mountain Movers*, Chapter Three for a brief biography of the saint-scholar.

therin; & partly from a resolution not to meddle with that subiect till I should haue tyme to go through with it. this last resolution I am willing now to breake: if I possibly can gette so much freedome of spirit & leisure as to utter though but Confusedly that which I conceiue. as for this Notion of Bishop Grossete it is but a parcell of the third degree of interpretation & except it bee otherwise grounded & exemplified it will neuer leade us to find out the Harmonie of outward & inward truths which hee aimeth at; the thinges which hee saith are truth for the most part: & me thinkes for those tymes hee is gone farre.'

In the same month, Durie replied to St. Amand, commenting briefly on the excerpt from Grosseteste his correspondent had copied and passed on to him. Rather wary of criticising so great an exegete, Durie explains to St. Amand where he differs from Grosseteste:

'In respect of the matter and affinity which it hath with some of my thoughts about that Subject & allthough I perceive partly by the discourse it selfe, partly by the Title of the Treaty whence it is transcribed which you call De Cessatione legalium, that hee speaketh of the Interpretacion of Scripture onely soe farr as it serveth for that theame which hee hath in hand yet something may bee gathered from it applyable to other matters, For his Rules which are given in the latter end how to interpret Allegorys have some truth & vse, all though it bee but obscurely & not fully opened, The matter which hee delivereth is not to bee Contradited, but yet not demonstratively proposed. For many hypotheses are taken as granted which would require a proofe if narrowly examined, but it is faire & probable in a Scholasticall Way & I thanke you for it.'

Durie's reference to 'which you call 'De Cessatione legalium' might indicate that Durie was not familiar with Grosseteste's work as *De Cessatione Legalium* is the correct title.[487] However, it appears that the earliest edition of that name first appeared in 1658 and the work was formerly merely a part of Grosseteste's collected writings with which Durie may have been familiar. However, Durie would have known or quickly recognised that Grosseteste was fond of the Aristotelian method of logical analysis against which Durie, following in Bacon's footsteps, was averse. Durie also notes that Grosseteste used the allegorical method against which he also warned. In short, Grosseteste's view of Biblical analysis in Durie's opinion was fine as far as it went but did not come up to Durie's own strict standards which sought to rule out the obscure and the hypothetical. Durie would

---

[487] Usually dated between 1231-1235.

have welcomed Grosseteste's attitude to a broader learning as the bishop wrote treatises on the nature of light, astronomy, psychology and mathematics and enquired into the whole realm of deductive knowledge. His scientific work would influence all-round scholar Roger Bacon (1214-1294), among many others. Though Durie felt Grosseteste took too much for granted and left too much unexplained,[488] St. Amand's letter reminded Durie of his promise to continue outlining his views so Durie recapitulated on the main points of his previous discourse before going on to expand on them. These, he gives as:

'(1) That a demonstrative method of Analysing Scripture should shew vnto vs the way how a mans vnderstanding may bee led infallibly by degrees (that is by an orderly Concatenacion of true thoughts) from one intellectuall object vnto another till it gather vp all the meaning expressed in the discourses of holy writte.

(2) That to lead the vnderstanding of a man by such a way of diving into truthes it must bee supposed & granted, that when the mind apprehendeth truely all the simple Axiomes of a discourse & is enabled to joyne all these axiomes together without errour as they are in the text set in relacion one to another that then the totall summe of thoughts resulting from such a meditacion cannot bee false.

(3) That to apprehend the simple axioms & joyne the same together, the text ought to bee set downe in write & articulately expressed according to the order of the Axioms & theire Coherences by particles which make them have a relacion together & all to theire joynt maine scope.

(4) That to meditate vpon this frame of Axiomes thus set downe the first Care & Caution must bee to avoide suddaine preconceptions which will readily arise & disorderly bee suggested to the vnderstanding through the quicknes of our imaginacions to doe which the conceiving faculty of the mind must suffer itselfe to bee led in every thing by the letter vnto the matter & becoming all together passive & captivated it must apprehend nothing but that which by a certaine rule the orderly frame of thoughts doth suggest to bee taken vp from the letter concerning the sense of the matter.'

This method of Scripture analysis must be quite unique in the writings of 17th century Puritans but Durie is writing less as an exegete and more as a pedagogue in methodology, providing tools for text comprehension and understanding. Durie therefore claims there are three stages in text inter-

---

[488] The text here used is from Ref: 1/41A-8B Blank, HP.

pretation. These are in regard to different objects: first the bare words; second the sentences and third the matters in the sentences. The right procedure is thus:

> i. The analysis of the words is to discern their literal meaning as they stand together in a single sentence.
>
> ii. The analysis of the sentence is to conceive their material sense as they stand as parts of a full discourse.
>
> iii. The analysis of the matter is to work out the spiritual meaning within the mysteries of God's Kingdom and the Gospel and how it might be discerned by faith as an eternal truth which works towards regeneration.

The reason for such an analysis is to first work out the basic and ordinary surface connotations regarding the sections before studying the deeper structures in meaning. This is not unlike the analytical and mathematical analysis of modern linguists such as Noam Chomsky's cognitive approach to generative, transformational, naturalistic and universal linguistics, believing in 'an innate set of linguistic principles shared by all humans'.[489] Durie's system, however, has more to do with matter than form and distinguishes more between the innate and the acquired than Chomsky's system.

The diversity of analytical methods and their interdependence

Durie raises the question why so many kinds and degrees of analysis have developed and what factors connect them. The answer, for him, is that Biblical texts offer such a diversity of intellectual and cognitive stimuli that various methods of analysis have of necessity been developed to avoid cognitive confusion and simply because man has been trained to think in that way. Grosseteste had, for instance, one system which had influenced subsequent theological practice greatly but Durie finds it wanting. His aim is thus to better Grosseteste and put his methods on a more practical and scientific basis, teaching that lexicology and syntax must be first correctly interpreted before their meaning can be ascertained. Words can mean one thing in a given context and carry another meaning in a further context. In-

---

[489] Chomsky's views tempted me to a study-in-depth of Applied and Social Linguistics at Uppsala and Duisburg universities and were of enormous importance in opening the doors of more profitable text critical studies for me. The quote is from *The Cambridge Dictionary of Philosophy*, 1999 edition.

deed, even in one context where the words mean exactly the same as in another, due to their word order, syntax and subject matter, they can convey quite different meanings. Durie points out that interpretation problems can be caused by the smallest elements in syntax and grammar such as full stops, commas etc.. Unless the syntax and contents are correctly discerned, one cannot hope to discover the meaning hidden in the construction. One of the classical classroom examples of this phenomenon (not given by Durie) is seen in the words 'The teacher says Thomas is a donkey.' Punctuated differently, as, for instance, 'The teacher', says Thomas, 'is a donkey', the meaning is radically altered. Durie's own individual use of punctuation also illustrates this point. He uses a semi-colon where contemporary authors use commas or full stops; separates clauses by capitalising governing pronouns without punctuation and often does not mark genitive nouns as such. He often ends a sentence without a full stop and begins a new sentence with a small letter. This causes interpretation and reading problems, at least for present day readers. Also his apparently random variations in spelling both of nouns and especially verbs may easily lead to lexical and grammatical confusion. In this, modern strictures and rules in lexicology, grammar, style and orthography assist one in putting Durie's system into practice. However, interpreting texts 'correctly' for Durie means mainly 'spiritually correct', and the 'hidden meaning' is what God wishes to reveal in the structure. For Durie, the spiritual meaning is the key to all meaning in the sense of 1 Cor. 2:13-14. Spiritual meanings can only be spiritually discerned by the spiritual but the way to this end must be opened for everyone.

Always striving to show how analysis must needs lead to synthesis in the process of Pansophism, Durie argues concerning the three stages in text interpretation listed above:

> 'For these 3 parts of Analyticall meditacion doe Harmonically answer to the three digestions which are in our naturall bodyes for the Sustentacion thereof by food, that even as the materiall food is dissolved to give our bodyes nourishment, soe the Spirituall food of knowledge is in like manner distributed and by the division of Gods word made a meanes of nourishment for our Soules vnto life Eternall; For in our naturall bodys the first digestion is when the gross substance of meate is dissolved into its Chilus & the Superfluityes are sent away into the draught this digestion is performed in the Stomacke. The Second is when out of the Chilus blood is made which the liver doth performe, & the third is when out of blood every part of the body taketh to it selfe, by its owne digestive quallity that nutriment whereof it doth stand in need, Soe out of Blood vitall Spirits are digested in the heart &

in the braine animall spirits & in the Spermaticall Vessels Sperme & in the Paps milk &c each member assimilating the Substance of blood vnto it selfe for its owne nutriment. Now as this falleth out in the Elementall food of our Bodys naturally without our knowledge, soe wee to feed our Soules with knowledge must distribute & digest the intellectuall food thereof by the like operacions vnderstandingly & this is to bee done by this threefold analyticall Meditacion of the text.'

Here, Durie's repeated mention of 'meditation' does not refer to a mere pondering over a matter but a gnosiological study and method of learning in the form of a *filum meditandi* to accompany his quest for knowledge expressed in his *filum Ariadnes* taking him through learning's labyrinth. This treatise is thus a more detailed development of his *Treatise on Education* of 1628 already mentioned. It is a method of progressing from the known to the hitherto unknown. After further comparing his ideas to food which gives nourishment to both body and mind, Durie offers general rules in a summary form which he promises to outline further. These are:

1. The person who meditates on a given text must be first taught how to organise his thoughts in an orderly way, and not allow random thoughts to interrupt this process.

2. One must learn to order thoughts so that one coherent conception might be seen to arise out of another logically leading the understanding to comprehend the whole.

3. One must learn to think in terms of simples to compounds and vice versa and understand the relation or subordination simples have one with another in the discourse analysed.

4. The manner of proceeding from compounds to simples or simples to compounds must be by no less infallible and demonstrable means than anything else conceived or practised in methods of analytical studies, or 'analyticall meditacion' in Durie's language. Rules must be observed in the same way in respect of their substance but differently in respect of the matter to which they are applied.

The mind must be taught how to order its thoughts to automatically find out the literal sense of any word considered alone or in relation to other words in the sentence joined together in an axiom and show by what evidence the true sense might demonstrably be conceived. Concerning the sentences, the mind must be trained to spot every shade of meaning which makes the utterance coherent and demonstrable. Then one must learn to develop one's thoughts from the outward or material sense of the sentence to the spiritual meaning it conveys and be able to demonstrate how one comes to a particular conclusion.

Durie ends the document explaining that he longs for time to compose a more profound treatise but is compelled to be always on the move with so very little leisure to write. He complains understandably enough:

> 'If the full declaracion of these poynts with the Illustracion thereof by Examples were set downe as I conceive it may bee done, perhaps your laudable desire to dive into this matter would receive Satisfaccion, but you know my State & distraccions & you see by the blotts of this writing what time I have to meditate & recollect my selfe in such waighty matters Since my coming from Brunswic immediately after the sight of your letter I begunne to sett these thoughts to paper, but before I could make halfe an end I was occasioned to make a journey from hence to Gluckestad to prosecute my negotiacion with his Majesty of Denmarke, there I had noe more time then to reade over what I had written & now I have in hast corrected some of the first expressions and added this list of Rules to the Discourse of the parts of the method that it may serve mee for a Taske against the next time of Leisure & that you may know the Summe of that which ought to bee explained in this method of Textuall Interpretacion. You cannot believe how I long to bee once at rest & free to my selfe that I may beate out this matter & perfect divers discourses which are begunne about it & it is a loathsome thing vnto my Spirit thus to handle this Subject abruptly & imperfectly But what can I doe? I must command my desires & possesse my Soule in patience till it please God to set mee a liberty & ease mee from the burden of other Cares & thoughts which give mee noe rest by reason of my present Condicion.'

Advising students how to study

In describing academic activities for the education of mankind, Durie deals mainly with teachers who are also ministers of the gospel because in those days this was the usual combination. In 1647, Durie received a number of letters from a student by the name of Smart who required detailed help with his studies as far as both the academic and spiritual side was concerned. These letters, with Durie's replies, grew into a pamphlet of some twenty pages with cover, which was probably never published. For archive purposes this correspondence was entitled simply *Dury's advice about studies in reference to the Ministry*.[490] True to his Body of Divinity and universal aims in learning, Durie expects Mr Smart to start on a wide vari-

---

[490] Ref: 68/4/1A-14B: 1B-14B BLANK, HP.

ety of studies which no university even today provides in one faculty and in one degree course. Durie wished to incorporate this wide variety into primary and secondary education but in most schools of his day, the teaching of alphabeticism, including reading and writing, simple literature, mathematics, the natural sciences, religion and sport as a comprehensive syllabus was still a novelty. In today's European schools pupils are usually taught these basic elements of general learning, though sadly still mostly as 'separate subjects'.

Durie commences his advice to Smart by saying:

> 'I suppose your aime is to fitte yourself to the worke of the Ministerie in the way of a Pastorall charge; and you are now at the vniversitie to gaine that part of Learning which is proper to Schollars; in order to that aime; my advice shall bee directed therefore to those two heads: first what you should doe in Reference to your Scholasticall; Secondly to your Pastorall or properly Ministeriall Studies.'

Durie recommends that Smart bases his academic pursuits on three pillars: languages; the Sciences; and world history. He must learn enough Latin to be able to speak, read and write fluently and study a wide variety of authors in Latin. He must also be able to discourse with other scholars in Latin and carry out his correspondence and enter into public debate in that language. If he cannot gain suitable tutors, he must work on his own translating backwards and forwards into and out of the languages, here especially Latin, until he is as skilled in the one language as the other. Durie expects Smart to be perfect at translating from Latin into English within two weeks but in translating from English into Latin, he gives no set time. He advises Smart to compare his own translations with those already published so as to observe and correct his own faults. The best of the old writers to follow, Durie believes, are Cicero, Cæsar; Terence, Salust, Livy and Quintilian and those of more recent times Erasmus, Muretus, Politianus, Baudius and Lipsius. Amongst theologians, he recommends 'Old Hieronimus,' Lactantius and Calvin's *Institutes*. Indeed, Durie finds in all Calvin's writings, the purest Latin, equal to all purposes. Concerning the Latin poets, Durie has some surprising and critical things to say:

> 'Amongst Latin Authors the Poets are to bee lookt upon that you may not bee altogether ignorant of their way expressing themselves, it appears that Paul (did) vouchsafe looke upon them by that which hee doth quote out of them in the Acts and in Titus (Acts.17. 28: Tit*u*s 1. 12.), so that a Schollar may and ought to acquaint himself with them chiefly when hee is of ripe Iudgment: and indeed none but these that are come to ripenes of judgment

ought to meddle with Poets; they are not food for childrens understanding; and chiefly the wanton, faboulous heathen poets, Doctors of Lustfull vanities, are meer poison to their Imaginations. Buchanan[491] is the only Poet which I would allow Christian Children to use; I mean his Psalmes, and there is none of the Ancients themselves that have better language than hee: Beza his Paraphrase on the Psalms[492] and Ionstons[493] may also bee put into their hands.'

Concerning Hebrew and Greek, the student must know enough to be able to understand the Old and New Testaments. When this aim is reached, he should read the Church Fathers and Nonnus' paraphrase of John. If leisure permits, he should go on to read Homer, Pindar and Hesiod. For the Greek, he should use Pasor's *Manual*,[494] the *Grammatica Clenardi cum Notis Antesignani*[495] and Scapula.[496] Buxtorf's Grammar and Dictionary[497] should be used for Hebrew studies. For Latin, Durie recommends Comenius' Janua and Calapine's Dictionary

For scholarly studies in the sciences, Durie recommends Logic, Rhetoric, Physics, Ethics, Politics, Metaphysics, Mathematics, Chronology, Geography and Astronomy, using Keckermann's[498] and Alsted's[499] works.

In his historical studies, the student should have an overall view of the world obtained from Sleidan's *de quatuor Summis Imperijs* as also Jonston's *Compendium* and *Universalis Historiae Profana Medullam Parei* or *Epitomen totius Mundi Historiarum Cluveri*. When these have been well-studied, the student can move on to *Medullam Historiae Ecclesiasticae Parei* and then read other works at leisure. These scholastic studies should

---

[491] George Buchanan (1506-1582). See his *Paraphrasis Psalmorum Davidis poetica ... auctore Georgio Buchanano, Scoto and Georgii Buchanani Scoti, Poetarum sui seculi facile principis, Opera Omnia.*

[492] See his *Psalmorum Davidis et aliorum Prophetarum.* Libri quinque.

[493] Arthus Johnston (1506-1582). See his *Psalmorum Davidis paraphrasis poetica et canticorum evangelicorum*, Aberdeen, 1637.

[494] George Pasor, Herborn scholar, London (NT)1644, Elzevir edition (NT and OT) 1664.

[495] Nicolaus Clenardo (1495-1543).

[496] Johann Scapula (c. 1540-c. 1600).

[497] *Johannis Buxtorfii P. Lexicon Chaldaicum, Talmudicum Et Rabbinicum.*

[498] Bartholomäus Keckermann (1572-1609). See his *Systema logicae, tribus libris adornatum, pleniore praeceptorum methodo, et commentariis scriptis ad praeceptorum illustrationem. Hanoviae.*

[499] Johann Heinrich Alsted (1588-1638). See his mammoth work *Encyclopaedia Cursus Philosophici.*

only take up half of each day with studies which fit one out for the ministry taking up the second part.

Concerning ministerial studies, Durie begins with:

i. The catechetical

Dury tells Smart that he should not only study the theology and practice revealed in the Scriptures concerning the ministry but study human sources on the subject and cull from them all teaching that may assist his calling as a minister. Here, he must consult not only those authors who have written since the Reformation but those of pre-Reformation divines. Durie divides the (then) modern writers into the catechetical, the practical and the polemic. The catechetical writers such as Johannes Wollebius (1566-1629), Amandus Polanus (1561-1610), William Bucanus (15?-1603), Zacharius Ursinus (1534-1583), William Ames (1576-1633) and John Calvin (1509-1564), handle the material briefly but systematically in compendium form. The practical writers seek to enforce the duties of conscience rather than knowledge of doctrine and the polemic writers strive to come to decisions concerning controversies but also touch on doctrine and practical matters. Durie believes that if one uses Wollebius, Calvin and Ames, one cannot go far wrong in catechetical works.

ii. The practical

Once the student has mastered the principles of theology and has a broad overview, one might take up controversial subjects but Durie advises Smart to deal with Practical Divinity first as this will help to deal with both basic and controversial theology. Dury takes it for granted that Smart is familiar with works on the subject in his own tongue but there are few works in Latin and advises his enquirer to make his own compendium on the methodology of the duties of the Christian life in the practice of piety. Here, he tells Smart:

> 'let Mr Perkins bee your cheife patterne to imitate, in his popular & plaine way of handling matters. In your practicall Common places, make a distinction of Cases of Conscience and their decisions from other matters, which are vndoubted truths in duetie; In the cleare matters of duty, I take notice of 3. things 1 of the nature of it. 2 of the Motives inducing to the observation theirof 3. of the Signes evidencing that observation or discovering the want thereof.

In the studie of Cases read 1ˢᵗ Mr Perkins Anatome of the Conscience then his treatises Imaginations of the hearte of man, and of the great Case of Conscience how man should know, that he is in the state of Salvation, to which affterwardes add the reading of Dikes deceitfullnes of the hart of man; and when you have attentively considered Mr Perkins more full treatise of the Cases of Conscience, which is extant in his first volume; proceed to meditation of Dr Ames his Cases, which are very briefly stated and resolved, to the heades, which he hath; and such others as yow may adde from other Casuists; all in that kind may be referred.'

iii. The polemic

After dealing in detail with Perkins, Smart will be prepared and ready for tackling polemic authors as all ministers must have some insight into the controversies of their age. Here again Durie returns to Polanus and Wollebius, two Reformers sadly forgotten by our modern age. In all this advice, Durie wishes to guide Smart through the methodology of learning rather than help him merely pick up facts. He wants Smart to be able to stand on his own feet when faced with controversy. Having now worked out a method of approach, Smart is now advised to go on to other authors, some who give general overviews and others who deal with a specific point of controversy. For a brief overview, Durie recommends the compendiums used at his alma mater Leiden, *Corpus Purioris Doctrinae professorum Leidensium* and the *Syntagmata Disputationum*. For rather deeper studies, he recommends the Common Place book of the Italian Peter Martyr (1499-1562) and the works of the Dutch Leyden theologian Antonius Walaeus (1573-1639) one of the compilers of the Canons of Dort. Durie recommends reading the larger works first and then the smaller merely to refresh the memory.

Concerning particular controversies, Durie says:

'As for particular Controversies handled at large; yow may fall upon the studie of them as yowr occasions shall require & your owne judgment shall guide yow, for by this tyme your judgment will be informed to discerne what is most expedient for yowr use, to bee insisted on in the ministerie; the Authors which have handled particular controversies at large against the Papists are Calvin, Beza, Sadeel, Mornæus, Whitaker, Iuell, Perkins, & others which tyme will shew yow. then also yow may learne to know those who have bestowed their gift against the Socinians, Arminians, Anabaptists, Lutheranes & other Sectaries of which I need not at all now to speak.'

Concerning ministerial studies of ancient works, Durie is rather briefer, dealing with the Fathers who were associated with the various church councils and the Schoolmen. He divides the Schoolmen into the *Summulistae* such as Thomas Aquinas in his *Summa*; then the *Casuists* and *Sentenystae* who comment on the 'Master of the Sentences'. A reference, no doubt, to Peter Lombard and his *Libri Quattuor Sententiarum* which still engages the minds of theological students. He feels that when Smart has reached this stage, he will be mature enough to go his own way.

Understanding the Scriptures aright

Durie firmly believed that a correct study and interpretation of Scripture both formal and spiritual was the key to understanding all literature whether occupational or recreational. Thus all human sciences must be studied in the light of Scripture because Scripture alone can lead one to faith according to the adage *Bonus Textualis Bonus Theologus*. The writings of men, he affirms, are to enlarge our learning but salvation comes only by the Word. So Durie tells Smart:

> 'Your maine studie then must bee that off the Scriptures wherin the Word of Truth is offered to us; that beleving therin, the spirit also may bee obtained, which will seale us up untill the day off our Redemption, & lead us in all Truth & Righteousnes, whilest wee are in this our Pilgimage.'

Now, however, Durie tells Smart that he will have to read the Scriptures in a two-fold way: as a normal Christian and as a Minister of the Word. Whereas the ordinary Christian studies the Word for his own spiritual benefit, the pastor must set aside special study times to 'dive into' (a common expression of Durie's when referring to obtaining knowledge of whatever kind) the text prayerfully and work out its every meaning and doctrine. As an ordinary Christian, one should read through the entire Bible within a year, reading morning passages from the New Testament and evening passages from the old. Durie especially recommends beginning each Bible study by reading a Psalm. At least once a week besides the Lord's Day certain passages should be learnt off by heart and the lessons deduced from the passages pondered over. This will, as Durie puts it 'bee a Settlement of our soule in the wayes of God'.

The principle study of Scripture for a minister is to be enabled so to understand the saving knowledge of God provided in the text that he can convey it to others but also so that he might reprove and convince gainsayers. The minister must be familiar with Christ and His work; understand how the iniquities of the world came to be and salvation from it and convey these truths to his flock. If a minister fails here, he will find that all his learning is an impediment to himself and others. 'Unsanctified knowledge doth puff up.' He tells Smart:

> 'the just shall live by Faith; the knowledge then of the Scriptures which is begotten in Faith, is that only which doth quicken the soule; now the object of Faith is the Testimonie of Iesus, & it being received, doth purifie the Conscience & Enliven the soule; with the light of life; which makes it conformable unto his Image; if then in your study yow doe not apply yowr whole attention to apprehend, search & discover the evidences of this light & life; as they are attested in the word, you will never bee proffitable unto others to manifest Iesus Christ unto them; & if yow make not him knowen to yowr hearers, yow will never bee approoved by him, or owned as one of his Ministers.'

Just as one learns to accept the words of Christ as the oracles of God and thus believed for their own sake, so must the student be resolved to be led by faith in the contemplation of them according to 2 Tim. 3:15. Smart must also beware of using reason as his measuring rod according to 2 Cor. 10:5, which teaches that as the Word is given by the Spirit, it can only be spiritually discerned. As Christ represents the fullness of knowledge and all Scriptures point to Christ all studies are futile if not Christ-centred.

Dury ends his advice to Smart by saying:

> 'God hath promised to all that beleive in Christ that his word & spirit shall not be wanting to them, Es: 59. 21. But yet he will have us to call upon him for wisdome Iames 1. 5. nor is it enough to Aske, but wee ought also to seek and knock Math 7. 7. 8; for hee that asketh receiveth, hee that seeketh findeth & to him that knocketh, it shall bee opened. Wee seeke by meditation & wee knock at the doore of the Kingdome, by practise & all this must bee done in Faith; & all with a reference to the Testimonie of Iesus. The prayer must bee made in Faith for the spirit; to bee able to observe what is Testified in the Word. the Meditation must bee ordered by the rule of faith to bee able to dive into the word and to search the depth thereof & the Practise must bee set affoot in the full assurance of Faith to obtaine an experimentall entry through Christ into his everlasting Kingdome, according to the Direction of the Word. The worke of spirituall meditation is properly that whereby the testimonie of Iesus is observed in the Word; this Meditation is to bee ordered by the rule off Faith where off the summe & substance is this Iohn: 20. 31.; that Iesus is the Christ the sonne of God, & that by beleeving in him (& knowing him with the Father (who hath sent him) Iohn 17. 3. to be the only true God, wee may have life eternall. To this scope all the Scripture is to bee

refferred, & by the Analogie of this Truth every thing delivered in the Word, is to bee vnderstood.'

In the above treatise, Durie refers a number of times to William Perkins (1558-1602). The Durie-Hartlib circle had reviewed and supported Perkins' works from the thirties through to the late fifties, especially in *Ephemerides* and Perkins' posthumous work *The Arte of Prophecying, or, A Treatise concerning the Sacred and Onely True Manner and Methods of Preaching* was eagerly read by the members. In the Hartlib Papers there is a detailed review of the book in Hartlib's hand where it touches on text analysis and interpretation. Perkins, however, goes a different way in his interpretation to that of both Bacon and Durie, though there is so much in common with them that Durie can be seen as taking a position between them.

Hartlib sums up Perkins' thoughts on analysis as being:

'1. To Read the Text distinctlie out of the Canonical Scriptures.

2. To giue the sense & vnderstanding of it by the scripture itself.

3. To collect a few & profitable doctrines out of the Natural sense.

4. To applie the doctrines rightly to the life & manners of men & specially to the hearers in a simple & plaine speech.'

Under his heading 'Interpretation and Division', Hartlib quotes Perkins as saying: 'Interpretation is the Opening of the wordes & sentences of the Scripture that one entire & Natural sense may appear. This sense is onely one & the summe is the Literal.' Perkins rejects the 'Papistes' allegorical interpretation such as when Melchisedech offered bread and wine he was teaching that the priest would offer up Christ in the Mass. The 'The Literal sense is heere true & cleere only', he says.

Though concentrating on expounding Scripture for preaching purposes only, Perkins' methods are also useful in separating the objective factual statement from the imaginative and poetic in any text to be studied, whatever its subject. Whilst warning against the false use of allegory and analogy, Perkins shows his wisdom and knowledge of the meta-language of grammar and syntax by warning against the wrong usage of 'Anthropapathia, Metonomie and Synechdoche' using many examples from Scripture. He also gives many examples to show how a special use of grammar, syntax, repetition, rhetorical questioning and other aids are used in the Scriptures to enhance its didactic and methodical teaching. Perkins also gives help in dealing with apparent textual contradictions and how to apply the text to the needs of man.

Durie gives a full-length overview of his analytical methods in his approach to a particularly difficult passage of Scripture in his preparatory analysis of Psalm 105 and especially verse 15, 'Touch not mine anointed, and do my Prophets no harm' which was a subject of much controversy in his day.[500] Of special interest here is how Durie prepares his own thoughts for undertaking such a study so that the text alone speaks irrespective of other influences:

'Worthy Friend,

You desired me, that I should Analyse the 105 Psalme, in hope, that by this meanes some Disputes, which are now on foot, concerning the 15th. verse thereof (Touche not myne anoynted, and doe my Prophets no harme) may bee cleared.

To give you Satisfaction herein, you must first knowe, what my Aime is in Analysing the Scripture, et how I proceede, to attaine unto that Aime. Secondly, how by a true Analysis of the Text Scripturall Doubtes should bee resolved.

The Aime, which I propose unto myselfe in Analysing Holy Scripture is, to discover the meaning of the Spirit, which speaketh therein, with all possible certaintye; taken from the Rationalitye of the Discourse, et the Analogie of Faith, wherein, besides the Literall Sense of every distinct Speech, the Materiall Coherence of the Sentences, doth manifest the Wisdome of the Speaker, et the Depth of his Sense.

The Way of proceeding, which I use, to make this Discovery, doth consist in 2. things.

1. I labour to Emptie my Mind from all Thoughts, which either I myselfe, or any other hath at any time had, or Suggested to mee of the Sense of the Place, which is to bee Analysed.

2. When my Mind is thus freed from all forestalled Notions, I Shape a Course of Meditation, which doth lead my reason to reflect upon all the Words et Matters conteined in the Text, as they stand in their proper Places, et as theie are Connected each unto another, by Severall Particles, which make divers Sentences one.

---

[500] Ref: 1/10/1A-6B, HP.

In this Meditation I take nothing upon trust, but all must result from a regular Methode et way of Contemplation, which is Demonstrative to the Vnderstanding of him, that doth vse it, because it inferres every Analyticall Proposition from an infallible Truth found in the Text, as a thing clearly foreknowen. For every thing, that is not begotten in the Minde a priori infallibili noto, et per immediatam Consequentiam, is not to bee allowed, as Valid or Solid in the way of Analysis; but whatsoever is thus begotten in the Mind, is Demonstrable, if it bee called in Doubt. Therefore, I intend to say nothing of this Psalme, which I shall not bee willing in a Rationall way to Demonstrate, that is, Demonstratively to Evince, if it bee called in doubt.

Now to apply such an Analysis to the clearing of Doubts, is no difficult matter; because if it doth leade the Vnderstanding in a Demonstrative way to the Apprehension of the true Sense of the Text, it will by the Evidence of that Sense take away Doubts, even as light doth Darkenes. Therefore the best way to have a Doubt cleered by this kind of Meditation, is, to conceale it to him, who is to meditate, least it might forestall his Mind, et not suffer it to proceed orderly in the Discoverye of the Trueth: or if hee needs must know it, then hee must, to resolve it, first set it wholly aside from his thoughts, till hee hath made his discovery according to the regular way; et then, when his discovery is ended, hee must compare the meaning, which is doubted of, with that, which hee hath discovered, and shew the agreement or disagreement of the one to the other: which I shall bee also willing to doe, whensoever you shall make the doubtfull Matter more distinctly knowen unto mee.

Having premised thus much concerning the Groundes of my way of Analysing, I will come to the Worke it selfe. Where first I will give you a Generall View of the whole Psalme in breife; and then come to the particular place, which is Disputable.'

This was the method Durie proposed to the synod of ministers and professors at Uppsala in 1636 which was rejected as being too 'scientific' and not doctrinal enough. Scripture, they argued, should be interpreted through the dogmas of the Church.

The place of the library and librarian in universal learning

For Durie, the library was the only real centre of learning and think-tank of his times. It was a clearing-house of information, knowledge and hands-on experience. There, the world-thought gathered could be processed, developed and re-cycled for the common good. During 1651, Durie was scandalised at the fact that over-enthusiastic Republicans and Levellers were taking their iconoclastic enthusiasm so far that they were plundering and destroying national treasures and centres of learning and turning buildings dedicated to the glory of God and former royal property into ruins, stables and barracks. The national libraries and public treasures were also in danger of being plundered and precious manuscripts burnt or sold. Durie had already worked closely in conjunction with Duke August of Brunswick in founding the celebrated Wolfenbüttel Library in the 1630s where Leibniz later studied and Lessing worked for many years as its Head Librarian. Repeatedly in the forties, he had emphasised the importance of libraries in the educational system. He thus demanded that the great Royal Library of King James and King Charles and the Royal private collections should remain as a national inheritance and its precious mss copied and published for research scholars. Early in 1650, he published his *The Reformed Librarie-Keeper* based on letters he had previously written on the subject. In Paul A. Nelles words, in his essay 'Libraries, books and learning, from Bacon to the Enlightenment', 'Durie's methodological treatise, the *Reformed Librarie-Keeper*, embodies his lifelong ambition to bring about a general reformation of learning under a pan-Protestant banner'.[501] After leading Parliamentarian, lawyer and scholar John Shelden had stopped the plundering and Bulstrode Whitelocke was given the job of protecting the Royal Library, Durie, who had already shown his proficiency in library management was given the post of Librarian of King Charles' Library in October 1650. It is obvious that Durie had suggested that a professional librarian should be employed for the task. The Hartlib Papers have preserved the initial motion placed before Parliament to use St. James' Chapel as the initial Royal Library site. The document is in Durie's hand and Turnbull suggests that it was Durie himself who put forward the motion which reads:

'Humble Motions

Concerning the Library at St. James

It is humbly desired for the Honour of this Commonwealth to manifest that the preseruation of learning is minded therein & that care is taken for the rare monuments therof.

1. That Mr. Patrick Young may bee ordered by the Parliament or Counsell of State to dispatch forthwith the printing of the septuagint copie of the Bible which is in his hands; and for the effecting of which hee hath receiued a thousand pounds and that the Originall Copie bee returned without delay into the Library to bee kept there.

---

[501] *The Cambridge History of Libraries in Britain and Ireland*, p.27.

2. That the Trustees for the selling of the Kings goods bee ordered to giue vp to the Counsell of State without delay the Catalogue and inventory which is made as it is now made of the bookes and medals belonging to the Library.

3. That the New Chappell at St. Iames bee fitted with all convenient speed for the vse of the Library; Lest the bookes as now they lye in confused heapes bee spoiled, and remaine still vseles. and that the Library keeper Mr. Dury bee put in a capacity to take the bookes and medals in his custody, by being lodged next vnto the said Chappell, in which hee is to keepe them.'[502]

Immediately on assuming his post, Durie converted derelict buildings, formerly used by Charles I, into library premises for all the royal books and had shelves built for their storage because they had formerly merely been placed on furniture or the floor. From then on Durie led Britain and Europe in his methods of cataloguing, processing and accessing books put on loan besides organising inter-library loans and a joint Europe-wide co-operation in Library Science.

Scott Mandelbrote, in his essay 'Professional collections libraries for scientists and doctors' states, 'One topic of discussion was the need to perfect catalogues and indices. Dury believed the task of the scientific librarian was to be 'a factor and trader for helpes to learning, a treasurer to keep them and a dispenser to apply them to use.'[503] Durie's very title of his book on library management, *The Reformed Librarie-Keeper: with a Supplement to the Reformed School, As subordinate to Colleges in Universities,* shows that Durie wishes to incorporate the nations libraries into the general educational system. As universities are, or should be, the centre of research, so too, they must be equipped with the means of such research. Thus Durie starts by complaining that libraries, churches and universities in most countries are seen as places of profit and gain and not as centres for the advancement of piety and learning. The aim of their stewards is to receive an easy subsistence and gain an importance over others which they in no wise earn. Especially librarians in universities are usually mere sinecurists or mercenaries and they have no interest in the books in their care apart from seeing that they are not stolen or sold by the borrowers. The libraries themselves encourage this as even the great Oxford library pays its librarian a mere pittance so they have no incentive to become agents for the advance-

---

[502] Ref: 5/1A-B, HP.
[503] *The Cambridge History of Libraries in Britain and Ireland,* p. 159. Sadly, Mandelbrote, as several other contributors to this important work, merely give secondary sources for their quotes. This quote is actually from page 18 of the 1650 publication of the *Reformed Librarie-Keeper.*

ment of learning. In undated letters to Hartlib, later taken up into Durie's Reformed Librarie-Keeper,[504] Durie says, 'Concerning the Librarie-Keeper's place, I forgot the last week to tell you that I had enquired of the Warden of the Colledge here what it was worth, hee tells me not of settled maintenance about 50 or 60 lib, but that accidents make it worth 100 at the most.' Durie explains here that 'accidents' means that the Librarian lets out rooms under his charge for a fixed charge, but elsewhere he refers to 'accidents' with books, leaving the reader to assume that the librarian has to secretly sell off books so that he can cover his own costs. Thus Durie argues that libraries must be run by qualified staff with a wage of at least £200 per annum. Libraries are not dead bodies to be guarded over but must be put into circulation and used thus people trained in the administration and organisation of such usage must be appointed. So, too, it would not suffice to train staff merely in administration. A Librarian must be a person of more than common education who knows how to use books to their fullest extent. Such a Librarian should never be there to keep the status quo in a library but to be always extending the stock, planning investment, encouragement of legacies and general state and private financing. He is a factor and trader in auxiliary media for learning.

It is thus necessary that the first duty to fall on a librarian is to prepare a catalogue of all the books, Durie says 'treasures' put in his care. Such catalogues should be divided both as to titles and subject matter. Such broad cataloguing should then be subdivided according to what language the works are in and what branches of a particular subject are covered. Catalogues should never be exhaustive just as shelves must never be complete. Space must be left in both for constant new entries and acquirements. Part of the cataloguing must include the departmentalising, processing, shelf-marking and accessing of books. It appears that Durie did not think of a numerical and alphabetical system of cataloguing like that of Melvil Dewey's Decimal system but considering that many great libraries of the world still use Durie's common-sense cataloguing system and have not yet come round to Dewey's system yet, it must be accepted that Durie was quite before his time. Indeed, Dewey's divisional system, as it is widely practiced, is most unsuited for interdisciplinary studies and has become far too bulky to be practical, especially after the advent of digitalised and online learning.[505] A further reform in classifying and cataloguing knowledge-engineering and information-management media is urgently needed.

---

[504] Ref: 47/14/1A-8B, HP.
[505] I speak as one who has studied Library Science and taught library staff for over 16 years and run school libraries.

It took Germany's libraries decades to work out a national catalogue and once the monster was created, it has been breaking at the stitching seams of usefulness ever since.

Durie planned to employ Government agents whose tasks were to search the libraries and publishing houses of the world with a view to purchasing needy works and copyrights for the English educational establishment and this work must be assisted by the librarians. Also each librarian should be diligent in trading superfluous books for others in other libraries and bookshops which are needed in the home libraries

Durie believed that no mere human could be absolutely trusted to work ideally on his own and do things to his maximum capacity. Thus Durie campaigned for Library Boards which supervised the libraries in their area and made sure that everything was working usefully and orderly. Hope was set in developing machines which would be more efficient and quicker than mere manual organisation. Librarians should be proficient in mathematics and good bookkeepers and take yearly stock of both their books and their expenditures regarding sales and new purchases. The best boards of supervision, Durie thought, should be made up of university professors who should spend a whole week every year going through the accounts of the librarians. Libraries are not just sources of knowledge but they must be successful commercial enterprises also, though not for individual gain. The professors must also give the librarians lists of works needed in their respective teaching areas. The library accounts must be published for general information and control.

All printers and publishers must be compelled to supply the libraries, free of charge, with new books which come on the market. These books are then passed on to the university professors who grade the books according to their suitability and give the librarians advice as to what their subject matter is and where they should be best recorded in the catalogues. Books rejected by the professors as not being useful should not be destroyed but recorded in a catalogue on their own and stored, to alter a modern key-word a little, in a 'bad book bank' as there are no books which provide absolutely no information or particles of knowledge or may become profitable at some time.

Durie makes a special appeal to Parliament to encourage, indeed enforce, his plan for libraries. He points out that the Oxford libraries could easily lead the world and that the libraries abroad, such as the one at Heidelberg had declined in their usage through lack of government and church support. Durie puts this down to the Continental libraries being left in the hands of a few idealists who were more collectors than supporters of universal learning and practical divinity. The talents in the libraries at their founding were quickly buried. Durie is saying that librarians come and go but a library must have a permanent apparatus behind it to make it a lasting enterprise. This can only happen when the state or some permanent trusteeship vouchsafes the permanency of the institution. Durie also criticises the Continental libraries because they are dependent on the changing religious convictions of the local dukes and thus no permanency is allowed them. Durie thus had a hard time with the so-called Puritans of his day who would not accept learning from sources which were considered 'papists'. The 'papists', too were reluctant to accept any scientific findings which were considered 'Protestant' or 'Mohamedan', thus there was little continuity in true, universal learning. Libraries are placed under God's stewards which are responsible to Him first and foremost to keep learning available to all mankind no matter what colour, class or creed they may belong. Learning is like commerce, Durie argues. It must always be practiced in a free-trade area. Protectionism and custom-barriers are equally dangerous in both spheres. Sadly, it is a common sight in today's market places to see libraries selling off precious stock for low prices because of new fashionable topics and themes taking over.

In 1892, *The Library*, a librarian magazine centred in London, brought out a reprint of Durie's Reformed Librarie-Keeper, as part of a series of older works on librarianship. The reprint has a very informative essay attached by an anonymous writer. Comments are based on a thorough study of the *Calendars of State Papers* which give profuse details of Durie's life and work. The writer feels that Durie made such little headway because of his political and religious comprehensiveness so that believers in black and believers in white could not appreciate him. He comments that Whitelocke was given responsibility over the King's library but was told by the Council to employ Durie as his Deputy whom Whitelocke described on July 30, 1650 as, 'Mr. Duery, a German by birth, a good scholar, and a great travellor and friend to the Parliament.' Whitelocke adds that he wanted to be 'less answerable' and so gave Durie the keys and told him to take over from Patrick Young, the King's librarian. From thence on, Durie is called 'Mr. Dury, the Library keeper' in the Calendars. We are informed in the introductory essay that, 'The excellence of Durie's treatise on library-management speaks for itself'.

The tone of *The Library* article reflects the respect shown to a pioneer librarian and colleague. This sober presentation, built on historical data only, is rather lacking in the 1983 reprint edited by Popkin and Wright mentioned in Chapter Five which was marred by the editors' millennial speculations. Popkin's interpretations have been already mentioned, but Popkin was not a professional librarian. However, Thomas F. Wright, Librarian and Assistant Director of the Clark collection of ancient and old mss and books, who gave Popkin first place in prefacing Durie's reprint, continues Popkin's millennial interpretations, even claiming that the office of a librarian had 'a sacramental nature' for Durie. Rather than keep to the sober account of how Durie came to be a librarian as stated on historical evidence by *The Library*, Wright airs the quite speculative idea that Durie's motives in writing his The Reformed Library-Keeper might have been 'impure' and merely a means to climb up the career ladder. He finds Durie's criticism of the low state of libraries 'obsessive' and tells us that Durie's 'larger vision' that underlies *The Reformed Librarie-Keeper* is 'now merely a historical curiosity.' Nevertheless, Wright believes that Durie's 'specific reforms' as opposed to his 'larger vision' are now accepted standards of modern librarianship. Wright does not explain what he means by 'a larger vision' and 'specific reforms' or how he is able to separate the one from the other.

Durie's teaching recommended by today's information processors and librarians

Since Popkins' and Wright's days, modern information processing and library management and outreach has improved with leaps and bounds. In 1994, *Information Processing and Management*, Pergamon Press, published a 12 paged article entitled *Some Schemes for Restricting and Mobilising Information in Documents: A historical Perspective*.[506] In this paper, W. Boyd Rayward of the University of New South Wales writes of 'the mobilising of information stored in documents to advance learning and social well-being'. The author claims that 'until recently, information storage and retrieval systems, of which the library is one of the oldest and most important examples, have not provided a direct solution to the problem of providing access to needed information.' He feels that a reformation in knowledge processing and immediate availability of input is faced with 'overwhelming technical and epistemological problems' but he suggests some 'speculative approaches' which might help to overcome such difficulties. These he divides into two categories, dealing rather briefly with 'contemporary' and at great length with the 'historical' which he finds more *avant-garde*. He sees a contemporary deficit in the administrative difficulty of processing documents to make them applicable to particular

---

[506] Vol. 30, No. 2, pp. 163-175, 1994.

modern needs and thus creating new documents out of old. In this, of course, Rayward is retracing Durie's steps in using a combination of new ideas improved by old books in order to write new books which would inspire even more new ideas. Rayward believes, however, that modern methods of knowledge management have made this process more complicated than ever.

Nowadays, Rayward explains, instead of having a Librarian, or like Durie, a Library Warden, who has a general overview of what is happening, we have specialised librarians, archivists, library and archive administrators, records managers and museologists, each with different objectives and tasks and each within a separate administration and organisation system. Thus instead of a fusion of methods of knowledge acquirement leading to a synergism and to universal learning, knowledge has become more diversified and less immediately accessible than ever. Rayward might also have added that the modern trend in library and archive management is to decentralise access and create specialised libraries and subject-orientated digitalised collections in different areas, thus creating new posts and complicating the actual appropriation of knowledge. Rayward, as Durie before him, is seeking to rectify the dysfunctional state of libraries as think-tanks and places where information can be gained swiftly and comprehensively from one major source.

So, to reform the modern chaos in knowledge management, Rayward takes a long and nostalgic look at past methods of regulating knowledge, starting with the Office of Publicke Addresse which was pioneered and organised by the Durie circle. Rayward relies closely on the works of Charles Webster and G. H. Turnbull here though they focused on Samuel Hartlib's presence in the circle as 'Agent of the Advancement of Universal Learning'. As demonstrated above, Hartlib was Durie's agent but not the main instigator and author in promoting Parliamentary and educational schemes for furthering knowledge. So, too, almost all Rayward's evidence is quoted from Durie's works, not Hartlib's. He thus uses Durie's 1642 *Reformation in Learning and Religion* and his 1647 account of the *Office of Publicke Adresse* besides his 1650 *Reformed Librarie-Keeper*, though he does not mention Durie's overview of knowledge-attainment in his *Advancement of Learning* of 1653. Perhaps he feels this was by Hartlib as indicated wrongly by Webster's unclear title.

Also, by leaning on Turnbull, and contrary to the evidence given in Chapter VII of this dissertation, Rayward assumes that Durie obtained his pansophism from Comenius and that Hartlib and Durie were Comenius' 'English disciples'. He even suggests that Comenius influenced Hartlib's and Durie's conception of the Office of Publicke Adresse, though Comenius openly rejected Durie's and Hartlib's idea of a central state system regulating the flow and use of centralised knowledge. Nevertheless, Rayward writes of Durie's proposals for a warden for the Office of Addresse of Accomodations, for which post, though Rayward does not mention it, Durie had recommended Hartlib. This warden should supervise, 'all manner of registers, inventories catalogues and lists'. Durie's proposals for an Office of Addresses of Communications based on the great Oxford libraries, also appeals to Rayward as Durie campaigns in his manual of library management to reduce and organise the diversity of matters and methods used in the sphere of learning. Rayward also comments most favourably on what he calls Durie's 'cry from the heart' in seeking 'the orderly and useful concatenation of human notions as they relate to their proper ends' and that then 'all the confusion and superfluity, which we groan under' could be avoided. Obviously Rayward thinks that the best way of moving forward is to look back for guidance to Durie. However, though Rayward quotes Durie's enthusiasm in working out all things in relation to their proper ends, he refrains from using Durie's *filum Ariadnes* to that end.

It is interesting to note that as soon as Rayward has dealt in several pages with Durie's pioneering ideas, he goes on to describe Leibniz as an 'imaginative and resourceful' librarian. He does not link or compare him with Durie which would have been a useful contribution in tracing the history of epistemology and gnosiology in library management and education, including Lessing's later contribution.

As indicated by Rayward's references to the Lending Library, none of Durie's ideas seems to have caught on in the modern world more than his teaching regarding the practical and most efficient use of libraries in information-engineering and a wholesome, practical education. Indeed, in 1999, Illinois University published an *Educational Technology Timeline* in which the sixth most important event in the history of mankind in education technology was given as 1651 when 'John Dury invented the modern library'. As Prof. Rayward taught there at the time, this comes as no surprise.

For one who is familiar with the library systems of Europe and the USA, and has taught library staff and run school libraries for many years, it is always refreshing to note that Durie is still honoured and followed by the profession as witnessed lately by Thomas Hapke at the modern University of Technology Library in Hamburg. On hearing of Hapke's cutting-edge research, I obtained a copy of his fine Power-Point lecture given at the July 2005 LIBER Conference, Groningen, entitled 'In formation' of better learning environments' with the added words set apart '. . . . is not enough'. Reading through his lecture with its well-chosen illustrations was quite a sensation as if Durie himself were giving the presentation as the terminology and ideas came so close to his. Under two illustrations, one engraved in ancient stone and one printed on a modern sign, declaring that the unlocking of the past is the key to the future, Hapke opens by quoting Durie's simple but explicit words from his *The Reformed Librarie-Keeper* of 1650, 'Librarie-keepers . . . ought to become agents for the advancement of universal learning . . . . his work then is to bee a Factor and Trader for helps to learning.' Next, now quoting Jean Marc Cote's and William F. Poole's ideas of 1899, Hapke emphasises in true Durie style that the scientific method of studying books should have an assured place in the university curriculum and will aid students in their studies throughout their lives. He explains the same 'recycling' method of library work which Durie used. Books are donated to the library where they are examined by the library staff and related to the need of the times. These are studied *in situ* or as loans and used to write further works which are, in turn, donated to the library. Hapke emphasises that true learning is active and incorporates the student's background, interests and private interpretations as he engineers his knowledge for further use in specific situational contexts.

Thus the libraries contribute to the social process which is part of community-creating life. Every university library, says Hapke, should reflect and present the change and diversity of its times but also provide a linking thread (*filum Ariadnes* again!) through its complexity. Whatever else happens in the knowledge process, knowledge must never be fragmented. Thus Hapke, like Durie, sees the library as having an environmental service, linked to the environment and the world's think tanks through its facilities, including, digitalised media. A library must be an actively functioning teacher in itself, otherwise, just as Durie says, it is a mere building with books. Library staff must help the student step by step through his courses in his quest for appropriating, amalgamating and using information. This will encourage the student to be a furtherer, manager and even creator of knowledge, at first though such means as wikis and weblogs and then on to larger works. Hapke is not a mere book worm but sees libraries as information centres combining old and new methods. Today's library cannot be conceived without USB-sticks, handhelds and laptops. Libraries are thus learning laboratories which connect information, recreation, teaching, contemplation and activation and not merely places where facts are supplied.

Libraries, Hapke continues, are places for individual, group and classroom study. Whilst studying education, this writer learnt from John Dewey (1859-1952) to place the library physically at the centre of class work, each classroom having immediate and direct access to the library via the opening of a door. By this means, pupils could research their projects during lessons. This was the pattern Durie proposed. So, too, the project teaching of Dewey can be traced back to that of Durie, with Hapke following in their wake. Hapke, here following Durie more closely than Dewey, even goes further and will have the library as a classroom in its own right. These 'classrooms' or group-study centres must be connected to what Hapke calls 'the clusters' in all the different rooms of the library by computers and other modern media. Online conferences should be no strangers to libraries. Hapke even goes so far as to see the need for libraries as a place for socialising, eating and drinking and having fun as all communication engenders knowledge.[507] Thus, rather than use the term 'teaching library' Hapke prefers to speak of the learning facilitating, enabling, experiencing and empowering library. Here, the student must learn what the misuses of intellectual property are, again completely in Durie's spirit, and rules concerning plagiarism and copyrights. Libraries are places where students gain information literacy and create, organise and shape their own information process, not forgetting its usefulness. Next, Hapke goes into great and lengthy detail into methods of engineering information which would break the bounds of this dissertation but his further pages are, nevertheless, a must for those concerned with knowledge organisation. Here, again, Hapke resorts to the *filum Ariadnes* and exhorts us to 'Grab the thread! 'Hapke ends with a quote from Nobel Prize winner, William Ostwald who said:

'It is not enough to found libraries. It is necessary . . . to instruct those eager for knowledge in the best methods of utilising their treasures.'

However, Hapke's vision differs in one major point from Durie's. It comes short of Durie's idea of the public good and sees knowledge engineering as being demand-oriented rather than need-oriented. Here, there is still room for improvement before Durie's standard is reached.

---

[507] Happily, our newly-built city library in Mülheim has incorporated a café-restaurant, a film theatre and a tourist information department with areas for socialising and a large multi-media department fitted out with almost living-room-type comfortable furniture. There is even a couch! The city provides free transport from all parts of Mülheim to and from the Library for library ticket holders. Sadly, fees have gone up two-hundred per-cent and more.

CHAPTER NINE

A Parliamentary Agency for the Advancement of Universal Learning

Early attempts at finding private sponsors for an agency for advancing learning

Throughout the 1630s, we find letter after letter from Durie's pen sent to wealthy people to solicit their help in setting up agencies in England and Europe for international correspondence regarding the inter-church and international advancement of learning and practical divinity. If people themselves could not help, he asked them to 'provoke others whome you know to be most able & fitt to give advise, that they would concurre with vs in the Counsells of Pacification & practicall divinity'.[508] Most of these letters refer to a person named 'Abureth' who is presented as worthy of support. Typical of these solicitations is a letter sent from Amsterdam to a wealthy person whose name has not been preserved, asking for help to set up an agency led by 'Mr Abureth' who had become poverty-stricken through his work of assisting scholars. Durie, writing under the pseudonym of Daniel Rhaetus, given to him by State Secretary Thurloe on his diplomatic missions, tells his correspondent:

> 'What greater worke of Christian charity can there bee, then to mainteyne and set out a worke, that is an vniversall Agent for all publicke endeavours in the communion of Saincts? Surely this is an obiect of true spirituall liberality, yf there be anie in the Church of God, for in such an Agency is the seed of all manner of vertue & knowledge sowen to all places, that the fruicts may spring vpp both now & hereafter to many generations. Therefore yf you would bee a meanes to acquaint some generous spiritts, that loue to doe good workes for the publicke state of Gods Church, of this opportunity which may be gayned to doe good service in mayntcyning mr Albureth for such his agency, I make noe doubt but you may bee an happie instrument, both of his comfort, & of much good towards others, therefore let mee in-

---

[508] Ref: 3/4/57A-60B, HP.

treat you, not for him alone, but for the benefit which may redound hereafter to Gods glory & the comfort of many.'[509]

The name 'Albureth' is also recorded in the minutes of the Durie-Hartlib circle entitled *Ephemerides* throughout the fifties. We read, for instance, in the 1655 entries:

'Albureth's designation.
　　To procure stipendiary intelligencers from several Princes, Cities, Commonwealths or kingdoms to reside with Albureth who vndertakes to furnish them with Intelligence and all other Accomodations and Communications in reference to the good of Mankind and their Masters and Principals who maintaine them.
　　Intelligencers of Forraigners.
　　Vpon condition that they may stand engaged to bee employed by Albureth according to their abilities and the occasions of the Agency for Vniversal learning, Arts and Industry. which is the only Gratitude desired by Albureth.
　　Albureth designations.
　　Any Intelligence though otherwise constant and good cannot possibly bee so advantageous either to forraigners or this Commonwealth as the living besides with such an Instrument as Albureth who may traine them vp for the Interest aforesaid and of the Publique Good.
　　The like may bee applied to both Vniversities for the through Advancement of the National Reformation.
　　The benefits of this designation will a hundred or a thousand fold requite the Charges or stipends which are given and allowed to the stipendiaries.'[510]

As this Mr Albureth does not appear outside of Durie's letters and *Ephemerides*, edited by Samuel Hartlib, I became suspicious that Hartlib was probably editing out his own name and supplying a pseudonym instead. This became evident when discovering copies of Durie's letters edited by Hartlib who had crossed out his own name and replaced it by 'Albureth'. Thus, when Durie says of 'Albureth', 'I must tell you, that without him I know not how to enterteine my correspondence in England, for he is the center of my correspondency. Therefore I am bound to consider & to take his case to heart very tenderly, not onely as he is a most worthy Christian deserving all love & compassion from every one, but cheifely as he is a faithfull solliciter of the communion of Sainets, & as I may soe say a publick Treasurer & dispensator of all spirituall obiects & enterprises

---

[509] Letter written 26th Nov. 1635, Ref: 3/4/39A-44B, HP.
[510] Ref: 29/5/1A-14B: 1B, HP.

amongst all the best men in Europe', he is writing about his good friend Hartlib.[511]

Hartlib battled on for years as the agent of both the Old and New World, collecting a huge treasure of knowledge sent in from his countless correspondents and distributing them to friends requiring the knowledge pooled in this way. Whether it was in the realms of history, politics, medicine, mechanical inventions, chemistry, alchemy, physics or languages ancient and modern, Hartlib proved to be a think-tank in his own person. Sadly, all Hartlib's records were lost soon after his death in 1662 but happily recovered in 1933, forming the basis of the present Hartlib Papers.

When Hartlib left Elbing in 1628 to act as agent for Durie, he was able to start an educational work at Greenwich College which was to be an international centre for the advancement of learning. Though this started off as a private enterprise, many efforts were made to have the college officially recognised by the state as an educational, theological and international think-tank for cooperative learning and what Durie called 'correspondency' or the exchange of ideas, leading also to a pan-European cooperation of the various Protestant churches. Though Durie and Hartlib gained backing from some fifty like-minded ministers, scholars, scientists and writers, these were more able to give professional advice rather than raise the amount of funds needed.

Whilst in Hamburg in 1639, Durie wrote his *A Summary Discourse concerning the work of Peace Ecclesiasticall, How it may concurre with the aim of a civill confederation amongst Protestants*, which he presented to Ambassador Sir Thomas Roe. This was eventually printed in 1641 with an Epistle Dedicatory to Roe. Here, Durie makes it quite clear that his plans for a Practical Divinity and joint learning programme extend beyond the ecclesiastical to the civil education of all Protestants. Indeed, Durie now claims:

'The aim of a civill Confederation, I suppose to be a purpose of joyning the Protestant States together in councels and actions of peace and war, tending to their mutuall preservation. That these two businesses may concurre as well as Religion and civill prudence are able to stand together, is out of all doubt: but what the first may contribute unto the last, and how the concurrence must be framed, are two things which are now to be thought upon.'

Then Durie outlines how it is squabbling over religion that has led to civil squabbles so unless there is no union of religious goals, there can be no

---

[511] Ref: 3/4/57A-60B, HP.

civil union. Furthermore, he maintains that the differences at stake in religious quarrels are not spiritual, religious or theological but always centred on worldly thought and behaviour where the common good is ignored. Durie saw no hope in his time that such unity could be attained by men merely discussing their problems together, though this might happen in a lengthy process of mutual good will. The world could not wait for that, so the Christian heads of state and churches must use their delegated authority to rule for peace and civil confederation. As the Thirty Years War was still in full force, Durie felt that Sweden and Germany must first establish concord in ecclesiastical and civil matters which could be achieved through a concurrence of politicians, ecclesiastical heads and the universities. From these sources, the common people should be educated in unionist thinking. All discussions and conclusions must be put in print for general information. This should lead to other states and Protestant churches joining in with the Swedish and German Protestant states to form a Protestant league of nations which Durie calls simply 'The Civill League'. Cases of conscience brought forward by those who would still differ, must be respected and such people be invited to work with the rest, both parties showing mutual respect but freedom of utterance. In all this, Durie was convinced that any stable ecclesiastical or civil body was to be preferred to chaos and general mal content and those that opted out of a general consensus of mutual toleration usually gave birth to further split-offs and rebellion.

Durie's *Discourse* was mainly designed for the Continental Protestant nations but in 1641 he turned to the British civil and ecclesiastical authorities, pleading for a similar action towards mutuality and tolerance. In 1641, Durie petitioned both Charles I and Parliament, explaining that he had been working in a 'private Theologicall way' not unknown to his majesty for ten years to promote an agency for correspondence and the union of the English and foreign Protestant churches. He further argues that such is the chaos and disunity in society that a joint synod must be called of all Protestant churches to work out a programme of unification for 'Evangelical correspondency for mutual edification, for healing of breaches, for taking away of scandals and for the advancement of the Gospel of Jesus Christ amongst Protestants' whether at home or abroad. So that King and Parliament would know what Durie had in mind, he included in his petition a paper entitled *A Memoriall Concerning Peace Ecclesiasticall amongst Protestants: Which John Dury offereth to Master Alexander Henderson, to bee sent or presented unto the General Assembly of the Church of Scotland.* Before Britain could act as a leader in Europe, he thought, they must be united civilly and ecclesiologically themselves. This is a very important document in working out Scotland's participation in Durie's work, particularly as Hetherington has argued that it was Alexander Henderson who took this initiative.[512] Durie pleaded with Henderson and his fellow Scottish delegates to unite with him, King and Parliament in procuring 'the means of true Christian learning, and holy knowledge'. The first step must be to end 'the ordinary Philosophicall-jangling School-Divinity' and devise a 'full body of practicall Divinity' for all those who seek the truth which is according to godliness, especially amongst young scholars and university students. Secondly, a system of Bible interpretation must be jointly worked out based on the literal and material sense of the text and not on the various traditions and externals of the churches. Thirdly, the advancement of Christ's Kingdom must be placed centrally in the work of the churches and the light revealed to Protestants in the gospel must be propagated amongst those in darkness and ignorance.

Durie had already received encouraging backing for his proposals from German divines and educationalists and the Scottish General Assembly had begun to correspond with him on ways and means of putting his ideas into practice. Thus Durie petitioned the King and Parliament again in 1642, outlining the progress made and asking that a planned public day of fasting should take up the theme of Protestant reconciliation and urging them again to consider setting up a national synod. This time, he attached a printed copy of his *Certaine Considerations, Shewing The necessity of a Correspondencie in Spiritual matters betwixt all Protestant Churches. An especiall means for effecting whereof, and healing our present breaches, would be a national Synod*. This is a heart-felt plea as Britain was now suffering under many intolerant displays in politics and church life. Durie urges Britain to endeavour to keep the unity of the Spirit in the bond of peace. In this pamphlet, Durie sees ahead to the state of affairs in the Commonwealth and warns his readers against making that a reality. Protestantism, he maintains, is bringing about its own ruin.

In the early forties, we also find Durie writing from The Hague, still urging Hartlib to keep up his pressure on their influential friend Pym to set up a Parliamentary agency on lines suggested by Durie for the advancement of religion and the support of Protestants abroad, especially those of the Palatinate, saying; 'for if they would maintaine but an Agent or two; or only yowr self to negotiat in the waye that I should shew yow; for the upholding of correspondency for that cause; I saye if they would but doe so much as would maintaine yow to bee a seruant of that house for the public interest of Religion for which it is persecuted they would doe themselues a

---

[512] See p. 38 ff. in this thesis.

great deale of credit & their cause in hand much good, & the house Palatin no small seruice'.[513]

With the advent of the Commonwealth and funds made available through the confiscation of Church and Royal property, enhanced by the spoils of war, Durie and his circle began to campaign in greater earnest for an increasingly more comprehensive agency owned and run by the state for the financing and organisation of religion and learning with Hartlib as its first major agent. The agency, however, should first work for a unification of the churches in England and Scotland, before opening their doers to the Continent. It was no use scrubbing the doorsteps of others when the home doorsteps were left unclean. During 1643, Durie published his *A Faithful and Seasonable Advice, Or, The necessity of a Correspondence for the advancement of the Protestant Cause, Humbly suggested to the great Council of England assembled in Parliament*.[514] In this work, Durie shows again how the state and Church must work together for the common good of the people. He refers to the colleges of the papists for *de propaganda fide* in which the more learned clergy are trained to combat Protestantism. When the papists, however, approach the Puritans with their propaganda, they find them so tattered and torn in their own theologies and church traditions that the papists have an easy task condemning them for their disorder. The setting up of such international institutes for the training of Christian thinkers and debaters should be a prime goal amongst Protestants. Thus Parliament ought to be pioneering such a work of education to stop a new Roman Catholic take-over.

Preserved in the Hartlib Papers is a list of small donations collected from the members of the Westminster Assembly in 1643 under the heading *The Names of those that haue subscribed the Role for the Advancement of a Spiritual Agency for the good of all Protestant Churches*. The twelve subscribers, however, were all self-offering members of Durie's circle. Now that Durie was a Member of the Westminster Assembly, even when he was still abroad more than in England, he could use his authority directly to promote his aims. In the fifties there were some efforts made by the state to take on the patronage of such an institution and help to fund it.[515] This was after at least ten petitions and memorandums had been read before Parliament, assisted by detailed instructions as to how the project

---

[513] 5th Sept. 1642, Ref: 2/9/24A-25B, HP.
[514] Sig. A1-A4, HP.
[515] Ref: 23/17/1A-2BA, HP.The subscribers are, in order of signing, Palmer, Witacker, Caryl, Carter, Case, Greenhill, Woodcocke, Ashe, Calamy, Harcourt, Brice and Pennington.

could be financed. Perhaps Durie and his friends took too much advantage of Parliamentary liberties as they not only petitioned for aid in setting up a state agency in England but also similar institutions, in teamwork with the Swedes in Germany. Durie claimed that the Commonwealth under its covenant with God was obliged to protect Protestants 'from the power of Anti-Christianity' worldwide.[516] He thus suggested setting up centres of contact and education abroad on the lines of the modern British Council and Goethe Institute. Enough money was there, he argued as all royal and Church funds and assets had been taken over by the Commonwealth government.

Obviously, Durie's and Hartlib's many appeals to Parliament in general and Cromwell in particular had a practical and utility background. Funds were needed, whatever their legal source might be. Durie explains himself in the longer, unpublished version[517] of *A further Discoverie of the Office of Addresse, in matters, of Communication for the Advancement of Divine and Human Learning*, written sometime in the forties:

> 'Although there were not any engagment upon our Leaders obliging them to advance the Meanes, of an Effectuall Reformation amoungst us; yet wee should think it our Dutie to make our Addresse in this & such like Motions vnto them; not only because the direction of Public Affaires, is committed unto their Trust; But because wee ought to respect them; and hope well of them, that to such as doe good; and studie to promote vertue, they will give praise; and whether they mind this part of their dutie or not; Wee shall in respect of the maine of our Worke, neither bee much encouraged, nor much discouraged at it. For as on the one hand wee take it to bee a dutie, not to neglect those that are in Authoritie; soe on the other hand, Wee know them to bee but men; nor doe wee build any hopes vpon the rewards or encouragments which they can give; but wee looke unto Him for whose sake, wee desire to serve the Public, & our expectation is the reward which he hath promised to the vpright in heart. All our Aime then, is to approve our Conscience unto him; & to purifie our soules from Earthly Qualities, that wee may be found Vessels of Honour in his House, fit to build it up unto his Glory.[518]

---

[516] See Durie's petition *A Proposition That the summe of 2000 lib. a yeare may bee set a part out of the Deane Chapters lands towards the erecting maintaining of an English colledge at Heidelberg: for the promoting of Religious Learning*, undated.

[517] As far as is known.

[518] Ref: 47/10/2A-55B: 55A, 55B. HP. Some scholars distinguish between the various agencies and offices mentioned in Durie's and Hartlib's correspondence put actually, it was all one project which grew in scope over the years.

Petitioning Parliament again concerning reforms in Church and State

In May 1647, John Durie petitioned Parliament again, this time with his *Considerations Tending To the Happy Accomplishment of Englands Reformation in Church and State*. The year had started with a Parliament divided over England's future with the defeat of the Royalists and the Scots' handing over Charles I to Parliament who promptly made him their prisoner, though he soon escaped and the 1648 Second Civil War began. Durie thought that as Parliament was ready to reform England from the roots to the branches, he ought to break a lance for his own ideas of reforming church and state through his educational policy of universal learning. Addressing the Members by the new popular term 'senators', Durie under-titled his petition with the words, 'Humbly presented to the Piety and Wisdom of the High and Honourable Court of Parliament'. For its publication, Samuel Hartlib provided an Introduction of a rather unfitting kind as he writes mostly about himself, refers to his thankfulness of being *sine invidia lucri*, which is rather odd, considering the letters he sent to Kings and Protector's asking to be given a pension, and that he had friends in Parliament. It serves in no way as an introduction to Durie's work. This is also the case concerning *A further Discoverie*, mentioned above, where Durie's opening words serve as a good introduction to the matter in hand but Hartlib eliminated these and prefaced the published edition of 1648 with his own personal autobiographical details which appear rather off the point. Perhaps an element of rivalry was developing between the friends.

Durie begins by paying Parliament the compliment of being 'more solemnly and strongly engaged to advance the Glory of God by the Reformation of this Church and State, than any other Protestants are.' This is merely to warm them to the idea that 'God hath put into the hands of Parliament sufficiently all the Meanes and Advantages that may enable them to discharge their duty in order to this engagement'. Durie tells Parliament that their move in putting the state under a National Covenant was one of the basic props of his life's work. Cromwell, however, never supported the idea of a Covenant as taught by Durie in his *A Summarie Platform of the heads of a Body of Practicall Divinity* as enthusiastically as Durie. Though Cromwell humoured the Scots for a number of years concerning accepting the Solemn League and Covenant so as to receive the benefits of having their armies on English soil, this interest soon waned. Durie, however, agreed with Parliament, as he says in the petition, in the practical outworking of their covenant teaching in supplying a common creed, a common catechism, a common order of worship, a common discipline and order and a common stand against error, profanity and the Church of Rome. He, however, wrote to William Hamilton, in a letter mentioned below, showing in what way he differed from the hard-line Presbyterian interpretation of the Covenant. After a very lengthy preamble, Durie gets down to outlining four points which he believes should lead to a special Parliamentary Office of Address being set up and how such an Office should be made practicable and successful. These are:

'1. What is meant by the Universal Kingdom of God, and by the Generall Communion of his Saints?

2. What the Particular Duties are whereby Gods Glory is to be Advanced in this Universal Kingdom and Gereral Communion?

3. What the Meanes are, by which God hath inabled our Leaders, and called them to the performance of these Duties?

4. And lastly, what the Way and Method of proceeding may be, to make Use of these Meanes, for the accomplishment of the Workes whereunto the Duties doe oblige Us? Which Way will end in an Office of Address, of whose Method and Usefulness is finally to be spoken.'

These problems are best solved by:

'1. The Reforming, Ordering and Constitution of Schooles.

2. The settling of Cources to Prevent or Remedy Publike Scandals and disturbances of the Peace in matters of Religious Concernments.

3. The maintaining of the Liberties which are void of offence in such as differ and walke orderly for edification.

4. The Advancement of Publike Helpes to Knowledge, and encouragements to Vertue towards those thatare within the Kingdome.

5. The Propagation of the Gospel towards those that are without, and void of the knowledge of Christ as Jewes, Turks, and Heathens.

5. The entertaining of Brotherly Correspondence, Intelligence and Commerce with Neighbour Churches, to trade in Spiritual Matters with them; for vthe Enlargement of Christs Kingdome, and the support of his Truth against the Enemies thereof.'

As Durie deals more practically with these points in his 1649 published work for the general public called *A Seasonable Discourse Written by Mr. John Dury upon The earnest requests of many*, his main views will be set out when considering that work below. However, there were a few elements in this 1647 petition which were outlined in more detail than in the 1649 work, so these will be dealt with briefly here. Durie is referring to the responsibility of a Christian state to watch over the civil and religious walk of its citizens. Concerning the youth, he pleads for a system of comprehensive education for all which should be well staffed, financed, regulated and supervised by professionals. Every child should have the widest and fullest education offered to him in so far as he can take advantage of it. This education should be seen as the basis of society. After the basic primary, secondary and tertiary education, all who have the strength and ability to be employed according to their education should be given such employment by the state and those who have not the strength and ability to perform useful work should be provided with sufficient means to live an honest life. For the sick and infirm, hospitals must be founded to care for them. In a Christian society, no one should know need. Durie had been closely in touch with Swiss cantons such as Zürich where, since the time of Bullinger, full employment had reigned and poverty as good as banished. All possible trades whether vulgar, agricultural, manufacturing, merchant, seafaring, commercial or administrative should be made available to those seeking employment. Those occupations which are unlawful, unprofitable or downright superfluous should be stamped out.

Concerning the responsibility of Parliament to care for the state in spiritual and practical issues, Durie starts off with the idea of an Office of Accommodations started by Charles I and continued by Cromwell for the regulating of Church and State and for explaining England's policy towards foreign nations. This had played, and was still to play, a major role in the debates between Anglicans, Presbyterians and Independents. Durie wished to extend its functions and also combine it with an 'Office for the Addresse of Communications' which he planned. He explains the difference as being:

> 'The Office of Bodily Addresses, should bee appointed to Meddle with all Outward Things concerning this present life, for the relation of men to each other in worldly Governments, and may be called the Addresse of *Accommodations*. Bur the Office of Spirituall Addresses should be appointed to meddle with all Inward things concerning the Soules of Men, and the Wayes whereby they may be helpful one to another in Matters relating the same, which may be called The Addresse of *Communications*. Their Main and

proper Objects of Employment will be different; but their Ends and Wayes to doe service will be the same, and some things Collaterall to their Main Objects, will be common to both, and and in these Collateral Matters, they should be appointed to keep Mutuall Correspondencey with each other for the Advancement of their Publik Services.'[519]

Such an Agency of bodily and spiritual addresses should be placed in a central, easily accessible venue which all men can freely visit giving information as to what they have to offer for the general edification, education and needs of mankind. This information should be recorded and made available to others who are looking for this or that information. This centre should also function as an employment agency or labour-exchange where employers can advertise for workers and the unemployed look for work. People should be able to put houses or property up for sale there and others be catered for who wish to buy property. The agency should function as a stock exchange and meeting place for merchants. Indeed, it should serve as a nodal point or bridgehead for every kind of human learning, business and enterprise. This centre should be fitted out with a library of informative works and journals covering all sources of knowledge besides, inventories, registers, catalogues, lists and other reference literature. It should be staffed by wardens who are experts in the various fields of research who know where to acquire information and how to make it easily available. The work of the wardens must be absolutely impartial. News of all inventions and new discoveries should be immediately posted at the Office. Those who profit financially from transactions at the Agency should donate to a fund which is used for the upkeep of the knowledge centre and for the development of ideas regarding the wider scope and usage of the agency and should be administrated by the Committee for the Rules of Reformation. Books of all financial transactions should be kept and presented every two or three months for inspection. At least annually, the agency should inform schools, public libraries and universities of all the new learning which has been recorded and committees should be set up composed of senior college heads etc., to process these findings. Those establishments of learning who profit from the information received must help with the financing. The main building should be situated in London but at least one branch should be established at Oxford. The agents, wardens, clerks and administrators should be provided with fitting accommodation and salaries. Trusts should be set up to raise money and legacies and donations encouraged.

---

[519] *Considerations tending to the happy accomplishment of England's Reformation*, p. 43.

It took a very long time for Durie's and Hartlib's plans of the thirties to be materialised but in 1648, the following 'memorial' was drawn up by the Durie circle, recommending Samuel Hartlib for the post of superintendent of a state agency for the advancement of universal learning under the title The Office of Public Address for Accommodation. The fact that it is called 'An other Memoriall', indicates that others had gone before. In fact, a rather impatient Durie now reminded Parliament that he had been petitioning them for ten years.

> 'An other Memoriall on the behalf of Master Hartlib, and his Negotiations for the generall good of the Kingdom.
>
> Amongst other ways, whereby the Good of the Kingdom, and the benefit of all Inhabitants thereof, may be greatly advanced, there is one very easie to be set afoot, which is called an Office of Addresse. Whereby an Orderly and effectuall Correspondencie and Agencie will be setled for the Advancement of Universall Learning, and all manner of Arts and Ingenuities.
>
> Whereby ready helps will be offered, to supply the wants, of every one without prejudice unto any.
>
> Whereby all manner of Commerce, will be mainly facilitated, And whereby every one will be easily Accommodated with such things as may be lawfully used, and are usefully communicable, unto every one, from each other in a well ordered Society or Common-wealth (as is more fully specified, and explained in the Printed Discourses that Describe the foresaid Office.)
>
> It is therefore most humbly desired, that the Parliament would be pleased to Resolve upon these following particulars, as the Matter of Ordinance to be passed by both Houses.
>
> 1 That Samuel Hartlib Esquire be appointed Superintendent Generall of an Offices of Addresse, instituted in the Kingdom of England, and the Dominion of Wales, with prohibition to all others whatsoever, to intermeddle with that businesse, either by imitating, or any other ways altering the said Offices, without permission and Deputation from the said Samuel Hartlib.
>
> 2 That in case no allowance be made for the said Samuel Hartlib in reference to the Agencie for Learning, that then the sum of two hundred pound per annum be allowed to him for his Superintendency of the said Office, either out of some place of profit at Oxford, according to the express Order of the House of Commons, or out of the Revenues of Deans and Chapters Lands, or by what other way, the Honorable Houses shall think more convenient.

A Parliamentary Agency for the Advancement of Universal Learning 343

3 That the said Superintendent, shall have power to demand for every Entry and Extract, the summe of two pence, or three pence at the most, (consideration being always had of such as are poor and unable to pay the said Dues) for Clerks and Registers wages, and defraying the other Charges incident to the Employment.

4 That a Convenient great House be allowed unto the said Samuel Hartlib to keep the said Office in (which is henceforth to be call'd and known by the name of the Office of Addresse) with consideration for the furniture thereof.

5 That in the Ordinance, Provisoes may be inserted, to impose somwhat by way of penalty on such as having entred their desires, into the Registers of the said Office, and received satisfaction in them, shall not within 24 hours (if it be not impossible so to do) cleer and discharge the said Registers, to the end that no further Addresses, be in vain made about the same businesse: And also that none shall be bound or oblieged to make use of this Office, by giving or taking out Memorials, further then of their own accord, they shall be willing.'

We know from Hartlib's Preface to Durie's *Reformed Librarie-Keeper*, written probably in 1650, that Hartlib appears to have received this post as he writes:

'I have been taught from within, to look up to God alone in well doing, till he bring his Salvation out of *Sion*: for, propagate this Salvation of his with my poor talents, and to stirre up others to contribute their help thereunto, is the utmost aim which I have in the Agency for Learning; wherein the goodnes of the Parliament hath owned me. And although, towards the businesse it self, nothing hath been further done then to name me for it; (*which for the time hath made my burdens somewhat heavier*) yet because my genius doth lead this way; and I hope still in God that he will not leave me without encouragements.'

Here, Hartlib is confessing that he has at last been appointed to this government post, but he has not yet seen anything of his promised salary. This did come with an initial generous grant to set up the work and eventually a pension for Hartlib, but the running of the agency was more or less left to private sponsors as it had been when purely in private hands. Happily, Oxford University, led by its Vice-Chancellor John Owen, also petitioned the government for a central agency for the advancement of religion and learning. Hartlib had to wait until 1656 before Cromwell gave the go-ahead for an adequate funding via monies gained in the Irish campaigns.[520]

Setting up a School Council to organise educational reform

Sometime in the late forties, a document was drawn up by the Durie circle for the founding of a school council for the advancement of learning. This paper was entitled *Councel for Schooles with an Appendix of an Agency of Learning to prepare for the Advancement of Vniversal Learning*. John Durie was to be the President of the institution and Councillors Dr Snell, Sir John Wollaston, Dr Bathurst, Adam Boreel, Aires, Needham, Heyling, Dr Cox and Sir Fr. Rethersole (name suggested by editor). Petty and Pell were to present to Parliament plans for the agency's financing and for buying land which should be farmed for the upkeep of the institution. Those named '*Commissioners for the Act of the Councel for schooling*' were Dury, Pell, Rand, Horne, Ravius, Needham and Milton. Collier was to be the secretary and then came the names of Heyling, Wall and Ezer Tonge (Tong, Tongue). It is not easy to find first names for all of these men who appear to have been chosen as possible lecturers. Durie was well-qualified in both ancient and modern languages, science and theology; John Pell had an international reputation in Mathematics, the natural sciences and political diplomacy and was one of the founding members of the Royal Society. There were two Rands, James and William in the Durie circle; both appear to have been scholars who worked for the spread of universal learning. As William stood close to Hartlib and Boyle and had studied medicine abroad and also translated for the Durie circle, he is probably the man named.

Durie had several associates named Horn or Horne but this person appears to be Thomas Horn 1610-1654, the educator who had worked closely with Hartlib and Durie for many years. The Ravius mentioned here is Professor Christian Ravius of Uppsala and Danzig, the Hebrew expert. The name Needham appears to be Marchmont Needham who was a close associate of the Durie circle. He was a journalist and author who produced a weekly news journal called *Mercurius*. He was a graduate of Oxford, having studied to become a teacher, lawyer and physician. He was also a member of one of the several 'Offices of Intelligence' set up in London. He was closely in touch with international affairs. John Milton, a close friend of Needham's, needs no introduction. The one direct reference to a

---

[520] See Records of State Payments to Hartlib found in the Bodleian ms Rawlinson, A 62, p. 5 & 37. Copy also in HP under same title but no Ref: mark. See also British Library, MSS 4196 f. 13A-B and 106 A-B.

'Collier' is found in a letter from Sir Cheney Culpeper to Hartlib where a merchant Collier is mentioned whose wife is a crypto-papist and rather troublesome.[521] There was also a Giles Collyer, pastor of the church in Blockley, Worcestershire, who stood close to the Durie circle. The Collier here mentioned is probably Jeremy Collier who translated one of Comenius' many introductions to his hoped for definitive work on pansophy, this one being called *A Patterne of Vniversal Knowledge Shadowing forth the largenesse dimension and vse of the intended Worke In an Ichnographical and Orthographical Deliniation* which the Hartlib Papers date around 1651.

Dr. Heyling, judging by his remarks in *Ephemerides*, appears to have been a scientist. Moses Wall was a Jewish merchant domiciled in England and appears to have been a very learned man who kept the Durie circle in touch with world Jewry. Wall wrote to Hartlib shortly after Cromwell's death saying:

'. . . . in the late Protectors days ther wer more good men persecuted in his almost fiue years of government, than were in almost fiue score years of our late Queen, & Kings, beginning with Elizabeth who came in Nov.19.1658. And as for the wars abroad, I am of his mind who sayth, That there was never so much war in the world to so little purpose; the good of mankind being very little, if at all minded. And after all disappointments from men, I come to be of the mind that Rabbi Ioannes was of, concerning his own people the Iews Quòd cùm Judæi aliàs ducibus ex captivitate fuerint liberati, redemptio ultima à deo sub propriâ personâ est explenda.'[522]

Ezerel (Ezer) Tonge was a minister of the gospel who was also a skilled botanist and a dabbler in eschatology. His name appears often in *Ephemerides*. There is an interesting document preserved in the Hartlib Papers entitled:

Articles tripertite

Agreed & Concluded, betwixt Iohn Sivertus Küffeler, Dr. of Physick;

Samuel Hartlib Esqr & Ezerel Tonge, Bachelor of Divinity.

this 20th Day of Iune. 1656.

---

[521] Ref: 13/198A-199B.
[522] Ref: 34/4/17A-18B. HP.

It is a contract drawn up by the three men so that Küffler might demonstrate certain experiments in the presence of Oliver Cromwell with a view to Cromwell patronising him and allow his family to settle in London. It is done in a very business-like way and ends with the words:

> 'Item, That the said Ezerel Tonge, in consideration of the præmises & out of his zeale to the Publique good of this Commonwealth & happinesse thereof, vnder his Highnesse Goverment, will lend vnto the said Iohn Kuffeler the summe of 100 lb. to bee paid vnto him the said Iohn or his assignes, in forme & manner following. viz: sixtie pounds the first payment thereof, the tenth day of Iuly next, & the summ of forty poundes, the residue of the said summe vpon the first day August next.'[523]

The grounds and method of reformation and its advancement

In Durie's *Seasonable Discourse* of 1649, Durie enlarges on his ideas stated before Parliament in his *Considerations* of two years earlier, dividing the work into two parts. The first he named: *What the Grounds and Method of our Reformation ought to be in Religion and Learning*. The second he called: *How even in these times of distraction, the Worke may be advanced*. He then dealt with the second part under two sub-headings, *By the knowledge of Orientall tongues and Jewish Mysteries* and *By an Agency for advancement of Universal Learning*.

Durie prefaces the work with an address from the people of Lincolnshire to General Fairfax concerning setting up schools in the county. The inhabitants requested:

> 'That some Publick Schooles for the better education and principling of youth in vertue and justice, would soberly be considered and settled, that so by not leaving them loose to themselves, and their carelesse Parents (the Laws being deficient to instruct them well when Children, though not to punish them for it when men) the may not remaine lyable, to be scourged for the faults of their naturall and civill Parents rather than their own, as they now do. Besides that, according to the structure this Generation propounds to build for the next, it may not againe incline to fall by its own weight, through negligence of timely preparing fit materials to support and confirme it.'[524]

---

[523] Ref. 26/49/1A-2B, HP.
[524] *Seasonable Discourse*, p. 1.

Durie uses these words to show that the whole nation is intent on reforming education by means private and public but though 'many stones have been moved about' nothing really constructive has been done and the nation appears to be losing its profession of true religion. This is because, Durie argues, ignorance of the true aims and rules of reformation prevails and there is too much self-seeking and party-mindedness in devising them. Educators lack positive and reliable principles in working out necessary aims and rules. Durie returns to his doctrine of the public good, deducing that no man without piety and the right use of reason can be happy. Without piety there is no enjoyment of God and without God-given reason, there can be no common interest in a public good.

Durie's ideas of right reason being a divine attribute have continued with us since Durie's pioneering works were written, being built on during the following centuries but rarely reaching the comprehensiveness of Durie's reforms. A case in point is the eighteenth centuries Gotthold Ephraim Lessing, the famous essayist, novelist, playwright and librarian at the Herzog August Library. Lessing's famous *Erziehung des Menschen Geschlechts* and *Nathan der Weise* show direct parallels with Durie. Lessing commences his Preface to his 'Erziehung' with a row of questions such as:

> 'Warum wollen wir in allen positiven Religionen nicht lieber weiter nichts, als den Gang erblicken, nach welchem sich der menschliche Verstand jedes Orts einzig und allein entwickeln können, und noch ferner entwickeln soll; als über eine derselben entweder lächeln, oder zürnen? Diesen unsern Hohn, diesen unsern Unwillen, verdiente in der besten Welt nichts: und nur die Religionen sollten ihn verdienen? Gott hätte seine Hand bey allem im Spiele: nur bey unsern Irrthümern nicht?'

This could have come from Durie's pen and certainly his sense of humour. Lessing's first three points are then:

> 1. Was die Erziehung bey dem einzeln Menschen ist, ist die Offenbarung bey dem ganzen Menschengeschlechte.

> 2. Erziehung ist Offenbarung, die dem einzeln Menschen geschieht: und Offenbarung ist Erziehung, die dem Menschengeschlechte geschehen ist, und noch geschieht.

> 3. Ob die Erziehung aus diesem Gesichtspunkte zu betrachten, in der Pädagogik Nutzen haben kann, will ich hier nicht untersuchen. Aber in der Theologie kann es gewiss sehr grossen Nutzen haben, und viele Schwierig-

keiten heben, wenn man sich die Offenbarung als eine Erziehung des Menschengeschlechts vorstellet.'

In his further discussion in 'Erziehung', however, Lessing leaves Durie by claiming that man's reason as the measure of all things, albeit with the underlining teaching that Reason is that spiritual work which Jesus referred to on promising that He would send the Spirit to enlighten mankind. Durie sees right reason as something which must be taught and developed to the common good before it can be practised and it remains a gift and not an inherent virtue or natural state.[525] First one must experience piety and then the means to make men rational on this basis is to advance the truth of learning. Thus seeking the public good is the same as asking how true religion and learning ought to be advanced. Even a pioneer behaviourist educationalist such as John Dewey, who has influenced this writer's educational thinking so much, combined metaphysical and psychological thinking with pragmatic action. Admittedly, Durie's basic conviction that universal learning points to the Creator and Giver of all knowledge and He is the Alpha and Omega within whom all knowledge finds its rightful place, still finds a most varied acceptance. However Durie's basic teaching that the total effect of universal learning is greater when applied interdisciplinary than the sum total of effects applied in separate 'subject' teaching, now meets universal agreement. If this is not done for the common good, then, for Durie, the rational has lost touch with the spiritual.

Thus, for Durie learning for the benefit of the public good is the outworking of grace in the life of a believer. Piety is necessary to discern the source of all knowledge and industry prompted by right reason is needed to pass on universal knowledge to all for the benefit of mankind. Durie believed that the chief responsibility in such a campaign for the public good was in the hands of the gospel ministry. A true minister will show his worthiness in doctrine and practice. In doctrine, he must prove that he is sound and knowledgeable and is gifted not only in public speaking but also in private conversation and counselling. In practice, the minister should conduct himself well, give evidence that he is walking with God and be able to lead his flock to God. The minister should thus have the two elements that Durie would wish of every educated person; however, he must excel in the doctrinal and the pastoral. As such a nicely balanced minister is rather an

---

[525] See my Trebytyg thesis *Gott, Offenbarung und Mensch in Lessings 'Nathan dem Weisen'* (Uppsala). After gaining my Uppsala degree, I had the privilege of sitting under Helmut Thielicke, a world authority on Lessing during a Kandidaten Jahr at Hamburg.

uncommon thing, Durie suggests that a central agency be appointed to oversee the appointment of ministers to make sure that each church receives the right kind of teaching. This idea was taken up by Cromwell who, after the Presbyterians lost their dominance, appointed a Board of Examiners named Triers composed of Presbyterians, Independents and Baptists to make sure that a church received the ministry it needed. Durie also suggests that, as the perfect minister is a rarity, someone should be appointed to the church who could assist him where his ability is lacking. However, Durie treads carefully here from his own experience as a lecturer in other people's parishes. He says honestly that this can be 'one of the greatest disturbances of publique edification which can befall unto a congregation'. So Durie emphasises that the pastor has the main responsibility over his flock and the 'Doctor' or lecturer should keep his place as a helper and supporter. However, in preaching, visiting, caring for the sick and sorrowing as also in catechising, the 'doctor' should work with but under the minister. Durie emphasises that the orderliness of a minister and his being able to work for the public edification is more important than the fitness of his qualifications or his painstaking attitude to his work. Durie, always a utilitarian, believes that spiritual results and an edified flock count more than anything else in the life of a minister. So, too, he has no use for ministers who cannot work with their colleagues, or cause public unrest. There must be *Antistites Publici ordinis & justitiae* who have their authority under God and they must be obeyed.

Not only should an agency be established for the appointment of pastors but one should be established also to deal with those ministers who become disorderly. Rules must be established both to prevent disorderliness in ministers and for dealing with them when they misuse their office. Attention must be paid to how ministers are called; how they are maintained; how they should perform their duties and how they should relate to their flocks and colleagues. Durie was no friend of a rigid division of Church and State. The conviction that England was a Christian country dominated all factors in the life of the English nation at the time. So, too, any disorder in any occupation was also thought to be a matter for the public magistrate who was responsible for the upkeep of public peace. Durie, however, wanted to be on the safe side and demanded a committee to control the appointments committee. The fact is that such committees set up became a law unto themselves and, as illustrated by the case of Church Historian and Anglican clergyman Thomas Fuller who had to appear before such a committee. One must here ask Socrates' question taken over by Juvenal, '*Quis custodiet ipsos custodes*'. Durie goes into this and believes that '*ab abusum non valet sonsequentia*'. Though no man is perfect, certain men must be picked who know and practice their duty as this is simply 'the done thing' in a Christian society and is for the common good. Durie is campaigning for the restoration of integrity in the powers that be, however small.

Concerning the pedagogical or scholastical function of learning

Durie emphasises once again that though men by nature have a reasoning faculty, it is only by education and exercise that they become masters of it. The greater the learning and greater the work for the common good which it enables, the greater heights one's reason attains. Thus, though the public ministry is the chief outward means of advancing piety towards God, and the Magistrate God's instrument for upholding moral virtues, education is the chief outward means of promoting right reason. The seed sown in education, Durie emphasises will be the quickest to take root and grow, quoting the old Seneca adage, '*Quo semel est imbuta recens, servabit odorem festa diu*' to back up his thoughts.

Durie defines the end of education as 'to fit every one for the industrie and employment in the society of men, whereunto by reason of his birth, he may have a right, or by reason of his natural parts, he may by others be called, or of his own accord lawfully apply himself.' In other words, the privileged have the means to be educated, so have they who are sponsored by others but also the person who shows industry and initiate in spite of an adverse background can attain academic success. Durie is as eager to have the latter encouraged as the other two categories of educational candidates. In order to implement the chances of education for all, Durie suggests there should be four different kinds of schools fitting pupils out for the various forms of employment in society and the various standards to be reached. These are a vulgar or plebeian school; a school for the gentry and nobility which must have places for the more intelligent of the vulgar; a school for perfecting the arts and sciences and a school for those who which to train themselves in Divinity. In other words, we have here, primary, secondary and tertiary education for those training as workers, administrators, employers or academics so that each will find the education he needs. Durie emphasises that he is not suggesting that all men have the same education but that all men need the education which their abilities demand. They must all, however, be given the chance to be educated to their full natural capacities. Those who are able to teach others must have the wider learning whether this be in the realms of their natural capacities or spiritual. He expects, however, that those following spiritual pursuits will have the most comprehensive education.

Durie pleads here for an emphasis on the academic schools in the natural sciences and theology because, if they could be perfected in his generation, they could found the two first schools and give them a higher standard than the ordinary primary and secondary schools of his day. Thus each generation would be able to introduce better and wider prospects for education. In this way, Durie seeks to reform education in the direction of universal learning. He realises that this will take several generations to materialise. So first we must breed reformed schoolmasters before we can talk of Reformed pupils and students. Indeed, without reformed schoolmasters as the products of higher education, there can be no reformed employers, reformed magistrates or even a reformed state.

Durie now looks at ways of means of succeeding in his suggested reforms. First one must show the public how dangerous, corrupt, and even hurtful, contemporary education is in failing to adequately foster piety and right reason. Secondly, the state must be made aware that schools are the seed-beds of all reformations be they in the Church or in the legislation or administration or in all public departments, indeed in the entire Commonwealth. Schools are nothing other than the corner-stone of society. Durie is convinced that the great corruption which there is in the Commonwealth is the result of impiety and lack of learning. Durie has criticised the monarchy of yesteryear harshly, but now he is castigating the very society that rebelled against the latter on the grounds that they were going to found a state centred in a Covenant with God, so that the nation would be one holy people and a Theocracy like Israel of old. So Durie says first, schoolchildren must be reformed in character and manners; second, the Arts and Sciences must be re-defined as to their scope and purpose and third, methods of training teachers must be reformed.

Schools must have piety, justice, temperance, faithfulness, truth and diligence in their curriculum and they must show how personal and social decay sets in when these are not practiced. The natural disposition of every child is impiety, folly, injuriousness, violence, excess, falsehood, untruth and laziness. If these evils are not stopped in the schools, the whole nation will perish.

The Arts and Sciences must be reformed in their basic aims, in their practice, in their rules and in their precepts. They should follow the two-fold path of godliness and the common relief of mankind from outward miseries. They are there for the benefit of sick minds and sick bodies.

Rules must be enforced which pursue no matters unless they can be demonstrated as true and which are homogeneous to the universal matter of learning. No art or science can be studied in a vacuum but each should be taught in its relationship to other branches of art and science until it is realised that all knowledge is homogeneous and has a common end and right use.

The reformed way of teaching the Arts and Sciences is, according to Durie:

'1. Things necessary and universall must be first taught universally; and then things severally usefull and profitable to the several ends of education in the Arts and Sciences sub-servient thereunto: where a main rule is to be observed, that superfluities be avoided. Durie adds Horace's adage to this, '*Sapientia prima est stultitia caruisse.*'

2. Every thing must be taught upon some fore-knowne Ground, as a consequence thereof: the fore-knowne Ground of all Rationall Matters are outward sense and fancy; and the fore-knowne Grounds of Divine Matters are Conscience, and the sence or experience of ones own thoughts in reference to God.

3. Every thing whereof the Ground is foreknown must be taught, first practically, and then Theoretically; Practically that is by an imitable example of that which is practicable therein, held forth by him that teacheth the fancy of him that is taught: and then Theoretically, the same thing is to be delivered unto his judgement: that is, he is to be taught the Rule and Reason of that practice, to let him see how, and why it answers the end wherefore it is done.

4. The Principles of Piety should be taught before the Principles of Reason in Practicall matters; and in Theoreticall the Rules of Rational Truths, should preceed the Rules of Religious Truths; for Divine Truths presuppose right Reason, and exalt it to Objects above sence and fancy, so then the will is first to be wrought unto the affections and duries of Piety, and then the understanding to the rules and exercises of Reason. These two, then, must gradually and hand in hand be led into perfections, because the will is a knowing, and the understanding a willing faculty, and both are the subjects of reason in their proper waies.

5. The Application of Naturall Principles, and Reasonings unto spiritual Objects, is a root of great confusion in Sciences; but if the distinction of naturall and spirituall be duly kept, and the true Harmony of the one to the other, with the proportion of reasoning answerable thereunto be observed, that will set us againe aright. Therefore, as we are to be taught how spirituall things

are to be discerned spiritually, and naturall things naturally, each in his distict, sphear and way of knowledge according to nhis kind: so we are not to be left ignorant of the harmonicall correspondency which is between them, and the use of Reason therein. By which Rule, School-Divinisty being examined, will be found very light in the Balance of the Sanctuary, and in like manner, much of that controversall Divinity, which is handled Scholastically in these our daies.

6. The whole way of teaching must be made free, igenious, and delightful; So then the merciniary way, whereunto Schoolemasters are forced, to betake themselves for want of a competent livelyhood, ought to be remedied by some laudable provision, and rewards for industry: and on the other side, the servile and blockish way of training up Scholars for fear of punishment, to get certaine lessons by rote, must be changed into a way of emulation and judgement.'[526]

Thereafter, Durie makes an appeal to possible patrons who would be interested in furthering his plans and explains that he has said thus far is merely what he can envisage happening under the present circumstances. He now goes on to announce his further ideas of introducing an advancement of knowledge in the oriental tongues which will help further piety and many spiritual graces and universal learning which will further the development of rationality. This latter advancement is the more important for Durie as universal learning combines all the objects of piety and all the objects of learning.

In his section 'Concerning oriental languages and Jewish mysteries', Durie is referring to the languages of the Old Testament which he sees as going back to the first utterances in the world and the first media of the oracles of God laying out the first principles of religion towards God. He believes also that the earliest teaching concerning justice, judgement, and prudence in economical and civil government is found in the records in these languages as is the history of all nations. The Jews were a privileged nation who passed on all these sources to the world. By learning the wisdom of the ancients, one can better understand the wisdom of all ages which make us wise unto salvation. It is thus wrong for a church to merely concentrate on the New Testament as it is not to be understood without the Old and vice versa. Those scoffers who say they accept the New Testament only are thus building on an imperfect faith, lacking the full wisdom of Christ the Messiah. Thus a knowledge of Hebrew, Aramaic and the history of Semitic languages is essential to universal learning, especially for those

---

[526] *Seasonable Discourse*, p. 12.

who are to teach others. This goes for the Jews of old, as also the Jews of the Diaspora such as Menasseh Ben Israel with whom Durie was in close touch. Durie was one of the major campaigners to have the Jews either settle again in either England the New Jerusalem, or in North America or be repatriated in Jerusalem.

From the Jews, Durie goes on to discuss how the Christian can follow God's command to go into all the world preaching the gospel if language study is not seen as a crucial part of universal learning. Always practical, Durie emphasises what a great boon language learning is to world trade. However, he obviously thinks of world trade because he associates the Jews with that occupation and he is soon back with the Jews again, showing how their future is closely tied up with that of Christians in prophetic fulfilment. Thus Durie would have Parliament set up schools for Oriental Studies for public lectures and academic studies. More research should be done into their ancient manuscripts and printing presses set up to make these available to the academic public. The New Testament should be printed in Hebrew for the benefit of the Jews. Grammars and textbooks must be authored for the English students of these languages besides English literature being spread abroad in foreign tongues. Thus Durie suggests that if the state provided but a thousand pounds a year for such enterprises, much could be done and this would encourage private people also to invest in such colleges. He hoped also to see libraries of oriental books set up and agents sent abroad to distribute copies of them. He points out that the Roman Catholics have colleges to propagate their faith and literature in foreign parts but such are lacking in England.

The need for a national curriculum for the advancement of universal learning

All these educational preparations for Durie are mere steps along the way to basing England's education on a national curriculum for the advancement of learning. Such a great reform is only possible if Parliament puts all the force of its power and provisions behind it. Durie is therefore adamant that such schools must be set up to give all the inhabitants of a nation in Covenant with God the chance of receiving an education worthy of a Christian calling. Such an Agency should not be one of dominance and control so much as one of negotiation and cooperation in finding out in either a public or private way how the nation is thinking and what contributions each has to give towards a common knowledge for the common good. Durie points out that there are so many societies for the promotion of this that and the other but they all devote all their energies to minute and special fields which are of no immediate use to the majority who do not share that society's sole interest. As long as there is a society of Man qua Man, then that society must be coordinated for the benefit of man and not split up as if mankind were a profusion of different animals, each in their own herd or flock. Man is not part of a herd of animals where the strongest prey on the weakest. He is a member of a society which can only remain and develop itself in the way God intended by building a single society of the strong and the weak, the wise and the foolish, the healthy and the sick for the benefit and mutual instruction of all in the ways of goodness. Durie uses the example of the Venice of his days, then the most settled and ancient republic in Europe, which has an agency where each citizen may register ways of promoting the public good and receive a reward in proportion to the usefulness of his contribution. Here, Durie mentions the basic ideas of Lord Verulam or Sir Francis Bacon who wrote extensively on the advancement of learning and the accumulation of knowledge. Turning back to Durie's *Conciderations* of 1647, we find that Durie is referring here to Bacon's *De Augmentis Scientiarum*.[527] Durie also refers in his *Conciderations* for the need to perfect Comenius' work on teaching methods and the grading of pupils according to age and abilities, as he does in his early forties work *A Brief Discourse Concerning the Accomplishments of our Reformers Shewing that by an Office of Addresse in Spiritual and Temporall Matters the Glory of God and the Happines of this Nation may bee Highly Advanced*. He omits this reference in his 1649 *Seasonable Discourse*, though he keeps the reference to Bacon, probably because of the cooling off between his circle and Comenius mentioned in the previous chapter on Comenius' relationships with Durie and Hartlib.[528] Bacon believed that his views of natural philosophy and education should be fostered by the state and become part of the political system of the country. Obviously, Durie has informed himself of such an interest on the part of Parliament and reminds them here that they had already set apart a 'Gentleman' (Hartlib?) to the furtherance of such aims and that:

> 'there is a Reserve of Means purposely kept to be employ'd for the Advancement of Religion and Learning', and we are inform'd that an Ordinance is drawing up for the effectuall disposall thereof towards those ends; seeing (I say againe) these things are so, we ought not to dispaire of some good issue at last; and therefore in reference to the Advancement of this Des-

---

[527] Available as a freebie to read online at Google Books.
[528] *Seasonable Discourse*, p. 21.

igne, which doth seeme already to be own'd and countenanc'd by Authority'.[529]

Durie goes on to argue for an extension of this admittedly rather vague enterprise of the government so that it extends beyond the range of the universities and embraces all educational establishments. Durie then again affirms his commitment to universal learning by saying that when he writes of education for all, he is referring to bounds of schooling that must be made 'as large as the borders of Rationality in Mankinde' otherwise we shall come short of the aim of what is meant by the advancement of learning.

Universities have their rightful place but no monopoly on learning

Once on the subject of the universities, Durie argues that it is wrong that they are so encouraged as to think they have a monopoly on the means of learning and rather than encourage the few subjects and professorships at the universities, there should be professorships created in all branches of the Arts and Science catering for the needs of all men who wish to obtain the greatest advantage in procuring the common good through a profound and wide education. Thus another of the multi-tasks of his Office of the Advancement of Universal Learning should be to examine all the current systems of education and repair their defects and widen their scope and work. Indeed, so intent was Durie on campaigning for Further Education in colleges and open lectures that he was severely criticised by some for ringing the death knolls of the universities. All these new professorships in new forms of educational establishments should be in regular consultation with one another and knew ways of universal learning worked out and then passed down to the more junior educational establishments. In principle, this was not new to the English teaching system. Lawrence Chaderton (c.1538-1640), called 'the pope of Cambridge Puritans', taught students until he was a 102 so that Cambridge stopped looking for successors proclaiming that he would outlive them all. When Mildmay founded Emmanuel College in 1584, Chaderton became its master, using the Zürich or 'conference' method of instruction. He abolished subject teaching and had all his tutors working in teamwork with the students on joint projects. One took care of the translation work, another led the students in grammatical analysis, yet another took over the exegesis and another dealt with the doc-

---

[529] Ibid, p. 21.

trines discovered. Chaderton's motto was the 'universities ought to be the seed and the fry of the holy ministry throughout the realm.'

Durie closes this work on a state-run educational agency by demanding:

1) That the Parliamentary agencies already formed and working should be extended as Durie suggests.
2) That trustees should be appointed amongst men of public trust and favour to superintend the new schools and be in charge of the salaries of ministers, professors and schoolmasters throughout the kingdom. They should also have an annual budget of £500 to £1,000 for encouraging the extension of learning.
3) These trustees should be empowered to receive donations and legacies from well-wishers.
4) The trustees must keep an exact and thorough account of all that they undertake and all their financial transactions and be at all times answerable to Parliament.
5) These trustees should elect out of their midst an agent who is responsible to them as their adjutant. He should serve as a go-between so that the trustees are always informed of what is happening at the grass roots.
6) The trustees are thus authorised by the supreme power of the kingdom to oversee all schools, schoolmasters and their lives and abilities and furnish them with the necessary aid needed in their teaching and educating.
7) The trustees should keep up correspondence through their agent both at home and abroad, recording all new developments in all fields of learning so that they might be incorporated into the curriculum.
8) To this end learned secretaries must be employed who know Latin and other foreign languages and clerks and translators employed to record the agent's findings. These, too, must be multi-lingual.
9) The agent must be given enough funds to pay for his travels, accommodation, entertaining of learned foreigners and research work over and above his salary.
10) A printing press must be set up and literature composed should be sent to all the schools and universities in the country as also to all the most learned citizens requesting their feedback in the interest of all.[530]

As Durie knew from personal experience during his many journeys that, 'many excellent feats of Learning in Men, and in Manuscripts lie dead and

---

[530] Ibid, p. 25-26.

buried in oblivion'. He now hoped that they would be rediscovered and used for the good of mankind.

Though Durie was often so occupied with the organisation and planning of his school system as a human enterprise, he never left the cause of God and truth out of his mind but ever saw the latter to be the right basis for the former. Thus, whenever sketching the rationality and empiricism of a matter, he always started with a description of the source of all rationality and observable facts. In his work, *A further Discovery of the Office of Address in matters, of Communication for the Advancement of Divine and Human Learning*, Durie deals with his theme theologically before dealing with it rationally and empirically, expressing his major wish to see the knowledge of the Lord cover the earth as water does the sea, writing:

> 'For wee believe that his Kingdome will be set up & that all such as are faithfull unto him for the Advancement thereof; shall bee accepted; & in the vse of their Talents sowing unto the Spirit, shall in due time reap from the Spirit the life & glorie, which is Everlasting. Wee expect also, that before this Kingdome of His Mediatorship between God and the Elect bee Ended, & given up unto the Father; the Restitution of all things shall be wrought in the Churches, & by the Church in the World. & therefore wee desire to sow our seed upon all waters, whiles wee have opportunity; that wee may bee Servants unto every one, in that which is good; & partake of the Gospell withall that are faithfull therin. And because wee judge the time to be neere at hand, Wee prepare ourselves; wee trimme our lampes, are willing to goe forth & desirous to meet the bridegroome, that wee may by our attendance upon him with our lights in our handes; increase the manifestation of his Glorie, Not that wee conceive our endeavours to bee of any worth in themselves, or that wee can lawfully as some doe, commend themselves, as if they had alreadie attained, & were made perfect (whose workes nevertheles are not yet, as wee suppose, tried by the fire), but that wee only presse towards the mark, for the price of the high calling of God in Christ Iesus, endeavouring to apprehend, that, for which also by him wee are apprehended; & whiles wee are in this tabernacle, wee shall count this our perfection, that wee are found in him by Faith; that wee know him & the power of his resurection; & that wee have fellowship with him in his sufferings and are made conformable unto his death. As for that inconceavable perfection, which some doe boast themselves of; that they are gone beyond Christs, & that they stand now alone in God, without him as their head, that they have their owne righteousnes for themselves, as hee had his; wee desire not to aime at it; but wee rather tremble at at the thought therof: & with horrowr lament that any should bee soe miserable as to set themselves in Lucifers roome to doe his worke with confidence; that is, to presume in their heart to trample vpon the Son of God; to debase him whom the Father hath set at his

owne right hand; and deservedly exalted above all Principality and Power, & every Name that is named in this world and in the world to come, and to dethrone him in their Imaginations, that they may set themselves above him. Farre be it from vs to pretend to any such perfection; & wo bee it to such as seek after it. All our desire, even to Eternitie, is to walk and dwell in the Light of the Lamb, to bee vnder him as the head, and not to be out, or above that place or station, whereunto wee are by him appointed: nor is it lawfull for vs (who are worthy of nothing) or for any creature to challenge any higher degree of blessednes, then what he hath promised freely to confer vpon vs; which is this; That having overcome wee shall sit with him vpon his Throne, even as he overcame, & is set downe with his Father on his Throne Rev.3.21.'[531]

The practical duties of an Office of Address

In *A Brief Discourse concerning the Accomplishment of our Reformation shewing that by an office of Address in spiritual and Temporal Matters the Glory of God and the Happiness of this Nation may be Highly Advanced*,[532] after dealing with the spiritual duties of the clergy, Durie turns, in detail, to the practical, every day duties of the state towards its subjects, saying:

'The State then of the Magistrat as a Magistrat doth beare the sword of Iustice to execute wrath upon evill doers, which sinne against the Lawes & Light of Nature: & he beareth the Scepter of Authoritie to reward & encourage those that doe well according to the same Light & Lawes. And if hee doth understand that his calling doth bind him not only to resist & banish evill out of the Commonwealth, but in it to further & maintaine all that is good: then his Care & Dutie should bee not only to rule men, so as he doth finde them, but hee should looke upon their wayes to order them, so as they should bee, to become partakers of that Happines, which this life doth affoord, wherunto hee is bound to give them Addresse.

His dutie then is to looke unto all; as well to the Direction of the Young Ones, as of those that are of Age; both in respect of their Civill & of their Religious Public Walking.

His Dutie toward the Young Ones, is to order the meanes of their Education aright, to which effect hee should see Schooles opened, provided with Teachers, endued with Maintenance; regulated with Constitutions; & hee should have Inspectors & Overseers to looke to the observance of good Orders in this Busines. The Schooles should bee of Foure severall kindes or Degrees. The First for the Vulgar, whose life is to bee mechanicall. The Sec-

---

[531] Ref: 47/10/2A-55B, HP.
[532] Ref: 17/10/1A-20B, HP.

ond for the Gentry & Nobles who are to beare Charges in the Common Wealth. The Third for Schollers who are to teach others Humane Arts & Sciences. And the Fourth for the Sonnes of the Prophets, who are a seminarie of the Ministerie. And the right ordering of these Schooles is to bee lookt upon as the Main Fundation of a Reformed Common Wealth without which no other worke of Reformation will ever bee effectuall.

His Dutie towards those that are of Age is to see that none who have strenght & abilities for emploiment, bee without necessarie relief. And to fullfill this part of his Dutie all vulgar Trades belonging to Husbandrie, to Manufactures, to Merchandise & Commerce by Sea or Land in the severall kindes of usefull Commodities; or Emploiments about Commodities & all Honorable Offices & Charges belonging to the Comonwealth in Generall, or to any part of it in Country & Citie in Particular; are to bee ranked in their proper places: & all the unlawfull & unprofitable wayes, wherby men or woemen get a livelihood, or spend their time in Idlenes in riot & vanitie, are to be taken notice of, that such Employments as foment naughty Superfluities causing pride & sinne to abound in a Nation, or such Persons as live disorderly & cannot bee reduced to any certain Employment, may bee banished the Common Wealth. Even as weeds are to be rooted up & cast out of a fruitfull garden.

Then to such as are not able for Age or otherwise to entertaine any employment, if they bee poore, relief is due unto them & the Rules by which Hospitalls are to bee ordered aright, will bee of singular use in the Reformation of this State.'[533]

Such a well-ordered state, however, cannot hope to arise where there is not a centralised national effort to foster universal learning and Practical Divinity in both young and old. Thus Durie declares: 'Therfore it belonges to none but to a Supreme Magistrat to establish such an Office, & to Order it to the proper Endes & Uses whereunto it should serve.'[534]

Durie's plans for such a grand central Office of Address, Communications and Correspondence were not merely designed for the running of schools but also for the total intercourse and inter-relationship of society. It should be open to everyone who wished to communicate anything to anybody, including employers seeking employees, there and employees seeking employment. Trade, commerce, the registering of patents, financial transactions, the recording of all public records, indeed everything appertaining to human spiritual, material and bodily conveniences and social needs. The Agency was to be a Post-House, Forum, Exchange, place of recreation, weekly lecture area for every man, think-tank, data base and lending li-

---

[533] *A Brief Discourse*, p. 5.
[534] Ibid, p. 13.

brary and above all other things, a spiritual temple. Wardens and other office bearers must be set up and financed whose administration powers concerning registering commodities, persons, employments, offices, and common and general necessary requisites of life prevented 'all danger of Abuses & make them Unblameable, Comfortably servicable to every use'. All must be recorded and catalogued for national and international use as the Agency was open to all foreigners and representatives of all cultures and societies. All this would assist England to become a country of complete and total reformation in religion and all human practices.

The central feature of this great administrative complex in which the administer stood side by side with the administrated, was the Great Library which should serve as a fulcrum and axis to all the business around it like the Queen bee in the centre of the hive. After regulating the financing of this mega-brain which Durie sees as being 'extraordinary expensive' yet manageable giving the right staff, Durie concludes with the words:

> 'Now to have the matter caried on easilie & without noise; It should not bee imparted unto many but unto such only as are truly zealous for the Glory of God, that are free from Self-endes & Partialitie & that Love Learning & have power with others in the Houses. If three or foure of these bee throughly possessed with this designe; & they can bee brought to lay there heads together, to move for the Erecting of such an Office in the Houses, & gette the Contrivement therof Referred, unto some few; who for Pietie, Prudencie & Learning are most commendable unto all; no doubt the Thing may bee speedily brought to passe, & a fundation laid which by the accomplishment of our Reformation will bee a Blessing unto all Posteritie: Wherunto my prayers shall bee offered as a daily sacrifice & what else God shall inable me to contribute; to whom the successe of all Our Wishes is to bee referred in Christ, to him bee Glory & Honour for ever. Amen!'[535]

Petitioning the Protector

Those of Durie's circle who wished for the state to pull its weight in the advancement of learning in the forties were disappointed in the fifties that more had been done theoretically for the cause than practically and initial monies coming from Parliament had been mostly down-payments with nothing following but empty promises. So a formal petition was made on Thursday 25. December 1656, introduced with the words:

'TO HIS HIGHNESSE THE LORD PROTECTOR
OF THE COMMONWEALTH OF ENGLAND

---

[535] Ibid, p. 19.

The humble Petition of diverse well affected & publicke spirited Persons. Sheweth. That Your Petitioners cannot but with all gratefullnesse mention & doe with all sincerity desire to acknowledge Your Highness great Care, for the preservation of Learning in this Nation. As also Your Highness extraordinary Endeavour for the mainteyning a Unity & Correspondency with Persons eminent for Abilityes, Learning & Piety beyond the Seas.'

The petitioners had done their homework and reminded Cromwell of the monies coming in to England as a result of the victories in Ireland and suggested that Cromwell could put them to good use in education for the support of learned men and the work of translating into and out of the English language. Their formal demands were:

'1. Entertainement to an Agent, to find out Men of Parts & Abilities to tender their severall Proposalls for the advancement of Learning to the Trustees, & keepe Correspondencies with such as reside in remote & forraigne places, & solliciting of all other businesses subordinate therevnto.

2. Entertainment of a Learned Secretary, for Latin & other vulgar Langvages one or more, to assist the said Trustees in those Affaires.

3. Rewards for some professed Intelligencers in forraigne Countries, residing in the best & most Centrall places imploying themselves to give notice of any thing singular in the places for Learning or Art.

4. Defraying the Postage of the Intelligencers & Correspondents.

5. The maintenace of some other Schollars of greater abilities to be imployed by way of Translations, Collections, Epitomizing, & Methodizing.

6. Defraying the charges of Paper & printing for publick & private Informations.

7. The purchasing & making of Mechanicall modells & workes.

8. The purchasing & making of Naturall experiments.

9. Of rarities & representations of all Common Naturall & Artificiall things.

10. Donatives & gratuities for Learned Men in want.

11. Rewards for painting & drawing designes vpon all Occasions.

The subsequent correspondence of the petitioners with Whitehall reveals that since the days of Bacon, little had been done in the country to forward

A Parliamentary Agency for the Advancement of Universal Learning 363

his reforms and especially the universities had been slow to rise to the challenge of reforming education. Indeed, Oxford had decided that it was no use teaching the natural sciences in schools. The petitioners thus complained:

> 'how little publicke Professors of sciences & other Schollars mainteined of Course in the Universities have really promoted the publicke good, it beeing too apparent, How little they have endeavoured that the knowledge of those things, which they profess might bee made more certaine & lesse full of idle dispute or contention. Or that the principles & Arts which they commonly teach might bee indeed of some solid vse, profitt, or service to mankind, noe choice or singular experiments in things Naturall or Artificiall very few or noe improvements for Arts for Education, or for the facilitating or Advancement of any Part of learning having vsually flowed from the Universityes or Publickly maintained Professors wants & deficiencies in the most parts of Learning being generally complained of among all Scholars. And if any thing singular in any of the particulars aforesaid have beene done. It hath binn rather the worke of some private Person then of those that are publickly mainteyned as Schollars. Thiese little being neverthelesse the uttmost that the ordinary Institutions for promotion of Learning have donn. It remaines, that either a further progresse for advancement of sciences & learning is not to bee expected or aimed at or some such course or Method in makeing vse of all such helpes for the advantage of it as Providence shall in his Wisdome offer opportunities for according to the severall Instances & particulars here inclosed must necessarily be incouraged & a foundation therefore of a revenue different from all the vsuall & common presidents must necessarily be laid.'[536]

After over a year of waiting, the day before Parliament opened, Cromwell himself replied positively to the petitioners, saying:

> 'Right Trusty & Well beloved.
>
> A Petition & Proposalls being by some well minded persons, lately presented to Us for the purchaseing (with such Debenters or other Publick faith Debts, as were properly satisfyable & chargeable vpon Ireland:) a certaine number of houses to the value of about 2000^{lbs}. a yeare in such Townes as are yet vndisposed of in Ireland & the said houses & annual revenue soe purchased by them fortwith to assigne & sett over to persons (to be approved by ourselfe) in Trust for the carrying on a forreigne Correspondency with

---

[536] See *Petition to Cromwell on Advancement of learning with Related Papers and Cromwell's Reply, 1656-1658*, Ref: 47/4/1A-7B, HP.

learned men, for the supplying & assisting alsoe such at home or abroad, whose learning Parts, studies or abilities have made them capable of being in some way or other extraordinary vsefull to the publique & for the doeing such other things as shall be thought most conduceing to the advancement in generall of learning, provided that for their better encouragement they might not pay above 5. or 6. yeares purchase for the said houses according to such survay, as shall be taken of this present value. And the said Proposalls vpon a reference & examination of them haveing been approved by vs & our Councell wee takeing into our further consideration that a revenue & Institution of this Nature though greatly, tending to the benefit & promotion of all manner of Learning hath not hitherto as wee remember bin founded at the charge of any within these 3. Nations, doe for these reasons judge it worthy of all encouragments willing & desiring that the same may likewise receive all due assistance & furtherance from your Lordshipps. And that therefore soe many houses not exceeding in the whole the said 2000^{lbs} a yeare as shall at 6. yeare purchase (according to the survey of the present value) amount to the Debenters & Certificats delivered in by the Petitioners or their Agents be forth with set out to them or whom they shall appoint in such Townes & after such manner as is more particularly prescribed & directed in the Order of vs & our Councell, your speedy dispatch herein will give a considerable advantage to the worke by the opportunity you will give the Petitioners to seeke a confirmation thereof in this present Parlament which wee for their further encouragement doe much desire

Whitehall 19 Ianuar. 1657/8'

Sadly, this letter was written in the last year of Cromwell's earthly life and it appears that nothing was done to carry out the Protector's wishes. Cromwell's last speeches in Parliament were really sermons in which Cromwell reviewed the work of Parliament as a fulfilling of Old Testament prophecy. They were a positive reviewing of the past rather than a reforming view of the future.[537]

---

[537] My four long essays during 2011 on *Oliver Cromwell: Rebel, Republican and Reformer* published in New Focus give a detailed account of Cromwell's life under these three headings.

CHAPTER TEN

Universal Reform through Practical Divinity

Proposing a platform for Practical Divinity

By 1653, Durie had been through turbulent times during his Parliamentary and Westminster Assembly activities and now hoped to settle down to a period of undisturbed writing on his favourite topic. In his 1653 work *On the Advancement of Learning*, written and published during the six-months of the Saints' Parliament, Durie wrote, as he had so often done in the thirties up to the middle forties, of the need for a Practical Divinity which would encourage a universal reform in piety and learning and serve as the basis of a national and international education. He had high hopes of success so wrote on his suggestions for a broad, interdisciplinary education, including the natural sciences:

> 'As concerning the Constitution of these Schooles in a Commonwealth, if it is the Common interest of all well ordered Societies, that all the members thereof should be usefull to the whole Body; and if no members can be counted usefull thereunto, but such as are intelligent and verteous; and if none attaine by nature without education, to so much understanding and vertue, as he will by the meanes of good teaching added unto nature; then it will follow, that none are to be counted faithfull to the welfare of the Societie, wherein they live, who would not have the care of Schooles to be a publick concernement of great moment. This care then ought to be for the erecting, maintaining, ordering, and overseing of them; and that these things may be done, the Trust of effecting the same is to be committed unto some, who Consciunably should mind the worke. And we blesse God, who hath put this care in the Parliaments heart, & by them in the hands of faithfull men, upon whom we shall daily pray for a blessing.'[538]

Sadly, the Saints Parliament turned truly into a Barebones Parliament[539] with no body, flesh and spirit to it and many hoped-for reforms were left as mere wishful thinking. In 1654, Durie published the first of two further

---

[538] *Some Proposals Towards the Advancement of Learning*, p. 8, Ref: 47/2/1A-12B, HP.
[539] Also called by this name because of the Member for London, Praise-God Barebones.

works specifically on universal learning called *A Summarie Platform of the heads of a Body of Practical Divinity*. He began the work with an introductory letter from Archbishop Ussher to his 'loving friend' dated December, 1653. This was a bold move on Durie's part as he was writing in Cromwellian days when Episcopalians were outlawed. This, however, is quite in accordance with Durie's own principle to be open to all Protestant churches, whatever the politicians thought. Ussher had, however, suffered much at the hands of the new regime and had become something of an outcast and had not been able to assist Durie as much as he had hoped. He tells Durie he would have acted, 'if God had been pleased to continue our Peace.' So, too, a number of would-be co-workers had died since Durie had introduced the project twenty years before. Ussher gave Durie the advice that he should not have organised such a large team to take on the work. This was a good point as the original would-be co-workers had later found themselves in different political and even military camps and it had proved impossible for them to work together. Now that Durie was hoping to go ahead again with his Practical Divinity, Ussher says it should be thus 'contracted to as few hands as may be.' The hands were now fewer than Ussher imagined and Durie was left to go it alone.

A Practical Divinity should be the whole doctrine of a life of Godliness in covenant with God

In his Preface, Durie says his aim is to hold forth 'the whole doctrine of the life of Godliness, in an exact description of all the Precognitions, Principles and Parts thereof; with a Resolution of the materiall doubts which may be incident thereunto.'

Concerning the precognitions, a usual 17th century term for premises, Durie means all that is reasonable and does not need to be deduced or believed as a dogma or oracle. These fall into six categories:

1. That there is a Supreme Being which men call God.

2. That this supreme power is to be worshipped, honoured and glorified by men.

3. That He is a rewarder of those who show Him such respect.

4. That the Old and New Testaments are the Word of God.

5. That they teach mankind the true way to seek God and

6. The time will come when God will make all men accountable for their relationship to Him.

Though nowadays few would agree that such 'precognitions' could be considered general, the religion, politics, philosophy and culture of Durie's day was centred on these basic, *a priori* fundamentals.

After establishing the history and characteristics of the canon, Durie goes on to discuss its 'principles'. These are, for Durie, truths taught which encourage a belief in the Scriptures as the Word of God and the way to true godliness. These Scriptural truths show how the covenant is revealed, made and confirmed and how man is motivated in his conscience to keep it. Concerning its tenor, man must be taught who the Persons are who take part in the covenant, namely God, mankind and Jesus Christ and that God is the Author of the Covenant as revealed in Scripture which outlines man's dependence on Him in His Covenant. Jesus Christ is the sole Mediator between God and man within this Covenant by virtue of His nature as God and man in one person and thus a true Medium and centre of all God's and man's properties. Christ is placed in His covenant function as Prophet, Priest and King of all the saints in Heaven and earth. for which His twofold state of life qualifies Him for eternity, this being His humiliation on earth and His exaltation in Heaven and His work of mediation in both these capacities.

The Covenant is directly contracted solely with Christ and with man only in, by and through Him. Thus we distinguish between the things promised and the terms by which they are promised in relation to Christ directly and to believers and professors indirectly.

The performance and accomplishment of what is to be done by both sides is two-fold: Christ, by His vicarious and substitutionary sufferings vouchsafed all the conditions of fulfilment for such as believe and profess His name and He thus secured the blessings of the Covenant directly and properly for them. Thus the Father by his power and glory made good unto Christ all His promises by raising Christ from the dead and setting him at His right hand and by giving Him all power in heaven and in earth to administer his own Testament by sending forth the Holy Spirit and the preaching of the gospel: In this administration of the Testament of Christ by the Spirit in the Gospel a general call is given and an offer of grace made by Christ on God's part unto all that hear the Gospel. This grace secures the terms of the Covenant to all believers, by their effectual calling and conversion unto God, and by their constant perseverance in grace unto the end. Believers are thus not to neglect the gathering of themselves together into one body, and by their mutual edification and growth through the unity of the Spirit, and the communion of holy duties strengthen one another in their enjoyment and use of Covenant blessings.

The motives which oblige men's consciences to entertain the offer are the happiness which is the lot of those in Covenant with God (Psalm 25:10), and the obligation which lies upon the conscience of men to obey God's commandments and calls and prepare them for the Day of Judgement

After learning what the Covenant is, Durie shows how the Covenant is confirmed via the manner of its institution through its doctrines appointed by God to place a seal on the reality of His working in the inner man. Following these doctrines equips us for a life confirmed in grace and godliness and provides us with all the benefits which God purposes for mankind in them.

Durie divides these confirming doctrines into substantial and circumstantial. The substantial part is the power and practice of all the truth whereby God is enjoyed in the Covenant relating to the inward and outward man of God. The inward man is the New Creature who must learn what regeneration of the soul is and how it is wrought by God's Spirit in fellowship with God. He must also learn how this differs from the unregenerate soul. To stabilise him on this path, he must know what the deceits of natural imagination and the whiles of Satan are and how to resist unclean things.

The outward man of God is the state of life in which the inward change makes us conformable to our heavenly calling by self-denial in respect of ungodliness and worldly lusts and self-resignation in offering up our ways to walk after the Spirit. Believers thus should keep a life of sobriety in respect to their neighbours and a life of righteousness in respect of God. The formal union of these inward and outward parts is in a life of universal obedience in which the whole man in his inward and outward acts follows the will of God according to the right interpretation of his commandments, keeping a spiritual watch over himself and others.

When Durie writes about the circumstantial part of the believer's life, he means the ordinary daily life of a believer who follows a particular education, trade or any other calling and his witness within that sphere. This includes all the various activities of both males and females socially, within the family and in their employment. Durie starts with blood relationships such as man and wife in founding a family, of their relationship to each other and their children and the relationship of brothers and sisters to one another. He then goes on to outline the society of masters and servants, Magistrates and subjects and proprietors and tenants. Then Durie deals with the relationship of church members to one another and to their church officers and the officers' relationship to one another.

The place of schools in confirming the Covenant in the life of the nation

Finally, Durie deals with educational reform as the way of realising his Practical Divinity. To him, the seed-bed of Christian culture, virtue and learning is not in the hands of the Church alone but the citizen's education in Practical Divinity and Universal Learning is best advanced through a co-operation between Church and State in the setting up of suitable schools, colleges and universities. He thus demanded:

1) A discernment of what school forms were suitable to the principles and life of Christianity.
2) Who should be entrusted in erecting and reforming such schools and to what degree is this necessary.
3) What should be the particular duties of schoolmasters and mistresses and pupils of both sexes.

Obviously, all people are not alike in their convictions and there will be cases of conscience concerning the feasibility and practicability of such suggestions. So Durie discusses the various problems schematically which could arise in the public mind concerning his suggestions for reform. These 'cases of conscience', he argues, must be dealt with in two ways to find general and specific solutions:

    1. In general, the Christian public should resolve their own doubts according to the principle of the analogy of faith, hope and charity and the general principles of the Covenant and the fundamental rules of that which pertains to godliness.

    Experienced Christians, whether they be teachers or not, should strive to help those having difficulties of conscience with the new kind of education according to the abilities of those who have scruples and according to the causes which have given rise to them.

    2. In problems arising in specific cases only, these should be ranked for special attention as to how they compare with the Body of Practical Divinity proposed and also scaled according to the Christian maturity of the doubters. Solutions found to the agreement of all should be incorporated

into the Practical Divinity handbook of motives and methods proposed so that immediate future reference may be made.[540]

The Reformed School of Practical Divinity

Perhaps Durie's most important work of concrete proposals for fostering Practical Divinity world-wide was his *The Reformed School*. My printed copy is dated 1651 but Webster believes that undated copies were printed either in 1649 or 1650, the 1651 copy printed with the Reformed Librarie-Keeper being a second edition.[541] Both books were part of a series produced by Durie and Hartlib on reforming institutions and occupations.

The Reformed School has a Preface written by Samuel Hartlib entitled 'The Publisher to the Reader'. Here Hartlib takes pride in having played a part in propagating Christ's 'Salvation out of Sion,' saying, 'to stirre up others to contribute their help thereunto, is the utmost aim which I have in the Agency for Learning; wherein the goodness of the Parliament hath owned me.' Actually, the idea was Durie's who had strongly recommended Hartlib for the post of Superintendent of such an agency. Durie had also suggested that Hartlib should receive a salary of up to £1,000 a year. This seems rather ambitious as it was equal to the wage of England's two major politicians, Lord Commissioners Lisle and Whitelocke, were being paid. However, Hartlib's appointment was seen as being that of a leading cabinet member who had responsibilities in all sections of the Government. The fact is that Hartlib was given a once only payment of some four hundred pounds to start on this work with repeated empty promises of more money to come.[542] Indeed, both Hartlib and Durie were repeatedly listed in Parliament as obtaining monies which were seldom forthcoming. In his preface, therefore, Hartlib expresses a hope that more initiative will come from Parliament than merely supporting him further in name only. Though Hartlib is obviously appealing for promised funding, complaining of his 'manifold private difficulties and public desertions' and his 'heavy burdons', he is not very diplomatic about it and castigates the contemporary English situation writing, 'whiles the Magistracy and Ministry is made an Object of violent contradictions, and therefore almost wholly put out of frame and made useless, as to the Reforming of vices in Church and Commonwealth; it cannot be expected although they be never so knowing and willing, that in the execution of their places, they should be able to bring matters to per-

---

[540] *A Summarie Platform*, p 8.
[541] See Webster, p. 139.
[542] See Webster pp. 46-52.

fection.' Actually, Hartlib is merely going the way of all educational reformers whose felt-duty is to point out what is wrong in society before going on to argue how things might be bettered. This was the 18th century strategy of William Cowper in his *Tirocinium, or A Review of Schools*. Dorothy Sayers in her Oxford University summer school paper of 1947, *The Lost Tools of Learning*,[543] severely criticises contemporary English education as if it were in the same sorry state as Hartlib and Durie found it.

However, Hartlib insists that with his preface he is taking the initiative of introducing reforming ideas on education whereas it was Durie who sent him the manuscript which is obviously a development of Durie's own ideas propagated since 1628. Hartlib's task was merely to affix an introductory preface, recommending the work. However, throughout most of his criticism of the 'strains and distempers' of the times, Hartlib preaches one lasting educational truth. It is not any particular school form which serves the pupils best but a good curriculum in the hands of good teachers eager to reform society and not merely to reflect it. Sadly, still today in Europe, new school forms are being introduced to solve old problems on an organisational basis only rather than one appertaining to education. Dorothy Sayers has assisted education by declaring the same truths, arguing for less organisation and fancy curricula and more solid practical education for life. Perhaps needless to say, Durie was not very pleased with Hartlib's survey of the contemporary educational system because it gave rise to criticism that the Durie circle thought universities superfluous. This problem will be discussed in Durie's *A Supplement to the Reformed School* after dealing with Durie's initial work.

Concerning an Association or Society for the Education of Children

Hitherto Durie had written about aims and curricula without much emphasis on precisely how the reform schools he favoured were to be managed and just how children were to be prepared for social and occupational integration. Now he begins by describing his Reformed School as a society or association in and of itself, representing all society as it should be. In looking to the future in preparation for an egalitarian education for both males and females, Durie relies on some old and highly debatable structures. He envisages his ideal school as a boarding school where both staff and pupils live in and form a close-knit society of their own. Indeed, in the highly Puritan spheres in which he lived, many were speaking of re-introducing

---

[543] Project Gutenberg, Canada E-Book.

methods hardly practiced since the Roman Catholic dominated mediaeval educational traditions. Since those days, Universal Learning and Practical Divinity had been ignored and isolated and disconnected 'subject' learning had taken their place leading to the dumbing down of education. Miss Sayers thus asks in the above mentioned lecture in true Durie style:

> 'Do you often come across people for whom, all their lives, a "subject" remains a "subject," divided by water-tight bulkheads from all other "subjects", so that they experience very great difficulty in making an immediate mental connection between, let us say, algebra and detective fiction, sewage disposal and the price of salmon, cellulose and the distribution of rainfall— or, more generally, between such spheres of knowledge as philosophy and economics, or chemistry and art?'

Durie, in a similar way to Miss Sayers who went back to mediaeval education in order to start reforming English education of the nineteen-forties, is going forwards by moving backwards and consolidating the ideas of a lost generation. He thus argues that the staff of a school must form a body of teachers who are on the school premises at all times for the sakes of their pupils whom they train in early years in moral sciences and virtues, going on to instruct them to play a responsible and successful part in the ordering of a future society. Here we have the basic idea of the educational plans of those who set up Oxford and subsequent boarding schools where the tutors also are in residence. Members of such a school staff which Durie calls an 'Association' or 'Society' must be:

1) Composed of independent persons who are free to dispose of themselves as they wish either by their own right or by their recommendation by others.
2) Those who join should not do so out of external or selfish reasons but with the sole aim of advancing the Christian life with all diligence and working for the public good. Teaching must be a calling rather than a mere 'occupation'.
3) The way of entering and leaving the association should be free and motives for doing so freely expressed and respected.[544]

In this way, Durie wanted his staff to be free from any external obligations or responsibilities and duties so that they could live for the benefit of the children to whom they were called.

---

[544] *Reformed School*. pp. 14-15.

We note here at once that Durie is speaking of both male and female teaching staff and children in general, both male and female. Indeed, the word 'children' had hardly been used in educational programmes hitherto. Up to then, education to university graduation level was principally a male enterprise, the far fewer girls' schools providing a limited sub-academic education with an emphasis on sewing and embroidery. This sufficed for girls to obtain a livelihood as a seamstress or governess but a true academic career was closed to them. Durie spells out the meaning of the word 'children' carefully by adding 'boys' and 'girls'. Furthermore, Durie uses the term 'persons' when speaking of the school staff and not merely 'men'. He only distinguishes between male and female teachers when speaking of their various duties in the boys' and girls' houses. The girls have a governess and the boys a governor or overseer. However, all children are to be trained to enter into society and succeed in society with equal chances. They are, however, all to be taught from the start that the advancement of goodness and reformation from vices is necessary to any stable society and will help them to manage their future lives as adults. As they grow older, their learning will be widened in proportion to their ages.

Concerning the duties of the teachers outside of class, Durie is, however, most elastic. The association in each house should organise daily joint-worship of staff and children but this should be 'according to the capacity and free willing inclinations of those that shall engage to entertain the same.' Organisation concerning the spiritual, material, social and educational needs of the school, including handicrafts and aiding the poor, should be planned by the entire association but 'according to the proportion which everyone shall be willing to enlarge himself in.' A table-society should be jointly set up to plan the diet of the pupils and a steward appointed to do the buying according to the stipulations of the society with whom he works out expenses and who regularly check his bookkeeping. Separate and regular staff conferences are to be held dealing with either the spiritual or the practical side of school life. Even here, Durie shows a great deal of acceptance concerning the initiative of each member of staff, saying concerning the regulating of outward affairs, 'nothing is to be counted a matter of common concernment, but that wherein everyone doth knowingly and judiciously profess himself to be concerned freely and willingly.' Each member of staff should be able to rely on any other members of staff at all times when advice and counsel is needed.

All the girls are to be lodged in the same building as the female staff with a senior teacher who helps each girl with her curriculum and timetable. The boys must live in a separate building under the inspection of their tutors who must be members of the school teaching body. These are under an Overseer who gives the tutors their tasks. The educational aim of the school is described by Durie for both boys and girls as:

> 'to train them up to know God in Christ, that they may walke worthy of him in the Gospell and become profitable instruments of the Common-wealth in their Generations. And in order to this, two things are to be taught them. First, the way of Godliness, wherein every day they are to be exercised, by prayers, reading of the word catecheticall Institutions, and other exercises subordinat unto the life of Christianity. Secondly, the way of Serviceableness towards the Society wherein they live, that they may be enabled each in their sex respectively, to follow lawfull callings for profitable uses; and not become a burden to their generation by living in Idleness and disorderlinesse, as most commonly those do which come from Schools of this age.'[545]

Teaching in the school must be based solely on what is useful to mankind and the practicing of employments approvable to godliness. All matters of show and appearance which people adopt to demonstrate their status as a learned being should be laid aside as the pupil's education develops. The girls must be taught not to titivate themselves with fine hair styles, make-up and dresses and 'bold behaviour'. Should they marry, they should be taught the abilities and graces of the ideal woman described by Solomon in Proverbs 31 which is a description of a family woman employed in commerce. The girls must be encouraged to develop all their intellectual abilities especially in languages and the sciences. Boys are to observe the same rules as girls in their decorum and curriculum and learn to reject all signs of disorderliness, vanity, pride and self-conceitedness. They must learn to be serviceable to their own families and neighbours and made ready to enter into any God-honouring occupation whether it be in, for instance, trade, husbandry, administration, seamanship or economics.

Concerning proficiencies and the means and parts of learning[546]

The true end of all human learning is to rectify the deficiencies in human nature. This means that:

1) Nothing is to be taught which is not directly serviceable to mankind and his natural happiness.

---

[545] Ibid, pp. 18-19.
[546] Ibid, p.38 ff.

2) Any other aim is to pervert the truth of science and the right methods of attaining it. Education is to remedy moral and social diseases, not cause them.
3) Nothing must be taught by rote but only introduced when pupils are ready to accept and comprehend it. Only fools learn without understanding.
4) All knowledge must be coordinated and nothing taught as a 'subject' in a vacuum. Knowledge is not merely like an encyclopaedia but like a watch in which all the wheels interact with one end in view. Knowledge which is merely 'by the book' with no practical and synthetic application makes a pupil useless and a burden to society.

The three means of learning are sense, tradition (handed down experience) and reason. Sense is place first as it conveys to the imagination the shapes and images of all things which the memory stores so that reason can make use of them. Tradition comes next because it is a communication of acquired knowledge regarding the items of the senses, thus supplementing our knowledge. According to Job 8.8,9, we ought to 'Enquire of the former Age, and be willing to make search of their Fathers; because we are but of yesterday and know nothing, and our dayes upon Earth are a shadow.' Reason is the third because it makes use of all the reports of our senses and other people's experiences. Without these, no inferences can be made which enlarge knowledge. With the assistance of these means we can progress in the advancement of learning whether in the Arts or Sciences.

Those Arts and Sciences which can be received by mere sense must be discussed first to make room for more intensive methodical work with more abstract items. Making work where it is not necessary is no help to wisdom. Such sense perceptions serve as a preparation to receiving traditional and rational knowledge. Sense is the servant of imagination; imagination of memory and memory of reason. In teaching arts and science, we must encourage the faculties to work in this order towards the ends to be obtained and only proceed in introducing new objects of learning when these are comprehendible through sense, imagination, memory and reason. Knowledge is only useful when it is comprehended in this way. Thus objects of learning must only then be introduced when the child has the mental and bodily maturity and ability to embrace them. If a child does not know the purpose and use of an object of learning then no true learning can take place. So, too, it is no use teaching by rules unless those rules are feasible and understandable and their aims can be realised at least in the mind. Abstract thinking must come after concrete thinking has been established.

It is thus absurd to teach logic and metaphysics when the pupil has no adequate perception or imagination to follow the reasoning.

First the child should learn the grounds and precepts of all profitable arts and sciences. This trains the ordering of the faculties and the right use of what is learnt. Languages must needs be taught which are necessary to further that knowledge. In order to further an understanding of arts and science beyond that conveyed in the mother tongue, Latin, Greek, Hebrew and related languages should be introduced. Durie sees the learning of tongues not as a source of happiness in itself but merely to understand what others say to us and how to interact meaningfully. Again, he is never for art for art's sake.

Rules of teaching according to the ordinary degree of children's natural capacities[547]

Before going on to gain knowledge via other tongues, the child must be thoroughly grounded in his own language first. A hundred years later, William Cowper was still complaining that English children were learning to debate in Latin who could not write a simple letter home to their mothers in plain English. Durie was proficient in English, German, French, Dutch, Latin, Hebrew and Greek besides a smattering of other languages, but he was often told to use Latin so that the learned could understand him. Latin renderings of scholars were made the basis for translations into the vernacular of other languages and not the vernacular to the vernacular. Even Durie's colleagues of the Westminster Assembly could not debate totally and freely in English and had to use Latin terms to describe the finer points of their arguments. Anyone reading Byfield's minutes of the Westminster Assembly's transaction, preserved in the Dr. Williams Library, London, will soon have enough material to write a philosophical, political and theological book of Latin Phraseology. Again Durie emphasises that nothing should be taught before the child is capable of fully understanding its purpose, application and use. Durie also applies this to language learning which he sees more as an application of memory rather than judgement by hearing and retaining what the constant speech custom of a particular nation is. Durie believed in learning a language by practicing it and not by rules. He again uses the word 'preposterous' of that method of teaching languages which presented rules before the language which they governed was learnt. First learn to speak and write the language and then deduce rules to facilitate further learning. Thus languages must be learnt situation-

---

[547] Ibid, 51 ff.

ally and in a meaningful context. Languages learnt outside the sphere of knowledge and truth they ought to confer is time wasted. This is why Durie wished to revolutionise the way English children learned to read and write as it was outside of any true socio-linguistic, practical context. Such teaching hinders the development of children when they are at their best learning age.

In all this, teachers must work hard doing three things. They must familiar themselves with the person and character of each pupil. Teaching is primarily personality relevant and teachers should not view pupils as similar 'objects' to be taught. If the teacher does not understand the child, the child will not understand the teacher. Next, the teacher should consider what is to be taught and how it can be put over to the individual capacities of the pupils. He must be quite clear whom and why he is teaching and to what ends. All superfluous material should be rejected. This is material, irrespective of its possible educational value which does not foster the apprehension of the pupils and affords them delight in learning. Yes, for Durie, education must be fun. Thus lessons to be learnt must not be disjointed from those who are to learn them and not be disjointed from what they have learnt before and what they are to learn afterwards in ever widening and deepening stages. Education is for the perfecting of mankind.

Until children can articulate themselves meaningfully in speech, they are to be considered as infants. This means children of up to four or five years of age. However, even before this time, the children should be encouraged to use their imagination and memory and be trained to be mature enough to start their elementary education. As far as grading children from infancy to the age of twenty is concerned, experience shows that such grades in learning or the stages in their capacities are:

> a. From four or five to eight or nine. Pedagogical aims in this stage are to encourage the use of sense, imagination and the beginning of memory.

> b. From eight or nine to thirteen or fourteen. This stage should afford tuition based on imagination, memory and the beginnings of reason. Now the pupil is no longer a child but a youth.

> c. From fourteen or fifteen to nineteen or twenty. The third stage provides all possibilities of reasoning, judgement and prudence, training the pupil to order himself aright before God and man. At this educational level, the previous teacher-pupil relationship should be abandoned and the teacher becomes a mentor but not without disciplining responsibilities.

Concerning the things to be taught within each degree of capacity, Durie has seven points to make concerning the first stage:

1) In the first degrees of teaching, nothing should be given the child which cannot pass through the doors of sense, imagination and a developing memory.
2) The pupil should now learn to speak his mother-tongue distinctly and to read in the same tongue readily, intelligibly and without an affected childish tone. He must read as in his natural speech.
3) The pupil must learn to write in his mother-tongue legibly but also begin the first stages of writing in a foreign tongue in the form of learning to write their alphabet in alternative scripts. He must progress from the known to the hitherto unknown.
4) Drawing lines and circles with the aid of rulers and compasses should be taught and the rudiments of painting using lines and curves.
5) Next, the significance of mathematics should not be neglected including numbers and their relationships. Comparative proportions and aids to measuring should be understood.
6) All things discernable to sense-perception must be named and described in speech and writing and black and white drawings of them made.
7) The pupil should be taught to comprehend and articulate data given him by the teacher and learn the general heads of the history and geography of the world and the historical and geographical background of the Scriptures and Church History. The main revolutions and radical changes made historically in Britain or one's mother-country should be known.

These things must be learnt before being placed after the age of eight or nine in the hands of further teachers (ushers), all members of the association.

Durie now surprisingly as if it were a second thought, suggests that the initial tuition be done in a nearby nursery outside of the association boarding school bounds and independent of the association school in administration but in cooperation with them as far as the training in general Christian behaviour is concerned.

Concerning the second stage, Durie finds that often the things learnt in the nursery section still appear to the pupil as 'a chaos or confused mass of notions in his head.' In the second stage, this confusion will be put into order and the memory more strongly exercised by the following means:

Universal Reform through Practical Divinity 379

1) Impressions are fixed on the children's memory by creative writing and art.
2) In observing all things natural and artificial information concerning them should be ordered according to their variety, coherence, differences, parts, actions, properties, uses and relevance to mankind in trades and manufacturing.
3) At this stage Hebrew Greek and Latin should be introduced. Items and their properties already known in English should now be classified similarly in the foreign languages learnt. The children should be taught to read and write in these languages only in as far as their experience goes. From now on, growth in using these languages will run parallel with things learnt to be expressed in the mother tongue.
4) This multi-lingual ability goes for all acquired knowledge so that even in mathematics the principle parts must be known in the four languages taught. Mathematics, however, should not be learnt in isolation from any other subject. Thus the child should learn:
    a) The geographical descriptions of the world and its kingdoms in globes and tables.
    b) The astronomical descriptions of the Heavens in globes and tables.
    c) The arithmetical rules of addition, subtraction, multiplication, division, fractions and proportions, but no further.
    d) The principles of geometry including lines, surfaces, bodies and rules of measuring the same and their proportions. Also methods of measuring land and the instruments involved in that study.
5) General rules concerning husbandry, gardening, hunting and fowling.
6) The anatomy of man through models and pictures of all his parts and their names in the foreign languages learnt.
7) The history of the monarchies of the world and the history of the Church since Christ's days.
8) A comparative study of the rudiments and grammar of the three foreign languages hitherto learned with their similarities and differences. Translations into and from the other languages studied.

During the third stage of learning, pupils of between thirteen or fourteen to nineteen or twenty must be taught all the useful arts and sciences which will fit them out for any employment in Church or Commonwealth. All the means of traditional and rational learning must be made available and reading be pursued in all branches of learning. This should include:

   a) The Latin agricultural authors such as Cato, Varro and Columella as an extension of what they have learnt concerning husbandry.

b) The natural history of Pliny and others together with studies of meteors, minerals and other natural geological and astrological phenomena.
c) Models and books on architecture, Engineering, fortifications, explosives, weapons, military discipline and navigation.
d) The Greek authors of moral philosophy such as Epictetus, Cebes, Arrianus, Plato, Xenophon and Plutarch should be studied and checked.
e) The doctrines of economics, civil government, natural justice and equity in international law, in fact all that relates to jurisprudence should be examined as also the Institutions of Justinian and the *Regulae Juris*.
f) All mathematical theories must be studied and methods of reforming them, together with optics and the use of optical instruments. The art of measuring via dials should be learned as also bookkeeping.
g) Part of the upper school's studies should be natural philosophy, medicine including pharmacy and the making up of drugs, distilling and chemistry.
h) A general knowledge of surgery and its tools and plasters and ointments.
i) The rules of logic, rhetoric, and poetry should be taught and the pupils trained in debate and well-ordered speaking and writing. They must be able to express themselves historically, philosophically, oratorically and poetically.
j) Directions must be given in the study of all human kind (nowadays we would call it psychology) and all that appertains to wisdom and prudence in human behaviour. Rules of judgement, discretion, prudence and civil conversation should be given the pupils who are to make a special study of Proverbs and Ecclesiastes.

Such well-trained universal students can thus be sent into the world ready to apply themselves to any employment or further study.

Durie adds that he has not mentioned a separate place for music whether vocal or instrumental as this belongs properly to the study of mathematics and recreation. Nor has he said much about reading Hebrew as this comes automatically in the study of the Old Testament with its exegesis, hermeneutics and literary analysis. Durie ends with the words:

> 'Thus I have done with all the matters which are to be taught to each degree of capacity within the period of the years appointed for their education: now followeth the Last point of this Method; how all this is to be taught and expedited within the time appointed with ease and delight.'

A Supplement to the Reformed School

Durie could not continue with his 'last point' or sequel to the *Reformed School* because certain misunderstandings had arisen concerning his work which Durie had not foreseen and his 'Supplement' dealt with these misunderstandings. The cry had been raised that Hartlib and Durie wanted to do away with he universities by presenting a view of education in schools which made universities superfluous. Durie's schools, it was argued, provide education up to the level of all academic occupations, so what further use would the state have for universities? Be this as it may, Durie had made it very clear in his essay, but obviously not clear enough for some, that he was laying a foundation for further studies and even studies to last a life-time. He had also written elsewhere on the need for a university and college education which taught academics to take on senior posts in teaching, pastoral work and the so-called secular occupations. He was not against a governing elite providing that they had gone through his school system first. The idea of disestablishing the universities had never even entered his head, nor could it be deduced from his writings in any way. Indeed, he suggests that those who think his schools provide all that is necessary for governing the world must have a very low opinion concerning how the present universities meet the higher needs of those in the service of the state, Church, education and occupations. He would have them raise their thoughts to not only a higher standard for schools but an even higher standard for the universities. The reform of universities must be at least proportionate to the reform of schools so that they might maintain a lead in education. Durie affirms that far from wishing to abolish the universities, he wished to make them 'a thousand times' more useful. However, in this work, he was dealing with schools only and not with universities.

Durie's ideas of an ever increasing absorbing of knowledge and its practical application amongst school children, he explains, was a preparation for all subsequent development of the personality and capacities of students going through further education. Indeed, he had argued elsewhere that learning should never stop and should be carried on through one's occupational life by means of public lectures and classes running parallel to the main task of earning a living. Each stage in education, however, must be built on the foundation of the stage before and in preparation for the next stage according to the Latin proverb, 'One cannot learn to swim without a cork'. School education is there to bring into society people with the ability to exercise themselves in all kinds of studies and the task of the university is to publish for the world matters not hitherto published, to reveal errors formerly thought to be true and supply solutions to the world's problems which will be serviceable to all sorts of professions. Universities must provide their students with the tools of research which enable them to discover 'things not hitherto found out by others; but which in probabilitie may bee found out by rational searching.' Furthermore, schools need oversight and guidance and must be fed with new discoveries. Such an oversight must be academically above the schools and the best place to foster such oversight is in the universities. Furthermore, one cannot automatically go from the school to take up leading offices in the Commonwealth. There must be special institutions which supply such training. Rather than abolish the Universities, Durie had stood up before Parliament and delivered a rousing appeal to the nation in his sermon of 26 November, 1645, entitled Israel's Call to March Out Of Babylon, saying, 'The Schooles of the Prophets, the Universities must be setled, purged and reformed with wholsom constituations, for the education of the sons of the Prophets, and the government of their lives and with the soundness and purity of spiritual learning, that they may speak the true language of Canaan, and that the gibberidge of Scholastical Divinity may be banished out of their society.'[548]

The truth is, says Durie, that universities are not up to the tasks demanded of them so they must be improved, not scrapped. Contemporary universities, Durie argues, encourage each to do his own but with every student working for his own ends in competition with others. Each scholar wants to be seen as possessing 'some exquisite pieces of Learning' and to be found thus academically 'extraordinarie'. This must stop. University work must be transparent and performed for the general good of the public and its further education. Its entire staff, like the staff in the school associations, must pull together and its findings not retained within the walls of such centres for public learning. Knowledge is never a private matter. Durie explains that foreign universities find English Dons quite as proficient as any other but they are of no practical use and thus good for nothing. They delight in living a retired and unsociable life without thought of using their knowledge for the preparation of mankind to live a life to the glory of God and the extension of Christ's kingdom.

How to find out the effectual way of advancing learning

As Durie refers back to his Reformed School in this work, it is taken for granted by scholars such as Webster that *Some Proposals towards the Ad-*

---

[548] *Israel's Call to march Out Of Babylon*, page 48.

vancement of Learning (1653) is the promised sequel to that work and therefore based on it. Webster claims that the text he uses from the *Hartlib Papers* 47/2 is 'the complete text of the only known copy of this work'[549]. He states in footnote 43 that, 'There is a discontinuity in the text at this point'. What appears to have happened is that Webster has copied the text from the Sheffield University records and then lost exactly two pages of it. He then had the text printed in his book without realising that Ref: 47/2/1A, No. 53 in the *Hartlib Papers* includes the lengthy passage between 1B and 2B which he has inadvertently left out.

The 'Honourable Committee' to whom Durie addresses the petition was most likely the Committee for the Advancement of Learning set up during the short Saint's (or Barebones) Parliament, established in July 1653. This Parliament was unelected and called by Cromwell as Commander in Chief of the army. Only men of Cromwell's choice took part in it. It was almost entirely a 'commoners' affair, academics and the nobility being few and far between. There were 125 members for England, five for Scotland and six from Ireland. However, representatives for Ireland and Scotland were not representative at all as they were chosen from English soldiers stationed there.

The Saints' Parliament at once began squabbling over what to abolish from the old regime. Ecclesiastical reforms such as those regarding tithing had to be postponed or cancelled because of lack of agreement. Though a Parliament of 'saints', church marriages were banned and marriage became a matter for the Justice of the Peace. Attendance increasingly dwindled and after six months, the members realised that they were not in a position to rule the country. In December 1653, the majority of members resigned and a furious Crowell expelled the rest. This was succeeded by the First Protectorate Parliament.

In his *Reformed School*, Durie had described his three-stage view of his ideal pre-university school, now he puts proposals before the Saint's Parliament for a reorganisation of the entire nation's educational systems. Durie thus suggests that first, the term learning must be defined and what the aims of such learning and methods of advancing it ought to be. By learning, Durie means the knowledge of divine and human things attainable by human industry and rational methods. This must be distinguished from knowledge which is not gained by rational means but by an experience of divine things taught by God's Spirit to those in Covenant with Him. This knowledge is available to all who seek it by prayer and medita-

---

[549] *Samuel Hartlib and the Advancement of Learning*, p. 165.

tion and communion with Christ to whom none can go unless the Father draws him. Here, Durie comments in a passage Webster had lost:

> 'We shall therefore not dare to undertake the advancement of this kinde, of learning by any humane industrie which God hath reserved for himselfe to teach, but the knowledge which is proportionate unto the rationall abilties of Mankind: & towards the attainement of which God hath put wayes and meanes into our hands: & upon the Industrious use of which meanes we find by ordinary Experience, that a blessing doth attend. this kinde of knowledge (we say) is within our reach, & by the meanes of Learning may be advanced.'

Durie emphasises that he is not talking about all that can be acknowledged as possible, and naturally feasible to human industry but that which is, the stage reached by the learner, useful and practical and necessary in laying the foundations of a thorough and lasting Reformation; and without which the safety of a well-functioning Christian constitution cannot be rationally transmitted to posterity. In order to reach this we must:

1) First reveal the numerous corruptions of true and profitable learning which have crept into the educational system and then remove them.
2) To search out and organise learning aids by which these corruptions may be rooted out and amended.
3) To search after the most expeditious way of utilising these aids.[550]

Concerning the first point, in order to discover how true and profitable learning has been corrupted; we must first know what true learning is and how far present education has departed from it. True learning is that which is demonstrable. Whoever accepts a thing as true only via a probable argument is no real searcher for truth and would appear willing to be deceived. Only things evidenced by the senses or shown to be concluded from foreknown principles and axioms which are assented to by all men are worthy of being accepted by reason. These are things either of nature, whereby we observe that what contains the whole also contains the parts, or in moral matters where we deduce, for instance, that when we find a just and faithful man, we can trust him. If things purporting to be natural or moral are not rationally deducible on such grounds, they cannot be accepted as a truth to be learnt.

Furthermore, profitable learning must have a direct tendency to benefit a man but also to fit him out for doing good and thus benefiting his genera-

---

[550] Also not found in Webster's publication.

tion. True and profitable learning teaches discernment and the will and affections to choose and follow those things which are necessary for human profit, both for the individual and all members of society. Knowledge, however, is in no wise true and profitable if it is not demonstrable as a fact. Otherwise, it might just as well be based on lying and unrighteousness. Sadly, not that it is in any way different today, much education in Durie's day was built on theory rather than fact. So Durie concludes that 'it may be demonstrated by dolefull Experience, & by the true Maximes of knowledge, that the Corruptions of all Learning are so universall, both in the matter and manner of teaching, that it is impossible to attaine to any certantie of truth, so long as we are trained up, in the ordinary course which is now in use.' Durie tells us that proof of what he says would fill a book but mentions works of Cornelius Agrippa, Francisco Sanches and Juan Luis Vives who have demonstrated at length what Durie is affirming.[551] Indeed, Durie goes so far as to say that if education was ransacked of its unproven theories, we would only have mathematics, arithmetic, geometry, geography, astronomy, optics and parts of music left which would not make up a tenth of learning necessary.

Durie, a classicist of note, writes that education in Latin, Greek and Hebrew literature is so bad that not one in a thousand attains any perfection in them as the way they are taught and what they are taught leaves the mind empty of any association with real life. Here Durie is thinking of hours of blind repetitions of vocabulary and grammatical paradigms void of all sense contents which still plague the learning of Classical languages. Happily, such as Cambridge University with their interactive multi-media Cambridge School Classics Project are at last pioneering a Latin which is fun to learn and a door to literature, history, geography, commerce and religion.

Durie castigates the faulty teaching of logic in schools and universities which has the very opposite aim (abstract thinking) to that which it is really designed for (concrete thinking). All reasoning is to find truth rather than be some unhelpful form of mental gymnastics which is only provable within the rules of the game but not with reference to the facts outside of it. Indeed, as Durie had experienced, the rules for the steps in attaining logical achievements are often devoid of the logic of the construction to be demonstrated. So, too, logic cannot go from the unknown to the known as it limits itself to the known or to that which all men recognise is a truth with-

---

[551] Durie has already explained in his *A Motion tending to the Publick Good* (letter dated 6 Jan. 1641/2) that a treatise on the corruption of learning in the contemporary educational system should be put into every teacher's hand.

out it having to be proved. For instance, showing that Socrates was a man and that he was mortal and even that all men are mortal, though they do not all act like Socrates, is hardly a serious step in discovering the unknown as the details are self-explanatory.

So, too, moral virtue which should be one of the main tasks of the school is totally neglected and its neglect leads to a debasing of character. Instead, pupils are placed under the cowardly rule of a rod-waving tyrant who beats all character out of the children thus creating rebels only instead of free, generous, modest, discreet, decent and virtuous members of society. Thus Durie concludes this section by writing:

> 'Thus the Memorie, the understanding of the Affections of Schollars in common Schooles, are for the most part by their very education, perverted from the true and profitable objects of knowledge & of Vertue, and either led forth, or suffered to fall into the habits of Error & vice, which bring forth the miseries, under which all the Societies of Mankind doe groane at this day.'[552]

This is why Durie told Smart in his *Advice about Studies* concerning reading the Bible:

> 'This daily reading of the word at least morning and evening is not all that is requisite of a Christian in this kind; but there ought to bee also some Exercise of the Iudgment & Memorie at certaine set tymes to collect Precepts and promises & doctrines and Exhortations out of it, & to get the same by heart: & this should bee at least once a weeke besides the Lords-day, that such choise Places as wee meet withall, & wherewith wee are most affected, may not bee lost, but noted and layd up in store in our heart to bee a settlement of our soule in the wayes of God.'

This spiritual work of memorising must, however, go hand in hand with the rational work of the mind which Durie outlines in his *Tractus de Memoria*, giving a rational, scholarly analysis of how the memory might be trained positively via *facillima impressione, fidelissima conseuisatione* and *promptissima recordatione*.[553] Thus he can tell Sir Cheney Culpeper:

> 'Thus then we see what the Acts of the mind of man are & how they are distinguished namely into the Acts of the spirit dwelling in the Conscience & into the Acts of the Rationall soule dwelling in the memorative vnderstanding & willing facultyes to which the whole sensuall life & all the Acts of the inward & outward sences are subordinate. The Relation wherein these Acts

---

[552] *Some Proposals*, p. 3A.
[553] Ref: 60/6/1A-16B, HP.

stand one to another in respect of the propertyes of these facultyes whence they proceede is this that the faculty of the spirit in the acts & enditements of the Conscience is supreme & predominant above all the rest: to which the Rationall faculty of the soule in the acts of Memory, vnderstanding & willing is imediately subordinate; & to these the acts of the imaginations & sensuall passions are subservient & submitted. And if this Relation & subordination be altered so that the sensuall should be predominant above the Rationall or the Rationall above the spirituall Acts, then all is out of order & a mans life is either Beastly or Divilish.'[554]

Reflections on how defects in learning may be rectified

Durie claims that in order to rectify the miserable state of education in his day, four major defects must be dealt with. These are the defects in precognitions through lack of preparation; the defects in the material used in learning; the defects in the methods of learning and the defects in the exercise of learning.

Concerning precognitions, Durie refers here to preliminary information and preparations leading to new knowledge being taught in the arts and sciences appertaining to the subject matter and the usefulness of the knowledge to be provided. The capacities of the pupils must be sounded out so that the lessons may be organised accordingly.

Concerning the materials of learning, there are four points to note:

First defects in teaching to read and write should be obliterated. The children must be taught to read and write in their mother tongue and then in Latin, Greek and Hebrew in more meaningful ways than hitherto practiced. This should be fact and reality orientated and not taught in a vacuum from other means of acquiring and maintaining knowledge by, for instance, relating writing and drawing. Children should learn to express truths not only through descriptive words but also descriptive art. For instance, a child should not only be able to explain to a French visitor the way, but draw a map of how he can best get there to accompany him. He should also be able to describe the place of destination so the French-speaker will recognise it when he gets there.

Secondly, unlike in England then, in the Low Countries, pupils are taught the rudiments of arithmetic and accounting alongside reading and writing so that the learning affect of reading and writing is extended and made more practical from the start. This is necessary because by the time a child is eleven or 12 years of age, he must be able to master addition, sub-

---

[554] Undated, Ref: 1/4/9A-18B, HP.

traction, division and the rule of proportions as a necessary basis for his next stage in learning.

Thirdly, the neglect of teaching concerning the knowledge of God as revealed in Scripture must be taught alongside other rudiments of learning. Producing atheists is denying the children a major stay in life and life's purpose. Again, this should be according to capacity only. Perfection in all realms of knowledge must be aimed at during the child's education. As things stood in Durie's days, he tells us, there is no effectual course taken to restrain dissoluteness and carnal liberties and to shame such as practise them. Those who pretend to live a spiritual life do not practise what they preach and there is much hypocrisy amongst Christians at work which is made evident in the nation's moral and civil conduct. Thus, 'upright men in publick places should be stirred up to strengthen the innocent against the Hypocrite.'

Fourthly, Durie wished to see pupils taught the catechetical doctrines of the churches, the absence of which teaching, he thought to be a grave defect. This should go hand in hand with a practice of natural truths and moral virtues.

Concerning defects in Natural Sciences, Medicine and Chemistry, Durie believed that all school children should be grounded in the natural sciences including medicine but there was a dearth of such teaching in contemporary schools. He listed the deficits in this sphere as indicating:

1) There is no current education in any school form which teaches a methodical use of reasoning and searching which facilitates looking into the nature and properties of everything.
2) Geometry, Geography, and Astronomy are not being taught by ocular demonstration but remain as Aristotle delivered them, buildings of mere notions in the air. Such branches of learning should be taught through hands-on field- work or at least in classroom laboratory work.
3) This goes also for husbandry, architecture, navigation and knowledge of minerals. Such learning without practical experience is useless and wholly abstracted from the things which are necessary for the life of mankind and civil society. This goes also for mathematics which is not related to practical use. Those who have been taught in this abstract way are in capable of civil conversation and employment and thus unprofitable both to themselves and to others.

Concerning defects in Social and Political Sciences, history and office work, Durie maintains:

Universal Reform through Practical Divinity

1) There is a grave lack of tuition in centres of learning regarding jurisprudence and equity and the duties of morality in general. All they are taught is self-lust and service to themselves. If others are brought into their perspective, it is only to use them for one's own ends. This is the root of all confusion and disorderliness in the Commonwealth.
2) There is also a great dearth in knowledge regarding the Constitution and the methods by which government is carried out. The pupils should be taught what the fundamental offices are and to what public use they are put and what laws regulate them. Without this knowledge a person can hardly be serviceable to his generation.
3) Skills relating to office work, secretarial duties and general administration should be taught in school where they are entirely lacking. Pupils receive no knowledge of how to transact business.
4) There is also a great lack of knowledge concerning worldwide history in schools and the various kinds of government that have been in force. Especially the reasons for the present political upheavals in Britain should be discussed in class.

Concerning defects in teaching how to discern spiritual matters, Durie says that such discernment is the third noble object of reason which helps us understand the natural and the moral. Should pupils be made aware that also spiritual truths are deducible from the grounds of reason, this will open to them 'a new well-spring of knowledge and of learning which God will in due time (we hope) bring to perfection.

Thus, Durie has dealt with the defects in the materials of learning put under his third major section he wishes to speak more of the defects of method. This, Durie argues would be a never-ending subject which he has already touched on in *The Reformed School*,[555] so he will merely deal with the fundamental defects here. Before doing so, however, he adds the great defect in education is going from one subject to another, ticking off each item once and for all and not bringing it in to play with newly learnt material and not realising that repetition and regular use are essentials of learning.

The need for a fundamentally different training for teachers

In his fourth major point, Durie declares that if such corruptions and defects are to be removed, schoolteachers must have a fundamentally different kind of training. Durie argues:

---

[555] *Reformed School*, page 39 ff.

'That through the care & by the inspection of such as manage the universall Trust of the Publick, such Sciences should be taught which will fit all men, according to their severall Conditions, to be good members of a Commonwealth; that is, to be intelligent and vertuous for themselves, & industrious to serve each other for a publick interest. The severall Ends then of teaching Sciences must be taken notice of, that the means necessary to reach them, may be made use of in the Schooles to advance learning. Now the ends of teaching are distinguisheable, chiefly by the severall qualifications, that are to be aimed at in those that are to be taught, which we conceive to be of two sorts: some are common to all, whereof none ought to be destitute; some are proper onely to some, & not requisite in all.'[556]

Durie thus starts with the common qualifications for all which are:

1) Every pupil should be able to read distinctly, and write accurately and legibly in his own mother tongue.
2) Pupils should be able to count by numbers and measure objects by their weight and dimensions of breadth, length, height and depth, that they may not be deceived by appearance only.
3) Every pupil should have a general notion of the world and the shape of its continents and be able to name their features.
4) Everyone should have an overview of the history of Gods works, how he made the world, and how He governs it.
5) Every pupil should be familiar with the history of the Church and what God expects of everyone in their Christian service.
6) All should be familiar with the basic skills of reasoning (logic).
7) Everyone should know the fundamental grounds of natural justice and equity, and the duties on which human societies are grounded.
8) They should all know the basic details of the history of their own country and its fundamental constitutions.
9) Each pupil must learn the art of defence and to understand the precepts of courage when it must be undertaken and he must learn how to avoid and settle quarrels with credit.

Durie adds that if anyone is wanting in any of these things, he will be less fit for any private or public service than if he possessed them. With people trained like this 'in a few yeares the generation of Common men in this Commonwealth, will be so changed that few Commoners in the world, or none in any Nation will be found like unto them, for publick usefulnesse.'

---

[556] *Some Proposals*, p. 10.

Qualifications which are not requisite for all in their service for the public are the mechanical, i.e. trades and crafts, and those of leadership on a national and local level. Trades and crafts come under the rubric 'sciences' for Durie in which category he includes all toilsome and corporal work which benefits the worker himself and others. These qualifications include:

1) The art of husbandry.
2) The art of navigation.
3) The art of minerals and mining.
4) The art of land surveying.
5) The art of architecture.
6) The art of painting.
7) The arts of working in metals whether by fire, or by tools, or both.

Those who are most skilled in these arts should be trained to teach them to others, so, over the years, perfecting the knowledge required for their practice.

Education for public offices and leadership

Now Durie speaks of what he calls the noble qualifications of learning which he distinguishes from the mechanical. Durie is thinking of training which prepares those capable for entering a public office in a ruling or serving capacity. These public areas he sees as caring for the citizens' bodily needs, the guarding of the citizens possessions; looking after the peace of the country; watching over human associations and those who care for the happiness of the citizens' minds. Of such training, Durie maintains:

1) It is requisite that those showing the correct capacities and calling should be educated in the science of Medicine in healing and strengthening the physical body. These must, however be thoroughly grounded in what we call today Physics, Chemistry, Mathematics, including Astronomy, Pharmacy and Surgery.
2) So, too, education should be made available for those who look after the safety and plenty of man's possessions, the laws concerning possessions, inheritance and purchase, trading and commerce and the defence of personal rights.
3) For the peace and prosperity of human associations, all the parts of Moral Philosophy must be studied as also the science of land and sea warfare.

4) For the accomplishment and happiness of the minds of men, specialists must be educated who either:
   a) Are trained to discern the nature, faculties and properties of the spirits of men and to what occupations they may be fittingly employed.
   b) Are trained in the the science of divine things so far as they are the object of reason, either in the interpretation of the text of the holy Scriptures, or in matters of moral divinity.

These members of the noble professions should be skilled in the pansophical use of reason in ordering human thoughts so as to search and find out that which is not discovered hitherto and can be known of truth in Nature. They must also know how to teach and exercise all men according to their capacities in all arts and sciences useful for human society. The last kind of person Durie wanted to educate was a one-track-minded specialist. The chief end then of human sciences is to produce pansophists, though it is not expected that such will devote their entire occupational career to all knowledge but use their inter-active universal knowledge as it reflects on their various occupational tasks.

Education for all children, youths and adults according to their abilities and calling

Three things are, however, still required to remove educational defects

   a) What distinctions and constitutions are necessary in the school system.
   b) What the course of teaching should be to further pansophy or universal learning.
   c) What teachers' duties and methods ought to be in their oversight of scholars so that they may leave their care fit for public employment.

To this end, there should be:

   a) Common Schools for all children throughout all the parts of the nation.
   b) Trade schools in convenient places, dealing with the exercise of mechanical sciences.
   c) Noble schools to fit out such as are capable of the best breeding to do that public service to which their genius leads them.
   d) Special teacher-training schools dealing with the science of teaching others. Durie calls these 'The Schools of the Prophets'.

The constitution of such schools in a Commonwealth should represent a common interest and all members should be useful to the entire body. No member can be considered useful who is not virtuous and trained to use his intelligence through good teaching added to his nature. Those who will not see that schools are a public concern of great magnitude are not faithful to the welfare of society and thus not useful to it. All citizens therefore should be concerned in erecting, maintaining, ordering, and overseeing schools and that these things must be put into the hands of a Trust. Durie sees no better Trust than Parliament itself and declares, 'And we blesse God, who hath put this care in the Parliaments heart, & by them in the hands of faithfull men, upon whom we shall daily pray for a blessing'. Sadly, Parliament looked on Durie's reforms enthusiastically for a very short time and the state agencies set up to enforce Durie's reforms were lasted as long as there was political union in Parliament which was seldom.

The problem is how progress is to be made in teaching right knowledge to the right candidates in the right environments, assuming the same chances for all. Durie's solution is:

1) If the teaching of knowledge in schools is to fit men out to be useful as virtuous, intelligent members of society, all must pull together in ensuring that education by common principles of right, reason and equity, all knowledge should be taught as fitting into the one serviceableness which each part owes to the other. This serviceableness should be the same throughout all schools because nothing breaks up society more than a diversity of breeding based on different principles.
2) If sciences (branches of knowledge) though distinct in their ends, are subordinate and subservient one to another in their use, it will follow, that knowledge should be taught for its usefulness and not for its theory which would be a corruption of useful teaching.
3) If one branch or part of science is considered for some purpose as being superior to another, this branch or part must not be taught until the supposed inferior parts are dealt with in lessons. No part of learning should be taught in theory until the way of using it is first understood by common rules of practice or customary habits.
4) Here, Durie gives as an example whereby a supposed 'superior' learning is taught void of any practical 'inferior' comprehension. This is the study of 'dead languages' such as Latin Greek and Hebrew. Of course, they are only dead if killed off by bad teaching. Grammarians and Classical scholars are thought to be learned who descant upon the meaning of words in isolation or the fine points of grammar. Durie emphasises that 'tongues are onely taught & learned to be helpes towards the com-

munication of Learning, & for mutuall Conversation; and therefore should not be taught otherwise, then by & with the knowledge of the things, for the communication of which they are sought after.' I remember the strong criticism I received from my Headmaster and colleagues, all Classists, at one Grammar School for teaching Hebrew in the language laboratory, readapting the 'Essential English' programmes I had authored for 'Essential Hebrew'. I was told it was 'not the done thing' and therefore, I should not do it.

5) Nothing should therefore be taught heterogeneously to the end and use for which a school is appointed. All the parts of learning to be delivered should be merged according to the order of their usefulness, and according to what has gone before and is to follow.

6) The teaching of theoretical contemplations of sciences as they stand in their ideas only, is no use to anybody but those trained in colleges to become teachers of others.

As contemporary teachers were, in Durie's opinion, not yet able to teach according to Durie's specifications, schools, 'must be so framed, & the method of their teaching and Gouvernement so ordered therein, that all their Actions at all times may be under some account, & lyable to their Rulers inspection & regulation.'

Durie claims that these are but brief and general methods of ensuring that the corruptions and defects in education should be removed. What remains is for the government to set up a new model of education from the bottom to the top with directories handed out to all teachers so that they might lead their pupils into all knowledge and virtue realising, 'For it is not enough for a workman to have good tooles to work withall, but he must also know how to use them.'

To this end, Durie recommends the compiling of better textbooks, library catalogues and the setting up of a learned press. A complete Body of Moral or Practical Divinity must be drawn up by the best authors. The marrow of the best of our predecessors in learning should be committed to books suitable for school use in Britain but also to be distributed throughout Europe according to the many requests of Continental colleagues. So, too, the great libraries which remain shut because of the political and military troubles which however, are easily opened by thieves and robbers, should be catalogued and opened for the general good of the public. Durie believed in a free press, controlled by a general oversight of state and public initiative and always campaigned for what he called 'a learned Presse' to play their part in the advancement of universal education. Durie was so beyond his age that he believed schools, libraries and the press could work together in advancing learning which would become self-financing.

How Reform must start at once

Durie's fourth major argument is that these reforms are mere suggestions for getting his plans started, believing that once underway, the movement would look after itself without too much legislation. At this initial stage, in order to overcome all difficulties, an Advisory Board must be set up of members who are well-grounded in universal learning and in a position to work out the necessary curricula for such schools and employ teachers worthy of their task.

Next, intelligent well-qualified people should be appointed to visit the schools superintend their progress and methods of teaching and to confer with and encourage the local teachers for the mutual advancement of their aims. Summed up, the Board's tasks would be:

1) To satisfy themselves concerning the models and heads of learning which they will undertake to advance.
2) When these models are ready, the Board should consider how many schools of each kind of learning and in what places of the nation they should be most conveniently erected.
3) When this is determined, plans must be laid concerning the manner of erecting these schools and directions given concerning the choice of teachers to be settled in them so that the employment of 'unworthy' teachers may be avoided.
4) When this is done, senior academics should be appointed in every Province in positions of Authority to supervise teaching methods and curricula and the general organisation of the schools. Concerning school supervision, Durie says that countries of the Continent of Europe such as The Netherlands, Germany and Switzerland are far in advance of Britain.
5) First, the common or mechanical schools should be constituted and then the noble schools should be built on the experience gathered from these concerning what needs to be bettered. If the noble schools and universities are started first, it would be like building a house roof first before foundations and walls are set up.
6) When the noble schools are established, these should be in a position to understand better, in what specific way they can further the common and general education in the lower schools.

7) However, the 'noble sciences' must not be confined to the universities alone as the setting up of such schools is open to anyone who can provide the right education and are willing to put themselves under the supervision of the Advisory Board.

8) After such necessary and profitable schools are constituted, then the country can be rid of dissolute snares set up for the children of the richer sort where they are taught singing, dancing, wantonness and lascivious. Durie was not a 'leveller' and decried riches but he could not stand the idle rich who were parasites on their country.

9) As for girls' education, this should be scrutinised by 'grave and vertuous Matrons' on the supervisors' staff, who understand what in Christianity is most useful and decent for them to be trained up in. Such education should not be designed to teach girls to think their only future lies in their becoming objects of lust or snares to young gentlemen but fit them out to play their part in a Christian Commonwealth as modest, discreet, and industrious household manageresses.

10) Some academies may also be built in which noblemen's sons may be trained in such knowledge as will fit them for public employments in both peace time and war time, at home or abroad, as occasion requites their services.

11) The monkish constitutions of the universities must be abolished whereby dons and students live a dronish life within themselves, pretending to uphold learning whereas they are no use to the Commonwealth, learning or the Church of God. They might be used in the sense of Durie's noble schools or colleges but the academic findings of the universities must be made available to all. Chancellors and fellows must be given public tasks in which they can exercise their learning and be in of immediate use to schools.

12) Besides perfecting that which is defective in universal learning both in divine and human matters, the chief use of universities should be to train teachers in all sciences, wisdom and virtue to enrich the schools of the nation, the churches and all public societies bent on working for the public good. Durie ends his presentation to Parliament by saying:

'Having now this long-wished for and seasonable opportunities offered to us, we have with all cheerfulness of mind, & due submission desired to tender these Proposalls unto the Honourable Committee for the advancement of learning: referring the event thereof unto their godly zeale, wisdome & prudence, & all their deliberations unto the grace of God, for whose direction upon them we shall not cease to pray.'[557]

Sadly, once more, as Durie was within inches of realising his life-long homes. The Saints' Parliament collapsed and with it most plans for educational reform. When we read William Cowper's proposals a hundred years later, they are almost identical, though not so thorough-going as Durie's, but sadly, likewise, unimplemented.

The intellectual and practical truths to be taught in a Body of Practical Divinity

Busy as always, with a variety of strenuous tasks, Durie became engaged in diplomatic service to Parliament and Cromwell, especially on the Continent so he could only return to the subject after completing a tour of the Continent in 1658. He then published his *The Earnest Breathings of Forreign Protestants, Divines and others: to the Ministers and other Able Christians of these three Nations, for a Compleat Body of Practical Divinity*. Durie wrote this work, like his earlier attempts, to encourage others to write on the subject rather than provide a definitive work. In his new, or rather, extended work, Durie makes a lengthy preamble, referring to the 1654 edition, pounding home the significance of Practical Divinity which introduces the churchgoer, pupil, student, minister, employer and teacher to universal learning.

Durie begins his *Earnest Breathings* with the same question as in his former work, that is, 'What is meant by a Body of Practical Divinity?' This time, he affirms that it is simply 'the revealed truths of God concerning the obedience of the faith which is to be yielded unto his will.' He sees this truth as being two-fold:

1) First, Divine truth refers to what is to be contemplated as the object of the understanding and remembrance. This contemplation leads to the conformity of our intellectual faculty to the testimony of God's word when understood correctly, thus working in the notions of the mind to beget knowledge. This is what Durie calls 'intellectual truth'. This is according to Christ's own words in John 8:31-32, 'If you continue in my word, ye shall know the truth.'
2) Secondly but not subordinately, Divine truth, as far as we are enabled to pursue it and partake of it, becomes the object of the will and affections

---

[557] Ibid, pp. 21-22.

and leads to a conformity of the purposes of our heart to that which is known to be God's will. It thus fosters the conviction of the conscience to beget resolutions and 'obediential performance'. This is what Durie calls 'practical truth'. This is in accordance with Christ's words in John 3:21, 'He that doeth truth, cometh to the light.' Thus both intellectual and practical truths are not born in human rationalism and idealism but in being open to the will of God as revealed in Christ. This is the start of universal knowledge.

So Durie argues that there are truths to be contemplated and truths to be done. The former forms virtue in the intellect and the latter puts virtue into practice. As darkness is the opposite of light, truth is opposed to all falsehood, ignorance and error so through Divine truth virtue is engendered and error put to flight. Durie can thus conclude that:

> 'Whether it be in the Theoretical or Practical matters, nothing is true Divinity, but that which is Divine truth; nor is anything a Divine truth but that which is manifested by the Word of God: the Word then to us, is the Standard of Truth.

Now although the Action of the understanding, must of necessity be Antecedent to all our Acts of truth, because the will is a knowing faculty, and cannot act orderly without the Understanding; yet the Theoretical truths notionally apprehended, bring the soul to no perfection of happiness, except they become fruitful in the actions of vertue. The Notional Science of all God's truth, and of his whole will, as it may be in the brain alone, and without the practice whereunto that Science doth oblige the heart, is more hurtfull than profitable to our felicity'.

Appropriating data in theory alone is not knowledge, but doers of Practical Divinity learn how to activate data knowingly and usefully

Here we note that Durie, who was quite opposed to mere rote learning and learning for learning's sake, sees true knowledge or Science as an appropriating and using of facts, not their encyclopaedic storing in the mind. Data alone is never full knowledge. If one cannot put a truth in one way or another into practice and use it for the cause of virtue in harmony with God's omniscient Being, it is only a half-truth. 'Half-knowledge' which is 'in the brain alone' can be, indeed, dangerous. It is interesting to compare Durie's use of the term 'science' with the contemporary usages of the term 'philosophy' in relation to education. He is obviously not using the term in the ancient way of knowledge in general but in the modern 'scientific' way of experimental and applied knowledge. Durie quotes here 2 Peter 2:21 and John 3:17 where we read that if we know useful things, happy are we who do them. Durie claims that he who keeps knowledge to himself, though he may know all mysteries, cannot be happy and cannot know God. Durie goes further and claims according to James 1:21, 25 that because activating knowledge of divine truths is the life of God in man, only the doer can be the true believer. Therefore practical truths encourage happiness more than theoretical because practicing truth is God working in us.

Durie sees Christ's work in the active believer as confirming to him all the promises He has given to those who walk by faith. This works in two ways:

a) By the truth of obedience, we shall be enabled to clear up doubts in intellectual matters because of our sharpened discernment. John 7:17, 'If any man will do the will of him that sent me, he shall know the doctrine, whether it be of God, or whether I speak of myself.'

b) To such who are obedient to the commandments of God, the Father and the Son will manifest to the soul their presence with him. John 14:21, 23, 'He that hath my commandments, and keepeth them, he it is that loveth me; and he that loveth me, shall be loved of my Father, and I will love him, and manefest my love unto him: and if any man love me, he will keep my words: and my Father will love him, and we will come unto him, and make our abode with him.'

Durie concludes from this that 'all truth, as it is the object of contemplation, is nothing else but a 'Preparative to, or a consequence of the Truth, which is the object of Action.' Only this leads to a life of happiness and godliness because God loves the cheerful doer of his will. Durie thus concludes thus concludes this section by saying:

'the study of Practical Divinity, is of farre greater concernment unto all, and far more to be heeded, esteemed, and entertained in the Schools of the Prophets, then the study of contemplative Mysteries and notions of Divinity; whereupon Controversal matters are ordinarily attendants. And feeling there are so many bodies and Systemes of Theoretical and Controversial matters, that it would be no easie task to any man to reckon them all up; and yet there is not so much as one compleat body or System of Practical Divinity found in all the Churches; wherewhereunto we see nevertheless, that all Theoretical Truths ought to be referred, and directed as to their end; it is evident that therein is there is a manefest defect, and that much is wanting hereby, to the increase of publique Edification, to the supply of Spiritual Consolation, and to the settlement of a sound Reformation in all the churches, which may be remedied by a Body of this nature.'

Thus for Durie, Practical Divinity is a full and orderly collection and disposition of all divine truths appertaining to godliness so that the man of God can be perfectly instructed with sufficient helps and directives to make him not only wise unto salvation but able also to perform all the tasks he has to do in every day life in God. As a good minister and teacher does everything decently and in order, so Durie offers the following suggestion to those who will take up the work of teaching according to Practical Divinity. First, the steps and parts of this teaching must be suitable and proportionate to the goal aimed at. Nothing should be brought into it which is not proper and useful to the attainment of a life of godliness, and nothing should be left out which is requisite and subservient for such an aim. This truth is the manifestation of the life of God in the soul of man through the knowledge of and obedience to Christ. This gives us light which makes us wise unto salvation and the power of life which enables us to work out our salvation by doing all our works in God. Thus the complete end of Practical Divinity is to teach men the wisdom which is profitable to their souls so that they may perform all their works walking in His light.

Precognitions, Principles and Parts:
Practical Divinity versus Case Divinity[558]

Durie now moves on to discuss the precognitions, principles and parts in more or less the same form and framework as in his *A Summarie Platform*, summing up the three stages as a. Precognitions: preparing the mind to think of a life of godliness; b. Principles: by which that life is begotten and; and c. Parts or acts: wherein that life consists. However, Durie gives far more space to discussing common doubts expressed concerning his views. He has just returned from three intensive, tiring, though triumphant, years seeking to win over the Swiss Protestant Cantons; the German Protestant principalities and kingdoms and the Dutch provinces, though the German and Dutch nobility were now hostile to the British Protector whom they called 'The King-Killer'. Though successful in convincing the Continent that Cromwell was serious in his desires for political, educational and ec-

---

[558] See Durie's appendix to *Earnest Breathings* entitled A letter written divers years ago by the Author of the foregoing Treatise to M. Samuel Hartlib, (concerning the difference of Practical and Case Divinity), pp. 50-52.

clesiastical cooperation, Dury had learnt that his policy of Practical Divinity was often pushed aside as the Continent now, after the Thirty Years War, thought more of stabilizing their countries politically rather than spiritually. He thus prefaces his remarks on precognitions by admitting that though his words might find immediate acceptance by unprejudiced minister-teachers, such are only a part of the instructing body and he must meet the objections of those who follow other systems.

In this issue, therefore, Dury urges his friends to add to the Body of Practical Divinity he wishes them to write, a lengthy Supplement or Appendix dealing with all inhibitions and counter arguments which might be collected. He saw these as coming mostly from those Puritans who had taken over the Aristotelian method of Systematic Theology in dealing with branches of Christian knowledge in isolation or with case-studies which Durie found contrary to sound, all-round universal learning. Here, though Durie never lost the support and friendship of Samuel Hartlib, his great friend could not agree with his strong criticism of case-law and the analytical study of knowledge. Hartlib's doctrine of Pansophy was more ideological than practical and Durie challenged its basic logic. Hartlib thought that subject-teaching by case-studies was the best way of cutting up knowledge to be fed to pupils during their first steps in learning. Durie found this would give pupils spiritual, methodical and educational indigestion because one must first know the source and purpose of learning and then work out from that basis rules which apply universally. In other words, didactics alone are of little use without method and goals being taught first. So, too, case studies, for Durie, as he told Hartlib in a sample appendix he enclosed on the subject, left the pupils with no idea why they were learning and what the various parts really signified.

Durie thus tells his friend that two things must be taken note of in learning. First what is essential, and then what is the means of reaching that end. Practical Divinity, as opposed to Case Divinity, 'containeth properly the determination of the End and means of all our actions, to show how they are subordinate to Godliness and the Rules whereby the actions are to be directed to their own proper ends.' Practical Divinity concerns the essential part of the whole being of man and the backbone of a Christian nation. The circumstantial or accidental results of this refer to the state of a Christian as he stands in this or that calling and occupation. For the latter, specific subject knowledge is required but it is only of practical use when knowledge of the essentials and means of Christian living according to the Word of God are understood and followed. Once the essentials are understood, it is up to every man to study his particular studies or calling to see where they might fit into his essential status as a Christian. He can then walk according to his conscience in the different occurrences of his life. Durie thus tells Hartlib:

> 'When these expresse determinations are set down in their natural order, then we have a Rule of understanding and conscience by which every man is able to direct himself afterwards in the several Occurrences as his occasions may fall out; for the spirit of obedience dwelling in his conscience, and being informed and strenthened in the Rule of the Word, will discern the duty which is most requisite to be performed in the particular occasion wherein a man is; Neither is it possible as I suppose, that all the incident cases of this nature can be truly determined, so that they will satisfie every mans conscience. For the different measures of knowledge and of the apprehensions of the Rule, make the conscience doubtful; And therefore, except the settled and infalible Rules be first received and proposed, all particular decisions of doubtful cases will become nothing else but a matter of inextricable dispute, by which means instead of a Body of Practical Truths, we shall have a new kind of Polemical Divinity in matters of Practice, because the preposterous course being taken to begin at doubt, before the true rule be known whereby to frame our life, we shall hardly ever finde the right way. For after that different opinions are once taken up in matters of doubt, we see how hardly they are laid down; and how that men before they will seem to have erred in the particular determination of the doubt, will sometimes strain the sense of many Principles as in matters of Theory the Papists do plainly. Therefore I think to begin with cases is a preposterous course every way.'[559]

Hartlib's thoughts break the *filum Ariadnes*

Here we have the most probable chief reason why there had been such a delay in getting a Practical Divinity finished. As is obvious from the text, Hartlib had insisted on merely gathering articles from various theologians on various subjects; talks given at meetings such as the Invisible Society's; and correspondence both received and sent. He planned thus to make an encyclopaedic compendium of Christian knowledge before going on to work out a more pansophical overview on this basis. This would account for the Hartlib Papers being preserved which deal with almost every subject under the sun but have no order, cross referencing, summing up or framework of any kind. This would scarcely suffice as an encyclopaedia of knowledge as even encyclopaedias have always some kind of framework and order, even if only alphabetical. Hartlib's approach is thus the very op-

---

[559] *Earnest Breathings*, p. 51.

posite of Durie's. The latter wanted stable terms of reference with which all case studies could be compared, amalgamated, synergised and thus find their rightful and useful place. Nowadays, happily, most school have such a system in their teaching-targets and curricula but we have still, at least in modern secondary school and university education of which this author has over 45 years experience, not reached Durie's standards whether the framework be Christian, humanistic or any other Weltanschauung. Education is and remains a broken *filum Ariadnes* in a badly lit labyrinth.

Durie shows that though he is thoroughly analytical in his method, in his treatment of the subject matter he is comprehensive and situational. He saw education, whether inside or outside of the ministry as problem- and project-orientated and emphasised its culminating effect on the learner and not its encyclopaedic, compartmentalised accumulation. So, too, Durie would not have a dichotomy between the essentials and circumstantials of education. All learning must be seen as fitting into a comprehensive plan and purpose.

Durie's last stand in England

Durie obviously wrote *Earnest Breathings* between Cromwell's fierce campaigns in Ireland and Scotland. Feeling that after the troubles in Ireland, peace would once again reign in the British Isles Dury again pleaded for a national body to foster the education of the nation along the lines suggested by him in his writings. Hartlib took a middle way and fostered private schools under part private and part state financing. However, he expected to be paid for his services by the state. Cromwell granted a salary to both Durie whom he employed directly and Hartlib who worked mostly as a lobbyist which was, however, only sporadically paid. Even that was stopped by Charles II along with all government backing for Hartlib and Durie's projects. Hartlib died in poverty in 1662 but Durie was given various forms of employment by the German Protestant princes until his death, usually given as 1680.

In his demand for parliamentary support, Durie differed radically from Comenius who detested state intervention in education. Durie felt that if a state professed to be Christian as did Britain, it must exercise the responsibility of teaching universal Christian learning. Indeed, in *Earnest Breathings*, Durie departs from his usual irenic spirit entirely and spends several pages in a devastating denouncement of Charles I and the prelates of the Church of England for not giving his views the support he had demanded and for not protecting the persecuted Protestants on the Continent. Charles and the Church of England's disestablishment, he argues, was the judgement of God. 'These sins,' he declares, 'have caused Christ to fall with his iron Rod upon them to dash them to pieces.' It was thus no wonder that Charles II, only two years later, refused to carry on Cromwell's financial support. Here we see a most frustrated, undiplomatic Durie who is apparently taking his last stand in striving to persuade the English Parliament to follow his course. He even risks a quarrel with the friend who had stuck by him through thick and thin for some thirty-four years. Nowhere else in the hundreds of published works from Durie's pen and the scores of letters and mss listed in my Bibliography did he allow his temper to overcome him and drive him to the precipitous edge of fanaticism as in his *Earnest Breathings*. However, in his last efforts to gain government backing in England, he was forgetting that it was Parliament who had repeatedly refused to allow Charles to assist the persecuted Palatinate and other Continental Reformed areas with money, ships and troops and at least three Archbishops, six bishops had some forty Anglican Doctors of Divinity had given Durie all the support they could in perilous times leading to rebellion and civil war. So, too, it must be realised that even in the face of Parliamentary opposition, Charles managed to send thousands of troops and gigantic gifts of money to assist the Continental Protestant principalities whereas Cromwell dispensed first with half of Parliament and then disbanded the Rump and made himself unpopular in Scandinavia, Holland, France, Germany, Portugal and Spain. Though Cromwell gave Durie more than an uncommon amount of support, his influence on the Continent gained the fear and respect of the Continentals rather than their friendship and sympathy and they felt that Cromwell had let them down in their campaign for religious freedom and educational reform. Though Switzerland remained faithful to Cromwell as a bulwark against France, the most powerful Continental powers turned from him after Charles' execution and especially during the middle 1650s. When Cromwell died in 1658, there was dancing in the streets throughout Europe but especially in the Netherlands, the Palatinate and Northern Germany.[560]

However, not anticipating the Scottish problems which were to darken Cromwell's final few years and feeling that after the Irish campaigns, peace was returning to England, Durie again strove to set up a central agency for the compiling of Practical Divinity literature for the English and Continental educational system. This time, he does not plead for a state organisation but asks for a committee of co-workers to be set up with two Directors and an Agent settled in London to serve as a sorting and transla-

---

[560] These matters are dealt with in more depth in my companion volume *John Durie, the Defragmenter of the Reformation*.

tion office. Now, Durie does not demand state financing but merely says of the Agent, 'his charges should be born.' He suggests the printing should be done at Geneva. There is such an air of melancholy in the final pages of Durie's 57 paged sketch of the kind of education he wants for the world that one realises that the author, now over sixty, is looking back on a life time's work which had inspired the kings, princes, educators and clergy of Europe but had seen so little practical outcome of it. It appeared to him, also, that the nation of his birth, Britain, had done very little indeed to further the cause of God and truth in the education of her people.

CHAPTER ELEVEN

Summing Up

Durie's Plans Seen as Realisable, Practical and Necessary in Twenty-First Century Thinking

Bringing the strands together

My aim in writing this thesis was to attempt to gather all the various strands of Durie scholarship under one common heading and demonstrate that only then could one begin to understand what Durie sought to accomplish in his long life of service to God and mankind to the honour of the One and the welfare of the other. In this closing chapter, I wish to sum up my evidence, arguments and conclusions and thus to demonstrate clearly that especially today, Durie's reforms in pansophical learning and practical divinity are found to be realisable, practical and even necessary in twenty-first century thinking.

Durie more than a sum total of parts

In my first chapter, I explained my motives in choosing both my subject, John Durie, and my topic, his pansophical doctrine, giving a swift overview to be complemented and deepened in the following chapters. Durie was shown to be a greatly gifted man whose multi-abilities had moved most subject-minded writers to dwell on merely one or a few of his talents and thus presented a largely limited, in fact, false picture, of their subject, his calling and purpose. Nor did they demonstrate Durie's all-round competence in all branches of learning. In this manner Durie was not seen to be the pansophist he was. My aim was to show that Durie was far more than the sum total of all these facetted presentations.

In my second chapter, Durie's life and work were depicted so that the studious reader would begin to see how greatly useful Durie was to his age but in a way that the future would remain ever influenced by him and, indeed, ever grateful to him for a constructive and practical teaching that has withstood time's decay. The chapter, showed too, how Durie's contemporaries, on the whole, were not yet ripe for Durie's teaching. He always, however, emphasised that the path of learning was a life-long, indeed eternal enterprise. Following the example of his Mentor, Christ, whom Durie saw as the God-Only-Wise and Creator and Finisher of faith and understanding, Durie presented his pansophical ideas of practical divinity and universal learning in a self-offering way to the people of his generation who mostly could not received them.

Chapters Three and Four presented an overview of major works, mostly of an academic order, written over the centuries in appreciation of Durie's contribution to learning, be it practical or theoretical. Most of these concentrated on Durie's inter-church work and were to a high degree positive with a few exceptions due to strictly held denominational axioms which Durie, as a man of no specific church party, could not accept. A minority of the forty or so works discussed dealt with Durie's epistemology and gnosiology and it is only when we come to the writers of this century, especially Léchot, that we find a more marked interest in Durie's practical divinity. The historical trend, nevertheless, is that more modern writers are moving their focus from Durie as an ecumenist to Durie as a pansophist. However, this means that Durie's teaching is still being dissected rather than synthesised.

The fifth chapter shows one modern development in Durie scholarship which is most important in gaining an overview of Durie's comprehensive work. Durie pioneered the opening of doors for Jews to enter into dialogue with the government and churches of England leading to a resettlement. He strove to have Jews take part in British university, college and school education and influence British culture, trade and commerce. He felt that no pansophy was possible for the West without the addition of the skills of the East. However, though modern Jewish appreciation of Durie is high, their interest in Durie is still restricted, keeping more to special Jewish topics than to the wide scope of Durie's many other undertakings. So, too, modern Jewish scholarship tends to relate Durie to specific, but hardly representative, movements in Jewish European history. Durie wished to open Britain to all Jews, providing they became peaceful, law-abiding citizens no matter whether they were Orthodox , Caraites, Kabbalistic or Messianic.

Developing the filum Ariadnes

My intention in the sixth chapter was to describe Durie's method of preparing Europe for the advancement of universal learning. We looked at the success Durie experienced in varying degrees in his ecumenical activities, especially in Germany. This work was designed to bring the Protestant churches nearer together in order to form a basis for much wider irenic cooperation in the pursuit of knowledge and practical divinity. Without the one, Durie saw no hope for the other.

We thus looked closer at Durie's first undertakings at a time when his generation was full of hope that a new era would set in. His international upbringing with his diversity of studies and his quickly acquired skills in languages helped form his vision of inter- European solidarity in the search for all things spiritual and knowledgeable. He began to write of his vision of a *filum Ariadnes*, a God-given directive to link, bind and unite all branches of learning on a world-wide basis. If God was for it, who could be against it? At the commencement of Durie's work, King Charles and Archbishops Abbott, Laud, Ussher and Spotiswoode were all looking for some degree of Protestant unity. Sweden's Gustav II Adolf was claiming to be the Protestant Emperor whose task was to force out a conservative Papacy, antagonistic to reforms, Durie felt he should utilise this unique opportunity as a means of linking Protestant Britain with Protestant Europe to further in a peaceful manner the universal learning and practical divinity which he was quickly developing. At Conferences such as Leipzig, Heilbronn, Thorn, Hanau and Frankfurt, he believed he had found ample proof that Britain and Europe were now in a position to work together for a common education for the common good. We then find Hartlib and Durie striving to support promising contemporaries who will go with them like Comenius but, as we saw, those who succeeded him such as Oldenburg, Jablonski and Leibniz did not quite have the same synergistic mind as Durie. They did not succeed in putting his ideas into full practice as they did not rely on the same motivation as Durie in his application of *ordo inversus* because of the three-fold, not one-fold, platform on which they worked. Now from the early thirties Durie became not only the 'solvent of religious disunity' as Rae describes him but St Augustine's *solvitur ambulando*, collecting knowledge through walking with God's Word, through God's garden of Europe, using the knowledge of the one to gain entrance to the knowledge of the other. This gave rise to Durie's numerous publications on international universal learning and practical divinity.

Between 1631 and 1634, England received a number of official requests for help in Continental education based on the practical divinity lines put forward by Dury at their diets and conferences. Therefore, Durie published concrete plans in his *Touching the Worke Of Pacification* which came out in March, 1634, containing his instruction for educating Protestant ministers, who then were in charge of the bulk of teaching, to educate the world. In his *A Motion Tending to the Public Good* of 1642, Durie worked out a further agenda, proclaiming an education for all, irrespective of gender, age or social status. It was to be an education for the needs of the whole man to serve the needs of the entire society, combining the spiritual with the physical. Practical Durie also added how to organise institutions giving such instruction and provide public lecture halls for the further education of the employed populace. His emphasis here was more on means and methods of learning and the instruction of parents and employers so that they might better instruct those in their care. Durie believed that all society must be instructed at the same time otherwise one sector would not be able to work with the other. True pansophy to Durie is not merely a combination of the various 'sciences' but a consolidation of all who are able to learn.

Next, Durie concerns himself with the curriculum necessary for universal learning in its religious, linguistic and scientific aspects. His new thrust in assisting learners of all ages to organise, synergise and apply their newly-gained knowledge demands a thorough-going reorganisation of the contemporary school system, including its methodology and its media.

Durie and Comenius: Two different approaches to universal learning

Chapter Seven was a most necessary chapter in evaluating the scope of Durie's work as hitherto, Jan Amos Comenius has been ranked as the one who most perfected the teaching of panoply in the educative system. A comparison with Durie was thus inevitable. So, too, though both men on the surface had roughly the same aims and ambitions, research into Comenius' life and work has been immense over the years and other candidates for the same or even greater fame have been quite elbowed out through neglect. The amount of elementary, secondary and grammar schools, colleges and universities carrying Comenius' name is enormous, thus emphasising Comenius' acceptance in modern education as second to none. Thus, Durie scholars have had a difficult time rescuing their subject from under Comenius' shadow where many believed he stood from the sixteen-twenties on. By using Durie's, Hartlib's and Comenius' own words, I have striven to show that such early influence is merely speculative and when we first read of a concrete encounter between the two men, it is the Bohemian who is soliciting assistance from the Scotsman. Both men, of course, did not stand alone but had their helpers and helpers' helpers. The difference was that Hartlib and the societies close to the Durie circle served as agents publishing the works of Durie's own genius whereas Comenius had to rely on expert help to fill the many breeches in his own education, especially in the sciences. Comenius emphasised the human reaching out for the divine, whereas Durie saw divinity upholding humanity. Of the two, Durie was more the comprehensive practitioner and the selfless realist in his quest for human good. Furthermore, Comenius never succeeded in formulating a true spiritual and intellectual panoply embracing all disciplines, synergising them from the start, as did Durie, and though both men emphasise the rationality of man, Comenius always saw this as a third column on which to build his ideas alongside God's Word and God's creation. Durie was far more Theo-centric, indeed Christo-centric, in his ideas, not wishing to exclude any part of knowledge in the great Oneness of universal learning. Comenius' source of knowledge based on three pillars cannot be seen as a synergistic, pansophical wisdom. Durie's calling was not to trace unity back to disunity but lead disunity back to unity of mind, thought, deeds and actions.

The idea that former scholars have put forward regarding the *Foedus Fraternum* between Hartlib, Durie and Comenius as being ample proof of Comenius' influence on the two other signatories has proved to be without substantial evidence. So, too, have the many speculations concerning the extent of Comenius' contributions to a country from whom he wished to learn rather than whom he wished to teach. Indeed modern writers such as Young maintain that Comenius was bullied into visiting England by Hartlib, not expecting to stay there for more than a few days and had no idea why he was being called there at all and what his role was supposed to be.[561] Moreover, Comenius told Hartlib that through his being invited to England, Hartlib had hindered Comenius from pursuing his quest for a pansophy. Comenius' later conviction that he was officially called to England by Parliament is seen to be without foundation, apart from it being the wish of preacher John Gauden. Young, too, also repeatedly hints at the fact that Comenius' contact with Durie and Hartlib was one of being taught, rather than one who taught.[562] The findings of this thesis, too, point in this direction. Comenius' breaking of the pact with his friends proved their meeting in England to have been a mutual disappointment. It certainly brought nothing new for Durie and though Comenius profited from it ideawise, he was highly dissatisfied with the degree of that profit.

---

[561] *Faith, Medical Alchemy and Natural Philosophy*, pp. 127-130.
[562] See Chapter Four, Panaceas of the Soul: Comenius and the Dream of Universal Knowledge in his *Faith, Medical Alchemy and Natural Philosophy*.

Durie the information manager

Moving on to Chapter Eight, we are given a detailed analysis of Durie's method of information management and knowledge engineering based on textual work, taking into consideration the pros and cons of different methods. The one Durie favours is simply retracing the stages, or footsteps, as he prefers to call them, in a writer's understanding or thinking, as he progresses in his argumentation, thus striving to think a writer's thoughts after him. Here, Durie is developing modern methods of psychological analysis but amalgamating them into his complete method of amassing knowledge to combine and use it with what has been previously learned, demonstrating that the method of ascertaining spiritual, sensual and bodily knowledge is one and the same. No step is to be taken until each step before has been perfectly understood. For Durie, there could be no existentialistic leap in the dark in the progress of learning as this would be a leap away from existence which provides knowledge. The way is to work from the simple to the complex, retracing one's steps to find out what went wrong if one can go no further.

In 1640, Durie wrote his *A Method of Meditation*, explaining more meticulously each step in the way to right, productive thinking. The same rules applied to the sensual should be applied to the rational and also the spiritual. However the first two should not overbalance the third and the spiritual without the rational and sensual cannot be utilized for the common good. Faith without works is void. The aims of all acts of the mind should be directed back to an Edenic perfection which finds man in union with God, exercising God's stewardship on earth. Thus the Paradise Lost will become a Paradise Regained, first in the Church and then, through the Church, to the world.

Here, again, Comenius' ideas as expressed in his *A Reformation of Schools*, which Hartlib brought out rather pre-maturely in 1642, are contrasted with those of Bacon and Durie. Comenius' work lacks didactic methodology in its basic theories and his views of teaching Latin so that the transfer of training can be applied to all venues lacks close argumentation. For Durie, all transfer of training is there where the balance of the sensual, rational and spiritual is kept and applied. The proof of the pudding is always in the eating. One's ultimate aim in education is not to propose premises and hypotheses but to reach a position whereby one can apply conclusions.

Durie had the rather embarrassing task of improving on great Grosseteste's method of text analysis. What he misses in Grosseteste is an orderly 'concatenation of true thoughts' with simple axioms being joined together in right order without admitting preconceptions and a too speedily coming to conclusions. He then concerns himself with analysing the many different analytical methods and to what extent their inter-dependency may be gauged. If analysis does not lead to synthesis, the methods are impractical and thus wrong.

After 1647, we find that Durie has found his 'Emile' and is coaching a young man who is appropriately called 'Smart' in how to study. First by considering a combination of languages with Hebrew and Greek, the sciences, world history and suitable literature before going on to take catechetical, practical and polemic courses, Smart is being prepared for a life of useful study and service. Above all, he must learn to understand the Scriptures aright. Then Durie covers the enormous importance of librarians and libraries to a student which takes us on to Duries own library reforms as outlined in his *Reformed Librarie-Keeper* and which are mentioned passim in so many other works. Here Durie is shown to be at the cutting edge of modern reforms in library and information management. Rayward's and Hapke's clear message is that we must get back to Durie's *filum Ariadnes* and 'Grab the thread'.

The duty of the Christian state to universalise learning

Chapter Nine on the setting up of A Parliamentary Agency for the Advancement of Learning refers to Durie's perhaps most ambitious project and describes the struggle Durie and Hartlib had through almost forty years of campaigning to persuade the state to take the initiative in fostering a universal education leading to qualifications in all trades and professions whether civil, ecclesiastical, governmental or in the public services. This occupational training, based on a thorough pansophic educational background, must be irrespective of social background and gender. Here, Durie was quite aware that money and birth still played a major role in choosing those who should lead the nation but argued that everyone should be given the same chance to climb the careers' ladder. All must be educated as far as their abilities go for the sake of the common good of all.

Durie goes into meticulous detail concerning how such an agency should be staffed, organised and financed and laid out plans for every single department. By touching the conscience of the government and showing them their responsibilities, Durie hoped to get things going. He was no stranger to their ways and enjoyed great respect in government circles so there were always people in high places ready to listen to him. Durie thus is careful to present the political advantages of his programme. Indeed, in his demands for an agency of learning with its various 'Addresses' of communication and accommodation, Durie was laying a foundation that no man had ever laid before or has laid since. Of course, now school councils, parent-teacher associations, school governors, and joint training courses, work-shops and conferences for all those connected with schools and colleges are part of our every day educational system, though years of participation in these organisations have shown this writer that we are still far from Durie's 'norms'. So, too, the partnership that Durie envisaged between governmental departments and private donors is still hard to realise in state school life.

Durie also spent much time in his works on his planned agency in warning against false reforms and pitfalls in the current views of education in his day, in his effort to make teaching 'free, ingenious and delightful'. So, too, Durie's demand for a national curriculum for the advancement of learning was a truly pioneering idea as also was his plans to reform each school grade from the elementary school to the universities. The latter gave Durie the most resistance, arguing that such a learning as Durie planned for all was for a mature elite and not for any Tom, Dick or Harry.

At last, however, Durie had to realise that he could not pull Britain with him. As so often happened in Durie's life, just when a goal seemed certain to be reached, something unexpected happened to shatter his hopes, mostly in the death of a supporter or sponsor such as Spence, Frederick V or Gustav Adolf. This time it was Cromwell. Just when the Protector had promised to back Durie's agency on a permanent basis through Parliament, and provide the necessary funds for maintaining it, Cromwell departed from this life. No one, who was in a position to finance it, was interested in Durie's project thereafter.

Practical Divinity, the crown of human learning

Chapter Ten deals with Durie's overall view of practical divinity. By the end of the forties, Durie realised that Ussher and other Puritans such as Gouge and Goodwin who had backed him in the early thirties would never be in a position to produce the definitive work they had pledged themselves to undertake. He thus collected together ideas that he had been advocating for some twenty-five years and produced his *Summarie Platform* and *Earnest Breathings*. His aim was to teach that a practical divinity is the whole doctrine of the life of godliness in covenant with God. Durie's covenant teaching was, however, radically different to the politico-religious teaching of the Presbyterians who separated a Covenant of Works from a Covenant of Grace. They presented these covenants as if they were a bilateral deal between England's governing parties, and God. Then they used this self-drawn-up covenant as a legal yoke to govern the people. The covenant which Durie taught showed the depths of man's fall and the height of his ascension in Christ which was entirely a covenant of grace and solely an act of the Godhead to redeem man. This was the doctrine of the English Reformers before it was radically split up and re-organised by Presbyterian politico-religious strategy to bind the people; their Solemn League and Covenant being, in fact, a Covenant of Works only.

Durie believed that neither the State, nor the Church nor the people were in a position to covenant with God in this way, so any covenant which could be of saving effect must be God's initiative alone. Indeed, Durie saw the Scriptures as teaching that the covenant was signed and sealed in Heaven without human help or interference. In explaining what the precognitions (or premises), the principles and parts of practical divinity are, Durie always starts with the Being of God and His Word and then moves on to man's responsibility to God and his fellow men. In these two books, he outlines man's covenant duties as God's stewards on earth to receive and pass on the offer of grace covenanted between the Father, Son and Holy Spirit on man's behalf. Its message was no less than Paradise Regained. Appropriating this gift of grace is the foundation of wisdom which provides a life in fellowship with the all-knowing God in the everyday life of a believer in what ever profession, trade or calling he might be preparing himself for or already following.

Thus, the duty of the church, school and government is to confirm the covenant of grace in the life of the nation which entails a co-operation between all parties. The educational establishments must therefore cater for as many courses as are necessary to prepare people for every honest profession in society by first providing a common education in universal learning and then specialising on that basis. There can thus be no doctor, scientist or tradesman who is not motivated in his occupation by a universal learning leading for the common good as it needs to be exercised in his particular profession. Such professions, however, would change as they became more and more based on a synergising of knowledge and methods of its practical application. Durie, however, insisted that no pupil or student should be pressurised into performing any practice of any knowledge against his or her conscience and the curriculum should be so organised that cases of conscience are respected. Each should be educated so that the candidate could freely participate in the tuition and progress into an occupation which is according to his conscience and choice. As a modern teacher, I realise with pain that we have not yet reached Durie's aim. Young girls are still compelled to take part in public or co-ed sports and swimming against their conscience and culture and, indeed, faith. Female heads must not be covered in class, not even with a beret, and both boys and girls are forced into one school form or another against their own wills or the wills of their parents. Medicine students are compelled to cut out the fruit of the womb, though this is viewed as murder by many of them. These are but a few of the cases of conscience ignored in modern education. For all such cases, Durie foresaw staff-meetings working out solutions to these problems. We might argue that times were different then, forgetting that there were Jews and Turks with their families in England at that time who also needed education, and most of Durie's solutions were plain common sense.

So Durie demands a complete reformation of schooling whereby the schools are considered as associations or societies in themselves. Their task is not to reflect society but to reform it. In all this, Durie speaks of 'children' rather than boys and girls. He believed in equal aims for all, though obviously they might take on different roles in society, made less different due to a common educational background of practical divinity and universal learning. Durie also left room for extra-curricular activities both for pupils and staff, encouraging hobbies, especially music, art and sport. The school should be, above all, a team in which each teacher or pupil felt he or she could rely on all.

Nothing is therefore to be taught which is not profitable to mankind and blind-alley scholarship is to be rejected. No education should be designed for individual gain or renown. Scientific enquiry must be entirely free and knowledge must be taught as a watch with integrating wheels, all serving a function and not as a lexicon which gives data in isolation. All must be taught along lines of sense, experience and reason and rules of learning must be geared to the ordinary degree of the pupils' natural capacities. Thus the teacher must have an intimate and comprehensive understanding of each pupil to be cared for. Next, Durie deals with the level of learning thought acceptable and necessary for each age and ability group and the skills to be taught. Lessons are not subject centred but centred on what duties in society the child is old enough, mature enough and has the capacities and motivation to perform.

In his *Supplement*, Durie deals with misunderstandings caused by his Reformed School, concerning, for example, the role of the universities in education. All these proposals Durie placed before the Saints' Parliament in 1653 but they did not approve of the way Durie thought a 'saint' should live and broke up in strife and confusion.

In the section on advice about studies, Durie gives his detailed conception of what a 'rounded off' education entails spending almost as much space on how things should not be done as how things should be done. Here, Durie castigates the lack of adequate training in professional and practical knowledge in England which does not prepare a child for future employment. He therefore pleads for a fundamentally different training for teachers, arguing that what use is a school form without reformed teachers and what use are the best school books if the teachers cannot use them? His long list of what he expects of the 'normal' school teacher would embarrass most of us who are in that profession. Durie's ideals for a basic 'mechanical' education go beyond what is classified as 'academic' today and his 'noble schools' were truly designed for world leaders. Perhaps this is why Durie called them 'The Schools of the Prophets'. His plans for teacher training colleges were fulfilled two centuries later and his trade schools, commercial colleges and institutes for further education have been realised in the last seventy-five years or so.

Durie insisted that the matter was so urgent that his reforms must start at once. No data must be appropriated in theory alone and all learned truths must be seen as objects of action. In comparing practical divinity with case divinity, Durie condemns the latter as piecemeal and patchwork learning with a bundle of incoherent parts which must not be mistaken for true learning. Here, in Durie's eyes, was the weak spot or failure of Hartlib's and Comenius' concepts. Happily, such weak spots are being gradually eliminated from our educational system, but like Rayward, we must look back to Durie to see how it ought to be done.

The voice of the synergistic pansophist John Durie speaks loudly today

That Durie's pansophic plans found little resonance in his own times, does not mean that he was a mere dreamer and dilettante as claimed even in some academic works. Durie's views found backing in the sporadically held Parliaments of England at least twice and his ideas for a governmental Ministry of Education still hold good. Far from being an enthusiast and theorist only, Durie's major aim was utility. He taught that if a theory is not demonstrably practicable, it must be rejected. Even if one comes up with a comprehensive plan to bring peace, prosperity, universal learning and millennial-like conditions to the earth; if there is no practical experience to build on and no one takes concrete steps to put such learning into practice, then this idea is a mere pipe-dream or a brown study. Thus, throughout the years, there has always been a band of faithful co-visionaries composed of irenists, educators, church historians, politicians, scientists and librarians who have seen Durie's achievements as a lamp to lighten and enlighten future times.

No contemporary of Durie's really shared his deep and wide understanding of synergistic pansophy and none of the other great pansophists in Britain or Continental Europe came up to his standards and methods of implementation in the following two centuries. He was a pioneer in seeing knowledge as a totality of realism, rationality and spirituality. However, Durie's ideas certainly did not die with his own death. As this thesis has shown, numerous scholars, some on the cutting-edge of Durie scholarship, have seen their subject as being a man before his times, that is a man for future times, when scholars and practitioners would be ready and able to appropriate his ideas. Even in the century following Durie's death, his ideas were eagerly taken over and made part of the ecclesiastical and educational theories of 18th century thinkers such as Mosheim, Jablonski, Leibniz and Lessing, though not with such single-mindedness, intensity, and inclusiveness. Since then, as shown in my overview of Durie scholarship, Durie's ideas and endeavours have outlived the passing challenges of the centuries and are coming into maturity in modern scholarship. This is because, with the passing of time, Durie's visions have become more and more relevant to modern theological, ecclesiological, political and scientific need. Durie's axioms, propositions, precepts and conclusions are being accepted today in a measure that perhaps only he envisaged. So, too, the present generation is adequately equipped to see the need for them and it has the ability, organisational capacities and technology to put them into practice in consolidated, world-wide action. Thus we find today, conferences being held in places as far apart as Israel's Jerusalem and England's Oxford centred in the relevance of Durie's teachings to our modern world. Typical of these modern studies are the works of some fifteen modern Jewish scholars, many of them named in this thesis, and the large circle of international scholars attached to St. Anne's, Oxford of whom Howard Hotson, Professor of Early Modern Intellectual History, Mark Greengrass and Pierre-Oliver Léchot are very productive examples. The selected number of modern publications listed in my bibliography, shows how numerous scholars are reassessing Durie's contribution to modern thought most positively. It is interesting to note how so many histories of learning technologies, such as the works of Professors Bertram Bruce[563] and W. Boyd Rayward, deal with Durie not only as the founder of the modern library but also as the founder of information processing and management. Indeed, whilst browsing the web during my writing of these last few sentences, I discovered an attractive, colourful 37 page PDF brochure published by a consortium of information managers who profess to be walking in the footsteps of John Durie, presented as the first man to describe the role of the information manager.[564]

In short, Durie is no longer seen as an idealist visionary, gazing centuries ahead, striving to discern the future by some special revelation of God. He was, indeed, a seer who trusted infinitely in the Maker, Coordinator and Synergist of all things, but with the difference that he did not imagine he was standing centuries before the realisation of his own thoughts but that he believed he was putting them into practice day by day in his own time. Throughout his self-offering life, he was a man with a slakeless thirst for knowledge and reform, ever learning and ever passing on what he had learnt for the common good of all. He was thus not only a man of his times but a man for all times. In this way, he was highly suited to develop a better and more comprehensive means of furthering church unity and universal learning than the *status quo* methods of his day. One might subjectively quarrel with Durie's 'naivety' in believing, but, objectively speaking, results count. One cannot, as a pastor, politician, scientist, employer of men and teacher, quarrel with the outcome of Durie's work which was entirely for the welfare of all men and the positive development of mankind.

Above all, Durie's conception of synergism is a leading thought in today's culture, commerce and science. In recent years, there has been an enormous synergising of subject teaching, information processing, healthcare; agro-chemistry, bio-science, nanotechnology, energy production, toxicology, medicine, surgery and mechatronics besides inter-church cooperation and amalgamation in the training of workers for the public good. Durie's 'properly rounded off academic education' is certainly proving the mother of modern industry and science. So, too, his dream of such a comprehensive, life-long education for males and females, young and old, rich and poor is certainly within the imagination if not the planning of modern education and employment thinkers.

Durie's ideas of inter-disciplinary learning and the merging of one science with another have really caught on to day. Previously educationalists

---

[563] See his Constructing a Once-And-Future History of Learning Technologies, in *The Journal of Adolescent and Adult Literacy* and other works.

[564] Catalogue.pearsoned.co.uk/assets/hip/gb/hip_gb_pearsonhighered/sa...

such as Comenius, Kinner, Klähr, Sander Scougal, Rae, Forster Watson and Webster have all witnessed to the age-less potentials in Durie's system. Today, Durie's educational conceptions are widely accepted in modern education. Leading educationalists such as Professor John White, of the Institute of Education, University of London, in his critical review of the UK government's Schools White Paper *The Importance of Teaching* of November 2010, claims that we have now at last come to 'A properly rounded academic education' in 'the post-Ramic age', and names Durie as a pioneer of this success.[565] As such modern studies are providing the foundations for most present-day educational schemes; we find their fruits in all walks of life and in the curricula of all training courses whether academic, manual, social or ecclesiastical. Durie's synergising reforms are appreciated today in all branches of modern human endeavours especially in education and tele-communications which form the basis of most modern knowledge. The World-Wide Web, Face-Book, tele-communications, cyber-space, and synergisation in all branches of science and education were all within the scope of Durie's practical vision of the future. Nothing which is developing in these fields nowadays would have surprised him. He would only have said, 'I told you so'. Google's internet slogans and aims make this obvious. Their sites claim that 'Google's mission is to organize the world's information and to make it universally accessible and useful. Google Book Search helps readers discover the world's books while helping authors and publishers reach new audiences.' This is nothing less, but also nothing more, than Durie's aims developed through his Agency for Universal Correspondence and Learning.

Concluding thoughts on Durie's synergised universal learning

One can therefore conclude that although there is still no world-wide synthesising of Christian doctrines, exegesis, traditions, worship, culture and science along the Biblical path to pansophy as pioneered by Durie, our modern age is certainly approaching such a situation. Durie's acceptance in the realms of education, library management, tele-communications, system integration and synergised learning is now enormous. It was Durie's plans to merge all branches of thinking, including all known knowledge be it religious, scientific, economic, educational, social or whatever for the benefit of all ages, ranks and orders, which was not clearly understood by Durie's contemporaries.

---

[565] A critical review of the UK government's November 2010 Schools White Paper *The Importance of Teaching*.

Nowadays, synthesised thinking is pervading society now in leaps and bounds. We now know that even two formerly considered opposites can be merged to make them more than doubly useful. Knowledge was always one and beneficial until human theologians, philosophers and scientists began to destroy it by their artificial, dissecting logic. They were like the proverbial clockmaker who thought by dismantling a complicated clock, he could make several new ones out of the wreck. Dissecting is merely another name for either killing or destroying. Today, even in toxic poisons, we know that two substances, formerly treated as killers, when merged, can save life or that two medicines when applied together have a more positive, total effect than when applied in separate, subsequent doses. In the Education & Reference Questions and Answers Web (EduQnA), downloaded in February, 2011, a request was aired for an antibiotic which exhibited the phenomenon of synergism. The answer given was that the two antibiotics sulfamethoxazole and trimethoprim can be synergised and synthesised and work two ways when thus combined. They work synergetically together by blocking a bacterial synthesis of nucleic acids and proteins essential to the growth of many bacteria judged to be harmful. The negative is thus made positive by synthesis.

One of the greatest successes of Durie in his campaign for a comprehensive education was that the Royal Society took up Durie's reasons for admitting the study of science into basic school education, not leaving it as Oxford told Durie, for mature academics as an intellectual pursuit *in vitro*. Now, at least, in the twenty-first century, there is talk of synthesis and synergism in all branches of learning, be it in the natural sciences; communication science; library science; the arts; medicine; engineering; ecology; education or the Public Services. In recent years, there has been an enormous synergising going on in health-care; agro-chemistry and bio-science. Furthermore, Durie's name is often associated with many of these reforms, though the amount of synergising still does not come up to Durie's vision. Durie teaches in his books on practical divinity that the total effects of universal learning is greater when applied inter-disciplinary than the sum total of effects applied in separate 'subject' teaching. This is especially so when one bears in mind Durie's basic conviction that universal learning points to the Creator and Giver of all knowledge and He is the alpha and omega within whom all knowledge finds its rightful place.

We find the need for inter-disciplinary work emphasised especially in the training of scientists, doctors and teachers. However, often nothing more is meant by the terms 'synthesis' and 'synergism' than either one branch of learning being considered in conjunction with those closely allied to it, or to describe one branch of learning which can best be applied practically when combined with another. A case in point here, as the Japanese have shown us during the past decades, is mechanical engineering combined with electronic engineering, which has obviously a wider practical use. Here, however, though a measure of synthesis has been gained, no true pansophical approach was even targeted. Nevertheless, even this is a quantum leap from the understanding of knowledge-engineering of yesteryear which did not follow such pioneersa as John Durie. More recent research in this field comes nearer to the Durie goal as illustrated by a paper entitled *Mechatronics Education – Synergising Integration of New Paradigm for Engineering Education* presented at the August 2010 National Congress of Mechanical Engineering at Campina Grande, Brazil. In this paper, illustrated by numerous power-point type diagrams, a post-graduate study group at the Federal University of Rio de Janeiro[566] seek to prove from economical needs and epistemological and ontological experience, that 'a combination of power electronics and microcontrollers in mechanical systems' is practicable and that knowledge should be pooled in various areas such as mechanics, electronics, computing and control which, when integrated make possible, 'the generation of simple, economical, reliable and versatile systems.' This is a step in the right direction, though Durie was against setting up particular paradigms because of their inward-looking nature and the fact that they defined limits in usage to a particular discipline only. Here, however, the fact that the South American scientists work from empiricism, epistemology and ontology rather than from abstract logic would have pleased Durie. That the scientists do not clearly define their epistemological and ontological grounds of knowledge before embarking on their trial-and-error experimentation would suggest that the 'philosophical' approach they speak of is still separate from their common sense of adding two and two together (mechanics and electronics) in a workable, utility way, thus creating *Mechatronics*.

Elsewhere, research into Environmental Science as a synergism of Information Technology, Biotechnology, Nanotechnology and Energy, as carried out at present in the Department of Physics and Materials Science at the University of Hong Kong here researchers are looking into what they call the 'ubiquitous factors' in each formerly supposed 'branch' of knowledge and are speaking of this as a 'frontier challenge'.[567] Again, this is merely thinking Durie's thoughts after him.

---

[566] Omar Legerke; Max Suell Dutra and Magda J. M. Tavera
[567] See University and Department websites.

Dr Roger A. Rosenblatt of the University Of Washington School Of Medicine writes in *Public Health Reports*[568] on the subject of Synergism in Medical Education and Service: He emphasises the need to train medical students in an ordinary, every-day community, caring for their needs instead of working in 'splendid isolation' on a university campus. This is quite according to Durie's ideal; he criticised universities for being ivory towers of learning and doing no direct good to the communities which they were supposed to be leading. For Rosenblatt, all curricula must be organised according to the medical needs of the particular community under their care. So, too, Rosenblatt is now replacing what can only be called factory medicine and specialist-only hospitalisation with the old, well-proven, family medicine and placing local medical care in the hands of doctors with a wider medical background and comprehensive, interdisciplinary background knowledge. Rosenblatt is bent on a recruiting programme which draws idealists and those who truly feel called to serve mankind rather than those who are in the profession for pecuniary interests. Rosenblatt concludes:

> 'Clearly, no one program operating in a vacuum would have had the impact of a combined assault from different but compatible directions. Synergy between medical education and those programs that deploy the resources which medical education creates is fundamental to bringing care to the underserved.'

Nor is Durie's constant complaint in the seventeenth century that 'one thing is still needed' in the 'combined assault' against faulty learning true, in general, of modern education. We occasionally hear from diverse media and religious, political, social, educational and juristic schools of thought that we live in a secular world which leaves God out of the gnosiological process. Such a removal from God is easier said than done. Our modern society, be it eastern or western, cannot be understood without the advancement of Christianity and the other great religions of the world, which have gone hand-in-hand with national and international reforms in all walks of life. In the history of mankind, there have been setbacks through tyranny, wars, revolutions, anarchy, poverty, hunger and drought. Nevertheless, these setbacks have left in their wake a deeper desire for world unity and a wish to recreate an Eden out of a ruined society. Surely the development of the United States of America and our own European Union, foreseen by our sixteenth century Reformers, testifies to this. Especially in

---

[568] January-February 1980, vol. 95, No. 1, pp. 12-15.

the education of mankind, Durie's Christian Pansophy of understanding all knowledge has been, and still is, supported by leading theologians, scientists, philosophers and men and women of letters who transmit, organise, engineer and develop knowledge. Here Christian mind-mappers, knowledge extenders and coordinators such as Alcuin, Aquinas, Albert the Great, Ockam, Charlton, Bullinger, Gessner, Mulcaster, Vives, de la Salle, Durie, Hartlib, Pell, Comenius, Cowper, Wesley, Kuyper, Pestalozzi, Fröbel and Sayers have been corner stones and bulwarks in reforming both spiritual and material education.

Though Durie would probably not have agreed with Minister of Education David Colart's view that Christian education is irreconcilable with a state school system, he would have agreed with his affirmation in his opening speech at the Christian Education Conference held at Gateway School, Harare, 2009 that, 'Real science is not only compatible with Christianity, but is still held by many educationalists, theologians, politicians, sociologists, scientists and men of letters world-wide.' Indeed whilst arguing that science and religion were natural allies and that 'good religion needs good science', Colart said:

> 'Christian education has a unique advantage over secular. It is based on the belief that God has revealed himself to humanity in two books. The first is His revelation in history and in the Person of His Son, which is found in the written record (the Bible); and the second is His revelation of Himself in the record of nature (Romans 1:20).'

Colart himself enjoyed a very comprehensive education but later specialised in applied law, not science, using his legal knowledge as a mediator of peace between disputing, and even warring, parties. One modern scientist of world fame however, who agreed with Colart concerning the origins of modern science and the goals of education was James H. H. Merriman (1915-1997). Trained by Sir Edward Victor Appleton[569] as a war-time communications expert, Merriman became Engineer-In-Chief and Senior Director of Engineering of British Telecom and occupied a chair as Professor of Electronic Science and Telecommunications at Strathclyde. Other posts he held were: Member of the Council of the Imperial College; President of the Institution of Electrical Engineers, Director of the Organisation and Methods Department at Britain's Treasury and Member of the Council

---

[569] (1892-1965). A scientist from Bradford, Yorkshire who gained the Nobel Prize for discoveries leading to the invention of radar. A boyhood hero of this writer who attended Appelton's old school, Hanson Grammar School, where my ideas of universal learning were first cultivated.

of the Spurgeon Theological Seminary. A man with the Christian ideals of a Durie, he deplored in a Hunter Memorial Lecture the fragmentation of religion and knowledge going on in modern church life, education and science, quoting Scotsman Henry Francis Lyte's hymn-line 'change and decay in all around I see'. In a 1969 Faraday Lecture, Merriman presented his plans for instant inter-communication through optical fibres (notice the *filum Ariadnes* again!). He planned think-tank computers to relay sight, sound, voices and music from all over the world, instantly and perpetually. In 1982, Merriman was asked to give his reason for his Pansophic, universal mentality in a film made by the Institution of Electrical Engineers. Without hesitation, the Christian universal thinker said, "It is the fear of the Lord and the concern for his creation that is the beginning of wisdom'. Thus the utility of Durie's practical divinity leading to universal, pansophic learning survives and even prospers today as truly divine knowledge begins to cover the earth as the waters cover the sea.

Appendix

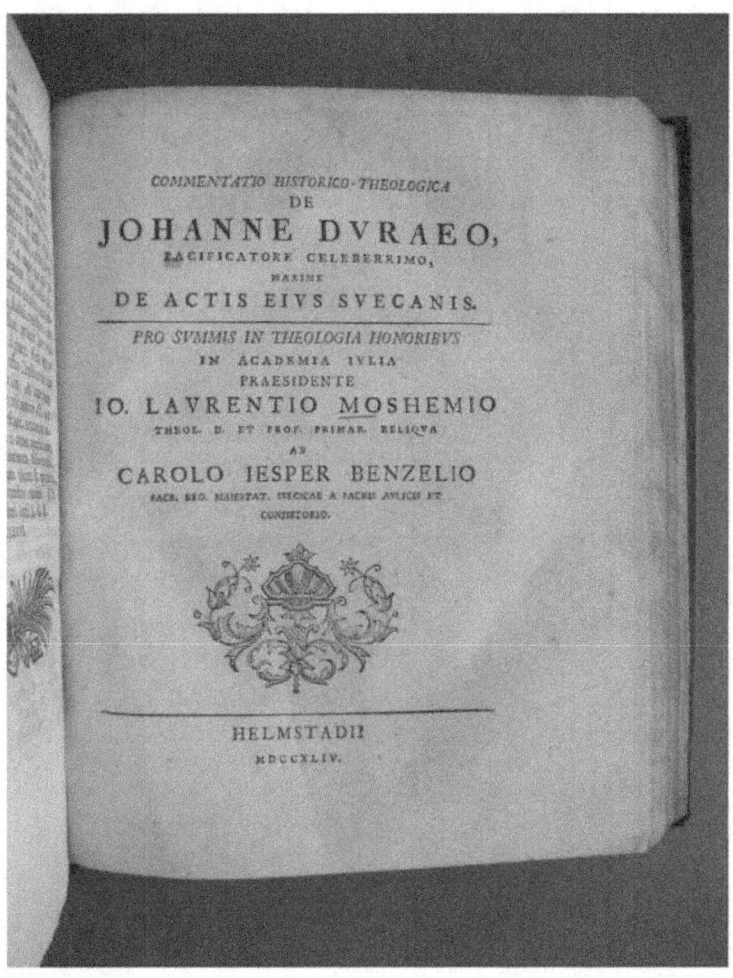

Courtesy of the Codrington Library, Oxford

DISSERTATIO HISTORICO - THEOLOGICA
DE
JOHANNE DVRAEO,
PACIFICATORE CELEBERRIMO,
MAXIME
DE ACTIS EIVS SVECANIS.

QVAM
CONSENSV VENERANDAE FACVLTATIS THEOLOGICAE
IN ILLVSTRI ACADEMIA IVLIA
PRAESIDENTE
MAGNIFICO PRORECTORE
IO. LAVRENTIO MOSHEMIO
S. S. THEOL. D. ET PROF. PRIMARIO, COLLEGIIQVE THEOL. SENIORE
SEREN. DVC. BRVNSV. ET LVNEB A CONSILIIS CONSISTOR ET ECCLES.
ABBATE MONASTER. VALLIS S. MARIAE ET LAPIDIS S MICHAELIS,
SCHOLARVM IN TERRIS GVELPHICIS EPHORO GENERALI,
ORDINIS SVI H. T. DECANO
PATRONO AC HOSPITE SVO OMNI HONORIS
CVLTV PROSEQVENDO
PRO
SVMMIS IN THEOLOGIA HONORIBVS
CONSEQVENDIS
IN IVLEO MAIORI
HORIS ANTE ET POMERIDIANIS CONSVETIS
D. XXIX. M. MAII MDCCXLIV.
PVBLICAE CENSVRAE SVBIICIET
CAROLVS IESPER BENZELIVS
SACR. REG. MAIEAT. SVECICAE A SACRIS AVLICIS ET
CONSISTORIO.

HELMSTADII
TYPIS PAVLI DIETERICI SCHNORRII
ACAD. TYPOGR.

Courtesy of the Herzog August Bibliothek

Appendix

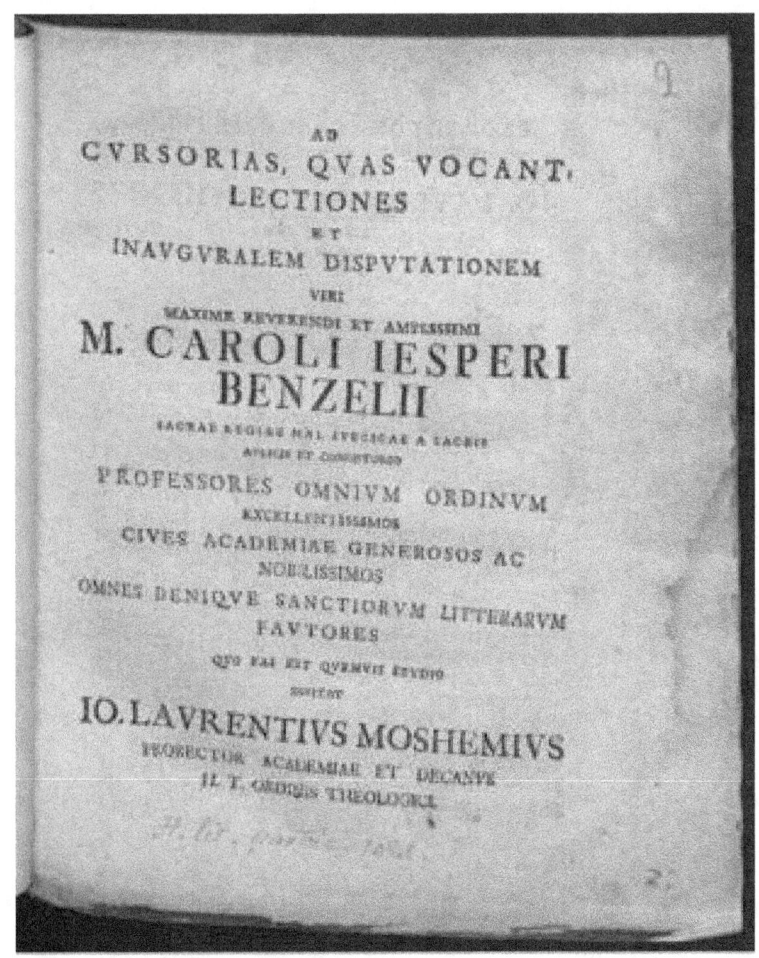

Title-page concerning Benzelius' inaugural Disputation

Bibliography

The major dated works of John Durie, including his reports and minutes used for this thesis in chronological order:

1618: *Exhortationis Summa; qvam pro consensu constituendo per Reformatas Ecclesias per Europam edidit pius qvidam Theologus nomine Fratrum Evangelicæ Professionis in Regno Poloniæ.* Ref: 20/11/1A-14B, HP.

1628: *Le Tres humble Supplication d'un vray Fidele presentee Au tresillustre & trespuissant Prince **Gustavus Adolphus** Par la grace de Dieu Roy des Swedois des Goths & des Wandales. Grand Duc de Finlande; Duc d'Esthone & de Carele & Seigneur d'Ingre etcæt: pour obtenir Aide & Assistance necessaire en temps opportun Afin de recercher[altered] & restablir la Paix Ecclesiastique parmi les Eglises Evangeliques a la gloire de Dieu & l'auancement du Salut de tous Chrestiens. Matth. 5. v. 9,* Ref: 19/9/1A-&B, HP.

1628: *De summa Curae Paedagogica seu Spirituali Agricultura*, undated but given the date 1628 by Turnbull, 1/27/1A-6B, HP.

1628: *Some Extracts of Mr Duries Letters concerning his Treatyse of education.* **Ref:** 1/12/1A-4B, HP. (This unfinished treatise gave rise to Durie's *De Summa Curae Paedagogica* and *De Morum Puerilium Disciplina*).

1631: *An Extract, out of the Nationall Synode, held by the Churches of France, at Charaton, in September, 1631*, undated. Shelfmark B237 Linc, pp. 259-260, Bod L, Special Collections.

1631?: *Brevis Informatio, De vero Scopo & Mediis propriis quibus Concordiam Euangelicam apud Ecclesias Protestantes prosequitur Johannes Duraeus.* Undated but contents suggest a very early date. HStA, 22a1, Nr. 10, Mappe 1.

1631: *Brevis Discursus De ista Conciliatione Religionum quæ instituta fuit Lipsiæ Anno 1631 Mense Martio inter Theologos Saxonicos & Brandenburgicos itemque Hassiacos,* Ref: 17/14/1/1A-16B, HP.

1631: *Colloquium Lipsiae habitum inter utriusque partis Theologos ad Consensum in Doctrina contestandum: cui subjungitur decretum ordinum Euangelicorum ad Concordiae Conatum promovendum & praemittitur extractum ex Epistola D. Joh, Bergii, ad Duraeum de Colloquii Instituti scopo & usu.* In *Irenicorum Tractatum, Prodromus*, VB 292, HStA.

1631: *Colloquium Lipsiae habitum anno 1631. Inter Lutheranos & Reformartos Theologos de reconciliandis Euangelicorum in Germania diffidiis.* Signed by J. Bergius, J. Crocius and T. Neuberger. In *Irenicorum Tractatum, Prodromus*, VB 292, HStA.

1631: *Extractum ex Epistola D. Dris. Joh Bergii ad Joh. Duraeum, qua cum Colloquii Lipsiae habiti Apographhum ei misit, Angliae Praesulibus & Theologis communicandum.* In *Irenicorum Tractatum, Prodromus*, VB 292, HStA.

1631: *Summa Copiæ Conventius habiti inter Theologos Protestantes Lipsiæ Mensi Martio Anno 1631. Ab uná Parte erant Doctores Lutherani Dr. Matthias Hoe Elect: Sax: Primarius Concionator Aulicus. Dr. Polycarpus Leiserus Superintendens et Th: Professor primarius Lipsiæ Dr. Henricus Hopfnerus itidem Professor Th: Lipsiæ. Ab aliá Parte erant Dr. Iohannes Bergius Concionator Aulicus Marchionis Brandenburgici. Dr. Theophilus Newburger Concionator Landtgravii Hassiæ*, Ref: 17/16/1A-8B, HP.

1631: *The Purpose, and Platforme of the Iourneyes that are vndertaken for the worke of Peace Ecclesiasticall and other profitable Ends.* 18/17/1A-4B: 1A-B, 4A-B BLANK. HP.

1632: *Narrative of Durie's German Travels*, Ref: 60/5 1A-8B, /B, 8B Blank, HP.

1632-33: *Mechlenburg, Acta des Landgrafen Wilh. von Hesse*, 1632 Dec. 8 – Jan. 8. HStA.

1633: *A Summarie Relation of that which John Durie hath Prosecuted in the Works of Ecclesiasticall Pacificacon in Germanie since ye Latter End of Julie 1631 till 26 September 1633*, presented, introduced and printed by C. A. Biggs in The Presbyterian Review, New York, Volume VIII, 1887, pp. 297-309. See also Westin's version in *Negotiations about Church Unity*, p. 264 ff., also version in Bod L.

1633: *Ecclesiarum Magnae Britanniae atq; Hyberniae Patronis & Antibus Primariis, Eximiis Dei servis atq; Ecclesiae Laborantis in Germania fautoribus Colendissimis* etc.. contained as a Preface in *The Earnest Breathings of Forreign Protestants etc.*, London, 1656, unpaged, Bod. L.

1634: *Responsio ad Quaestiones Paracevasticas, De Unione Evangelicorum ab Ecclesiarum Transylvaniae Pastoribus & Professoribus exhibita.* Printed with *Concordiae Inter Evangelicos querendae Consilia*, Bod L.

1634: *Touching the work of pacification*, Ref: 1/9/1A-6B, HP.

1634: *Decretum Ordinum Euangelicorum Francofurti factum*, with delegates' signatures, in *Irenicorum Tractatum, Prodromus*, VB 292, HStA.

1635: *Proposition Concerning Ecclesiastical Peace*, Ref: 9/1/121A-126B, HP.

1636: *Consultatio Theologjca de Tollendis in Negotio Pacjs Ecclesiasticæ tractando difficultatibus QVAS Rev. admod. in Christo Pater Dom. Iohann. Rudbeckius S.S. Theol. Doctor et in Diæcesj Arosiensj Epjscop. ejusdemque locj Capjtulares Spectatissimj proposuerunt Próposita submissaque gravissimis ipsorum Iudicijs à Iohanne Duræo Ecclesiaste Scoto-Britanno.* Ref: 19/11/80A-87A, HP.

1636: *De pacis ecclesiasticæ rationibus inter evangelicos usurpandis et de theologorum fundamentali consensu in colloquio Lipsiensi inito ... Johannis Davenantii ... Thomæ Mortoni ... Josephi Halli ... sententiæ, I. Duræo ab ipsis ad ecclesiarum evangeliarum ædificationem promovendam traditæ* Amsterdam, Bod L.

1636: *Duraei epistola ad episcopum & Capitulum Stregneuse* d. 2 Octob. 1636, Benzelius p. 136ff..

1636: *Hypomnemata de studio pacis ecclesiasticae*, Amsterdam, Bod L.

1636: *Motives to induce the Protestant princes to mind the works of peace ecclesiasticall amongst themselves*, Amsterdam, Bod L.

1636?: *Conditiones Quae ad Concordiam Sanciendam inter Ecclesias Evangelicas fuerunt propositae Iohanni Duraeo ab Acad Vpsaliensis Ven.da Facult. Theologica.* HA, 22a1, Nr. 10, Mappe 1, p. 26 ff.

1636: *Irenicum Theologorum Scopus, qui et Iohanni Duraeo, hactenus in Germania et alibi versanti fuit propositus*. Undated but registered in the Uppsala city archives on 10.9. 1636. Full text also available in Westin's second collection of Durie documents.

1637: *Against Images*, Ref: 68/1A-12B, HP.

1637: *Capita rerum, in quibus Duraei fidem suam Holmiae obstrinxit Comiti Forbesio*, Benzelius p. 138 ff..

1637: *Consultatio Theologica De via Qvâ pacis Ecclesiasticæ studia, atque Deliberationes, inter Ecclesias Evangelicas ad optatum perduci qveant euentum: Submissa Iudicijs Rev. admodum in Christo Patris, Domini Laurentij Paulinj, SS. Theolog. Doctoris et Episcopi Strengnensis meritissimi Et Capitularium Ecclesiæ Cathedralis Strengnensis ipsi adjunctorum à Iohanne Duræo Ecclesiastæ Scoto-Britanno*. 4 files, 19/11/22A-30A: 22A-B BLANK, HP. Written in 1636. Benzelius, p. 92 also provides a copy.

1637: *EXPLICATIO Phrasium qvarundam In Dogmate de Sacra Domini Cæna Occurrentium Quas Rever. Facultas Theologica Acad. Ubsaliensis annotauit; ut difficultatem monstraret, propter qvam nondum ei satis liqveat qvomodo Ecclesiæ Reformatæ atque Augustanæ Consensionem in Religione Evangelica profiteri qveant; Secundum tenorem sententiæ qvam ipsis Nomine Aberdoniensium Theologorum obtulit Iohannes Duræus Ecclesiastes Britannus Proposita eidem Rever. Facultati ab Eodem Ioh. Duræo ad ulteriorem consensionem hac in re testandam. Anno 1637. die. 19. Decembr*. Ref: 19/11/1A-10A, HP.

1637: *Gratiam & Pacem â Deo Patre & D:no N:ro Jes. Christo. Amen. Reverendiss:e in Chr:o Pater ac Rev:di admodum Doctissimique Professores Academici*, Oxenstierna Collection in the Riksarkiv and Westin's John Dury in Sweden, pp. 65-66.

1637: *Historica Relatio Colloquij habitj Holmiæ 1637*, Iulij 10. inter Theologos Suecos, et Ioh. Duræum. Ref: 19/11/1A-11B: 1B, 2B, HP, also reprinted in Benzelius, p. 152 ff.

1637: *Idæa specialior Tractatuum De medijs Ecclesiasticæ Concordiæ suscipiendorum â Iohanne Duræeo; Oblata Reverendis in Academia Vbsaliensi Facultatis Theologicæ Professoribus; ut apud se deliberent, An,*

Quandò, Quatenus, Vbi, Quousque & Quomodò, conducibile futurum sit Evangelio Christi ut illa in effectum deducantur Communi piorum Consilio; Ref: 19/5/1A-10B: 1A-B, HP.

1637: *Iudicum Cleri Suecici de negotio Dvraei ex Suecico Latine conversum, Exhibitum d. XI. Iulii 1637*, Benzelius, 160 ff.

1637: *Memoriale Quod Reverensiss: is & Eximijs Ecclesiae Svecanae Antistitibus atque Theologis Holmiae congregatis, cum debita observantia offert Johannes Duraeus Ecclesiastes Sc. Brit:us.* Copy in the Oxenstierna Collection in the Riksarkiv and in Westin's John Durie in Sweden Collection, pp. 48-50.

1637: *Propositio Arosiensi Capitulo oblata,* Ref: 19/11/12A-21B, HP.

1637: *Relatio de colloquio Duraei cum episcopis Suecucis & Cleri delectis Ex tabulari Consistorii regni*, Benzelius p. 146 ff..

1637: *Reverendae in Academia Ubsaliensi Facultati Theologicae oblata â Johanne Duraeo Propositio*, Oxenstierna collection, Riksarkiv, undated but Westin dates it April, 1637 because of the contents. See Westin, *John Durie in Sweden*, pp. 40-42.

1637: *Status Diffidi exorti inter Reverend. Virum Dom. Ioh. Rudbeckius Episcopum Arosiensem, & Ioh. Duraeum Ecclesiasten protestanttes sollicitatorem publicum*, Benzelius, 167 ff..

1638?: *A Christian Vow To be made in these tymes of trouble by all such as deplore the decayes of the Church & the confused diversities of Religions amongst Christians*, Ref: 1/26/ 1A-2B, HP. Different versions at 68/2/1, undated. Klähr gives 1638.

1638: *Consilia Theologica qvæ Iohannes Duræus, Ecclesiastes Britannus in negotio Pacis Ecclesiasticæ inter Evangelicos Theologos ulterius perseqvendo sibi observanda proposuit, Qvæque omnibus in Ecclesia Svecana pié Doctis debitâ cum observantiâ per Reverendissimum Dominum Archiepiscopum, et honorandos Theologos Vbsalienses consideranda offerre cupit, Vt apud animum suum mitigare velint Censuræ gravitatem, qvam de se in Comitiis Holmiæ habitis anno 1638*, Ref: 19/2/1A-4B, HP.

1638: *De pace inter evangelicos procuranda sententiæ quatuor quarum tres a Reverendis Dominis Episcopis Tho. Dunelmensi. Io. Sarisburiensi.*

Ios. Exoniensi. Vltima ab eximijs quibusdam in Gallia theologis conscripta est. Traditæ pridem fuerint Johanni Duræo Scoto viro docto ac prudenti qui in opere hoc pijssimo jam per aliquot annos non infeliciter desudavit. Prodeunt vero hæ (præsertim tres priores) istis Amstelodami antea? editis non paulo pulchiores, utpote quæ ab autoribus revisæ sunt, nec non proprijs ipsorum manibus tam auctæ tum emendatæ. Accessit syllabus brevis Dorum qui de hac argumente antehac scripserunt. Londini, Per G. Miller pro Gualtero Hammond & prostane venales per Bernardum Langford juxta pontem Holborne sub signo Biblij MDCXXXVIII. Bod L.

1638: *Necessariæ et Modestæ EXCUSATIONES Quas Iohannes Duræus Ecclesiastes Britannus offert eâ quâ decet observantiâ considerandas Ecclesiæ Suecanæ Episcopis et Clero, ut apud animum suum mitigare velint censuræ gravitatem quam de instituto et actionibus suis tulerunt in Comitijs* Anno 1638. Ref. 19/3/1A-7A. Document divided between 4 files; HP.

1638: *To the Archbishop and Theological Faculty of Uppsala*, Oxenstierna Collection and Westin's John Durie in Sweden, pp. 121-125.

1638: *Votum Quod Johannes Duraeus, in Suecia decumbens, paulo ante suum ex ea discessum, concepit, & obtulit illustri Dn. Cancellario Oxenstierna, ut via convenienti, praecipuis Regni Suecani Theologis insinuaretur*, in *Irenicorum Tractatum, Prodromus*, VB 292, HStA.

1639: *Acta Tractatuum Johan. Duraei cum Daniae Theologis, ubi agitur de concordiae quaerendae fundamentis & Methodo ad quam se Duraeus solemni voto in Suecia concepto obstrinxerat*, in *Irenicorum Tractatum, Prodromus*, VB 292, HStA.

1639: *Apographum*, in *Irenicorum Tractatum, Prodromus*, VB 292, HStA.

1639: *An Information Concerning the meanes of Peace Ecclesiasticall*, Bod L.

1639: *Inscriptio, illustri magnifico Domino, Domino Dietlovio Reventlaw, Domino de Retz & Ziefendorff/ Serenissimi Regis Daniae Archivi Germanici Cancellario, Domino suo colendo*, in *Irenicorum Tractatum, Prodromus*, VB 292, HStA.

1639: Inscriptio erat Serenissimo potentissimoque Principi ac Domino, Domino Christiano IV, in *Irenicorum Tractatum, Prodromus*, VB 292, HStA.

1639: *Motives to Induce the Protestant Princes to mind the worke of peace Ecclesiasticall among themselves*, Bod L.

1639: *Syllabus documentorum, quorum exemplaria Illustri Domino Reverentlaw transmissa fuerunt 21 Aprilis anno 1639. una cum praecodenti epistola.* (Lit. B.-D.) Irenicorum Tractatuum, IX B 2562, HStA.

1640(?): *Discource on a Method of Meditation*, Ref: 26/4/1A-10B, HP.

1641: *A Briefe Relation of That which hath been lately attempted to procure Ecclesiasticall Peace amongst Protestants*, London. Bod L.

1641: *A Copy of a Petition As it was tendered by Mr, Dury to Gustavus, the late King of Sweden*, Bod L.

1641: *A memorial concerning Peace Ecclesiastical amongst Protestants by John Dury*, London. Bod L.

1641: *A Proposition That the summe of 2000 lib. a yeare may bee set a part out of the Deane & Chapters lands towards the erecting & maintaining of an English colledge at Heidelberg: for the promoting of Religion & Learning*, Ref: 67/19/1A-2B, HP.

1641?: *De Studio Comeniano Consultationes atque Exercitationes*, Ref: 7/71/1A-9A in two files, HP.

1641: *To the King's most Excellent Magesty: or to his Magesties Commisioner and to his Reverend and loving Brethren in Christ, the PASTORS and ELDERS of the Kirk, of Scotland met together at their generall Assembly appointed to be held at Saint Andrews in July Anno*, London. Bod L.

1641: *Tract on Church Government*, Ref: 68/9/1A-4B, HP.

1641: *A peace-maker without partiality and hypocrisie. Or The gospel-way to make up the present breaches of brotherhood, and heale the divisions, whereby some of the reforming professors and ministers of the kindome at* *the time, sadly dishonour their profession, mainley obstruct our reformation, utterly destroy the safe constitution both of church and state. Wherein are handled, 1. How the meanes of Christian peace, as well civill as ecclesiasticall, may bee found and ought to bee followed, both by pastors and people. 2. What are the speciall lets of Ecclesiasticall reconciliation, and what the causes of divisions are, and how to be remedied. 3. What are the grounds, termes and motives of brotherly unitie and forbearance, which the ministers and members of the churches of England ought ot professe and practise one towards another for the gospels sake*, printed by R. Cotes for John Bellamy, at the three Golden Lions in Cornhill neer the Royall Exchange, London, 1648, Bod L.

1641: *A Petition to the Honourable House of the Commons in England Now Assembled in Parliament.* Bod L.

1641: *A Summarie Discourse Concerning the Work of Peace Ecclesiaticall. How it may concure with the aim of a civil confederation amongst Protestants: Presented to the consideration of my Lord Ambassadour Sr. Thomas Rowe, etc., at Hamburg in the year 1639*, Cambridge, Bod L.

1641: *Certain briefe treatises, written by diverse learned men, concerning the ancient and moderne government of the church. : Wherein, both the primitive institution of episcopacie is maintained, and the lawfulnesse of the ordination of the Protestant ministers beyond the seas likewise defended. The particulars whereof are set downe in the leafe following, Martin Bucer 1491-1551.; John Rainolds 1549-1607; James Ussher 1581-1656.; Edward Brerewood 1565?-1613.; John Dury 1596-1680.; Leonard Lichfield d. 1657*, printed by Leonard Lichfield, printer to the University, Oxford Anno Dom.. Bod. L.

1641: *Consultatio theologica: super negotio pacis ecclesiasticæ promovendo, exhibita submissaq, judicio reverendæ facultatis theologicæ in Academia Regia Upsaliensi: cui addita est propositio de quærendæ concordiæ principiis, conventui Holmensi ab eodem oblata, nec non ejusdem ad Synodos Belgicas epistola, excudebat* G.M. pro Andrea Crooke, Londini. Bod L.

1641: *John Dury, his Petition to the Honourable House of commons in England, now assembled in Parliament*, London. Bod L.

1641: *Motives to induce the Protestant princes to mind the works of peace ecclesiasticall amongst themselves*, London, Bod L.

1641: *Petition to the English Clergy in Convocation*, Ref: 6/4/103A-108B, HP.

1642: *A Faithfvll and seasonable Advice, OR, The necessity of a Correspondencie for the advancement of the Protestant Cause. Humbly suggested to the great Councell of England assembled in Parliament*, Hartlib Papers, A1-A4, Wing Number: H986, Thomas Tracts: E.87(14), Feb. 6.

1642: *A Motion tending to the Publick Good of this Age*, London, Sparke, Microfilm, Bayerische Staatsbibliothek, 80328 München. Also to be found in full in Charles Webster's Samuel Hartlib and the Advancement of Learning, Cambridge.

1642: *Certaine Considerations shewing the necessity of a Correspondencie in spirituall matters betwixt all Protestant Churches: an especiall meanes for effecting whereof and healing our present breaches would be a Nationall Synod*, printed for Wil. Hope, London. Bod L.

1642: *England's Thankfulnesse, or, an Humble Remembrance Presented to the Committee for Religion in the High Court of Parliament etc.*. Turnbull suggests it was written by Durie, Webster by Hartlib. Taken from Webster's *Samuel Hartlib and the Advancement of Learning*.

1642: *Foederis fraterni Ad mutuam in publico Christianismi bono promovendo aedificationem sancte in conspectu Dei initi*. Pact signed by Durie, Comenius and Hartlib, and later by William Hamilton, 7/109/1A-2B, HP.

1643: *A copy of Mr. John Duries letter presented in Sweden to the truly noble and religious Lord Forbes: briefely intimating, the necessity of a common, fundamentall confession of faith amongst those Christians that receive the holy scriptures as the only rule of faith and practise, and in the scriptures, have the same apprehension of the tenour of Gods evangelicall covenant in Christ. The possibility of framing such a confession of faith, which infallibly shall be approved (by Gods grace) by all those that agree in these two fore-named principles. The manner of introducing this confession amongst them. Published by Samuell Hartlib. For the better improvement of Great Brittain's solemne covenant, and the advancement of truth, holinesse and peace amongst all Protestant churches. Licensed and entred* *according to order*, with Samuel Hartlib, Printed by G.M. for Thomas Vnderhill. Bod L.

1643: *A memorial concerning PEACE Ecclesiastical amongst Protestants: which John Dury offered to Master Alexander Henderson, to bee sent or presented unto the General Assembly of the Church of Scotland*, 1641. Bod L.

1643: *The copy of a letter written to mr. Alexander Hinderson*, Lond. Bod L.

1644: *An epistolary discourse wherein (amongst other particulars) these following questions are briefly resolved. I. Whether or no the state should tolerate the independent Government? II.If they should tolerate it, how farre, and with what limitations? III. If they should tolerate it, what course should be taken to bring them to a conformity with the Presbyterials? Written by Mr. John Dury. To Mr. Tho. Goodwin. Mr. Philip Nye. Mr. Samuel Hartlib. Published by a friend, for more common use.* London : Printed for Charles Greene, and are to be sold at his shop in Ivie Lane. Bod L and HStA.

1644?: *An Extract of a letter, being a Memorial from Mr John Durie concerning the Independents, undated, Hartlib Papers,* Ref: 1/19/1A-4B: 3B-4B, HP. Undated.

1645: *Good Covnsells for the Peace of Reformed Churches*, (John Dury; John Davenant.; Thomas Morton; Joseph Hall; James Ussher), Bod L. (See 1654 for further edition).

1645: *Madam, although my former freedom in writing might rather give me occasion to beg pardon for a fault committed ...*, London, Bod L.

1645: *Madam, ever since I had a resolution to make a change in my life by marriage ...* London, Bod L.

1646: *Israels call to march out of Babylon unto Jerusalem: opened in a sermon before the Honourable House of Commons assembled in Parliament, Novemb. 26, 1645, being the day of publique humiliation*, printed by G.M. for Tho. Vnderhill, at the signe of the Bible in Wood-street, London, Bod L.

1646: *Some few considerations propounded, as so many scruples by Mr. Henry Robinson in a letter to mr. John Dury upon his epistolary discourse. With Mr. Dureys answer thereunto*, London. Bod L.

1647: *Considerations Tending To The Happy Accomplishment Of England's Reformation in Church and State Humbly Presented to the Piety and Wisdome of the High and Honourasble Court of Parliament*, May, 1647, Hartlib Papers, Wing Number H981, Thomason Tracts, E. 389(4).

1647: *A model of Church Government or, The grounds of the spiritual frame and government of the house of God*, London, Bod L.

1647: *Advice Concerning Studies for Entering the Ministry*, Ref: 68/4/1A-14B, HP.

1648: *A further discovery of the Office of Public Address for Accommodation*, London, (by Durie or Hartlib), Ref: 14/2/3/1A-19B, HP. See a lengthier version in the list of Durie's undated works below. The shorter version for printing appears to have been heavily edited by Hartlib.

1648: *A Peace Maker Without Partiality and Hypocrisie*, London, 1648, Bod L.

1648: *Satans stratagems, or The Devils cabinet-councel discovered: whereby he endevors to hinder the knowledg of the truth ... wherein is laid open an easie way to end controversies in matters of conscience ... together with arguments to each book ...* London: Printed by John Macock, and are to be sold by G. Calvert, Bod L.

1648: *A Case of Conscience resolved: Concerning Ministers meddling with State Matters in their sermons, and how far they are obliged by the Covenant to interpose in the Affairs of Civil Government*, March 15, Imprimatur, Joseph Cayl, London. See below for a second extended edition. Reprinted in Harleian Miscellany, vol. 6, pp. 196-212.

1649: *A Seasonable Discourse written by John Dury upon the earnest request of many, briefly showing these particulars etc* April 24th, Bod L.

1649: *Considerations Concerning the Present Engagement Whether it May Lawfully be Entered into*, yea or no? London, 1649, reprinted by The Rota, University of Exeter, 1979. Also in Webster and Bod L.

1650: *A Pack of Old Puritans Maintaining the Unlawfulness inexpediency of Subscribing the new Engagement*, London, 1650, Bod L.

1650: *The Reformed Librarie-Keeper*, Augustan Reprint Society, publication number 220, 2005, Guttenberg online books.

1650: *A case of conscience concerning ministers medling with state matters in or out of their sermons resolved more satisfactorily then heretofore.: Wherein amongst other particulars, these matters are insisted upon, and cleared. 1 How all controversies and debates among Christians ought to be handled regularly, and conscionably to edification by those that meddle therewith. 2 What the proper employments are of Christian magistrates, and Gospel-Ministers, as their works are distinct, and should be concurrent for the publick good at all times. 3 What the way of Christianity is, whereby at this time our present distractions, and publick breaches may be healed: if magistrates and ministers neglect not the main duties of their respective callings. Where a ground is layed to satisfie the scruple of the Demurrer, and of the Grand Case of Conscience*, printed by Francis Neile for Richard Wodenothe at the Signe of the Star under Peters Church in Cornhill, London, Bod L.

1650: *A second parcel of obiections against the taking of the engagement answered, or, The doubts which som godlie ministers in som neighbor counties entertained upon that subject: as they were proposed in several letters to, and resolved by J.D. whereunto is occasionably annexed a discoverie of the weakness of the plea of the Cheshire and Lancashire ministers for non-subscribing*, printed by Will. Du-Gard, London. Bod L.

1650: *Considerations Concerning the present Engagement: Whether it may be lawfully be taken YEA or NO?* Fourth enlarged edition, London. Bod L.

1650: *Ievves in America, or, Probabilities that the Americans are of that race. With the removall of some contrary reasonings, and earnest desires for effectuall endeavours to make them Christian*, printed by William. Hunt. for Tho. Slater, and are be to sold at his shop at the signe of the Angel in Duck lane, London. Bod L

1650: *Just re-proposals to humble proposals. Or An impartiall consideration of, and answer unto, the humble proposals, which are printed in the name of sundry learned and pious divines, concerning the Engagement which the Parliament hath ordered to be taken: Shewing, how farre those*

proposals are agreeable to reason, to Christianity and to policie. How the proposers thereof may receive satisfaction therein, in all these respects. Hereunto are added, The humble proposals themselves; because they are not currantly to be found. Written by John Dury. January 7. 1650. Imprimatur, Joseph Caryl, printed by J.C. for Richard Wodenothe, at the Starre under St. Peters Church in Cornhill, London. Bod L.

1650: *The Unchanged, Constant and single-hearted Peacemaker, drawn forth into the world. Or a Vindication of Mr. John Dury from the aspersions cast upon him in a nameless pamphlet called, The time-serving Proteus and ambidexter divine, uncased to this world: Wherein the two letter written seventeen years ago the one to Joseph Hall, then Bishop of Exeter, the other to William Laud, then Arch-bishop of Canterbury, are cleared from the most false and injurious interpretations put upon them. Entered according to the late Act concerning printing,* London. Bod L.

1650: *Two treatises concerning the matter of the Engagement: The first of an unknown author, excepting against Mr. Dureus Considerations for the taking of the Engagement, to shew the unsatisfactoriness thereof. The second of Mr. Dureus maintaining the satisfactoriness of his considerations against the unknown authors exceptions*, printed by J. Clowes for Richard Wodenothe London. Bod L.

1651: *Clavis apocalyptica: or, a prophetical key: by which the great mysteries in the revelation of St. John and the prophet Daniel are opened; it beeing made apparent that the prophetical numbers com to an end with the year of our Lord, 1655. Written by a Germane D. and now translated out of High-Dutch. In two treatises. 1. Shewing what in these our times hath been fulfilled. 2. At this present is effectually brought to pass. 3. And henceforth is to bee expected in the years neer at hand. With an introductorie preface,* printed by William Du-Gard for Thomas Matthewes, and are to bee sold by Giles Calvert, at the Black-Spread-Eagle at the West-end of St Paul's, London. Bod L.

1651: *Conscience eased: or, the main scruple which hath hitherto stuck most with conscionable men, against the taking of the Engagement removed: Where amongst other things is shewed, first, how farre the oath of allegiance, and the nationall League and Covenant are obligations; either in their legall intents unalterable or at this time no more binding and alterable. Secondly. How farre in a free people the subordinate officers of the state, have a right to judge of the proceedings of a king in that state.*

Thirdly, how Zedekia'es case in breaking his oath to the king of Babylon, and our case in making use of our freedome from the oath of allegiance, and supremacie to the king of England doe differ, printed for T.H. in Russell-street, neere the Piazza of the Covent-Garden, London. Bod L.

1651: *The Reformed School: and the Reformed Librarie-Keeper (Supplement)*, London, 1651, microfilm, Duisburg-Essen UB.

1651: *The Revelation reveled: By two apocalyptical treatises. Shewing. I. How neer the period of the time is, wherein the mysterie of God shall bee fulfilled. II. What things are already fulfilled, and what shall shortly follow thereupon, as they are foretold in the Revelation. Translated out of High-Dutch. With an introductorie preface, shewing that besides the accomplishment of the particular historical events, spoken of in the Revelation, which are com, ... there is a deeper mysterie, and matter of more necessarie and profitable knowledg, to bee reflected upon in the words of this prophesie; whereof also a summarie and a key, ... to bee thought upon by all the Godlie-wise in the three nations*, printed by William Du-Gard, and are to bee sold by Rob. Littleberrie at the sign of the Unicorn in Little Britain, London. Bod L.

1652: *Digitus dei: nevv discoveryes: with sure arguments to prove that the Jews (a Nation) or people lost in the world for the space of near 200 years, inhabite now in America; how they came thither; their manners, customs, rites and ceremonies; the unparallel'd cruelty of the Spaniard to them; and that the Americans are of that race. Manifested by reason and scripture, which foretell the calling of the Jewes; and the restitution of them into their own land, and the bringing back of the ten tribes from all the ends and corners of the earth, and that great battell to be fought. With the removall of some contrary reasonings, and an earnest desire for effectuall endeavours to make them Christians. Whereunto is added an epistolicall discourse of Mr John Dury, with the history of Ant: Monterinos, attested by Manasseh Ben Israell, a chief rabby.* Thomas Thorowgood, John Dury and Manasseh ben Israel, printed for Thomas Slater, and are to be sold at his shop at the signe of the Angell in Duck-Lane, London. Bod L.

1652: *Eikonoklastes, ou, Réponse au livre intitulé Eikon basilike, ou, Le pourtrait de Sa Sacrée Majesté durant sa solitude & ses souffrances*, A Londres: Par Guill. Du-Gard ..., et se vend par Nicolas Bourne ... (John Milton translated by John Dury). Bod L.

1652: *The reformed spiritvall husbandman: with an humble memorandum concerning Chelsy Colledge, and a correspondencie with forreign Protestants*, printed for Richard Wodenothe, and are to be sold at his shop, London. Bod L.

1653: *Some Proposalls Towards the Advancement of Learning*, HP, Tract XLVII, 2, Ref: 47/2/1A-12B, No. 53 and Webster, *Samuel Hartlib and the Advancement of Learning*, CUP, 1970.

1654: *A demonstration of the necessity of settling some Gospel-government amongst the churches of Christ in this nation: held forth in an answer to a querie whereby Mr. Saltmarch did once endeavour to hinder the settlement of all church-government in the nation : written in the year 1646, and now published for the present use of these times, wherein it may be seasonable to be taken into consideration for the preventing of further confusion and disorder amongst the professors of the Gospell*, printed for Richard Wodnothe, London. Bod L.

1654: *A Summarie Platform of the Heads of a Body of Practical Divinity which the Ministers of the Protestant Churches abroad have sued for and which is farther enlarged in a Treatise intitled An Earnest Plea for Gospel-Communion, etc.*, London. Bod L.

1654: *Concordiæ inter evangelicos quærendæ consilia, quæ ab ecclesiæ in Transylvania evangelicæ pastoribus & scholæ Albæ Juliacensis Professoribus in synodo congregatis approbata fueruent an. M DC XXXIV. Et tunc ipsorum nomine Johanni Duræo transmissa, ad promovendam evangelicarum ecclesiarum unionem, cujus tum se præstabat sollicitatorem. nunc autem primùm publici juris fiunt ab eodem ad instaurandum pristinos in eadem concordia quærendâ conatus, & ad exploranda super hisce consiliis piè doctorum Judicia*, London. Bod L.

1654: *Descriptio Scopi quem in Irenico Studio Secatur, Johannes Duraeus*. First part hand-signed by Durie as *verbi Dei Minister*, second part print signed by Johannes Jacobus Huldricus 5. June, 1654. Third Part print-signed by both 9. June 1654. HA, 22a1, Nr. 10, Mappe 1, p. 85 ff. Printed with:

1654: *Uberior Scopi Declaratio*, in *Irenicorum Tractatum, Prodromus*, VB 292, HStA.

1654: *Good counsells for the peace of reformed churches*, (John Dury; John Davenant.; Thomas Morton; Joseph Hall; James Ussher), Oxford Oxfordshire: Printed by Leonard Lichfield for William Webb 1641. Printed for Richard Wodenothe, London. Bod L.

1654: *An Earnest plea for Gospel Communion In the Ways of Godliness: Sued for by the Protestant Churches in Germany*, London. Bod L. Also Ref: 11/3/2A-B, HP.

1654: *Irenicum, in quo casus conscientiæ præcipui de viis quærendæ & constituendæ inter Ecclesius evangelicas religiosæ pacis breviter proponuntur & deciduntur* [by J. Dury and W. Bedell], Lond.. Also HStA, 22 a1, Nr. 10, Mappe Nr.1.

1654: *Irenicum: in quo casus conscientiæ inter ecclesias evangelicas pacis, breviter proponuntur & decidunter, ad exploranda super iis piè doctorum judicia, vel ad obtinendum super corum decisione corundum consensum*, Londini: *Impensis Richardi Wodenothe*. Bod L.

1654: *Irenicum, In quo Casus Conscientiae praecipui, de viis querendae & constituendae inter Ecclesias Evangelicas Religiosae Pacis*, London, HStA, 22a1, Nr. 10, Mappe 1, pp. 19-26.

1655: *Ad Ministerium Heidelbergense*, Ref: 20/11/85B-88A,HP.

1655: *Brevis relatio. De progressu negotiationis agitae à I. D. pro Reconciliatione Ecclesiarum Protestantium. Inde ab Anno 1660. ad Annum 1665*, HStA, 22a1, Nr. 10 Mappe 1, p. 15 ff.

1655: *Bewegliche Vrsachen, welche die fürnembsten Häupter der Republick, die Diener des Worts vnd Professores der Hohen-Schulen in Engelland bewegt haben, ein Religions-Correspondentz mit den Protestierenden ausserhalb gros Britannien zu suchen. Ein Religions-Correspondentz mit den Protestierenden ausserhalb gros Britanien zu suchen*, HStA, 22a1, Nr. 10, Mappe 1, p. 60 ff.

1655: *Apographum Epistolæ. Domino Doctori IOHANNI CROCIO MISSÆ*, Ref: 20/11/81A-85A, HP.

1655: *Epistolæ Circularis sive Informatoriæ Theologis per Germaniam & Belgium mittendæ Apographum*, Ref: 20/11/81A-85A, HP.

1655: *Declaratio Ecclesarum & Academiaru Helvetiae Reformatae.* 15. April, 1655, Zürich. Title and date in Durie's hand. HStA, 22a1, Nr 10, Mappe 1, pp. 28-30.

1655: *Judicium Ecclesiae & Academiae Genevensis, de Concordiae Ecclesiasticae inter Evangelicos studio, Tiguri, Typis Johannes Caspari Suterl.* HStA, 22a1, Nr. 10, Mappe 1.

1656: *A Case of Conscience, whether it be lawful to admit Jews into a Christian Common-Wealth? Resolved by John Dury*, London. Reprinted in Harleian Miscelany, vol. 6., pp. 438-444,1810, also Bod L.

1656: *Syllabus Documentorum, que ab Ecclesiis & Magistratibus per Helvetiam & Germaniam Evangelicis* etc. HStA, 22a1, Nr. 10, Mappe 1. p. 11 ff.

1656: *Supplementum Syllabi: Documenta à Ministris & Theologis tradita haec sunt.* HStA, 22a1, Nr, 10, Mappe 1. p. 17 ff.

1656?: *De modo procedendi, quo inter evangelicos unio obtineri poterit.* Hand signed by Durie. Undated, HStA, 22a1, Nr 10, Mappe 1.

1656?: *Syllabus documentorum: quae ab ecclesiis & magistratibus per Helvetiam & Germaniam euanglicis, ad concordiae ecclesiasticæ studium inter sese & apud exteros suis suffragiis excitandum & promovendum tradita sunt*, London? It appeared before the following suplement. HStA, 22a1, Nr. 10, Mappe Nr. 1. p. 11 ff.

1656: *Supplementum Syllabi: Documenta*, HStA, 22a1, Nr. 10, Mappe Nr. 1, p. 17ff.

1656: *Certain Positions Concerning The Fundamentals of Christianity, Which bringe Salvation to all that entertain them.* Ref: 14/2/2/1A-6B, HP.

1656-58: *Petition to Cromwell on Advancement of Learning with Related Papers and Cromwell's Reply*, Ref: 47/4/1A-7B, HP.

1657: *An Answer to the Proposall of Doubts, made by Mr. Hamilton. Concerning his Engagement with Mr. Durye and Mr. Hartlib, to prosecute public aimes*, Ref: 9/11/31A-34B, HP.

1657: *A Summarie Account of Mr John Dury's Former and latter Negotiations For the procuring of true Gospell Peace, with Christian Moderation and Charitable Unity amongst the Protestant Churches, and Academies*, London, Microfilm, Bayerische Staats Bibliothek.

1657: *The effect of Master Dury's negotiation for the uniting of Protestants in a Gospell interest in brief is this etc.* Ref: 14/2/1A-6B, 1A-B, 6A-B Blank, HP. Printed edition in Bod L but undated.

1657: Correspondence to and from Durie in Latin and French. England Nr. 89. HStA.

1657: *Akten des Kasselischen Geheimerates Dauber: Schreiben des Herrn Jean Duré aus Westminster. Betr. Ablehnung der ihm durch das engl. Parlament angebotenen Königswürde durch Cromwell. Duraeus Bemühungen um e. Zusammengehen des Protectors mit e. Partei in Deutschland*, 4 f England, Nr. 98, HStA

1657: *Certain Positions Concerning The Fundamentals of Christianity which bringss Salvation to all that entertain them*, London. Ref: 14/2/2 1A-6B, HP.

1658: *A true relation of the conversion and baptism of Isuf the Turkish chaous, named Richard Christophilus In the presence of a full congregation, Jan. 30. 1658. in Covent-Garden, where Mr. Manton is minister.* Imprimatur, Edm. Calamy, printed by S. Griffin, and are to be sold by John Rothwell at the Fountain in Cheapside, and Thomas Vnderhill at the Bible in Pauls Church-yard London. Bod. L.

1658: *An information concerning the present state of the Jewish nation in Europe and Judea: wherein the footsteps of Providence preparing a way for their conversion to Christ, and for their deliverance from captivity are discovered*, with Henry Jessey and Petrus Serrurier printed by R.W. for Thomas Brewster London. Bod. L.

1658: *The Earnest Breathings of Forreign Protestants, Divines and others: to the Ministers and other Able Christians of these three Nations, for a Compleat Body of Practical Divinity*. Bod L.

1659: *Extracts of correspondence with Parliament*, England Nr. 59, HStA.

1659: *Epistola veridica ad homines Philoprōteuontas; cui additur oratio pro statu ecclesi fluctuantis qu ex quavis regione vacillat & periclitatur dum clavum teneant qui arte sacro-nauticâ minimè polleant.* Londini excusum: s.n. anno Domini.

1659: *The Interest of England in the Protestant Cause*, London, Bod L.

1660: *A declaration of John Durie, a minister of Jesus Christ to witness the gospell of peace: wherein he doth make known the truth of his way and comportment in all these times of trouble: and how he hath endeavoured to follow peace and righteousness therein innocently towards all that the offences taken against him, through the mis-construction of some, of his actions may be removed and the work of peace and unity amongst the Protestant churches at home and abroad advanced in due time.* London. Bod L.

1660(?): *Some Proposals concerning The Happie Settlement of the Nation*, Ref: 53/29/1A-2B, HP.

1660: *The plain way of peace and unity in matters of religion*, London, Microfilm-Ausg. E 1808. 1. hbz, 2002-2007, SUB, Göttingen, also Bod L.

1661: *Judicium*, Utrecht. Signed by Gilbertus Voetius, Andreas Essenius and Mattias Nethenius on 7/17 September. In Durie's hand, Ysenburg Collection, Repositor VI, p. 589, Section 26, 201, 1654-1670, Nr. 18.

1661: *A discourse concerning liberty of conscience:In which are contain'd proposalls, about what liberty in this kind is now politically expedient to be given, and severall reasons to shew how much the peace and welfare of the nation is concern'd therein*, printed for Nathaniel Brook, and are to be sold at his shop at the Angel in Cornhill London. Bod L.

1661: *Memoriale De Medijs Ecclesiastica pacis* in Durie's hand, Ysenburg Collection, Repositor VI, p. 589, Section 26, 201, 1654-1670, No. 15.

1662: *Copie D'une Lettre escrite a un prince de L'Empire; ou Brieve Information du Commencement, du Progres & de l'Estat present de la Negotiation De Jean Dureus, avec les Eglises Protestantes.* Zürich, HA, 22a1, Nr. 10, Mappe 1, p. 69 ff.

1662: *Irenicorum tractatuum prodromus*, HStA, Shelfmark VB 292 u.

1662: *Admodum Referendi*, letter von Büdingen 'Oblatum Budingen 17/27 Feb., Ysenburg Collection, Repositor VI, p. 589, Section 26, 201, 1654-1670, No. 14.

1663: *Informatio De Progressu Studij Ecclesiis communicandae*, HA, 22a1, Nr 10, Mappe 1. p. 67 ff. The Yssenburg copy, No. 24, has a covering letter and is dated 1664.

1664: *Brieve Deduction Du Progress de la Negotion pour L'union Euangelique des Eglises Protestantes, Depuis 'l'An 1660 inseques à l'An 1664*. HStA, 22a1, Nr. 10, Mappe 1., p. 75 ff.

1664: *Informatio De ulteriori progressu studij Irenici Ecclesiis communicandae*, HA, 22a1, Nr.10, Mappe 1, p. 66 ff.

1665: *Brevis Relatio. De Progressu Negotiationis agitae à I.D. Pro Reconciliatione Ecclesiarum Protestantium. Inde ab Anno 1660 ad Annum 1665*. HLA, 22a1, Nr. 10, Mappe 1.

1667: *De Mediis ad Scopum Evangelicae Unionis Obtinendum Reqvisitis*, undated but found between Duries letters for 1667 in 22a1, Nr. 10, Mappe 1. HStA, Probably earlier.

1669: *Carmen Gratulatorium In Reditum Serenissimae Matris Serenissimique Filii Celsissimorum Hassiae Principium cum Serissima Sponsa Churlandica Cassellas, Cassel*, IXB 2562, HStA.

1670: *Brevis Narratio de iis, quae in negotio irenico acta fuerunt Gothae.*

1670: *Memoriale of a conference held in Cassel, 28/Sept./8 Oct, 1670*, Schloß Ysenburg und Büdingen Records Repositor VI, p. 589, Section 26, 201, 1654-1670, Nr. 25.

1671: *Extractum ex harmonia Confessionum*, HStA, VB, 293ag.

1671: Duraeus Gothaer Verhandlungen, including the handwritten *Acta Gothana* containing *Brevis Narratio*; *Memoriale*; *Dissertatio De Informatione*; *Maximae*; *Nomine*; *Annotata ad Scriptum* (1670); *Propositio* on the Lord's Supper signed 31st Oct. 1670 with Durie's Hebrew slogan ירלא; *Extractum ex Epistola*, 1670; *De Causa Protestantium communi* with ירלא; *De veritate salutari*; *De Methodo & Modo Consultandi in Negotio Irenico*, a statement undersigned by Durie, November, 1670. In the same folder 22a1,

Nr 10, Mappe 2 we find also two letters in Durie's hand dated 1671; a two-page *Memoriale* dated 28 Sept. to 8 Oct. 1776; a document for Durie from Johann Helwig Schutz dated 22 Nov. 1670 from a gathering of theologians at Cassel and a letter from Christian Albrecht to Durie dated 30. Oct. 1670. HStA.

1672: *Acta Collationis Amicae Antehac Privatim per literas institutae*. VB 293, HStA.

1672: *Brevis disquisitio de Doctrinis Veri Christianismi Fundamentalibus, Cassel, 1672*, HStA, VB 293 ak.

1672: *Lettre de Mr. Duraeus a S.E. Mr. le Comte de la Gardie, Chancelier du Royaume de Suede*, Benzelius 180 ff..

1676: *Rayons de L'Esprit de Grace Donnant Conseil, Lumiere, vie & consolation a l'ame fidele, Iean Dure*, HAB, Digital Library, 1263.6 Theol.

Published Collections of Durie's correspondence used in this thesis:

1628-1634: Documents and Letters Written by John Dury, Westin, Gunnar (ed.) in *Negotiations about Church Unity*, Uppsala, 1932, pp. 187-305.

1636-1638: Documents and Letters 1636-1638, Westin, Gunnar (ed.). in *John Durie in Sweden,*. Uppsala, 1936, pp. 5-165.

1636-1638: Turnbull, G. H. (ed), Letters Written by John Dury in *Kyrkohistorisk Årsskrift*, 1949, Band 49, pp. 204-251.

1636-1672: Benzelius reproduces a number of Durie's letters, especially to Matthiae and the Swedish bishops.

1638-1661: Eekhof, Utrecht (ed), *De Theologische Faculteit Te Leiden in de 17de Eeuw*, 1921, pp. 205-206; 349-357.

1654-1659: Vaughan, Robert (ed.), *The Protectorate of Oliver Cromwell and the State of Europe . . . Illustrated in a Series of Letters*, ii vols., Durie's letters to Pell i. pp. 116; 136; ii. pp. 173; 195; 209; 214; 261.

Undated works by John Durie either printed or published on the HP CDs

A Brief Discourse concerning the Accomplishment of our Reformation shewing that by an office of Address in spiritual and Temporal Matters the Glory of God and the Happiness of this Nation may be Highly Advanced, Ref: 17/10/1A-20B, HP.

A Demonstration that the Lutherans are not Idolaters, and that it is not vnlawfull to resort vnto their publicke meetings, 68/6/1A-10B, HP.

A Discourse concerning the Queries of the House of Commons to the Assembly of Divines, Ref: 17/9/1A-10B, HP.

A Further Discovery of the Office of Addresse, in matters, of Communication for the Adbancement of Divine and Humans Learning, Ref: 47/10/2A-55B: 55A, 55B, HP.

A Large Epistle touching peace Unity & Charity, Ref: 17/17/1A-20B: 1B, HP.

A Proposition that the summe of 2000 lib. a yeare may bee set a part out of the Deane & Chapters lands towards the erecting & maintaining of an English colledge at Heidelberg for the promoting of Religion & Learning, Ref: 67/19/1A-2B, HP.

An Analysis of the 105th Psalm, Ref: 1/10/1A-6B, HP.

Brevis Discursus de Fundamentalibus verae Religionis Capitibus, ex quibus confessionem fidei Christinae confici convenit, Præfatio ad Dn. Forbesium, undated, Ref: 17/12/1A, HP.

Brevis Informatio, de vero Scopo & Mediis propriiis quibus Concordiam Euangelicam apud Eclesias Protestantes prosequitur Johannes Duraeus. HLA, 22a1, Nr. 10, Mappe 1, p. 58 ff., pagination displaced in collection, so might be earlier.

Circa hoc Diploma, Schloß Ysenburg und Büdingen Records Repositor VI, p. 589, Section 26, 201, 1654-1670, Nr. 11.

Concerning the Question Whether it bee lawfull to admit Iewes to come into a Christian commonwealth, Ref: 68/8/1A-2B, HP.

Conditiones Que Ad Concordiam Sanciendam inter Ecclesias Evangelicas fuerunt propositae Iohanni Duraeo Ab Acad. Vpsaliensis Ven.da Facult. Theologica.

Considerations touchant Le Vray Interest des Estats Protestants. Undated but placed in Durie's records for 1654 though the pencelled pagination (3ff.) suggests an earlier position in the collection. HSA, 22a1, Nr. 10, Mappe 1.

De deliberatione Rev: et Clariss. D. Duræi, de Medijs ad Scopum Vnionis Evangelicæ obtinendum necessarijs: Iudicium Fraternum. Vir Reverende et Clarissime. D. et Frater colendissime, Ref: 20/11/56B-61A, HP.

De Mediis ad Scopum evangelicae Reqvisitis. Signed by Durie. Undated, Ysenburg Collection, Repositor VI, p. 589, Section 26, 201, 1654-1670, No. 5.

De Modo Procendi, Qvo inter evangelicos unio obtineri poterit, HStA, 22a1, Nr. 10, Mappe 1, pp. 7-11, with monogram.

Declaratio Amplissimorum Helvetiae, Reformatae Magistratum, super negiotio Pacificatorio, Reverendi & Clarissimi D. Duraei, undated, Ysenburg Collection, Repositor VI, p. 589, Section 26, 201, 1654-1670, No. 7.

Hypomnema de Negotiatione Pacifica â Johanne Duraeo suscepta:Vt intelligantur cause que ipsum permoverunt ad rem agitandam; Et Media quibus ad umbilicum per Dei gratiam poterit perduci. VB 291 db, HStA.

Memo on the Conversion of the Jews. Ref. 25/4/1A-4B.

Proposition Concerning Ecclesiastical Peace, Ref: 9/1/108 A-B, HP.

Reasons Why the State should not suffer the Office of public Entries or Adresses to bee in any other hand but such as they shall appoint to haue it, Ref: 63/7/2A-3B, HP.

Restaurationis Universalis Cynosura & Amussis id est Descriptio Summaria Scopi, Mediorum ac Methodi, ad qvem dirigendus qvibus promovendus, & per qvam perficiendus est Conatus illorum (si qvi sint Qvi Reformationem Universalem vereque Christinam per homines idoneos, id est Sinceros Christianismi professores moliuntur Matth. 3. v. 3., Ref: 17/19/1/1A-8B: 1B, HP.

Specimen Speculationis siue Meditationis Geneticæ, Ref: 24/18/1A-12B, HP.

The meanes of Ecclesiastical Peace and Reconciliation amongst Protestants, Rawlinson, A.427, Bod. L.

Tractus de Memoria, Ref: 60/6/1A-16B, HP.

Schloß Ysenburg und Büdingen Records Repositor VI, p. 589, Section 26, 201, 1654-1670, in numbered order as per folder.

1) Conference records signed by imperial delegates (copy) September 1634 after Nordlingen. The Count of Ysenburg was banished.
2) *Pensa and Postulata* in Durie's hand, signed by Duraeus.
3) *Judicium Ecclesiae & Academiae Genevensis, de Concordiae Ecclesiasticae inter Evangelicos studio, Tiguri, 1655.*
4) *Descriptio Scopi quem in Irenico studio sectatur* (Huldricus and Durie. (also signed by Durie). 1654. Also in HStA.
5) *De Mediis ad Scopum evangelicae Reqvisitis.* Signed by Duraeus. Undated.
6) *De modo procedendi*, hand signed by D. Also in HStA.
7) *Declaratio Amplissimorum Helvetiae, Reformatae Magistratum, super negiotio Pacificatorio, Reverendi & Clarissimi D. Duraei*, undated.
8) *Conditiones* (Uppsala) undated. Also in HStA.
9) *Disertatio Brevis de Medijs Necesarijs*, undated. Also in HStA.
10) Letter written in Durie's hand from Hanover, 23 July 1655 to Duke Johann Ernst of Ysenburg and Büdingen.
11) *Circa hoc Diploma.*
12) Document dated 1662. (correspondence between ducal brothers on topics not connected directly with Durie's work.
13) A letter beginning 'Hochgebornen', dated February, 1662 but illegible.
14) *Admodum Referendi*, letter von Büdingen 'Oblatum Budingen 17/27 Feb. 1662. Handwritten by Duraeus when Graf Ysenburg's guest.
15) Notes for a conference dated May 6/16, 1661, *Memorale De Medijs Ecclesiastica pacis* in Durie's hand. 2 and a half pages of notes (fo-

lio).with main points in Roman numerals and sub-points in Arabic numerals. Preparations for for discussions amongst Protestant leaders in Schloß Ysenburg.

16) Utrecht *Judicium* signed by Gilbertus Voetius, Andreas Essenius and Mattias Nethenius on 7/17 September, 1661. (Copy in Durie's hand).
17) Copy of the findings of various sittings of conferences called by the Elector of Brandenburg including pastors from Duisburg, France and Belgium such as Rouyer. Includes Zacharias Streso from Moers. Parts dated variously throughout 1661. All the different parts of Frederick Wilhelm's realm represented. *Consilia Theologica ad Concordiam Evangelicam inter Ecclesias Protestantes promovendam.* Sends views of the various places he has visited. Copied in Durie's hand. Leading signatories Johannes Hundius, Georgius Henricy à Lahr; Abrahamus Brckius; Johannes Jarubus?? Zellerus.
18) *Judicium* signed by J, Caspari Wigandi, Nicolaus Emmelig, Gotthard Schäffer, Adan Hattstemig, Philippus Capsius.at the Solms castle, 27 Jan 1662.
19) *Judicium & Responsum* in Durie's hand, Actum Braunfels in Comitatu Solms, 23, Jan. 1662.
20) Unreadable note dated 18 Feb, 1662.
21) To the ministers of Ysenburg and Budingen. *Informatio De Progressu Studij Irenica Ecclesiis communicanda*, August 1663 with handwritten covering letter and dedication. Sent from Geneva dated 7/17 March (old and new style) Geneva, 1664.
22) Letter written in French by scribe from Lausanne 23/April/9 May, 1664, but dated and signed in Durie's hand. Possibly to Graf Ysenburg as the letter appears to have been received in Büdingen.
23) Letter in other hand to Graf Ysenburg signed Johannes Ax??. Dated 15 May, 1664.
24) *Informatio De ulteriori progresu studij Irenici Ecclesiis communicanda, Anno 1664 in Julio.* 2 copies. Brief letter to Duke Johan Ernst in French in Durie's hand dated 23/August, 1664.
25) *Memoriale* of a conference held in Cassel, 28/Sept./8 Oct, 1670

Original hand written mss, printed works, conference minutes and contemporary copies found in HStA, Marburg.

A single archived page number can denote two to four pages according to folding, so the actual pages are far more than given.

Durie documents Shelfmark Pkt 22a1, Nr. 10:

Mappe 1. Mainly printed works which are listed above. Documents in Durie's hand are pages 1-2 (3 pages in all) and pages 44-45 (3 pages). All further folders contain solely hand written documents.

Mappe 2, pages 5-30.

Mappe 3, pages 29-37.

Mappe 4, pages 26-37; 45-52; 54-62; 74-77; 98-99; 103-104; 107-114; 119-131; 134; 141-142; 145; 164-206; 211-220; 223-245.

Mappe 5, pages 13-20; 23-25; 29-44.

Politische Akten nach Phillip d. Gr. 1567-1821. Shelfmark 4f:

England, 88; 89; 90; 110; 165; 289.

Mecklenburg, 57.

Original hand written mss, printed works, conference minutes and contemporary copies found in the Bodleian Library, Oxford.

Codices Rawlinsoni Fasciculus Primus, Catal. Codd, MSS. Bibl. Bodl. 427, Hearne Collection, 16 Durie mss.

Codices Rawlinsoni, Facsiculus Secundus, C. 911. Codex chartaceus, in 4to, saec. xvii, ff. 728. manibus variis exartus, containing 63 paragraphs concerning separate and bundled works from Durie's pen, revealing several hundred documents in all.

See OLIS and SOLO catalogues for some 100 further titles as also relevant works under Samuel Hartlib, Comenius etc.. SOLO is being completed.

Use of the Swedish Archives

At the Riksarkiv, Stockholm, I found a parcel labelled foreign church correspondence with the Svenska Kyrka between 1640-1655 and a parcel dealing with Gustav Adolf's and Christina's correspondence between 1633 and 1654. There was a letter from Durie to Oxenstierna marked E 589 but also many letters to and from Oxenstierna to do with Sir James Spens, Elbing and the work of Christian union. Several of these are in Durie's hand.

At the Carolina Rediviva, I found the files:

Handlingar till Sveriges politiska Historia (E). See esp. E437.

Er. Ekholms Anteckningar i Sverige's Historia (N). See esp. N53 to Dannhauer and Oxenstierna.

E. Ehrensteens Handlingar III (E III).

Johan Mattiae (G). G 360 gives Oxenstierna's Letter of Recommendation to Durie and letters to Matthiae.

Nordin. Ecclesiastika Handlingar 1624-1647 (N1910)

These contained eight letters in all from Durie written between 1642 and 1663 and seven letters from Cromwell dated between 1655 and 1656.

At the Domkapitel collections from Uppsala and Strängnäs (Mattiae's bishopric), I read *Protokoll med Bilagor* (Minutes and Appendices) (huvudserie) A1 for the relevant dates, these being:

Vol. 3:   1641-1645 1646-1648

Vol. 4:   1649-1664

In A1:2, I found one letter from John Durie which was dated 10th Sept. 1636 which had either been put in by chance or the archivist thought that Durie had written 1636 for 1663.

Durie researchers may avoid searching through the following collections as they contain little of interest to their subject:

Inkomma kungliga brev och regeringsskrivelser, Vol. 1 – 1521-1679 (listed as E1)

Inkomma allmänna skrivelser, Vol. 1 – 1610-1649; Vol. 2 – 1650-1656

Protocollum Consistorii Ecclesiastici Ubsaliensis Anno 1643-1551

Looking through EI:1-26 and EII: 12, I found one letter from John Durie dated 1638 26/2 in EI:2, Letter 61.

In ms Palmsk. 105 there is a letter from Durie to King Charles dated 1673.

In *Kunglig. Brev 1566-1670*, there is one letter from Durie to the King marked E. 81:2.

The relative poverty of material in the Swedish archives was explained to me as being due to the fact that much seventeenth century material was not catalogued and still may be found in loose piles of unsorted documents. A further reason was that in 1697, the state and church records were partly destroyed by a large fire in the Tre Kronor Castle in Stockholm where most of Durie's correspondence and works would have been kept. So, too, when Queen Christina abdicated and went to Rome, she took whole libraries and archives with her in order to set up a Swedish research centre in the Italian capital. As she looked to Durie as her mentor, she could well have taken his records with her. However, Benzelius has preserved much of Durie's Swedish work and Westin and Turnbull have made huge collections from many sources.

I have used the British Library records sparsely as much was on micro-film (for instance, the Sloane mss) and could be digitalised easier elsewhere. The HAB provides a good online and postal service but contain duplicates available cheaper through libraries and archives of which I am a member such as the Carolina Rediviva, All Souls, Bodleian, Duisburg UB and the Mülheim Media House.

Sixteenth to Eighteenth Century Documents and Works consulted (originals, copies, reprints and microfilms)

Anonymous, *A pack of old Puritans, maintaining the unlawfulness & inexpediency of subscribing the new engagement .... With mr. John Dury's considerations and just reproposals concerning it*, London, 1650, Bod L.

Bacon, Francis, *The Advancement of Learning*, transcribed from the 1893 Cassell & Company edition by David Price, Project Gutenberg E-Book, 2004.

Bayne, Peter (ed.), *Documents Relating to the Settlement of the Church of England by the Act of Uniformity of 1662*, London, 1862.

Baxter, Richard et. al.. The judgement and advice of the Assembly of the Associated Ministers of Worcester, Aug. 6th 1658 concerning the endeavours of ecclesiasticall peace, and the waies and means of Christian unity, which Mr John Durey doth present, sent unto him in the name, and by the appointment of the aforesaid Assembly, 1658.

Braine, John, *Dr. Durie's Defence of the Present Ministry*, 1649.

Bray, Gerald (ed.), *Documents of the English Reformation*, James Clarke & Co., 1994.

Calixtus, Georg, *Georg Calixtus Briefwechsel: In einer Auswahl aus wolfenbüttelschen Handschriften'*, Google Books.

Bruce, John (ed), *The Calendar of State Papers, Domestic Series, of the Reign of Charles I*. vol. 4, 1629-1631; vol. 5, 1631-1633; vol. 6, 1633-1634; vol. 7, 1634-1635; vol. 8, 1635; vol. 9. 1635-1636; vol. 10, 1636-1637; vol. 11, 1637; vol. 12, 1637-1638.

Burton, Thomas, *Diary of Thomas Burton Esq. Member in the Parliaments of Oliver and Richard Cromwell from 1656 to 1659*, 4 vols, London, 1828.

Cardwell, Edward, *Documentary Annals of the Reformed Church of England*, 2 vols, Oxford University, 1844.

Carlyle, Thomas (ed), *Oliver Cromwell's Letters and Speeches with Elucidations*, (5 vols), Chapman and Hall, 1871.

Comenius, Johann Amos, eds, Nordström, Stig and Sjöstrand, Wilhelm, *Comenius' Självbiografi, Continuatio Admonitionis Fraternae de temperando Charitate Zelo cum fideli Dehortatione à Pantherina Indole & à Larvis, Joh. Comeni ad S. Maresium*: etc., Original work 1669, facsimilie with commentary, Stockholm, 1975.

Comenius, Johann Amos, *Jana Amosa Komenského: Korrespondence*, 1892.

Comenius, Johann Amos, *Vorspiele, Prodromus Pansophiae*: Vorläufer der Pansophie (ed. Herbert Hornstein, mit Übersetzung), Pädagogischer Verlag Schwann, Düsseldorf, 1963.

Copia Literarum Synodi Herbornensis, 1633, Ref: 59/10/82A-91B bis: 91B, HP.

Cromwell, Oliver, Oliver Cromwell's letter to Landgrave William concerning Durie's work in uniting Lutherans and Reformed, HStA.

Davenant, Bishop John et al., *Good Counsells for the Peace of Reformed Churches by some Reverend and Learned Bishops and other Divines*, Translated out of Latin, Oxford, 1641: Containing:

The Opinion of the Right Reverend Father in God John Davenant Bishop of Salisbury to his Learned and Worthy Friend Mr John Dury.

The Opinion of the Right Reverend Father in God Thomas Morton Bishop of Durham, Concerning the Peace of the Church.

The Opinion of the Right Reverend Father in God Joseph Hall Bishop of Exeter.

The Opinion of the most Reverend Father in God James Usher, Lord Archbishop of Armagh and Primate of Ireland, with some other Reverend Bishops in Ireland, May 14, Anno 1634.

The Judgement of the same Right Reverend Father, the Lord Arch-Bishop of Armagh, delivered in a sermon of his preached before King James at Wanstead, June 20th 1624.

The Opinion of some Famous Divines of the French Church.

Early English Books 1641-1700, Film R361, 1136, W1293-W2166. Courtesy of Bayer. Staatsbibliothek.

Elzevir, Isaac (Printer), *Acta Synodii Nationalis, ... Dordrechti*, 1620.

Erdmannsdörffer, B. (ed.), *Urkunden und Aktenstücke zur Geschichte des Kurfürsten Friedrich Wilhelm Von Brandenburg*, Vierte Band, Berlin, 1877.

Evelyn, John, *The Diary of John Evelyn*, London, 1559.

Fuller, Thomas, The Church History of Britain From the Birth of Jesus Christ Untill the Year M.D.C.XLVIII., London, 1656.

Gardiner, Samuel Rawson (ed.), *Letters and Papers Illustrating the Relation Between Charles the Second and Scotland in 1650*, Edinburgh, 1894.

Gardiner, Samuel Rawson (ed.), *Documents relating to the proceedings against William Prynne, in 1634 and 1637*. With a biographical fragment by the late John Bruce, Printed for the Camden Society, 1877.

Gardiner, Samuel Rawson (ed.), *The Constitutional Documents of the Puritan Revolution 1625-1660*, Clarendon Press, 1906.

Grotius, Hugo (Hugo de Groot), *Hugonis Grotii ad Ioh. Oxenstierna et Ioh. Adl. Salvium, et Iohannis Oxenstierna ad Cerisantem*, Halemi, 1829.

Grotius, Hugo (Hugo de Groot), *The Truth of the Christian Religion in Six Books* (A seventh is added by L. E. Clerk), London, 1729.

Hall, Bishop Joseph, *A Recollection of such Treatises as haue bene hertofore seuerally published and are nowe reuised, corrected, augmented. By Jos: Hall Dr of Divinity with addition of some others not hitherto extant*, London.

Hartlib, Samuel (Compiler), *The Hartlib Papers, A Complete Text and Image Database of the Papers of Samuel Hartlib (c. 1600-1662)*, Sheffield University, 2 CDs, 2002.

Hartlib, Samuel, *The Reformed Husband-Man*, London 1651, Micro-film R 361-741, Bayerische Staatsbibliothek.

Heylin, P., *Cyprianus Anglicus: Or the History of the Life and Death, Of The Most Reverend and Renowned Prelate William By Divine Providence, Lord Archbishop Of Canterbury*, London, 1668,

Hillerbrand, H. J. (ed.), *The Reformation in its Own Words*, SCM Press, 1964.

Journal of the House of Commons, vol. 7, 1651-60, 1802.

Keeble, N. H. and Nuttall, Geoffrey F (eds), *Calendar of the Correspondence of Richard Baxter*, vol. 1, 1638-1660. Only summaries and extracts.

Kidd, B. J., *Documents Illustrative of the Continental Reformation*, Oxford, Clarendon Press, 1911.

Laud, Archbishop William, *The Works of the Most Reverend Father in God William Laud D.D.*, Oxford, 1860.

Members of the University of Oxford, To the Supreame Authority the Parliament of the Commonwealth of England, undated, Ref: 47/19/1A-6B.

Milton, Anthony (ed.), *The British Delegation and the Synod of Dort (1618-1619)*, Church of England Record Society 13, Boydell Press, 2005.

Oldenburg, Henry, *The Correspondence of Henry Oldenburg*, (eds Hall and Hall), 13 vols., Taylor and Francis, London and Philadelphia, 1986.

Petty, Sir William, The Advice of W. P. to Mr Samuel Hartlib, for the Advancement of some particular parts of learning, London, 1648. Reprinted in *Harleian Miscellany*, vol. 6, pp. 141-157, 1810.

Printed Papers on the Founding of a University in London, 1647, Ref: 47/20/1/2A, HP.

Robinson, Henry, *An ansvver to Mr. John Dury his letter which he writ from the Hague, to Mr. Thomas Goodwin. Mr. Philip Nye. Mr. Samuel Hartlie: Concerning the manner of the reformation of the church, and answering other matters of conseqvence. And King James his judgement concerning the Book of Common Prayer*, printed Anno Dom. London, 1644.

Sandys, Sir Edwin, *Europae Speculum or a Survey of the State of Religion in the Western Parts of the World*, London, 1673.

Terry, Charles Sanford, *Papers Relating to the Army of the Solemn League and Covenant 1643-1647*, 2 vols, 1917.

Tudur-Jones R., et al (eds), *Protestant Nonconformist Texts 1550-1700*, Vol. 1, Ashgate, Aldershot,1988.

Vaughan, Robert, *The Protectorate of Oliver Cromwell, and the State of Europe During the Early Part of the Reign of Louis XIV*, 2 vols., Henry Colburn, London, 1838. Contains seven letters from Durie to Pell besides Pell's correspondence with Dury and others.

Wall, van der, Ernestine, *The Dutch Hebraist Adam Boreel and the Mishnah Project: Six Unpublished Letters (Durie-Boreel)*, LIAS 16 (1989) 2, pp. 239-263, Leiden University.

Wall, van der, Ernestine, *Three Letters by Menasseh Ben Israel to John Durie* (original letters with commentary), *Nederlands Archief voer kerkegeschiedenis 65 (1985)*, Leiden, p.p. 46-53.

Wallmann, Johannes (ed.), *Philipp Jacob Spener: Briefe aus der Frankfurter Zeit 1666-1686*, 4 vols., J. C. B. Mohr (Paul Siebeck) Tübongen, 1992.

Whitfield, H.; Ed. Calamy et al, A Narrative of the Late Proceedings at Whitehall, Concerning the Jews, London 1656. Reprinted in *Harleian Miscellany*, pp. 445-454, 1810.

William VI, Landgrave, *Schreiben an den Protektor v. England Oliver Cromwell, 28 April, 1656*, 4f England, Nr 88, HStA.

Wood, Anthony A., *Athenae Oxonienses*, vol. 2., with *Fasti Oxonienses*, First Part, edited by Phillip Bliss (1813-1820), Anglistica & Americana Reprint, Georg Olms Verlag, Hildesheim, 1969.

Dissertations

Arnold, Georg Heinrich, *Historia Joannis Duraei, qua ea inprimis, quae P. Baelius et G. Arnoldus tradiderunt/diligentius investigantur et explicantur praeside Jo. Christophoro Colero ... publica excussa a Georgio Henrico Arnoldo, Vitembergae* : Creusigius,1716. HAB.

Auzière, Louis, *Essai Historique sur les Facultés de Théologie de Saumur et de Sedan*. Thèse Présentée a la Faculté de Théologie de Strasbourg, pour Obtenir le Grade de Bachelier en Théologie, G. Silbermann, 1836.

Brauer, Karl, *Die Unionstätigkeit John Duries unter dem Protektorat Cromwells*, Marburg University, 1907.

Batten Joseph Minton, *John Dury – Advocate of Christian Reunion*, Chicago University, 1930.

Benzelius, Carl Jesper, *Dissertatio Historico-Theologica De Johanne Dvraeo, Pacificatore Celeberrimo, Maxime De Actis Eivs Svecanis / Qvam ... In Illvstri Academia Ivlia Praesidente Magnifico Prorectore Io. Lavrentio Moshemio ... Pro Svmmis In Theologia Honoribvs Conseqvendis In Ivleo Maiori Horis Ante Et Pomeridianis Consvetis D. XXIX. M. Maii MDCCXLIV. Pvblicae Censvrae Svbiiciet Carolvs Iesper Benzelivs*.

Bowman, Jacob N., *The Protestant Interest in Cromwell's Foreign Relations*, Inaugural Dissertation, Ruprecht-Karls-Universität zu Heidelberg, 1900.

Hållander, Tore, *Vägen in i sockenkyrka: De uppländska vallonernas religiösa assimilation 1636-1696*, Uppsala Universität, 2000.

De Vries, Peter, *Die mij heeft liefgehad: De Betekenis van de Gemeenschap met Christus in de Theologie van John Owen (1616-1683)*, doctoral dissertation Theologische Universiteit Christlijke Gereformeerde Kerken in Nederland te Apeldoorn, 1999.

Jones, Guernsey, *The Diplomatic Relations between Cromwell and Charles X. Gustavus of Sweden*, inaugural dissertation for the degree of Doctor of Philosophy, submitted to the Philosophical Faculty of the University of Heidelberg, 1897.

Kotljarchuk, Andrej, *In the Shadows of Poland and Russia: The Grand Duchy of Lithuania and Sweden in the European Crisis of the mid-17th Century*, Södertörns högskola, 2006.

Lackmann, Adam Heinrich, *Epistolae diversi argumenti maximam partem a Variis ad clarissimum multorumque meritorum Virum Lucam Los-*

sium illustris Lycei apud Luneburgenses dum viveret Pro-Rectorem & post eum â Duraeo, Langwedelio, Boeclero, Portnero, Berneggero, Freinshemio aliisque ad alios exaratae, partim excerptae, & in compendium redactae, partim vero integrae ex autographis descriptae / Nunc primum in lucem protraxit ac Dissertationem de multiplici Eruditorum studio epistolis hactenus impenso praemisit Adamus Henricus Lackmannus, Hamburgi: Felginer,1728, HAB.

Léchot, Pierre-Oliver, *Un christianisme 'sans partialité': Irénisme et méthode chez John Dury (v. 1600-1680)*, a 591 page extended edition of his doctoral thesis presented to the Protesatant Theological Faculty of Geneva in September 2009. Published by Honoré Champion Éditeur, Paris, 2011.

Meyfarto, Johanne Matth. *Dissertatio Academica de concilianda Pace inter Ecclesias per Germaniam Evangelicas*, Erfurt, 1636. HA, 22a1, Nr 10, Mappe 1, p. 32-43. Four pages per numbered sheet.

Meisner, Johann, *Irenicum Duraeanum De Articulis Fidei Fundamentalibus, Et Consensu Ac Dissensu Inter Lutheranos ac Reformatos* / In Academia Wittebergensi Explicatum a Johanne Meisnero, D. & Prof. Publ., Wittebergae: Mevius; Schumacherus; Wittebergae: Schrödterus,1675, HAB.

Menk, Gerhard, *Die Hohe Schule Herborn in ihrer Frühzeit (1684-1660): Ein Beitrag zum Hochschulwesen des deutschen Kalvinismus im Zeitalter der Gegenreformation*, Wiesbaden, Johann Wolfgang Goethe-Universität, 1971, extended 1981.

Neval, Daniel A, *Comenius' Pansophie: Die dreifache Offenbarung Gottes in Schrift, Natur und Vernunft*, TVZ, 2007. Unvollendete Habilitationsschrift, Zürich University.

Pick, Peter Richard, *Interjection of Silence: The Poetics and Politics of Radical Protestant Writing 1642-1660*. PhD thesis presented to Birmingham University, Department of Humanities, 2000.

Scougal, Harry J., *Die pädagogischen Schriften John Durys (1590-1680): Ein Beitrag zur Geschichte der englischen Pädagogik*, Jena University, 1905.

Van Duinen, The 'Junto' and its Antecedents; The Character and Continuity of Dissent under Charles I from the 1620s to the grand Remonstrance. A thesis in fulfilment of the Requirements of Doctor of Philosophy, School of History and Philosophy, University of New South Wales, 2009.

General and specific works related to Durie's life and times

A Romish Recusant, *A life of Archbishop Laud*, London, 1894.

Abbott, W. C., *A Bibliography of Oliver Cromwell*, Cambridge and Harvard, 1969 reprint.

Adair, John, *Puritans: Religion and Politics in Seventeenth Century England and America*, Sutton Publishing, 1998.

Adamson, John William, Pioneers of Modern Education 1600-1700, Cambridge University Press, 1921.

Ainslie, James L., *The Doctrines of Ministerial Order in the Reformed Churches of the 16th and 17th Centuries*, T & T. Clark, 1940.

Anonymous, *The Persecutions in Scotland 1603-1685*, Local History Series No. 15, G. C. Book Publishers Ltd, Wigtown, 1995.

Ashley, Maurice, *Charles I and Oliver Cromwell: A study in contrasts and comparison*, Methuen, London, 1987.

Ashley, Maurice, *Oliver Cromwell and the Puritan Revolution*, The English Universities Press, 1972.

Askew, Reginald, *Muskets and Altars: Jeremy Taylor and the Last of the Anglicans*, Mowbray, 1997.

Aylmer, G. E., *The Struggle for the Constitution 1603-1689*, London, 1968.

Backer, Derek (ed), *The Materials, Sources and Methods of Ecclesiastical History*, Barnes & Noble, 1975.

Barteleit, Sebastian, *Toleranz und Irenik: Politisch-Religise Grenzsetzungen im England deer 1650er Jahre*, Mainz, 2003.

Barnett Smith, G., *History of the English Parliament*, 2 vols., Ward, Lock, Bowden & Co., 1892.

Batten, Joseph Minton, *John Dury, Advocate of Christian Reunion*, Chicago, 1944.

Bäumker, Franz, Geschichte des brandenburgischen Staates in seiner äußern und innern Entwicklung, Paderborn, 1857.

Beeke, Joel, *Gisbert Voetius: Towards a Reformed Marriage of Knowledge and Piety*, Reformation Heritage Books, 1999.

Beveridge, W., *A Short History of the Westminster Assembly*, Edinburgh, 1904.

Blair, William, *Archbishop Leighton*, London, 1874.

Blunt, J. H., *The Reformation of the Church of England*, 2 vols., vol. 1, 1514-1547; vol. 2, 1547-1662, London, 1882.

Bourne, E. C. E., *The Anglicanism of William Laud*, SPCK, London, 1947.

Brandes, Friedrich, *Geschichte der evangelischen Union in Preußen*, Erster Theil, Gotha, 1872.

Breslow, Marvin Arthur, *A Mirror of England: English Puritan Views of Foreign Nations 1618-1640*, Harvard University Press, 1970.

Brook, Benjamin, *The Lives of the Puritans*, vol. 3, Soli Deo Gloria, 1994.

Brown, John, *The English Puritans*, Cambridge, 1912.

Brown, Kieth M., *Kingdom or Province? Scotland and the Regal Union, 1603-1715*, Macmillan, 1992.

Brown, Michael J., *Itinerant Ambassador: The Life of Sir Thomas Roe*, The University Press of Kentucky, Lexington, 1970.

Bryant, Arthur, *King Charles the Second*, Longmans, Green and Co, 1946.

Buchan, John, *Oliver Cromwell*, The Reprint Society, London, 1941.

Butler, D., *The Life and Letters of Robert Leighton*, London, 1903.

Campbell, Douglas, *The Puritan in Holland, England and America*, 2 vols., 1893.

Carpenter, Edward, *Cantaur: The Archbishops in their Office*, Cassell, 1971.

Carr, J. A., *The Life and Times of James Ussher, Archbishop of Armagh*, London, 1895.

Carruthers, S. W., *The Everyday Work of the Westminster Assembly*, Philadelphia, 1943.

Cnattingius, Hans, *Den Centrala Kyrkostyrelsen i Sverige 1611-1636*, Uppsala, 1939.

Cohn, Norman, *The Pursuit of the Millenium*, London, 1957.

D'Aubigne, J. H. Merle, *The Protector: A Vindication*, Sprinkle Publications, 1983.

Davies, E. T, *The Political Ideas of Richard Hooker*, London, SPCK, 1946.

Davies, Horton, *The Worship of the English Puritans*, Morgan, PA, Soli Deo Gloria, 1997.

Davis, Godfrey, *The Early Stuarts 1603-1660*, Oxford, 1952.

De Witt, J. R., *Jus Divinum: The Westminster Assembly and the Divine Right of Church Government*, J. H. Kok N. V. Kampen, 1969.

Dewar, Michael W., *They Subdued Kingdoms*, Focus Christian Ministries Trust, undated.

Dictionaire historique et critique, Duraeus (Jean) Théologien Protestant, 1740, pp. 333.334.

Dircks, H., *A Biographical Memoir of Samuel Hartlib, Milton's Familiar Friend; with Bibliographical Notices of Works Published by Him*, London, John Russell Smith, 1865.

Dodwell, C. R., *The English Church and the Continent*, London, 1959.

Dooyeweerd, Herman, *The Christian Idea of the State*, New Jersey, 1978.

Doran, Susan and Durston, Christopher, *Princes, Pastors and People: The Church and Religion in England 1529-1689*, London and New York, 1991.

Dowding, William Charles, *The Life and Correspondence of George Calixtus*, Oxford and London, 1863.

Duke, Alastair (et al. eds.) *Calvinism in Europe 1540-1610: A Collection of Documents*, Manchester University Press, 1997.

Edwards, William, *Notes on European History*, 4. vols, London, 1948.

Elison, James, *George Sandys: Travel, Colonialism and Tolerance in the 17th Century*, Studies in Renaissance Literature, vol. 8, D. S. Brewer, 2002.

Fabian, Bernard, (Hrsg), *Handbuch der historischen Buchbestände in Deutschland*, Digitalisiert von Günter Kükenshöner, Hildersheim: Olm Neue Medien, 2003. See chapter: Libraries in the British Isles and their German Holdings.

Ferguson, Sinclair B., *John Owen on the Christian Life*, BOT, Edinburgh, 1987.

Firth, Charles, *Oliver Cromwell and the Rule of the Puritans in England*, London, 1925.

Fischer, Th. A., *The Scots in Germany, Being a Contribution Towards the History of the Scots Abroad*, Otto Schulze & Co., Edinburgh, 1902.

Fleming, J. R., *The Story of Church Union in Scotland: Its Origins and Progress 1560-1929*, James Clarke & Co, 1929.

Förster, Winfried, *Thomas Hobbes und der Puritanismus*, Berlin, 1969.

Fraser, Antonia, *Cromwell Our Chief of Men*, Book Club Associates, 1973.

Gardiner, Samuel Rawson, *The History of the Commonwealth and Protectorate 1649-1660*, 2 vols, Longmans, Green, and Co., 1894.

Geneva, Ann, *Astrology and the Seventeenth Century Mind: William Lilly and the Language of the Stars*, Manchester University Press, 1995.

Gilmour, Robert, *Samuel Rutherford: A Study Biographical and somewhat Critical, in the History of the Scottish Covenant*, Edinburgh and London, 1904.

Göransson, Sven, *Allmän Kyrkohistoria*, Teologiska Institution, Uppsala, undated.

Göransson, Sven, *Den Europeiska Konfessionspolitiken Upplösning 1654-1660*, Uppsala and Wiesbaden, 1956.

Göransson, Sven, *Ortodoxi och Synkretism i Sverige 1647-1660*, Uppsala, 1950.

Green, Mary Anne Everett, *Elizabeth Electress Palatine and Queen of Bohemia*, Revised by S. C. Lomas, Methuen & Co, London, 1909.

Greengrass, Mark et al (eds), *Samuel Hartlib and Universal Reformation: Studies in Intellectual Communication*, Cambridge University Press, 1994.

Gustafsson, Berndt, *Svensk Kyrkohistoria*, Verbum, Stockholm, 1957.

Guthry, Henry, *The Memoirs of Henry Guthry, Late Bishop of Dunkeld*, Glasgow, 1747.

Hadjiantoniou, George A., *Protestant Patriarch: The Life of Cyril Lucaris, Patriarch of Constantinople*, John Knox Press, Richmond, 1961.

Harte, Walter, *The History of the Life of Gustavus Adolphus, King of Sweden, Sirnamed, The Great*, Vol. I., London, 1759.

Haykin, Michael A, G, *'To honour God': The Spirituality of Oliver Cromwell*, Joshua Press, Dundas, 1999.

Henke, Ernst Ludwig Theodor, *Georg Calixtus und Seine Zeit*, 3 vols., Halle, 1853-1856.

Hering, Carl Wilhelm, Geschichte der kirchlichen Unionsversuche seit der Reformationen bis auf unsere Zeit, Leipzig, 1836-1838. Erster und zweiter Band.

Hetherington, W. M., *History of the Westminster Assembly*, Edinburgh, 1843.

Hibbard, Caroline M., *Charles I and the Popish Plot*, University of North Carolina, 1983.

Hidson, Edward (ed.), *Introduction to Puritan Theology*, Grand Rapids, 1976.

Hill, Christopher, *God's Englishman: Oliver Cromwell and the English Revolution*, Book Club Edition, 1970.

Hill, Christopher, *The English Bible and the Seventeenth-Century Revolution*, Penguin Books, 1994.

Hintze, Otto, *Die Hohenzollern und ihr Werk*, Berlijn, 1916.

Holmquist, Hjalmar, *Svenska Kyrkans Historia 1611-1632*, Uppsala 1938.

Holstun, James, *Pamphlet Wars: Prose in the English Revolution*, Frank Cass, 1992.

Hotson, Howard, Philological pedagogy in reformed central Europe between Ramus and Comenius: a survey of the continental background of the 'Three Foreigners', in *Samuel Hartlib and Universal Reformation: Studies in Intellectual Communication*, Cambridge University Press, 1994, eds M. Greengrass, M. Leslie, and T. Raylor, 29-50.

Huntley, Frank Livingstone, *Bishop Joseph Hall 1574-1656: A biographical & critical study*, D. S. Brewer Ltd, Cambridge, 1979.

Hutton, William Holden, *A History of The English Church: From the Accession of Charles I. to the Death of Anne*, Macmillan, 1903.

Hyamson, A. M., *A History of the Jews in England*, Chatto & Windus, London, 1908.

Ives, E. W. (ed.), *The English Revolution 1600-1660*, Edward Arnold, 1968.

Jones, John, *Bishop Hall, His Life and Times*, Seeley and Son, London, 1826.

Jones, Richard Foster, *The Seventeenth Century*, Stanford University Press, 1951.

Katz, David S., *Philosemitism and the Readmission of the Jews to England, 1603-1655*, Oxford, 1982.

Katz, David S. and Israel, Jonathan I, (eds), *Sceptics, Millenarians and Jews*, Brill, Leiden, 1990.

Keller, Ludwig, *Comenius und die Akademien der Naturphilosophen des 17. Jahrhunderts*, Berlin, 1895.

Kittel, Helmuth, *Der Calvinismus in Westeuropa*, Leipzig, undated.

Kjöllerström, Sven, *Kräkla och Mitra*, Gleerups Förlag, 1965.

Klueting, Hans, (Hg), *Irenik und Antikonfessionalismus im 17. und 18. Jahrhundert*, Georg Olms Verlag, Hildesheim, 2003.

Knox, E. A., *Robert Leighton: Archbishop of Glasgow*, James Clarke & Co., 1930.

Knox, R. Buick, *James Ussher: Archbishop of Armagh*, University of Wales Press, 1967.

Koser, Reinhold, *Der Große Kurfürst und Karl X von Schweden*, HZJB, 1914.

Kvačala, Johann, *J. A. Comenius*, Berlin, 1914.

Lamont, William, *Puritanism and historical controversy*, UCL Press, 1996.

Le Bas, Charles Webb, *The Life of Archbishop Laud*, London, 1836.

Leibniz, Gottfried Wilhelm, *Philosophischer Briefwechsel*, Leibniz-Forschungsstelle der Universität Münster, Erster Band 1663-1685, Akademie Verlag, 2006.

Leube, Hans, *Kalvinismus und Luthertum im Zeitalter der Orthodoxie*, 1. Band, *Der Kampf um die Herrschaft in protestantischen Deutschland*, 1928.

Lewis, Peter, *The Genius of Puritanism*, Carey Publications, 1979.

Lindhart, Poul Georg, *Skandinavische Kirchengeschichte seit dem 16. Jahrhundert*, Vandenhoek & Ruprecht in Göttingen, 1982.

Lutzow, Count Francis, *A History of Bohemian History*, Heineman, 1899.

M'Crie, Thomas, *Life of Andrew Melville*, William Blackwood, London and Edinburgh, 1856.

Macgregor, Janet G., *The Scottish Presbyterian Polity: A Study of its Origins in the Sixteenth Century*, Oliver and Boyd, 1926.

Mackenzie, Agnes Mure, *The Scotland of Queen Mary and the Religious Wars 1513-1638*, Oliver and Boyd Ltd., 1957.

Magee, Glenn, Alexander, *Hegel and the HermeticTradition*, Cornell University Press, 2001.

Mandelbrote S, 'John Dury and the Practice of Irenism', in N. R. Aston (ED.), *Religious Changes in Europe (1650-1914), Essays for John McManners*, Oxford, Clarendon Press, 1997, p. 41-58.

Martin, Hugh, *Puritanism and Richard Baxter*, SCM Press Ltd, London, 1954.

Masson, David, *The Life of John Milton: Narrated in Connection with the Political, Ecclesiastical and Literary History of his Time*, Boston 1859.

Metzler, Ed, *The Impact of Israel on Western Philosophy*, Baalschem Press, Herborn, 1993.

Meyer, R. W., *Leibnitz and the Seventeenth-Century Revolution*, Chicago, 1952.

Milton, Anthony, *Catholic and Reformed: The Roman and Protestant Churches in English Protestant Thought 1600-1640*, Cambridge University Press, 1994.

Milton, Antony, 'The Unchanged Peacemaker'? John Dury and the politics of Irenicism in England, 1628-1643." In *Samuel Hartlib and Universal Reformation: studies in intellectual communication*, ed. M. Greengrass, 95-117. Cambridge: Cambridge University Press, 1994.

Moeller, Wilhelm, *History of the Christian Church*, 3 vols., London, 1898.

Morrill, John, *The Nature of the English Revolution*, Longman, 1993.

Mosheim, *Institutes of Ecclesiastical History*, Reid Edition, London, 1849.

Murdoch, Steve (ed.), *Scotland and the Thirty Years War, 1618-1648*, Brill, Leiden, 2001.

Murdoch, Steve, *Network North: Scottish Kin, Commercial and Covert Associations in Northern Europe, 1603-1746*, Brill, Leiden, 2006.

Murray, Iain H., *The Puritan Hope*, Edinburgh, 1975.

Murray, Iain H., *The Reformation of the Church*, Banner of Truth Trust, Edinburgh, 1965.

Neal, Daniel, *The History of the Puritans*, Klock and Klock reprint of Thomas Tegg and Son edition 1837, 3 vols., 1979.

Nippold, Friedrich (Herausgeber), *Berner Beiträge zut Geschichte der Schwitzerischen Reformationskirchen*, Bern, 1884.

Norlin, Theodor, *Svenska Kyrkans Historia efterr Reformationen*, Första Bandets Första Afdeling, Lund, 1864.

Palmer, Tony, *Charles II*, Cassell, London, 1979.

Paul, Robert S, The Lord Protector: Religion and Politics in the Life of Oliver Cromwell, Lutterworth Press, 1955.

Peacey, Jason, *Politicians and Pamphleteers: Propaganda During the English Civil Wars and Interregnum*, Ashgate, 2004.

Pennington, Donald and Thomas, Keith (eds.), *Puritans and Revolutionaries: Essays in Seventeen-Century History Presented to Christopher Hill*, Oxford, 1978.

Peronnet, Michel (ed), *Naissance et Affirmation de L'Idee de Tolerance XVIe et XVIIIe siècle*, Universite de Montpellier III, 1987. See essays 'John Durie ou Dury (1595-1680) Apôtre de la Réunion Protestante', pp. 132-144 and 'Le Chevalier Edwin Sandys 1561-1629) et John Durie (1595-1680)', pp. 145-156.

Pettegree, Andrew, *Emden and the Dutch Revolt: Exile and the Development of Reformed Protestantism*, Clarendon Press, 1992.

Popkin, Richard H., Hartlib, Dury and the Jews, in *Samuel Hartlib and Universal Reformation: Studies in Intellectual Communication*, Cambridge University Press, 1994, eds M. Greengrass, M. Leslie, and T. Raylor, 118-136.

Pursell, Brennan C., *The Winter King: Frederick V. of the Palatinate and the Coming of the Thirty Years War*, Aldershot: Ashgate, 2003.

Rae, Thomas H. H., *John Dury and the Royal Road to Piety*, Peter Lang, Frankfurt, Berlin, 1998.

Rae, Thomas H. H., *John Dury: Reformer of Education*, Marburg/ Lahn, 1970.

Reid, James, *Memoirs of the Westminster Divines*, BOT reprint, 1982.

Reilly, Tom, *Cromwell: An Honourable Enemy*, Phoenix Press, London, 1999.

Romish Recusant, *Life of Archbishop Laud*, London, 1894.

Rosenkranz, Albert, *Abriss Einer Geschichte Der Evangelischen Kirche Im Rheinland*, Presseverband der Evangelische Kirche in Rheinland, 1960.

Rouse, Ruth und Neill, Stephen Charles, *Geschichte der Ökumenischen Bewegung, 1517-1948, Göttongrn, 1957*, 2 vols.

Schaff, Philip, <u>The Creeds of Christianity with A History and Critical Notes in Three Volumes</u>, Vol. III, The Evangelical Protestant Creeds with Translations, New York, 1877.

Schaller, Klaus, *Johann Amos Comenius: Ein pädagogisches Porträt*, Belz UTB, 2004.

Schäufele, Wolf-Friedrich, ‚Erzbischof William Wake von Canterbury (1657-1737) und die Einigung der europäischen Christenheit', in: Heinz DUCHHARDT; Gerhard MAY (eds.), *Union – Konversion – Toleranz. Dimensionen der Annäherung zwischen den christlichen Konfessionen im 17. und 18. Jahrhundert* (Veröffentlichungen des Instituts für Europäische Geschichte Mainz; Beiheft 50), Mainz 2000, S. 301.

Schendell, Werner, *Wilhelm von Oranien Befreier der Niederlande*, Gustav Kiepenheuer Verlag, 1935.

Schiller, Friedrich, *Geschichte des 30 Jährigen Kriegs*, Bertelsmann, Mohn & Co., Gütersloh. 1966.

Schrey, Prof. Helmut, *Das verlorene Paradies: Auf dem Wege zu Milton's 'Fit Audience though Few'*, St Augustin, 1980.

Schröder, Christel Mattias (ed.), *Klassiker des Protestantismus*, Direkt Media, Digitale Bibliothek 127, Berlin, 2005.

Scott, Eva, *Die Stuarts*, München, 1936.

Shaw, William A., *A History of the English Church During the Civil Wars and Under the Commonwealth*, 2 vols., Longmans, Green and Co., 1900.

Simpkinson, C. H., *William Laud, Archbishop of Canterbury 1573-1645*. London, 1894.

Snow, W. G. Sinclair, *The Times, Life and Thought of Patrick Forbes, Bishop of Aberdeen 1618-1635*, S.P.C.K., London, 1952.

Spalding, Ruth, *The Improbable Puritan: A Life of Bulstrode Whitelocke 1605-1675*, London, 1975.

Sprunger, Keith L., *Dutch Puritanism: A History of English and Scottish Churches of the Netherlands in the Sixteenth and Seventeenth Centuries*, Brill, Leyden, 1982.

Strasser, O. E. et al, *Geschichte des Protestantismus in Frankreich und den Niederlanden*, Vandenhoek & Ruprecht in Göttingen, 1975.

Sykes, Norman, *Old Priest and New Presbyter*, Cambridge, 1956.

Tatham, G. B., *The Puritans in Power*, CUP, 1913.

Thomson, J. M., *Lectures on Foreign History*, Oxford, 1951.

Thulin, Oskar (ed.), *Reformation in Europa*, Berlin, 1967.

Toon, Peter, *God's Statesman: The Life and Work of John Owen*, Paternoster Press, Exeter, 1971.

Toynbee, Margaret, *King Charles I*, International Profiles, 1968.

Trevor-Roper, Hugh, *Archbishop Laud 1573-1645*, Macmillan, London, 1940.

Trevor-Roper, Hugh, *The Crisis of the Seventeenth Century: Religion, the Reformation and Social Change* (Indianapolis: Liberty Fund, 2001).

Turnbull G. H., *Hartlib, Dury and Comenius, Gleaning from Hartlib's Papers*, Liverpool-London, Liverpool University Press, 1947.

Turnbull, G. H., *Samuel Hartlib: A Sketch of his Life and his Relation to J. A. Comenius*, Oxford University Press, 1920.

Underdown, David, *Pride's Purge. Politics in the Puritan Revolution*, Oxford, 1971.

van 't Spijker W., et al., *Het Puritanisme: geschiedenis, theologie en invloed,* 's-Gravenhage, Boekencentrum, 2001.

Vladimir, J. (ed.), *Internationale Wissenschaftliche Konferenz Comenius' Erbe und die Erziehung des Menschen für das 21. Jahrhundert: Comenius als Theologe*, Prague, 1992.

von Bischofshausen, Sigismund Freiherrn. *Die Politik des Protectors Oliver Cromwell in der Auffassung und Thätigkeit seines Ministers des Staatssecretärs John Thurloe*, Innsbruck, 1899.

Walker, James, *The Theology and Theologians of Scotland, 1560-1750*, Edinburgh, 1982 reprint.

Wallmann, Johannes, *Der Pietismus*, Vandenhoek & Ruprecht in Göttingen, 1990.

Walsh, Walter, *England's Fight with the Papacy*, Nisbet, London, 1912.

Webster, Charles, *Samuel Hartlib and the Advancement of Leaning*, CUP, 1970.

Webster, Charles, *The Great Instauration: Science, Medicine and Reform 1626-1660*, New York, 1975.

Webster, Tom, *Godly Clergy in Early Stuart England: The Caroline Puritan Movement c. 1620-1643*, CUP, 1997.

Wedgwood, C. V., *The Thirty Years War*, Jonathan Cape, 1956.

Wedgwood, C. V., *The Trial of Charles I*, The Reprint Society, London, 1964.

Welsby, Paul A., *George Abbot The Unwanted Bishop 1562-1633*, SPCK, London, 1962.

Westin, Gunnar, *Negotiations About Church Unity 1628-1634: John Durie, Gustavus Adolphus and Axel Oxenstierna*, Uppsala, 1932.

Westin, Gunnar, *Svenska Kyrkan och de Protestantiska Einheitssträvandena under 1630-Talet*, Uppsala, 1934.

Westminster Conference Papers, *The Christian and the State in Revolutionary Times*, WCP, 1975.

Whyte, Alexander, Samuel Rutherford and Some of His Correspondents, Oliphant, Anderson and Ferrier, 1894.

Wordsworth, John, *The National Church of Sweden*, Hale Lecture 1910, Mowbray and Co., London, 1811.

Young, John T., *Faith, Medical Alchemy and Natural Philosophy: Johann Moriaen, Reformed Intelligencer, and the Hartlib Circle*, Aldershot, 1998.

Published magazine, journal and review essays dealing with John Durie's life and times

Abbott, Wilbur, C., John Dury, *The American Historical Review*, 1945, Issue. 50, pp. 317-319.

Aldridge, Richard, 'John Locke (1632-1704), *courtesy of PROSPECTS: the quarterly review of education*(Paris, UNESCO: International Bureau of Education), vol. 24, no. 1/2, 1994, p. 61–76. © UNESCO: International Bureau of Education, 1999.

Anonymous, John Durie's Reformed Librarie-Keeper and its Author's Career as a Librarian, The Library, vol. 4, Oxford University Press, 1892, pp. 81-89.

Asch, Ronald, G., Die englische Republik und die Friedensordnung von Münster und Osnabrück, *Historische Zeitschrift*, Beiheft, new series vol. 26, 1998, pp. 421-443.

Bain, John A., Gunnar Westin, Svenska Kyrkan och de protestantiska enhetssträvande under 1630-talet, Lundaquistska Bokhandeln, Uppsala, *The Expository Times*, Vol. 46, No. 11, 1935, p. 524.

Baird, H. M., Notes on Theological Education in the Reformed Churches of France and French Switzerland, The Presbyterian Review, vol. 1, 1880, N.Y., pp. 85-103.

Batten, J. M., John Dury, Advocate of Christian Reunion, *Church History: Studies in Christianity*, American Society of Church History, vol. 1, No. 4., pp. 222-231.

Berg, J. van den, and **Wall**, Ernestine van der, (eds), 'Jewish-Christian Relations in the Seventeenth Century: Studies and Documents', Kluver Academic Publishers, Dordrecht, undated, first 94 pages only.

https://openaccess.leidenuniv.nl/bitstream/1887/.../1/3_908_005.pdf.

Bergmann, W., Zum Gebrauche des Wortes 'Pansophia' vor Comenius, *Monatsheft der Comenius Gesselshaft für Kultur und Geistesleben*, Band 5, H. 7/8, 1896, pp. 210-221.

Brandes, Friedrich H., John Dury and His Work for Germany, *Catholic Presbyterian*, July 1882, pp. 22-32; August 1882 (continued) pp. 91-101.

Briggs, C.A., 'The Work of John Durie in Behalf of Christian Union in the Seventeenth Century', *Presbyterian Review*, No 30, April 1887, pp. 297-309.

Büsser, Prof. Fritz, Johann Heinrich Hotinger und der 'Thesaurus Hottingerianus', *Zwingliana*, XXII, 1995, pp. 85-108.

Carlson, Martin E., Johannes Matthiae and the Development of the Church of Sweden During the First Half of the Seventeenth Century, American Society of Church History Quarterly, Red Bank, NJ, CUP, pp. 289-309, 1944.

Cogley, Richard W., ''The Most Vile and bararous Nation of the World': Giles Fletcher the Elder's The Tartars Or, Ten Tribes (ca. 1610)', *Renaissance Quarterly*, 58 (2005): pp. 781-814.

Cook, Daniel J., Leibniz on 'prophets', prophecy, and revelation, , 45, 2009, pp. 269-287.

Cook, Sarah Gibbard, The Congregational Independents and the Cromwellian Constitutions, *Church History*, vol. 46, Sept. 1977, No. 3, pp. 335-357.

Davies, Godfrey, John Dury, Advocate of Christian Union, J. Minton Batten, University of Chicago Press, 1944. In *The English Historical Review*, Oxford University Press, 60, 237, pp. 254-256, 1945.

Dickson, Donald R., The Hartlib Papers: A Complete Text and Image Database of the Papers of Samuel Hartlib (c.1600-1662), *Seventeenth Century News*, vol. 62, 384, pp. 165-169, College Starion, Texas, 2004.

Eijnatten, van, Joris, Lodestar of Latitude: Gerard Brandt's *Peaceable Christian* (1664), Irenicism and Religious Dissent, http://ads.ahds.ac.uk/catalogue/adsdata/PSAS.

England, Church of, Project Canterbury, The Church of England and the Church of Sweden. Report of the Commission Appointed by the Archbishop of Canterbury. In Pursuance of Resolution 74 of the Lambeth Conference of 1908, On the Relation of the Anglican Communion to the Church of Sweden. Appendix I. Sketch of the history of the Swedish Church by Chancellor E. R. Bernard, *The Young Churchman*, Milwaulkee, 1911.

Erlandson, Seth, Lutherdomens första tid i Sverige, *Tidskriften Biblicum*, nr. 6, 1979, p. 7 ff..

Fissel, Mark Charles, The Winter King, *Seventeenth Century News*, vol. 62, 384, pp. 249-252, College Station, Texas, 2004.

Forster, Leonard, Philip von Zesen, Johann Heinrich Ott, John Dury, and Others, Unpublished Comeniana, *The Slavonic and East European Review*, Leeds, Bd 32, 1953/54, pp. 475-489.

George, Timothy, War and Peace in the Puritan Tradition, *Church History*, vol. 53, Dec. 1984, No. 4, pp. 492-503.

Gibson, Kenneth, John Dury's Apocalyptic Thought: A Reassessment, *Journal of Ecclesiastical History*, Vol. 61, No. 2, April 2010, pp. 299-313.

Healey, Robert M., The Jew in Seventeenth-Century Protestant Thought, *Church History*, vol. 46, March 1877, No.1, pp. 63-79.

Himmelreich, Fr., Die Einigungsbestrebungen des Johannes Duraeus zwischen den evangelischen Konfessionen und die Klassen des Solmser Landes, *Monatshefte für rheinische Kirchengeschichte*, Jg. 28, 1934, PP. 305-310. Contains contemporary letters about and from Durie.

Hof, W.J. op 't, De internationale invloed van het Puritanisme, from *Het Puritanisme: geschiedenis, theologie en invloed* / W. van 't Spijker, R. Bisschop, W.J. op 't Hof. ('s-Gravenhage, Boekencentrum, 2001), p. 271-384, Boekencentrum | Claves pietatis, 2007.06.15; versie 1.0, Onderzoeksarchief / Research Archive Nadere Reformatie, Nummer B01001994.

Houston, Chloë, Could "Eutopian politics (...) never be drawn into use?" Utopianism and radicalism in the 1640s, University of Reading, *Cromohs Virtual Seminars*, 2006-2007.

Hyamson, Albert M., The lost tribes and the Return of the Jews to England, *Transactions of the Jewish Historical Society of England*, vol 5, 1903, pp. 114-147.

Johnson, Ronald A. P., 'For Such a Time as This': John Dury, Jean-Baptiste Stouppe, and Cromwellian Diplomacy, *Selected Annual proceedings of the Florida Conference of Historians*, 15, (2008) 95-101.

Klähr, Th., Johannes Duraeus, *Monatsheft der Comenius-Gesellschaft für Kultur und Geistesleben*, 1897, Band 6, pp. 65-76, 191-203.

Krupp, Antony, Cultivation as Maturation: Infants, Children, and Adults in Alexander Baumgarten's Aesthetica, *Monatsheft für deutschsprachige Literature unf Kultur*, Vol. 98, No. 4, pp 524-538.

Lamont, William, The Left and Its Past: Revisiting the 1650s, *History Workshop Journal*, vol. 23, Nr. 1, OUP, 1987, pp. 141-153.

Landwehr, Hugo, Johannes Duraeus' Unionsverhandlung mit Kurbrandenberg, *Zeitschrift für Kirchengeschichte*, Band 10, 1886, pp. 463-489.

Lasker, Daniel J., Karaism and Christian Hebraism: A New Document, *Renaissance Quarterly*, 59 (2006) pp. 1089-1116.

Levy, S., John Dury and the English Jewry, *Transactions of the Jewish Historical Society of England*, vol. 4, 1899-1901, London, pp. 76-82.

Lindeboom, Dr. J., Johannes Duraeus en Zijne Werkzaamheid in Dienst Van Cromwell's Politik, *Nederlands archief voor kerkgeschiedenis,*

Dutch Review of Church History, vol. XVI, 1921, Leiden, pp. 241-268.

McDayter, Mark, The Haunting of St. Jame's Library: Librarians, Literature, and The Battle of the Books, *Huntington Library Quarterly*, vol. 66, No.1/2 (2003), pp 1-26.

Menk, Gerhard, Die Hohe Schule Herborn, Der Deutsche Kalvinismus und die Westliche Welt, Sonderdruck aus *Jahrbuch der Hessischen Kirchengeschichtlichen Vereinigung*, 35. Band, Hessisches Staatsarchiv, Marburg, 1984.

Menk, Gerhard, Die Hohe Nassauische Schule, *Der Convent*, December, Jahr 30, Heft 12, 1979, pp. 291-295.

Menk, Gerhard, Die Herborner Pädagogik und Comenius, *Der Convent*, Jahr 30, Heft 12, December, 1979, pp. 296-303.

Menk, Gerhard, Das Restitutionsedikt und die Kalvinistische Wissenschaft: Die Berufung Johann Heinrich Alsteds, Philipp Ludwig Piscators und Johann Heinrich Bisterfelds nach Siebenbürgen, Sonderdruck aus *Jahrbuch der Hessischen Kirchengeschichtlichen Vereinigung*, 1980.

Nellen, Henk, Hugo Grotius Political and Scholarly Activities in the Light of His Correspondence, *Grotiana*, 26-28, 2005-2007, pp. 16-30.

Nischan, Bodo, John Bergius: Irenicism and the Beginning of Official Religious Toleration in Brandenburg-Prussia, *Church History*, vol. 51, Dec. 1982, No. 4, pp. 389-404.

Nischan, Bodo, The 'Franco Panis:' A Reformed Communion Practice in Late Reformation Germany, *Church History*, vol.53, March 1984, No. 1, pp. 17-29.

O'Brian, Matthew, The Winter King: Frederick V of the Palatinate and the Coming of the Thirty Years' War by Brennan Pursell, Aldershot: Ashgate, 2003. Department of History, *Rutgers University Review*, H-German, September, 2004.

Odlozilik, Otakar, We live in the Seventeenth Century, *The Educational Forum*, Vol. V., Nr. 1., November, Indianapolis,1940, pp. 5-16.

Petröczi, Eva, Samuel Hartlib, A 'Man for All Countries', including Hungary and Transylvania, Károli Gáspár University of the Hungarian Reformed Church, Hungary, courtesy of www.theroundtable.ro.

Popkin, Richard Henry, "The End of the Career of a Great 17th Century Millenarian - John Dury." In *Pietismus und Neuzeit*, ed. M. Brecht, 1988, 203-220.

Popkin, Richard Henry, The Fictional Jewish Council of 1650: A Great English Pipedream, *Hîstôrya yêhûdît*, Haifa, vol. 5, No. 2, Fall 1991, pp. 7-22.

Popkin, Richard Henry, The First College for Jewish Students, *Revue des études juives*, Peeters, Paris, 1984, pp. 351-364.

Popkin, Richard Henry, The Lost Tribes, the Caraites and the English Millenarians, *The Journal of Jewish Studies*, Oxford, 1986, Issue 37, 213-227.

Popkin, Richard Henry, James R. Jacob. Henry Stubbe, Radical Protestantism and the Early Enlightenment, review, *Journal of the History of Philosophy*, 24, 2, 1986.

Popkin, Richard Henry, Three English Tellings of the Sabbatai Zevi Story, *Jewish History*, vol. 8, Numbers 1-2.

Roberts, Prof. M., The Political Objectives of Gustavus Adolphus in Germany 1630-1632, in Transactions of the Royal Historical Society, Cambridge, 5th series, vol. 7, pp. 19-46, 1957.

Sander, Friedrich, Comenius, Duraeus, Figulus. Nach Stammbüchern der Familie Figulus-Jablonski, in *Monatshefte der Comenus-Gesellschaft*, Dritte Band, 1894, Heft 9 und 10, pp. 307-326.

Schapiro, B. J., Latitudinarianism and Science in Seventeenth-Century England, *Past & Present, A Journal of Historical Studies*, vol. 40, 1968, pp. 16-41., Oxford University Press.

Selected Annual Proceedings of the Florida Conference of Historians, Vol. 15, Feb. 2008, p. 77, Purdue University.

Shen, H. *Milton and Old English* (pdf) *www.sisins.zju.edu.cn/*.

Spinka, Matthew, John Dury, the Peacemaker, *Christian Union Quarterly* XIII, Chicago, III, 1924, pp.

Sprunger, Keith L., English and Dutch Sabbatarianism and the Development of Puritan Social Theology (1600-1660), Church History, vol. 51, March 1982, No. 1, pp. 24-29.

Sprunger, Keith L., Letters on Toleration: Dutch Aid to Persecuted Swiss and Palatine Mennonites 1615-1699. By Jeremy Dupertuis Bangs. Rockport, Maine: Picton Press. 2004. Pp. 489. With CD-ROM of transcriptions, in *The Mennonite Quarterly Review* 289, 2004. Goshen College, the Associated Mennonite Biblical Seminary and the *Mennonite Historical Society* Volume LXXX, April 2006 Number Two.

Sprunger, Keith L., Other Pilgrims in Leiden: Hugh Goodyear and the English Reformed Church, *Church History*, vol. 41, March 1972, No. 1, pp. 46-60.

Stimson, Dorothy, Comenius and the Invisible College, *Journal of the History of Science Society*, Cornell University, Chicago, 23, 2, 1935, pp. 373-388.

Stisser, Karl Adolf, Ökumenische Verhandlungen in Hildesheim i. J. 1640: Johannes Duraeus und Georg Calixt am Hof Herzog Georgs, *Alt Hildesheim: Jahrbuch für Stadt and Stift Hildesheim*, Stadtarchiv Hildesheim, 1988, Issue 59, pp. 79-91.

Stupperich, Robert, Evangelisches Konzil. Forderungen und Pläne luth. Theologen und Politiker im 16. und 17. Jahrhundert, *Neue Zeitschrift für Systematische Theologie und Religionsphilosophie*. Volume 3, Issue 3, Pages 296–314, 1961, published online: 19/10/2009

Sunshine, Glenn S, Scotland and the 30-Years' War, *The Sixteenth Century Journal*, vol. 35, No. 1, pp. 199-201, Kirksville Mo., 2004.

Tighe, W. J., William Laud and the Reunion of the Churches: Some Evidence from 1637 and 1638, *The Historical Journal*, 30, 3 (1987), pp. 717-727.

Tollin, H., Johannes Duraeus in *Geschichtsblätter für Stadt und Land Magdeburg*, Jahrgang 1897, pp. 227-285.

Turnbull, G. H., Samuel Hartlib's Influence on the Early History of the Royal Society, *Notes and Records of the Royal Society of London*, 1953, pp. 101-130.

Wake, Archbishop W. and Jablonsky D. E., Protestant Union in the 18th Century, *The Savonic and East European Review*: SEER/ publ. for the Modern Humanities Research Association and the School of Slavonic and East European Studies, University of London, vol. 13, No. 37, pp. 119-126.

Wall, van der, Ernestine, The Dutch Hebraist Adam Boreel and the Mishnah Project, LIAS 16 (1989) 2.

Wall, van der, Ernestine, *A Precursor of Christ or a Jewish Impostor? Petrus Serrarius and Jean de Labadie on the Jewish Messianic Movement around Sabbatai Sevi*, openaccess.leidenuniv.nl/bitstream/1887/12129/1/3_908_17pdf. pp. 109-124.

Walton, Annette, Paper Bullets: Being a briefe Studie of the wayes in which Propaganda has been utilised by Gouernments, in times both moderne and ancient, *Exposition*, Trinity, 2010, **Oxford**.

Watson, Foster, John Dury I. The Public Good and Education, *The Educational Review*, vol. 1, pp. 769-776, 1899, London.

Watson, Foster, John Dury II. Seasonable Discourse, *The Educational Review*, vol. 2, pp. 216-223, 1900, London.

Wies-Campagner, Elizabeth, Messianismus und die Entdeckung Amerikas : Menesse Ben Israel, *Internet Zeitschrift für Kulturwissenschaft*, 16, März 2005.

Wilensky, M. L., 'Thomas Barlow's and John Dury's attitude towards the readmission of the Jews to England,' Part 1, *The Jewish Quarterly Review* 50 (1959): 167-175.

Wilensky, M. L. 'Thomas Barlow's and John Dury's attitude towards the readmission of the Jews to England, Part 2, *The Jewish Quarterly Review* 50, no. 3 (1960): 256-268.

Windsor, Graham, The Reunion Views of Archbishop Ussher and his Circle, *Churchman*, 77/3, 1963.

Biography of John Durie

John Durie (1599-1680), the son of a Scottish minister exiled by James VI, was brought up in France and the Netherlands. Whilst a student he campaigned to unite the Protestant churches through joint ecclesiastic, political and educational schemes, particularly moved by the efforts in Poland to unite the Bohemian Brethren with the various Polish Protestant churches. This produced his first known writing on the subject in 1618. After teaching and lecturing in France and Germany, he was encouraged in 1630 by Governor Oxenstierna and Ambassador Sir Thomas Rowe, to obtain official credentials from King Charles and the English Church for his irenic and educational work. Armed with such authority, Durie toured Europe, working for pan-European cooperation. His friend Samuel Hartlib stayed behind in England as his agent and coordinator. After the Rebellion, Durie became a member of the Westminster Assembly, supported by leading theologians, scientists, writers and social reformers. Cromwell appointed Durie to teach the King's children and reform the library system. He sent Durie as his personal ambassador to Sweden, the Netherlands, Germany and Switzerland to campaign for political, ecclesiastical and educational cooperation with Britain.

Durie believed that all wisdom reflects the being of the God-only-wise (Rom. 16:27) and a Christian education in godly wisdom was the major way of preparing the nations for a selfless life of service for the public good and the glory of God. He thus drew up plans for an educational revolution based on international think-tanks. This entailed founding schools Europe-wide for all classes of people irrespective of social standing, age or gender, taught by interdisciplinary methods which he termed Pansophy, Universal Learning or Practical Divinity. Education must mean training the whole being to utilize all knowledge and to free the pupil from departmentalized thinking and action. Specialising only made sense after a thoroughly integrated and synergized general education. Durie's reforms were geared not only to children's needs but to those of parents, teachers, pastors, employers and administrators.

Modern commentators on Durie see him as a man long before his time. He is acknowledged as the initiator of synthesized and synergized all-round education; the creator of modern Library Science; the first true Ecumenist and the founder of knowledge engineering and information management.

Biography of George M. Ella

George M. Ella, born February 1939 in Yorkshire, England, has lived most of his life on the European Continent. He is a retired Senior Civil Servant formerly employed in teaching, post-graduate teacher-training, chairing examination boards and curricula work. He holds degrees from London, Hull, Uppsala, Essen, Duisburg and Marburg universities with doctorates in English Literature and Theology. Dr. Ella has written regularly since the seventies for a number of magazines and newspapers and published numerous books on Church History, including biographies of William Cowper, William Huntington, James Hervey, John Gill, Augustus Montague Toplady, Isaac McCoy and Henry Bullinger besides works on doctrine and education. He is currently finishing the third volume of his series 'Mountain Movers'; a biography of John Durie; a work on Law and Gospel and further study material for the Martin Bucer Seminar. Dr. Ella is still internationally active as a lecturer and is a Vice-President of the Protestant Reformation Society. He is keenly interested in missionary work and has written on the spread of the Gospel amongst the Samë people of Lapland, the people of India and the Native Americans. This present volume follows Dr. Ella's 'The Covenant of Grace and Christian Baptism', also published by the Martin Bucer Seminar.

George Ella is married to Erika Ella, née Fleischman, a former government administrator, and they have two sons Mark (41), Director of a Polytechnic College in Bremerhaven and Robin (39), Leading Senior Physician in a newly-built Geriatric and Psychiatric clinic in Dessau.

www.ingramcontent.com/pod-product-compliance
Lightning Source LLC
Chambersburg PA
CBHW052047290426
44111CB00011B/1647